Taxation

Companion Website

For open-access **student resources** specifically written to complement this textbook and support your learning, please visit **www.pearsoned.co.uk/melville**

Lecturer Resources

For password-protected online resources tailored to support the use of this textbook in teaching, please visit **www.pearsoned.co.uk/melville**

Taxation

Finance Act 2017

Twenty-third edition

Alan Melville
FCA, BSc, Cert. Ed.

Harlow, England • London • New York • Boston • San Francisco • Toronto • Sydney • Dubai • Singapore • Hong Kong
Tokyo • Seoul • Taipei • New Delhi • Cape Town • São Paulo • Mexico City • Madrid • Amsterdam • Munich • Paris • Milan

PEARSON EDUCATION LIMITED
KAO Two
KAO Park
Harlow
CM17 9NA
United Kingdom
Tel: +44 (0)1279 623623
Web: www.pearson.com/uk

First published 1995 (print)
Twenty-third edition published 2018 (print and electronic)

ISBN: 978-1-292-20080-4 (print)
978-1-292-20081-1 (PDF)
978-1-292-20082-8 (ePub)

British Library Cataloguing-in-Publication Data
A catalogue record for the print edition is available from the British Library

Library of Congress Cataloging-in-Publication Data
A catalog record for the print edition is available from the Library of Congress

10 9 8 7 6 5 4 3 2 1
21 20 19 18 17

Front cover image: © Getty Images

Print edition printed and bound by Ashford Colour Press Ltd, Gosport

NOTE THAT ANY PAGE CROSS REFERENCES REFER TO THE PRINT EDITION

Contents

Part 2 Capital Gains Tax

Preface

The main aim of this book is to describe the UK taxation system in sufficient depth and with sufficient clarity to meet the needs of those undertaking a first course of study in taxation. The book has not been written with any specific syllabus in mind but should be useful to anyone who is studying taxation as part of a university or college course in accounting, finance or business studies. The book should also be of value to students who are preparing for the taxation examinations of the professional accounting bodies. A list of relevant examinations is given on the back cover of the book.

Every effort has been made to explain the tax system as clearly as possible. There are numerous worked examples and each chapter (except Chapter 1) concludes with a set of exercises which thoroughly test the reader's grasp of the new topics introduced in that chapter. The book also contains four sets of review questions, drawn mainly from the past examination papers of the professional accounting bodies. The solutions to most of these exercises and questions are located at the back of the book but solutions to those exercises and questions marked with an asterisk (*) are provided in a separate Instructor's Manual.

This twenty-third edition includes the provisions of Finance Act 2017, which is based upon Finance (No. 2) Bill 2017. This Bill was fast-tracked through Parliament before the June 2017 general election and omitted many of the proposals made in the March 2017 Budget. The remaining Budget proposals are explained in the relevant chapters of this book, but it is made abundantly clear that these are merely proposals and have not yet been enacted. Some of the more significant areas affected are:

- The timetable for the Making Tax Digital (MTD) project (Chapter 1)
- A planned reduction in the dividend allowance (Chapter 2)
- The property and trading income allowances (Chapters 5 and 9)
- The cash basis for property income (Chapter 5)
- Corporation tax loss reliefs (Chapter 26)
- Corporate interest relief restrictions (Chapter 28)
- The deemed domicile rules (Chapter 32).

The Government has stated that there will be a Summer Finance Bill but (at the time of writing) it is not known which measures will be included in this Bill and whether the implementation date of any of them will be delayed. An analysis of the Summer Finance Bill will be made available as soon as possible on the website which accompanies this book. The website address is www.pearsoned.co.uk/melville.

Alan Melville
June 2017

Acknowledgements

I would like to thank the following accounting bodies for granting me permission to use their past examination questions:

- Association of Chartered Certified Accountants (ACCA)
- Chartered Institute of Public Finance and Accountancy (CIPFA)
- Association of Accounting Technicians (AAT).

I must emphasise that the answers provided to these questions are entirely my own and are not the responsibility of the accounting body concerned. I should also point out that the questions which are printed in this textbook have been amended in some cases so as to reflect changes in taxation law which have occurred since those questions were originally published by the accounting body concerned.

I would also like to thank the Office for National Statistics for granting me permission to reproduce the table of Retail Price Indices given in Chapter 24.

Please note that, unless material is specifically cited with a source, any company names used within this text have been created by me and are intended to be fictitious.

Alan Melville
June 2017

Summary of Tax Data

Income Tax

	2017-18	2016-17
TAX RATES AND BANDS		
Basic rate	20%	20%
Higher rate	40%	40%
Additional rate	45%	45%
Basic rate limit	£33,500†	£32,000
Higher rate limit	£150,000	£150,000
Starting rate for savings	0%	0%
Starting rate limit for savings	£5,000	£5,000
Personal savings allowance (maximum)	£1,000	£1,000
Dividend allowance	£5,000‡	£5,000‡

† Basic rate limit applicable to non-savings income of Scottish taxpayers in 2017-18 is £31,500

‡ Rates of tax on dividends in both years are 7.5%, 32.5% and 38.1%

	2017-18	2016-17
ALLOWANCES	£	£
Personal allowance	11,500	11,000
Marriage allowance	1,150	1,100
Blind person's allowance	2,320	2,290
Married couple's allowance:		
Born before 6 April 1935	8,445	8,355
Minimum amount	3,260	3,220
Income limit for basic personal allowance	100,000	100,000
Income limit for married couple's allowance	28,000	27,700
CAR AND FUEL BENEFIT		
Not exceeding 50g/km	9%	7%
51g/km to 75g/km	13%	11%
76g/km to 94g/km	17%	15%
95g/km	18%	16%
Each additional 5g/km	+1%	+1%
Maximum charge	37%	37%
Amount used in car fuel benefit calculation	£22,600	£22,200
PENSION SCHEMES	£	£
Annual allowance	40,000	40,000
Lifetime allowance	1,000,000	1,000,000

Capital Allowances

Writing Down Allowance (WDA)	
Main pool of plant and machinery	18%
Special rate pool of plant and machinery	8%
Annual Investment Allowance (AIA)	
AIA annual limit from 1 January 2016	£200,000
AIA rate	100%
First Year Allowance (FYA) on qualifying plant and machinery	
Low emission cars	100%
Gas refuelling equipment†	100%
Energy saving or water efficient technology	100%
Zero-emission goods vehicles	100%

† *The Government has proposed that expenditure on charging points for electric vehicles should also be eligible for a 100% FYA.*

National Insurance Contributions

	2017-18	*2016-17*
CLASS 1		
Lower earnings limit (weekly)	£113	£112
Primary threshold (weekly)	£157	£155
Upper earnings limit (weekly)	£866	£827
Secondary threshold (weekly)	£157	£156
Upper secondary threshold (weekly)	£866	£827
Employee contributions		
Rate on earnings between primary threshold and UEL	12%	12%
Rate on earnings beyond UEL	2%	2%
Employer contributions		
Rate on earnings beyond secondary threshold	13.8%	13.8%
CLASS 1A		
Rate	13.8%	13.8%
CLASS 2		
Weekly contribution	£2.85	£2.80
Small profits threshold	£6,025	£5,965
CLASS 3		
Weekly contribution	£14.25	£14.10
CLASS 4		
Lower profits limit	£8,164	£8,060
Upper profits limit	£45,000	£43,000
Rate on profits between lower and upper limit	9%	9%
Rate on profits beyond upper limit	2%	2%

Capital Gains Tax

	2017-18	*2016-17*
Standard rate†	10%	10%
Higher rate†	20%	20%
Entrepreneurs' relief rate	10%	10%
Entrepreneurs' relief lifetime limit	£10,000,000	£10,000,000
Annual exempt amount	£11,300	£11,100

† *Taxable gains on the disposal of residential property are taxed at 18% and 28%*

Corporation Tax

Financial Year	*FY2017*	*FY2016*	*FY2015*	*FY2014*
Main rate	19%	20%	20%	21%
Small profits rate	-	-	-	20%
Lower limit	-	-	-	£300,000
Upper limit	-	-	-	£1,500,000
Marginal relief fraction	-	-	-	1/400

Note:
The main rate for FY2018 is 19%.

Inheritance Tax

Date of transfer	*Nil rate band*	*Rate on life-time transfers*	*Rate on death*	*Lower rate*
6 April 2006 to 5 April 2007	0 - £285,000	20%	40%	-
6 April 2007 to 5 April 2008	0 - £300,000	20%	40%	-
6 April 2008 to 5 April 2009	0 - £312,000	20%	40%	-
6 April 2009 to 5 April 2012	0 - £325,000	20%	40%	-
6 April 2012 to 5 April 2018	0 - £325,000	20%	40%	36%

Note:
The main residence nil rate band for 2017-18 is £100,000.

Value Added Tax

Standard rate†	20%	(from 4 January 2011)
Reduced rate	5%	
Registration threshold	£85,000	(from 1 April 2017)
Deregistration threshold	£83,000	(from 1 April 2017)

†*Standard rate 17.5% prior to 4 January 2011*

Part 1

INCOME TAX AND NATIONAL INSURANCE

Chapter 1

Introduction to the UK tax system

Introduction

The purpose of this first chapter is to provide an overview of the UK tax system. The principal UK taxes are introduced and classified and the main sources of taxation law are explained. This chapter also deals with:

(a) the structure and functions of Her Majesty's Revenue and Customs (HMRC) which is the organisation responsible for the administration of the UK tax system

(b) the annual procedure which is used to determine the tax liability of an individual.

The chapter concludes by distinguishing between tax avoidance and tax evasion.

UK taxes

The UK taxation system is composed of a number of different taxes, some of which are *direct* taxes and some of which are *indirect* taxes:

(a) Direct taxes are charged on income, profits or other gains and are either deducted at source or paid directly to the tax authorities. The main direct taxes which are payable by individuals are income tax, capital gains tax and inheritance tax. The main direct tax payable by companies is corporation tax. All of these taxes are administered by HM Revenue and Customs (HMRC), which was formed in April 2005 when the Inland Revenue and HM Customs and Excise were merged. National Insurance contributions, which can also be looked upon as a form of direct taxation, are administered by the NICs and Employer Office of HMRC.

(b) Indirect taxes are taxes on spending. They are charged when a taxpayer buys an item and are paid to the vendor as part of the purchase price of the item. It is then the vendor's duty to pass the tax on to the tax authorities. Indirect taxes include value added tax (VAT), stamp duty, customs duties and the excise duties levied on alcohol, tobacco and petrol. The only indirect tax considered in this book is VAT, which is also administered by HM Revenue and Customs.

Sources of tax law

There is no single source of UK tax law. The basic rules are laid down in Acts of Parliament but it is left to the courts to interpret these Acts and to provide much of the detail of the tax system. In addition, HMRC issues a variety of statements, notices and leaflets which explain how the law is implemented in practice. These statements have no legal backing but they explain the tax authorities' interpretation of the law and will be adhered to unless successfully challenged in the courts.

Statute law

The basic rules of the UK tax system are embodied in a number of tax *statutes* or Acts of Parliament. The main statutes currently in force for each tax are as follows:

Tax	*Statute*	*Abbreviation*
Income tax	Capital Allowances Act 2001	CAA 2001
	Income Tax (Earnings and Pensions) Act 2003	ITEPA 2003
	Income Tax (Trading and Other Income) Act 2005	ITTOIA 2005
	Income Tax Act 2007	ITA 2007
National Insurance	Social Security Contributions and Benefits Act 1992	SSCBA 1992
Capital gains tax	Taxation of Chargeable Gains Act 1992	TCGA 1992
Inheritance tax	Inheritance Tax Act 1984	IHTA 1984
Corporation tax	Taxation of Chargeable Gains Act 1992	TCGA 1992
	Capital Allowances Act 2001	CAA 2001
	Corporation Tax Act 2009	CTA 2009
	Corporation Tax Act 2010	CTA 2010
Overseas aspects of tax	Taxation (International and Other Provisions) Act 2010	TIOPA 2010
Value added tax	Value Added Tax Act 1994	VATA 1994
Administration of }	Taxes Management Act 1970	TMA 1970
the tax system }	Customs and Excise Management Act 1979	CEMA 1979

These statutes are amended each year by the annual Finance Act, which is based upon the Budget proposals put forward by the Chancellor of the Exchequer. Some of the tax statutes provide for the making of detailed regulations by *statutory instrument*. A statutory instrument (SI) is a document which is laid before Parliament and then automatically becomes law within a stated period unless any objections are raised to it.

European Union law

Membership of the European Union (EU) involves adherence to EU law†. Member states are not required to adopt a common system of taxation but some parts of the UK system are nonetheless influenced by EU requirements. At present, the main impact is on VAT, where the prevailing legislation takes the form of EU Directives. These are binding on the UK and dictate the results which the internal legislation of the UK must bring about.

Additionally, EU "State aid" approval must sometimes be sought for amendments to UK tax-advantaged schemes such as the Enterprise Investment Scheme (see Chapter 6) or the R&D tax credits scheme (see Chapter 23). Furthermore, decisions made in the European courts may trigger changes to UK tax law, as occurred in relation to the tax treatment of the losses of overseas subsidiary companies (see Chapter 32).

† *In view of the Referendum result on 23 June 2016, it seems safe to say that EU influence over the UK tax system will eventually cease to exist.*

Case law

Over the years, taxpayers and the tax authorities have frequently disagreed over the interpretation of the tax Acts. As a result, many thousands of tax cases have been brought before the courts. The decisions made by judges in these cases form an important part of the tax law of the UK and some of the more significant cases are referred to in this book.

Statements made by the tax authorities

The main statements and other documents produced by HM Revenue and Customs as a guide to the law on taxation are as follows:

(a) **Statements of Practice**. A Statement of Practice (SP) sets out the HMRC interpretation of tax legislation and clarifies the way in which the law will be applied in practice. For example, SP 4/97 (the fourth SP issued in 1997) deals with the taxation treatment of commissions, cashbacks and discounts.

(b) **Extra-Statutory Concessions**. An Extra-Statutory Concession (ESC) consists of a relaxation which gives taxpayers a reduction in liability to which they are not entitled under the strict letter of the law. In general, concessions are made so as to resolve anomalies or relieve hardship. For example, ESC A91 deals with the taxation treatment of living accommodation provided by reason of employment.

A process of giving statutory effect to certain ESCs is currently underway. This is generally being done by means of statutory instruments.

(c) **Announcements**. Announcements (and other notices and documents) are issued by HMRC throughout the year on a wide variety of tax-related subjects. Of especial interest are the documents which are issued on Budget day and which provide a detailed explanation of the Budget proposals.

(d) **Internal Guidance Manuals**. HMRC produces a comprehensive set of internal tax manuals for the guidance of its own officers. These manuals may be accessed on the HMRC website (see below).

(e) **Explanatory publications**. Leaflets, factsheets and booklets are aimed at the general public and explain the tax system in non-technical language. These can usually be accessed online, though some are still available in printed form.

Most of the above information is now available on the HMRC website, the address of which is www.gov.uk/government/organisations/hm-revenue-customs.

The tax year

The changes to the tax system that are proposed in the annual Budget speech† are usually intended to take effect as from the start of the next *tax year*. Tax years for individuals and for companies are identified as follows:

(a) For individuals, a tax year runs from 6 April to the following 5 April. For instance, tax year 2016-17 began on 6 April 2016 and ended on 5 April 2017. Tax years are also referred to as *fiscal years* or *years of assessment*.

(b) For companies, a corporation tax *financial year* runs from 1 April to the following 31 March and is identified by the year in which it begins. For instance, the financial year referred to as FY2016 began on 1 April 2016 and ended on 31 March 2017.

This book takes into account the provisions of Finance Act 2017 (which is based on the March 2017‡ Budget) and describes the UK taxation system for fiscal year 2017-18 and corporation tax financial year FY2017.

† *The Budget traditionally takes place in March but is now being moved back to the Autumn of the previous year. The final Spring Budget occurred in March 2017. The first Autumn Budget will occur in Autumn 2017 and will lay out the Government's tax plans for the following tax year.*

‡ *Many of the proposals made in the March 2017 Budget were removed from the ensuing Finance Bill so as to expedite the Bill's progress through Parliament before the general election of June 2017. At the time of writing, it seems likely that these proposals will be re-introduced and will form the basis of a second Finance Act in 2017. Further information will be made available on the website which accompanies this book. The address is www.pearsoned.co.uk/melville.*

Structure of HM Revenue and Customs

Her Majesty's Revenue and Customs (HMRC) consists of a large body of civil servants headed by the *Commissioners for Revenue and Customs*. The Commissioners are appointed by Her Majesty The Queen in accordance with recommendations made by the *Treasury*. This Government department has overall responsibility for the public finances of the UK and is managed by the *Chancellor of the Exchequer*. The main duties of the Commissioners for Revenue and Customs are as follows:

(a) to implement the law relating to direct and indirect taxation

(b) to provide advice to the Chancellor of the Exchequer on taxation matters

(c) to administer the divisions and offices into which HMRC is organised.

The routine work of HMRC is carried out by officials known as *Officers of Revenue and Customs*. With regard to direct taxation, the main function of these officials is generally to check a taxpayer's own self-assessment of the tax liability (see below) and then to ensure that the correct amount of tax is paid. The functions of HMRC with regard to indirect taxation (and VAT in particular) are explained later in this book (see Chapter 30).

HMRC has specialist offices which deal with such matters as pension schemes, charities and so forth but most of the day-to-day work relating to direct taxation takes place in local area offices. These offices are responsible for routine assessment and collection and for ensuring that taxpayers comply with tax regulations. At present, HMRC has 170 local offices but these are to be consolidated into 13 regional centres over the next ten years.

Support for taxpayers who need help with their tax affairs is provided by means of specialist expert advice either given over the telephone or delivered by mobile advisors at convenient locations in the community or at a taxpayer's home or workplace.

Administration of the tax system

The remainder of this chapter describes the administration system which is used to assess an individual's liability to income tax and capital gains tax in each tax year. This system is known as "Self Assessment". Under this system, the taxpayer (*not* HMRC) is primarily responsible for ensuring that:

(a) the tax liability for each tax year is properly assessed, and

(b) the correct amount of tax is paid on the due date or dates.

Later chapters of this book explain the administration systems which are used for the purposes of corporation tax, inheritance tax and VAT.

Self Assessment

If an individual's tax liability for a tax year cannot be collected entirely by deduction at source (see Chapter 2) or via the PAYE system (see Chapter 7), then the liability must be formally assessed. The starting point in the assessment process is usually the completion of a *self assessment tax return*. The annual procedure is as follows:

(a) Tax returns†‡ are normally issued in April each year to those taxpayers who are likely to need them. Each tax return includes a formal notice requiring a return to be made and delivered to HMRC. Paper tax returns are not sent to taxpayers who submitted the previous year's return electronically (see below) but such taxpayers are still sent a notice requiring a return to be made and can request a paper tax return if they so wish. Returns can also be downloaded and printed from the HMRC website.

† *As from tax year 2016-17, HMRC is empowered to make an assessment of an individual's income tax or capital gains tax liability without that person being first required to complete a tax return. This "simple assessment" procedure may be used where HMRC already has sufficient information about the individual to make the assessment.*

‡ *By 2020, the Government intends to replace tax returns with online "digital tax accounts" as part of the "Making Tax Digital" project (see later in this chapter).*

(b) The main paper tax return consists of a basic eight-page form. There are also several sets of supplementary pages, each dealing with a different type of income or gains (e.g. income from self-employment). Taxpayers are required to complete only those supplementary pages that are relevant to their circumstances.

(c) A short tax return (STR) is available for taxpayers with straightforward tax affairs.

(d) Rather than completing a paper tax return, taxpayers can file returns electronically by means of the internet and are encouraged to do so. Approximately 90% of self assessment tax returns are in fact filed electronically.

(e) The information requested in a tax return relates to the tax year just ended. For example, the tax returns issued in April 2017 required taxpayers to declare their income and gains for tax year 2016-17.

(f) A tax return must be completed in full. It is not permissible to omit figures or to make entries such as "see accounts" or "as submitted by employer". Unless asked to submit accounts or other supporting documentation with the return, a taxpayer is under no obligation to do so. However, it is necessary to retain all supporting documentation in case HMRC enquires into the accuracy of a return.

(g) If a main tax return is submitted on paper, the taxpayer has the option of calculating his or her own tax liability (using "tax calculation summary" pages) and submitting this calculation to HMRC as part of the return. HMRC will calculate the tax liability for taxpayers who do not take up this option or for those who submit the short tax return (which does not include a self-calculation facility). However, if a paper return is submitted late (see below), HMRC does not guarantee to advise the taxpayer of the liability in time for the correct amount of tax to be paid on the correct date.

If a tax return is filed electronically, the tax liability is calculated by computer software. In all cases, the resulting assessment is referred to as a "self-assessment".

(h) Self assessment tax returns must normally be filed (i.e. submitted to HMRC) on or before the following dates:

- for paper returns, 31 October following the end of the tax year
- for returns filed electronically, 31 January following the end of the tax year.

However, if the return notice is issued after 31 July following the end of the tax year (but not after 31 October) the taxpayer has three months from the date of the notice to submit a paper return. The deadline for electronic filing in such a case remains at 31 January. If the notice is issued after 31 October, the taxpayer has three months from the date of the notice to submit the return either on paper or electronically.

(i) Penalties are imposed if a return is filed late. Furthermore, the submission of a late return may mean that the tax liability for the year is not determined until after the due date of payment (see below). A taxpayer who pays tax late will incur interest and may also incur a late-payment penalty (see Chapter 15).

(j) The 31 January which follows the end of a tax year is known as the "filing date" for that year. For example, the filing date for tax year 2017-18 is normally 31 January 2019. However, if a return notice is issued after 31 October, the filing date becomes the date which falls three months after the issue date of the notice.

(k) HMRC is empowered to correct a tax return (so as to rectify obvious errors or omissions or anything else that is believed to be incorrect) within nine months of the date on which the return is filed. Similarly, the taxpayer has the right to amend his or her tax return within 12 months of the filing date for that return.

(l) A taxpayer who has paid an amount of tax but now believes that this tax should not have been paid (a situation that could be caused by an error in a tax return) may make a claim for recovery of the overpaid tax. Such a claim must be made within four years of the end of the tax year to which it relates. Depending upon the circumstances of the case, HMRC may or may not accept the claim.

(m) The tax due in relation to a self-assessment is normally payable as follows:

  (i) A first payment on account (POA) is due on 31 January in the tax year to which the self-assessment relates.
  (ii) A second POA is due on the following 31 July.
  (iii) A final balancing payment is due on the following 31 January.

  For example, the tax due in relation to a 2017-18 self-assessment would normally be payable on 31 January 2018 (first POA), 31 July 2018 (second POA) and 31 January 2019 (balancing payment). Further information is given in Chapter 15 of this book.

(n) An employed taxpayer whose balancing payment does not exceed £3,000 may ask that this should be collected via the PAYE system (see Chapter 7). In such a case, taxpayers who file their returns electronically are advised to do so by 30 December so as to give HMRC sufficient time to make the necessary arrangements.

Notification of chargeability to tax

An individual who has not received a notice to submit a tax return, but has taxable income (or gains) of which HMRC is not aware, must notify HMRC of his or her chargeability to tax within six months of the end of the tax year in which the income arises. However, notification of chargeability is *not* required if *all* of the following conditions are satisfied:

(a) the individual has no capital gains
(b) the individual is not a higher-rate taxpayer (see Chapter 2)
(c) all of the individual's income has been subject to deduction of income tax at source (see Chapter 2) or has been dealt with via the PAYE system (see Chapter 7)
(d) the individual is not liable to a high income child benefit charge (see Chapter 7).

An individual who fails to notify chargeability within the permitted six-month period will incur a penalty (see Chapter 15).

Determinations

If an individual fails to submit a tax return by the required filing date for that return, an Officer of Revenue and Customs may make a determination of the tax due, calculated according to "the best of his information and belief". There is no right of appeal against a determination and the tax due cannot be postponed. A determination can be displaced only if the individual files the required return.

Enquiries

HMRC may "enquire" into any tax return. The usual reason for opening an enquiry is the suspicion that something is wrong with the return. However, some enquiry cases may be selected at random and HMRC is under no obligation to justify the opening of an enquiry or to state whether or not the case has been chosen randomly. Note that:

(a) If a tax return is filed by the due date, an enquiry cannot usually begin more than 12 months after the date on which the return is filed. This means that the "enquiry window" for a return which is filed early closes correspondingly early.

(b) If a return is filed late or is amended after the date on which the return was due to be filed, the enquiry window is extended until the quarter day which follows the first anniversary of the date on which the return or amendment was filed. For this purpose, the quarter days are 31 January, 30 April, 31 July and 31 October.

EXAMPLE

In April 2017, HMRC issues a notice requiring an individual to submit a tax return for the year 2016-17. The return is submitted electronically to HMRC on 8 December 2017.

(a) State the date by which any enquiry into the above return must begin.

(b) How would the situation differ if the return was submitted on 1 March 2018?

Solution

(a) The return is filed before the due date (31 January 2018). Any enquiry must begin within 12 months of the date that the return is filed (i.e. by 8 December 2018).

(b) The return is filed late. Any enquiry must begin by the quarter day which follows the first anniversary of the date that the return is filed (i.e. by 30 April 2019).

Discovery assessments

HMRC may raise a "discovery assessment" if it is discovered that full disclosure has not been made in a tax return and tax has been lost as a result.

The time limit for making a discovery assessment is normally four years after the end of the tax year concerned. This increases to six years if the taxpayer has been negligent and 20 years if the taxpayer has been dishonest.

Record keeping

Taxpayers are required to keep proper records so that they can make a correct tax return and (if necessary) substantiate the figures entered on the return. A taxpayer who is in business or who lets property must normally preserve these records for five years after the 31 January which follows the end of the tax year concerned. Otherwise, records must be preserved for 12 months after the 31 January which follows the end of the tax year. For example, records for tax year 2017-18 must normally be retained until 31 January 2024 by a taxpayer who is in business or who lets property and until 31 January 2020 otherwise.

Appeals

Taxpayers have the right of appeal in relation to a number of HMRC decisions. For example, a taxpayer may appeal against a discovery assessment or against an HMRC amendment to a self-assessment. The main features of the appeals system are as follows:

(a) An appeal must be sent to HMRC in writing within 30 days of the disputed decision.

(b) The taxpayer may also apply to postpone payment of all or part of any tax which is payable as a result of the decision, though interest will continue to accrue on the postponed amount until the appeal is settled. However, postponement is generally not available if the appeal relates to the use of a tax avoidance scheme covered by the DOTAS rules (see below) or in connection with arrangements which have been counteracted by HMRC under the GAAR (see below).

(c) On receiving an appeal, HMRC considers the taxpayer's reasons for disputing the decision. Most appeals are settled by discussion and agreement at this stage.

(d) If the taxpayer and HMRC are unable to agree, the taxpayer will be offered an internal review of the decision. A taxpayer who wishes to accept this offer must normally do so within 30 days. An internal review is carried out by an HMRC officer who has not previously been involved with the disputed decision and is usually completed within 45 days. The review officer then writes to the taxpayer to inform him or her of the review's conclusions.

(e) A taxpayer who rejects the offer of an internal review may appeal to a tribunal within 30 days of the date of the offer letter. Otherwise, an appeal to a tribunal may be made within 30 days of the date of the review conclusion letter.

(f) Most appeals are dealt with by the Tax Chamber of the First-tier Tribunal. However, more complex appeals may be heard by the Tax and Chancery Chamber of the Upper Tribunal. The Upper Tribunal also hears appeals against First-tier Tribunal decisions.

(g) If either HMRC or the person concerned is dissatisfied with a decision made by the Upper Tribunal, a dispute on a point of law may be referred to the Court of Appeal.

(h) The costs of bringing an appeal before the First-tier Tribunal are usually fairly modest. Parties bear their own costs and so a taxpayer who loses an appeal is not normally required to pay HMRC's costs (unless the taxpayer has acted wholly unreasonably). The costs of taking an appeal to higher authority can be very high and an unsuccessful taxpayer may be required to pay HMRC's costs in defending the appeal as well as his or her own costs.

Tax evasion

Taxpayers are required to provide information which is correct and complete. Dishonest behaviour (e.g. concealing a source of income) is known as *tax evasion* and is against the law. On summary conviction in a magistrates' court, an offender may be imprisoned for up to six months. If the conviction is obtained on indictment in a higher court, the maximum prison term is seven years. In either case, a fine of any amount may also be imposed.

Tax avoidance

Taxpayers are entitled to organise their financial affairs in such a way that their tax burden is minimised. This perfectly legal activity is known as *tax avoidance*. For example, a taxpayer might legally avoid income tax and/or capital gains tax by moving funds into a tax-efficient investment (see Chapter 6). Tax avoidance (which is legal) should be sharply contrasted with tax evasion (which is not).

Tax avoidance is acceptable within limits but, over the years, tax advisors have shown great ingenuity in devising very complex and highly artificial tax avoidance schemes to exploit "loopholes" in the tax system. These schemes often result in a significant loss of tax revenue until eventually blocked by specific anti-avoidance legislation. So as to limit the effectiveness of tax avoidance schemes, a regime known as DOTAS (Disclosure of Tax Avoidance Schemes) has been introduced which requires certain disclosures by those who devise such schemes or use them. A brief summary of the requirements is as follows:

(a) Those who promote and market schemes which bear certain "hallmarks" of tax avoidance are required to provide HMRC with details of each scheme. Promoters must provide a description of the scheme, including details of its tax consequences and the statutory provisions on which it relies. The scheme is then registered by HMRC and is allocated a registration number.

(b) Taxpayers using such a scheme are required to quote the registration number of the scheme in their tax returns. Taxpayers who develop their own "in-house" tax avoidance schemes must provide details of each scheme directly to HMRC.

These rules are intended to provide HMRC with advance warning of tax avoidance schemes, so enabling swifter and more effective investigation and counteraction.

General anti-abuse rule (GAAR)

Finance Act 2013 introduced a "general anti-abuse rule" (GAAR) into UK tax law. This rule applies to income tax, capital gains tax, inheritance tax, corporation tax and certain indirect taxes. The aim of the GAAR is to counteract tax advantages arising from abusive tax arrangements. Tax arrangements are defined as "abusive" if they cannot be regarded as reasonable in relation to the relevant tax law, having regard to whether the arrangements:

(a) are consistent with the principles on which the relevant tax law is based
(b) involve any contrived or abnormal steps
(c) are intended to exploit any shortcomings in the tax law.

The GAAR empowers HMRC to make "just and reasonable" adjustments to counteract the tax advantages that would otherwise arise from tax arrangements that are deemed to be abusive. These adjustments may involve increasing a taxpayer's tax liability or imposing a tax liability where otherwise there would be none. However, before making any such adjustments, HMRC must comply with the following procedure:

(a) If an officer of HMRC considers that a tax advantage has arisen as a result of abusive tax arrangements, the taxpayer concerned must be provided with a written notice to that effect. The notice must explain why HMRC considers the arrangements to be abusive and must set out the proposed counteraction. The taxpayer then has 45 days in which to make written representations in response to this notice.

(b) If, after considering any representations received from the taxpayer, HMRC still believes that counteraction should be taken, the matter must then be referred to the GAAR Advisory Panel (an independent panel established for this purpose). The taxpayer must be notified that the matter is being referred in this way and then has 21 days in which to make written representations to the Advisory Panel.

(c) The GAAR Advisory Panel considers the tax arrangements concerned and produces an opinion notice, stating whether or not (in the opinion of the Panel members) the arrangements are abusive. HMRC must then issue a notice to the taxpayer, setting out whether the tax arrangements are to be counteracted.

(d) A penalty† will generally apply in cases where abusive tax arrangements have been successfully counteracted by means of the GAAR. The penalty is equal to 60% of the additional tax payable as a result of the counteraction (see Chapter 15).

Taxpayers may appeal against an HMRC decision to counteract tax arrangements. When considering such an appeal, the tribunal or court must take into account the opinion expressed by the GAAR Advisory Panel.

† *The Government intends to introduce a penalty for the "enablers" of tax avoidance schemes which are defeated by HMRC. The amount of such a penalty would be equal to 100% of the fees charged by the "enabler" to clients who used the scheme in the hope of gaining a tax advantage.*

Making Tax Digital (MTD)

The Government has announced that it intends to replace tax returns with online "digital tax accounts". These accounts will be phased in over the next three years and will be pre-populated with information already held by HMRC (e.g. employment income, pensions income, bank interest received etc.). Taxpayers will be able to visit their digital accounts at any time and, in many cases, will not need to submit any information to HMRC at all.

Self-employed taxpayers and those with income from property will be required to use MTD-compliant accounting software to record their income and expenditure and to update their digital tax accounts every three months. However, there will be an exemption from quarterly reporting for taxpayers with business or property income which does not exceed a specified threshold (currently expected to be £10,000). There will also be an MTD exemption for taxpayers who are "digitally excluded", either on religious grounds or because of their age, disability or location.

The proposed MTD timetable envisages that businesses and landlords with annual turnover which exceeds the VAT threshold (currently £85,000 (see Chapter 29)) will be required to start quarterly reporting as from April 2018. The proposed start date is April 2019 for those with turnover not exceeding the VAT threshold. It is also expected that MTD will be introduced for companies as from April 2020.

The HMRC Charter

The HMRC Charter sets out the rights and obligations of taxpayers. The Charter explains what the taxpayer can expect from HMRC and what HMRC expects from the taxpayer. In summary, the taxpayer can expect:

- to be treated even-handedly and with respect and to be treated as honest
- to receive help and support from HMRC
- to be tackled if he or she breaks or bends the rules of the tax system
- that HMRC will be professional and act with integrity
- that HMRC will protect taxpayer information and respect taxpayer privacy
- that the costs of dealing with HMRC will be kept as low as possible.

In return, HMRC expects taxpayers to be honest, to take care to get things right and to treat HMRC staff with respect.

The Adjudicator

An independent and impartial Adjudicator considers complaints made by taxpayers who are not satisfied with the quality of the service they have received from HMRC. The Adjudicator writes an annual report and makes recommendations for improvements to HMRC procedures and practices. The Adjudicator is not empowered to hear tax appeals.

Summary

- The main direct taxes are income tax, CGT, inheritance tax and corporation tax. Indirect taxes include VAT, stamp duty and excise duties.
- Taxation law is a combination of statute law and case law. Statements made by the tax authorities provide information on the authorities' interpretation of the law.
- The fiscal year runs from 6 April to the following 5 April. The corporation tax financial year runs from 1 April to the following 31 March.
- Individuals who fall within the scope of the Self Assessment system are normally required to submit an annual tax return. Paper returns must be filed by 31 October following the end of the tax year. Returns submitted electronically must be filed by the following 31 January.
- A taxpayer who has not received a tax return notice, but has taxable income or gains of which HMRC is not aware, must notify HMRC of his or her chargeability to tax within six months of the end of the tax year in which the income arises.
- If a tax return is submitted by the required filing date, HMRC cannot initiate an enquiry into the return more than 12 months after the date on which the return is submitted. Discovery assessments may be made after the enquiry window has closed if it is discovered that the taxpayer has not made full disclosure of all relevant facts.
- Tax appeals which cannot be settled by agreement between the taxpayer and HMRC are dealt with by a two-tier tribunals system.
- Tax evasion involves dishonest conduct by the taxpayer and is illegal. Tax avoidance involves the sensible arrangement of the taxpayer's affairs so as to minimise the liability to tax and is legal. However, abusive tax avoidance schemes may fall foul of the general anti-abuse rule (GAAR) and be counteracted by HMRC.
- Digital tax accounts are set to replace tax returns by 2020. Self-employed taxpayers and landlords will generally be required to keep electronic records of their income and expenditure and to update their digital tax accounts at quarterly intervals.

Chapter 2

Introduction to income tax

Introduction

Income tax assessments are computed for a tax year (or "year of assessment") and are based on the taxpayer's total income for the year from all sources, ignoring any income which is exempt from income tax. This chapter explains the main features of an income tax computation, in preparation for the much more detailed information which is provided in subsequent chapters.

Most of the primary legislation relating to income tax used to be located in the Income and Corporation Taxes Act 1988, but this legislation has mostly been rewritten and moved to more recent statutes. Income tax legislation can now be found mainly in the Income Tax (Earnings and Pensions) Act 2003, the Income Tax (Trading and Other Income) Act 2005 and the Income Tax Act 2007, as amended by subsequent Finance Acts.

Taxable persons

Individuals who are resident in the UK for a tax year are generally charged to income tax on all of their income for that year, including both income arising in the UK and income arising overseas. However, there are two main exceptions to this general rule:

(a) Some forms of income are exempt from income tax altogether (see below).

(b) UK residents who are not UK-domiciled (i.e. whose permanent home is not the UK) may claim that their overseas income should be subject to UK income tax only to the extent that the income is remitted to the UK. However, this may lead to an additional tax charge of £30,000 or more in some cases (see Chapter 32).

Individuals who are not UK residents are liable to pay income tax on their UK income only (see Chapter 32). Income tax is payable by:

(a) adults, on their own income and on their share of the income of a partnership

(b) children, if they have sufficient income to pay tax (see below)

(c) trustees, on the income of a trust or settlement

(d) personal representatives, on income arising from the estate of a deceased person.

Child's income derived from parent

If an unmarried minor child receives investment income which is derived from a parent, this income is treated for tax purposes as the income of the parent, not the child, unless the amount involved does not exceed £100 (per parent per child) in the tax year. This prevents parents from transferring income-bearing assets to a child so as to take advantage of the child's personal allowance (see Chapter 3).

However, income which is derived from parental contributions to a Child Trust Fund account or a Junior ISA (see Chapter 6) does not count towards the £100 limit.

Exempt organisations and individuals

Most organisations are generally exempt from income tax, subject to various restrictions and exceptions. Certain individuals are also exempt. Exempt organisations and individuals include the following:

(a) companies, which are liable to corporation tax rather than income tax

(b) clubs and societies, which are also liable to corporation tax

(c) registered pension schemes

(d) registered charities (on income used for charitable purposes)

(e) representatives of foreign countries (e.g. ambassadors)

(f) visiting members of foreign armed forces (on their service pay and on income arising from a source outside the UK).

Classification of income

Income is classified for income tax purposes into a number of types or categories, each with its own set of rules for calculating the amount of income of that type arising in a tax year. These rules are located in the Income Tax (Earnings and Pensions) Act 2003 and in the Income Tax (Trading and Other Income) Act 2005. The main classes of income which are subject to income tax are as follows:

Statute	*Type of income*	*Chapter of this book*
ITEPA 2003	Employment income	Chapters 7-8
	Pensions	Chapter 7
	Social security income	Chapter 7
ITTOIA 2005	Trading income	Chapters 9-13
	Property income	Chapter 5
	Interest	Chapter 6
	Dividends	Chapter 6
	Miscellaneous income	Chapter 6

Each of these classes of income is considered in some detail in later chapters of this book.

Exempt income

Certain types of income are specifically exempt from income tax and should be completely ignored when preparing an income tax computation. Some of the more important sources of exempt income† are as follows:

(a) Exempt savings and investment income (see Chapter 6):
- income from Individual Savings Accounts
- income from National Savings Certificates
- interest arising from a Save As You Earn arrangement linked to a tax-advantaged employee share option scheme (see Chapter 7)
- income from investments held in a Child Trust Fund account
- dividends on shares held in a Venture Capital Trust (subject to conditions)

(b) Exempt employment income (see Chapter 7):
- certain minor benefits provided by employers for their employees
- bonus payments of up to £3,600 per annum received by employees of companies controlled by an employee ownership trust
- the first £30,000 of "ex gratia" compensation received for loss of employment
- certain lump sums payable under registered pension schemes (e.g. a lump sum payable at the commencement of a pension)
- the operational allowance paid to UK armed forces serving in specified locations

(c) Exempt property income (see Chapter 5):
- income of up to £7,500 per annum received under the "rent-a-room" scheme

(d) Other exempt income:
- winnings from betting, competition prizes and premium bond prizes
- maintenance payments (see Chapter 4)
- income from scholarships
- wound and disability pensions
- certain social security benefits (e.g. child benefit‡ and housing benefit)
- income from the sale of electricity generated by home microgeneration systems
- most commissions, discounts and cashbacks received by ordinary retail customers
- damages or compensation received for personal or professional injury
- receipts (not exceeding specified limits) from foster care and other qualifying care
- certain payments made to individuals who adopt children.

† *The Government has proposed that property or trading income of less than £1,000 for the year should be exempt from income tax as from tax year 2017-18 (see Chapters 5 and 9).*

‡ *Although child benefit is exempt from income tax, a taxpayer who receives child benefit and has an income exceeding £50,000 p.a. may be subject to an income tax charge known as the "high income child benefit charge" (see Chapter 7).*

Structure of an income tax computation

In order to calculate a taxpayer's income tax liability for a tax year it is necessary to bring together *all* of the taxpayer's income into a single income tax computation. The structure of this computation is specified in the Income Tax Act 2007. A typical computation for the year 2017-18 might appear as follows:

		£
Business profits		54,410
Loan interest taxed at source (pre-tax equivalent)		640
Bank interest received		60
Total income		55,110
Less: Tax reliefs		1,200
Net income		53,910
Less: Personal allowance		11,500
Taxable Income		42,410
Income tax		
33,500†	@ 20%	6,700.00
8,210	@ 40%	3,284.00
500	@ 0%	0.00
200	@ 40%	80.00
42,410		10,064.00
Less: Tax reductions		0.00
Tax borne		10,064.00
Add: Tax withheld on payments		0.00
Tax liability for the year		10,064.00
Less: Tax paid by deduction at source		128.00
Tax payable		9,936.00

† *This figure would be different for a Scottish taxpayer (see later in this chapter).*

All of the terms used in this computation are explained in detail in this chapter and in later chapters. For now, the main features of the computation are as follows:

(a) The taxpayer's "total income" for the year is calculated by adding together income from all sources, including the pre-tax equivalent of any income from which tax has been deducted at source but excluding income which is exempt from income tax.

(b) Relief for certain payments made by the taxpayer (see Chapter 4) together with certain loss reliefs (see Chapters 5 and 12) and relief for certain pension contributions (see Chapter 14) are deducted from total income, giving "net income".

(c) Any personal allowance available to the taxpayer is deducted from net income to give "taxable income". The personal allowance for tax year 2017-18 is usually £11,500, ensuring that those on very low incomes are not liable to income tax. However, the allowance is reduced (possibly to zero) for those on high incomes (see Chapter 3).

(d) Income tax is charged on the taxable income, using the rates of tax in force for the year. The amount of tax calculated in this way is then subject to a number of adjustments and the result is the tax payable to HM Revenue and Customs.

(e) The *tax borne* by the taxpayer is the amount of income tax suffered for the year. This may be different from the *tax liability*, which is the amount of tax which must be accounted for to HMRC and the *tax payable* which is the tax remaining to be paid after deducting any tax already paid for the year. These distinctions will become clearer in the course of the next two chapters.

A formal tax computation is not required for every taxpayer. For example, a computation is not usually required for an individual whose income is derived entirely from employment, since the correct amount of tax is normally deducted automatically by the PAYE system (see Chapter 7). However, the only way to calculate the income tax liability in more complex cases is to prepare a tax computation.

Married couples and civil partners

Married couples are taxed independently, which means that the husband's income and the wife's income are taxed completely separately. This is also the case for same-sex civil partners who have entered into a legally-recognised civil partnership.

If a married couple (or civil partners) have income which is derived from an asset held in their joint names, such as interest on a joint bank account, the amount of that income will normally be divided between them equally for tax purposes. But if the source of income is genuinely held between them in some other proportion, the couple may make a declaration to that effect and the income will then be divided between them as appropriate.

Dividends from jointly owned shares in close companies (see Chapter 27) are always taxed according to the actual proportions of ownership of the shares.

Rates of income tax for 2017-18

An individual's taxable income is taxed according to the rates of income tax in force for the year in question. *For non-Scottish taxpayers*, the main income tax rates and thresholds for tax year 2017-18 are as follows:

First £33,500 of taxable income	20% (the "basic rate")
Next £116,500 of taxable income (up to £150,000)	40% (the "higher rate")
Remaining taxable income after the first £150,000	45% (the "additional rate")

Note that:

(a) The point at which basic rate tax gives way to higher rate tax is known as the "basic rate limit". For non-Scottish taxpayers in 2017-18, this limit is £33,500 and the first £33,500 of taxable income is referred to as the "basic rate band". Similarly, the figure of £150,000 is known as the "higher rate limit" and taxable income lying between £33,500 and £150,000 may be referred to as the "higher rate band".

(b) Savings income and dividend income are treated specially, as explained below.

(c) Calculations are made to the nearest pound when calculating taxable income. The amount of tax due on that income is calculated to the nearest penny in this book but HMRC will generally accept calculations made to the nearest pound.

Scottish taxpayers

As from tax year 2017-18, Scotland Act 2016 gives the Scottish Parliament full control over the income tax rates and thresholds which should apply to the non-savings income of Scottish taxpayers†. The term "non-savings income" refers to income which is neither savings income nor dividend income (see later in this chapter) and encompasses mainly income from employment or self-employment and income from property.

For 2017-18, the Scottish Parliament has retained the same income tax rates as in the rest of the UK but has determined that the basic rate limit for Scottish taxpayers should be £31,500 rather than £33,500. This limit applies only when calculating the income tax due on the non-savings income of a Scottish taxpayer. The higher rate limit for Scottish taxpayers is £150,000, as in the remainder of the UK.

† *Scottish taxpayers are broadly defined as those who live in Scotland. Please see the Appendix at the end of this chapter for more information.*

EXAMPLE 1

Calculate the 2017-18 income tax liability of a non-Scottish taxpayer with taxable income (i.e. income remaining after deducting any available personal allowance) of:

(a) £11,250 (b) £32,900 (c) £44,836 (d) £231,400

Assume that none of the income is derived from savings or dividends. How would these income tax liabilities differ in the case of a Scottish taxpayer?

Solution

Non-Scottish taxpayer:

(a) £11,250 @ 20% = £2,250.00.

(b) £32,900 @ 20% = £6,580.00.

(c) £33,500 @ 20% + 11,336 @ 40% = £11,234.40.

(d) £33,500 @ 20% + £116,500 @ 40% + £81,400 @ 45% = £89,930.00.

Scottish taxpayer:

(a) £11,250 @ 20% = £2,250.00.
(b) £31,500 @ 20% + £1,400 @ 40% = £6,860.00.
(c) £31,500 @ 20% + 13,336 @ 40% = £11,634.40.
(d) £31,500 @ 20% + £118,500 @ 40% + £81,400 @ 45% = £90,330.00.

Welsh taxpayers

As from tax year 2019-20, Wales Act 2014 gives the National Assembly for Wales the right to set Welsh rates of income tax. The rates of income tax which apply to the non-savings income of Welsh taxpayers† will be derived by subtracting 10p in the pound from the basic rate, higher rate and additional rate which apply in the remainder of the UK (other than Scotland) and then adding the Welsh rates set for that year for the purpose of calculating the Welsh basic rate, the Welsh higher rate and the Welsh additional rate.

† *Welsh taxpayers are broadly defined as those who live in Wales. The definition of a Welsh taxpayer is very similar in principle to the definition of a Scottish taxpayer (see the Appendix at the end of this chapter).*

Income taxed at source

Certain types of income are *taxed at source*, which means that basic rate income tax is deducted from the income before the taxpayer receives it. In tax year 2017-18, the main types of income normally received net of basic rate tax are:

(a) debenture and other loan interest† paid by UK companies
(b) interest on UK government securities ("gilt-edged" securities) if the taxpayer applies to receive this interest with tax deducted at source
(c) the income element of a purchased life annuity (as long as the annuity has not been purchased with assets held under a registered pension scheme)
(d) patent royalties.

† *Bank and building society interest is now paid gross (i.e. without deduction of tax at source).*

Income which has been taxed at source must still be included in the taxpayer's income tax computation, despite the fact that tax has already been paid. This may seem unnecessary but there are two good reasons for including such income in the tax computation:

(a) It is important to derive correct figures for the taxpayer's "total income" and "net income", as will become clearer in later chapters.
(b) The basic rate tax which has been deducted at source might be inadequate or might be excessive, depending upon the taxpayer's individual circumstances. The only way to check this is to aggregate the income concerned with all of the taxpayer's other income in a single tax computation.

In a tax computation, all income must be shown "gross". In other words, the amount of income shown must be the amount of the income *before* any income tax was deducted at source. When the tax liability has been calculated, tax paid by deduction at source is subtracted and the taxpayer is then required to pay only the balance of the liability. A tax refund is given if tax deducted at source exceeds the tax liability for the year.

If income is taxed at source, the amount received by the taxpayer is often referred to as the "net" amount of the income. This usage of the term "net" must be distinguished from the entirely different usage of the same term in the Income Tax Act 2007, which defines "net income" as being equal to a taxpayer's total income less tax reliefs.

Grossing up

If income has been received net of basic rate (20%) income tax, the gross amount of the income can be ascertained by multiplying the amount received by 100/80. This calculation is often referred to as "grossing up". When wages and salaries are received net of income tax, the gross pay and the amount of tax deducted can be ascertained by examining the end-of-year certificate supplied by the taxpayer's employer (see Chapter 7).

Savings income

The tax liability on a taxpayer's "savings income" is calculated differently from the tax liability on non-savings income. The main categories of savings income are:

(a) interest received from banks, building societies and NS&I, plus interest received on gilt-edged securities and corporate bonds (e.g. debentures and loan stocks)

(b) the income element of purchased life annuities (other than annuities from registered pension schemes, which are treated as non-savings income)

(c) certain foreign income (see Chapter 32).

But savings income does *not* include dividends received. The tax regime which applies to dividends is explained later in this chapter.

An important difference between the taxation of savings income and non-savings income is that savings income which falls into the first £5,000 (for 2017-18) of taxable income is taxed at the *starting rate for savings* of 0%, so that such income is tax-free. If a taxpayer has both savings income and non-savings income, it is necessary to split taxable income between these two categories before the tax liability can be calculated. Note that:

(a) Non-savings income is regarded as the bottom layer or "slice" of taxable income and savings income is regarded as a higher layer. This means that the basic rate band is made available to non-savings income in priority to savings income.

(b) Tax reliefs and the personal allowance are set against income in the way which gives the lowest tax liability. These deductions should be made from non-savings income in priority to savings income, as non-savings income cannot benefit from the 0% rate.

(c) The figure of £5,000 (for 2017-18) is known as the *starting rate limit for savings*. If a taxpayer's taxable income includes non-savings income of at least this amount, then the starting rate will not be available at all. Otherwise, some or all of the taxpayer's savings income (if any) will fall into the first £5,000 of the basic rate band and will be taxed at the starting rate for savings of 0%.

Personal savings allowance

ITA 2007 provides that taxpayers are entitled to a personal "savings allowance" (PSA) of up to £1,000 for tax year 2017-18. In general, this means that the first £1,000 of savings income included in taxable income is taxed at the "savings nil rate" of 0%. However, the PSA is lower than £1,000 in some cases (see below).

It is important to realise that the PSA is *not* used against any savings income which falls within the first £5,000 of taxable income and so already benefits from the starting rate for savings. The PSA is used only against savings income which falls beyond the first £5,000 of taxable income. Therefore a taxpayer with non-savings income of £nil in 2017-18 and a PSA of £1,000 will pay 0% income tax on the first £6,000 of taxable savings income. Note the following important points relating to the PSA:

(a) A taxpayer's PSA for 2017-18 is £1,000 unless:

  (i) taxable income for the year exceeds the basic rate limit (but does not exceed the higher rate limit) in which case the PSA for the year is £500

  (ii) taxable income for the year exceeds the higher rate limit, in which case the PSA for the year is £nil.

  The basic rate limit for 2017-18 is normally £33,500† (see above) and the higher rate limit is normally £150,000. However, these figures are both increased if the taxpayer makes Gift Aid donations in the year (see Chapter 4) or makes pension contributions that are "relieved at source" (see Chapter 14).

  † *In the case of Scottish taxpayers, a basic rate limit of £33,500 is used both for the purpose of determining the amount of the PSA to which the taxpayer is entitled and when calculating the amount of income tax due on savings income. This is despite the fact that a basic rate limit of only £31,500 is used when calculating the tax due on the non-savings income of a Scottish taxpayer. The intention of this rule is to ensure that the amount of income tax payable on the savings income of a Scottish taxpayer is the same as would be payable if he or she were not a Scottish taxpayer.*

(b) Although savings income falling within the PSA is effectively tax-free, the income concerned is still part of the taxpayer's taxable income for the year. This is significant when determining whether taxable income exceeds the basic rate limit or higher rate limit (see above) and may also be significant when calculating the taxpayer's entitlement to personal allowances (see Chapter 3). The same point applies to savings income which is taxed at the starting rate for savings.

EXAMPLE 2

Calculate the personal savings allowance available in 2017-18 to a taxpayer with taxable income for the year (i.e. net income less any available personal allowance) of:

(a) £20,000 (b) £33,501 (c) £63,000 (d) £375,000

Assume that there are no Gift Aid donations or pension contributions during the year.

Solution

(a) Taxable income does not exceed £33,500, therefore the PSA is £1,000.

(b) Taxable income exceeds £33,500 but does not exceed £150,000. Therefore the PSA is £500. Exceeding the basic rate limit by £1 has reduced the PSA by £500.

(c) Taxable income exceeds £33,500 but does not exceed £150,000. The PSA is £500.

(d) Taxable income exceeds £150,000, therefore the PSA is £nil.

EXAMPLE 3

In 2017-18, Robert has business profits of £39,700 and receives bank interest of £1,250. His personal allowance is £11,500. Calculate Robert's income tax liability for the year.

Solution

	Total £	*Non-savings* £	*Savings* £
Business profits	39,700	39,700	
Bank interest	1,250		1,250
Total income	40,950	39,700	1,250
Less: Personal allowance	11,500	11,500	
Taxable income	29,450	28,200	1,250

Income tax due				
Non-savings income	: Basic rate	28,200	@ 20%	5,640.00
Savings income	: Nil rate	1,000	@ 0%	0.00
	: Basic rate	250	@ 20%	50.00
		29,450		
Tax liability				5,690.00

Notes:

(i) Taxable income includes non-savings income of more than £5,000. Therefore the starting rate for savings is not available.

(ii) Taxable income does not exceed £33,500, so the PSA is £1,000. Savings income of £1,000 is taxed at the savings nil rate. The remaining £250 is taxed at basic rate.

EXAMPLE 4

In 2017-18, Roberta has rental income of £15,700 and receives building society interest of £1,100. Her personal allowance is £11,500. Calculate the income tax liability for the year.

Solution

	Total	*Non-savings*	*Savings*
	£	£	£
Income from property	15,700	15,700	
Building society interest	1,100		1,100
Total income	16,800	15,700	1,100
Less: Personal allowance	11,500	11,500	
Taxable income	5,300	4,200	1,100

Income tax due				
Non-savings income	: Basic rate	4,200	@ 20%	840.00
Savings income	: Starting rate	800	@ 0%	0.00
	: Nil rate	300	@ 0%	0.00
		5,300		
Tax liability				840.00

Notes:

(i) The non-savings income occupies £4,200 of the basic rate band. This allows £800 (£5,000 – £4,200) of the savings income to be taxed at the starting rate of 0%.

(ii) Taxable income does not exceed £33,500, so the PSA is £1,000.

(iii) The remaining £300 of savings income (£1,100 – £800) does not exceed £1,000, so this is taxed at the savings nil rate.

EXAMPLE 5

In 2017-18, Kenneth (who is not a Scottish taxpayer) has business profits of £44,200 and bank interest of £980. His personal allowance for the year is £11,500. He makes no Gift Aid donations or pension contributions during 2017-18. Calculate Kenneth's income tax liability for the year. Also explain how this liability would differ for a Scottish taxpayer.

Solution

	Total	*Non-savings*	*Savings*
	£	£	£
Business profits	44,200	44,200	
Bank interest	980		980
Total income	45,180	44,200	980
Less: Personal allowance	11,500	11,500	
Taxable income	33,680	32,700	980

Income tax due				
Non-savings income	: Basic rate	32,700	@ 20%	6,540.00
Savings income	: Nil rate	500	@ 0%	0.00
	: Basic rate	300	@ 20%	60.00
	: Higher rate	180	@ 40%	72.00
		33,680		
Tax liability				6,672.00

Notes:

(i) Taxable income includes non-savings income of more than £5,000. Therefore the starting rate for savings is not available.

(ii) Taxable income exceeds £33,500 so the PSA is £500 and the first £500 of savings income is taxed at the savings nil rate.

(iii) There is now £300 (£33,500 – £32,700 – £500) of the basic rate band remaining so the next £300 of the savings income is taxed at basic rate and the remaining £180 is taxed at the higher rate..

Scottish taxpayers

If Kenneth were a Scottish taxpayer, the computation would differ in only one respect. The taxable non-savings income of £32,700 exceeds the Scottish basic rate band of £31,500 by £1,200, so tax due on the non-savings income would be calculated as (£31,500 × 20%) + (£1,200 × 40%). This would increase the total tax liability by £240 to £6,912.

It is important to appreciate that none of this has any effect on the amount of tax due on the savings income. The PSA is still determined by comparing total taxable income with £33,500 (not £31,500). And the amount of the basic rate band remaining for the savings income is also determined by reference to a basic rate band of £33,500 (not £31,500).

EXAMPLE 6

In 2017-18, Philip (who is not a Scottish taxpayer) has business profits of £240,235 and receives building society interest of £1,600. His personal allowance for the year is zero. He makes no Gift Aid donations or pension contributions during 2017-18. Calculate his income tax liability for the year.

Solution

	Total	*Non-savings*	*Savings*
	£	£	£
Business profits	240,235	240,235	
Building society interest	1,600		1,600
Total income	241,835	240,235	1,600
Less: Personal allowance	0	0	
Taxable income	241,835	240,235	1,600

Income tax due

Non-savings income	: Basic rate	33,500	@ 20%	6,700.00
	: Higher rate	116,500	@ 40%	46,600.00
	: Additional rate	90,235	@ 45%	40,605.75
Savings income	: Additional rate	1,600	@ 45%	720.00
		241,835		
Tax liability				94,625.75

Notes:

(i) Non-savings income occupies the whole of the basic band so the starting rate for savings is not available.

(ii) Taxable income exceeds the higher rate limit so the PSA is £nil.

(iii) The whole of the bank interest is taxed at the additional rate of 45%.

(iv) In the case of a Scottish taxpayer, an extra £2,000 (£33,500 - £31,500) of the non-savings income would be taxed at 40% rather than 20%. This would increase the tax liability by £400 to £95,025.75.

EXAMPLE 7

In 2017-18, Philippa has business profits of £8,000. She also receives bank interest of £380 and net loan interest of £36,680. Her personal allowance is £11,500 and she makes no Gift Aid donations or pension contributions during 2017-18.

Calculate the income tax payable by Philippa for the year. Does it matter whether or not she is a Scottish taxpayer?

Solution

	Total	*Non-savings*	*Savings*
	£	£	£
Business profits	8,000	8,000	
Bank interest	380		380
Loan interest £36,680 x 100/80	45,850		45,850
Total income	54,230	8,000	46,230
Less: Personal allowance	11,500	8,000	3,500
Taxable income	42,730	nil	42,730

Income tax due				
Savings income	: Starting rate	5,000	@ 0%	0.00
	: Nil rate	500	@ 0%	0.00
	: Basic rate	28,000	@ 20%	5,600.00
	: Higher rate	9,230	@ 40%	3,692.00
		42,730		
Tax liability				9,292.00
Less: Tax deducted at source (£45,850 – £36,680)				9,170.00
Tax payable				122.00

Notes:

(i) Taxable income does not include any non-savings income. Therefore the first £5,000 of savings income is taxed at the starting rate.

(ii) Taxable income exceeds the basic rate limit (but not the higher rate limit) so the PSA is £500 and the next £500 of savings income is taxed at the savings nil rate.

(iii) The next £28,000 (£33,500 – £5,500) of the savings income is taxed at the basic rate and the remaining £9,230 is taxed at the higher rate.

(iv) Taxable income does not include any non-savings income. So the computation is the same, whether or not Philippa is a Scottish taxpayer.

Dividend income

The income tax liability on a taxpayer's dividend income is calculated differently from the liability on non-savings income or savings income. The main points are as follows:

(a) Dividends are treated as the top slice of taxable income, ranking above both non-savings and savings income.

(b) Dividends which fall into the basic rate band† are generally taxed at the "dividend ordinary rate" of 7.5%. Dividends which fall into the higher rate band are generally taxed at the "dividend upper rate" of 32.5%. Any dividends which lie above the higher rate limit are generally taxed at the "dividend additional rate" of 38.1%.

(c) However, taxpayers are entitled to a tax-free "dividend allowance" of £5,000‡ for the year, which means that the first £5,000 of dividends included in taxable income are taxed at the "dividend nil rate" of 0%. Unlike the personal savings allowance (see above) which is reduced for higher-rate and additional-rate taxpayers, the dividend allowance is £5,000 in all cases.

(d) As stated earlier in this chapter, tax reliefs and the personal allowance are set against income in the way which gives the lowest income tax liability. In most cases, these deductions should be made against non-savings income in priority to savings income and against savings income in priority to dividends.

(e) Although dividend income falling within the £5,000 dividend allowance is tax-free, the income concerned is still part of the taxpayer's taxable income for the year. This may be significant when determining whether a taxpayer's taxable income exceeds the basic rate limit or higher rate limit (which affects entitlement to the PSA) and when calculating the taxpayer's entitlement to personal allowances (see Chapter 3).

† *In the case of Scottish taxpayers, a basic rate limit of £33,500 (not £31,500) is applied when calculating the amount of income tax due on dividend income in 2017-18. This ensures that the amount of income tax payable on the dividend income of a Scottish taxpayer is the same as would be payable if he or she were not a Scottish taxpayer.*

‡ *The Government has proposed that the dividend allowance should be reduced to £2,000 as from tax year 2018-19.*

Dividends from UK-REITs

A UK company which is a property investment company may elect to become a UK Real Estate Investment Trust (UK-REIT). Dividends received from a UK-REIT, to the extent that they derive from the company's tax-exempt property income or gains, are subject to a different tax regime than the one which is described above. Such dividends are received net of basic rate (20%) income tax and are treated as property income (see Chapter 5).

The examples and exercises in this book all assume that any dividends received are received from companies other than UK-REITs. A fuller description of the tax regime which relates to UK-REITs is given in Chapter 23.

EXAMPLE 8

In tax year 2017-18, Christopher has rental income of £24,590. He also receives bank interest of £1,050 and dividends of £204,100. His personal allowance for the year is zero and he makes no Gift Aid donations or pension contributions during 2017-18. Calculate his income tax liability for the year.

Solution

	Total	*Non-savings*	*Savings*	*Dividends*
	£	£	£	£
Income from property	24,590	24,590		
Bank interest	1,050		1,050	
Dividends	204,100			204,100
Total income	229,740	24,590	1,050	204,100
Less: Personal allowance	0	0		
Taxable income	229,740	24,590	1,050	204,100

Income tax due				
Non-savings income	: Basic rate	24,590	@ 20%	4,918.00
Savings income	: Basic rate	1,050	@ 20%	210.00
Dividend income	: Nil rate	5,000	@ 0%	0.00
	: Ordinary rate	2,860	@ 7.5%	214.50
	: Upper rate	116,500	@ 32.5%	37,862.50
	: Additional rate	79,740	@ 38.1%	30,380.94
		229,740		
Tax liability				73,585.94

Notes:

(i) Taxable income includes non-savings income of more than £5,000. Therefore the starting rate for savings is not available.

(ii) Taxable income exceeds the higher rate limit so the PSA is £nil. The whole of the bank interest is taxed at the basic rate of 20%.

(iii) The first £5,000 of the dividends is taxed at the nil rate. There is now £2,860 of the basic rate band remaining (£33,500 – £24,590 – £1,050 – £5,000) and therefore the next £2,860 of the dividends is taxed at the dividend ordinary rate of 7.5%.

(iv) Dividends of £116,500 which fall into the higher rate band are taxed at the dividend upper rate of 32.5% and the final £79,740 of the dividends is taxed at the dividend additional rate of 38.1%.

(v) Taxable income does not include more than £31,500 of non-savings income. So the computation is the same, whether or not Christopher is a Scottish taxpayer.

EXAMPLE 9

In 2017-18, Charlie's income consists of a pension of £16,750, bank interest of £195 and dividends of £4,600. His personal allowance is £11,500. Calculate his income tax liability for the year.

Solution

	Total	*Non-savings*	*Savings*	*Dividends*
	£	£	£	£
Pension	16,750	16,750		
Bank interest	195		195	
Dividends	4,600			4,600
Total income	21,545	16,750	195	4,600
Less: Personal allowance	11,500	11,500		
Taxable income	10,045	5,250	195	4,600

Income tax due				
Non-savings income	: Basic rate	5,250	@ 20%	1,050.00
Savings income	: Nil rate	195	@ 0%	0.00
Dividend income	: Nil rate	4,600	@ 0%	0.00
		10,045		
Tax liability				1,050.00

Notes:

(i) Taxable income includes non-savings income of more than £5,000. Therefore the starting rate for savings is not available. However, taxable income does not exceed the basic rate limit so the PSA is £1,000. Since savings income is only £195, this is all taxed at the savings nil rate of 0%.

(ii) The dividends of £4,600 fall within the dividend allowance of £5,000 and are all taxed at the dividend nil rate of 0%.

(iii) The computation is the same, whether or not Charlie is a Scottish taxpayer.

EXAMPLE 10

In 2017-18, Sue receives bank interest of £6,000 and dividends of £12,500. She has no non-savings income.

(a) Calculate Sue's income tax liability assuming that her personal allowance of £11,500 is set first against the savings income.

(b) Now re-calculate the liability assuming that the personal allowance is set first against the dividend income.

Solution

(a) If the personal allowance is set first against savings income, taxable income will consist solely of dividends of £7,000. The income tax liability will be (£5,000 × 0%) + (£2,000 × 7.5%) = £150.

(b) If the personal allowance is set first against the dividends, taxable income will consist of savings income of £6,000 and dividends of £1,000.The first £5,000 of the savings income qualifies for the starting rate for savings and the remaining £1,000 is covered by the PSA. So there is no tax to pay on the savings income. Since the dividends do not exceed the dividend allowance of £5,000, there is no tax to pay on the dividends either. Therefore Sue's total tax liability for the year will be £nil.

In general (as stated above) tax reliefs and the personal allowance should normally be set against savings income in priority to dividend income. However, in this case, setting the personal allowance first against the savings income means that the opportunity to benefit from the starting rate for savings is lost. Setting the personal allowance first against the dividend income (which the law allows) results in a tax saving of £150.

Summary

- In general, income tax is chargeable on all of the income of UK residents and on the UK income of non-residents.
- Income is classified into a number of categories, each of which has its own rules for determining the amount of assessable income in a tax year. However, certain types of income are specifically exempt from income tax.
- To calculate a taxpayer's income tax liability it is necessary to bring together all of the taxpayer's income into a single computation. The gross equivalent of any income received net of income tax must be included in the computation.
- Husbands, wives and civil partners are assessed to income tax independently.
- In 2017-18, the main rates of income tax are the basic rate of 20%, the higher rate of 40% and the additional rate of 45%. Savings income which occupies the first £5,000 of the basic rate band is taxed at the starting rate for savings of 0%.
- In 2017-18, basic rate taxpayers are entitled to a personal savings allowance (PSA) of £1,000. The PSA is £500 for higher rate taxpayers and £nil for additional rate tax-payers. Savings income falling within the PSA is taxed at the savings nil rate.
- In 2017-18, the first £5,000 of dividends included in taxable income are taxed at the dividend nil rate. Dividends after the first £5,000 are taxed at 7.5% in the basic rate band, 32.5% in the higher rate band and 38.1% otherwise.
- *For Scottish taxpayers*, the basic rate limit used when calculating the tax due on non-savings income in 2017-18 is £2,000 lower than elsewhere in the UK.

Appendix

Definition of a Scottish taxpayer

In general terms, a Scottish taxpayer is an individual who lives in Scotland. Whether the individual identifies as Scottish is irrelevant. Nor does it matter whether the individual works in Scotland. This means that employers elsewhere in the UK must apply Scottish rates of income tax to any of their employees who live in Scotland (see Chapter 7).

It will usually be obvious whether or not an individual is a Scottish taxpayer. But it may be necessary to apply a number of tests in more complex cases. An individual is treated as a Scottish taxpayer for a tax year if he or she is UK resident in that year (see Chapter 32) and satisfies any of the following criteria:

(a) the individual has a "close connection" with Scotland, usually through having only a single UK place of residence (which is in Scotland) and living there for at least part of the tax year in question, or

(b) the individual does not have a close connection with any other part of the UK and spends more days of the tax year in Scotland than in any other part of the UK, or

(c) the individual is a Scottish Parliamentarian (e.g. an MP for a Scottish constituency or a member of the Scottish Parliament).

Note that the status of the individual has to be determined for whole tax years and it is not possible to be a Scottish taxpayer for only part of a tax year. Furthermore, it is quite feasible that an individual could be a Scottish taxpayer in one tax year but not in the next tax year (e.g. by moving away from Scotland).

Exercises

It should be assumed in all of these exercises that the taxpayer makes no Gift Aid donations or pension contributions during tax year 2017-18.

2.1 Calculate the income tax liability for 2017-18 of a non-Scottish taxpayer with a taxable income (after deducting any available personal allowance) of:

(a) £1,830 (b) £32,300 (c) £67,833 (d) £320,000.

Assume that none of the income is derived from savings or dividends. How would these liabilities differ in the case of a Scottish taxpayer?

2.2 Calculate the 2017-18 income tax liability of a non-Scottish taxpayer with income for the year as follows:

(a) Business profits of £27,105 and bank interest of £720.

(b) Business profits £44,150, building society interest £930 and bank interest £570.

(c) Net loan interest of £130,604.

Assume a personal allowance of £11,500 in cases (a) and (b) and £nil in case (c). How would these liabilities differ in the case of Scottish taxpayers?

2.3 Stephanie (who is not a Scottish taxpayer) has the following income in 2017-18:

	£
Income from self-employment	28,880
Rents received	15,730
Bank interest	200
Dividends	250

Compute Stephanie's income tax liability for the year, assuming that the rents received are not within the "rent-a-room" scheme and that Stephanie is entitled to the personal allowance of £11,500.

2.4 Ernest (who is not a Scottish taxpayer) has a retirement pension in 2017-18 of £51,890 and bank interest of £620. His personal allowance for the year is £11,500. Compute Ernest's income tax liability for the year. What difference would it make if Ernest had received dividends of £620 instead of the bank interest?

***2.5** Ivan's income for the tax year 2017-18 is as follows:

	£
Part-time salary	15,985
Net interest on gilt-edged securities	1,360
Premium bond prize	50
Dividends	18,560

His personal allowance for 2017-18 is £11,500. Compute the income tax payable by Ivan for the year.

***2.6** Mary's income for tax year 2017-18 consists of business profits of £26,920, dividends received of £124,460 and rents received of £3,750. Her personal allowance for the year is £nil. Calculate Mary's income tax liability for 2017-18, assuming that the rents received are not within the "rent-a-room" scheme.

Chapter 3
Personal allowances

Introduction

One of the factors which must be taken into account when preparing an income tax computation is the taxpayer's entitlement to *personal allowances*. Most taxpayers can claim only the basic personal allowance but there are extra allowances for blind taxpayers and for older married couples. The purpose of this chapter is to describe the allowances that are available in 2017-18 and to explain the way in which each allowance is dealt with in an income tax computation.

It is important to appreciate that personal allowances are indeed "personal". If all or part of a personal allowance cannot be used by the person to whom it is available, then any unused part of the allowance is generally lost. Excess allowances cannot normally be transferred to anyone else and cannot be carried back to previous years or forward to future years. However, some limited provisions exist for transferring allowances between spouses or civil partners (see later in this chapter).

Personal allowances for 2017-18

The personal allowances for tax year 2017-18 are as follows:

	£
Allowances which are deducted from income	
Personal allowance	11,500
Blind person's allowance	2,320
Allowances which are "tax reducers"	
Married couple's allowance:	
Born before 6 April 1935	8,445
Minimum amount	3,260
Marriage allowance	1,150
Income limit for basic personal allowance	100,000
Income limit for married couple's allowance	28,000

The circumstances in which each of these allowances may be claimed (and the way in which each allowance is given effect in an income tax computation) are explained below.

Personal allowances may be claimed by UK residents and by certain non-residents. The main classes of non-resident who may claim personal allowances and set these allowances against their UK income are:

(a) nationals of the European Economic Area (EEA), which comprises all EU states plus Norway, Iceland and Liechtenstein
(b) residents in the Isle of Man or the Channel Islands
(c) persons who used to reside in the UK but now reside abroad for health reasons
(d) Crown servants, ex-Crown servants (and their widows/widowers)
(e) missionaries.

The personal allowance (PA)

Anyone who is entitled to claim personal allowances may claim at least the basic personal allowance. This allowance is deducted from the taxpayer's income when computing his or her income tax liability. The basic personal allowance for 2017-18 is £11,500 but this is reduced (possibly to zero) if the taxpayer has income exceeding £100,000 (see below).

The personal allowance is fully available in the tax year in which a taxpayer is born or dies, apart from being reduced as usual if income for that year exceeds £100,000.

Reduction in the basic personal allowance

The amount of the basic personal allowance for a tax year is reduced if the taxpayer's "adjusted net income" for the year exceeds £100,000. Adjusted net income is defined as the taxpayer's net income less the grossed-up amount of any Gift Aid donations made during the year (see Chapter 4) and the gross amount of any pension contributions relieved at source during the year (see Chapter 14).

If adjusted net income exceeds £100,000, the basic personal allowance is reduced by one-half of the excess. Therefore the allowance is reduced to zero in 2017-18 if adjusted net income is £123,000 (£100,000 + (2 × £11,500)) or more.

It is worth noting that the gradual withdrawal of the personal allowance means that a taxpayer with income in the range £100,000 to £123,000 can be subject to a marginal rate of income tax of 60%. This surprising result is illustrated in the following example.

EXAMPLE 1

Ben (who is not a Scottish taxpayer) has business profits of £110,520 in 2017-18. He has no other income and makes no Gift Aid donations or pension contributions. Calculate the amount of his 2017-18 personal allowance and show that a £100 increase in his profits would result in a £60 increase in his income tax liability for the year.

Solution

(i) Ben's adjusted net income is £110,520. This exceeds £100,000 by £10,520. So the personal allowance for the year is £6,240 (£11,500 – 1/2 x £10,520).

(ii) If profits increased by £100, adjusted net income would exceed £100,000 by £10,620 and the personal allowance would be £6,190 (£11,500 – 1/2 x £10,620).

(iii) The income tax computations are as follows:

	Profits £110,520	*Profits £110,620*
	£	£
Business profits	110,520	110,620
Less: Personal allowance	6,240	6,190
Taxable income	104,280	104,430
Income tax due		
£33,500 @ 20%	6,700.00	6,700.00
£70,780 @ 40%	28,312.00	
£70,930 @ 40%		28,372.00
Tax liability	35,012.00	35,072.00

Note:

A £100 increase in profits causes a £50 reduction in the personal allowance. So taxable income increases by £150 and the income tax liability rises by (£35,072.00 – £35,012.00) = £60, which is 60% of the £100 increase in income.

Marriage allowance

Subject to certain conditions, an individual may elect to transfer part of his or her personal allowance to a spouse or to a civil partner. The "transferable amount" is 10% of the basic personal allowance for the year (i.e. £1,150 in 2017-18). HMRC refers to this transferable amount as the "marriage allowance", although this term is not used in the legislation. The main conditions which must be satisfied are as follows:

(a) The transferor is entitled to the basic personal allowance for the year.

(b) The transferor's taxable income for the year does not exceed the basic rate limit and this will remain the case after the transfer is made. Similarly, the taxable income of the spouse or civil partner must also not exceed the basic rate limit.

As explained in Chapter 2, the basic rate limit for 2017-18 is normally £33,500†, but this figure is increased if the taxpayer makes Gift Aid donations (see Chapter 4) or makes pension contributions that are relieved at source (see Chapter 14).

(c) Neither the transferor nor the spouse or civil partner claims the married couple's allowance (MCA) for the year (see below).

† *For Scottish taxpayers, the basic rate limit used for this purpose is the basic rate limit applicable to non-savings income (£31,500 for 2017-18).*

A marriage allowance election must be made within four years of the end of the tax year to which it relates. If such an election is made, the personal allowance of the transferor is reduced by the transferable amount but the personal allowance of the spouse or partner is *not* increased. Instead, the income tax liability of the spouse or civil partner is reduced by the transferable amount multiplied by the basic rate of income tax (20% in 2017-18). In other words, the marriage allowance acts as a "tax reducer" (see below).

It is important to note that the marriage allowance is *not* an extra allowance. It is merely an opportunity to transfer part of the personal allowance to a spouse or civil partner. This may be of benefit to taxpayers with a low income who cannot use the whole of their personal allowance. It is also important not to confuse the marriage allowance with the married couple's allowance (MCA) which is available to older couples (see below).

EXAMPLE 2

A husband and wife both claim the basic personal allowance in 2017-18. The husband's total income for tax purposes is £10,400 and the wife's income is £30,000. None of their income is derived from savings or dividends. Calculate the combined tax liability of the couple for the year if:

(a) no election is made to transfer part of the personal allowance

(b) the husband elects to transfer part of his personal allowance to his wife.

Solution

(a) The husband's income is exceeded by his PA of £11,500 so his tax liability is £nil. His wife's tax liability is (£30,000 – £11,500) × 20% = £3,700.

(b)

	Husband	*Wife*
	£	£
Total income	10,400	30,000
Less: PA (Husband £11,500 – £1,150)	10,350	11,500
Taxable income	50	18,500
Income tax at 20%	10.00	3,700.00
Less: Marriage allowance £1,150 @ 20%		230.00
Tax liability	10.00	3,470.00

Note:

The combined tax liability of the couple is £3,480, a saving of £220.

Blind person's allowance (BPA)

The blind person's allowance (£2,320 in 2017-18) may be claimed by registered blind persons. This allowance is deducted from income and is given in full in the tax year in which the taxpayer is first registered as a blind person.

Any unused part of the BPA can be transferred to the taxpayer's spouse or civil partner, even if that spouse or partner is not a registered blind person.

Tax reducers

The personal allowance and the blind person's allowance are deducted from income when calculating taxable income. By contrast, the "marriage allowance" (see above) acts as a "tax reducer". The transferred allowance is ignored until the amount of tax due on the spouse or civil partner's income has been calculated but then this liability is reduced by 20% of the transferred amount. Similarly, the married couple's allowance (the only other allowance available in 2017-18) is a tax reducer. If MCA is claimed, the taxpayer's income tax liability is reduced by *10% of the amount of the allowance*. Note that:

(a) Certain payments and some types of investments made by a taxpayer also act as tax reducers (see Chapters 4 and 6).

(b) The amount of tax borne can never be reduced to less than zero as a result of the tax reduction process. If available tax reductions exceed the tax due on taxable income, there is no repayment of the excess. Any unused part of a tax reduction is generally lost. However, the tax reduction relating to the MCA may be transferred between spouses or civil partners in certain cases (see below).

Married couple's allowance (MCA)

The married couple's allowance is available to a legally married couple who live together for at least part of the tax year, *so long as at least one of the spouses was born before 6 April 1935*. MCA is also available to civil partners, so long as at least one of the partners was born before 6 April 1935. Note the following points:

(a) MCA is not available to a couple who are separated for the whole of the tax year.

(b) The amount of the MCA for 2017-18 is £8,445, giving a maximum tax reduction of £844.50 (£8,445 @ 10%).

(c) For couples who were married before 5 December 2005, MCA is generally claimed by the husband. However, the couple may elect that the MCA should instead be claimed by the spouse with the higher net income. Such an election must be made before the start of the first tax year in which it is to have effect and then applies to all subsequent tax years. The election is irrevocable.

(d) For couples who marry on or after 5 December 2005 (and for civil partners) the MCA is claimed by the spouse or partner with the higher net income.

(e) The MCA is reduced if the *claimant's* adjusted net income exceeds a specified limit (£28,000 in 2017-18). If adjusted net income exceeds this limit, the MCA is reduced by one-half of the excess. But the MCA is never reduced to less than a specified minimum amount (£3,260 in 2017-18).

It is noteworthy that the other spouse's (or other partner's) income is not taken into account for this purpose, even if the MCA is available because of that spouse's or partner's age rather than because of the claimant's age.

EXAMPLE 3

Calculate the MCA available for 2017-18 in the following situations:

	Husband	*Wife*
(a)	Born 5 July 1938, income £19,100	Born 1 March 1935, income £12,450.
(b)	Born 3 May 1933, income £28,110	Born 7 September 1938, income £nil.
(c)	Born 4 June 1934, income £39,480	Born 8 October 1939, income £13,950.
(d)	Born 16 November 1939, income £nil	Born 9 July 1934, income £49,300.

In each case, MCA is claimed and the stated income figure is the adjusted net income. All of the couples were married before 5 December 2005 and none of them have elected that MCA should be claimed by the spouse with the higher net income.

Solution

(a) The husband is entitled to an MCA of £8,445 because his wife was born before 6 April 1935. The MCA is available in full because his income does not exceed the £28,000 limit.

(b) The husband is entitled to the MCA because he was born before 6 April 1935. But his income exceeds £28,000 by £110, so the MCA is reduced by £55 (1/2 × £110) to £8,390 (£8,445 – £55).

(c) The husband is entitled to the MCA because he was born before 6 April 1935. His income exceeds £28,000 by £11,480. A reduction of £5,740 (1/2 × £11,480) would give an MCA of only £2,705 (£8,445 – £5,740) but the MCA is never reduced to less than the minimum amount of £3,260. Therefore an MCA of £3,260 is available.

(d) The husband is entitled to an MCA of £8,445 because his wife was born before 6 April 1935. His income does not exceed the £28,000 limit so the MCA is available in full. Because the husband is the claimant, his wife's income is not taken into account at all when calculating the MCA, even though (in this case) the MCA is available only by virtue of her age (not his).

Allocation of the MCA

The tax reduction relating to the MCA is normally set against the tax liability of the *claimant*, but note that:

(a) The couple may elect jointly that the tax reduction relating to the MCA minimum amount (£3,260 for 2017-18) should be set against the tax liability of the claimant's spouse or civil partner.

(b) The claimant's spouse or civil partner may elect unilaterally that the tax reduction relating to 50% of the MCA minimum amount (£1,630 for 2017-18) should be set against his or her tax liability.

(c) If either spouse or partner is unable to use their MCA-related tax reduction in full or in part, the unused part may be transferred to the other spouse or partner.

The elections described in (a) and (b) must normally be made before the start of the tax year to which they relate, but they can be made during the tax year if this is the year of marriage or the year in which a civil partnership is registered. If either of these elections is made, any remaining part of the MCA is dealt with in the claimant's tax computation.

The transfer described in (c) must be claimed within four years of the end of the tax year to which it relates.

Year of marriage and year of separation or death

In the tax year in which a marriage occurs or a civil partnership is registered, MCA is calculated as usual but is then reduced by 1/12th for each full tax month which elapses between the start of the year and the date of the marriage or registration. A tax month runs from the 6th of one month to the 5th of the next month. An election to transfer all or 50% of the MCA minimum amount to the claimant's spouse or partner in the year of marriage or registration applies to that amount reduced in the same proportion as the MCA itself.

MCA is available in full in the tax year in which a couple separate or in which one of them dies (subject to the usual restriction if the claimant's income exceeds the limit).

EXAMPLE 4

Calculate the MCA available in 2017-18 to a husband and wife (both born in August 1934) who each have an adjusted net income not exceeding £28,000 and who marry on:

(a) 23 June 2017 (b) 4 April 2018

Solution

(a) Two full tax months have passed since the start of the tax year (6 April 2017 to 5 May 2017 and 6 May 2017 to 5 June 2017). So the MCA is £8,445 x 10/12 = £7,038.

(b) The MCA is £8,445 x 1/12 = £704.

EXAMPLE 5

Calculate the income tax liability for 2017-18 of a husband and wife (both born in March 1935) given the information shown below. In each case, an election has been made for 50% of the tax reduction relating to the MCA minimum amount to be set against the tax of the claimant's spouse. None of the income is derived from savings or dividends.

(a) Married July 1960; husband's income £28,060, wife's income £22,250.

(b) Married 1 October 2017; husband's income £20,625, wife's income £16,695.

(c) Married July 1960 but husband dies on 12 October 2017; husband's income £13,085, wife's income £23,255. The couple have not elected that MCA should be claimed by the spouse with the higher net income.

In each case, the stated income figure is the taxpayer's net income (i.e. total income less tax reliefs) and adjusted net income is the same as net income.

Solution

	(a)	(b)	(c)
	£	£	£
HUSBAND			
Net income	28,060	20,625	13,085
Less: Personal allowance	11,500	11,500	11,500
Taxable income	16,560	9,125	1,585
Income tax due @ 20%	3,312.00	1,825.00	317.00
Less: MCA £6,785 @ 10%	678.50		
MCA £3,975 @ 10%		397.50	
MCA £6,815 @ 10% = £681.50			317.00
Tax liability	2,633.50	1,427.50	nil
WIFE			
Net income	22,250	16,695	23,255
Less: Personal allowance	11,500	11,500	11,500
Taxable income	10,750	5,195	11,755
Income tax due @ 20%	2,150.00	1,039.00	2,351.00
Less: MCA £1,630 @ 10%	163.00		
MCA £951 @ 10%		95.10	
MCA £1,630 @ 10% + £364.50			527.50
Tax liability	1,987.00	943.90	1,823.50

Notes:

(i) In case (a), the husband's income is £60 over the income limit, so the MCA is reduced to £8,415 (£8,445 – 1/2 x £60). MCA of £1,630 (one-half of the minimum amount) is claimed by the wife, leaving £6,785 for the husband.

(ii) In case (b), the available MCA is 7/12 x £8,445 = £4,926. The wife claims 7/12 x £1,630 = £951, leaving £3,975 for the husband.

(iii) In case (c), the MCA is available in full in the year of the husband's death. £1,630 is claimed by the wife, leaving £6,815 for the husband. The tax reduction that he cannot use (£364.50) is transferred to his wife.

Summary

- All UK residents and certain non-resident taxpayers are entitled to claim at least the basic personal allowance. But this allowance is reduced if the taxpayer's adjusted net income for the year exceeds £100,000. The amount of this reduction is equal to one-half of the excess and the personal allowance can be reduced to zero.
- An individual may transfer 10% of the basic personal allowance to a spouse or civil partner as long as neither party has taxable income which exceeds the basic rate limit. The tax liability of the transferee is reduced by 20% of the amount transferred.
- The blind person's allowance is granted to registered blind persons. Any unused part of this allowance can be transferred to the person's spouse or civil partner.
- The married couple's allowance is available to a legally married couple who live together for at least part of the tax year, so long as at least one of the spouses was born before 6 April 1935. MCA is also available to civil partners.
- MCA is reduced if the claimant's adjusted net income exceeds a specified limit. But the MCA is never reduced to less than a specified minimum amount.
- In certain circumstances, all or part of the MCA may be transferred to the claimant's spouse or partner if an appropriate claim or election is made.
- The personal allowance and the blind person's allowance are deducted from the taxpayer's net income when computing taxable income. The MCA reduces tax borne by 10% of the amount of the allowance.
- Personal allowances which cannot be used in the tax year to which they relate are lost. There is no provision for carrying unused allowances backwards or forwards.

Exercises

It should be assumed in all of these exercises that the taxpayers concerned make no Gift Aid donations or pension contributions during tax year 2017-18.

3.1 Calculate the basic personal allowance available in 2017-18 to a taxpayer with adjusted net income of:

(a) £90,000 (b) £108,000 (c) £130,000.

3.2 Pamela's salary in 2017-18 is £105,000. She has no other income for the year and she is not a Scottish taxpayer.

(a) Calculate her income tax liability for 2017-18.

(b) Re-calculate her income tax liability as it would have been if her salary for the year had been £20,000 higher.

(c) Explain how the difference between these two tax liabilities arises.

3.3 Calculate the married couple's allowance available to the following couples in 2017-18, assuming that they were married before 5 December 2005 and that they have not elected for MCA to be claimed by the spouse with the higher net income:

(a) Husband born 1931, income £19,200; wife born 1932, income £29,500

(b) Husband born 1929, income £28,040; wife born 1934, income £10,070

(c) Husband born 1934, income £34,400; wife born 1939, income £20,000

(d) Husband born 1936, income £17,900; wife born 1933, income £46,700.

In each case, the stated income figure is the adjusted net income.

3.4 Calculate the tax liability for 2017-18 of a husband and wife (both born in 1933), given the information shown below. No elections have been made in relation to the married couple's allowance and none of the income is derived from savings or dividends.

(a) Married in 1956; husband's income £18,140, wife's income £19,440

(b) Married 17 August 2017; husband's income £9,500, wife's income £15,375

(c) Married in 1956 but husband dies on 16 September 2017; husband's income to date of death £11,835, wife's income for the year £19,305.

In each case, the stated income figure is the taxpayer's net income (i.e. total income less tax reliefs), MCA is claimed and adjusted net income is the same as net income.

3.5 Toby is a widower. He was born in August 1932. His wife was born in June 1933 but she died in March 2017. Toby's income for 2017-18 is as follows:

	£
Retirement pension	10,480
Income from purchased life annuity (net)	912

Calculate the amount of income tax repayable to Toby for 2017-18.

3.6 Brian and Danny are civil partners. They were both born in 1974 and they both claim the basic personal allowance for 2017-18. Brian's total income for 2017-18 is £25,000 and Danny's total income for the year is £4,000. None of their income is derived from savings or dividends.

(a) Calculate their income tax liabilities if Danny does not make an election to transfer part of his personal allowance to Brian.

(b) Calculate their income tax liabilities if Danny does make the election.

(c) How would the situation change if Brian's total income were £50,000?

3.7 Richard was born on 5 April 1935. His wife, Patricia, was born on 5 October 1938. They were married in 1968. Their income for 2017-18 is as follows:

	£
Richard:	
Business profits	32,560
Patricia:	
Dividends received	3,600

Calculate their income tax liabilities for 2017-18.

***3.8** A married man (born 3 November 1934) died on 8 July 2017. He received a retirement pension of £12,730 between 6 April 2017 and the date of his death. His wife (born 12 August 1940) had no income whilst her husband was alive but received a pension of £18,685 between 8 July 2017 and 5 April 2018. They were married in 1970 and made no elections in relation to the married couple's allowance.

Calculate their income tax liabilities in 2017-18.

***3.9** Bill was born in 1978. He is married to Hazel who was born in 1982. Neither of them is a Scottish taxpayer. In 2017-18, Bill had business profits of £47,550 and received dividends of £5,200. Hazel received a salary of £220,570 and bank interest of £3,040.

Calculate their income tax liabilities for the year.

Chapter 4

Payments and gifts eligible for tax relief

Introduction

Certain payments and gifts made by a taxpayer are eligible for tax relief. Some of these are subtracted from the taxpayer's total income when computing his or her tax liability. Others act as tax reducers and are relieved by reducing the amount of tax payable on the taxpayer's taxable income. A special tax regime applies to charitable donations which fall within the "Gift Aid" scheme.

The purpose of this chapter is to identify the main types of payments and gifts which attract tax relief in these ways and to explain how relief is given for each. However, this chapter does *not* deal with:

(a) payments and gifts which are deductible when computing a taxpayer's income from either employment (see Chapter 7) or self-employment (see Chapter 9)

(b) pension contributions (see Chapter 14).

Payments and gifts deductible from total income

The following payments and gifts are deductible from a taxpayer's total income for the tax year in which the payment or gift is made:

(a) eligible interest payments

(b) certain "annual payments"

(c) gifts of listed shares or securities to a charity

(d) gifts of land or buildings to a charity.

Each of these is explained later in this chapter. As indicated in Chapter 2, the income which remains after these items (and certain other reliefs) have been subtracted from total income is referred to by Income Tax Act 2007 as the taxpayer's "net income".

Tax relief for these payments and gifts is given at "marginal rate" (i.e. at the highest rates of income tax to which the taxpayer is liable). Deducting them from total income will automatically give the right amount of relief, since the effect of the deduction is to reduce the amount of taxable income which falls into the upper tax bands.

Payments made gross or net

Most of the payments which are deductible from total income are made gross (without deduction of income tax). However, certain payments are required by law to be paid net, after deduction of basic rate income tax (see later in this chapter).

Payments made gross are deducted from the taxpayer's total income when computing his or her income tax liability, but it is tempting to ignore any payments made net since the taxpayer has already taken tax relief at source. However, the tax deducted at source is always calculated at the basic rate (20% for 2017-18) and this will not give the right amount of relief to a taxpayer whose highest rate of tax is not the basic rate. The only way to be sure that the right amount of tax relief is given for a payment made net is to:

(a) calculate the gross amount of the payment (net payment × 100/80)

(b) subtract the gross figure from the taxpayer's total income

(c) increase the taxpayer's income tax liability by the amount of basic rate tax which was deducted from the payment when it was made.

In effect, the person making the payment is regarded as having collected basic rate income tax from the recipient on behalf of HM Revenue and Customs and must therefore account to HMRC for this tax as part of his or her income tax liability. Note the following points:

(a) This treatment of payments made net of tax is entirely consistent with the treatment of income received net of tax (see Chapter 2). Income received net is shown gross in the taxpayer's income tax computation and the amount of tax deducted at source is subtracted when calculating tax payable. Similarly, payments made net are shown gross in the taxpayer's income tax computation and the amount of tax deducted at source is added when calculating tax payable.

(b) Basic rate tax must be deducted at source from certain payments which are allowable when computing a taxpayer's income from self-employment (see Chapter 9). In this case, to ensure that tax relief is not given twice, these payments are not also deducted from total income. However, the amount of tax deducted at source must still be accounted for to HMRC and this is achieved by adding this amount to the taxpayer's income tax liability for the year.

EXAMPLE 1

(a) Bob has total income of £21,445 in 2017-18. None of his income is derived from savings or dividends and he claims the basic personal allowance. During the year he makes a payment which is deductible from total income of £200 (paid gross).

(b) Cathy's circumstances are precisely the same as Bob's except that her payment is required by law to be made net of basic rate tax, so she pays a net amount of £160.

Compute Bob and Cathy's income tax liabilities for 2017-18. Does it seem to make any difference whether a deductible payment is made gross or net?

Solution

	Bob	*Cathy*
	£	£
Total income	21,445	21,445
Less: Payment	200	
Payment £160 x 100/80		200
Net income	21,245	21,245
Less: Personal allowance	11,500	11,500
Taxable income	9,745	9,745
Income tax		
£9,745 @ 20%	1,949.00	
£9,745 @ 20%		1,949.00
Tax borne	1,949.00	1,949.00
Add: Tax deducted from payment	0.00	40.00
Tax liability	1,949.00	1,989.00

Note:

Bob has made a payment of £200 and has a tax liability of £1,949.00, a total of £2,149.00. Cathy has made a payment of £160 and has a tax liability of £1,989.00, again a total of £2,149.00. Apart from the timing of the cash flows involved, it makes no difference whether a deductible payment is made gross or net and this is evidenced by the fact that tax borne is the same for both taxpayers.

Higher rate and additional rate taxpayers

If a taxpayer pays income tax at the higher rate or additional rate (or at the dividend upper rate or dividend additional rate) a payment or gift which is deductible from total income will effectively cost the taxpayer less than it would cost a basic rate taxpayer. This is because tax relief is given at marginal rate. The method of computation described above will ensure that the correct amount of tax relief is given.

EXAMPLE 2

Derek's total income for 2017-18 is £63,310 (entirely non-savings) and he makes a gross deductible payment of £3,000 in the year. He is not a Scottish taxpayer and he makes no Gift Aid donations or pension contributions. Show his income tax computation:

(a) with the deductible payment (b) as it would have been without the payment.

How much has the payment effectively cost him? How much would it have cost him if his total income for the year had been £163,310? And in what ways would the situation have differed if his total income for the year had been £115,000?

Solution

				Income £63,310		*Income £163,310*	
				(a)	(b)	(a)	(b)
				£	£	£	£
Total income				63,310	63,310	163,310	163,310
Less: Payment				3,000		3,000	
Net income				60,310	63,310	160,310	163,310
Less: Personal allowance				11,500	11,500	0	0
Taxable income				48,810	51,810	160,310	163,310
Income tax							
	33,500	33,500	@ 20%	6,700.00	6,700.00		
	15,310	18,310	@ 40%	6,124.00	7,324.00		
	48,810	51,810					
	33,500	33,500	@ 20%			6,700.00	6,700.00
	116,500	116,500	@ 40%			46,600.00	46,600.00
	10,310	13,310	@ 45%			4,639.50	5,989.50
	160,310	163,310					
Tax liability				12,824.00	14,024.00	57,939.50	59,289.50

Notes:

(i) With total income of £63,310, Derek's income tax liability for the year is reduced by £1,200 if he makes the £3,000 payment, so in fact it costs him only £1,800. In effect, tax relief has been given at 40%, which is Derek's highest rate of tax.

(ii) With total income of £163,310, Derek's tax liability is reduced by £1,350 if he makes the £3,000 payment, so it now costs him only £1,650. Tax relief has been given at 45%, which is Derek's highest rate of tax. The personal allowance is zero in this case because adjusted net income greatly exceeds £100,000 (see Chapter 3).

(iii) With total income of £115,000, the £3,000 payment reduces Derek's net income to £112,000 so his personal allowance is £5,500 (£11,500 – 1/2 x £12,000). Without the payment, the personal allowance is only £4,000 (£11,500 – 1/2 x £15,000). Therefore the combination of the £3,000 payment and the extra personal allowance of £1,500 reduces taxable income by £4,500.

Since Derek's highest rate of tax in this case is 40%, he saves income tax of £1,800 (40% of £4,500). A tax saving of £1,800 on a payment of £3,000 amounts to an effective rate of tax relief of 60%. This exceptionally high rate of tax relief will always occur if a taxpayer has adjusted net income (for 2017-18) which lies between £100,000 and £123,000 (see Chapter 3).

Dividend ordinary rate taxpayers, 0% taxpayers and non-taxpayers

A taxpayer whose highest rate of income tax is the dividend ordinary rate is entitled to tax relief on deductible payments and gifts at that rate only (7.5% in 2017-18). Similarly, a non-taxpayer (whose income does not exceed the personal allowance) or a taxpayer whose highest rate is either the starting rate for savings, the savings nil rate or the dividend nil rate (all of which are 0% in 2017-18) is not entitled to any tax relief at all. But the method described above will ensure that tax relief (if any) is always given at the correct rate.

EXAMPLE 3

Esmé receives dividends of £17,000 in 2017-18 and has no other income. She makes a gross deductible payment of £100 during the year and claims only the basic personal allowance. Calculate Esmé's tax liability for the year:

(a) with the deductible payment (b) as it would have been without the payment.

How would the situation differ if her dividend income had been £1,000 lower?

Solution

			Dividends £17,000		*Dividends £16,000*	
			(a)	(b)	(a)	(b)
			£	£	£	£
Dividends received			17,000	17,000	16,000	16,000
Less: Payment			100		100	
Net income			16,900	17,000	15,900	16,000
Less: Personal allowance			11,500	11,500	11,500	11,500
Taxable income			5,400	5,500	4,400	4,500
Income tax						
5,000	5,000	@ 0%	0.00	0.00		
400	500	@ 7.5%	30.00	37.50		
5,400	5,500					
4,400	4,500	@ 0%			0.00	0.00
Tax liability			30.00	37.50	0.00	0.00

Notes:

(i) With dividends of £17,000, Esmé's highest rate of tax is the dividend ordinary rate. If she makes the payment, her tax liability is reduced by £7.50 (7.5% of £100 = £7.50).

(ii) With dividends of £16,000, Esmé's highest rate of tax is the dividend nil rate and her tax liability is zero with or without the payment. She is entitled to tax relief at 0% (i.e. no tax relief at all) and so the payment costs her the full £100.

Eligible interest payments

The interest paid on certain loans is deductible from a taxpayer's total income. This interest is generally paid gross. The main types of eligible loan are:

(a) A loan to purchase plant or machinery which is necessarily acquired for use in the taxpayer's employment. Interest on such a loan is eligible for relief in the tax year in which the loan is taken out and the next three years. This relief is not available in relation to the purchase of a mechanically propelled vehicle or a cycle.

(b) A loan to purchase plant or machinery for use in the business of a partnership in which the taxpayer is a partner. Interest on such a loan is eligible for tax relief if it is paid no later than three years after the end of the period of account in which the loan was made.

(c) A loan to purchase ordinary shares in a close company (see Chapter 27), so long as the taxpayer owns at least 5% of the company's ordinary share capital or works for the greater part of his or her time in the management of the company.

   This relief also applies to the purchase of shares in companies which are resident in the European Economic Area (EEA) and which would have been regarded as close companies if they had been resident in the UK.

(d) A loan to purchase shares in an employee-controlled company that is resident in the UK or elsewhere in the EEA, or to purchase an interest in a partnership.

(e) A loan to pay inheritance tax. The interest on such a loan is eligible for tax relief if it relates to a period ending within 12 months of the date that the loan was made.

Note that interest which is paid wholly and exclusively for business purposes is treated as a business expense and is deducted when calculating the business profits charged to income tax as trading income (see Chapter 9). In this case, the interest is not deductible from total income.

Limit on income tax reliefs

Finance Act 2013 introduced a limit on the amount of tax relief that may be deducted from a taxpayer's total income when calculating his or her net income. This limit applies only to certain types of tax relief and is mainly concerned with reliefs available in relation to trading losses (see Chapter 12). However, the eligible interest payments listed above also fall within the scope of this rule.

In general terms, the total of the reliefs to which the limit applies cannot exceed the greater of £50,000 and 25% of the taxpayer's total income. A more detailed explanation of the limit on income tax reliefs is given in Chapter 12 of this book.

Annual payments

ITA 2007 requires that certain "annual payments" made by an individual should be made net of basic rate income tax. One example of this is the payment of royalties to a person who holds intellectual property as an investment. Tax relief on a qualifying annual payment may be obtained in one of two ways. Either:

(a) the gross amount of the payment may be deductible when calculating the taxpayer's trading profits for income tax purposes (see Chapter 9), or

(b) if the payment is not deductible when calculating trading profits, the gross amount of the payment is relieved instead by deduction from the taxpayer's total income†.

In either case, the amount of tax deducted at source from the payment must be accounted for to HMRC by being added to the taxpayer's income tax liability for the year concerned.

† *Patent royalties can no longer be relieved by deduction from total income. So if patent royalties are not deductible when calculating trading profits, they will not be relieved at all.*

Gifts of shares or property to charity

A gift of listed shares or securities made to a charity attracts tax relief in the same way as a deductible payment. The amount of the gift is taken to be the market value of the shares on the date of the gift, plus any incidental costs borne by the donor and less the value of any benefits received by the donor in consequence of making the gift. Gifts of land or buildings to a charity are also eligible for relief.

This income tax relief is in addition to the relief from capital gains tax which arises when assets are given to charities (see Chapter 17).

EXAMPLE 4

In 2017-18, a taxpayer who pays income tax at 45% and capital gains tax at 20% gives listed shares with a market value of £20,000 to a charity. There are no incidental costs of disposal and the taxpayer receives no benefit in consequence of making the gift. A capital gain of £12,000 would have been charged to capital gains tax if the shares had been sold. In effect, how much does this gift cost the taxpayer?

Solution

Assuming that 45% income tax would have been paid on at least £20,000 of taxable income if the gift had not been made, income tax saved is £9,000 (45% of £20,000). CGT of £2,400 (20% of £12,000) is also saved. The total tax saving is £11,400. This amounts to tax relief at a total rate of 57% and the gift has effectively cost the taxpayer only £8,600.

Payments which are tax reducers

The following payments are granted tax relief by means of a reduction in the income tax liability of the taxpayer who makes the payment:

(a) certain alimony or maintenance payments (as long as either the payer or the recipient was born before 6 April 1935)

(b) interest on a loan secured on the taxpayer's main residence and used to purchase a life annuity (so long as the loan was taken out before 9 March 1999).

If such a payment is made gross, a tax reduction at the relevant rate (see below) is given in the payer's income tax computation. This tax reduction takes priority over tax reductions for the marriage allowance or the married couple's allowance (see Chapter 3). No refund is available if available tax reductions exceed the tax due on the payer's taxable income.

If such a payment is made net, it should be *entirely omitted* from the taxpayer's income tax computation, since precisely the right amount of tax relief has already been given at source and there is nothing more to be done.

Maintenance payments

Maintenance payments consist of periodical payments made:

(a) by one of the parties to a marriage or civil partnership (or a former marriage or civil partnership) for the maintenance of the other party, at a time when:

  (i) the couple are no longer living together, and

  (ii) the party for whose benefit the payment is made has not entered into a new marriage (or civil partnership)

(b) by one parent of a child to the other parent, made for the child's maintenance and at a time when the two parents are not living together.

Tax relief is available to a person who makes maintenance payments if at least one of the parties or parents was born before 6 April 1935 and the payments are made under either a court order, a legally binding agreement or an assessment made under the Child Support Act 1991. The income tax regime which applies to such payments is as follows:

(a) Maintenance payments are made gross, without any deduction of tax at source.

(b) In 2017-18, a taxpayer making qualifying maintenance payments is entitled to a tax reduction equal to 10% of the *lower* of:

  (i) the payments made by the taxpayer which fall due in the tax year, and

  (ii) the minimum married couple's allowance (£3,260).

(c) The recipient of maintenance payments is not liable to pay income tax on them.

Loans used to purchase a life annuity

Tax relief is available† in relation to the interest paid on the first £30,000 of a loan taken out *before 9 March 1999* and which was:

(a) made to a taxpayer aged 65 or over at the time that the loan was made, and

(b) used to purchase a life annuity, and

(c) secured on the taxpayer's main residence.

Such arrangements are often referred to as *home income plans*.

Tax relief takes the form of a tax reduction equal to 23% of the qualifying interest. This rate of relief remains at 23% (the basic rate of income tax for tax year 1998-99) even though the basic rate has now fallen to only 20%. If the interest is paid gross, relief is given in the payer's tax computation. If the interest is paid net it should be entirely omitted from the payer's tax computation, as explained above.

† *The Government has decided not to withdraw this tax relief from 6 April 2019 (as had originally been intended).*

Gifts of pre-eminent property to the nation

Subject to certain conditions, an individual who makes a gift of "pre-eminent property" to the nation (e.g. a work of art) is entitled to a total tax reduction equal to 30% of the value of that property. This total tax reduction may be split across the tax year in which the gift is made and the following four tax years in any way that the individual wishes. For instance, the total tax reduction of £300,000 relating to a gift with an agreed value of £1m made in tax year 2017-18 could be allocated as follows:

(a) the entire £300,000 could be allocated to 2017-18, or

(b) £60,000 could be allocated to each tax year from 2017-18 to 2021-22 inclusive, or

(c) the £300,000 could be allocated to the five tax years in any other way at all (including a nil allocation in some years).

The tax reduction allocated to a tax year is normally set first against the individual's income tax liability for that year. If this liability is less than the tax reduction, the balance is then set against the individual's capital gains tax liability. However, the individual may choose to reverse this order if he or she so wishes.

Note that a similar tax relief is available to *companies* which make a gift of pre-eminent property to the nation (see Chapter 23).

Gift Aid

The Gift Aid scheme provides a tax incentive for individuals and companies to make charitable donations. The way in which the scheme applies to individuals is explained here. The way in which the scheme applies to companies is explained in Chapter 23.

This scheme applies to any charitable donation (including donations made to community amateur sports clubs) so long as:

(a) the donor is a UK resident or a non-resident with income or gains charged to UK tax

(b) the donation takes the form of a gift of money and this gift is not repayable to the donor, is not covered by the payroll giving scheme (see Chapter 7) and is not deductible when computing the donor's income from any source

(c) the donor receives no benefit at all from making the gift, or receives a benefit which does not exceed the following limits:

 (i) 25% of the amount of the gift, if the gift does not exceed £100
 (ii) £25, if the gift exceeds £100 but does not exceed £1,000
 (iii) 5% of the amount of the gift, if the gift exceeds £1,000

 subject to a limit of £2,500 on the value of the benefits which the donor may receive in any one tax year as a consequence of donations to any one charity

(d) the donor makes a Gift Aid declaration with regard to the donation.

If these conditions are satisfied, the gift is treated as if made net of basic rate tax and the charity can recover the tax deemed to have been deducted at source. For instance, a £20 gift would be treated as a gross gift of £25 (£20 × 100/80) less tax deducted of £5. In this case, the charity would receive £20 from the donor and a further £5 from HMRC.

Gift Aid relief for donors

Gift aid donations are *not* shown in the donor's tax computation, but the following provisions apply:

(a) The donor must pay income tax and capital gains tax equal to at least the amount of tax deemed to have been deducted from the gift. If this is not the case, then the donor's entitlement to personal allowances is restricted to ensure that this amount of tax is in fact paid. If the restriction of personal allowances does not give the required result, the donor is charged to income tax at the basic rate on as much of the gift as is necessary to ensure that the required amount of tax is paid.

(b) The donor's basic rate limit and higher rate limit are both increased by the gross amount of the gift, so ensuring that relief at the higher rate or additional rate is automatically given to higher rate and additional rate taxpayers.

Carry-back of Gift Aid relief

The donor may elect that a qualifying Gift Aid donation should be treated for tax purposes as if paid in the previous tax year. Such an election must be made on or before the date that the tax return for the previous tax year is submitted and no later than the 31 January which follows the end of that year.

EXAMPLE 5

In 2017-18, Owen (who is not a Scottish taxpayer) makes qualifying Gift Aid donations totalling £360. He has no capital gains tax liability for the year. Show his income tax computation if his only income for the year consists of business profits of:

(a) £27,825 (b) £11,715 (c) £246,090.

Solution

	(a)	(b)	(c)
	£	£	£
Business profits	27,825	11,715	246,090
Less: Personal allowance	11,500	11,265	0
Taxable income	16,325	450	246,090

Income tax

(a)	(b)	(c)		(a)	(b)	(c)
16,325	450	33,950	@ 20%	3,265.00	90.00	6,790.00
		116,500	@ 40%			46,600.00
		95,640	@ 45%			43,038.00
16,325	450	246,090				
Tax liability				3,265.00	90.00	96,428.00

Notes:

(i) The donations of £360 are grossed-up to £450 (£360 x 100/80) and are treated as if paid net of 20% tax. Deemed tax deducted is £90.

(ii) In case (a), Owen's income tax liability exceeds £90 so there is no more to be done.

(iii) In case (b), Owen's income tax liability will be only £43 if the full personal allowance is given i.e. (£11,715 – £11,500) = £215 x 20% = £43. This falls short of the required £90 by £47. Therefore he must pay a further £47 of income tax. This is achieved by reducing his personal allowance by £235 to £11,265.

(iv) In case (c), Owen's basic rate limit is increased by £450 to £33,950 and his higher rate limit is increased by £450 to £150,450. This moves £450 of taxable income from additional rate to basic rate and saves tax of £112.50 (£450 x 25%). In summary, the charity receives £450 but the cost to Owen is only £247.50 (£360 – £112.50). Total tax relief is therefore £202.50 (i.e. £450 x 45%).

Summary

- Certain payments and gifts made by a taxpayer are either deducted from total income or act as tax reducers. Payments which are deducted from total income must always be shown gross in the income tax computation. Any tax which was deducted when the payment was made is added to the tax liability of the payer.
- If a payment which ranks as a tax reducer is made gross, the appropriate tax reduction is given in the payer's tax computation. But payments of this type that are made net should be omitted from the computation entirely.
- The main deductible payments are eligible interest payments and certain annual payments. A charitable gift consisting of listed shares or securities or comprising land and buildings may also be deducted from total income.
- Qualifying maintenance payments of up to the amount of the minimum married couple's allowance are relieved at 10%. This relief is available only if either the payer or the recipient was born before 6 April 1935.
- Interest paid on a home loan taken out before 9 March 1999 and used to buy a life annuity is relieved at 23%.
- The Gift Aid scheme covers charitable donations which satisfy certain conditions. Qualifying donations are deemed to have been made net of basic rate tax.
- A taxpayer making a Gift Aid donation must pay income tax and CGT of at least the amount of tax deemed to have been deducted from the donation. Higher rate and additional rate taxpayers obtain higher and additional rate relief on such donations.

Exercises

4.1 Mabel has total income of £26,205 in 2017-18, none of which is derived from savings or dividends. During the year she makes a net deductible payment of £200. Show her income tax computation for the year.

4.2 Paul (who is not a Scottish taxpayer) has total income of £48,890 in 2017-18, none of which is derived from savings or dividends. During the year he pays gross eligible interest of £1,600. Show his income tax computation:

(a) with the interest payment (b) as it would be without the interest payment.

How much has the interest effectively cost him?

4.3 Rose is single and has total income of £11,250 in 2017-18. She makes a gross deductible payment of £25 during the year. Show her income tax computation for the year and determine the amount of tax relief given in relation to the payment.

4.4 At what rate of income tax is each of the following types of payment relieved in tax year 2017-18?

(a) interest on a qualifying home loan used to buy an annuity

(b) interest on a loan used to buy an interest in a partnership

(c) qualifying maintenance payments

(d) a gift of pre-eminent property to the nation.

4.5 A taxpayer with no capital gains tax liability makes a qualifying Gift Aid donation of £960 in tax year 2017-18. Explain:

(a) why this donation is worth more than £960 to the charity which receives it

(b) why this donation might cost the taxpayer more than £960

(c) why this donation might cost the taxpayer less than £960.

4.6 In 2017-18, Raj has dividend income of £58,400. He has no other income. He makes a qualifying Gift Aid donation of £440 during the year. Show his 2017-18 income tax computation.

4.7 Matthew (who was born on 1 May 1934) dies on 23 December 2017. His only income in tax year 2017-18 is a retirement pension of £29,260. He made a Gift Aid donation of £200 in July 2017. His wife has income from property of £20,895 and no other income. In August 2017 she gave listed shares to charity with a market value of £500.

They were married for many years and made no elections with regard to the married couple's allowance. Calculate their tax liabilities for 2017-18.

***4.8** Pauline (born May 1937) marries Adrian (born March 1935) on 17 October 2017. Their income for 2017-18 is as follows:

	£
Pauline:	
Retirement pension	15,000
Building society interest	3,025
Adrian:	
Income from property	39,600
Dividends received	6,750

During 2017-18, Adrian pays maintenance of £4,000 to his former wife, as required by a court order. She has not remarried.

Show Pauline's and Adrian's income tax computations for 2017-18.

***4.9** Geoffrey's income for 2017-18 consists of a salary of £114,600 and dividends received of £4,400. He makes qualifying Gift Aid donations of £7,200 during the year. He is not a Scottish taxpayer.

Calculate Geoffrey's 2017-18 income tax liability. How would the liability differ for a Scottish taxpayer?

Chapter 5

Income from property

Introduction

An individual's income from property is charged to income tax in accordance with the rules of the Income Tax (Trading and Other Income) Act 2005. The main purpose of this chapter is to explain those rules and to show how a taxpayer's UK property income is calculated. Income from overseas property is considered separately in Chapter 32.

Definition of property income

ITTOIA 2005 states that income tax is charged on the profits of a property business. This statute also states that a UK property business consists of a business which is carried on for generating income from land which is situated in the UK and that "generating income from land" means "*exploiting an estate, interest or right in or over land as a source of rents or other receipts*". This is a fairly broad definition but, in practice, the main classes of property income are:

(a) rents

(b) lease premiums (if the length of the lease does not exceed 50 years)

(c) amounts receivable in respect of rights of way, sporting rights etc.

(d) income from the letting of fixed caravans or permanently moored houseboats.

Dividends received from a UK Real Estate Investment Trust (UK-REIT) are also treated as property income to the extent that they are derived from the company's tax-exempt property income or gains (see Chapter 23). Such dividends are received net of basic rate income tax and rank as non-savings income (see Chapter 2).

Despite the use of the word "business" above, income from property is almost always treated as *unearned* income. The only occasion on which property income is treated as earned income is when the income derives from the commercial letting of furnished holiday accommodation (see later in this chapter). The distinction between earned and unearned income may be especially important if the taxpayer is hoping to obtain tax relief on pension contributions (see Chapter 14).

Basis of assessment and allowable expenditure

A taxpayer's property income for a tax year is normally calculated on the accruals basis† in accordance with generally accepted accounting practice (GAAP). However, short lease premiums (see later in this chapter) are subject to a special tax regime.

Expenditure incurred wholly and exclusively for the purposes of a property business is deducted when computing property income. This "wholly and exclusively" rule is copied from the rules relating to trading income (see Chapter 9). The types of expenditure which are likely to be deductible when computing property income include the following:

(a) repairs and maintenance (excluding improvements) and insurances

(b) the cost of providing services to tenants

(c) administrative and management costs, including bad debts incurred

(d) rent paid to a superior landlord (if the property is sub-let)

(e) business rates, water rates or council tax (if paid by the landlord)

(f) interest payable on a loan to buy or improve the property concerned (see below).

If a property is partly let and partly owner-occupied, the proportion of the expenditure which relates to the letting of the property is deductible when computing property income, as long as this proportion can be determined with reasonable accuracy.

When a taxpayer rents out more than one property, it is *not* necessary to calculate the profit (or loss) for each property individually. In each tax year, total property expenditure is deducted from total rental income, giving a single profit (or loss) figure for the year.

† *The Government has proposed that (as from tax year 2017-18) the profit of a property business should normally be calculated on the cash basis. On this basis, income is taxed in the year of receipt and expenditure is deductible in the year of payment. The cash basis for property income would operate in much the same way as the cash basis for trading income (see Chapter 9) but would not apply to property businesses with receipts for the tax year in excess of £150,000. Landlords with receipts not exceeding this threshold in a tax year could elect to apply GAAP for that year (rather than the cash basis) if they so wished.*

Tax relief for interest payable

As from tax year 2017-18, new rules are being phased in that restrict tax relief on interest payable (and other finance costs) in relation to "buy-to-let" loans on residential property. For tax year 2020-21 and later years, tax relief on such interest will be restricted to basic rate and the interest will no longer be deductible when computing property income. In the transition period, the percentage of interest payable for each year that may be deducted when computing property income is as follows:

2017-18 75% *2018-19* 50% *2019-20* 25%

The remainder of the interest for the year acts as a tax reducer (see Chapters 3 and 4) and is relieved at basic rate (currently 20%). As from tax year 2020-21, none of the interest payable for the year will be deductible from property income. All of it will be treated as a tax reducer relieved at basic rate. However, the available tax reduction in any tax year is limited to basic rate income tax on the *lower* of:

(a) the amount of interest for that year that is not deductible when calculating property income (e.g. 25% of the interest for 2017-18)

(b) the taxpayer's property income for the year, less any losses brought forward

(c) the taxpayer's adjusted total income for the year.

For this purpose, "adjusted total income" is defined as the taxpayer's net income for the tax year (apart from savings income and dividend income) less any personal allowance or blind person's allowance to which the taxpayer is entitled.

If the available tax reduction for a year is based upon either (b) or (c) above, then the excess of (a) over the amount on which the tax reduction is based is carried forward to the following tax year and is included in (a) for that year.

Note that these rules do *not* apply to furnished holiday lettings (see later in this chapter).

Capital expenditure

Capital expenditure is normally not deductible when computing property income but tax relief may be obtained on certain types of capital expenditure as follows:

(a) Capital allowances (see Chapter 11) may be claimed in relation to the acquisition of plant and machinery for use in the repair, maintenance or management of property which is let to tenants†.

(b) As from 6 April 2016, "replacement domestic items relief" is available for the cost of replacing certain items provided for domestic use in let residential property, including furniture and furnishings, household appliances and kitchenware. Note that:

 (i) Relief is available only when an "old item" is replaced by a "new item". There is no relief for the original cost of acquiring the very first item in a chain of items (e.g. the first washing machine installed in the property).

 (ii) If the new item is substantially the same as the old item which it replaces, the full cost of the new item is deductible when computing property income. Otherwise, the deduction from property income is restricted to that part of the cost of the new item that does not exceed the expenditure which would have been incurred on an item substantially the same as the old item.

 (iii) The deductible cost of the new item is increased by any disposal costs relating to the old item but reduced by any disposal proceeds of the old item.

 (iv) Replacement domestic items relief is available whether or not the property is let furnished. But the relief is *not* available if "rent-a-room" relief applies or in the case of furnished holiday lettings (see later in this chapter).

† *Capital allowances are not available in relation to plant and machinery provided for use by the tenants in let residential property.*

EXAMPLE 1

Ryan owns a house which he lets to a tenant. Rent is payable monthly in advance on the 6th day of each month. For some years the rent has been fixed at £7,200 per annum but this was increased to £7,800 per annum with effect from 6 December 2017. The rent due on 6 March 2018 was not paid until 7 April 2018.

Ryan's only property expenditure in 2017-18 was mortgage interest of £3,200. Compute his property income for the year (assuming that the cash basis does not apply).

Solution

On the accruals basis, rents for the year are £7,400 [(£7,200 x 8/12) + (£7,800 x 4/12)]. Deductible interest is £2,400 (75% × £3,200) so property income is £5,000. The remaining interest of £800 will be relieved as a tax reducer at 20% (as long as Ryan has adjusted total income for the year of at least £800).

EXAMPLE 2

Ursula owns a flat which was let to a tenant for the whole of tax year 2017-18 at a rental of £200 per week. Her expenditure during the year was as follows:

	£
Insurance	380
Repairs and maintenance	1,150
Replacement of sofa	729

The new sofa is superior to the sofa it replaced (and which was scrapped). It would have cost only £399 to have bought a new sofa which was equivalent in quality to the old one. Compute property income for 2017-18 (assuming that the cash basis does not apply).

Solution

		£	£
Rents for the year £200 x 52			10,400
Less:	Insurance	380	
	Repairs and maintenance	1,150	
	Replacement of domestic item	399	1,929
Property income			8,471

Property income allowance

The Government has proposed that, *as from tax year 2017-18*, gross property income of up to £1,000 per annum (before deduction of expenses) should be tax-free. If this figure is exceeded, the taxpayer will have the right to elect that he or she should be taxed on the excess of gross income over £1,000 (with no deduction for expenses). Otherwise, property income will be calculated by deducting expenses from gross income in the usual way.

Losses

If a taxpayer's gross property income for a tax year is exceeded by the allowable expenditure, then the taxpayer has incurred a loss and taxable property income for the year is £nil. The loss is carried forward and relieved against the first available property income arising in subsequent tax years. Strictly speaking, relief is given by deduction from the taxpayer's total income (see Chapter 2), but the amount of relief given in any tax year cannot exceed the property income for that year.

Any loss incurred on an individual property in a tax year will automatically be set against profits arising on other properties in the same year, since property income and expenditure is generally pooled to give an overall profit or loss for the year.

EXAMPLE 3

Sandra's entire income is derived from the letting of property. Her income and expenditure in tax years 2015-16 through to 2017-18 are as follows:

	2015-16	*2016-17*	*2017-18*
	£	£	£
Total rental income	49,320	51,400	76,100
Total allowable expenditure	78,510	25,430	17,540

Compute her net income for each year.

Solution

	2015-16	*2016-17*	*2017-18*
	£	£	£
Total rental income	49,320	51,400	76,100
Total allowable expenditure	78,510	25,430	17,540
Property income/(loss)	(29,190)	25,970	58,560
Total income	0	25,970	58,560
Less: Losses b/f	-	(25,970)	(3,220)
Net income	0	0	55,340

Note:

The 2015-16 loss must be set against the first available property income in subsequent years. This means that Sandra's net income for 2016-17 is reduced to £nil and that her personal allowance for that year is unused. However, it may be possible to transfer 10% of her 2016-17 personal allowance to a spouse or civil partner (see Chapter 3).

Lease premiums

A premium is a lump sum paid by a tenant to a landlord on the grant of a lease. The income tax treatment of lease premiums is as follows:

(a) Premiums arising on the grant of a "long lease" (a lease of more than 50 years) are not charged to income tax at all.

(b) Premiums arising on the grant of a "short lease" (a lease of 50 years or less) are charged to income tax in the tax year in which the lease is granted. However, the amount of the premium is reduced for this purpose by 2% for each year of the lease except for the first year.

Note that these provisions apply only to the *grant* of a new lease, not to the *assignment* of an existing lease. Note also that lease premiums arising on the grant of a lease may give rise to a capital gains tax liability (see Chapter 19).

EXAMPLE 4

In tax year 2017-18, a landlord receives a premium of £36,000 when granting a 25-year lease to a tenant. How much of this premium is chargeable to income tax?

Solution

£36,000 – (24 × 2% × £36,000) = £18,720.

Relief for premiums paid

A tenant who pays a premium on being granted a short lease may obtain tax relief on the premium paid in one of two ways:

(a) If the tenant uses the property for business purposes, he or she may claim an annual deduction from trading profits. This is equal to the amount of the premium on which the landlord is charged to income tax, divided by the lease duration (see Chapter 9).

(b) If the tenant sub-lets the property and receives a premium from the sub-lessee, then the assessable amount of the premium received is reduced† by:

$$\text{Landlord's income tax assessment on premium paid} \times \frac{\text{Duration of sub-lease}}{\text{Duration of head-lease}}$$

If this reduction cannot be made in full (either because the premium received is too small or because no premium was received at all) the excess is spread evenly over the period of the sub-lease and set against the rents due from the sub-lessee.

† *It appears that this reduction would not be available under the cash basis (see earlier in this chapter) although the tenant could obtain the reduction by opting for the accruals basis.*

EXAMPLE 5

Susan is granted a 20-year lease on a property, paying a premium of £76,000. Explain how tax relief will be given in relation to this premium if:

(a) she uses the property for trading purposes, or

(b) she grants a sub-lease to Timothy for five years, receiving a premium of:

(i) £25,000 (ii) £10,000

(assume that the cash basis does not apply).

Solution

(a) The amount assessable to income tax on Susan's landlord is £47,120 (£76,000 less 38% of £76,000). If Susan uses the premises for trading purposes she will be able to claim an annual deduction of £2,356 from her trading profits for each of the next 20 years (£47,120 divided by 20 = £2,356).

(b)

	(i)	(ii)
	£	£
Premium received	25,000	10,000
Less: 2% x 4 x £25,000	2,000	
2% x 4 x £10,000		800
	23,000	9,200
Less: Premium paid £47,120 x $\frac{5}{20}$ = £11,780	11,780	9,200
Assessable premium	11,220	nil

In case (ii), the reduction available in relation to the premium paid cannot be made in full. The amount unrelieved is £2,580 (£11,780 – £9,200). There will be no income tax assessment on the premium received in this case and a deduction of £516 will be made from Susan's property income for each of the five years of the sub-lease (£2,580 divided by 5 = £516).

Reverse premiums

A "reverse premium" is a premium paid by a landlord to a potential tenant so as to induce that tenant to take out a lease. From the point of view of the tenant†, a reverse premium is a receipt which is chargeable to income tax. If the rented premises are used for business purposes, the amount received is treated as trading income (see Chapter 9). Otherwise the amount received is treated as property income. In both cases, the timing of the tax charge will usually follow accepted accountancy practice, so that the tax liability arising on the receipt of a reverse premium will probably be spread over the period of the lease.

† *As regards the landlord, the payment of a reverse premium is usually treated as enhancement expenditure for capital gains tax purposes (see Chapter 18).*

"Rent-a-room" relief

If a taxpayer lets furnished accommodation which forms part of his or her main residence, gross annual rents not exceeding a specified limit (£7,500 for 2017-18) are exempt from income tax. However, the taxpayer may elect to ignore this exemption and to apply the usual property income rules instead. This might be beneficial if the rents were exceeded by expenses, so that a loss could be claimed.

If gross rents for a tax year exceed the limit, rents less expenses are assessed to income tax in the normal way. However, the taxpayer may elect to be assessed instead on the excess of gross rents over the limit, without deducting expenses of any kind.

Both of the elections referred to above must be made by 31 January in the second tax year following the tax year to which the election relates. The first election applies only to the year for which it is made. The second election applies to all subsequent tax years until a year arises in which gross rents do not exceed the limit (or the election is withdrawn).

EXAMPLE 6

In 2017-18, Victor rents out a room in his house and receives rents of £8,150. He incurs allowable expenses of £820. No "rent-a-room" elections are currently in force. What elections (if any) should he make?

Solution

The rent-a-room exemption does not apply since gross rents exceed £7,500. If Victor does nothing, he will be charged to income tax on property income of £7,330 (£8,150 – £820).

If he elects to be assessed on the excess of gross rents over the rent-a-room relief limit, his property income for tax purposes will be only £650 (£8,150 – £7,500). He should make this election and he has until 31 January 2020 to do so.

Furnished holiday lettings

Subject to certain conditions, income derived from the "commercial letting of furnished holiday accommodation" is treated for most tax purposes as if it were trading income. The main beneficial effects of this treatment are as follows:

(a) The income is regarded as earned income when determining the extent to which tax relief is available in relation to pension contributions (see Chapter 14).

(b) Capital allowances may be claimed in respect of plant and machinery (including furniture) which is provided for use by tenants (see Chapter 11).

(c) Business-related capital gains tax reliefs may be available (see Chapter 22).

At one time, losses incurred in relation to furnished holiday lettings (FHL) were relieved as if they were trading losses (see Chapter 12) but this is no longer the case.

FHL conditions

Letting qualifies as the commercial letting of furnished holiday accommodation if *all* of the following conditions are satisfied:

(a) The property concerned is situated in the UK or elsewhere in the European Economic Area (see Chapter 3) and is let furnished with a view to profit.

(b) The property is available for letting to the general public as holiday accommodation for at least 210 days in the tax year and is actually let for at least 105 days, ignoring any periods of "longer-term occupation" (i.e. periods of more than 31 consecutive days during which the accommodation is in the same occupation).

(c) The property is not in longer-term occupation for more than 155 days in the tax year.

A taxpayer with furnished holiday lettings both in the UK and elsewhere in the EEA is treated as having two separate FHL businesses. All qualifying property in the UK forms one FHL business. All qualifying property elsewhere in the EEA forms a separate FHL business. A loss incurred in either of these FHL businesses may be set only against income arising from the same FHL business.

If a property qualifies as furnished holiday accommodation in one tax year, the taxpayer who owns the property may elect to treat the property as continuing to qualify for up to two further tax years (the "period of grace") even though it does not satisfy the 105-day condition in those years. Such an election may not be made for a tax year if an averaging election is made in respect of the same year for the property concerned (see below).

Averaging

A taxpayer who owns two or more properties, each of which qualifies for FHL purposes except that at least one property does not satisfy the 105-day condition, may claim that all of these properties should be treated as furnished holiday accommodation as long as their average number of days let is at least 105 days.

An averaging claim must be made by 31 January in the second tax year following the tax year to which the election relates.

EXAMPLE 7

Yvonne owns four cottages, all let furnished with a view to profit. None of the cottages is ever let to the same tenant for more than 31 consecutive days. In 2017-18 the number of days each cottage was available for letting and the number of days actually let were:

	Days available	*Days actually let*
Cottage A	220	115
Cottage B	240	85
Cottage C	190	148
Cottage D	250	103

Show Yvonne's potential averaging claims.

Solution

Cottage C cannot be treated as furnished holiday accommodation since it does not pass the 210-day test. Cottages A, B and D all pass this test but only Cottage A also passes the 105-day test. Without any averaging claims, therefore, only Cottage A will be regarded as furnished holiday accommodation. Possible averaging claims are:

(a) Average Cottage A with Cottage B. This is no use since the average number of days let is only 100.

(b) Average Cottage A with Cottage D. This would be beneficial since the average number of days let is 109.

(c) Average Cottage A with Cottage B and Cottage D. This is no use since the average number of days let is only 101.

Therefore, Yvonne should claim that Cottage A should be averaged with Cottage D, in which case both cottages would qualify as furnished holiday accommodation.

Summary

- Income tax is charged on the profits of a business which is carried on for the purpose of generating income from land situated in the UK. Income from property is treated as unearned income unless it arises from furnished holiday lettings.
- Property income is generally calculated on the accruals basis, but the Government has proposed that the cash basis should apply to smaller property businesses. Expenditure incurred wholly and exclusively for the purposes of a property business is deducted when computing property income.
- Capital allowances may be claimed on plant and machinery used in the maintenance of let property. Tax relief is also available for the cost of replacing domestic items provided for use by tenants.
- Losses incurred by a property business are carried forward and set against the first available property income arising in subsequent years.
- A premium received on the grant of a lease is charged to income tax if the lease does not exceed 50 years. The assessable amount is the amount of the premium less 2% for each year of the lease except the first.
- Rent-a-room relief is available if a taxpayer receives rents of up to £7,500 p.a. from the letting of furnished rooms in his or her main residence.
- Under certain conditions, the letting of furnished property qualifies as the commercial letting of furnished holiday accommodation. This offers a number of tax benefits.

Exercises

It may be assumed in these exercises that the cash basis does not apply and that property income is calculated on the accruals basis.

5.1 Andrew owns a house which he lets to tenants. Rent is payable quarterly in advance on 1 January, 1 April, 1 July and 1 October. The rent was £8,000 per annum until it was increased to £8,800 per annum with effect from 1 January 2018. Rent received by Andrew during 2017-18 was as follows:

	£
2 July 2017	2,000
30 September 2017	2,000
3 January 2018	2,200
	6,200

Andrew did not receive the payment due on 1 April 2018 until 7 April 2018. Compute his property income for 2017-18, working to the nearest month and assuming that the only expenditure incurred during the year was buy-to-let mortgage interest of £4,100.

5.2 Simon owns an apartment which he lets to tenants. The apartment was let throughout tax year 2017-18 at a weekly rental of £320. The expenses incurred by Simon in relation to this apartment during 2017-18 were as follows:

	£
Advertising for new tenant	135
Repairs and maintenance	590
Insurance costs	730
Replacement of refrigerator	325
Interest on buy-to-let mortgage	3,420
Capital repayments on buy-to-let mortgage	2,160

The new refrigerator is very similar in all respects to the old one which was provided at a cost of £270 several years previously and has now been scrapped. Costs of £10 were incurred in order to transport the old refrigerator to the local recycling centre.

Compute Simon's property income for 2017-18 and explain how this computation would differ if the tax year concerned was 2018-19 instead of 2017-18.

5.3 In 2017-18, a landlord receives a premium of £12,000 when granting a lease to a tenant. Compute the amount of this premium which is chargeable to income tax if the length of the lease is:

(a) 60 years

(b) 50 years

(c) 20 years.

5.4 In 2017-18, Jasper is granted a 10-year lease on a property, paying a premium of £15,000. He uses the property for trading purposes. Compute the tax relief which he will be allowed in respect of the lease premium.

5.5 Georgina owns three holiday flats, all of which she lets furnished with a view to profit. None of the flats is ever let to the same tenant for more than 31 consecutive days. In 2017-18 the number of days for which each flat was available for letting, and the number of days actually let, were:

	Days available	*Days actually let*
Flat 1	210	99
Flat 2	220	107
Flat 3	252	109

Show Georgina's potential averaging claims.

***5.6** In 2017-18, Peter is granted a 12-year lease on a property, paying a premium of £40,000 to his landlord. He immediately grants a 4-year sub-lease to Paula, receiving a premium of £14,000. Calculate the income tax assessment on the premium received by Peter.

***5.7** Melissa owns a house which she lets to tenants. The house was let throughout tax year 2017-18 at a rent of £600 per month. Her allowable expenditure in 2017-18 was £900 and she had property losses brought forward from 2016-17 of £6,550. Her other income in 2017-18 was as follows:

	£
Retirement pension	15,980
Building society interest	1,730

Compute Melissa's income tax liability for the year.

Chapter 6

Income from savings and investments

Introduction

The main purpose of this chapter is to explain the tax treatment of income arising from savings and investments. The main options available to a taxpayer who wishes to save or invest are to deposit money in bank and building society accounts or to invest in shares and securities. Each of these courses of action has its taxation implications and this chapter explains those implications.

This chapter also briefly considers the taxation of income from trusts and settlements and the tax treatment of certain miscellaneous sources of income.

Interest received

Interest received by a taxpayer is charged to income tax by the Income Tax (Trading and Other Income) Act 2005. This Act states that tax is charged on the full amount of interest arising in the tax year and that interest "arises" when it is paid to the taxpayer or when it is credited to the taxpayer's account. Accrued interest is ignored when computing the amount of interest arising in a tax year. Note that:

(a) Interest ranks as savings income and so any interest which falls into the first £5,000 of taxable income (in 2017-18) is taxed at the starting rate for savings of 0%. Basic rate taxpayers are also entitled to a personal savings allowance (PSA) of £1,000. This is reduced to £500 if taxable income exceeds the basic rate limit and to £nil if taxable income exceeds the higher rate limit. Interest which falls within the PSA in 2017-18 is taxed at the savings nil rate of 0% (see Chapter 2).

(b) In general, no expenses are allowed against this form of income. However, taxpayers who make loans through "peer-to-peer" platforms may offset any bad debts incurred on such loans against the interest received.

Interest from banks and building societies (and NS&I) is now received gross, with no tax deducted at source. As from 6 April 2017, interest received from unit trusts and investment trusts and interest on peer-to-peer loans is also received gross. But certain other types of interest (see Chapter 2) are received net of basic rate income tax. When preparing an income tax computation, the gross equivalent of any interest received net of tax should be included in total income. The tax suffered by deduction at source is then subtracted from the income tax liability when calculating the amount of tax payable for the year.

Self-certification

Basic rate income tax is still deducted at source from the income element of purchased life annuities (see Chapter 2). However, a UK-resident individual who is unlikely to be liable to income tax for a tax year may supply a certificate to this effect (form R89) to the payer of the annuity. Such individuals then receive their interest gross. This avoids the need to claim a repayment of overpaid tax from HMRC at the end of the tax year.

EXAMPLE 1

In 2017-18, Alfred had business profits of £15,870 and received net debenture interest of £1,520. He acquired the debentures on 1 July 2017 and accrued interest (gross) on 5 April 2018 was £950. Calculate the income tax payable for the year.

Solution

	Total	*Non-savings*	*Savings*
	£	£	£
Business profits	15,870	15,870	
Debenture interest £1,520 x 100/80	1,900		1,900
Total income	17,770	15,870	1,900
Less: Personal allowance	11,500	11,500	
Taxable income	6,270	4,370	1,900

Income tax due				
Non-savings income	: Basic rate	4,370	@ 20%	874.00
Savings income	: Starting rate	630	@ 0%	0.00
	: Nil rate	1,000	@ 0%	0.00
	: Basic rate	270	@ 20%	54.00
		6,270		
Tax liability				928.00
Less: Tax deducted at source (£1,900 – £1,520)				380.00
Tax payable				548.00

Note:

Non-savings income occupies £4,370 of the basic rate band. This allows £630 of savings income to be taxed at the starting rate of 0%. Taxable income does not exceed the basic rate limit, so the PSA is £1,000. Accrued debenture interest is ignored.

Accrued income scheme

The accrued income scheme exists in order to prevent a form of tax avoidance known as "bondwashing". Bondwashing involves selling securities "cum interest" (so that the buyer of the securities will receive the next interest payment) just before an interest payment is due. The price paid by the buyer reflects the fact that the sale is cum interest and so the seller of the securities is not disadvantaged. However, the effect of the transaction from the tax point of view is that the seller has converted what would have been income into a capital gain. Since capital gains arising on the disposal of certain securities are exempt from capital gains tax (see Chapter 20) the seller appears to have avoided tax.

The accrued income scheme overcomes this potential loss of tax by charging the seller income tax on the interest which has accrued up to the date of the sale. The buyer of the securities is entitled to tax relief on the same amount and this is given by deduction from the next interest payment the buyer receives. Similar arrangements apply if securities are transferred "ex interest" (so that the seller will receive the next interest payment). In this case, the buyer is taxed on the interest accruing from the date of the sale to the date of the next interest payment and the seller is entitled to tax relief on the same amount.

The accrued income scheme applies to securities such as gilts, local authority bonds and company debentures. It does not apply to ordinary or preference shares. Transfers made by individuals who have not held securities with a total nominal value exceeding £5,000 in the current tax year or in the preceding tax year are excluded from the scheme.

Dividends received

Dividends received are charged to tax by the Income Tax (Trading and Other Income) Act 2005. Income tax is charged on the amount of dividends received in the tax year, with no adjustment for any accrued dividends. No expenses are allowed against dividend income.

For 2017-18, the first £5,000 of dividends included in taxable income are taxed at the dividend nil rate. Any further dividends are taxed at the dividend ordinary rate (7.5%), the dividend upper rate (32.5%) or the dividend additional rate (38.1%). Note that:

(a) The "dividend allowance" of £5,000 applies also to dividends received from overseas companies (see Chapter 32).

(b) Any capital gain which arises on a disposal of shares is generally subject to capital gains tax (see Chapter 20).

Tax-efficient investments

A taxpayer who is seeking a tax-efficient means of investing in an interest-bearing account or in shares and securities may invest in any of the following:

(a) an Individual Savings Account (ISA)

(b) the Enterprise Investment Scheme (EIS)

(c) a Venture Capital Trust (VCT)

(d) a Child Trust Fund (CTF).

Each of these forms of investment is considered below. Further tax-efficient investment opportunities are offered by the Community Investment Tax Credits (CITC) scheme and by investments which qualify for Social Investment Tax Relief (SITR). The main features of each of these schemes are explained on the website which accompanies this book. The website address is www.pearsoned.co.uk/melville.

Individual Savings Accounts

Individual Savings Accounts (ISAs) may be held by individuals who are at least 16 years old and resident in the UK. The residence requirement is waived in the case of Crown servants serving overseas and their spouses (or civil partners). The main features of these tax-free accounts are as follows:

(a) ISAs are of two main types†. These are "cash ISAs" and "stocks and shares ISAs". Money invested in a cash ISA is held in a savings account. Money invested in a stocks and shares ISA is used by the ISA provider to acquire stocks and shares on the saver's behalf. These stocks and shares may be listed on a stock exchange anywhere in the world. However, it is now permissible for a stocks and shares ISA to hold some cash on deposit. Savers under the age of 18 may invest in a cash ISA only.

† *As from 6 April 2016, there is a third type of ISA (the "innovative finance ISA"). Money invested in such an ISA is used to make peer-to-peer loans.*

(b) Each tax year, a saver may invest in only one ISA of each type. Savers may start fresh ISAs each year or may invest in ISAs started in previous years.

(c) The maximum amount ("subscription limit") which a saver may invest in ISAs during tax year 2017-18 is £20,000. This may be allocated in any way between the different types of ISA. There is no lifetime limit on the amount that may be saved in ISAs, nor is there a minimum level of saving.

(d) Some or all of the money saved in cash ISAs in previous tax years may be transferred to stocks and shares ISAs (or vice versa). Savers may also transfer *all* of the money saved in a cash ISA in the current year to a stocks and shares ISA (or vice versa).

(e) Interest and dividends arising from ISAs are exempt from income tax. Capital gains (and losses) arising from ISAs are exempt from capital gains tax.

(f) Withdrawals may be made from an ISA without loss of tax relief. ISA providers are now able to offer savers the flexibility of withdrawing cash from an ISA and then replacing it later in the same tax year, without this replacement counting towards the subscription limit for the year concerned.

(g) The surviving spouse or civil partner of an ISA saver who dies is granted an extra ISA allowance equal to the value of the deceased person's ISA savings on death. This allowance must be used within a specified time period.

(h) "Help to Buy" ISAs provide a tax-free bonus of up to £3,000 to savers who use the amount saved to buy their first home. "Lifetime" ISAs are available to savers under the age of 40. Up to £4,000 p.a. can be saved in such an ISA until the age of 50 and a bonus of 25% is added to the amount saved. However, withdrawals before the age of 60 incur a withdrawal charge of 25% unless the funds are used to buy a first home.

Note that ISAs were relaunched as NISAs (New ISAs) on 1 July 2014 and all existing ISAs became NISAs on that date. However, the term "ISA" is still widely used.

EXAMPLE 2

For each of the following savers, identify the further ISA investments that may be made during tax year 2017-18:

(a) Alexander saves £500 in a cash ISA on 26 April 2017.

(b) Bianca saves £6,000 in a stocks and shares ISA on 21 May 2017.

(c) Jon saves £1,000 in a cash ISA on 17 June 2017 and £8,000 in a stocks and shares ISA on 4 August 2017.

Solution

(a) £19,500 (£20,000 – £500) may be saved, in either the same cash ISA or a stocks and shares ISA or an innovative finance ISA (or in a combination of these).

(b) £14,000 (£20,000 – £6,000) may be saved, in either the same stocks and shares ISA or a cash ISA or an innovative finance ISA (or in a combination of these).

(c) £11,000 (£20,000 – £9,000) may be saved, in either the same cash ISA or the same stocks and shares ISA or an innovative finance ISA (or in a combination of these).

Junior ISAs

Junior ISAs (JISAs) are available to children under 18 who are UK resident and do not have a Child Trust Fund account (see below). JISAs are tax-free and investments may be made in cash or in stocks and shares. Funds invested in a JISA are owned by the child but are locked in until he or she reaches the age of 18.

The maximum amount that can be invested in a JISA in 2017-18 is £4,128. Note that:

(a) The fact that a child has a JISA does not prevent that child from also having an adult ISA as from the age of 16, in which case the existence of the JISA has no impact upon the adult ISA subscription limits.

(b) Any income derived from parental contributions to a JISA does not count towards the £100 limit relating to income derived from a parent (see Chapter 2).

Enterprise Investment Scheme

The Enterprise Investment Scheme (EIS) was established in 1994 to provide a means of encouraging investment in industry. The main features of the EIS are as follows:

(a) Income tax relief is available to taxpayers who subscribe for newly-issued ordinary shares in qualifying companies. Broadly, these are unlisted trading companies with less than 250 employees (less than 500 for "knowledge-intensive" companies) which have a permanent establishment in the UK and which have gross assets not exceeding £15m immediately before the share issue and not exceeding £16m immediately after it. The company must normally have been trading for no more than seven years (ten years for knowledge-intensive companies) and the total amount raised under the EIS and other venture capital schemes in the 12 months to date must not exceed £5m.

(b) The total amount of the tax-advantaged investments which a company may receive under the EIS and other venture capital schemes such as the SEIS and the VCTs scheme (see below) is capped at £12m (£20m for knowledge intensive companies).

(c) Income tax relief takes the form of a reduction in the amount of tax due on the taxpayer's taxable income. This tax reduction is equal to 30% of the amount invested in qualifying companies during the tax year and takes priority over the tax reductions relating to certain payments (see Chapter 4) and the MCA (see Chapter 3).

(d) A taxpayer's EIS investments of up to £1 million in each tax year are eligible for tax relief. Any of the EIS investments made in a tax year may be carried back and treated as if made in the previous year, but the total EIS investment that can attract income tax relief in any one tax year is subject to the £1 million limit.

(e) The taxpayer must not be connected with the company at any time during the two years prior to the date of the investment and the three years following that date. Broadly speaking, an individual is connected with a company for this purpose if he or she is an employee of the company or, together with associates, owns more than 30% of the company's ordinary shares.

(f) Dividends received on the shares are subject to income tax in the usual way.

(g) Any capital gain arising on the eventual disposal of the shares is exempt from CGT but any loss arising on the disposal is eligible for relief. A loss may be relieved:

    (i) as a capital loss, in the usual way (see Chapter 17), or
    (ii) against the taxpayer's total income of the year in which the loss is incurred or the previous year (see Chapter 12).

    When calculating the allowable loss, the shares are deemed to have been acquired for their issue price, less the tax reduction obtained when the shares were purchased.

The taxpayer must retain the shares for a minimum holding period of at least three years or both the income tax and capital gains tax reliefs are lost.

Seed Enterprise Investment Scheme

The Seed Enterprise Investment Scheme (SEIS) was launched in April 2012 as a means of encouraging investment in start-up companies. The main features of the scheme are:

(a) Subject to certain conditions, tax relief is available to investors who subscribe for ordinary shares in a company which is carrying on a new business. A new business is one which started no more than 2 years before the share issue.

(b) The company concerned must be an unlisted trading company with a permanent establishment in the UK. The company must have fewer than 25 employees and its total assets must be less than £200,000 before the SEIS investment is made. Also, the amount of all SEIS investment received by the company in the three years to the date of the latest investment must not exceed £150,000.

(c) During the period from the company's incorporation until the third anniversary of the share issue, the investor must not own 30% or more of the company's share capital. Also, the investor cannot be an employee of the company (other than a director).

(d) Tax relief takes the form of an income tax reduction equal to 50% of the amount invested up to a limit of £100,000 per annum. Relief is withdrawn if the shares are disposed of within 3 years. As with the main EIS, any SEIS investments made during a tax year may be carried back and treated as if made in the previous year.

(e) Any capital gain arising on the eventual disposal of the shares is exempt from CGT but any loss arising on the disposal is eligible for relief. Furthermore, the gain arising on the disposal of *any* asset may be reduced for tax purposes by 50% of the amount invested through the seed EIS during the year in which the disposal occurs.

The scheme was scheduled to end on 5 April 2017 but has now been extended indefinitely.

Venture Capital Trusts

A Venture Capital Trust (VCT) is a company which is approved as such by HM Revenue and Customs. The main conditions which must be satisfied before HMRC approval can be obtained are as follows:

(a) The company's ordinary shares must be listed on an EU stock exchange.

(b) Its income must be derived wholly or mainly from shares or securities and no more than 15% of this income may be retained by the company.

(c) At least 70% of its total investments must consist of "qualifying holdings" and at least 70% of these holdings must consist of "eligible" shares. Broadly, shares or securities owned by a VCT rank as qualifying holdings if they were newly issued to the VCT and are shares or securities of a company which would be a qualifying company for the purposes of the EIS (see above). Eligible shares exclude redeemable shares.

(d) No holding in any one company (other than in another VCT) can represent more than 15% of a VCT's investments. At least 10% of a VCT's investment in a company must be held in the form of eligible shares.

Income tax relief is available to taxpayers who subscribe for newly-issued shares of a VCT. This takes the form of a tax reduction equal to 30% of the amount invested, subject to an investment limit of £200,000 per tax year. This reduction takes priority over the tax reductions relating to certain payments made by the taxpayer (see Chapter 4) and the tax reduction relating to the MCA (see Chapter 3). To qualify for income tax relief, the taxpayer must hold the shares for a minimum holding period of at least five years.

Dividends on the first £200,000 of VCT shares acquired in each tax year are exempt from income tax and any capital gain or loss arising on the disposal of these shares is exempt from capital gains tax, regardless of whether or not the shares have been held for the minimum holding period.

Child Trust Funds

Child Trust Fund accounts were introduced in 2005 as a tax-efficient means of building up a fund of assets for a young person to use (or re-invest) at the age of 18. The scheme involved the establishment of a CTF account for each child born on or after 1 September 2002. The Government would contribute funds into each CTF account and additional contributions could be made by the child and by his/her family and friends.

However, the Child Trust Funds scheme has now been wound down. Children born in 2011 or later do not qualify for CTF accounts and all Government contributions to existing accounts have ceased. But existing CTF accounts remain open and these accounts continue to offer the following tax advantages:

(a) Additional contributions may still be made into a CTF account. These contributions do not attract tax relief in themselves. But income and gains arising from CTF investments are tax-free and no tax liability arises when a CTF account reaches maturity on the child's 18th birthday.

The maximum amount (the "subscription limit") that may be invested in a CTF in tax year 2017-18 is £4,128.

(b) Any income derived from parental contributions to a CTF account does not count towards the £100 limit relating to income derived from a parent (see Chapter 2).

Note, however, that no funds may be withdrawn from a CTF account until maturity.

Income from trusts and settlements

A trust or settlement is an arrangement whereby property is held by persons known as *trustees*, for the benefit of other persons known as *beneficiaries*. Trusts fall into two main categories, as follows:

(a) If one or more persons are entitled to receive all of the income which is generated by the trust property, then those persons are "life tenants" and the trust is a "trust with an interest in possession".

(b) If there is no life tenant and the trustees have the discretion to distribute as much or as little of the trust income to the beneficiaries as they see fit, the trust is referred to as a "discretionary trust".

Trust taxation is a very complex matter and a full study of the subject is beyond the scope of this book. However, an introduction to trust taxation is given below.

Trusts with an interest in possession

For tax year 2017-18, the trustees of a trust with an interest in possession are liable to income tax at the dividend ordinary rate (7.5%) on the trust's dividend income and at the basic rate (20%) on all of its other income. Note that:

(a) The tax liability of the trustees is never calculated at the starting rate for savings, the higher rate, the additional rate or the dividend upper and additional rates. Trustees are not entitled to the personal savings allowance or the dividend allowance, so the savings nil rate and dividend nil rate (see Chapter 2) are both unavailable.

(b) The general expenses of administering the trust are *not* allowed when computing the income tax liability of the trustees. However, expenses which relate to specific items of trust income (e.g. expenses normally deductible from property income) are set against that income.

(c) The trustees' tax liability is calculated without deduction of personal allowances.

(d) Relief is given for income tax deducted at source (if any).

The income which remains after tax and all expenses have been deducted (including general administration expenses) is paid to the life tenants and is dealt with in their personal tax computations. In those computations:

(a) trust non-savings income and trust savings income are treated as income received net of basic rate tax

(b) trust dividend income is treated as dividend income received net of tax calculated at the dividend ordinary rate.

The general administration expenses of the trust are deemed to have been paid first out of dividend income, then out of savings income and then out of non-savings income.

EXAMPLE 3

An interest in possession trust with one life tenant has the following income in 2017-18:

	£
Rents receivable	30,200
Loan interest received (net)	7,200
Dividends received	1,600

Expenses were incurred in the year as follows:

	£
Property expenses	6,900
Administration expenses	2,120

(a) Compute the trustees' income tax liability for 2017-18.

(b) How much income does the life tenant receive from the trust in 2017-18 and how will this be treated in his or her personal tax computation?

Solution

	Total	*Non-Savings*	*Savings*	*Dividends*
	£	£	£	£
Property income £30,200 – £6,900	23,300	23,300		
Interest received £7,200 x 100/80	9,000		9,000	
Dividends received	1,600			1,600
	33,900	23,300	9,000	1,600
Income tax @ 20%	(4,660)	(4,660)		
Income tax @ 20%	(1,800)		(1,800)	
Income tax @ 7.5%	(120)			(120)
Income after tax	27,320	18,640	7,200	1,480
Administration expenses	(2,120)		(640)	(1,480)
Income after tax and expenses	25,200	18,640	6,560	0

(a) The trustees' tax liability for the year is £6,580 (£4,660 + £1,800 + £120). The £1,800 of tax deducted at source (£9,000 – £7,200) is deducted, leaving tax payable by the trustees of £4,780.

(b) The income of the life tenant is:

	Gross	*Tax deducted*
	£	£
Non-savings £18,640 x 100/80	23,300	4,660
Savings £6,560 x 100/80	8,200	1,640
Total	31,500	6,300

The gross income will be included in the life tenant's computation for 2017-18. The tax deducted at source will be subtracted when computing tax payable for the year.

Discretionary trusts

In general, the income tax liability of the trustees of a discretionary trust is calculated at the "dividend trust rate" on dividend income and at the "trust rate" on all other income. For tax year 2017-18, these rates are 38.1% and 45% respectively. However, these rates do not apply to income which has been used to fund the expenses of administering the trust. Such income is taxed at the dividend ordinary rate (7.5%) or the basic rate (20%), depending upon the type of income involved.

Also, the first £1,000 of the income of a discretionary trust is not taxed at the special trust rates but is instead charged to tax at the income tax rate which generally applies to the class of income concerned (i.e. the dividend ordinary rate or the basic rate). When identifying the first £1,000 of a trust's income, non-savings income is considered first, then savings income, then dividends.

Any payments which are made to beneficiaries are deemed to have been made net of tax at the trust rate (45%) and must therefore be grossed-up at 100/55 in their personal income tax computations. The amount of tax which is deemed to have been deducted from such payments is assessable on the trustees, but only to the extent (if any) that it exceeds the trustees' "tax pool". Broadly, this comprises the sum of:

(a) any tax suffered by the trustees at the trust rate (45%)

(b) any tax suffered by the trustees at the dividend trust rate (38.1%)

(c) any tax suffered by the trustees at the basic rate (20%) or at the dividend ordinary rate (7.5%) on the first £1,000 of trust income.

Trusts with vulnerable beneficiary

A special tax regime applies to trusts with a vulnerable beneficiary. This tax regime ensures that the tax liability of this type of trust is reduced to the amount of tax that would have been payable if the trust income and gains had accrued directly to the beneficiary concerned.

A "vulnerable beneficiary" may be either a disabled person or (in certain instances) a minor. Trustees who wish to claim the special tax treatment available under this regime must make an appropriate election to HM Revenue and Customs. Once made, such an election is irrevocable.

EXAMPLE 4

Assume that a discretionary trust has the same income and expenses in 2017-18 as the trust described in the above example. Assume also that a payment of £8,250 was made to a beneficiary during the year.

(a) Compute the trustees' income tax liability for 2017-18.

(b) Show how the £8,250 received by the beneficiary will be treated in his or her personal tax computation.

Solution

	Total	*Non-Savings*	*Savings*	*Dividends*
	£	£	£	£
Property income £30,200 – £6,900	23,300	23,300		
Interest received £7,200 x 100/80	9,000		9,000	
Dividends received	1,600			1,600
	33,900	23,300	9,000	1,600
First £1,000 of trust income:				
Income tax at 20% on £1,000	(200)	(200)		
Remainder of trust income:				
Income tax @ 7.5% on £1,600	(120)			(120)
Income tax @ 20% on £800	(160)		(160)	
Income tax @ 45% on £8,200	(3,690)		(3,690)	
Income tax @ 45% on £22,300	(10,035)	(10,035)		
Income after tax	19,695	13,065	5,150	1,480
Administration expenses	(2,120)		(640)	(1,480)
Income after tax and expenses	17,575	13,065	4,510	0

Note:

The administration expenses of £2,120 are deemed to have been paid out of the trust's after-tax income, first out of dividends (£1,480) and then out of savings income (£640). As £640 of net savings income has been used for this purpose, gross savings income of £800 is taxed at only 20% and not at the special rate of 45%.

(a) The trustees' tax liability is £14,205 (£200 + £120 + £160 + £3,690 + £10,035). The tax deducted at source of £1,800 is subtracted, leaving tax payable by the trustees of £12,405. This consists of £10,235 payable on the non-savings income, an extra 25% (45% – 20%) on the £8,200 of savings income which is taxed at the trust rate (25% × £8,200 = £2,050) and £120 on the dividend income.

(b) The payment of £8,250 is grossed-up at 100/55, giving gross income of £15,000. This income is included in the beneficiary's tax computation for 2017-18 and the £6,750 of tax deducted at source is subtracted when computing tax payable for the year. The trustees' tax pool is £13,925 (£10,035 + £3,690 + £200). This exceeds £6,750 and so there is no further assessment on the trustees in relation to this payment.

Miscellaneous income

ITTOIA 2005 charges income tax on certain types of miscellaneous income to the extent that this income is not already taxed under another heading. Categories include income from intellectual property, income from films or sound recordings, income from telecommunications rights and any other income which is not otherwise charged to tax.

A loss arising under one of these categories during a tax year is relieved against the first available miscellaneous income of the same type in that year or in future years.

Summary

- Income tax is payable on the interest actually received by a taxpayer during the tax year. Most interest is now received gross but any interest received net is grossed up in the tax computation. Tax deducted at source is then subtracted from the income tax liability. Income tax is also payable on dividends received.
- Individual Savings Accounts (ISAs) provide a tax-free means of either saving cash or investing in stocks and shares. Junior ISAs are available to children. As from 1 July 2014, ISAs were relaunched as NISAs (New ISAs).
- The Enterprise Investment Scheme (EIS) provides tax reliefs to those who subscribe for the newly-issued ordinary shares of qualifying unlisted UK trading companies. The Seed Enterprise Investment Scheme (SEIS) provides tax reliefs to investors who subscribe for newly-issued ordinary shares in start-up companies.
- Subject to certain conditions, tax relief is available in relation to an investment in a Venture Capital Trust (VCT).
- Child Trust Fund (CTF) accounts provide a tax-free means of building up a fund of assets for a young person born between 1 September 2002 and 31 December 2010.
- Trustees must account for income tax on the income of a trust. The administration expenses of the trust are not allowed when computing the trustees' income tax liability. Special rates of tax apply to the income of a discretionary trust.
- Certain forms of miscellaneous income are charged to income tax.

Exercises

6.1 Edward has the following income in 2017-18:

	£
Bank interest	2,250
Loan stock interest (net)	14,520
Dividends received	50,600

He makes £800 of Gift Aid donations during 2017-18. Compute the amount of income tax payable for the year.

6.2 Anne's income for 2017-18 is as follows:

	£
Bank interest:	
Interest on deposit account	480
Interest credited to cash ISA	83
Dividends received	650
Retirement pension	10,886

Compute her income tax liability for the year.

6.3 Outline the income tax advantages of investing in:

(a) the Enterprise Investment Scheme

(b) the Seed Enterprise Investment Scheme

(c) a Venture Capital Trust.

6.4 Outline the main features of Individual Savings Accounts.

6.5 Bernice (who is not a Scottish taxpayer) has the following income in 2017-18:

	£
Business profits	102,850
Building society interest	410
Dividends received	7,240

She makes a qualifying EIS investment of £20,000 in May 2017. Compute her income tax liability for 2017-18, assuming that there are no Gift Aid donations or pension contributions during the year.

***6.6** An interest in possession trust with two life tenants has the following income in tax year 2017-18:

	£
Rents received	12,620
Bank deposit interest	1,240
Gilts interest received gross	1,800
Dividends received	14,480

Property expenses incurred in the year were £2,220 and general administration expenses amounted to £1,850.

(a) Compute the trustees' income tax liability for 2017-18.

(b) Assuming that the trust income is divided equally between the two life tenants, calculate each life tenant's income from the trust in 2017-18.

Chapter 7

Income from employment (1)

Introduction

Income from employment is charged to tax in accordance with the rules of the Income Tax (Earnings and Pensions) Act 2003. The main purpose of the next two chapters of this book is to introduce these rules and to explain how an individual's income from employment is calculated for tax purposes.

This chapter begins by distinguishing between employment and self-employment and then deals with various aspects of the taxation of employment income, including the basis of assessment, non-taxable employment income and deductible expenses. There is also a brief description of the Pay As You Earn (PAYE) system which is used to collect both income tax and National Insurance contributions from employees. The chapter concludes by outlining the features of a number of tax-efficient employee incentive schemes. The tax treatment of benefits in kind is explained in the next chapter.

These two chapters are concerned with employees whose duties are performed wholly within the UK. The taxation of overseas earnings is considered in Chapter 32.

Employment and self-employment

As will become clear in subsequent chapters, self-employed people enjoy tax advantages in comparison with employees. Two of the main advantages of being self-employed are:

(a) A much wider range of expenses is allowed against the income of self-employed people than against the income of employees (see Chapter 9).

(b) Self-employed people (see Chapter 15) generally pay their income tax much later than employees, who pay income tax under the Pay As You Earn system.

It is usually quite obvious whether someone is employed or self-employed but sometimes there are borderline cases. For example, it may be extremely difficult to distinguish between an employee with a number of part-time jobs and a self-employed person with a number of clients. In such cases, the taxpayer will usually wish to claim self-employed status, whilst HMRC will often insist that the taxpayer should be treated as an employee.

The key test to be applied when trying to establish a taxpayer's status in cases like these is concerned with the nature of the contract between the taxpayer and the person who is paying for the work done by that taxpayer. There are two possibilities:

(a) If it can be shown that a *contract of service* exists, then the taxpayer is regarded as an employee who is in service to an employer.

(b) If it can be shown that a *contract for services* exists, then the taxpayer is regarded as a self-employed person who is rendering services to a client.

A great deal of case law has accumulated on this subject over the years and several criteria have been established which may be used to distinguish between the two types of contract. The main criteria are as follows:

(a) **Control**. The more control that the person who is paying for the work has over the person who is doing the work, the more likely it is that a contract of service exists. Employees are usually unable to choose whether or not to do certain work, how to do the work, when to do the work or where to do the work. Self-employed people are usually able to decide these matters for themselves.

(b) **Remuneration and financial risk**. Employees usually receive a regular wage or salary; they are paid whether or not their employer is making a profit and do not risk their own capital in the business. Self-employed people are normally paid a separate fee for each job they do; they may make losses as well as profits and may lose their capital if their business fails.

(c) **Equipment**. In general, employees do not provide their own equipment but self-employed people do.

(d) **Work performance and correction**. Employees are usually expected to do their work themselves. If they make mistakes they will correct the work during working hours and get paid for both the original work and the corrections. Self-employed people often delegate their work to staff or subcontractors. If the work done is unsatisfactory, the client will not expect to pay for it to be corrected.

(e) **Holidays and sickness**. Employees are likely to receive holiday pay and sick pay from their employers. Self-employed people are paid by their clients only for the work that they do and do not get paid when on holiday or when ill.

(f) **Exclusivity**. In general, an employee is employed by just one employer and is an integral part of that employer's business. Self-employed people normally have a number of clients and are not integral to any of their clients' businesses.

There are exceptions to all of the general statements given above and therefore these criteria should be applied with caution. It is vitally important to consider the facts of each case as a whole† and not to rely upon just one criterion when trying to decide whether a taxpayer should be regarded as employed or self-employed.

† *This point is illustrated by the leading case of Hall v Lorimer (1993) which forms the subject of Exercise 7.6 at the end of this chapter.*

Personal service companies

One way in which an individual might seek to avoid being classed as an employee is to form a company (a "personal service company") and then hire out his or her services in the name of that company. Anti-avoidance legislation (the "IR35" legislation) exists to thwart this kind of disguised employment. The main features of this legislation are as follows:

(a) The legislation applies to "relevant engagements" where a worker provides services to a client through an intermediary (usually a company) in circumstances such that the income arising from the engagement would have been treated as income from employment if it had not been for the presence of the intermediary.

(b) If an intermediary receives income from relevant engagements during a tax year and this income (less any deductible expenses) is greater than the worker's employment income from the intermediary in that year, then the excess is treated as a deemed salary payment made on the last day of the year. This deemed payment is subject to both income tax and National Insurance contributions, collected via PAYE.

(c) The deductible expenses referred to above include all expenses generally deductible from employment income, plus any employer's pension and National Insurance contributions made by the intermediary, plus a further flat-rate 5%† of the income arising from relevant engagements (to cover running costs of the intermediary).

(d) If the worker is paid a dividend by the intermediary, the amount of any deemed salary payment may be set against this dividend so as to avoid double taxation.

† *This 5% deduction does not apply in the case of public sector engagements and the public sector engager is responsible for deducting and paying the necessary employment taxes and NICs.*

Managed service companies

Managed service companies (MSCs) are similar to personal service companies in that they act as intermediaries through which the services of workers are provided to end clients. However, whilst a personal service company is usually controlled by the individual who formed it, an MSC is a mass-marketed service company set up and controlled by an MSC provider. A number of workers (typically ten to twenty) may become shareholders in an MSC, which then offers their services to clients.

Anti-avoidance legislation has been introduced to ensure that income received by individuals who provide their services through MSCs is treated as employment income for tax purposes. MSCs are required to operate the PAYE system (see below) to collect income tax and National Insurance contributions in relation to such income.

Agency workers

If an individual has a contract with an agency, under which the individual renders services to a client, and these services are subject to "supervision, direction or control" by any person, the worker will generally be treated as an employee. Anti-avoidance legislation exists to prevent agency working being used to disguise employment as self-employment.

Basis of assessment

An individual's employment income for a tax year is the income actually received in that tax year (the "receipts basis"). This is not necessarily the same as the income *earned* during the year. Employment income is deemed to be received on the *earliest* of:

(a) the date that the income is actually received by the employee

(b) the date that the employee becomes entitled to receive the income

and, for a company director only:

(c) the date that the income is credited to the director in the company's records

(d) the end of a period of account, if the amount of the director's income for that period is determined before it ends

(e) the date that the amount of the director's income for a period of account is determined, if this falls after the end of that period.

EXAMPLE 1

Barry (who is not a director) receives an annual salary of £45,000. His bonus for the year to 31 March 2017 was £7,350, received in May 2017. His bonus for the year to 31 March 2018 was £7,900, received in May 2018. Compute his employment income for 2017-18.

Solution

Employment income for 2017-18 is £52,350 (£45,000 + £7,350). The bonus received in May 2017 is taxed in 2017-18, even though it was earned before the year began.

Employment income

The term "employment income" includes practically anything that could conceivably be received by an employee in respect of an employment (e.g. wages, salaries, bonuses, commissions, fees, expense allowances, payments on the termination of employment, pensions arising from an employment and benefits in kind). Also, certain social security benefits† are taxed in the same way as employment income, including:

(a) the state retirement pension
(b) the job seeker's allowance (up to a specified maximum amount)
(c) statutory sick pay, maternity pay and paternity pay.

Note that it is not necessary for the employee to receive the income directly from the employer. So long as the income in question is received as a result of employment it is taxable as employment income, no matter who has paid it. For example, a waiter's tips are taxable, even though these are paid by customers rather than by the employer.

†A special tax treatment now applies to child benefit (see later in this chapter).

Non-taxable employment income

Certain forms of income from employment are exempt from income tax. These include:

(a) trivial benefits in kind costing £50 or less (see Chapter 8)

(b) free or subsidised meals in a staff canteen, if available to all employees

(c) a party or similar function paid for by the employer, so long as the function is open to staff generally and the cost does not exceed £150 per head, but note that:

  (i) if a function costs over £150 per head, the whole cost is taxable

  (ii) if there is more than one function in the year and their total cost exceeds £150 per head, functions totalling £150 or less per head are exempt but any other functions are taxed in full (unless covered by the trivial benefits exemption)

(d) the provision of a parking space at or near the employee's place of work

(e) the provision of a taxi home for an employee who is occasionally required to work later than usual and until at least 9pm (but no more than 60 journeys per year)

(f) the payment by an employer of the costs of an employee's journey home if the employee regularly travels to work in a shared car, but is prevented from travelling home in the shared car because of unforeseen and exceptional circumstances

(g) "green commuting" benefits paid for by the employer and used by employees for travel between home and work, including the provision of:

- bicycles and cycling safety equipment loaned to employees
- works buses with a seating capacity for nine or more passengers
- subsidies to public bus services

(h) contributions by an employer towards the additional household costs incurred by an employee who works at home (supporting evidence of these costs being required only if the contributions exceed £4 per week)

(i) approved mileage allowances (see below)

(j) payment of an employee's "incidental overnight expenses" (e.g. the cost of telephone calls home) when the employee is away from home overnight on business, of up to £5 per night for stays within the UK or up to £10 per night for stays outside the UK

(k) reasonable removal expenses (up to £8,000) paid by an employer when an employee first takes up an employment or transfers to a new location within the organisation

(l) awards of up to £5,000 made under a staff suggestion scheme

(m) non-cash long-service awards, so long as the award is in respect of at least 20 years of service, does not cost the employer more than £50 per year of service and no such award has been made to the employee in the previous ten years

(n) non-cash gifts received by virtue of the employment from someone other than the employer, so long as the value of the gifts from any one source amounts to no more than £250 in the tax year and the gifts are not made in recognition of the performance of particular services in the course of the employment

(o) reasonable gifts made by employer to employee in a personal capacity rather than as remuneration for services rendered (e.g. a wedding present)

(p) the provision of work-related training courses for an employee and payments of up to £15,480 per academic year made to an employee who is attending a full-time course at a recognised educational establishment

(q) the provision of retraining courses for employees who will be leaving the employment within the next two years or for past employees who have left the employment within the previous 12 months

(r) the provision of one mobile telephone (or smartphone) for an employee's use

(s) the provision of job-related living accommodation (see Chapter 8)

(t) the provision of workplace childcare, sports or recreation facilities

(u) up to £55 per week of childcare if the employer contracts directly with an approved childminder or provides childcare vouchers (reduced to only £28 per week for higher-rate taxpayers and £25 per week for additional-rate taxpayers who joined employer-supported childcare schemes on or after 6 April 2011)†

(v) the provision of eye tests and spectacles for VDU use, one health screening and one medical check-up per year and medical treatment costing up to £500 per year to help an employee return to work after a period of absence caused by illness or injury

(w) bonus payments of up to £3,600 per year received by the employees of a company controlled by an employee ownership trust

(x) an employer's contributions to a registered pension scheme (see Chapter 14).

† *With the introduction of the Government "tax-free childcare" scheme in 2017, no new members will be allowed to join employer-supported childcare schemes after April 2018. But existing members will be able to stay in their employer's scheme if they so wish.*

‡ *The Government has proposed that up to £500 per tax year of employer-provided pensions advice should be exempt from income tax as from 6 April 2017.*

Approved mileage allowances

Employees who use their own vehicles on business may receive mileage allowances from their employers. These allowances are tax-free so long as they do not exceed the HMRC approved mileage allowance payment (AMAP) which is calculated by reference to a table of approved mileage rates. For 2017-18, these rates are:

	first 10,000 miles in tax year	*each mile over 10,000 miles*
Motor cars and vans	45p per mile	25p per mile
Motor cycles	24p per mile	24p per mile
Bicycles	20p per mile	20p per mile

If the mileage allowances paid to an employee exceed the amount calculated using these rates, then the excess is taxable. On the other hand, if the mileage allowances paid to an employee are less than the amount calculated using these rates, the deficit is a deductible expense. Tax relief cannot be claimed for any costs above the AMAP rate.

Employers may also pay employees up to 5p per mile tax-free for each passenger carried on a business trip. However, employees cannot claim tax relief if the employer pays less than this (or pays nothing at all).

EXAMPLE 2

Julie uses her own car when travelling on her employer's business. In 2017-18 she drives 12,000 business miles. Explain the taxation implications if her employer pays her:

(a) 47p per mile (b) 37p per mile (c) None.

Solution

(a) Having driven 12,000 business miles in the year, Julie may receive a tax-free mileage allowance of up to £5,000 ((10,000 × 45p) + (2,000 × 25p)). She actually receives £5,640 (12,000 × 47p) so her taxable mileage allowance is £640.

(b) Julie receives £4,440 (12,000 × 37p) and therefore she has a deductible expense of £560 (£5,000 – £4,440) which may be set against her income from employment.

(c) If Julie receives nothing, she has a deductible expense of £5,000.

Deductible expenses

If an employee incurs an expense in connection with his or her employment, then one of two situations may arise:

(a) The employee pays the expense and is not reimbursed by the employer. In this case, as long as the expense is deductible (see below), the amount of the expense will be subtracted from the employee's income for tax purposes.

(b) The employer reimburses the employee or pays the expense directly. In this case, as long as the expense is either:

    (i) an expense that would have been deductible if it had been paid by the employee without reimbursement, or

    (ii) an expense which has been calculated in an "approved way"

    then the amount paid by the employer is exempt from income tax and is not treated as part of the employee's income from employment. Otherwise, the amount paid by the employer is treated as employment income for tax purposes. The employee may then try to claim a deduction (if possible) for the expense concerned.

An expense is calculated in an "approved way" if it has been calculated in accordance with HMRC regulations. One example of such an expense is a meal allowance paid to an employee who is required to travel for business purposes. Regulations stipulate that such meal allowances are approved if they do not exceed specified amounts varying from £5 to £25 per day, depending upon the duration and timing of the business travel on that day.

Expenses incurred by an employee are deductible (or "allowable") for tax purposes only if they fall into one of the following categories:

(a) contributions to an occupational pension scheme, if deducted from the employee's pay by the employer (see Chapter 14)
(b) subscriptions to relevant professional bodies
(c) donations made under a payroll giving scheme (see later in this chapter)
(d) travel and subsistence expenses necessarily incurred in the performance of the duties of the employment (see below)
(e) other expenses incurred wholly, exclusively and necessarily in the performance of the duties of the employment.

The "wholly, exclusively and necessarily" rule is applied very stringently. In particular, the "necessarily" part of the rule means that an expense will not be allowed unless it can be shown that the duties of the employment concerned could not be performed (by anyone) if the expense were not incurred.

Travel between home and work

As stated above, travel and subsistence expenses are allowable for tax purposes only if they are necessarily incurred in the performance of the duties of the employment. This means that the cost of travel between home and work is normally disallowed on the grounds that the duties of the employment do not begin until the employee arrives at work. However, the following costs of travel between home and work are allowable:

(a) travel and subsistence costs incurred by a "site-based" employee (i.e. an employee who has no normal place of work) when travelling between home and the site
(b) travel and subsistence costs incurred by an employee who has a normal place of work, when undertaking business journeys which start from home
(c) travel and subsistence costs incurred by an employee who is seconded to a temporary place of work, so long as it is expected that he or she will return to the normal place of work within 24 months.

EXAMPLE 3

In which of the following cases will the expenses described be deductible from the employee's income for tax purposes?

(a) A bank manager voluntarily pays an annual subscription to a London club. He uses the club only for the purpose of meeting the bank's clients.
(b) A workman is required to provide his own tools and protective clothing.
(c) A clerk pays to attend a college course in the evenings, so as to gain qualifications and improve her career prospects.

(d) The finance director of a company pays an annual subscription to the Institute of Chartered Accountants.

(e) A barrister living and practising in London is appointed Recorder of Portsmouth. He pays his own train fares between London and Portsmouth.

Solution

(a) The bank manager uses the club wholly and exclusively for business purposes, but it is not necessary for him to be a member of the club in order to perform his duties. Therefore the cost of the subscription will be disallowed. The facts of this case are similar to those of *Brown* v *Bullock* (1961).

(b) The cost of necessary tools and protective clothing will be allowed. In some cases, HMRC has agreed flat-rate allowances with the relevant trade union or association for expenses such as tools, protective clothing, uniforms and laundry costs.

(c) Whilst attending college, the clerk is not performing the duties of her employment. Therefore the cost of the college course will be disallowed. The facts of this case are similar to those of *Blackwell* v *Mills* (1945).

(d) Relevant professional subscriptions of this nature are specifically allowed by statute. Therefore the cost of the subscription will be allowed.

(e) The duties of the employment are carried out entirely in Portsmouth. Whilst travelling from London, the barrister is not performing those duties so the expense will be disallowed. The facts of this case are similar to those of *Ricketts* v *Colquhoun* (1935).

Entertaining expenses

In general, entertaining expenses are not allowable against employment income and an employee who is obliged to defray such expenses personally cannot claim a deduction for them. However, if an employer either:

(a) reimburses an employee for entertaining expenses incurred, or
(b) pays the employee a specific entertaining allowance

then the entertaining expenses incurred by the employee may be set against the sums received from the employer. This rule is subject to the overriding rule that the entertaining expenses must be incurred wholly, exclusively and necessarily in the performance of the duties of the employment.

Payroll giving scheme

Employees whose employers operate an approved "payroll giving scheme" may make charitable donations by requesting that the donations should be deducted from their gross earnings. Income tax is then payable on the earnings which remain *after* the donations have been deducted, thus providing tax relief. The employer passes the donations on to an approved charity.

Payments made on termination of employment

Payments received by an employee on the termination of employment† fall into three distinct categories:

(a) **Fully exempt**. The following termination payments are exempt from income tax:

- (i) payments made on the death of the employee
- (ii) payments made to the employee because of injury or disability
- (iii) lump sum payments under registered pension schemes.

(b) **Fully taxable**. If an employee receives a termination payment which does not fall into any of the categories listed above and which is made by way of reward for the employee's services, then the payment is fully taxable in the year in which it is received. This applies if the employee was contractually entitled to the payment or if there was a reasonable expectation that the payment would be made.

(c) **Partially exempt**. Payments made at an employer's discretion ("ex gratia" payments) to compensate an employee for loss of employment are exempt from income tax if the total amount received does not exceed £30,000. Any excess over £30,000 is taxed in the year in which it is received. However, the £30,000 threshold is reduced by any statutory redundancy pay (SRP) that the employee also receives, even though SRP is itself exempt from income tax.

The taxable part of a partially exempt termination payment is treated as the top slice of income, ranking above both savings income and dividends. This provision ensures that a termination payment does not move savings income and dividends into higher tax bands. Prior to 2016-17 this was beneficial. But with the recent changes to the structure of tax rates, the "highest part" rule can now have an adverse effect (see example below). It remains to be seen whether this rule will be amended in due course.

† *The Government has proposed a number of amendments to the tax rules relating to termination payments and these are due to take effect as from April 2018. However, the first £30,000 of "ex gratia" payments will continue to be exempt from income tax.*

EXAMPLE 4

Henrietta (who is not a Scottish taxpayer) is made redundant in March 2018. She receives statutory redundancy pay of £2,500 and an ex gratia compensation payment of £40,000 from her employer. Her only other income in 2017-18 consists of her salary of £35,180 and dividends received of £9,400. Calculate her income tax liability for 2017-18.

Solution

The exempt part of the ex gratia payment is £27,500 (£30,000 – £2,500). The remaining £12,500 is taxable and is treated as the top slice of Henrietta's income. The income tax computation for the year is as follows:

	Total	*Non-savings*	*Dividends*	*Compensation*
	£	£	£	£
Salary	35,180	35,180		
Dividends received	9,400		9,400	
Compensation £40,000 – £27,500	12,500			12,500
Total income	57,080	35,180	9,400	12,500
Less: Personal allowance	11,500	11,500		
Taxable income	45,580	23,680	9,400	12,500

Non-savings income and dividend income fall entirely into the basic rate band, leaving £420 (£33,500 – £23,680 – £9,400) of this band for the compensation. The remainder of the compensation is taxed at the higher rate.

Income tax due

Basic rate band	: Non-savings	23,680	@ 20%	4,736.00
	: Dividends	5,000	@ 0%	0.00
	: Dividends	4,400	@ 7.5%	330.00
	: Compensation	420	@ 20%	84.00
Higher rate	: Compensation	12,080	@ 40%	4,832.00
		45,580		
Tax liability				9,982.00

Notes:

(i) If the compensation payment had not been treated as the top slice of income, all of the dividends would have been moved out of the basic rate band and £4,400 of these dividends would have been taxed at the dividend upper rate of 32.5%. However, an extra £9,400 of the compensation would have been taxed at the basic rate of 20%. So the "highest part" rule has increased the tax liability by (£9,400 x (40% – 20%)) – (£4,400 x (32.5% – 7.5%)) = £780.00.

(ii) Any tax paid by means of the PAYE system would be deducted when computing tax payable.

High income child benefit charge

Child benefit is a social security benefit which is not taxable. However, a taxpayer who has adjusted net income (see Chapter 3) in excess of £50,000 per annum and receives child benefit (or whose partner receives child benefit) may be subject to the "high income child benefit charge". This income tax charge is equal to 1% of the child benefit award for each £100 of income between £50,000 and £60,000. The charge on taxpayers with income of more than £60,000 is 100% of the child benefit award.

This charge applies only to taxpayers whose income exceeds £50,000 for the tax year. If both of the partners to a domestic partnership have income exceeding £50,000, the charge applies only to the partner with the higher income.

The PAYE system

Under the Pay As You Earn (PAYE) system, employers are required to deduct income tax and National Insurance contributions from their employees when paying them their wages and salaries. The amounts deducted from employees, together with the secondary National Insurance contributions payable by the employer (see Chapter 16) must be paid to HMRC within 14 days of the end of the tax month in which the employees are paid (or 17 days if payment to HMRC is made electronically). A tax month runs from the 6th of one month to the 5th of the next month. Therefore employers generally make a payment to HMRC on or before the 19th (or 22nd) of each month. However, employers whose payments to HMRC do not exceed an average of £1,500 per month are allowed to make quarterly payments.

The PAYE system applies to all payments which are assessable as employment income, including wages, salaries, bonuses, commissions etc. The system also covers:

(a) payments consisting of assets which are readily convertible into cash, such as shares or other commodities, but excluding "own company" shares which are provided by the employer under an approved share scheme (see later in this chapter)

(b) vouchers exchangeable either for cash or for readily convertible assets

(c) remuneration schemes involving trade debts, whereby employers assign trade debts to employees, who then receive cash when the debts are settled.

Benefits in kind (see Chapter 8) are usually brought within the scope of PAYE by making an adjustment to the employee's tax code (see below).

Tax codes

The PAYE system is based upon the concept of "tax codes". HMRC issues a tax code for each employee for each tax year, representing the amount which the employee may earn in that year before becoming liable to income tax. The tax code takes into account a number of factors which may affect an employee's income tax liability, including:

(a) the personal allowances to which the employee is entitled

(b) the employee's expenses and tax reliefs (e.g. payments deductible from total income)

(c) adjustments made in order to collect tax on benefits in kind†

(d) adjustments for tax overpaid or underpaid in previous years, including tax debts of up to £17,000 (with or without the taxpayer's consent) and self assessment balancing payments of up to £3,000 (see Chapter 15).

The tax code allocated to an employee is equal to one-tenth of the aggregate of the above items, rounded down to a whole number.

† *Until 2016-17, HMRC could not determine the amount of an employee's benefits in kind until these were reported by the employer on form P11D at the end of the year (see below). However, employers are now able (voluntarily) to quantify certain benefits in kind themselves and then collect tax on these benefits in real time through the PAYE RTI system (see later in this chapter).*

EXAMPLE 5

Henry is single and claims only the basic personal allowance. He makes a deductible payment of £100 per annum and pays an allowable subscription of £85 per annum. His taxable benefits in kind for 2017-18 are expected to be £500. Determine his tax code for 2017-18, assuming that his income for the year is not expected to exceed £100,000.

Solution

By virtue of his personal allowance, deductible payment and allowable expenses, Henry is entitled to earn £11,685 (£11,500 + £100 + £85) in the year before paying tax. But some of this will be set against his benefits in kind of £500, leaving only £11,185 to set against his salary. So his tax code for the year is "1118" (i.e. one-tenth of £11,185, rounded down to a whole number).

The same result would be obtained if the aggregate figure (£11,185) were anywhere in the range £11,180 to £11,189, so tax codes are not precise. But dividing the aggregate figure by ten results in only one-tenth as many different tax codes as would be obtained otherwise and cuts down the size of the tax tables used by employers (see below).

Tax code suffixes

A tax code may also have a suffix comprising a letter of the alphabet. The most common suffix is L which stands for "low" and indicates that the employee is entitled to the basic personal allowance (currently £11,500). So Henry's full tax code in the above example would actually be "1118L". Other suffixes include:

M - the employee's spouse or civil partner has elected to transfer part of his/her personal allowance to the employee

N - the employee has elected to transfer part of his/her personal allowance to a spouse or civil partner.

Code BR instructs the employer to deduct basic rate tax from all payments made to the employee. Code NT instructs the employer not to deduct tax from the employee at all. Codes prefixed† with the letter K are negative codes, used mainly for employees whose taxable benefits in kind exceed their allowances. Tax on the excess benefits is collected by increasing the amount of tax charged on the employee's wage or salary.

One purpose of tax code suffixes is to facilitate the recoding exercise which is needed whenever personal allowances increase. When this happens, HMRC may (for example) simply instruct employers to increase all L codes by the amount required to reflect the increase in the basic personal allowance, so avoiding the need to recode every employee in the country individually.

† *The tax codes of Scottish employees are prefixed with the letter S and employers are required to apply Scottish rates of income tax to such employees, whether or not the employer is located in Scotland (see Chapter 2).*

Operation of the PAYE system

Employers who operate manual payroll systems (now rare) are issued with sets of tax tables which enable them to calculate the amount of income tax that should be deducted from an employee in a given week or month. The main tables used are:

Table A This table (also known as the Pay Adjustment Table) contains pages for each week or month of the year and shows, for each tax code, the amount of tax-free pay to which the employee is entitled for the year to date. In effect, the table spreads an employee's allowances evenly over the year, giving 1/12th of the allowances per month or 1/52th of the allowances per week.

Table B This table (also known as the Taxable Pay Table) is used to look up an employee's income tax liability for the year to date, after the entitlement to tax-free pay has been taken into account.

In outline, the procedure followed for each employee in each week or month is:

(a) The employee's tax code is looked up in Table A, which shows the amount of tax-free pay to which the employee is entitled for the year to date.

(b) This is then subtracted from the employee's gross pay for the year to date giving the employee's taxable pay for the year to date.

(c) The employee's taxable pay for the year to date is then looked up in Table B, which shows the tax due for the year to date. Further tables are used if the employee is a higher rate taxpayer.

(d) Finally, the tax paid to date by the employee in previous weeks or months is subtracted from the tax due for the year to date, giving the employee's income tax liability for the current week or month.

The entire system is cumulative and requires employers to keep track of each of their employees' gross pay and income tax paid to date (i.e. since the beginning of the tax year on 6 April). Employers are provided with deductions working sheets (form P11) which facilitate the accumulation of the necessary "to date" figures.

In computer-based payroll systems (which are now used by nearly all employers) the tax tables become computer files and the weekly or monthly procedure is carried out by computer software. However, the operation of the PAYE system does not change in principle when a manual payroll system is replaced by a computer-based system.

PAYE forms

P2 A notice of coding, sent by HMRC to both the employer and the employee.

P11 Deductions working sheet (see above).

P11D An end-of-year return showing an employee's benefits in kind and expenses for the year. Forms P11D must be submitted to HMRC by 6 July following the end of the tax year. Employees must be provided with copies by the same date.

P45 A four-part form used when an employee leaves an employment, showing the employee's tax code, gross pay to date and tax paid to date. Part 1 of the form is sent to HMRC and the other three parts are given to the leaving employee. The employee gives parts 2 and 3 to his or her new employer who retains part 2 and sends part 3 to HMRC. The employee retains part 1A.

P46 A form providing details of a new employee who does not have a P45 from a previous employment. Sent to HMRC by the employer.

P60 Certificate of gross pay and tax deducted, given to employees by employers at the end of the tax year. Forms P60 must be provided to employees by 31 May following the end of the tax year.

Notes:

(a) Online filing of "in-year" forms P45 and P46 via the RTI system (see below) is now mandatory. End-of-year P11Ds may also be filed online.

(b) Employers are allowed to provide P60s to their employees by electronic means, as long as the employees concerned are able to access their P60s easily and securely.

(c) Employers with 250 or more employees are required to make their PAYE payments to HMRC by electronic means.

Real Time Information

The PAYE Real Time Information (RTI) system was introduced during tax year 2013-14 and is now in use by virtually all employers. This system requires employers to send data about their employees' pay and deductions (income tax and NICs) to HMRC at the time that the employees are paid. Online data transmission is mandatory.

Before the advent of RTI, it was necessary for employers to send end-of-year forms to HMRC showing each employee's gross pay, tax paid and NICs for the year. RTI removes the need for these forms, since the necessary data is automatically submitted to HMRC during the tax year each time that the employee is paid. Furthermore, information about starters and leavers is transmitted as part of the RTI process, so there is no longer any need for employers to submit forms P45 and P46 to HMRC separately.

As from tax year 2016-17, employers may also (voluntarily) deal with most† benefits in kind through the PAYE RTI system. If an employer chooses to do this, information about an employee's benefits in kind is submitted in real time to HMRC and there is no need to supply form P11D at the end of the tax year.

† *Voluntary "payrolling" of benefits in kind is not applicable to living accommodation or beneficial loans (see Chapter 8) so P11Ds are still required for employees who receive these benefits.*

Construction industry scheme

The construction industry scheme (CIS) may apply when a contractor makes payments to a subcontractor under a contract relating to construction operations. Subcontractors who rank as employees are dealt with via the PAYE system in the usual way, but it has proved necessary to introduce a special scheme in relation to subcontractors who do not rank as employees, so as to counter tax evasion. The main features of the CIS are as follows:

(a) Subcontractors are required to register as such with HMRC. They may apply to be paid gross by the contractors for whom they work or they may register to be paid under deduction of tax. In order to qualify for gross payment, a subcontractor must be running a business which:

   (i) is carried on in the UK and has a bank account (the "business test")
   (ii) has a construction turnover of at least a specified amount (the "turnover test")
   (iii) has complied with all of its tax obligations (the "compliance test").

   For sole traders, the "specified amount" referred to above is £30,000 per annum. For partnerships and companies, the specified amount is the *lower* of £100,000 and the figure obtained by multiplying £30,000 by the number of partners or directors.

(b) Subcontractors must give contractors their name, unique taxpayer reference and National Insurance number when they enter into a contract. The contractor then contacts HMRC to check on the subcontractor's status. This process is known as "verification".

(c) If the subcontractor is registered with HMRC, the contractor will be told either to pay the subcontractor gross or to apply the standard rate of deduction (20%). However, any payment which represents a reimbursement of the cost of materials supplied by the subcontractor is excluded from the amount which is subject to deduction of tax.

(d) If the subcontractor is not registered with HMRC, the contractor will be told to apply a higher rate of deduction (30%) when making payments to that subcontractor.

(e) Within 14 days of the end of each tax month, contractors must provide a statement to each subcontractor from whom a tax deduction has been made, showing details of the payments made and the amounts deducted.

(f) Also within 14 days of the end of each tax month, contractors must send a return to HMRC showing all of the payments made to subcontractors during the month, whether paid gross or under deduction of tax. Online filing of these CIS returns is now mandatory.

(g) All deductions made from subcontractors during a tax month must be paid over to HMRC within 14 days of the end of the tax month. Three further days are allowed if payment is made electronically.

Employee incentive schemes

An employee incentive scheme provides financial incentives for employees to improve their work performance. The main types of scheme which currently have income tax implications are:

(a) share incentive plans (SIPs)
(b) approved share option schemes
(c) enterprise management incentives (EMIs).

A brief description of each of these types of scheme is given below.

Share incentive plans

Share incentive plans (SIPs) offer employees a tax-efficient way of acquiring shares in the companies for which they work. SIPs were originally known as all-employee share ownership plans (AESOPs). The main features of these plans are as follows:

(a) Companies which set up a SIP may offer their employees:

   (i) *free shares* in the company worth up to £3,600 per annum per employee
   (ii) the opportunity to use salary of up to £1,800 per annum to buy *partnership shares* in the company (without having to pay either income tax or NICs on the salary used for this purpose)
   (iii) up to two free *matching shares* for each partnership share bought by an employee.

   This means that (in 2017-18) an employee paying income tax at the basic rate could acquire up to £9,000 worth of shares at a cost of £1,440 (80% × £1,800). The cost would be reduced to £1,080 (60% × £1,800) for an employee paying tax at the higher rate and only £990 (55% × £1,800) for an employee paying tax at the additional rate. There would also be a saving in National Insurance contributions (see Chapter 16).

(b) The company may offer free shares only, partnership shares only, free shares and partnership shares only, partnership shares and matching shares only, or all three of these types of shares.

(c) Subject to certain conditions, the plan may link the provision of free shares to the achievement of employee performance targets.

(d) In general, all employees must be eligible to participate in the plan. However, the plan may specify that employees do not become eligible until they have been employed by the company (or employed by the group, in the case of a group of companies) for a qualifying period of not more than 18 months.

(e) The plan may allow (or may compel) dividends arising on an employee's shares to be reinvested tax-free in further *dividend shares*.

(f) All of an employee's shares leave the plan when he or she ceases to be employed by the company (or group). The plan rules may specify that employees who leave within three years should forfeit their free and matching shares. Additionally, employees may take some or all of their shares out of the plan as follows:

Free/matching shares	:	at any time after the end of the holding period specified by the plan, which must be between three and five years
Partnership shares	:	at any time (though any related matching shares may be forfeited if this occurs within three years)
Dividend shares	:	at any time after three years.

(g) If free, matching or partnership shares leave the plan within three years, a charge to income tax and NICs arises based on the market value of the shares when leaving the plan. If the shares leave the plan after three years but in less than five years, this charge is based upon the *lower* of the market value of the shares when originally awarded and the market value of the shares when leaving the plan.

(h) If dividend shares leave the plan within three years, a tax charge arises on a *notional dividend* equal to the cash dividend which was used to acquire the shares.

(i) No tax charge arises if shares of any type leave the plan after five years (or earlier if caused by the employee's retirement or by death, injury, disability or redundancy).

(j) Employees who keep their shares in the plan until they sell them incur no liability to capital gains tax. Employees who take their shares out of the plan and sell them later pay CGT on any increase in value since the shares were taken out.

Approved share option schemes

In general, a charge to income tax (and NICs) may arise if an employee who works for a company is granted an option to buy shares in that company. The charge arises when the option is exercised and is based upon the market value of the shares obtained, less the amount paid for the shares and less the amount (if any) which was paid to acquire the option. However, this charge can be avoided if the option falls within an approved share option scheme. Approved schemes are of two main types:

(a) **Savings-related share option schemes**. Under a savings-related scheme, employees are granted an option to buy shares and then save through a tax-free savings scheme in order to raise funds to exercise the option. The amount saved must be no more than £500 a month and the savings contract may last for three or five years. The scheme must be open to all employees who have worked for the company for a specified qualifying period (which cannot exceed five years). The price at which employees are given the option to buy shares must be at least 80% of the shares' market value at the time that the option is granted.

(b) **Company share option plans**. These schemes are less restrictive than savings-related schemes. The company can select the employees to whom it would like to offer share options and can set these employees performance targets which must be achieved before the options will be made available. The price at which an option may be exercised must not be manifestly less than the market value of the shares at the time that the option is granted and options must normally be exercised no earlier than three years and no later than ten years after they are granted. However, options may be exercised within three years of being granted if an employee's participation in the scheme ends through injury, disability, redundancy or retirement. There is an upper limit of £30,000 on the value of the shares (at the time of the grant) for which an employee may hold options at any one time.

If a share option is granted under an approved scheme of either type and all necessary conditions are satisfied, then no income tax or NICs are payable on either the grant of the option or the exercise of the option. For capital gains tax purposes (see Chapter 18) the allowable cost of shares acquired under an approved share option scheme is the price actually paid for the shares by the employee.

Enterprise management incentives

Enterprise management incentives (EMIs) offer trading companies that have a permanent establishment in the UK the chance to reward selected employees with tax-free share options. In order to be eligible, a company must have fewer than 250 employees and gross assets not exceeding £30 million. The main features of the EMIs scheme are:

(a) The scheme allows a qualifying company to grant share options to any employee who works at least 25 hours per week for the company, or (if less) for at least 75% of his or her working time. The company may select the employees to whom it wishes to grant options and may award different amounts to different employees.

(b) Employees who own more than 30% of the company's ordinary share capital are excluded from the scheme.

(c) If the company so wishes, options may be granted to acquire shares at less than their market value at the time of grant or even at nil cost.

(d) No charge to income tax (or NICs) arises when an option is granted under the scheme. When the option is exercised, no charge arises if the shares are acquired at not less than their market value at the time of grant. Otherwise, a tax charge arises based on the *lower* of:

 (i) the excess of the market value of the shares at the time that the option was granted over the amount (if any) paid to acquire them

 (ii) the excess of the market value of the shares at the time that the option is exercised over the amount (if any) paid to acquire them.

(e) There is an upper limit of £250,000 on the value of the shares (at the time of grant) for which an employee may hold unexercised options that have been granted under the EMIs scheme. At any time, the total value of the shares for which options have been granted, but not yet exercised, cannot exceed £3 million.

(f) The sale of shares which were acquired under the scheme is a chargeable disposal for capital gains tax purposes, but such a disposal is generally eligible for entrepreneurs' relief (see Chapter 22).

Employee shareholder status

Employees who adopt "employee shareholder" status forfeit some of their employment rights (e.g. the right to claim unfair dismissal) in return for shares in their company with a value of between £2,000 and £50,000. The first £2,000 worth of shares acquired in this way are not subject to income tax or NICs†. Furthermore, any gains made on the disposal of the shares are not generally chargeable to capital gains tax† (see Chapter 17).

† *These exemptions apply only to shares acquired under an employee shareholder agreement which was entered into before 1 December 2016.*

Summary

- Criteria have been established which distinguish employment from self-employment.
- Employment income is taxed on the receipts basis.
- Income tax is payable on practically all of the income received in respect of an employment, including benefits in kind. However, some minor items of employment income are exempt from income tax.
- In general, an employee's expenses are allowed only if they are incurred wholly, exclusively and necessarily in the performance of the duties of the employment.
- Any amount to which an employee is contractually entitled on the termination of employment is fully taxable. Certain termination payments (e.g. on death or injury) are fully exempt. Ex gratia termination payments are partially exempt.
- The PAYE system is used to deduct both income tax and NICs from employees' wages and salaries.
- The construction industry scheme (CIS) may apply when payments are made by a contractor to a sub-contractor in connection with a construction contract.
- Certain employee incentive schemes offer tax advantages. Share incentive plans provide employees with a tax-efficient means of acquiring shares in the companies for which they work. Share options may be granted tax-efficiently to employees by means of approved share option schemes and enterprise management incentives.

Exercises

7.1 List the criteria which might be used to distinguish employment from self-employment.

7.2 Malcolm's gross annual salary is £57,500. He also receives an annual bonus based on his employer's profits for the calendar year. His bonus for the year to 31 December 2016 was £8,350 (which he received on 9 April 2017). His bonus for the year to 31 December 2017 was £9,570 (which he received on 18 April 2018). Malcolm is not a company director. Calculate his employment income for 2017-18.

7.3 Which of the following forms of income from employment would be exempt from income tax in 2017-18?

(a) Free meals in the company canteen.

(b) Removal expenses of £4,500.

(c) £1,000 given to an employee on reaching 25 years of service with his employer.

(d) A canteen of cutlery given to an employee on his marriage.

(e) A mileage allowance of 35p per mile given to an employee who drives her own motor car for 2,500 business miles per year.

(f) A payment of £5 per week made to a homeworker to cover the additional costs of working from home.

7.4 Which of the following expenses incurred by an employee would be deductible when computing employment income for tax purposes?

(a) Travel between work and home.

(b) Travel between work sites.

(c) Professional subscriptions.

(d) Protective clothing.

(e) A suit to wear at the office.

(f) Entertaining expenses.

***7.5** On 21 March 2018, Penny is made redundant by her employer. She receives statutory redundancy pay of £4,750 and an ex gratia payment of £32,000 from her employer as compensation for loss of employment. Her only other income in tax year 2017-18 is her salary of £41,415 and building society interest of £1,000. She is not a Scottish taxpayer.

Calculate Penny's income tax liability for 2017-18.

***7.6** Ian is a freelance television technician. In a typical tax year he works for approximately 20 separate TV companies. None of his engagements with any of these companies lasts for more than 10 days at a time. All of his work is performed at studios owned by the TV companies, using very expensive equipment also owned by these companies.

The TV companies initially book his services by telephoning him at his home (where he has an office) and then send a confirmation letter giving the dates of the engagement and the amount of the agreed fee. Ian's work is very skillful and he is required to do this work himself. He is not allowed to subcontract the work to anyone else.

Is Ian employed or self-employed?

Chapter 8

Income from employment (2)

Introduction

As explained in Chapter 7, the term "employment income" includes any benefits in kind which an employee might receive. Benefits in kind consist of income received in the form of goods or services (rather than money) and include items such as living accommodation, company cars and interest-free loans. The purpose of this chapter is to explain how an employee's benefits in kind are calculated for tax purposes.

Benefits in kind

As a general rule, employees are charged to income tax on the cost to their employer of providing benefits in kind. The cost of providing a benefit is normally the additional cost borne by the employer as a consequence of providing that benefit. This rule was established in the case of *Pepper* v *Hart* (1992) which concerned the provision of school places for the children of masters at the school. It was held that the cost of this provision for tax purposes should consist only of the additional costs borne by the school (e.g. extra food and laundry costs) rather than the average cost per pupil which would be obtained by dividing the total running costs of the school by the total number of pupils. However, there are special rules for calculating the taxable benefit in kind in relation to:

(a) living accommodation provided for an employee's use

(b) assets loaned to the employee for private use

(c) ancillary services connected with living accommodation

(d) cars and fuel provided for private use

(e) vans provided for private use

(f) beneficial loans.

These special rules are explained later in this chapter.

Note that no taxable benefit arises if an employer provides an employee with a benefit in kind and the cost of this benefit would have been a deductible expense if the employee had met this cost personally (see Chapter 7).

Trivial benefits

As from tax year 2016-17, there is an exemption from income tax (and NICs) for "trivial" benefits in kind, which satisfy certain conditions. The main conditions are:

(a) the cost of providing the benefit does not exceed £50

(b) the benefit is not cash or a cash voucher

(c) the benefit is not provided in recognition of particular services performed by the employee in the course of the employment.

If trivial benefits are provided to the directors of a close company (see Chapter 27), the exemption is capped at £300 per director per tax year. Note also that:

(a) If the cost of a benefit in kind exceeds £50, the full amount of the benefit is taxable (not just the excess over £50).

(b) Non-cash vouchers (e.g. gift vouchers which can be exchanged for goods but which cannot be converted into cash) are eligible for the trivial benefits exemption if all of the necessary conditions are satisfied.

(c) If a benefit is eligible for another exemption, that exemption and the trivial benefits exemption are applied in the way that is most favourable to the employee. This may be relevant in the case of parties or similar functions provided by an employer for the benefit of employees (see Chapter 7). However, if another exemption exempts only *part* of the cost of a benefit, the excess cost is not eligible for the trivial benefits treatment, even if that excess is less than £50.

EXAMPLE 1

In tax year 2017-18, an employer provides employees with a party at Christmas and a dinner dance in the summer. Calculate the taxable benefit if the cost to the employer of these two functions (per employee) is:

(a) £60 and £80. (b) £45 and £120 (c) £75 and £100.

What would the tax situation be if there had been only one function during the tax year costing £200 per employee?

Solution

(a) The total cost does not exceed £150 (see Chapter 7) so there is no taxable benefit.

(b) The total cost exceeds £150. The most favourable treatment is to use the £150 rule to exempt the £120 function and then use the trivial benefits rule to exempt the £45.

(c) The £150 rule can be used to exempt the £100 function. But the remaining £75 is not trivial and is a taxable benefit.

If there had been only one function costing £200, this would not be exempt under either the functions rule or the trivial benefits rule and so the entire £200 would be taxable.

Vouchers for goods or services

Employees are charged to tax on the cost to their employer of providing vouchers which may be exchanged for goods or services. But no liability arises if a voucher is used to provide a benefit that would otherwise be exempt from tax. Note that:

(a) Entertainment and hospitality vouchers provided by a person other than the employer or someone connected with the employer are exempt from income tax unless provided as a reward for specific services rendered by the employee.

(b) The provision of a cash voucher results in a taxable benefit equal to the amount of cash into which the voucher can be converted.

Fair bargain rule

In general, no taxable benefit arises if an employee acquires goods or services from his or her employer at the same price (and on the same terms) as would apply if those goods or services were sold to a member of the public. This is known as the "fair bargain" rule.

However, this rule does *not* apply to living accommodation, cars and vans provided for private use and beneficial loans. In each of these cases, the taxable benefit is calculated according to special rules set out in ITEPA 2003 and these rules take into account any payment made by the employee. This may result in a charge to tax even if the employee pays the same price for the item concerned as would be paid by a member of the public.

Living accommodation

In general, a taxable benefit arises if an employer provides living accommodation for an employee. The rules are as follows:

(a) In the case of accommodation which is owned by the employer, the employee is taxed on the "annual value" of the accommodation. In practice, this is taken to be the accommodation's rateable value, which was used in the calculation of domestic rates before these were abolished. The rateable value of properties constructed since the abolition of domestic rates has to be estimated.

(b) In the case of accommodation rented by the employer, the employee is taxed on the greater of the rent paid by the employer and the accommodation's annual value.

In either case, the taxable benefit in kind is reduced by any contribution made by the employee. Accommodation costing the employer more than £75,000 is regarded as "expensive" and gives rise to an increase in the taxable benefit. This increase is calculated by applying an appropriate percentage to the amount by which the cost of the accommodation exceeds £75,000. Note the following points:

(a) The "appropriate percentage" used for this purpose is the same as the official rate of interest used in beneficial loan calculations (see later in this chapter) as that rate stood at the beginning of the tax year for which the benefit is being calculated.

(b) The cost of providing accommodation is generally equal to the purchase price of the property, *plus* the cost of any improvements made to the property before the start of the tax year concerned, *less* any capital contribution made by the employee.

(c) But if the property was acquired by the employer more than six years before it was made available to the employee, the cost of providing the accommodation is taken to be its market value on the date that it was first occupied by the employee, *plus* the cost of any improvements made since that date but before the start of the tax year concerned, *less* any capital contribution made by the employee.

EXAMPLE 2

As from 1 January 2017, an employee is provided by his employer with the use of a house which has an annual value of £5,300. The following information is relevant:

(a) The employer bought the house in 2014 at a cost of £270,000 and spent £35,000 on improvements in 2015. A further £10,000 was spent on improvements in July 2017.

(b) The employee pays £3,000 per annum to his employer in relation to this benefit.

Calculate the taxable benefit in 2017-18, assuming that the official rate of interest as at 6 April 2017 was 2.5% per annum.

Solution

	£
Annual value	5,300
Add: 2.5% x (£270,000 + £35,000 – £75,000)	5,750
	11,050
Less: Employee contribution	3,000
Taxable benefit	8,050

Job-related accommodation

If accommodation provided by an employer for an employee is "job-related", then no taxable benefit arises. Accommodation is job-related if:

(a) it is necessary for the employee to reside in the accommodation for the proper performance of his or her duties (e.g. a caretaker who is required to live in a caretaker's flat on an employer's premises)

(b) the accommodation is provided for the better performance of the employee's duties and it is customary for such accommodation to be provided (e.g. a clergyman who lives in a vicarage provided by an employer)

(c) there is a special threat to the employee's security and the accommodation is provided as part of security arrangements.

Assets loaned to the employee for private use

If an employer lends an asset to an employee for private use, the employee is taxed each year on 20% of the value of the asset on the date of the loan. If the asset is subsequently sold or given to the employee, tax is also charged on the *greater* of:

(a) the market value of the asset when sold or given to the employee, less any amount paid for the asset by the employee, and

(b) the market value of the asset when first loaned to the employee, less the amounts already assessed to tax during the period of the loan, less any amount paid for the asset by the employee.

The loan of a bicycle and cycling safety equipment is exempt from tax if used wholly or mainly for travel between home and work.

EXAMPLE 3

On 6 April 2015, an employer purchases a music system for £800 and immediately lends the system to an employee for his private use. The system remains in the employee's possession until 6 October 2017 when the employee buys it from his employer for £100, its market value on that day being £240. Calculate the taxable benefit in kind for tax years 2015-16 to 2017-18 inclusive.

Solution

			£
2015-16	20% of £800		160
2016-17	20% of £800		160
2017-18	20% of £800 x 6/12	80	
	plus, the greater of:		
	(i) £240 – £100 = £140		
	(ii) £800 – £160 – £160 – £80 – £100 = £300	300	380
Total benefit assessed to tax over period of the loan			700

Ancillary services connected with living accommodation

An employee who is provided with living accommodation is charged to tax not only on the accommodation itself but also on the cost to the employer of providing any "ancillary services" in connection with that accommodation. Ancillary services include such items as heating and lighting, repairs and maintenance and cleaning. The provision of furniture for the employee's use is also included under the heading of ancillary services and is taxed as a loaned asset (see above). Note that:

(a) The taxable benefit in relation to ancillary services is reduced by any contribution made by the employee towards the cost of those services.

(b) If the accommodation is job-related, the taxable benefit with regard to ancillary services cannot exceed 10% of the employee's net earnings for the year, less any contribution made by the employee. Net earnings are defined for this purpose as total earnings for the year (apart from the ancillary services) less allowable expenses.

EXAMPLE 4

In 2017-18, an employer provides living accommodation for an employee. The employer also provides the following services in connection with this accommodation:

	£
Heating, lighting and cleaning	1,890
Repairs and maintenance	1,235
Loan of furniture, cost to the employer	13,000

The employee contributes £100 per month towards these services and has net earnings for the year (excluding the ancillary services) of £42,500. Compute the taxable benefit.

Solution

If the accommodation is not job-related, the taxable benefit is £4,525 (£1,890 + £1,235 + 20% of £13,000, less £1,200). If the accommodation is job-related, the taxable benefit is limited to 10% of £42,500, less £1,200 = £3,050.

Cars provided for private use

An employee is taxed on the provision of a motor car unless the car is totally unavailable for the employee's private use. The taxable benefit is based upon the list price of the car when new (even if the employer bought the car for less than list price or bought it second-hand) and is adjusted according to the car's level of carbon dioxide emissions. The main features of the method of computation are as follows:

(a) The price of the car for the purpose of calculating the benefit in kind is the sum of:

   (i) the list price of the car when new, including standard accessories

   (ii) the cost of all optional accessories (other than mobile telephones) fitted to the car before it is made available to the employee

   (iii) the cost of any optional accessories (other than mobile telephones) costing £100 or more and fitted to the car after it is made available to the employee.

   Accessories which are designed for use only by a disabled person are ignored when calculating the price of the car. This exemption extends to any accessories required because of the employee's disability (e.g. power steering) and is not limited just to accessories designed for use solely by the disabled. A similar exemption applies to security enhancements (e.g. armour plating) for employees who can demonstrate that their employment creates a threat to their personal security.

(b) The taxable benefit is based upon the price of the car, less any capital contribution (up to a maximum of £5,000) made by the employee towards the car's cost.

(c) If the car is a "classic car", the car's market value at the end of the tax year is used instead of list price when calculating the taxable benefit. A classic car is one which is over 15 years old at the end of the tax year and has a market value at the end of the year exceeding £15,000 and exceeding the price calculated at (a) above.

(d) The taxable benefit for a tax year is calculated by applying a percentage to the figure calculated at (b) above. The applicable percentage depends upon the car's level of carbon dioxide emissions (rounded down to the nearest 5g/km if over 95g/km). For petrol-driven cars in 2017-18 this percentage is computed as follows:

Carbon dioxide emissions	*Applicable percentage*
Not exceeding 50g/km	9%
51g/km to 75g/km	13%
76g/km to 94g/km	17%
95g/km	18%
each additional 5g/km	1% increase

The percentage is increased by a further 3% for diesel-driven cars†, but the maximum applicable percentage is 37% in all cases.

† *This 3% supplement will apply until April 2021 (not April 2016 as previously announced).*

(e) *In 2018-19*, the applicable percentages will increase by two percentage points, except that the increase will be 4% for cars with emissions not exceeding 50g/km and 3% for cars with emissions of 51-75g/km.

In 2019-20, the applicable percentages will increase by three more percentage points.

In 2020-21, it is proposed that the applicable percentage for a car with emissions not exceeding 50g/km should be based on the car's electric range, that several new bands should be introduced for cars in the 51-94g/km range and that the percentages for cars with emissions exceeding 94g/km should be increased by one percentage point.

(*The maximum percentage will remain at 37% in all of these years*).

(f) If a disabled employee is obliged by his or her disability to drive a car with automatic transmission, the taxable benefit is based upon the price (if lower) and emission rating (if lower) of the equivalent car with manual transmission.

(g) If a car is made available to the employee for only part of the year, the benefit in that year is reduced proportionately, depending upon the number of days for which the car is made available. This also applies if the car is unusable for a continuous period of at least 30 days in the year.

(h) Finally, the taxable benefit is reduced by any contribution which the employee pays to the employer for private use of the car (as long as this contribution is paid by the end of the tax year‡ to which it relates).

‡ *It is proposed that this should be changed to 6 July following the end of the tax year.*

EXAMPLE 5

(a) Throughout the whole of tax year 2017-18, Lucy is provided by her employer with a car with a list price of £15,400. She contributed £2,000 towards the car's cost and she pays £300 per annum to her employer for private use of the car. Calculate the taxable benefit arising in 2017-18 if the car is petrol-driven and has an emission rating of:

(i) 48g/km (ii) 63g/km (iii) 77g/km (iv) 129g/km (v) 202g/km

Re-calculate the taxable benefit in each case if the car is diesel-driven.

(b) During 2017-18, Luke is provided by his employer with the use of a petrol-driven car first registered in 2014 with a list price at that time of £21,000. His employer bought the car for £16,700 in 2016. The car's emission rating is 146g/km. Calculate the taxable benefit in 2017-18 if:

(i) the car is available to Luke throughout the entire year
(ii) the car is made available to Luke only from 6 November 2017.

Solution

(a) Lucy's capital contribution reduces the price of the car to £13,400 and her annual contribution of £300 (if paid before the end of the tax year) reduces the benefit accordingly. If the car is petrol-driven, the taxable benefit in each case is as follows:

(i) 9% x £13,400 = £1,206, less £300 = £906.
(ii) 13% x £13,400 = £1,742, less £300 = £1,442.
(iii) 17% x £13,400 = £2,278, less £300 = £1,978.
(Note that 77g/km is not rounded down to 75g/km.)
(iv) 18% + 6% = 24% x £13,400 = £3,216, less £300 = £2,916.
(The car's emission rating is rounded down to 125g/km. This exceeds 95g/km by 30g/km, which is 6 multiples of 5g/km.)
(v) 37% x £13,400 = £4,958, less £300 = £4,658.

If the car is diesel-driven, the applicable percentage is increased by a further 3% (but cannot exceed 37%). The revised taxable benefit in each case is:

(i) 9% + 3% = 12% x £13,400 = £1,608, less £300 = £1,308.
(ii) 13% + 3% = 16% x £13,400 = £2,144, less £300 = £1,844.
(iii) 17% + 3% = 20% x £13,400 = £2,680, less £300 = £2,380.
(iv) 18% + 6% + 3% = 27% x £13,400 = £3,618, less £300 = £3,318.
(v) 37% x £13,400 = £4,958, less £300 = £4,658.

(b) The fact that Luke's employer bought the car for £16,700 is irrelevant. The benefit is based on the list price of the car and the applicable percentage is 28% (18% + 10%).

(i) 28% x £21,000 = £5,880.
(ii) 28% x £21,000 = £5,880 x 5/12 = £2,450.

Pool cars

A "pool car" is one which satisfies all of the following criteria:

(a) it is available for use by more than one employee and is not ordinarily used by one employee exclusively.

(b) it is not normally kept at an employee's residence overnight.

(c) any private use by an employee is merely incidental to its use for business purposes.

If all these criteria are satisfied, no taxable benefit will arise in relation to the car.

Fuel provided for private use

The taxable benefit described above covers the cost of providing the car itself, together with the costs of road fund licence, insurance and maintenance. But a separate taxable benefit arises if the employer also provides the employee with fuel for private motoring. Fuel benefit for a tax year is calculated by applying the same percentage as was used in the calculation of the car benefit to a fixed amount set by the Government for that tax year. *For 2017-18 this amount is £22,600*. The charge is reduced proportionately if the car is not made available to the employee for the whole of the tax year and is normally reduced if the employee receives fuel for private use for only part of the year. However, a full year's tax charge arises if fuel for private use ceases to be provided at some point during the tax year but is then provided again later in that same year.

It is important to appreciate that the taxable fuel benefit is *not* reduced by any partial contribution which the employee makes towards the cost of private fuel. There is no taxable benefit if the employee pays the full cost of all private fuel. Otherwise, the benefit is calculated as above, ignoring any partial contribution towards fuel costs.

EXAMPLE 6

Throughout 2017-18, Miranda was provided by her employer with a petrol-engined car for both business and private use. The car had an emission rating of 144g/km and Miranda's employer paid all running costs. The cost of the fuel supplied for private motoring was £1,795. Calculate her taxable fuel benefit in 2017-18 if:

(a) she contributed nothing towards private fuel

(b) she reimbursed her employer for the cost of all private fuel

(c) she reimbursed her employer £1,750 towards the cost of the private fuel.

Solution

(a) 18% + 9% = 27% x £22,600 = £6,102.

(b) £nil, since the employer pays for no private fuel at all.

(c) Miranda's contribution is less than 100% and so the taxable benefit is £6,102.

Vans provided for private use

No taxable benefit arises if a motor van is made available to an employee mainly for business use and the employee is not allowed to use the van for private journeys other than ordinary commuting between home and work. But if a motor van is made available with no restrictions as to private use, the employee is normally liable to income tax on a taxable benefit (for 2017-18) of £3,230. Note that:

(a) The taxable benefit is reduced proportionately if the van is made available to the employee for only part of the tax year and is also reduced by any amount which the employee pays to the employer for private use of the van.

(b) A further taxable benefit arises if the employer provides fuel for private use, with no reduction for any partial contribution made by the employee towards the cost of such fuel. The amount of this taxable benefit for 2017-18 is £610.

(c) No taxable benefit arises in relation to a heavy goods vehicle (a van weighing more than 3,500kg) unless the vehicle is used wholly or mainly for private purposes.

The taxable benefit arising in relation to a "zero-emission" van in 2017-18 is equal to 20% of the charge for conventionally-fuelled vans. This percentage will increase to 40% in 2018-19, 60% in 2019-20, 80% in 2020-21, 90% in 2021-22 and then to 100% in 2022-23 and subsequent years.

Beneficial loans

A beneficial loan is one that is granted by an employer to an employee (or to a relative of the employee) either interest-free or at a low rate of interest. A loan is deemed to be made at a low rate of interest if the rate charged is less than the "official rate". Employees are taxed on the difference between the interest actually payable to the employer and the interest that would have been payable at the official rate. Note that:

(a) Loans made in the ordinary course of the employer's money-lending business and made on the same terms and conditions as loans made to the general public are ignored when calculating the benefit arising in connection with low-interest loans.

(b) Loans which qualify for tax relief (see Chapter 4) are also ignored.

(c) A loan made to a relative of an employee is ignored if it can be shown that the employee derives no personal benefit from the loan.

(d) No taxable benefit arises if the total amount outstanding on all beneficial loans made to an employee, apart from those covered by (a), (b) and (c) above, does not exceed £10,000 at any time during the tax year.

If any loan made by an employer to an employee (whether beneficial or not) is wholly or partly written off, the amount written off is generally charged to income tax in the tax year in which the write-off takes place. However, no taxable benefit arises if a loan is written off on the death of the employee.

EXAMPLE 7

Adam has the following four loans from his employer:

(a) A £36,000 loan at interest of 1% p.a. to enable Adam to buy his own home.

(b) An interest-free season ticket loan of £6,000.

(c) A £15,000 personal loan at interest of 2% p.a.

(d) A £5,000 loan to buy equipment for use in his employment.

The full amount of each loan was outstanding at 6 April 2017 and no repayments were made during 2017-18. Calculate Adam's taxable benefit in 2017-18 (assuming an official rate of interest of 2.5% per annum).

Solution

The £5,000 loan is a qualifying loan and is ignored. The remaining loans total more than £10,000 and so give rise to taxable benefits. The amount assessed to tax is:

	£
£36,000 x (2.5% – 1%)	540
£6,000 x 2.5%	150
£15,000 x (2.5% – 2%)	75
	765

Beneficial loans which vary during the year

In the above example, it was assumed that the amount of the loans did not vary during the tax year. However, if the amount of a beneficial loan does vary during the year, the taxable benefit can be calculated in one of two ways:

(a) **Normal method**. The amount of the loan at the start of the tax year (or when the loan began, if later) and at the end of the tax year (or when the loan ended, if earlier) are averaged and multiplied by the average official rate for the year. If the loan began or ended during the year, the result of this calculation is multiplied by the number of months for which the loan was outstanding in the year and divided by 12.

Interest actually paid by the employee (if any) is then subtracted, giving the taxable benefit.

(b) **Alternative method**. Interest at the official rate is calculated precisely on the day-to-day outstanding balance. Any interest paid by the employee is then subtracted, giving the taxable benefit.

The first method is easier and is generally used. However, either the employee concerned or HMRC may insist that the alternative method should be used. The employee will presumably do so if this results in a lower taxable benefit. HMRC may do so if it appears that the normal method is being deliberately exploited for tax avoidance purposes.

Salary sacrifice

An optional remuneration (or "salary sacrifice") agreement allows employees to give up part of their salary in exchange for benefits in kind. Until 6 April 2017, such an agreement could generate a tax saving if the benefits concerned were exempt from tax or if the value of the benefits for tax purposes was less than the amount of salary foregone.

However, as from 6 April 2017, the taxable value of benefits in kind provided through salary sacrifice agreements is fixed at the *greater* of:

(a) the value of those benefits calculated in the normal way, and
(b) the amount of salary which has been sacrificed.

This rule applies even if the benefits in question are normally exempt from tax. But certain benefits are specifically excluded from the rule, including employer-provided pensions and pensions advice, childcare, cycle to work benefits and the provision of cars with emissions not exceeding 75g/km.

As a transitional measure, existing salary sacrifice agreements are protected from this treatment until 6 April 2018, except for agreements involving cars, accommodation and school fees, which are protected until 6 April 2021.

Summary

- Employees are taxed on the cost to their employer of providing benefits in kind. But trivial benefits costing no more than £50 are exempt from tax.
- The taxable benefit arising in relation to living accommodation is generally based on the annual value of the property concerned. The benefit increases if the property cost more than £75,000. No taxable benefit arises if the accommodation is job-related.
- An asset loaned to an employee gives rise to an annual taxable benefit equal to 20% of the value of the asset on the date of the loan. A further benefit may arise if the asset is subsequently sold or given to the employee.
- Employees are taxed on any ancillary services provided in connection with living accommodation. The tax charge is capped if the accommodation is job-related.
- The amount of the taxable benefit arising in relation to a motor car provided to an employee for private use depends primarily on the car's list price and its carbon dioxide emissions. A further benefit will arise if the employee is also provided with fuel for private motoring.
- If an employee is provided with a beneficial loan, the employee is generally taxed on the difference between the loan interest actually payable (if any) and the interest that would have been payable at the official rate.

Exercises

8.1 Kim lives in a house provided by her employer. The house cost her employer £242,500 in 2015 and a further £27,500 was spent on improvements in 2016. The house has a gross rateable value of £3,700 and it has been agreed with HMRC that there is 12% business use. Kim pays rent of £400 per month to her employer. Compute the taxable benefit in 2017-18 (assuming that the official rate of interest is 2.5% per annum).

8.2 Throughout 2017-18, Niall is provided by his employer with a diesel-engined motor car which had a list price of £24,200 when new and has an emission rating of 157g/km. Niall's employer pays all of the car's running expenses including fuel for private use. Compute the taxable benefit in 2017-18.

8.3 On 1 June 2017, Stephen was provided by his employer with an interest-free loan of £20,000. He repaid £5,000 of this loan on 1 January 2018 and repaid another £3,000 on 1 March 2018. Compute the taxable benefit in 2017-18 using:

(a) the normal method
(b) the alternative method.

Assume that the official rate of interest is 2.5% per annum. Perform all calculations to the nearest month and to the nearest pound.

***8.4** Emma is the sales director of a company. She earns an annual salary of £95,000 together with a bonus (received in September each year) based on the company's profits for the accounting year ending on the previous 30 June. She also receives a general expenses allowance of £8,000 per annum, which she uses for business travel and entertaining. The company provides her with a new BMW motor car every two years and pays all running costs. She has an interest-free loan from the company of £20,000 and the company pays her annual subscription to a private medical insurance scheme, costing £1,850. Explain the taxation implications of each of the elements of Emma's remuneration package.

***8.5** Jim is the managing director of a company and earns a basic salary in 2017-18 of £225,000. He receives benefits from the company during the year as follows:

(a) He is provided with the use of a company house which has an annual value of £9,750 and which cost his employer £350,000. Jim makes no contribution towards the cost of the house or towards its running costs which cost the company £3,450 in 2017-18. The company has also furnished the house at a cost of £28,500. Jim's occupation of the house is not job-related.

(b) He is provided with a petrol-engined company car which had a list price when new of £45,000 and which has an emission rating of 133g/km. The company pays all running costs.

(c) He is provided with a company loan of £50,000 on which he is charged interest at 0.75% per annum.

Calculate Jim's taxable benefits in 2017-18 (assume an official rate of interest of 2.5% per annum).

Chapter 9

Income from self-employment: Computation of income

Introduction

This is the first of five chapters which deal with income from self-employment. The profits of a self-employed person are charged to income tax by the Income Tax (Trading and Other Income) Act 2005 and the main purpose of this chapter is to show how those profits are calculated for tax purposes. Subsequent chapters deal with related topics such as tax relief for capital expenditure, the tax treatment of trading losses and partnerships.

A self-employed person may be conducting a trade or may be exercising a profession or vocation. However, the profits of trades, professions and vocations are all taxed in accordance with the same set of rules. Therefore, in this chapter and in subsequent chapters, references to "trades" and "trading" should be assumed to include professions and vocations. Similarly, the terms "trader" and "sole trader" will be used to refer to any self-employed person, regardless of whether that person is actually conducting a trade or is in fact exercising a profession or vocation.

The badges of trade

ITTOIA 2005 states that the trading profits of a person who is resident in the UK are chargeable to income tax wherever the trade is carried on. The trading profits of a non-UK resident are generally chargeable to income tax only if the trade is carried on wholly or partly in the UK (see Chapter 32). When deciding whether or not a person is trading it is necessary to make two important distinctions:

(a) the distinction between employment and self-employment (see Chapter 7)

(b) for a taxpayer who sells goods or other assets, the distinction between trading activities (which give rise to trading profits) and non-trading activities (which will usually fall within the scope of capital gains tax).

Section 989 of the Income Tax Act 2007 states that a "trade" includes "*any venture in the nature of trade*". This circular definition is of little real help and therefore it has been left largely to the courts to decide whether or not a given activity constitutes trading.

The main criteria which have arisen from case law decisions and which may be used to distinguish between trading and non-trading activities are known as the "badges of trade". They are as follows:

(a) **Subject matter of the transaction**

If a taxpayer sells assets of a type which might normally be acquired for personal enjoyment or held as a source of income, this may suggest that any profit arising on their sale should be treated as a capital gain rather than a trading profit.

But if the assets concerned do not provide personal enjoyment and do not yield income, it would seem that the only way in which they could be turned to advantage is by selling them. In these circumstances, any profit arising on their sale might be treated as a trading profit. In *Martin* v *Lowry* (1926), the taxpayer bought and sold a huge quantity of war surplus linen. In *Rutledge* v *CIR* (1929), the taxpayer bought and sold one million toilet rolls. In both of these cases, it was held that the subject matter of the transaction was such that the activity must be construed as trading.

(b) **Length of the period of ownership**

Trading stocks are normally retained for only a short period before being sold, whereas assets acquired for personal use or as a source of income are generally retained for longer. Therefore, if assets are bought and sold within a short space of time it is more likely that any profit made will be treated as a trading profit.

(c) **Frequency of transactions**

The more often that a taxpayer repeats a certain type of transaction, the more likely it is that the activity will be construed as trading. In *Pickford* v *Quirke* (1927), the taxpayer bought a cotton mill and sold off its assets at a profit. This was the fourth time that the taxpayer had carried out this particular type of transaction and therefore he was held to be trading.

(d) **Supplementary work**

A taxpayer who buys an asset, performs work on the asset so as to make it more saleable and then sells the asset is more likely to be regarded as trading than someone who simply buys and sells an asset without performing any supplementary work. In *Cape Brandy Syndicate* v *CIR* (1921), a group of individuals bought a large quantity of brandy which they first blended and then sold. They were held to be trading.

(e) **Reason for the sale**

The circumstances which have prompted the sale of an asset might be taken into account when deciding whether trading has occurred. A sale necessitated by a sudden urgent need for cash is less likely to be regarded as a trading activity than a sale made in the normal course of events.

(f) **Motive**

The presence of a profit motive in the mind of the taxpayer when acquiring an asset provides strong evidence of trading. In *Wisdom* v *Chamberlain* (1969), the taxpayer acquired silver bullion to counter the effects of a possible devaluation of the pound. His only motive was to sell the silver at a profit. He was held to be trading.

However, this test is not always conclusive. After all, many investments are bought at least partially with a view to their eventual sale at a profit and yet such profits are generally treated as capital gains. This point emphasises the need to consider the evidence provided by *all* of the badges of trade (not just one) when trying to decide whether or not trading has occurred.

Since trading requires the presence of a profit motive when the asset was acquired, the sale of an asset originally acquired by inheritance or by gift (or in any way otherwise than by purchase) is very unlikely to be construed as trading.

The calculation of trading profits

The computation of a self-employed person's trading profit begins with the net profit shown by that person's accounts. For tax purposes, trading profits are normally calculated in accordance with generally accepted accounting practice, which means that income and expenditure should be measured on the accruals basis†.

It is usually necessary to make a number of adjustments to the net profit shown by the accounts in order to arrive at the trading profit for tax purposes These adjustments can be summarised as follows:

		£	£
Net profit shown by the accounts			xxx
Add:	Expenditure shown in the accounts but not deductible for tax purposes	xxx	
	Trading income not shown in the accounts	xxx	xxx
			xxx
Less:	Expenditure deductible for tax purposes but not shown in the accounts	xxx	
	Non-trading income shown in the accounts	xxx	xxx
Trading profit adjusted for tax purposes			xxx

Each of these adjustments is explained in this chapter.

† *Small businesses (with receipts not exceeding a stipulated threshold) may now choose to adopt the cash basis when calculating their profits for tax purposes. Furthermore, all businesses have the option of using simplified fixed rate deductions to calculate some of their expenses (whether or not the cash basis is adopted). An explanation of the cash basis rules and the rules relating to simplified expenses is given at the end of this chapter.*

Deductibility of expenditure

In general, expenditure is deductible (allowable) when computing trading profits only if it is incurred *wholly and exclusively for the purposes of the trade*. This rule is not as restrictive as the "wholly, exclusively and necessarily" rule applied to the expenses of an employee (see Chapter 7) but it does have the following implications:

(a) Expenditure which has no connection with the trade is disallowed (the "remoteness test"). In *Strong & Co of Romsey Ltd* v *Woodifield* (1906), damages paid by a brewery to a hotel guest injured by a falling chimney were disallowed. These damages were incurred by the brewery in its capacity as a property owner, not in its capacity as a trader, and therefore failed the remoteness test.

(b) Expenditure which serves both a business purpose and a private purpose cannot be allowed in full (the "duality test"). If the expenditure can be apportioned with reasonable accuracy, then the private element is disallowed. However, in *Mallalieu* v *Drummond* (1983), the cost of black clothing worn in court by a lady barrister was wholly disallowed, since it was not possible to apportion the cost of the clothing between the part which satisfied professional standards of dress and the part which simply provided warmth and decency.

Even if expenditure passes both of these tests it may still be disallowed by statute.

Disallowed expenditure

Certain classes of expenditure are disallowed (either by statute or by case law) when computing trading profits. If any of these types of expenditure have been deducted in the accounts of a self-employed person, then the amount of the expenditure must be "added back" to the profit shown by the accounts in order to arrive at the trading profit for tax purposes. The main classes of disallowed expenditure are identified below.

Capital expenditure

Capital expenditure is specifically disallowed by ITTOIA 2005 but the Act does not provide a definition of the term "capital". Consequently, there is a great deal of case law on this subject, much of which is concerned with distinguishing between repairs (which are allowable) and improvements (disallowed as capital expenditure). In *Atherton* v *British Insulated & Helsby Cables Ltd* (1926), it was stated that capital expenditure is such that it brings an "enduring benefit" to the business, and this test is still widely used. The following capital-related expenses are also disallowed:

(a) legal or professional fees incurred in relation to an item of capital expenditure

(b) depreciation and amortisation charges (and losses on disposal of non-current assets) although capital allowances may be available instead (see Chapter 11).

Even repairs may be disallowed if they relate to a newly acquired asset and the repairs are required in order to put the asset into usable condition. In *Law Shipping Co Ltd* v *CIR* (1923), the costs of putting a newly acquired ship into seaworthy condition were disallowed for this reason. However, repairs to a newly acquired asset which was usable before the repairs were carried out are generally allowed. In the case of *Odeon Associated Theatres Ltd* v *Jones* (1971), repairs to cinemas which had been bought in a state of disrepair (but were nonetheless usable) were allowed.

In general, a repair restores an asset to its original condition, whereas an improvement makes the asset better than it was originally. The use of modern materials in the course of a repair may give the impression of an improvement, but the work will still be classed as a repair unless the asset's functionality has been enhanced. On these grounds, HMRC now takes the view that the replacement of old windows by modern double-glazed windows should normally be classed as a repair rather than an improvement.

Appropriations of profit

Appropriations of profit made by the owner of a business (whether these are described as drawings, owner's salary or anything else) are disallowed. The owner's personal income tax payments and personal National Insurance contributions are also disallowed.

Provisions

Provisions are allowed so long as they are in respect of revenue expenditure and are made in accordance with generally accepted accounting practice. However, a provision will be disallowed if it cannot be estimated with sufficient accuracy.

Transfers to a *general* provision for doubtful debts (which is perhaps more correctly referred to as an "allowance" rather than a "provision") are disallowed when computing trading profits, since the amount involved is insufficiently accurate. The same is true of transfers to other general provisions (e.g. a general stock provision). However, transfers to *specific* provisions are normally allowable.

Entertainment and gifts

The cost of business entertainment (e.g. customer entertaining) is disallowed. Staff entertaining costs are allowable but the employees concerned may incur an income tax liability if the amount involved exceeds specified limits (see Chapter 7). The cost of gifts is also disallowed, other than:

(a) gifts to employees, if made wholly and exclusively for trade purposes

(b) samples of trading stock given to the public so as to advertise the business

(c) gifts to customers which display a conspicuous advertisement for the business, cost no more than £50 per customer per year and do not consist of food, drink or tobacco

(d) gifts of trading stock (or inventory) or used plant and machinery to designated UK educational establishments, charities or community amateur sports clubs

(e) gifts to charities, if made wholly and exclusively for trade purposes (e.g. a reasonably small gift to a local charity which attracts favourable publicity and which enhances the public image of the business concerned).

Charitable donations made within the Gift Aid scheme are given tax relief under the Gift Aid rules and are disallowed when computing trading profits (see Chapter 4).

Political donations

Political donations and subscriptions are usually not allowed. But political donations which result in a definite benefit to the trade may be allowed. In *Morgan* v *Tate & Lyle Ltd* (1954), the costs of a political campaign against nationalisation were allowed on the grounds that the campaign was waged for the survival of the trade.

Non-trade bad debts

Bad debts incurred in the course of trade are allowable. But loans written off are generally not allowable unless:

(a) the taxpayer is in the business of lending money and the loan concerned was made in the course of trade, or

(b) the loan was to an employee and was made by reason of the employment and for trade purposes; in this case, the amount of the written-off loan will usually be taxable on the employee as income from employment (see Chapter 8).

Transfers to a *specific* bad debts provision (or allowance) are allowable but transfers to a *general* provision are usually disallowed, as stated earlier. Bad debts recovered and reductions in a specific bad debts provision are both treated as trading income.

EXAMPLE

A sole trader's nominal ledger contains the following bad and doubtful debts account for the year ended 30 June:

	£	£		£	£
Trade debts written off		812	Allowances b/f at 1 July:		
Staff loan written off		50	General	432	
			Specific	312	744
Allowances c/f at 30 June:					
General	459		Trade debt recovered		42
Specific	288	747	Income statement		823
		1,609			1,609

The staff loan written off was not made for trade purposes. How much of the £823 charged to the income statement for the year should be added back when computing trading profits for tax purposes?

Solution

The figure of £823 charged to the income statement can be analysed as follows:

	£
Trade debts written off, less trade debts recovered (£812 – £42)	770
Staff loan written off	50
Increase in general allowance (£459 – £432)	27
Decrease in specific allowance (£312 – £288)	(24)
	823

The £50 staff loan written off and the £27 increase in general allowance are disallowed, so a total of £77 should be added back when calculating the trading profits for tax purposes.

Fines and penalties

Fines or penalties incurred because of infringements of the law are not regarded as trading expenses and are disallowed. An exception occurs if an employer pays parking fines incurred by employees whilst on their employer's business. Such payments are usually allowed when computing trading profits but may then be assessed on the employees as income from employment.

Criminal payments

A payment is disallowed if the making of the payment in itself constitutes a criminal offence (e.g. a bribe). Payments to blackmailers or extortionists are also disallowed.

Allowable expenditure

As explained earlier, expenditure is allowable when computing trading profits if it has been incurred wholly and exclusively for the purposes of the trade and is not specifically disallowed by statute. Apart from the disallowed items listed above, most of the expenditure shown in a typical income statement (or profit and loss account) will probably be allowable but the following points should be noted:

(a) **Interest**. Interest, including credit card and overdraft interest, is allowable if it is incurred for trade purposes. But interest paid on overdue tax is disallowed.

(b) **Legal and professional fees**. Legal and professional fees relating to capital expenditure are specifically disallowed (see above), but fees incurred for other trade purposes are normally allowable. For example, fees are allowed if incurred in connection with such matters as the collection of trade debts, the raising of loan finance, the renewal of a short lease (a lease of up to 50 years), a legal action for breach of contract or the preservation of trading rights.

Audit and accountancy fees incurred in relation to the preparation of accounts and the agreement of tax liabilities are normally allowed. Fees incurred in relation to a tax investigation by HMRC are incurred in the role of taxpayer rather than trader and are generally disallowed unless no profit adjustment arises from the investigation. The cost of tax appeals is disallowed, even if successful.

(c) **Short lease premiums**. A premium paid for the grant of a short lease of business premises (50 years or less) is discounted according to the length of the lease and is then allowed in equal annual instalments over the period of the lease (see Chapter 5). A reverse premium received by a tenant using premises for business purposes is taxable as trading income.

(d) **Damages**. Damages and compensation payments are allowed if incurred for the purposes of the trade.

(e) **Value added tax**. If a trader pays VAT in relation to an item of expenditure and is unable to reclaim that VAT (see Chapter 30), the amount of VAT suffered will be allowable so long as the item of expenditure is itself allowable.

(f) **Trade subscriptions**. Subscriptions payable to professional and trade associations are generally regarded as having been incurred for the purposes of the trade and are allowable. Political subscriptions are generally disallowed.

(g) **Employees' remuneration**. Employees' remuneration is allowable if it is genuinely expended for business purposes. In the case of *Copeman* v *Flood (William) & Sons Ltd* (1941), it was held that large salaries paid to family members could be allowed only to the extent that they were expended for trading purposes. Employer's National Insurance contributions (see Chapter 16) are also allowable.

Remuneration which is not actually paid to employees within nine months of the end of the period of account in which it is accrued is disallowed in that period but allowed in the period of payment.

Employers' contributions to registered pension schemes (see Chapter 14) are allowed in the *period of account in which they are paid*.

Redundancy payments and compensation payments made for loss of employment are generally allowable. On a cessation of trade, contractual redundancy payments, statutory redundancy payments and non-contractual redundancy payments of up to three times the statutory amount are all allowed.

The cost of educational courses provided for employees is allowable if incurred for trade purposes. The cost of retraining employees who are about to leave (or have recently left) is allowed subject to certain conditions. The cost of temporarily seconding an employee to a charity or educational establishment is allowable.

(h) **Staff defalcations**. Losses caused by the dishonesty of an employee are normally allowable. But, following the decision in *Curtis* v *J & G Oldfield Ltd* (1925), the defalcations of a person having control over the business (e.g. a business partner) are not allowed.

(i) **Travel expenses**. The cost of business travel is allowable but the cost of travelling between home and work is generally disallowed. In *Newsom* v *Robertson* (1952), the travelling expenses of a barrister between his home and his chambers were disallowed. But in *Horton* v *Young* (1971), the travelling expenses of a self-employed bricklayer between his home and the sites at which he worked was allowed, on the grounds that his business was conducted from his home.

As explained at the end of this chapter, unincorporated businesses may choose to use the "fixed rate deduction scheme" to calculate the expenses allowed in relation to a motor vehicle. No other motor expenses or capital allowances may then be claimed in relation to the vehicle concerned.

(j) **Leased cars**. The amount of the lease rental payments allowed in relation to a leased car is restricted if the car has an emission rating which exceeds 130g/km. The restriction takes the form of a disallowance of 15% of the lease rental payments, but this does not apply if the car is leased for no more than 45 days.

(k) **Patent royalties**. Patent royalties that are paid for trade purposes are allowable. The cost of registering a patent (or trademark) is also allowable.

(l) **Pre-trading expenditure**. Expenditure incurred during the seven years before starting to trade is treated as if incurred on the first day of trading and is allowable so long as the expenditure is of a type which would normally be allowable.

Expenditure not shown in the accounts

The most common example of allowable expenditure not being shown in the accounts of a business is the trader's claim (if any) to capital allowances (see Chapter 11).

Another instance of allowable expenditure not shown in the accounts is a premium paid for the grant of a short lease. As explained earlier, part of such a premium is deductible from trading income in equal annual instalments over the lease period. If the premium is being amortised in the accounts, the amortisation charges are added back and the allowable amount of the premium (see Chapter 5) is deducted instead.

Adjustments relating to income

Most of the adjustments required when calculating trading profits for tax purposes are concerned with business expenditure. But further adjustments might be necessary in relation to the income of the business. These adjustments are as follows:

(a) **Non-trading income shown in the accounts**. Any non-trading income which is shown in the accounts of a business must be deducted when computing trading profits. The main categories of non-trading income which might be found in the accounts of a business are:

(i) income which is taxed under another heading (e.g. interest, property income)

(ii) profits on the disposal of non-current assets; these are normally depreciation adjustments but a genuine gain may be chargeable to capital gains tax

(iii) decreases in general provisions or allowances.

(b) **Trading income not shown in the accounts**. The most common example of trading income being omitted from the accounts of a business occurs when the owner of the business appropriates trading stock (or inventory) for his or her personal use. This is referred to as "own consumption".

In this situation, generally accepted accounting practice (GAAP) suggests that the cost of the goods concerned, less any contribution made by the owner, should be credited to the income statement. But ITTOIA 2005 requires that own consumption of trading stock is accounted for at *market value*. This means that the profit of the business for tax purposes should be increased by the *selling price* of the goods, less any contribution made by the owner. For this purpose, "trading stock" consists of goods that are sold in the ordinary course of trade (including partially manufactured stock) but does not include raw materials (which are accounted for at cost).

This rule puts onto a statutory basis the view that was originally expressed in the famous case of *Sharkey* v *Wernher* (1955). In this case, horses were transferred from a farm to the owner's private stables and it was held that the profits of the farm should be increased, for tax purposes, by the full market value of those horses.

Post-cessation receipts

Post-cessation receipts are sums received after a person permanently ceases trading and which arise from the carrying on of the trade prior to cessation. Such receipts fall within the scope of ITTOIA 2005 and are treated as trading income.

Deductions are allowed for any expenses incurred which would have been deductible in calculating the profits of the trade if it had not ceased.

Trading income allowance

The Government has proposed that, *as from tax year 2017-18*, gross trading income of up to £1,000 per annum (before deduction of expenses) should be tax-free. If this figure were exceeded, the taxpayer would have the right to elect that he or she should be taxed on the excess of gross income over £1,000 (with no deduction for expenses). Otherwise, trading income would be calculated by deducting expenses from gross income in the usual way.

This "trading income allowance" would be of benefit to "micro-entrepreneurs" with very low amounts of trading income. If an individual's gross trading income for the year did not exceed £1,000, there would be no need to declare this income to HMRC or to pay tax on it. Individuals with income which exceeded the allowance would be able to calculate their profit by simply deducting £1,000 from the gross income figure.

A similar allowance has been proposed in relation to property income, also as from tax year 2017-18 (see Chapter 5).

Cash basis and simplified expenses

As stated earlier in this chapter, small unincorporated businesses may choose to calculate their profits for tax purposes on the cash basis. If this basis is applied, taxable profits for an accounting period are simply the difference between income actually received in the period and expenses actually paid. There is no need to adjust for receivables, payables or inventories. Nor is there any need to distinguish between capital expenditure and revenue expenditure. The main features of the cash basis are as follows:

(a) For this purpose, a small business is one which has total receipts in the accounting period that do not exceed a stipulated threshold for the tax year in which the profits for that period are taxed (see Chapter 10). The threshold for tax year 2017-18 is £150,000 (reduced proportionately for periods of less than 12 months).

(b) Use of the cash basis is entirely optional. In general, eligible businesses may start or stop using the cash basis whenever they wish. Once a small business starts using the cash basis it may continue to do so in subsequent years even if its receipts exceed the threshold in those years. However, businesses must stop using the cash basis when their receipts exceed twice the threshold (i.e. £300,000).

(c) Receipts are defined as all amounts received in connection with the business during the accounting period, including disposal proceeds of non-current assets.

(d) Expenses are defined as any payments made during the accounting period wholly and exclusively for business purposes, including capital expenditure. However, there are special rules relating to certain types of expenses. In particular:

   (i) Expenditure on buying a motor car is not deductible as an expense. Businesses may choose to claim fixed rate deductions in relation to their motor expenses (see below) and these include an element of depreciation. But if the fixed rate deductions are not claimed, the business may claim capital allowances in relation to the purchase of a motor car (see Chapter 11).

   (ii) No deduction is allowed for capital expenditure which does not qualify as plant and machinery (e.g. the cost of acquiring land and buildings).

   (iii) Loan interest is allowable up to a maximum of £500.

(e) In the case of a VAT-registered business (see Chapter 29) receipts and expenses may be recorded either including or excluding VAT. If VAT is included, then any VAT refunds received from HMRC are treated as receipts and any VAT payments made to HMRC are treated as expenses.

(f) Businesses which choose to adopt the cash basis are prohibited from claiming capital allowances (see Chapter 11) except in relation to motor cars.

(g) If a business which is using the cash basis incurs a trading loss, that loss can only be carried forward and set against any profits arising from the same trade in subsequent years. "Sideways relief" (see Chapter 12) is not available.

Simplified expenses

As stated earlier in this chapter, *any* unincorporated business may choose to use the "fixed rate deduction scheme" when calculating certain expenses for tax purposes. This scheme is available whether or not the business is small and whether or not it has adopted the cash basis. The expenses concerned are as follows:

(a) **Motor expenses**. Motor expenses in relation to a car, goods vehicle or motor cycle may be calculated with reference to specified mileage rates. At present, these are the same as the employee AMAP rates (see Chapter 7). If a fixed rate deduction is made in relation to a vehicle, no other expenses (or capital allowances) may be claimed in relation to the vehicle and use of the fixed rate deduction scheme is then compulsory for that vehicle in all future periods.

(b) **Use of home for business purposes**. A self-employed person who uses his or her home for business purposes may claim standard deductions based upon the number of hours spent working at home. These vary from £10 per month to £26 per month and cover expenses such as heat, light and power. A separate deduction may be claimed for the business proportion of telephone and broadband/internet costs.

(c) **Business premises used partly as a home**. If business premises are used partly as a home, the private proportion of expenses incurred in relation to the premises may be calculated as a fixed amount based upon the number of occupants. For instance, if there are two occupants, the private element is a standard £500 per month.

Summary

- A set of criteria known as the "badges of trade" may be used to distinguish between trading activities and non-trading activities.
- Expenditure is deductible when computing trading profits only if it is incurred wholly and exclusively for the purposes of the trade. Expenditure which is not so incurred is disallowed. Certain categories of expenditure are disallowed by statute.
- Any disallowed expenditure shown in a trader's accounts must be added back to the profit shown by those accounts when computing the trading profit for tax purposes.
- If the owner of a business takes trading stock for personal use, the full market value of that stock (less any amount paid by the owner) must be added to the net profit shown by the accounts when computing the trading profit.
- Non-trading income included in the accounts of a business must be deducted from the net profit shown by those accounts when computing the trading profit.
- Certain small businesses may choose to adopt the cash basis when calculating their profits for tax purposes. Unincorporated businesses may also apply simplified fixed rate deductions in relation to some of their expenses.

Exercises

It may be assumed in these exercises that (unless stated otherwise) the businesses concerned have not adopted the cash basis and do not use fixed rate deductions to calculate any of their expenses.

9.1 List and explain the six badges of trade.

9.2
(a) State the general rule which governs whether or not expenditure is deductible when computing trading profits.

(b) Explain the "remoteness" test and the "duality" test and the consequences which ensue if an item of expenditure fails either of these tests.

9.3 Which of the following items of expenditure would be allowed when computing trading profits?

(a) the salary paid to a sole trader's wife

(b) a Gift Aid donation

(c) a new machine bought for use by an engineering business

(d) diaries costing £3 each given to customers

(e) the cost of the annual staff outing to Blackpool

(f) the black suit worn at work by a self-employed undertaker

(g) the legal costs of acquiring new freehold premises

(h) a subscription to the local chamber of commerce

(i) cases of wine costing £49.99 each given to customers at Christmas

(j) the legal costs of suing a trade debtor for non-payment.

9.4 Julian, a self-employed shopkeeper, takes goods costing £30 from his trading stock for his own personal use. If he had sold the stock to a customer he would have charged £45. When computing his trading profit, what adjustment would need to be made to the net profit shown by his accounts if:

(a) he pays nothing for the goods?

(b) he puts £30 of his own money into the till so as to pay for the goods?

(c) he puts £45 of his own money into the till?

9.5
(a) A motor car with a retail price of £21,000 is leased for four years at a cost of £300 per month. The car is used only for trade purposes and has an emission rating of 152g/km. How much of the monthly charge should be disallowed when calculating trading profits?

(b) A sole trader is granted a 15-year lease on premises which he uses for business purposes. He pays a premium of £15,000 and writes off £1,000 per year in his business accounts. How much of the £1,000 should be disallowed each year when calculating trading profits?

9.6 Linda's income statement for the year ended 31 March 2018 is as follows:

	£	£
Sales		82,500
Less: Cost of sales		37,200
Gross profit		45,300
Add: Rents receivable	1,200	
Bank interest receivable	80	
Profit on sale of non-current asset	310	1,590
		46,890
Less: Wages and salaries	22,620	
Business rates and insurance	1,750	
Heating and lighting	2,170	
Repairs and renewals	4,280	
Telephone	880	
Motor expenses	3,250	
Sundry expenses	1,650	
Bad and doubtful debts	640	
Credit card interest	120	
Loss on sale of non-current asset	70	
Depreciation	2,500	39,930
Net profit for the year		6,960

Notes:

(a) Linda draws a salary of £200 per week from the business. This is included in the wages and salaries figure.

(b) Repairs and renewals are as follows:

	£
Decoration of business premises	400
Installation of new improved heating system	3,800
Minor repair	80
	4,280

(c) It has been agreed with HMRC that one-quarter of telephone costs and one-fifth of motor expenses relate to private use.

(d) Sundry expenses include business entertaining of £520.

(e) Trade debts written off in the year amount to £440 and £200 has been set aside as a general allowance (or provision) for bad and doubtful debts.

Compute Linda's trading profit (before deduction of capital allowances) for the year ended 31 March 2018.

***9.7** Imran owns a business which operates from rented premises. He has a 10-year lease on the premises and paid a premium of £7,000 in order to obtain the lease. His income statement for the year to 31 December 2017 is as follows:

	£	£
Gross profit for the year		52,618
Add: Interest receivable	212	
Surplus on sale of office equipment	300	512
		53,130
Less: Wages (see Note 1)	19,280	
Rent, rates and insurance (see Note 2)	6,915	
Electricity	4,328	
Telephone (see Note 3)	1,650	
Repairs (see Note 4)	2,286	
Printing and advertising	1,250	
Motor expenses (see Note 5)	5,712	
Legal and professional expenses (see Note 6)	3,000	
Sundry expenses (see Note 7)	4,777	
Bad and doubtful debts (see Note 8)	860	
Bank charges and interest	2,765	
Lease premium amortisation	700	
Depreciation	8,749	62,272
Net profit/(loss) for the year		(9,142)

Notes:

1. Wages include £5,800 for Imran's wife (who works part-time for the business) and £1,000 for his son (a student who does not work for the business at all). Also included in wages are Imran's personal income tax and personal National Insurance contributions totalling £3,524.
2. Insurance includes Imran's private medical insurance premium of £405.
3. It has been agreed that one-sixth of telephone costs relate to private use.
4. Repairs include £750 for the cost of essential repairs to a newly-acquired second-hand forklift truck which could not be used until the repairs had been carried out.
5. Motor expenses are as follows:

	£
Vehicle servicing and repairs	1,165
Fuel and oil	2,815
Loss on disposal of motor vehicle	422
Road fund licences and insurance	610
Fine for speeding by Imran	700
	5,712

It has been agreed that one-tenth of motor expenses relate to private use.

6. Legal and professional expenses comprise legal fees of £850 (renewal of Imran's 10-year lease), debt collection fees of £1,250 and accountancy fees of £900.

7. Sundry expenses are:

	£
Business entertaining	3,320
Staff Christmas dinner	312
Subscription to trade association	350
Donation to political party	200
Miscellaneous small items (all allowable)	595
	4,777

8. Trade debts of £500 were written off during the year. The general allowance for doubtful debts was reduced by £100 and the specific allowance for doubtful debts was increased by £460.

9. During the year, Imran appropriated trading stock costing £220 from the business for personal use, paying £220 of his own money into the business bank account. His gross profit percentage on turnover is 20%.

Compute Imran's trading profit (before deduction of capital allowances) for the year to 31 December 2017.

***9.8** Ewan began trading on 1 April 2017. A brief summary of his income statement for the year to 31 March 2018 (prepared on the accruals basis) is as follows:

	£	£
Sales		68,750
Less: Cost of sales:		
Purchases	29,220	
Less: Inventory at 31 March 2018	6,190	23,030
Gross profit		45,720
Less: Expenses		18,760
Net profit for the year		26,960

Notes:

1. Trade receivables at 31 March 2018 were £5,840. Trade payables were £3,650. Accrued expenses were £830 and prepaid expenses were £310.
2. Expenses include motoring costs of £3,120 and loan interest of £600. There were no accruals or prepayments in relation to either of these expenses at the year end. Ewan drove 12,400 business miles during the year.
3. Equipment costing £4,500 and a motor car costing £14,200 were bought in April 2017. Depreciation of £900 and £3,550 respectively is included in expenses.

Calculate Ewan's trading profit for tax purposes, on the assumption that he decides to use the cash basis and claims a fixed rate deduction in relation to his motor expenses.

Chapter 10

Income from self-employment: Basis periods

Introduction

Income tax is charged for tax years (or "years of assessment") which run from 6 April to the following 5 April. It would therefore be convenient if all self-employed people were required to choose 5 April as their annual accounting date, so that the trading income for each tax year could easily be identified. However, self-employed people are free to choose any accounting date they wish and so it is necessary to devise some means of establishing a link between the periods of account for which trading profits are calculated and the tax years in which those profits are charged to tax.

The Income Tax (Trading and Other Income) Act 2005 states that "*the profits of a tax year are the profits of the basis period for the tax year*". The main purpose of this chapter is to explain the rules which are used to determine the basis period for a tax year.

The current year basis

The main principle of the self-employed basis period rules is that the basis period for a tax year is "*the period of 12 months ending with the accounting date in that tax year*". This is known as the "current year basis" (CYB). On this basis, the profits that are taxed in a tax year are normally the profits of the accounting year which ends in the tax year.

However, special rules apply when a business starts trading, ceases trading or changes its accounting date (see below).

EXAMPLE 1

(a) A trader prepares accounts to 31 December each year. Identify the basis period for tax year 2017-18.

(b) A trader prepares accounts to 30 September each year. For which tax year will the accounting year to 30 September 2018 be the basis period?

Assume in both cases that the special rules which are used on commencement, cessation or change of accounting date do not apply in any of the years concerned.

Solution

(a) The accounting year which ends during tax year 2017-18 is the year to 31 December 2017. Therefore this is the basis period for 2017-18. In other words, the profits of the year to 31 December 2017 are charged to income tax in tax year 2017-18.

(b) The accounting year to 30 September 2018 ends during tax year 2018-19 and is therefore the basis period for 2018-19. In other words, the profits of the year to 30 September 2018 are charged to income tax in tax year 2018-19.

Commencement of trade

Special rules are used to determine basis periods for the first two tax years when a new business starts trading. The first tax year in which trading profits are taxed is the tax year in which trade commences. When this tax year has been identified, basis periods for the opening tax years are determined in accordance with the following rules:

Tax year		*Basis period*
1		Date of commencement to the following 5 April (the "actual basis")
2	*either*	(a) 12 months to the accounting date in the second tax year (if possible)
	or	(b) The first 12 months of trading (if the accounting date in the second tax year is less than 12 months after commencement)
	or	(c) The actual tax year from 6 April to 5 April (if there is no accounting date in the second tax year)
3 etc.		Current year basis.

Note the following points:

(a) The basis period for the first tax year will often be less than 12 months long but the basis period for the second tax year will always be 12 months long.

(b) Basis periods for the opening tax years may overlap to some extent and therefore some of the profits made in the early years of trading may be the subject of more than one tax assessment (see below).

(c) If necessary, the trading profits for early periods of account are apportioned on a time basis in order to compute the amount of profit arising in each basis period.

(d) ITTOIA 2005 states that apportionments should be made by reference to the number of *days* in the period concerned, but adds that any other reasonable method of apportionment will be accepted so long as it is applied consistently. In practice, such calculations are usually made to the nearest month and this is the approach adopted in this book.

EXAMPLE 2

Identify basis periods for the first four tax years in each of the following situations:

(a) Vera starts trading on 1 January 2016, preparing accounts annually to 31 December.

(b) Wilbur starts trading on 1 October 2016. He chooses 30 June as his annual accounting date and prepares his first accounts for the nine months to 30 June 2017.

(c) Yasmin starts trading on 1 February 2016. Her annual accounting date is 30 April and she prepares her first accounts for the 15 months to 30 April 2017.

Solution

(a)	2015-16	Actual	1 January 2016 to 5 April 2016
	2016-17	12 months to a/c date in year 2	year to 31 December 2016
	2017-18	CYB	year to 31 December 2017
	2018-19	CYB	year to 31 December 2018
(b)	2016-17	Actual	1 October 2016 to 5 April 2017
	2017-18	First 12 months	1 October 2016 to 30 September 2017
	2018-19	CYB	year to 30 June 2018
	2019-20	CYB	year to 30 June 2019
(c)	2015-16	Actual	1 February 2016 to 5 April 2016
	2016-17	Actual	6 April 2016 to 5 April 2017
	2017-18	CYB	1 May 2016 to 30 April 2017
	2018-19	CYB	year to 30 April 2018

Notes:

(i) For Wilbur, the accounting date which falls into the second tax year (30 June 2017) is less than 12 months after commencement, so it is not possible to tax the profits of the 12 months to that accounting date. Therefore the basis period for the second tax year is Wilbur's first 12 months of trading.

(ii) For Yasmin, no accounting date falls into the second tax year. So she is taxed on the actual profits made during that tax year. Note also that the accounting date which falls into the third tax year marks the end of a 15-month period of account, so the basis period for that year does not coincide with a period of account.

Overlap profits

If a business chooses 5 April as its annual accounting date, the basis periods used in the opening tax years will not overlap at all. Otherwise, opening basis periods will overlap and some profits will form the basis of more than one tax assessment. Such profits are known as "overlap profits".

ITTOIA 2005 states that accounts prepared to 31 March or to the 1st, 2nd, 3rd or 4th of April will usually be treated as if they were prepared to 5 April, so as to avoid very short overlap periods and very small amounts of overlap profits.

EXAMPLE 3

Albert begins trading on 1 May 2016 and has adjusted trading profits as follows:

	£
15 months to 31 July 2017	16,800
year to 31 July 2018	21,600

Compute Albert's trading income for each of the first three tax years and also calculate the amount of any overlap profits.

Solution

Albert's first period of account is 15 months long and his first basis period comprises the 11 months from 1 May 2016 to 5 April 2017. Trading income for the first three tax years is as follows:

Year	*Basis*	*Basis period*	*Workings*	*Trading income*
				£
2016-17	Actual	1/5/16 to 5/4/17	£16,800 x 11/15	12,320
2017-18	12 months to a/c date in year 2	1/8/16 to 31/7/17	£16,800 x 12/15	13,440
2018-19	CYB	y/e 31/7/18		21,600

The overlap period consists of the eight months from 1 August 2016 to 5 April 2017, which are common to the basis periods for 2016-17 and 2017-18. Overlap profits are therefore £8,960 (£16,800 x 8/15).

Overlap relief

In general, overlap profits which arise in the opening years of a business are relieved by deduction from the trading profits that are charged to tax in the final tax year when trade ceases. Note the following points regarding "overlap relief":

(a) Overlap relief ensures that, over the entire lifetime of a business, the total of the trading profits which are charged to tax is equal to the total of the adjusted trading profits for each period of account.

(b) Overlap profits are not index-linked. Therefore the real value of overlap relief is eroded by inflation, especially in the case of businesses which trade for many years.

(c) If overlap profits exceed the trading profits which are charged to tax in the final tax year, the resulting loss is eligible for tax relief (see Chapter 12).

However, if a business changes its accounting date at some point during its lifetime, it is possible that some of the overlap profits arising in the opening years may be relieved by deduction from the trading profits that are taxed in the year of the change. It is also possible that further overlap profits might arise on a change of accounting date (see later in this chapter).

Cessation of trade

A cessation of trade occurs when the owner of a business retires or sells the business or dies. The final tax year in which trading profits are taxed is the tax year in which the cessation occurs. The basis period for this final tax year is determined as follows:

(a) If a business commences trading and ceases trading in the same tax year, the basis period for that year consists of the entire lifespan of the business.

(b) If a business ceases trading in its second tax year, the basis period for that year runs from 6 April at the start of the year up to the date of cessation. This rule overrides the usual commencement rules for the second tax year.

(c) Otherwise, the basis period for the final tax year runs from the end of the basis period for the previous tax year up to the date of the cessation. This basis period may be less than, equal to or more than 12 months in length.

If the final set of accounts prepared for a business covers a period which is of more than 12 months, it is possible that no accounting date at all falls into the penultimate tax year (the last year but one). This makes it impossible to apply the usual current year basis in that year. In these circumstances, the basis period for the penultimate tax year is the 12 months up to the normal accounting date falling in that year.

It is important to appreciate that income tax is charged on the owner of a business and not on the business itself. Therefore a change in the ownership of a business is treated for tax purposes as a cessation of one business followed by the commencement of another.

EXAMPLE 4

Carmen starts trading on 1 July 2016 and chooses 30 June as her annual accounting date. Identify the basis periods for her last two tax years if she ceases trading as follows:

	Date of cessation	*Final set of accounts*
(a)	31 March 2017	9 months to 31 March 2017
(b)	30 June 2017	year to 30 June 2017
(c)	30 June 2021	year to 30 June 2021
(d)	31 May 2021	11 months to 31 May 2021
(e)	30 April 2021	22 months to 30 April 2021

Solution

(a) Trade both commences and ceases in 2016-17. The basis period for this single tax year is the entire lifespan of the business i.e. 1 July 2016 to 31 March 2017.

(b) The cessation occurs in the second tax year. Basis periods are:

2016-17	Actual	1 July 2016 to 5 April 2017
2017-18	6 April to date of cessation	6 April 2017 to 30 June 2017

(c)	2020-21	CYB	y/e 30 June 2020
	2021-22	End of previous basis period up to date of cessation	y/e 30 June 2021
(d)	2020-21	CYB	y/e 30 June 2020
	2021-22	End of previous basis period up to date of cessation	1 July 2020 to 31 May 2021
(e)	2020-21	12 months to normal a/c date	1 July 2019 to 30 June 2020
	2021-22	End of previous basis period up to date of cessation	1 July 2020 to 30 April 2021

EXAMPLE 5

Damien starts trading on 1 July 2012 and chooses 31 December as his annual accounting date. He ceases trading on 30 September 2017 and has the following results:

	Adjusted trading profit
	£
6 months to 31 December 2012	8,400
year to 31 December 2013	9,200
year to 31 December 2014	10,500
year to 31 December 2015	7,500
year to 31 December 2016	6,400
9 months to 30 September 2017	5,800

Compute Damien's trading income for each tax year and show that the total of this income is equal to the total of the adjusted trading profits listed above.

Solution

Year	*Basis period*	*Workings*	*Trading income*
			£
2012-13	1/7/12 to 5/4/13	£8,400 + 3/12 x £9,200	10,700
2013-14	y/e 31/12/13		9,200
2014-15	y/e 31/12/14		10,500
2015-16	y/e 31/12/15		7,500
2016-17	y/e 31/12/16		6,400
2017-18	1/1/17 to 30/9/17	£5,800 – overlap relief £2,300	3,500
			47,800

The overlap period is from 1 January 2013 to 5 April 2013 (3 months) and the overlap profits are £2,300 (£9,200 x 3/12). The total of the trading income which is charged to tax is £47,800, the same as the total of the adjusted trading profits.

Change of accounting date

If a business changes its annual accounting date from one date (the "old date") to another date (the "new date"), special rules are used to determine the basis period for the year of change. The year of change is defined as the first tax year in which accounts are *not* made up to the old date or *are* made up to the new date (or both). There will be a change of basis period for a year of change so long as the following conditions are satisfied:

(a) The first set of accounts made up to the new date does not cover a period of more than 18 months.

(b) Notice of the change of accounting date is given to HMRC in a tax return which is not filed late.

(c) Either:

  (i) None of the previous five tax years has been a year of change resulting in a change of basis period, or

  (ii) HMRC is satisfied that the change of accounting date has been made for genuine commercial reasons and not for tax avoidance purposes.

If all of these conditions are satisfied, the basis period for the year of change is determined as follows:

(a) The "relevant period" is identified as the period beginning immediately after the end of the basis period for the previous tax year and ending with the new date in the year of change.

(b) If the length of the relevant period is less than 12 months, the basis period for the year of change is the 12 months to the new date in the year of change.

(c) If the length of the relevant period is not less than 12 months, the basis period for the year of change is the relevant period itself.

(d) In consequence, the basis period for a year of change will always be of at least 12 months' duration.

If all of the required conditions are *not* satisfied, the basis period for the year of change is the 12 months to the old date in that year. However, the following tax year is then regarded as a year of change (the taxpayer being treated as though this were the first year in which the new date had been used) and a change of basis period will occur in that year if all of the conditions are satisfied in relation to that year. A change of accounting date can be carried forward indefinitely in this way until such time as the necessary conditions for a change of basis period are satisfied.

If a taxpayer regularly prepares accounts to a particular *day* in the year (e.g. the last Saturday in June) rather than a particular *date*, the fact that the accounting date will change slightly in each year does not trigger the change of accounting date rules.

EXAMPLE 6

(a) Gary began trading many years ago, preparing accounts to 30 September each year. He decided to change his accounting date to 30 June and the first accounts made up to the new date were for the period from 1 October 2016 to 30 June 2017. The conditions necessary for a change of basis period were all satisfied. Identify the basis periods for years 2015-16 to 2018-19 inclusive.

(b) Audrey began trading on 1 January 2014, preparing accounts to 31 December each year. She decided to change her accounting date to 31 March and the first accounts made up to the new date were for the period from 1 January 2016 to 31 March 2017. The conditions necessary for a change of basis period were all satisfied. Identify the basis periods for years 2013-14 to 2018-19 inclusive.

(c) Grant began trading many years ago, preparing accounts to 30 June each year. He decided to change his accounting date to 31 December and the first accounts made up to the new date were for the period from 1 July 2017 to 31 December 2017. The conditions necessary for a change of basis period were all satisfied. Identify the basis periods for years 2016-17 to 2019-20 inclusive.

(d) Clare began trading on 1 March 2013, preparing accounts to 31 January each year. Her first accounts were for the period to 31 January 2014. She decided to change her accounting date to 30 April and the first accounts made up to the new date were for the period from 1 February 2016 to 30 April 2017. The conditions necessary for a change of basis period were all satisfied. Identify the basis periods for years 2012-13 to 2018-19 inclusive.

Solution

(a) The year of change is 2017-18 (the first year in which the old date was not used and the new date was used). The basis period for 2016-17 ended on 30 September 2016, so the relevant period is from 1 October 2016 to 30 June 2017. This is less than 12 months long so the basis period for 2017-18 is the 12 months to 30 June 2017. Basis periods for 2015-16 to 2018-19 are:

2015-16 year to 30 September 2015
2016-17 year to 30 September 2016
2017-18 year to 30 June 2017
2018-19 year to 30 June 2018

Note that there is an overlap between the basis periods for 2016-17 and 2017-18. The treatment of overlap profits on a change of accounting date is explained below.

(b) The year of change is 2016-17 (the first year in which the old date was not used and the new date was used). The basis period for 2015-16 ended on 31 December 2015, so the relevant period is from 1 January 2016 to 31 March 2017. This is not less than 12 months in length so the basis period for 2016-17 is the same as the relevant period. Basis periods for 2013-14 to 2018-19 are:

2013-14	1 January 2014 to 5 April 2014
2014-15	year to 31 December 2014
2015-16	year to 31 December 2015
2016-17	1 January 2016 to 31 March 2017
2017-18	year to 31 March 2018
2018-19	year to 31 March 2019

(c) The year of change is 2017-18 (the first year in which the new date was used). The basis period for 2016-17 ended on 30 June 2016, so the relevant period is from 1 July 2016 to 31 December 2017. This is not less than 12 months in length so the basis period for 2017-18 is the same as the relevant period. Basis periods are:

2016-17	year to 30 June 2016
2017-18	1 July 2016 to 31 December 2017
2018-19	year to 31 December 2018
2019-20	year to 31 December 2019

(d) The year of change is 2016-17 (the first year in which the old date was not used). The basis period for 2015-16 ended on 31 January 2016, so the relevant period is from 1 February 2016 to 30 April 2016. This is less than 12 months long so the basis period for 2016-17 is the 12 months to 30 April 2016, even though this accounting date was not used in 2016-17. Basis periods for 2012-13 to 2018-19 are:

2012-13	1 March 2013 to 5 April 2013
2013-14	1 March 2013 to 28 February 2014
2014-15	year to 31 January 2015
2015-16	year to 31 January 2016
2016-17	year to 30 April 2016
2017-18	year to 30 April 2017
2018-19	year to 30 April 2018

There is an overlap between the basis periods for 2015-16 and 2016-17 (as well as the usual overlaps arising on the commencement of trade).

Overlap profits on a change of accounting date

If a change of accounting date results in profits being taxed more than once, these overlap profits are added to any earlier overlap profits which arose in the opening years or on a previous change of accounting date. The total overlap profits are then carried forward for relief on cessation or on a subsequent change of accounting date.

On the other hand, if the basis period for a year of change exceeds 12 months, a part of the overlap profits brought forward from previous years may be relieved in the year of change. The amount to be relieved is calculated according to the following formula:

$$\text{Amount relieved} = A \times \frac{B - C}{D}$$

where: A = Total overlap profits brought forward and not yet relieved
B = Length of the relevant period
C = 12 (or 365 if daily apportionments are being used)
D = Total length of the overlap period(s) to which the total overlap profits brought forward relate.

EXAMPLE 7

(a) Byron began trading on 1 November 2013, preparing accounts to 31 October each year. He decided to change his accounting date to 31 August and the first accounts made up to the new date were for the period from 1 November 2015 to 31 August 2016. The conditions necessary for a change of basis period were all satisfied. The adjusted trading profits for Byron's first five periods of account were as follows:

	£
Year to 31 October 2014	24,000
Year to 31 October 2015	36,000
Period to 31 August 2016	32,000
Year to 31 August 2017	42,000
Year to 31 August 2018	48,000

Compute Byron's trading income for years 2013-14 to 2018-19.

(b) Michelle began trading on 1 January 2014, preparing accounts to 31 December each year. She decided to change her accounting date to 28/29 February and the first accounts made up to the new date were for the period from 1 January 2017 to 28 February 2018. The conditions necessary for a change of basis period were all satisfied. The adjusted trading profits for Michelle's first five periods of account were:

	£
Year to 31 December 2014	9,120
Year to 31 December 2015	10,500
Year to 31 December 2016	23,360
Period to 28 February 2018	28,780
Year to 28 February 2019	32,540

Compute Michelle's trading income for years 2013-14 to 2018-19.

Solution

(a) The year of change is 2016-17 (the first year in which the old date was not used and the new date was used). The basis period for 2015-16 ended on 31 October 2015, so the relevant period is from 1 November 2015 to 31 August 2016. This is less than 12 months in length so the basis period for 2016-17 is the 12 months to 31 August 2016. Trading income for 2013-14 to 2018-19 is:

Year	Basis period	Workings	Trading income
			£
2013-14	1/11/13 to 5/4/14	£24,000 x 5/12	10,000
2014-15	y/e 31/10/14		24,000
2015-16	y/e 31/10/15		36,000
2016-17	y/e 31/8/16	(£36,000 x 2/12) + £32,000	38,000
2017-18	y/e 31/8/17		42,000
2018-19	y/e 31/8/18		48,000

There are overlap profits of £10,000 (5 months) on the commencement of trade and a further £6,000 (2 months) on the change of accounting date. Total overlap profits carried forward are £16,000 (7 months).

(b) The year of change is 2017-18 (the first year in which the old date was not used and the new date was used). The basis period for 2016-17 ended on 31 December 2016, so the relevant period is from 1 January 2017 to 28 February 2018. This is not less than 12 months in length so the basis period for 2017-18 is the relevant period itself. Trading income for 2013-14 to 2018-19 is:

Year	Basis period	Workings	Trading income
			£
2013-14	1/1/14 to 5/4/14	£9,120 x 3/12	2,280
2014-15	y/e 31/12/14		9,120
2015-16	y/e 31/12/15		10,500
2016-17	y/e 31/12/16		23,360
2017-18	1/1/17 to 28/2/18	£28,780 – overlap relief £1,520	27,260
2018-19	y/e 28/2/19		32,540

There are overlap profits of £2,280 (3 months) on the commencement of trade. The relevant period is 14 months long, which exceeds 12 months by 2 months. Overlap relief in the year of change is calculated as £2,280 x 2/3 = £1,520. Overlap profits carried forward are £760 (1 month).

Transitional overlap relief

The basis period rules now in use were introduced by Finance Act 1994. Businesses which existed before 6 April 1994 used to be assessed on the *preceding year basis*, which meant that the basis period for a tax year was the accounting year ending in the *previous* tax year. The switch to the current year basis for these businesses occurred as from 1997-98.

One aspect of this transition which will remain relevant for many years is that these older businesses (which cannot claim overlap relief in the normal way) are eligible for *transitional overlap relief* on a change of accounting date or on the cessation of trade. An explanation of transitional overlap relief is provided on the website which accompanies this book. The website address is www.pearsoned.co.uk/melville.

Averaging of trading profits for farmers and creative artists

Certain trades, professions and vocations are more likely than others to experience profits which fluctuate considerably from one period to the next, giving rise to corresponding fluctuations in the trading income which is charged to tax. In particular, this problem may affect farmers and market gardeners (who are at the mercy of the weather) and creative artists (with profits derived from literary works, musical works etc.).

ITTOIA 2005 allows farmers, market gardeners and creative artists to smooth out fluctuating profits by making a claim for *averaging*. As from tax year 2016-17, the profits of farmers and market gardeners may be averaged over two consecutive years or over five consecutive years. The profits of creative artists may be averaged over two consecutive years only. Note the following points in relation to the averaging process:

(a) Trading profits may be averaged over two consecutive tax years if the trading profit for one of those years is less than 75% of the trading profit for the other year (or if the trading profit for one of the years is £nil)†.

(b) *For farmers and market gardeners only*, trading profits may be averaged over five consecutive tax years if one of the following is less than 75% of the other:

   (i) the average of the trading profits for the first four of those five years, and
   (ii) the trading profit of the fifth year

   or if the trading profit for at least one of the five years is £nil.

(c) If a loss has been incurred in any of the years which are involved in an averaging claim, this loss counts as a trading profit of £nil for averaging purposes. The loss is then eligible for tax relief (see Chapter 12).

(d) An averaging claim may not be made in relation to the tax year in which trade commences or the tax year in which trade ceases.

(e) In the case of two-year claims, it is permissible for the earlier of those two years to be a year for which an averaging claim (either two-year or five-year) has already been made. Similarly, in the case of five-year claims, it is permissible for any of the first four years to which the claim relates to be a year for which an averaging claim (either two-year or five-year) has already been made. But overlapping claims of this nature must be made in chronological order.

(f) An averaging claim must be made by the first anniversary of the 31 January which follows the later of the tax years to which the claim relates. For example, a two-year averaging claim which relates to 2016-17 and 2017-18 (or a five-year claim which relates to 2013-14 through to 2017-18) must be made by 31 January 2020.

† *Prior to tax year 2016-17, a form of "marginal relief" was available if the trading profits of one of the tax years to which a two-year averaging claim related were between 70% and 75% of the trading profits of the other year. But this marginal relief has now been abolished.*

EXAMPLE 8

The recent adjusted trading profits of a self-employed farmer (who began trading many years ago) are as follows:

	£
year to 30 November 2016	54,200
year to 30 November 2017	18,640

He has no other income. May an averaging claim be made for these two years and would the farmer benefit from such a claim? If so, what is the time limit for making this claim?

Solution

The tax years in question are 2016-17 and 2017-18. The lower of the two profit figures is £18,640 and this is less than 75% of £54,200 (i.e. £40,650) so an averaging claim may be made. If such a claim is made, the farmer's trading income for both 2016-17 and 2017-18 will be revised for tax purposes to £36,420 (the average of £54,200 and £18,640). The farmer would benefit from this claim in the following ways:

(a) the likelihood of paying 40% tax for 2016-17 would be removed, so reducing the total income tax liability for the two years, and

(b) the farmer's cash flow situation would be improved, since the 2016-17 tax liability would be reduced and the 2017-18 tax liability would be increased.

The time limit for making the claim would be 31 January 2020.

EXAMPLE 9

A creative artist has been self-employed for many years. Adjusted trading profits/(losses) in recent years are as follows:

	£
year to 31 September 2013	43,000
year to 31 September 2014	28,440
year to 31 September 2015	(5,400)
year to 31 September 2016	13,800
year to 31 September 2017	21,600

Calculate the artist's trading income for 2013-14 to 2017-18 inclusive, assuming that all possible averaging claims are made.

Solution

2013-14 and 2014-15

£28,440 is less than 75% of £43,000 (i.e. £32,250) so an averaging claim may be made. Averaging gives revised trading income of £35,720 in each year.

2014-15 and 2015-16

Revised trading income for 2014-15 is £35,720. Trading income for 2015-16 is £nil, so an averaging claim may be made. Averaging gives revised trading income of £17,860 in each year.

2015-16 and 2016-17

Revised trading income for 2015-16 is £17,860. Trading income for 2016-17 is £13,800. This is not less than 75% of £17,860 (i.e. £13,395) so averaging is not possible.

2016-17 and 2017-18

£13,800 is less than 75% of £21,600 (i.e. £16,200) so an averaging claim may be made. Averaging gives revised trading income of £17,700 in each year. Trading income figures for tax years 2013-14 to 2017-18 are now:

	£
2013-14	35,720
2014-15	17,860
2015-16	17,860
2016-17	17,700
2017-18	17,700 (which may perhaps be averaged with 2018-19).

EXAMPLE 10

A market gardener began trading many years ago and has been making good profits for many years. However, adverse weather conditions in 2017 caused his profits to fall very sharply in that year. Adjusted trading profits for the most recent five years are as follows:

	£
year to 30 December 2013	47,800
year to 30 December 2014	52,750
year to 30 December 2015	52,750
year to 30 December 2016	41,100
year to 30 December 2017	2,300

He has no other income. The trading profits of 2014 and 2015 were averaged in a previous averaging claim. Identify any further averaging claims that might now be made.

Solution

A two-year averaging claim could be made in relation to 2016 and 2017. This would revise trading income for 2016-17 and 2017-18 to £21,700 per year and save basic rate tax in 2016-17. It would also avoid a waste of personal allowances in 2017-18.

But a better option might be to make a five-year claim. The average profit of the years 2013 to 2016 inclusive is £48,600 and the profit of £2,300 in 2017 is far less than 75% of this, so the claim may be made. A five-year claim would revise trading income to £39,340 per year and save higher rate tax in each of the first three years covered by the claim.

Summary

- Trading profits are charged to income tax on the current year basis. This means that the basis period for a tax year is normally the accounting year which ends in that tax year. However, special basis period rules apply in the opening and closing tax years of a business and on a change of accounting date.
- The first tax year in which trading profits are taxed is the tax year in which trade commences. The basis period for the first tax year runs from the date of commencement to the following 5th April.
- If there is an accounting date in the second tax year and this date is at least 12 months after commencement, the basis period for the second tax year is the 12 months to that accounting date. But if this accounting date is not at least 12 months after commencement, the basis period for the second tax year is the first 12 months of trading.
- If there is no accounting date in the second tax year, the basis period for that tax year is the actual tax year from 6th April to the following 5 April.
- Overlap profits arising in the opening years of a new business are relieved either on the cessation of trade or on a change of accounting date. However, further overlap profits may arise on a change of accounting date
- The final tax year in which trading profits are taxed is the tax year in which trade ceases. In general, the basis period for the final tax year runs from the end of the basis period for the previous tax year up to the date of the cessation.
- Special rules are used in order to determine the basis period for the tax year in which a business changes its accounting date.
- Subject to certain conditions, farmers and market gardeners and creative artists may claim that the trading income of two consecutive tax years should be averaged. As from 2016-17, farmers and market gardeners may make a five-year averaging claim.

Exercises

10.1 Under the *current year basis*, for which tax years would the following accounting years form the basis period?

(a) year to 31 October 2017
(b) year to 31 March 2018
(c) year to 30 April 2019
(d) year to 5 April 2019

10.2 Frank began trading on 1 July 2015. Identify the basis periods for his first four tax years if he:

(a) chooses 30 June as his annual accounting date and prepares his first accounts for the year to 30 June 2016

(b) chooses 30 April as his annual accounting date and prepares his first accounts for the 22 months to 30 April 2017

(c) chooses 30 April as his annual accounting date and prepares his first accounts for the 10 months to 30 April 2016.

Also identify any overlap periods which arise in each case.

10.3 Greta commences trading on 1 January 2016 and chooses 30 June as her annual accounting date. Her first accounts are made up for the 18 months to 30 June 2017 and show an adjusted trading profit of £27,300. Compute Greta's trading income for the first three tax years and calculate the amount of any overlap profits.

10.4 Hitesh has been trading for many years, preparing accounts to 31 January each year. His last full year of trading is the year to 31 January 2017. Identify the basis periods for the last three tax years in each of the following cases:

	Date of cessation	*Final set of accounts*
(a)	31 May 2017	4 months to 31 May 2017
(b)	31 March 2018	14 months to 31 March 2018
(c)	30 April 2018	15 months to 30 April 2018

10.5 Phillip starts trading on 1 June 2013 and ceases trading on 31 July 2018. He has adjusted trading profits as follows

	£
1 June 2013 to 30 September 2014	28,800
year to 30 September 2015	19,900
year to 30 September 2016	14,300
year to 30 September 2017	13,800
1 October 2017 to 31 July 2018	11,100

Compute Phillip's trading income for all tax years.

***10.6** Ivy begins trading as a farmer on 1 January 2015, making up annual accounts to 31 December. Her adjusted trading profits/(losses) in the opening years are as follows:

	£
year to 31 December 2015	31,600
year to 31 December 2016	15,400
year to 31 December 2017	(12,900)

(a) Compute Ivy's trading income for the first four tax years, assuming that no averaging claims are made.

(b) Compute Ivy's revised trading income for the first four tax years, assuming that all possible averaging claims are made.

***10.7** Ken starts trading on 1 October 2012 and chooses 30 April as his accounting date. He ceases trading on 31 January 2018 and has adjusted trading profits as follows:

	£
7 months to 30 April 2013	3,500
year to 30 April 2014	18,480
year to 30 April 2015	17,700
year to 30 April 2016	27,900
year to 30 April 2017	28,200
9 months to 31 January 2018	17,300

Compute Ken's trading income for all tax years.

***10.8** Belinda began trading on 1 March 2013 and chose 31 December as her accounting date. Her first accounts were for the period to 31 December 2013. She eventually decided to change her accounting date to 31 May and the first accounts made up to the new date were for the 17 months to 31 May 2017. The conditions necessary for a change of basis period were all satisfied. The adjusted trading profits for her first five periods of account were as follows:

	Adjusted trading profit
	£
1 March 2013 to 31 December 2013	43,700
year to 31 December 2014	52,590
year to 31 December 2015	54,300
1 January 2016 to 31 May 2017	71,060
year to 31 May 2018	68,200

Compute Belinda's trading income for 2012-13 to 2018-19 inclusive, showing the amounts of any overlap profits or overlap relief.

***10.9** Roger began trading on 1 January 2011, preparing accounts to 30 April each year. His first accounts were for the 16 months to 30 April 2012. In 2014 he decided to change his accounting date to 30 June. The first accounts made up to the new date were for the 14 months to 30 June 2014 and the conditions necessary for a change of basis period were all satisfied. Roger ceased trading on 31 May 2017. His adjusted trading profits were as follows:

	Adjusted trading profit
	£
1 January 2011 to 30 April 2012	33,920
year to 30 April 2013	29,700
1 May 2013 to 30 June 2014	33,300
year to 30 June 2015	41,600
year to 30 June 2016	37,900
1 July 2016 to 31 May 2017	23,500

Compute Roger's trading income for all tax years.

Chapter 11

Income from self-employment: Capital allowances

Introduction

Capital expenditure is generally not deductible when computing trading income but certain types of capital expenditure attract tax relief in the form of standardised depreciation allowances known as *capital allowances*. The purpose of this chapter is to define the categories of capital expenditure which are eligible for capital allowances and to explain how capital allowances are calculated for each of these categories.

Eligible expenditure

In order to be eligible for capital allowances, capital expenditure must usually fall into one of the following categories:

(a) plant and machinery
(b) patent rights
(c) know-how
(d) research and development
(e) renovation of business premises.

This chapter is primarily concerned with plant and machinery, which is the most important category. However, the other categories are considered briefly at the end of the chapter.

Chargeable periods

Capital allowances are calculated in respect of *chargeable periods*. For income tax purposes, each period of account generally ranks as a chargeable period and so there is usually one capital allowances computation per period of account. Note that:

(a) The capital allowances for a period of account are treated as a trading expense and are deducted when computing the adjusted trading profit for that period. The basis period rules are applied to the trading profit *after* deduction of capital allowances.

(b) A period of account lasting for more than 18 months is subdivided into one or more 12-month chargeable periods with (possibly) a short chargeable period at the end. Capital allowances are calculated separately for each of these chargeable periods and then aggregated to give the capital allowances due for the whole period of account.

(c) The chargeable periods of *companies*, which pay corporation tax rather than income tax, are determined according to a different set of rules (see Chapter 23).

EXAMPLE 1

Lee begins trading on 1 January 2017 preparing accounts to 31 December each year. His adjusted trading profit for the year to 31 December 2017 (before capital allowances) is £21,000 and capital allowances of £1,200 are claimed for that year. Compute his trading income for 2016-17 and 2017-18.

Solution

The adjusted trading profit for the year to 31 December 2017 (after deduction of capital allowances) is £19,800. Therefore trading income for the first two tax years is as follows:

Year	*Basis*	*Basis period*	*Workings*	*Trading income*
				£
2016-17	Actual	1/1/17 to 5/4/17	£19,800 x 3/12	4,950
2017-18	12 months to a/c date in year 2	y/e 31/12/17		19,800

Plant and machinery

Capital Allowances Act 2001 (the main statute concerned with capital allowances) does not provide a definition of the term "plant and machinery". Therefore it has been left mainly to case law to decide whether or not any given item should qualify as plant and machinery and so attract capital allowances. In *Yarmouth* v *France* (1887) it was stated that plant and machinery includes:

> "*whatever apparatus is used by a businessman for carrying on his business, not his stock in trade which he buys or makes for sale, but all his goods and chattels, fixed or moveable, live or dead, which he keeps for permanent employment in his business*".

It is fairly clear that machinery of all types, motor vehicles and items such as office furniture and equipment all qualify as plant and machinery but difficulties arise in connection with expenditure on buildings and fixtures to buildings. Much case law has been concerned with the distinction between:

(a) assets which perform an *active function* in the carrying on of the business (i.e. the apparatus *with which* the business is carried on), and

(b) assets which perform a *passive function* in the carrying on of the business (i.e. the setting *in which* the business is carried on).

Assets in the first of these categories qualify as plant and machinery whilst assets in the second category do not, but the distinction between the categories can be a very fine one. Some of the more important case law decisions are as follows:

Held to be plant and machinery:

(a) a dry dock built for the repair and the maintenance of ships, in *CIR* v *Barclay Curle & Co Ltd* (1969)

(b) a swimming and paddling pool, in *Cooke* v *Beach Station Caravans Ltd* (1974)

(c) a concrete grain silo, in *Schofield* v *R & H Hall Ltd* (1974)

(d) decorative display screens placed in the window of a building society's offices and incorporating the name of the building society, in *Leeds Permanent Building Society* v *Proctor* (1982)

(e) moveable office partitions, in *Jarrold* v *John Good & Sons Ltd* (1962)

(f) display lighting in a store window, in *Cole Brothers Ltd* v *Phillips* (1982)

(g) light fittings and pictures on the walls of a hotel, in *CIR* v *Scottish and Newcastle Breweries Ltd* (1982)

(h) storage platforms built in a warehouse, in *Hunt* v *Henry Quick Ltd* (1992)

(i) a barrister's law books, in *Munby* v *Furlong* (1977)

(j) a synthetic football pitch, in *CIR* v *Anchor International Ltd* (2005).

Held *not* to be plant and machinery:

(a) prefabricated school buildings, in *St John's School* v *Ward* (1974)

(b) a moored ship used as a restaurant, in *Benson* v *The Yard Arm Club Ltd* (1979)

(c) a petrol station forecourt canopy, in *Dixon* v *Fitch's Garage Ltd* (1975)

(d) a football stand, in *Brown* v *Burnley Football and Athletic Co Ltd* (1980)

(e) a false ceiling built to hide electrical conduits, in *Hampton* v *Fortes Autogrill Ltd* (1979)

(f) a false ceiling, mezzanine floors, staircases, decorative floor and wall tiles all used to create ambience in a restaurant, in *Wimpey International Ltd* v *Warland* (1988)

(g) golf putting greens, in *Family Golf Centres Ltd* v *Thorne* (1998).

In an attempt to clarify the distinction between buildings and plant, Capital Allowances Act 2001 provides a detailed list of types of expenditure on buildings or structures which are statutorily excluded from qualifying as plant. The Act also provides a detailed list of types of expenditure on buildings or structures which are not statutorily excluded from qualifying as plant and may therefore qualify if permitted by case law.

Expenditure statutorily deemed to be plant and machinery

By statute, expenditure of the following types always qualifies as plant and machinery:

(a) expenditure on the thermal insulation of a building
(b) expenditure on assets necessary to safeguard personal security
(c) expenditure on "integral features" of a building or structure (see below)
(d) expenditure on computer software
(e) expenditure on building alterations, incidental to installation of plant and machinery.

These types of expenditure all qualify as plant and machinery despite the fact that some of them would normally be disqualified by the rule excluding expenditure on buildings.

Capital allowances on plant and machinery

With some exceptions (see later), capital allowances are not calculated individually for each item of plant and machinery acquired by a business. Instead, expenditure on plant and machinery is pooled together and capital allowances are calculated with reference to the value of the pool. In fact, there are two pools to consider. These are:

(a) **Main pool**. This is the pool to which most general plant and machinery is allocated (e.g. factory machines, office equipment etc.). Motor vans, motor cycles and lorries are also allocated to this pool. The situation with regard to motor cars† is as follows:

   (i) In general, cars with emissions which do not exceed 130g/km (*110g/km as from 6 April 2018*) are allocated to the main pool. Cars with higher emissions than this are allocated to the special rate pool (see below).

   (ii) However, "low emission" cars (currently defined as those with emissions not exceeding 75g/km) are eligible for a 100% first year allowance and do not join any pool (see later in this chapter).

   † *A special treatment is accorded to cars acquired before 6 April 2009 and costing more than £12,000. This rule is now falling into disuse but is explained briefly later in this chapter.*

(b) **Special rate pool**. This is a pool of assets arising from any or all of the following:

   (i) the acquisition of motor cars with emissions exceeding 130g/km

   (ii) the acquisition or replacement of certain "integral features" of a building; these are listed in CAA 2001 as electrical systems, water systems, heating and cooling systems, lifts, escalators/moving walkways and external solar shading

   (iii) expenditure on the thermal insulation of a building and on solar panels

   (iv) expenditure on assets with a working life of 25 years or more ("long-life" assets) but only if the business spends more than £100,000 a year on such assets.

The rate of capital allowances to which a business is entitled in relation to an item of plant and machinery depends upon the pool to which the item is allocated, as explained below.

Writing down allowance (WDA)

In general, a business may claim a *writing down allowance* for each of its pools of plant and machinery in each chargeable period. The procedure for computing the amount of the writing down allowance for each pool is as follows:

(a) The written down value (WDV) of the pool at the end of the previous chargeable period is brought forward.

(b) The cost of any plant and machinery which has been acquired during the chargeable period but which is not the subject of a claim for either first year allowance or annual investment allowance (see below) is added to the pool. Items of plant and machinery owned by the trader personally and then brought into the business at a later date are treated as if purchased at their market value on that date.

Plant and machinery acquired by hire purchase is treated as if bought for its cash price. A similar treatment applies to assets acquired under "long funding leases". In broad terms, these are finance leases with a term of more than five years.

(c) If any pool items have been disposed of during the chargeable period a disposal value is subtracted from the pool, equal to:

   (i) sale proceeds, if the asset is sold in the open market

   (ii) market value on the date of disposal, if the asset is given away or sold for less than market value

   (iii) scrap value or compensation received, if the asset is scrapped or destroyed.

But if the disposal value exceeds the original cost of the item, only the original cost is subtracted from the pool. The profit on the disposal may give rise to a capital gains tax liability (see Chapter 19).

(d) The available writing down allowance (WDA) is then calculated as a percentage of the pool balance. The applicable percentages are currently as follows:

Main pool	18% per annum
Special rate pool	8% per annum

Note that WDA is calculated at a percentage rate *per annum*. This refers to the length of the chargeable period for which capital allowances are being claimed and WDA is scaled up or down accordingly if the length of this period is not 12 months.

(e) The WDA claimed for the chargeable period is subtracted from the pool, leaving a WDV which is carried forward to the next period. This WDV will then attract WDAs in future chargeable periods (even if all the plant and machinery has now been sold).

It is not mandatory to claim the maximum WDA available for a chargeable period and a trader with low profits (or a loss) may wish to claim less than the maximum, usually to avoid wasting personal allowances. The effect of such a claim is to increase the WDVs carried forward, thus increasing the allowances available in future chargeable periods.

EXAMPLE 2

Joanne started a business on 1 May 2016, preparing accounts to 31 December each year. Her first accounts were for the period to 31 December 2016. During this period and during the year to 31 December 2017 she bought and sold plant and machinery as follows:

		£
8 May 2016	Bought motor car (emissions 130g/km)	8,600
27 October 2016	Bought motor car (emissions 120g/km)	10,400
31 July 2017	Sold motor car bought in May 2016	6,620
31 July 2017	Bought motor car (emissions 145g/km)	14,200

Prepare her capital allowances computation for the first two chargeable periods.

Solution

	Main pool	*Special rate pool*	*Allowances*
	£	£	£
1/5/16 - 31/12/16			
Additions (£8,600 + £10,400)	19,000		
WDA @ 18% x 8/12	2,280		2,280
WDV c/f	16,720		
Total allowances			2,280
y/e 31/12/17			
WDV b/f	16,720		
Additions		14,200	
Disposals	(6,620)		
	10,100		
WDA @ 18%	1,818		1,818
WDA @ 8%		1,136	1,136
WDV c/f	8,282	13,064	
Total allowances			2,954

Notes:

(i) The motor cars bought for £8,600 and £10,400 enter the main pool because they have emissions not exceeding 130g/km.

(ii) WDA is scaled down by 8/12 for an eight-month period.

(iii) The motor car bought in 2017 for £14,200 enters the special rate pool because it has emissions which exceed 130g/km.

(iv) Total capital allowances are £2,280 for the eight months to 31 December 2016 and £2,954 for the year to 31 December 2017.

Changes in the rate of WDA

When changes are made to the rates of WDA, the WDAs available for a chargeable period which spans the date of the change have to be calculated at "hybrid" rates. The most recent occasion on which this occurred was 6 April 2012, when the rate of WDA in the main pool fell from 20% to 18% and the rate of WDA in the special rate pool fell from 10% to 8%.

Further details and a number of worked examples may be found on the website which accompanies this textbook. The website address is www.pearsoned.co.uk/melville.

Small pools of plant and machinery

If the balance in the main pool or special rate pool before calculating WDA is £1,000 or less, the business may claim a WDA of any amount up to the amount of that balance. This rule means that it is not necessary for businesses to carry forward very small pool balances for many years, claiming ever diminishing WDAs in each chargeable period.

Businesses with a balance of £1,000 or less in the main pool or special rate pool can claim a WDA of less than the full balance if they so wish.

EXAMPLE 3

Patrick prepares accounts to 31 August each year. The written down value of his main pool of plant and machinery after deducting capital allowances for the year to 31 August 2016 was £1,900. There were no acquisitions during the year to 31 August 2017 but an item of plant that had been acquired for £3,000 in 2013 was sold in May 2017 for £1,250.

Prepare a capital allowances computation for the year to 31 August 2017, assuming that maximum allowances are claimed.

Solution

	Main pool	*Allowances*
	£	£
y/e 31/8/17		
WDV b/f	1,900	
Disposals	(1,250)	
	650	
WDA	650	650
WDV c/f	0	
Total allowances		650

Note:

WDA for the year would normally have been 18% × £650 = £117, leaving a WDV carried forward of £533. However, since the WDV of the pool before calculating WDA is less than £1,000, a WDA of £650 may be claimed, leaving a WDV carried forward of £nil.

Annual investment allowance (AIA)

Expenditure on plant and machinery (other than motor cars) of up to a specified maximum amount each year is eligible for a 100% annual investment allowance (AIA). As from 1 January 2016, the AIA maximum is £200,000 per annum and this figure is expected to remain unchanged until at least 2020. Prior to 1 January 2016, the AIA annual maximum changed fairly frequently, as follows:

	£
6 April 2008 to 5 April 2010	50,000
6 April 2010 to 5 April 2012	100,000
6 April 2012 to 31 December 2012	25,000
1 January 2013 to 5 April 2014	250,000
6 April 2014 to 31 December 2015	500,000
1 January 2016 onwards	200,000

The main features of the annual investment allowance are as follows:

(a) An AIA of 100% may be claimed in relation to qualifying expenditure that does not exceed the AIA maximum for the period. If expenditure exceeds the AIA maximum, the excess enters the appropriate pool and is eligible for WDAs in the usual way.

(b) A business may allocate the AIA between items of expenditure in any way that it chooses. For example, if £160,000 is spent on main pool items and £80,000 is spent on special rate pool items in a year in which the AIA maximum is £200,000, £80,000 of the AIA might be allocated to the special rate pool and the remaining £120,000 to the main pool. This would maximise allowances for the period, since the main pool attracts WDA at 18% whilst the special rate pool attracts WDA at only 8%.

A business which spends no more than the AIA maximum amount on special rate items each year might use this approach to avoid having a special rate pool at all. But a special rate pool is unavoidable if the business acquires motor cars with emissions exceeding 130g/km, since cars are not eligible for AIA.

(c) The AIA maximum amount is increased or reduced proportionately for chargeable periods of more or less than 12 months in duration.

(d) A business is not required to claim the full AIA to which it is entitled. Any qualifying expenditure which is not the subject of a claim for AIA enters the appropriate pool and is eligible for WDAs.

(e) When an item of plant and machinery which has been the subject of an AIA claim is subsequently disposed of, the item's disposal value is subtracted from whichever pool the item would have joined if the AIA claim had not been made.

(f) If a person controls more than one business, these businesses are entitled to only one AIA between them if they are "related". Businesses are related if they are conducted from shared premises or if their activities are within the same EU classification.

Periods straddling a date on which the AIA maximum is increased

If a chargeable period straddles a date on which the AIA annual maximum is increased, special rules are used to calculate the maximum AIA available for that period. These rules were most recently invoked for periods straddling 6 April 2014† (when the AIA annual maximum increased from £250,000 to £500,000). Maximum AIA for a chargeable period which straddles 6 April 2014 (working to the nearest month) is:

$$(£250{,}000 \times m/12) + (£500{,}000 \times n/12)$$

where "m" and "n" are the number of months in the period falling respectively before and after 6 April 2014. But the AIA that may be claimed in relation to expenditure incurred in the part of the period that falls before 6 April 2014 is restricted to £250,000 (scaled up or down pro rata if the chargeable period is not exactly 12 months long).

† *Similar rules applied to previous occasions on which the AIA maximum was increased.*

Periods straddling a date on which the AIA maximum is decreased

If a chargeable period straddles a date on which the AIA annual maximum is decreased, special rules are used to calculate the maximum AIA available for that period. These rules were most recently invoked for periods straddling 1 January 2016† (when the AIA annual maximum decreased from £500,000 to £200,000). Maximum AIA for a chargeable period which straddles 1 January 2016 (working to the nearest month) is:

$$(£500{,}000 \times m/12) + (£200{,}000 \times n/12)$$

where "m" and "n" are the number of months in the period falling respectively before and after 1 January 2016. But the AIA that may be claimed in relation to expenditure incurred in the part of the period falling after 31 December 2015 is restricted to (£200,000 × n/12).

† *Similar rules applied to previous occasions on which the AIA maximum was decreased.*

EXAMPLE 4

Sam began trading on 1 December 2015 and prepared his first accounts for the 17-month period to 30 April 2017. His expenditure on plant and machinery (other than motor cars) in the period was £300,000, of which £25,000 was spent on 1 December 2015 and the remaining £275,000 was spent on 1 April 2016.

(a) Calculate the maximum AIA available for the 17 months to 30 April 2017.

(b) Calculate the AIA that may be claimed for the period.

Solution

(a) The maximum AIA available is £308,333 [(1/12 × £500,000) + (16/12 × £200,000)]. But no more than £266,667 (16/12 × £200,000) may be claimed in relation to expenditure incurred on or after 1 January 2016.

(b) £291,667 (£25,000 + £266,667).

EXAMPLE 5

(a) Sharon started a business on 1 July 2016. She chose 31 March as her accounting date and her first accounts covered the period from 1 July 2016 to 31 March 2017. During this period she bought plant and machinery as follows:

		£
1 July 2016	Bought plant	6,000
19 August 2016	Bought motor car (emissions 122g/km)	8,400
17 March 2017	Bought motor van	13,000

She claims maximum capital allowances in all chargeable periods. Prepare a capital allowances computation for the nine months to 31 March 2017.

(b) Sharon's purchases and sales of plant and machinery during the year to 31 March 2018 are as follows:

		£
8 April 2017	Bought plant	5,990
30 June 2017	Sold plant (original cost £3,500 on 1/7/16)	2,640

Prepare a capital allowances computation for the year to 31 March 2018.

Solution

(a)

		Main pool	*Allowances*
		£	£
1/7/16 - 31/3/17			
Additions not eligible for AIA		8,400	
WDA @ 18% x 9/12		1,134	1,134
		7,266	
Additions qualifying for AIA	19,000		
AIA @ 100%	19,000	-	19,000
WDV c/f		7,266	
Total allowances			20,134

Notes:

(i) The motor car is allocated to the main pool since it has emissions not exceeding 130g/km. Cars are not eligible for AIA.

(ii) WDA is scaled down by 9/12 for a nine-month chargeable period. The fact that the motor car was purchased part of the way through the period is irrelevant.

(iii) The AIA maximum for this nine-month period is (9/12 × £200,000) = £150,000. Sharon's expenditure of £19,000 is within this maximum.

(iv) A motor van is not a motor car and is therefore eligible for AIA.

(v) Total capital allowances for the period are £20,134.

(b)

		Main pool	Allowances
		£	£
y/e 31/3/18			
WDV b/f		7,266	
Disposals		(2,640)	
		4,626	
WDA @ 18%		833	833
		3,793	
Additions eligible for AIA	5,990		
AIA @ 100%	5,990	-	5,990
WDV c/f		3,793	
Total allowances			6,823

Notes:

(i) The AIA maximum for the year is £200,000. Sharon's qualifying expenditure of £5,990 is within this maximum, so AIA of £5,990 may be claimed.

(ii) Total capital allowances for the year are £6,823.

First year allowance (FYA)

A first year allowance of 100% is available in relation to certain classes of expenditure on unused (not second hand) plant and machinery. Unlike WDAs and the AIA, FYAs are not scaled up or down for chargeable periods of more or less than 12 months in duration. The main first year allowances (FYAs) are currently as follows:

(a) Expenditure on a motor car with emissions that do not exceed 75g/km (*reduced to 50g/km for cars acquired after 31 March 2018*) is eligible for a 100% FYA as long as the expenditure is incurred on or before 31 March 2021.

(b) Expenditure on plant and machinery for use in the refuelling of vehicles with natural gas, biogas or hydrogen fuel is eligible for a 100% FYA as long as the expenditure is incurred on or before 31 March 2018†.

(c) Expenditure on zero-emission goods vehicles is eligible for a 100% FYA as long as the expenditure is incurred on or before 6 April 2018.

(d) Expenditure incurred on certain classes of energy-saving and water-efficient plant and machinery also qualifies for a 100% FYA.

When an item of plant and machinery which has been the subject of a claim for a 100% FYA is disposed of, the disposal value of the item is deducted from whichever pool the item would have entered if that claim had not been made.

† *The Government has proposed that expenditure incurred between 23 November 2016 and 5 April 2019 on charging points for electric vehicles should also be eligible for a 100% FYA.*

EXAMPLE 6

Ian owns a large manufacturing business and prepares accounts to 31 December each year. The written down value of his main pool of plant and machinery after deducting capital allowances for the year to 31 December 2016 was £116,250. There was no special rate pool on that date. Purchases and sales of plant and machinery for the year to 31 December 2017 were as follows:

		£
9 April 2017	Bought factory electrical systems	138,300
17 May 2017	Bought plant	114,450
5 June 2017	Bought car (emissions 70g/km)	12,700
25 August 2017	Sold plant bought for £11,000 in 2016	12,500
31 October 2017	Bought car (emissions 133g/km)	14,000

The electrical systems bought in April 2017 qualify as "integral features" of a building for capital allowances purposes. Prepare a capital allowances computation for the year to 31 December 2017, assuming that maximum allowances are claimed.

Solution

		Main pool	*Special rate pool*	*Allowances*
		£	£	£
y/e 31/12/17				
WDV b/f		116,250		
Additions not eligible for AIA		52,750	14,000	
Disposal		(11,000)		
		158,000		
WDA @ 18%		28,440		28,440
WDA @ 8%			1,120	1,120
		129,560	12,880	
Additions eligible for AIA	200,000			
AIA @ 100%	200,000	-		200,000
Additions eligible for 100% FYA	12,700			
FYA @ 100%	12,700	-		12,700
WDV c/f		129,560	12,880	
Total allowances				242,260

Notes:

(i) The AIA maximum for the year of £200,000 could be allocated in any way between the expenditure of £138,300 on electrical systems and the expenditure of £114,450 on general plant. Capital allowances for the year are maximised if the AIA is allocated first to the expenditure of £138,300, since this expenditure would otherwise enter the special rate pool and be eligible for WDA at a lower rate than in the main pool.

(ii) Setting the AIA first against the expenditure of £138,300 leaves £61,700 available to set against the expenditure of £114,450. The balance of £52,750 is not eligible for AIA and therefore enters the main pool.

(iii) The disposal value of the plant sold in August 2017 is restricted to original cost.

(iv) The car bought in June 2017 has emissions not exceeding 75g/km, so it is eligible for a 100% FYA.

(v) The car bought in October 2017 has emissions exceeding 130g/km, so it is allocated to the special rate pool.

(vi) Total capital allowances for the year are £242,260.

Balancing allowances and charges

If the disposal value of the plant and machinery disposed of during a chargeable period exceeds the balance of expenditure in the relevant pool before disposals are deducted, this indicates that the capital allowances given to date exceed the depreciation which has actually occurred. In these circumstances, the written down value of the pool is set to zero and a *balancing charge* is made, equal to the amount of the excess. A balancing charge is a negative capital allowance which is *added* to trading profits for tax purposes.

Balancing adjustments are also required when a business ceases trading (see later in this chapter) or when a non-pooled asset is disposed of. Non-pooled assets are assets which are treated individually for capital allowances purposes (see below). When a non-pooled asset is disposed of, a balancing adjustment is required so as to ensure that the total capital allowances granted in respect of the asset are exactly equal to its depreciation. If the asset's disposal value exceeds its WDV brought forward, a *balancing charge* is made, equal to the excess. If the asset's WDV brought forward exceeds disposal value, a *balancing allowance* is given, equal to the excess.

Non-pooled assets

Certain items of plant and machinery are not brought into the main pool or the special rate pool. Instead, these items are treated individually for capital allowances purposes, each item having its own "single asset pool". The items in question are:

(a) assets with some private use

(b) short-life assets.

(c) expensive motor cars acquired before 6 April 2009

The treatment of each of these items is explained below.

Assets with some private use

Any asset which is partly used for private purposes by the owner of a business is dealt with in a single asset pool. Capital allowances in relation to such an asset are calculated in the usual way and are deducted in full when calculating the WDV of the asset, but only the business proportion of these allowances may then be claimed. Note that:

(a) A balancing allowance or charge will arise on the disposal of an asset which is held in a single asset pool. The taxpayer may claim only the business proportion of any balancing allowance which arises in these circumstances and is taxed on only the business proportion of any balancing charge.

(b) Capital allowances are available in full on assets used for private purposes by an *employee* of the business, but the employee may then be assessed to income tax on a benefit in kind (see Chapter 8).

EXAMPLE 7

Allan prepares accounts to 5 April each year. His acquisitions and disposals of plant and machinery in the years to 5 April 2017 and 2018 include the following:

		£
8 April 2016	Bought Audi motor car (emissions 118g/km)	17,500
12 May 2016	Bought computer system	3,000
27 March 2018	Sold Audi motor car	14,950
27 March 2018	Bought BMW motor car (emissions 141g/km)	24,000

Private use of both cars is agreed to be 30%. There is 25% private use of the computer system. Compute the capital allowances available in relation to each of these items for the years to 5 April 2017 and 2018, assuming that Allan's entitlement to AIA in both years is fully used against other assets.

Solution

	Audi (30% p.u.)	*Computer (25% p.u.)*		*Allces*
	£	£		£
y/e 5/4/17				
Additions	17,500	3,000		
WDA @ 18%	3,150		x 70%	2,205
WDA @ 18%		540	x 75%	405
WDV c/f	14,350	2,460		
Total allowances				2,610

	Audi (30% p.u.)	Computer (25% p.u.)	BMW (30% p.u.)		Allces
	£	£	£		£
y/e 5/4/18					
WDV b/f	14,350	2,460			
Addition			24,000		
Disposal	(14,950)				
Balancing charge	(600)			x 70%	(420)
WDA @ 18%		443		x 75%	332
WDA @ 8%			1,920	x 70%	1,344
WDV c/f		2,017	22,080		
Total allowances					1,256

Notes:

(i) The Audi motor car has emissions which do not exceed 130g/km, so WDAs on this car are calculated at 18% p.a.

(ii) The BMW has emissions which exceed 130g/km, so WDAs on this car are 8% p.a.

Short-life assets

A trader may elect that an asset (other than a car) which would normally join the main pool should instead be treated as a short-life asset. If this "de-pooling" election is made, the asset is treated on an individual basis, and then:

(a) if the asset is not disposed of within eight years of the end of the period in which it is acquired, it is transferred to the main pool at its written down value at the end of those eight years and the short-life election will have had no effect

(b) if the asset is disposed of within the eight-year period, a balancing allowance will be given (or a balancing charge will be made).

Making a short-life election in relation to an asset which is likely to be sold for less than its WDV within eight years will generate a balancing allowance on disposal, so ensuring that capital allowances are given as quickly as possible. There is (of course) no point in making such an election if a 100% AIA is available in relation to the asset. Note that:

(a) A short-life election relating to expenditure incurred during a chargeable period must be made by 31 January in the second tax year following the tax year in which the chargeable period ends.

(b) One effect of a short-life election is that the asset concerned is kept out of the main pool. This increases the likelihood that disposals from that pool will have a disposal value which exceeds the pool balance, so triggering a balancing charge (see earlier in this chapter). This factor should be borne in mind when making a short-life election.

EXAMPLE 8

Anita starts trading on 1 July 2017, preparing accounts to 30 June. Her only acquisitions and disposals of plant and machinery in the first three years of trading are as follows:

		£
1 July 2017	Bought general plant	205,000
1 July 2017	Bought office machine	140,000
31 March 2020	Sold office machine	35,000

Her AIA for the year to 30 June 2018 is set against the £205,000 expenditure on general plant. Compute capital allowances for the first three chargeable periods assuming that:

(a) she does not make any short-life elections

(b) she makes a short-life election with regard to the office machine.

Solution

(a)		*Main pool*	*Allowances*
		£	£
y/e 30/6/18			
Additions not eligible for AIA		145,000	
WDA @ 18%		26,100	26,100
		118,900	
Additions eligible for AIA	200,000		
AIA @ 100%	200,000	-	200,000
WDV c/f		118,900	
Total allowances			226,100
y/e 30/6/19			
WDV b/f		118,900	
WDA @ 18%		21,402	21,402
WDV c/f		97,498	
y/e 30/6/20			
WDV b/f		97,498	
Disposal		(35,000)	
		62,498	
WDA @ 18%		11,250	11,250
WDV c/f		51,248	

Notes:

(i) AIA Maximum for the year to 30 June 2018 is £200,000.

(ii) Total expenditure is £345,000. Subtracting the AIA of £200,000 leaves £145,000 to enter the main pool.

(iii) It has been assumed that the rate of WDA in the main pool will continue to be 18% p.a. until at least 30 June 2020.

(b)		*Main pool*	*SL asset*	*Allowances*
		£	£	£
y/e 30/6/18				
Additions not eligible for AIA		5,000	140,000	
WDA @ 18%		900	25,200	26,100
		4,100		
Additions eligible for AIA	200,000			
AIA @ 100%	200,000	-		200,000
WDV c/f		4,100	114,800	
Total allowances				226,100
y/e 30/6/19				
WDV b/f		4,100	114,800	
WDA @ 18%		738	20,664	21,402
WDV c/f		3,362	94,136	
y/e 30/6/20				
WDV c/f		3,362	94,136	
Disposal			(35,000)	
Balancing allowance			59,136	59,136
WDA @ 18%		605		605
WDV c/f		2,757		
Total allowances				59,741

Notes:

(i) Total allowances for the years to 30 June 2018 and 30 June 2019 are unaffected by the short-life election. But total allowances for the year to 30 June 2020 are increased by £48,491 (£59,741 – £11,250) if the short-life election is made.

(ii) However, if the short-life election is made, WDVs carried forward reduce by £48,491 (£51,248 – £2,757). This reduces future capital allowances.

Expensive motor cars acquired before 6 April 2009

Prior to 6 April 2014, motor cars acquired before 6 April 2009 and costing more than £12,000 ("expensive cars") were dealt with on an individual basis. WDA was calculated at the same rate as in the main pool but was restricted to a maximum of £3,000 per annum.

In general, any unrelieved expenditure remaining in relation to such a car was transferred to the main pool at the beginning of the first chargeable period starting on or after 6 April 2014. However, this transfer did not occur for cars with an element of private use. Such cars remain in a single asset pool and continue to attract main rate WDAs (restricted for private use) until disposal.

Allowances on cessation of trade

When a business ceases trading and all of the plant and machinery is disposed of, capital allowances for the final chargeable period are computed as follows:

(a) Any items acquired in the final period are added into the relevant pool.

(b) No WDA, AIA or FYA is given in the final chargeable period.

(c) The disposal value of each pool (including single asset pools) is subtracted from the balance of unrelieved expenditure, giving rise to balancing allowances or balancing charges. Assets taken over personally by the trader are treated as if sold for their market value on the date they are taken over.

The balancing adjustments normally made on a cessation of trade can be avoided if the business is taken over by a connected person (e.g. the trader's spouse, civil partner or other relative) as long as an election to this effect is made by both parties. If such an election is made, the plant and machinery concerned is treated as if it had been sold by the trader to the connected person "*at a price which gives rise to neither a balancing allowance nor a balancing charge*". Effectively, the plant and machinery pools are transferred to the new owner at their WDVs for tax purposes.

EXAMPLE 9

Jake has been trading for many years, preparing accounts to 30 September each year. The written down value of his plant and machinery at 30 September 2016 was:

	£
Main pool	11,350
Motor car (20% private use by Jake)	13,200

Jake bought plant costing £1,150 in October 2016. This was his only transaction in plant and machinery until 30 June 2017, when he ceased trading and closed down his business. On that date, all of the items in his main pool were sold for a total of £12,850 (all items were sold for less than cost) and his car was sold for £12,000. Prepare Jake's capital allowances computation for the 9 months to 30 June 2017.

Solution

	Main pool	Motor car (20% private)	Allowances
	£	£	£
1/10/16 - 30/6/17			
WDV b/f	11,350	13,200	
Additions	1,150		
	12,500		
Disposals	(12,850)	(12,000)	
Balancing allowance/(charge)	(350)	1,200 x 80% = 960	610

Miscellaneous capital allowances

Capital allowances are available in relation to some miscellaneous categories of capital expenditure. These include expenditure on:

(a) patent rights

(b) know-how

(c) research and development.

Furthermore, capital allowances may also be available in relation to expenditure on the renovation of business premises. Each of these matters is considered briefly below.

Patent rights

The treatment of purchased patent rights acquired for trade purposes is as follows:

(a) Patent rights are pooled together. The patent rights pool is adjusted in each chargeable period for acquisitions and disposals and then WDA is calculated at 25% per annum on the reducing balance.

(b) WDA is proportionately increased or decreased if the chargeable period is of more or less than 12 months.

(c) As with plant and machinery, disposal value is restricted to original cost.

(d) If the disposal value of a patent exceeds the balance of unrelieved expenditure in the pool, a balancing charge is made and the pool value is set to zero.

(e) On cessation of trade, there will be a balancing allowance if the patents are sold for less than the balance of unrelieved expenditure in the pool. There will be a balancing charge if the patents are sold for more than the balance of unrelieved expenditure.

Know-how

"Know-how" is defined as industrial information and techniques of use in either:

(a) the manufacturing or processing of goods or materials

(b) the working of mineral deposits

(c) agricultural, fishing or forestry operations.

All expenditure on know-how is pooled and capital allowances are calculated in much the same way as for patent rights. However, if know-how is sold for more than original cost, the disposal value used in the capital allowances computation is the *full sale proceeds*. Depending upon the balance of unrelieved expenditure in the pool prior to the disposal, this will either create a balancing charge or restrict the value of subsequent WDAs. In either case, the profit made on the disposal is (in effect) treated as trading income.

Research and development

Capital expenditure on research and development related to the claimant's trade attracts a first year allowance of 100%. Any proceeds subsequently received on the disposal of a research and development asset are treated as a trading receipt.

Business premises renovation allowance

For expenditure incurred before 6 April 2017, a 100% allowance known as the Business Premises Renovation Allowance (BPRA) is available in relation to capital expenditure on the renovation of certain business premises. In order to qualify for BPRA, the premises must be located in a disadvantaged area and must have been vacant for at least a year.

BPRA was originally available in relation to qualifying expenditure incurred on or after 11 April 2007 and the scheme was expected to last for five years. However, the BPRA scheme was later extended for a further five years until 5 April 2017.

Summary

- Capital allowances are granted for chargeable periods. For income tax purposes, each period of account usually ranks as a chargeable period, but periods of account lasting more than 18 months are divided into two or more chargeable periods.
- In order to qualify as plant and machinery, an asset must perform an active function in the trade, not merely provide the setting in which the trade is carried on. There is extensive case law in relation to this distinction.
- With some exceptions, expenditure on plant and machinery is pooled together for capital allowances purposes. Most general plant and machinery is allocated to the main pool but certain items are allocated to the special rate pool.
- Motor cars with emissions in excess of 130g/km are allocated to the special rate pool. Cars with lower emissions are generally allocated to the main pool but cars with emissions not exceeding 75g/km attract a 100% FYA.
- Writing down allowances (WDAs) on plant and machinery are calculated at 18% per annum in the main pool and 8% per annum in the special rate pool. WDA is scaled up or down accordingly if the chargeable period is not exactly 12 months long.
- The first £200,000 per annum of expenditure on plant and machinery (other than motor cars) is eligible for a 100% annual investment allowance (AIA). The "AIA maximum amount" of £200,000 is scaled up or down accordingly if the chargeable period is not exactly 12 months long.
- A first year allowance (FYA) of 100% is available in relation to certain classes of expenditure on plant and machinery. These include low emission cars, gas refuelling equipment, zero-emission goods vehicles and energy saving technology.
- An asset which is used only partly for business purposes is dealt with in a single asset pool. Capital allowances are calculated in the usual way and are deducted in full when calculating the WDV of the asset, but only the business proportion of these allowances may be claimed.
- Short-life assets are allocated to single asset pools. A balancing allowance or charge will arise if a short-life asset is disposed of within eight years of the end of the period in which it was acquired.
- Balancing allowances and balancing charges will arise on a cessation of trade unless the business is taken over by a connected person.
- Capital allowances are also available in relation to qualifying expenditure incurred on patent rights, "know-how", research and development and (until 6 April 2017) certain business premises renovations.

Exercises

It should be assumed in all of these exercises that maximum capital allowances are claimed.

11.1 Maurice prepares accounts to 5 April each year. The written down value of his main pool at 5 April 2017 was £10,300. There was no special rate pool. His purchases and sales of plant and machinery during the year to 5 April 2018 were as follows:

		£
7 April 2017	Bought plant	600
11 April 2017	Sold machinery (original cost £4,000 in 2016)	4,200
11 July 2017	Bought motor car (emissions 124g/km)	8,000
1 November 2017	Bought machinery	400
12 January 2018	Sold equipment (original cost £7,000 in 2014)	3,000

Compute the capital allowances which may be claimed for the year to 5 April 2018, assuming no private use of any of the assets.

11.2 Laura started a business on 1 May 2016, preparing accounts to 30 April. Her adjusted trading profit for the year to 30 April 2017 (before deduction of capital allowances) was £263,150. Her purchases of plant and machinery during the year were as follows:

		£
1 May 2016	Bought machinery	113,000
1 May 2016	Bought motor car (emissions 148g/km)	15,000
12 July 2016	Bought machinery	25,700
27 February 2017	Bought machinery	74,800

Compute her trading income for the first two tax years, assuming 40% private use of the car by Laura. Also compute the amount of any overlap profits.

11.3 Norma has prepared a set of accounts for the nine-month period to 31 December 2017. The written down value of her plant and machinery at 31 March 2017 was as follows:

	£
Main pool	178,400
Toyota motor car (50% private use by Norma)	18,200

Plant and machinery transactions during the period to 31 December 2017 were:

		£
17 April 2017	Bought plant	64,450
1 May 2017	Sold Toyota motor car	15,000
1 May 2017	Bought Saab motor car (emissions 120g/km)	29,600
4 June 2017	Bought motor van	14,500
12 October 2017	Bought Ford motor car (emissions 72g/km)	11,600
3 November 2017	Bought Peugeot motor car (emissions 136g/km)	15,400
1 December 2017	Sold plant (original cost £10,000 in 2013)	3,400

There was 50% private use (by Norma) of the Toyota and Saab motor cars. Prepare a capital allowances computation for the period to 31 December 2017.

***11.4** Talat owns a large retail business and prepares accounts to 31 December each year. The written down value of his plant and machinery after deducting capital allowances for the year to 31 December 2016 was as follows:

	£
Main pool	113,210
Special rate pool	9,900
VW motor car (30% private use by Talat)	14,500

He had the following transactions during the year to 31 December 2017:

		£
6 January 2017	Sold VW motor car	17,200
6 January 2017	Bought BMW motor car (emissions 124g/km)	32,000
1 April 2017	Sold plant (original cost £1,000 in December 2016)	1,150
23 May 2017	Bought lifts and air conditioning systems	100,850
12 June 2017	Bought plant	112,550
5 October 2017	Sold main pool car (original cost £7,500 in 2014)	3,000
5 October 2017	Bought car (emissions 131g/km)	8,200
18 November 2017	Sold plant (original cost £4,200 in 2012)	1,310

The lifts and air conditioning systems bought in May 2017 qualify as "integral features" for capital allowances purposes. Private use by Talat of the VW and BMW motor cars has been agreed with HMRC to be 30%.

There were no capital transactions between 1 January 2018 and 31 March 2018, when Talat ceased trading and sold his business. The plant and machinery was disposed of (on 31 March 2018) as follows:

(i) All of the plant and machinery other than motor cars was sold for £240,000. This consisted of £150,000 for main pool items and £90,000 for special rate items. All items were sold for less than original cost.

(ii) Talat took over the BMW car. Its market value on 31 March 2018 was £25,000.

(iii) The only other car remaining was the one acquired in October 2017 and Talat gave this to his brother, who will be using it for private purposes. The market value of the car on 31 March 2018 was £6,300.

Prepare the capital allowances computations for the year to 31 December 2017 and for the period from 1 January 2018 to 31 March 2018.

***11.5** Raymond started trading on 1 October 2016. He chose 31 March as his accounting date and his first accounts were for the period from 1 October 2016 to 31 March 2017. His purchases and sales of plant and machinery during the first two accounting periods were as follows:

		£
1 October 2016	Bought machinery	130,000
1 October 2016	Bought motor van (emissions 212g/km)	16,200
12 December 2016	Bought motor car (emissions 173g/km)	18,600
18 January 2017	Bought office equipment	4,800
4 February 2017	Bought motor car (emissions 122g/km)	9,200
12 April 2017	Sold car bought in February 2017	9,600
12 April 2017	Bought motor car (emissions 130g/km)	15,500
25 November 2017	Sold machinery (cost £11,500 in October 2016)	8,300
3 February 2018	Bought machinery	30,000

There was 25% private use (by Raymond) of the motor car purchased in December 2016 but there was no private use of any of the other assets.

Required:

Prepare a capital allowances computation for the period to 31 March 2017 and for the year to 31 March 2018.

Chapter 12

Income from self-employment: Trading losses

Introduction

If a self-employed person's adjusted trading profit for a period of account is negative, then a trading loss has been incurred. This has two main consequences:

(a) the person's trading income for the relevant tax year is set to £nil

(b) tax relief may be claimed in respect of the loss.

Several forms of tax relief are available and each involves offsetting the loss against other income or gains of the person concerned, so reducing the amount of tax payable on that other income or on those gains. The main purpose of this chapter is to explain the features of each of the tax reliefs available in relation to a trading loss.

This chapter also explains a restriction which applies to the total amount of certain tax reliefs (mainly loss reliefs) that may be claimed by an individual in a tax year.

Relief for trading losses

The rules which grant tax relief in relation to trading losses are located in the Income Tax Act 2007. This Act provides the following main reliefs:

(a) **Carry-forward trade loss relief**. A trading loss may be carried forward to the future and set against future profits of the same trade. This is the relief which takes effect if no other tax relief is claimed in relation to a trading loss.

(b) **Trade loss relief against total income**. A trading loss may be set against the trader's total income for a period of up to two years.

(c) **Early trade losses relief**. This is a special tax relief which concerns trading losses incurred in the early years of trading.

(d) **Terminal trade loss relief**. This is a special tax relief which concerns trading losses incurred in the final year of trading.

Each of these forms of loss relief is described below.

Carry-forward trade loss relief

Unless a trader claims any other form of loss relief in relation to a trading loss, the loss is automatically carried forward and relieved against future trading profits. It is important to note the following points:

(a) Carry-forward relief is given against future *trading profits* only, not against any other form of income.

(b) Furthermore, relief is given only against future trading profits arising from *the same trade* as that in which the loss was incurred. So if a trader ceases one trade and commences another, the losses of the old trade cannot be carried forward and relieved against the future profits of the new trade. Similarly, if a trader carries on two trades simultaneously, a loss incurred in one of the trades cannot be carried forward and relieved against the future profits of the other trade.

(c) Relief must be given against the *first available* trading profits arising in the future. The maximum possible relief must be taken in each year until the loss is fully relieved, even if this leaves insufficient income to absorb personal allowances.

(d) Strictly speaking, relief is given by deduction from the trader's total income when computing his or her net income (see Chapter 2). But the amount of relief given in any tax year cannot exceed the trading profits for that year.

EXAMPLE 1

Carla incurred a trading loss of £42,000 in the year to 30 June 2015. Her trading profits for the following three years (adjusted for tax purposes) are as follows:

	£
year to 30 June 2016	15,000
year to 30 June 2017	26,000
year to 30 June 2018	60,000

Carla's only other income consists of property income of £2,400 per annum. Assuming that the trading loss is carried forward, calculate her net income (i.e. total income less reliefs) for tax years 2015-16 to 2018-19 inclusive.

Solution

	2015-16	*2016-17*	*2017-18*	*2018-19*
	£	£	£	£
Trading income	nil	15,000	26,000	60,000
Income from property	2,400	2,400	2,400	2,400
Total income	2,400	17,400	28,400	62,400
Less: Trading losses b/f	-	15,000	26,000	1,000
Net income	2,400	2,400	2,400	61,400

Notes:

(a) Trading income for 2015-16 is £nil as there is a loss in the basis period for that year.

(b) The trading loss carried forward is relieved against future trading profits (not against the property income) and maximum relief must be given in each year. This results in a waste of personal allowances in 2016-17 and 2017-18. Carla would probably prefer to carry forward the loss in its entirety to 2018-19, where it could be put to good use and save tax at the higher rate, but this is not permissible.

Capital allowances

As explained in Chapter 11, any capital allowances claimed for a period of account are treated as a trading expense of that period. Therefore capital allowances are included automatically in the calculation of a trading loss.

It is important to remember that it is not mandatory to claim the maximum capital allowances available for a chargeable period. If a trading loss has been incurred it may be advisable to claim less than the maximum capital allowances (or even none at all) so as to avoid wasting personal allowances when the trading loss is relieved. Disclaimed capital allowances are not lost permanently, since higher WDVs are carried forward than would otherwise have been the case and this results in higher capital allowances in future years.

EXAMPLE 2

Colin's adjusted trading profits/(losses) for the years to 31 August 2016 and 2017 are:

	Before capital allowances	*Capital allowances available*	*After capital allowances*
	£	£	£
year to 31 August 2016	(8,900)	3,900	(12,800)
year to 31 August 2017	20,200	7,200	13,000

He is single and has no other income. If the trading loss is carried forward for relief against future trading profits, should Colin claim maximum capital allowances in these two years?

Solution

If Colin claims maximum capital allowances in both years, relief in 2017-18 for trading losses brought forward will be £12,800. This will almost entirely absorb the trading profit of £13,000 assessed in that year, leaving only £200 against which to set the personal allowance, most of which will therefore be wasted.

It would be better to claim no capital allowances at all for the two years. The trading loss brought forward from 2016-17 would then be £8,900 and this would be relieved against the trading profit of £20,200 in 2017-18, leaving income of £11,300 against which to set Colin's personal allowance. There would be minimal waste of personal allowances and the capital allowances available to Colin in future years would be increased.

Trade loss relief against total income

As illustrated earlier, carrying trading losses forward for relief against future profits of the same trade does not always provide the most satisfactory form of loss relief. Problems associated with carry-forward relief include:

(a) Loss relief is delayed until sufficient profits arise from the same trade in future years (if, indeed, they ever do).

(b) The trader has no control over the amount of relief given in each year and therefore personal allowances may be wasted.

(c) If tax rates are falling, relief may be given at a lower rate than the rates which were in force when the loss was incurred.

An alternative form of loss relief which overcomes some of these problems is "trade loss relief against total income". This tax relief allows trading losses to be set against the trader's total income for a period of up to two years. It is important to note that:

(a) The trader is under no obligation to make a claim to set trading losses against total income. If no such claim is made, trading losses are automatically carried forward for relief against future trading profits.

(b) Any unrelieved losses remaining after a claim has been made to set trading losses against total income are automatically carried forward.

(c) Trading losses may be set against the trader's total income only if the business is being carried on "on a commercial basis" and "with a view to the realisation of profits". Furthermore, trading losses may not be set against total income if they arise in consequence of tax avoidance arrangements.

(d) In the case of *farmers and market gardeners*, a loss is usually not eligible for relief against total income if losses (calculated without regard to capital allowances) have also been incurred in each of the previous five tax years.

(e) If a claim is made to set trading losses against total income, relief is given by deducting the amount of the claim from the trader's total income when calculating his or her net income (see Chapter 2). Relief is given against non-savings income, savings income and dividends in the way which results in the lowest tax liability.

(f) ITA 2007 uses the term "sideways relief" to refer to the relief of trading losses against total income. This term is also used in connection with early trade losses relief. The amount of sideways relief which may be claimed by a "non-active" trader in relation to a trading loss is limited (see later in this chapter).

Note also that trade loss relief against total income is one of the tax reliefs that is subject to a restriction on the total amount of certain income tax reliefs that may be claimed by an individual in a tax year (see later in this chapter).

Relieving a trading loss against total income

ITA 2007 states that relief against total income is available if a person who carries on a trade makes a trading loss "in the tax year". In most cases, the amount of the trading loss in a tax year is defined as the amount of the loss which was incurred in the basis period for that year. However, in order to prevent double counting, a trading loss incurred in an overlap period is treated as a loss of the earlier tax year only.

A trading loss incurred in a tax year may be set against the total income of:

either (i) the tax year in which the loss is incurred

or (ii) the previous tax year

or (iii) both of these years (if the loss is large enough for this).

A claim to set a trading loss against total income must be made by 31 January in the second tax year following the year in which the loss was made. For example, a claim in relation to a loss incurred in 2017-18 must be made by 31 January 2020. Note that:

(a) The trader can decide whether to make a claim for one of the available years, for both of these years, or for neither year. But partial claims are not allowed. A claim to set a trading loss against total income must be for as much of the loss as can be relieved, even if this sets the loss against income which would otherwise have been taxed at 0% (e.g. savings income within the personal savings allowance) or leaves insufficient income to absorb personal allowances.

However, if a claim is made for both years, the trader can decide whether to claim maximum relief in the year of the loss (relieving the remainder of the loss in the previous year) or vice versa.

(b) A trading loss may be set against the total income of the previous tax year whether or not the loss-making trade was being carried on in that year.

(c) If a trader claims that two trading losses should be set against the total income of the same tax year (one claim for a loss incurred in that tax year and another claim for a loss incurred in the following tax year) then the claim in respect of the current year's trading loss takes priority.

EXAMPLE 3

Ashok has been trading for many years, preparing annual accounts to 31 July. Recent trading profits/(losses), adjusted for tax purposes, are as follows:

	£
year to 31 July 2015	32,400
year to 31 July 2016	12,000
year to 31 July 2017	(9,500)

He has income from property amounting to £8,000 per annum and he claims only the basic personal allowance. Identify the claims which he could make in relation to the trading loss incurred in the year to 31 July 2017. Which of these loss relief claims (if any) might be recommended?

Solution

Ashok's trading income is:

Year	*Basis period*	*Trading income*
		£
2015-16	y/e 31/7/15	32,400
2016-17	y/e 31/7/16	12,000
2017-18	y/e 31/7/17	nil

He could make a claim to relieve the trading loss of £9,500 against his total income for 2017-18 only, 2016-17 only, both of these years, or neither year:

(a) A claim for 2017-18 only would relieve £8,000 of the loss against his other income, leaving no tax liability for the year and losses of £1,500 to carry forward against future trading profits. This would be a waste, since the other income of £8,000 would in any case have been covered by the personal allowance.

(b) A claim for 2016-17 only would relieve the entire loss against that year's total income of £20,000 (£12,000 + £8,000), leaving income of £10,500 (£20,000 – £9,500) from which to deduct the personal allowance. There would be some minor wastage of the personal allowance but the tax liability for 2016-17 would become zero. This seems to be a fairly efficient way of relieving the loss.

(c) A claim for both years is pointless, since:
   (i) a claim giving relief in 2016-17 first would leave no losses to relieve in 2017-18
   (ii) a claim giving relief in 2017-18 first results in a waste of the personal allowance for that year (see above).

(d) A claim for neither year would result in the entire loss being carried forward. This would mean that loss relief would be delayed until such time as sufficient profits of the same trade arose in future years.

On balance, a claim to set the trading loss against total income of 2016-17 might be recommended. This claim combines early relief of the loss with a very small wastage of the personal allowance. The claim would have to be made by 31 January 2020.

However, this claim would relieve the loss at only 20%. If the first available future profits from the same trade are expected to be very high, it might be better to carry the loss forward and possibly obtain relief at a higher rate.

Relieving trading losses against capital gains

If a claim is made to set a trading loss against the total income of a tax year (or if no such claim is made because total income for that year is zero) the trader concerned may claim that any unrelieved part of the loss should be set against his or her capital gains. Such a claim must be made by 31 January in the second tax year following the tax year in which the trading loss was incurred. This relief is considered further in Chapter 17.

Early trade losses relief

Losses incurred in the early years of trading may (just like other trading losses) be carried forward against future trading profits or set against the trader's total income. But, in addition to these forms of tax relief, ITA 2007 allows trading losses incurred in *any of the first four tax years* to be set against the trader's total income of the three previous tax years. This is another form of "sideways relief" (see above). Note that:

(a) If this relief is claimed in relation to a trading loss, the loss is relieved against the trader's total income of the previous three tax years, *beginning with the earliest year*. For example, an early years trading loss incurred in 2017-18 could be set against the trader's total income of 2014-15, 2015-16 and 2016-17, in that order.

(b) A claim for early trade losses relief applies to *all* of the three years concerned. The trader cannot specify the years in which relief is to be given or the amount of relief to be given in each year. The maximum possible relief must be given in each year.

(c) Relief is given by deducting the amount of the trading loss from total income. Relief is given against non-savings income, savings income and dividends in the way which results in the lowest tax liability.

(d) A loss incurred in an overlap period is treated as *a loss of the earlier tax year only*. This rule ensures that a loss is relieved only once.

(e) Early trade losses relief is not available in relation to a trading loss unless the trade is carried on "on a commercial basis" with a reasonable expectation of profits.

(f) A claim for early trade losses relief must be made by 31 January in the second tax year following the loss-making tax year. The claim *cannot* be extended so as to set any unrelieved trading losses against capital gains.

Early trade losses relief is subject to a restriction on the total amount of income tax reliefs that may be claimed by an individual in a tax year (see later in this chapter).

Non-active traders

There is a limit of £25,000 on the amount of sideways relief which may be claimed by a "non-active" trader in relation to a trading loss. A non-active trader is a person who carries on a trade but is not personally engaged in the activities of that trade for at least 10 hours per week. The £25,000 limit applies to the *total* amount of the following reliefs:

(a) trade loss relief against total income
(b) early trade losses relief
(c) relief for trade losses against capital gains.

However, this limit does not affect the giving of sideways relief against profits of the same trade. So if (for example) a trade loss is carried back and set against total income of the previous year, the £25,000 limit does not apply to the amount of the loss (if any) which is set against profits of the same trade made in that previous year.

EXAMPLE 4

Carl begins trading on 1 July 2016 and chooses 30 June as his accounting date. His tax-adjusted trading profits/(losses) for the first two accounting years are as follows:

	£
year to 30 June 2017	(49,200)
year to 30 June 2018	(12,400)

Now that he is self-employed, Carl has no other income. Prior to becoming self-employed his only income was from employment, as follows:

	£
2013-14	23,900
2014-15	24,760
2015-16	25,920
2016-17 (to 30 June 2016)	8,180

Assuming that Carl makes all possible early trade losses claims, calculate his net income (i.e. total income less reliefs) for years 2013-14 to 2016-17 inclusive.

Solution

The losses which are eligible for early trade losses relief are:

Year	*Basis period*	*Workings*	*Trading loss* £	*Early trade losses claim*
2016-17	1/7/16 to 5/4/17	£(49,200) x 9/12	(36,900)	13-14 *to* 15-16
2017-18	y/e 30/6/17	£(49,200) – overlap £(36,900)	(12,300)	14-15 *to* 16-17
2018-19	y/e 30/6/18		(12,400)	15-16 *to* 17-18

Trading income for 2016-17 through to 2018-19 is of course £nil. If all possible early trade loss claims are made, net income for years 2013-14 to 2016-17 is:

	2013-14 £	*2014-15* £	*2015-16* £	*2016-17* £
Employment income	23,900	24,760	25,920	8,180
Trading income	-	-	-	0
Total income	23,900	24,760	25,920	8,180
Less: Early trade losses:				
2016-17 loss	(23,900)	(13,000)		
2017-18 loss		(11,760)	(540)	
2018-19 loss			(12,400)	
Net income	-	-	12,980	8,180

Terminal trade loss relief

In normal circumstances, a trader who incurs a trading loss may choose between carrying the loss forward against future profits of the same trade or relieving the loss against total income. But if a trading loss is incurred in the final year of trading, the first of these alternatives is not available since there can be no future profits against which to set the trading loss. In order to remedy this situation, ITA 2007 provides a tax relief known as "terminal trade loss relief" which permits a trading loss incurred in the last 12 months of trading to be set against the trading profits (if any) of the tax year in which the cessation occurs and the previous three tax years.

Calculating the terminal loss

The "terminal loss" eligible for terminal trade loss relief is the trading loss incurred in the final 12 months of trading, excluding any part of that loss which has already been relieved in other ways (i.e. by deduction from total income). The terminal loss is calculated by adding together the following components:

(a) the actual trading loss incurred from 6 April to the date of the cessation

(b) the actual trading loss incurred from a date 12 months before the date of the cessation to the following 5 April

(c) any available overlap relief (see Chapter 10).

If either (a) or (b) is a profit, this counts as a zero in the calculation of the terminal loss.

EXAMPLE 5

Andrea ceases trading on 31 October 2017. Her adjusted trading profits/(losses) for the closing periods of account are as follows:

	£
year to 31 December 2015	6,600
year to 31 December 2016	2,400
10 months to 31 October 2017	(22,500)

Overlap profits of £3,200 arose when Andrea commenced trading. Calculate the terminal loss, assuming that no claims are made to set trading losses against total income.

Solution

		£
Trading loss 6/4/17 to 31/10/17	£(22,500) x 7/10	(15,750)
Trading loss 1/11/16 to 5/4/17	£2,400 x 2/12 + £(22,500) x 3/10	(6,350)
Overlap relief		(3,200)
Terminal loss		(25,300)

Relieving the terminal loss

As stated above, the terminal loss may be relieved against the trading profits of the year of cessation and the three tax years preceding the year of cessation. Note that:

(a) Relief is given in later years first. For example, a terminal loss arising as a consequence of a business ceasing to trade during 2017-18 would be set against the trading profits of 2017-18, 2016-17, 2015-16 and 2014-15, in that order.

(b) The maximum possible relief must be given in each tax year.

(c) Strictly speaking, relief is given by deduction from the trader's total income. But the amount of relief given in any tax year cannot exceed the trading profits for that year.

EXAMPLE 6

Brendan ceases trading on 30 September 2017. His recent trading profits/(losses) are:

	£
year to 31 January 2015	24,700
year to 31 January 2016	12,500
year to 31 January 2017	2,100
8 months to 30 September 2017	(21,840)

He has no other income. Overlap profits of £4,700 arose when Brendan began trading and no claims are made to set Brendan's trading loss against his total income. Calculate the amount of the terminal loss and show how this may be relieved.

Solution

The calculation of the terminal loss is as follows:

		£
Trading loss 6/4/17 to 30/9/17	£(21,840) x 6/8	(16,380)
Trading loss 1/10/16 to 5/4/17	£2,100 x 4/12 + £(21,840) x 2/8	(4,760)
Overlap relief		(4,700)
Terminal loss		(25,840)

The terminal loss may be relieved as follows:

	2014-15	*2015-16*	*2016-17*	*2017-18*
	£	£	£	£
Trading income	24,700	12,500	2,100	nil
Less: Terminal trade loss relief:				
(i) in 2016-17			(2,100)	
(ii) in 2015-16		(12,500)		
(iii) in 2014-15	(11,240)			
Net income	13,460	-	-	-

Post-cessation trade relief

Post-cessation expenses which were not provided for in the final accounts of a business are relieved first against any post-cessation receipts (taxed as trading income). Post-cessation expenses that cannot be relieved in this way and that fall into certain categories may be relieved against the taxpayer's total income for the tax year in which the expenses are incurred. The expenses concerned are:

(a) the costs of remedying defective work done whilst the business was operating

(b) bad debts which were not provided for in the accounts of the business, together with associated debt collection costs.

If the taxpayer's total income for a tax year is insufficient to absorb all of the post-cessation expenses eligible for relief in that year, the excess expenses may be set against the taxpayer's capital gains for the year. Expenses incurred more than seven years after cessation are not eligible for post-cessation trade relief.

Transfer of a business to a company

If the owner of a business transfers that business to a limited company, there is a change in the legal ownership of the business and the vendor is deemed to have ceased trading. In consequence, any trading losses sustained by the vendor before the date of the transfer cannot be carried forward and set against the company's trading profits.

Such trading losses might be relieved by deduction from the taxpayer's total income for the year of the loss and/or the previous year. Terminal loss relief might also be available. But a further tax relief is offered by ITA 2007, which provides that:

(a) if a business is transferred to a limited company wholly or mainly in exchange for shares in that company, and

(b) the vendor of the business continues to hold those shares, and

(c) the company continues to carry on the transferred business

then the vendor may set unrelieved trading losses against the first available income that he or she receives from the company (e.g. dividends or director's fees).

Losses on shares in unlisted trading companies

A person who subscribes for newly-issued shares in certain unlisted trading companies and then incurs a capital loss on the disposal of those shares may claim that this capital loss should be set against his or her total income as if it were a trading loss. This relief is generally available only if the company concerned is of a type which would qualify for the purposes of the Enterprise Investment Scheme (see Chapter 6).

Limit on income tax reliefs

Finance Act 2013 introduced a limit on the amount of tax relief that an individual may deduct from total income. This limit applies to the *aggregate* amount of certain specified reliefs. The main reliefs to which the limit applies are:

(a) Trade loss relief against total income
(b) Early trade losses relief
(c) Post-cessation trade relief
(d) Relief for losses on shares in unlisted trading companies
(e) Relief for eligible interest (see Chapter 4).

The total amount of the above reliefs which may be deducted from total income in a tax year is equal to the *greater* of £50,000 and 25% of the individual's "adjusted total income" for the year concerned. Note the following points:

(a) Adjusted total income is defined as the individual's total income for the year, less the gross amount of any pension contributions that are not relieved through a net pay arrangement (see Chapter 14). Any charitable donations made under a payroll giving scheme are added back when computing adjusted total income.

(b) An individual who claims more than one of the above reliefs may decide the order in which they are given. For instance, an individual with both trade losses and eligible interest might prioritise the interest, since relief for this will be lost if it cannot be given in the year concerned, whereas unrelieved trade losses are carried forward.

(c) The limit does not apply to trade losses caused by overlap relief. Nor does it restrict the extent to which trade losses can be deducted from profits of the same trade.

The limit on income tax reliefs does not affect the amount of relief for trading losses that may be set against an individual's capital gains.

Summary

- A trading loss may be carried forward and relieved against future profits of the same trade. This will happen if no other form of tax relief is claimed in relation to the loss.

- A trading loss may be relieved against total income for the year of the loss and/or the previous year. Any part of a trading loss which remains unrelieved after a claim has been made to set that loss against total income may be set against capital gains.

- A trading loss incurred in any of the first four tax years may be set against the trader's total income of the three previous tax years.

- A trading loss incurred during the final 12 months of trading may be set against the trading profits of the tax year in which trade ceases and the previous three tax years.

- If a business is transferred to a company, the unrelieved trading losses of the vendor may (subject to certain conditions) be set against the first available income which the vendor receives from the company.
- Capital losses incurred on the disposal of shares in certain unlisted trading companies may be treated as trading losses.
- The total amount of certain specified income tax reliefs (mainly loss reliefs) that may be claimed in a tax year is capped at the greater of £50,000 and 25% of the taxpayer's adjusted total income for the year.

Exercises

12.1 Sally, who has been trading for many years, incurs an adjusted trading loss of £40,000 in the year to 31 December 2017.

(a) What is her trading income for 2017-18?

(b) If she makes no claim in relation to her trading loss, how will it be relieved?

(c) How will the loss be relieved if she does make a claim?

12.2 Jane is self-employed. Her recent adjusted trading profits/(losses) are:

	£
year to 31 May 2014	(18,860)
year to 31 May 2015	4,710
year to 31 May 2016	6,210
year to 31 May 2017	14,810

Jane has other income of £10,000 per annum. Assuming that the trading loss is carried forward and set against future trading profits, calculate her net income (i.e. total income less reliefs) for tax years 2014-15 through to 2017-18.

12.3 Marcus begins trading on 1 January 2016 and has the following results:

	Adjusted trading profits/(losses) before capital allowances	*Capital allowances claimed*
	£	£
year to 31 December 2016	17,720	6,460
year to 31 December 2017	(7,480)	2,320

He has no other income.

(a) Compute his trading income (before loss relief) for 2015-16 to 2017-18.

(b) Identify the claims that could be made in relation to the trading loss, assuming that early trade losses relief is <u>not</u> claimed. Which (if any) of these claims should be recommended?

12.4 Nathan begins trading on 1 October 2015, making up accounts to 31 December each year. His first two sets of accounts show the following adjusted trading losses:

	£
15 months to 31 December 2016	(56,850)
year to 31 December 2017	(32,660)

He has had no other income since becoming self-employed. Before this, his only income consisted of employment income, as follows:

	£
2012-13	25,100
2013-14	25,250
2014-15	26,400
2015-16 (to 30 September 2015)	13,450

Assuming that all possible early trade losses relief claims are made, calculate Nathan's net income (i.e. total income less reliefs) for years 2012-13 to 2015-16.

***12.5** Olive ceases trading on 31 May 2017. Her recent adjusted trading profits/(losses) are:

	£
year to 30 June 2013	37,450
year to 30 June 2014	39,190
year to 30 June 2015	16,120
year to 30 June 2016	(6,840)
11 months to 31 May 2017	(36,300)

Overlap relief of £7,140 is available. Calculate the terminal loss and show how this would be relieved, assuming that Olive has savings income of £10,000 per annum and that no claims are made to set trading losses against total income.

***12.6** Craig began trading on 1 August 2015 and has the following results:

	Adjusted trading profits/(losses) before capital allowances	*Capital allowances claimed*
	£	£
year to 31 July 2016	5,460	1,140
year to 31 July 2017	(27,400)	1,920

Before commencing to trade, Craig had only investment income. He sold all of his investments in October 2016 (realising a large capital gain) so as to raise extra working capital for his own business. His income from investments in recent years has been:

	£
2013-14	9,150
2014-15	9,940
2015-16	7,190
2016-17 (to October 2016)	2,510

(a) Compute Craig's trading income for 2015-16 to 2017-18.

(b) Explain the trading loss reliefs available to Craig. Which would you recommend?

Chapter 13

Income from self-employment: Partnerships

Introduction

The purpose of this chapter is to explain the taxation treatment of individuals who are members of a partnership. Most of the information given in the previous four chapters with regard to the computation of trading profits, basis periods, capital allowances and trading loss reliefs is applicable to partners as well as to sole traders. The main new factor which arises when dealing with partnerships is the problem of calculating each partner's share of the partnership profit or loss for taxation purposes and much of this chapter is devoted to that problem.

Note that a Limited Liability Partnership (LLP) which is regulated by the Limited Liability Partnership Act 2000 and which carries on a trade or profession is generally dealt with for tax purposes as a partnership rather than as a company.

Principles of partnership taxation

Under the partnership tax rules, a partnership is not regarded as a separate entity for taxation purposes and the partnership itself is not charged to tax. Instead, the profits of the partnership are allocated between the partners and then each partner is taxed as an individual. In detail, the procedure for each tax year is as follows:

(a) The partnership submits a tax return to HMRC. This return provides information on the profit or loss for the period of account ending in the tax year and gives details of the profit-sharing agreement in force during that period. The return is also used to:

 (i) claim capital allowances for the period of account, both on partnership assets and on individual partners' assets

 (ii) claim relief for any business expenses incurred by partners personally.

(b) The adjusted trading profit or loss of the partnership is calculated in the usual manner. Any drawings or other appropriations of profit made by the partners are disallowed. Capital allowances on partnership assets are treated as a trading expense.

(c) The adjusted trading profit or loss is then allocated between the partners according to the profit-sharing agreement in force during the period of account. If the agreement changes during the period of account, it is necessary to time-apportion the profit or loss, applying the old agreement to the pre-change profit or loss and the new agreement to the post-change profit or loss.

(d) Any capital allowances claimed on an individual partner's assets and any expenses incurred personally by a partner are deducted from the relevant partner's share of the adjusted trading profit or added to that partner's share of the adjusted trading loss.

(e) Partners are then assessed to tax individually, as if each partner's share of the partnership's trading profit or loss had arisen from a trade carried on by that partner alone. In effect, each partner is treated as a sole trader who:

   (i) begins trading when joining the partnership

   (ii) has the same periods of account as the partnership (except that a partner who joins or leaves the partnership part-way through a period of account will have an individual period of account which begins or ends part-way through a partnership period of account)

   (iii) ceases trading when leaving the partnership.

(f) Each partner is solely responsible for the tax due on his or her share of the partnership profit. Partners must include their share of the partnership profit or loss in their own tax returns and in their self-assessment calculations.

EXAMPLE 1

Tom, Dick and Harry begin trading as a partnership on 1 January 2016, sharing profits in the ratio 3:2:1. With effect from 1 January 2017, they agree that Harry should receive a salary of £20,000 per annum, that partners should be entitled to 4% per annum interest on capital and that remaining profits should be shared in the ratio 5:3:2. The adjusted trading profits of the partnership are:

	£
y/e 31 December 2016	90,000
y/e 31 December 2017	110,000

Fixed capitals are Tom £50,000, Dick £60,000, Harry £80,000. Compute each partner's trading income for 2015-16, 2016-17 and 2017-18.

Solution

The allocation of trading profit for each period of account is:

	Tom	*Dick*	*Harry*	*Total*
	£	£	£	£
y/e 31/12/16				
Profit (shared 3:2:1)	45,000	30,000	15,000	90,000
y/e 31/12/17				
Salary	-	-	20,000	20,000
Interest on capital	2,000	2,400	3,200	7,600
Remainder of profit (shared 5:3:2)	41,200	24,720	16,480	82,400
	43,200	27,120	39,680	110,000

Each partner is treated as a sole trader, commencing trade on 1 January 2016, making up accounts to 31 December and with trading profits for the first two accounting years as shown above. The trading income of each partner is:

Tom

Year	*Basis period*	*Workings*	*Trading income*
			£
2015-16	1/1/16 to 5/4/16	£45,000 x 3/12	11,250
2016-17	y/e 31/12/16		45,000
2017-18	y/e 31/12/17		43,200

Dick

Year	*Basis period*	*Workings*	*Trading income*
			£
2015-16	1/1/16 to 5/4/16	£30,000 x 3/12	7,500
2016-17	y/e 31/12/16		30,000
2017-18	y/e 31/12/17		27,120

Harry

Year	*Basis period*	*Workings*	*Trading income*
			£
2015-16	1/1/16 to 5/4/16	£15,000 x 3/12	3,750
2016-17	y/e 31/12/16		15,000
2017-18	y/e 31/12/17		39,680

Note:

In each case, the overlap period is from 1 January 2016 to 5 April 2016. Overlap profits are Tom £11,250, Dick £7,500 and Harry £3,750. These overlap profits will be relieved when the relevant partner leaves the partnership (or on a change of accounting date).

Notional profits and losses

If the effect of accounting for partners' salaries or interest on capital is to allocate a trading loss to an individual partner, even though the partnership as a whole has made a trading profit, that partner's share of the trading profit is set to £nil and his or her "notional loss" is allocated between the remaining partners in proportion to their original profit allocations.

A similar procedure is followed if a partner is allocated a "notional profit" in a year in which the partnership as a whole has sustained a trading loss.

EXAMPLE 2

(a) Lock, Stock and Barrel are in partnership, making up accounts to 30 June each year. Their profit-sharing agreement specifies that Lock and Barrel should receive annual salaries of £20,000 and £24,000 respectively and that remaining profits or losses should be divided equally. The partnership has an adjusted trading profit of £26,000 in the year to 30 June 2017. Show how this will be allocated between the partners.

(b) Rod, Pole and Perch are in partnership, also making up accounts to 30 June each year. Their profit-sharing agreement specifies that Perch should receive an annual salary of £25,000 and that remaining profits or losses should be shared in the ratio 3:2:1. The partnership has an adjusted trading loss of £5,000 in the year to 30 June 2017. Show how this will be allocated between the partners.

Solution

(a)

	Lock	*Stock*	*Barrel*	*Total*
	£	£	£	£
Salaries	20,000	-	24,000	44,000
Remainder (£26,000 – £44,000)	(6,000)	(6,000)	(6,000)	(18,000)
	14,000	(6,000)	18,000	26,000
Stock's notional loss divided in the ratio 14,000:18,000	(2,625)	6,000	(3,375)	-
Allocation of trading profit	11,375	-	14,625	26,000

(b)

	Rod	*Pole*	*Perch*	*Total*
	£	£	£	£
Salaries	-	-	25,000	25,000
Remainder (£5,000 + £25,000)	(15,000)	(10,000)	(5,000)	(30,000)
	(15,000)	(10,000)	20,000	(5,000)
Perch's notional profit divided 15,000:10,000	12,000	8,000	(20,000)	-
Allocation of trading loss	(3,000)	(2,000)	-	(5,000)

Change in partnership composition

A change in partnership composition occurs if a new partner joins a partnership (or joins a sole trader to form a partnership) or if an existing partner dies or leaves the partnership. A change in composition has no tax effect on those persons who:

(a) were carrying on the trade beforehand (either alone or in partnership), and
(b) continue to carry on the trade after the change (either alone or in partnership).

Such persons are taxed on the current year basis as if the change had not taken place. But new partners have commenced trading and are subject to the commencement rules, whilst leaving partners have ceased trading and are subject to the cessation rules.

EXAMPLE 3

Red and White begin trading as a partnership on 1 October 2014, sharing profits equally. On 1 January 2016, they agree to admit Blue as a partner and to share profits in the ratio 3:2:1. The adjusted trading profits of the partnership are:

	£
y/e 30 September 2015	105,000
y/e 30 September 2016	120,000
y/e 30 September 2017	135,000

Compute each partner's trading income for the years 2014-15 through to 2017-18.

Solution

The allocation of trading profit for each period of account is:

	Red	*White*	*Blue*	*Total*
	£	£	£	£
y/e 30/9/15 (shared equally)	52,500	52,500	-	105,000
y/e 30/9/16				
1/10/15 - 31/12/15				
£120,000 x 3/12 (shared equally)	15,000	15,000	-	30,000
1/1/16 - 30/9/16				
£120,000 x 9/12 (shared 3:2:1)	45,000	30,000	15,000	90,000
	60,000	45,000	15,000	120,000
y/e 30/9/17 (shared 3:2:1)	67,500	45,000	22,500	135,000

For tax purposes, each partner is now treated as a sole trader and is assessed on his or her share of the partnership trading profit. The position of each partner is as follows:

(a) Red began trading on 1 October 2014, preparing accounts to 30 September. Each period of account is of 12 months' duration. Profits are £52,500 for the year to 30 September 2015, £60,000 for the year to 30 September 2016 and £67,500 for the year to 30 September 2017.

(b) White began trading on 1 October 2014, preparing accounts to 30 September. Each period of account is of 12 months' duration. Profits are £52,500 for the year to 30 September 2015, £45,000 for the year to 30 September 2016 and £45,000 for the year to 30 September 2017.

(c) Blue began trading on 1 January 2016, preparing accounts to 30 September. The first accounts cover the nine-month period from 1 January 2016 to 30 September 2016 with profits of £15,000. Profits are £22,500 for the year to 30 September 2017.

Each partner's trading income is as follows:

Red

Year	*Basis period*	*Workings*	*Trading income*
			£
2014-15	1/10/14 to 5/4/15	£52,500 x 6/12	26,250
2015-16	y/e 30/9/15		52,500
2016-17	y/e 30/9/16		60,000
2017-18	y/e 30/9/17		67,500

White

Year	*Basis period*	*Workings*	*Trading income*
			£
2014-15	1/10/14 to 5/4/15	£52,500 x 6/12	26,250
2015-16	y/e 30/9/15		52,500
2016-17	y/e 30/9/16		45,000
2017-18	y/e 30/9/17		45,000

Blue

Year	*Basis period*	*Workings*	*Trading income*
			£
2015-16	1/1/16 to 5/4/16	£15,000 x 3/9	5,000
2016-17	1/1/16 to 31/12/16	£15,000 + 3/12 x £22,500	20,625
2017-18	y/e 30/9/17		22,500

Note:

In the case of Red and White, the overlap period is from 1 October 2014 to 5 April 2015 and each partner has overlap profits of £26,250. In the case of Blue, there is an overlap period from 1 January 2016 to 5 April 2016 and another overlap period from 1 October 2016 to 31 December 2016. Overlap profits are £5,000 + (£22,500 x 3/12) = £10,625.

Non-trading income

A partnership which has trading income may also have non-trading income. For partnership tax purposes, non-trading income falls into two categories:

(a) **Taxed income**

For this purpose, "taxed income" is defined as income from which tax has already been deducted at source (e.g. loan interest from a company) and dividends received. The amount of any taxed income arising in a period of account is divided between the partners in profit-sharing ratio and then each partner's share is apportioned between tax years and assessed to tax on the actual basis.

It is acceptable to allocate taxed income between tax years on the receipts basis if this would be more appropriate than time-apportionment.

(b) **Untaxed income**

For this purpose, "untaxed income" is defined as non-trading income which is not taxed income (e.g. income from property and bank or building society interest). The amount of any untaxed income arising in a period of account is allocated between the partners in profit-sharing ratio and is then assessed to tax using *the same basis periods as those used for the trading income*. The basis periods that would normally be applied if the income were received by an individual rather than a partnership are totally ignored. If this treatment results in non-trading income being taxed twice when a partner starts trading, overlap relief is available.

If a partnership does not carry on a trade or profession, the treatment described at (a) above applies to *all* of the partnership's non-trading income.

EXAMPLE 4

Hook, Line and Sinker begin trading as a partnership on 1 July 2015, sharing profits equally. The chosen accounting date is 30 June and the first accounts are made up for the year to 30 June 2016. In addition to its trading income, the partnership has non-trading income as follows:

	y/e 30/6/16	*y/e 30/6/17*
	£	£
Income from property	7,500	9,000
Net loan interest received from a company	2,400	3,600

(a) Compute each partner's income from property for tax years 2015-16, 2016-17 and 2017-18.

(b) Compute the gross amount of loan interest on which each partner is taxed in tax years 2015-16 and 2016-17.

Solution

(a) Each partner is allocated property income of £2,500 in the year to 30 June 2016 and £3,000 in the year to 30 June 2017. Property income per partner for each tax year is as follows:

Year	*Basis period*	*Workings*	*Property income*
			£
2015-16	1/7/15 to 5/4/16	£2,500 x 9/12	1,875
2016-17	y/e 30/6/16		2,500
2017-18	y/e 30/6/17		3,000

Each partner is entitled to overlap relief of £1,875.

(b) Each partner is allocated net loan interest of £800 in the year to 30 June 2016 and £1,200 in the year to 30 June 2017. When grossed-up at 100/80, these figures become £1,000 and £1,500 respectively. Therefore the gross interest on which each partner is taxed in each tax year (assuming time-apportionment) is as follows:

Year	*Workings*	*Savings income*
		£
2015-16	£1,000 x 9/12	750
2016-17	(£1,000 x 3/12) + (£1,500 x 9/12)	1,375

The remaining 3/12ths of the interest received during the year to 30 June 2017 will be taxed in 2017-18, along with the first 9/12ths of any interest received net in the year to 30 June 2018.

Trading losses

As explained above, a trading loss is allocated between the partners in the same way as a trading profit. In general, each partner is then entitled to precisely the same loss reliefs as a sole trader (see Chapter 12) with regard to his or her share of the loss.

EXAMPLE 5

Game, Set and Match begin trading in partnership on 1 August 2015, preparing accounts to 31 January each year and sharing profits equally. With effect from 1 March 2016, they agree to share profits in the ratio 1:2:2. The adjusted trading profits/(losses) of the partnership are as follows:

	£
period to 31 January 2016	43,050
y/e 31 January 2017	21,600
y/e 31 January 2018	(7,420)

Compute each partner's trading income for tax years 2015-16, 2016-17 and 2017-18 and explain how the trading loss incurred in the year to 31 January 2018 will be treated.

Solution

The allocation of trading profit or loss for each period of account is:

	Game	*Set*	*Match*	*Total*
	£	£	£	£
period to 31/1/16 (shared equally)	14,350	14,350	14,350	43,050
y/e 31/1/17				
1/2/16 - 29/2/16				
£21,600 x 1/12 (shared equally)	600	600	600	1,800
1/3/16 - 31/1/17				
£21,600 x 11/12 (shared 1:2:2)	3,960	7,920	7,920	19,800
	4,560	8,520	8,520	21,600
y/e 31/1/18 (shared 1:2:2)	(1,484)	(2,968)	(2,968)	(7,420)

Each partner's trading income is as follows:

Game

Year	*Basis period*	*Workings*	*Trading income*
			£
2015-16	1/8/15 to 5/4/16	£14,350 + 2/12 x £4,560	15,110
2016-17	y/e 31/1/17		4,560
2017-18	y/e 31/1/18		nil

Set

Year	*Basis period*	*Workings*	*Trading income*
			£
2015-16	1/8/15 to 5/4/16	£14,350 + 2/12 x £8,520	15,770
2016-17	y/e 31/1/17		8,520
2017-18	y/e 31/1/18		nil

Match

Year	*Basis period*	*Workings*	*Trading income*
			£
2015-16	1/8/15 to 5/4/16	£14,350 + 2/12 x £8,520	15,770
2016-17	y/e 31/1/17		8,520
2017-18	y/e 31/1/18		nil

Notes:

(i) The basis period for 2015-16 for each partner includes two months out of the year to 31 January 2017. The profit for these two months is calculated by taking 2/12ths of the partner's profit for that year. In the case of Game (for example) it would be wrong to take £600 + (1/11 x £3,960) as the profit of the period from 1/2/16 to 5/4/16.

(ii) Each partner has overlap profits, calculated in the usual way.

(iii) Each partner may choose individually how to relieve his/her share of the trading loss incurred in the basis period for 2017-18. Possibilities include carry-forward against future trading profits, loss relief against total income or an early trade losses claim.

Treatment of certain interest as a loss

As explained in Chapter 4, certain types of loan interest are deductible from a partner's total income when computing his or her net income. The eligible loans are:

(a) a loan to purchase plant or machinery for use in the business of a partnership

(b) a loan to purchase an interest in a partnership.

If a partner's total income is insufficient to deduct such loan interest in full, the excess interest may be treated as a trading loss for the purposes of carry-forward trade loss relief and terminal trade loss relief (see Chapter 12).

Restrictions on trade loss relief for certain partners

Income Tax Act 2007 contains anti-avoidance rules which restrict the amount of tax relief that may be given for trading losses incurred by partners. These rules restrict the amount of sideways relief and capital gains relief that may be claimed by partners. As explained in Chapter 12, the term "sideways relief" refers to the relief of trade losses against total income, including early trade losses relief. The main restrictions are as follows:

(a) A limited partner or a member of an LLP is denied sideways relief or capital gains relief for a trading loss incurred in a tax year to the extent that the loss exceeds the partner's "contribution to the firm" as measured at the end of the basis period for that year. For this purpose, a partner's "contribution" is broadly equal to the amount of capital which the partner has contributed to the partnership, plus any share of profits that have not been withdrawn†.

(b) Similarly, a "non-active" partner (one who is not personally engaged in the activities of the trade for at least ten hours per week) is denied sideways relief or capital gains relief for a trading loss incurred in an "early tax year", to the extent that it exceeds his or her contribution to the firm. For this purpose, an early tax year is defined as the tax year in which the partner began trading or one of the next three tax years†.

(c) Furthermore, the total amount of sideways relief and capital gains relief given in relation to trading losses incurred by a limited partner or non-active partner is capped at £25,000 per tax year.

(d) Finally, trading losses incurred by any partner may not be set against total income or capital gains if the losses arise in consequence of tax avoidance arrangements.

† *When comparing a trading loss with a partner's contribution, the contribution is first reduced by any previous trading losses for which sideways relief or capital gains relief has been claimed.*

Note that the restrictions on sideways relief do *not* restrict the extent to which a trading loss may be relieved against the partner's profits from the loss-making trade. For example, if a trading loss is relieved against total income of the previous tax year, there is no restriction on the amount of the loss which may be set against the partner's trading profit from the partnership in that year. The aim of the anti-avoidance rules is to restrict the extent to which losses may be relieved against other forms of income.

Summary

- Each partner is taxed individually on his or her share of a partnership profit and each partner is solely responsible for his or her own tax liability.
- The adjusted trading profit of a partnership is allocated between the partners in accordance with the profit-sharing agreement for the period of account in which the profit arises. Notional profits and losses allocated to a partner are redistributed among the remaining partners.
- In effect, each partner is treated as a sole trader who begins trading when joining the partnership, has the same accounting dates as the partnership and ceases trading when leaving the partnership.
- The tax treatment of the non-trading income of a partnership depends upon whether the income ranks as taxed income or untaxed income and whether or not the partnership also has trading income.
- The trading losses of a partnership are allocated between the partners. Each partner may then choose individually how to relieve his or her share of the loss.

Exercises

13.1 Nickleby, Copperfield and Drood have traded as equal partners for many years, making up accounts to 31 December each year. As from 1 April 2017 they agree to share profits in the ratio 1:2:2. The adjusted trading profit for the year to 31 December 2017 is £183,000. Show how this profit is allocated between the partners.

13.2 Pickwick, Snodgrass and Tupman are in partnership, making up accounts to 31 March annually. Each partner receives 6% interest on fixed capital. Pickwick and Tupman are entitled to annual salaries of £40,000 and £30,000 respectively. Remaining profits or losses are divided equally. Fixed capitals are Pickwick £60,000, Snodgrass £100,000 and Tupman £50,000. The adjusted trading profit for the year to 31 March 2018 is £62,500. Show how this profit is allocated between the partners.

13.3 Dodson and Fogg began trading in equal partnership on 1 July 2014. On 1 July 2015, they admitted Jackson as a partner and agreed to share profits in the ratio 5:4:1. The adjusted trading profits of the partnership are:

	£
year to 30 June 2015	68,000
year to 30 June 2016	88,000
year to 30 June 2017	116,000

Compute each partner's trading income for 2014-15 through to 2017-18.

13.4 Wardle, Jingle and Trotter began trading on 1 October 2015, preparing accounts to 30 September each year and sharing profits in the ratio 7:2:1. Results for the first two years of trading are as follows:

	y/e 30/9/16	*y/e 30/9/17*
	£	£
Trading profit	117,460	136,540
Bank interest received	200	220
Loan interest received net (net amount)	992	1,088

(a) Compute each partner's trading income for 2015-16, 2016-17 and 2017-18.

(b) Compute each partner's bank interest for 2015-16, 2016-17 and 2017-18.

(c) Compute the gross amount of loan interest on which each partner is charged to tax in 2016-17.

***13.5** Cluppins and Raddle form a partnership on 1 November 2013, preparing accounts to 31 May each year. Bardell is admitted as a partner on 1 January 2015. Cluppins leaves the partnership on 29 February 2016 and Winkle is admitted as a partner on 1 March 2016.

Profits and losses are shared as follows:

Cluppins and Raddle	1:2
Cluppins, Raddle and Bardell	7:8:5
Raddle, Bardell and Winkle	4:3:1

Adjusted trading profits are:

	£
1 November 2013 to 31 May 2014	60,000
year to 31 May 2015	120,000
year to 31 May 2016	30,000
year to 31 May 2017	80,000

Calculate each partner's trading income for 2013-14 through to 2017-18, identifying any overlap periods and profits.

Chapter 14

Pension contributions

Introduction

The most tax-efficient way of providing for a pension is to make contributions into a registered pension scheme. This might be an occupational pension scheme sponsored by an employer, a public service pension scheme established by the Government or a personal pension scheme taken out with a bank or insurance company. The main purpose of this chapter is to explain the tax reliefs which are available in relation to contributions made into registered pension schemes.

Registered pension schemes

The tax regime which now applies to pension schemes has been in effect since 6 April 2006 and was established by Finance Act 2004. This Act defines a pension scheme as "*a scheme ... to provide benefits to or in respect of persons -*

(a) on retirement,

(b) on death,

(c) on having reached a particular age,

(d) on the onset of serious ill-health or incapacity, or

(e) in similar circumstances."

A pension scheme may be either a "defined benefits" scheme or a "money purchase" scheme. In a defined benefits scheme, the benefits payable to a member are calculated by reference to earnings or length of service or some other such factor. An example of a defined benefits scheme is an occupational pension scheme in which an employee's pension rights are based upon his or her final salary. In a money purchase scheme, the benefits payable to a member are calculated by reference to the size of the pension fund built up during the member's working life.

Registration

A pension scheme which is registered with HMRC is known as a "registered pension scheme" and qualifies for various tax reliefs and exemptions. An application to register a pension scheme may be made if the scheme satisfies certain conditions and is either:

(a) an occupational pension scheme, or
(b) a public service pension scheme, or
(c) a pension scheme established by an insurance company, bank or similar institution.

An occupational pension scheme is one established by an employer or employers so as to provide benefits to employees. A public service pension scheme is (broadly) one established by the Government. The tax advantages of registration include:

(a) The scheme's investment income is exempt from income tax. Any capital gains made on the disposal of scheme investments are exempt from capital gains tax.
(b) Contributions made by scheme members attract tax relief (see below).
(c) Contributions made by employers attract tax relief (see below).
(d) Although pensions are chargeable to income tax, lump sums paid to scheme members on the commencement of a pension are generally exempt from income tax, subject to the operation of the "lifetime allowance" (see below).

Except on ill-health grounds, a registered pension scheme must not allow members to take any pension benefits until they reach normal minimum pension age. This rose from 50 to 55 as from 6 April 2010. However, there is no requirement that members should actually retire before benefits are taken. Therefore, a member of an occupational pension scheme could draw a pension from his or her employer's scheme whilst continuing to work for that employer. Pension benefits must normally begin by the age of 75.

Unregistered pension schemes

A registered pension scheme must comply with many regulations with regard to its investments, the payments it makes to its members and a number of other matters. A pension scheme which does not wish to register is under no compulsion to do so and therefore these regulations can be avoided. However, unregistered schemes do not qualify for any of the tax reliefs and exemptions enjoyed by registered schemes.

National Employment Savings Trust (NEST)

The National Employment Savings Trust (NEST) is a state-sponsored pension scheme which is intended to act as a default scheme for those employees whose employers do not offer an occupational scheme. For taxation purposes, NEST is treated as an occupational pension scheme and can therefore register with HMRC.

Tax relief for contributions by scheme members

An individual may belong to as many pension schemes as he or she wishes and may make unlimited pension contributions. However, there are limits on the amount of contributions which can attract tax relief.

To be eligible for tax relief, an individual's contributions must be "relievable pension contributions" made into a registered pension scheme and the individual must be a "relevant UK individual" who is an "active member" of that scheme. Note that:

(a) Relievable pension contributions are contributions paid by the scheme member or by a third party on his or her behalf, excluding contributions made after the age of 75 and excluding employer contributions.

(b) An individual is a relevant UK individual for a tax year if *at least one* of a number of conditions is satisfied. The main conditions are that:

  (i) the individual has UK earnings that are chargeable to income tax for the year (i.e. income from employment or self-employment)

  (ii) the individual is resident in the UK at some time during the year.

  Income derived from the commercial letting of furnished holiday accommodation ranks as self-employment income for this purpose (see Chapter 5).

(c) An active member of a registered pension scheme is an individual who is accruing benefits under that scheme.

Tax relief can be claimed for a contribution only in the tax year in which payment is made. There are no provisions for carrying contributions back to previous tax years or forward to subsequent tax years.

Limit on tax relief

The maximum amount of pension contributions on which an individual can claim tax relief in any tax year is the *greater* of:

(a) 100% of the amount of the individual's UK earnings for the year that are chargeable to income tax

(b) the "basic amount", which is currently set at £3,600 (gross).

If an individual's earnings for a tax year are less than the basic amount, tax relief on the amount of any contributions beyond the level of earnings and up to the basic amount is available only if these contributions are made to a pension scheme which operates tax relief at source (see below).

EXAMPLE 1

Gordon is self-employed and a member of a registered pension scheme. His trading income for tax year 2016-17 is £27,800 but this falls to only £2,500 in 2017-18.

(a) How much may Gordon contribute to his pension scheme in each year ?

(b) How much of these contributions would attract tax relief?

Solution

(a) Gordon may make unlimited contributions to his pension scheme in both years.

(b) He may claim tax relief on contributions of up to £27,800 in 2016-17 and £3,600 in 2017-18 (assuming that the pension scheme operates tax relief at source).

Refund of excess contributions

If an individual makes pension contributions in a tax year which exceed the maximum amount on which tax relief can be claimed, then the excess contributions may be refunded (if the individual so wishes). Such a refund of pension contributions is known as a "refund of excess contributions lump sum".

A refund of excess contributions lump sum is not subject to income tax. This reflects the fact that the contributions which are being refunded by the pension scheme did not attract tax relief in the first place.

Methods of giving tax relief

There are three methods by means of which tax relief is given on member's pension contributions. The method adopted in any particular case will depend upon the type of pension scheme concerned and cannot be chosen by the member. The three methods of giving tax relief are as follows:

(a) **Relief at source**. If relief at source applies, the member's pension contributions are paid net of basic rate tax (20%) and the pension scheme administrator recovers the tax deducted at source from HMRC. Also, the member's basic rate limit and higher rate limit are both increased by the gross amount of the contributions, so ensuring that relief at the higher rate or additional rate is automatically given to higher rate and additional rate taxpayers. This is similar to the way in which higher and additional rate relief is given on Gift Aid donations (see Chapter 4). Another similarity with Gift Aid donations is that the member's "adjusted net income" (see Chapter 3) is reduced by the gross amount of the contributions.

If a scheme member makes pension contributions in excess of the maximum amount on which tax relief can be claimed (see above) and relief at source applies, the excess net contributions are treated as if they were actually gross contributions on which no tax relief is available.

(b) **Net pay arrangements**. The net pay arrangement applies if an employer deducts an employee's contributions to an occupational pension scheme from the employee's pay before operating the PAYE system. This automatically gives tax relief at the employee's marginal rate of income tax.

(c) **Relief on making a claim**. If it is not possible to use relief at source or the net pay arrangement, tax relief on a member's pension contributions is given by deducting those contributions from total income when computing the member's income tax liability for the year. This might apply (for example) in the case of contributions to a retirement annuity contract. Retirement annuity contracts were at one time an important means of providing for a pension but it has not been possible to take out a new retirement annuity contract since 30 June 1988. However, contributions may still be made in relation to contracts which were in existence at that date and retirement annuity contracts which have now become registered pension schemes are not obliged to operate relief at source.

EXAMPLE 2

(a) Wesley has no income at all for tax purposes in 2017-18. He belongs to a registered pension scheme which operates relief at source and he makes pension contributions during 2017-18 which are all eligible for tax relief. Compute the maximum amount of his net contributions in the year.

(b) Alana is self-employed. She has trading income of £62,000 in 2017-18 and no other income. She belongs to a registered pension scheme which operates relief at source and she makes contributions of £500 per month (gross) to this scheme in 2017-18. Explain how tax relief will be given in relation to these contributions.

(c) Bruce is self-employed and a member of a registered pension scheme to which he pays net contributions of £320 per month. His trading income for 2017-18 is £2,750 and he has no other earnings. Explain the tax treatment of his pension contributions for the year.

(d) Charlotte is employed at an annual salary of £24,000. She pays 7% of her salary each month into her employer's occupational pension scheme (which is a registered scheme). Explain how tax relief will be given in relation to her pension contributions.

Solution

(a) Gross contributions of up to £3,600 are eligible for tax relief in the year. Deducting basic rate (20%) tax relief at source gives maximum net contributions in the year of £2,880. Wesley is entitled to basic rate tax relief on these contributions even though he is a non-taxpayer.

(b) Alana pays net contributions of £400 per month (80% of £500). Her basic rate band will be extended by £6,000 (12 x £500) so she will pay higher rate tax on £6,000 less of her income than would otherwise have been the case.

(c) Bruce is entitled to tax relief in 2017-18 on contributions of up to £3,600 (the greater of £2,750 and £3,600). Maximum net contributions are £2,880 (80% of £3,600). He has made payments totalling £3,840 (12 x £320) so excess contributions are £960. He will be treated as though he had made gross contributions of £4,560 (£3,600 + £960) with basic rate tax of £720 (20% of £3,600) deducted at source. This gives net contributions of £3,840. His pension scheme will recover £720 from HMRC.

(d) Charlotte earns £2,000 per month and makes monthly pension contributions of £140 (7% of £2,000). Her employer will deduct these contributions from her salary before operating the PAYE system, so she will pay income tax on only £1,860 per month.

Tax relief for contributions by employers

In general, contributions made by an employer into a registered pension scheme are deductible when computing the employer's trading profit for tax purposes. This is subject to the overriding condition that the contributions must be made wholly and exclusively for trade purposes. Note the following points:

(a) The amount of contributions which may be deducted when computing the trading profit for a period of account is usually the amount of the contributions *actually paid* by the employer in that period. However, "spreading" provisions may apply to especially large contributions (see below).

(b) There is no upper limit on the amount of contributions which may be deducted when computing an employer's trading profits. This is in contrast to the situation with regard to an individual's own contributions, which are subject to a limit on the amount which may attract tax relief in each tax year (see above).

(c) Contributions made by an employer in respect of an employee are disregarded when computing the *employee's* income for tax purposes.

Spreading of relief

If there is an unusually large increase in an employer's pension contributions between one period of account and the next, tax relief on excess contributions may be spread over a number of periods. Assuming that the current period and the previous period are of equal length, the required procedure is as follows:

(a) The contributions made by the employer in the current period are compared with those for the previous period. Certain contributions made in the current period are disregarded when making this comparison (e.g. contributions paid into the scheme so as to fund cost-of-living increases in current pensions).

(b) If the amount of contributions in the current period is more than 210% of the amount for the previous period, then there is an excess and this may need to be spread.

(c) The excess is equal to the contributions made in the current period less 110% of the contributions made in the previous period. Spreading does not apply if this is less than £500,000. Otherwise, tax relief on the excess contributions is spread as follows:

Amount of the excess	*Tax relief spread equally over*
£500,000 to £999,999	current period and next period
£1,000,000 to £1,999,999	current period and next two periods
£2,000,000 or more	current period and next three periods

A further adjustment is required if the current period and previous period are of unequal length. Spreading does not apply if the employer made no contributions at all in the previous period (e.g. if a new scheme has been established in the current period).

EXAMPLE 3

During the year to 31 May 2017, an employer made contributions of £400,000 into a registered pension scheme. Explain how tax relief will be given on the contributions made during the year to 31 May 2018 if the amount of these contributions is:

(a) £800,000 (b) £920,000 (c) £1,000,000 (d) £2,640,000

Solution

(a) The current year contributions are 200% of those for the previous year. This does not exceed 210% so spreading does not apply. Tax relief on contributions of £800,000 will be given in the year to 31 May 2018.

(b) Current year contributions are 230% of those for the previous year but the excess of current year contributions over 110% of previous year contributions is only £480,000. This is less than £500,000 so spreading does not apply. Tax relief on contributions of £920,000 will be given in the year to 31 May 2018.

(c) Current year contributions are 250% of those for the previous year. The excess of current year contributions over 110% of previous year contributions is £560,000. This is between £500,000 and £999,999 so the excess must be spread equally over the current period and the next period.

Tax relief on contributions of £720,000 (£440,000 + £280,000) will be given in the year to 31 May 2018 and tax relief on the remaining £280,000 of contributions will be given in the year to 31 May 2019.

(d) Current year contributions are 660% of those for the previous year. The excess of current year contributions over 110% of previous year contributions is £2,200,000. This exceeds £2,000,000 so the excess must be spread equally over the current period and the next three periods.

Tax relief on contributions of £990,000 (£440,000 + £550,000) will be given in the year to 31 May 2018. Relief on contributions of £550,000 will be given in each of the three years to 31 May 2019, 2020 and 2021.

Annual allowance charge

If an individual is a member of one or more registered pension schemes, an income tax charge (the "annual allowance charge") arises if the "total pension input amount" for that individual in a tax year exceeds the annual allowance for the year. The annual allowance for tax year 2017-18 is normally £40,000. However, this figure is reduced by £1 for every £2 by which the individual's "adjusted income" exceeds £150,000, subject to a minimum annual allowance of £10,000. Note the following points:

(a) For this purpose, "adjusted income" is broadly equal to the individual's net income for the year (see Chapter 2) *plus* any pension contributions relieved either through net pay arrangements or on making a claim (see earlier in this chapter) *plus* any employer pension contributions.

(b) The maximum reduction of £30,000 (reducing the annual allowance from £40,000 to the minimum of £10,000) occurs when an individual's adjusted income for the year is £210,000 or greater, since (£210,000 – £150,000) ÷ 2 = £30,000.

(c) The annual allowance is *not* reduced (even if adjusted income exceeds £150,000) if the individual's "threshold income" for the year does not exceed £110,000. For this purpose, "threshold income" is broadly equal to the individual's net income for the year *less* the gross amount of any pension contributions relieved at source.

(d) This "tapering" of the annual allowance did not apply in years prior to 2016-17.

If an individual's total pension input amount for a tax year exceeds the annual allowance for the year, the excess is charged to income tax at marginal rate (i.e. as if the amount of the excess were an additional slice of income on top of the individual's income from all other sources). This tax charge falls upon the individual concerned.

Pension input amount

An individual's total pension input amount for a tax year is found by calculating the pension input amount for each registered pension scheme to which the individual belongs and then aggregating these figures. Pension input amounts are calculated as follows:

(a) **Money purchase schemes**. The pension input amount for a tax year in relation to a money purchase scheme is equal to the total relievable contributions made by or in respect of the individual during that year†, plus any employer contributions.

(b) **Defined benefits schemes**. The pension input amount for a tax year in relation to a defined benefits scheme is equal to the increase in the value of the individual's pension rights under the scheme during that year†. For this purpose, the value of an individual's pension rights on a specified date is equal to:

  (i) the amount of any lump sum which would be payable to the individual if he or she became entitled to payment of it on that date, *plus*

(ii) 16 times the amount of the annual pension which would be payable to the individual if he or she became entitled to payment of it on that date.

Before calculating the increase in value of an individual's pension rights under a defined benefits scheme, the value of those rights at the start of the year are adjusted for inflation. This adjustment reflects the annual increase in the Consumer Prices Index up to the September prior to the start of the tax year concerned.

There is no pension input amount for a tax year in respect of a pension scheme if the individual (in consequence of severe ill health) becomes entitled before the end of that year to all of the benefits which may be provided under the scheme. Nor is there any pension input amount for a tax year if the individual dies before the tax year ends.

† *Prior to 2016-17, pension input amounts were calculated for "pension input periods" which did not often coincide with tax years. But pension input periods are now aligned with the tax year.*

Carry forward of unused annual allowance

An individual whose pension input amount for a tax year is less than his or her annual allowance for that year (possibly tapered as from 2016-17) has "unused annual allowance" for the year concerned. This is not necessarily wasted, since unused annual allowance may be carried forward for up to three years, so making it less likely that an annual allowance charge will apply in those years. Note the following points:

(a) The individual must have been a member of a registered pension scheme during a tax year in order to carry forward unused annual allowance from that year.

(b) The current tax year's annual allowance must be set first against the total pension input amount for that year. Unused annual allowance from the three previous tax years may then be taken into account, beginning with the earliest of those years. For instance, an individual whose pension input amount for tax year 2017-18 exceeds his or her annual allowance for the year may use unused annual allowance brought forward from 2014-15, 2015-16 and 2016-17, in that order.

(c) The calculation of the amount of unused annual allowance from the previous three years (that may be carried forward to the current year) takes into account the fact that any unused annual allowance in those years may have been "used up" in an intervening tax year in which pension input amount has exceeded the annual allowance.

EXAMPLE 4

Calculate the annual allowance available in 2017-18 (including unused annual allowance brought forward) to an individual with total pension input amounts as follows:

2014-15 £25,000 2015-16 £62,000 2016-17 £31,000

The annual allowance has been £40,000 since 2014-15. Assume that the individual's "adjusted income" does not exceed £150,000 in any year.

Solution

Unused annual allowance is £15,000 in 2014-15 and £9,000 in 2016-17. But pension input amount for 2015-16 exceeds the annual allowance by £22,000 and this uses up the £15,000 brought forward from 2014-15. So the annual allowance available in 2017-18 is £49,000 (current year £40,000 plus £9,000 brought forward from 2016-17).

EXAMPLE 5

Diane is self-employed and a member of three registered pension schemes. Her pension input amounts for 2017-18 for each of these schemes are as follows:

Scheme A:	£12,500
Scheme B:	£4,400
Scheme C:	£11,600

Diane's "adjusted income" for 2017-18 is £206,000 and her marginal rate of income tax for the year is 45%. Her "threshold income" for 2017-18 exceeds £110,000. Compute the annual allowance charge for the year, assuming that there is no unused annual allowance to bring forward from the previous three years.

Solution

Diane's adjusted income for 2017-18 exceeds £150,000 by £56,000. Therefore her annual allowance for the year is £12,000 (£40,000 – 1/2 × £56,000). Total pension input amount is £28,500. This exceeds the annual allowance by £16,500, so Diane's annual allowance charge for the year is £16,500 @ 45% = £7,425.

EXAMPLE 6

Compute the annual allowance charge payable by each of the following employees for tax year 2017-18, assuming in each case that "adjusted income" for the year does not exceed £150,000 and that there is no unused annual allowance brought forward. Also assume that the Consumer Prices Index (CPI) rose by 3% in the year to September 2016.

(a) Jill belongs to a money purchase scheme. Her relievable contributions for 2017-18 are £15,000. Her employer's contributions for the year on her behalf are £30,000. Jill's taxable income for 2017-18 is £84,000.

(b) Eric's scheme is a defined benefit scheme. When he retires he will receive an annual pension equal to 1/80th of his final salary for each year of pensionable service. He will also receive a lump sum equal to 3/80ths of final salary for each year of pensionable service. Eric had completed 22 years of pensionable service by the start of 2017-18 and his salary was £72,000 per annum. His salary rose to £76,000 by the end of the tax year. His taxable income for 2017-18 is £67,500.

Both Jill's and Eric's pension contributions are relieved by means of the net pay arrangement. Neither of them made any Gift Aid donations during 2017-18.

Solution

(a) Total pension input amount for the year is £45,000 and this exceeds the 2017-18 annual allowance by £5,000. With a taxable income of £84,000, Jill's marginal rate of income tax for the year is 40%. Therefore the annual allowance charge payable for 2017-18 is £2,000 (£5,000 × 40%).

(b) If Eric became entitled to payment of his pension and lump sum at the start of the tax year, he would receive an annual pension of £19,800 (£72,000 x 22/80) and a lump sum of £59,400 (£72,000 x 66/80). The value of his pension rights at the start of the year is therefore £376,200 (£59,400 + (16 x £19,800)). Increasing this figure by 3% to reflect the change in CPI gives £387,486.

If Eric became entitled to payment of his pension and lump sum at the end of the tax year, he would receive an annual pension of £21,850 (£76,000 x 23/80) and a lump sum of £65,550 (£76,000 x 69/80). The value of his pension rights at the end of the year is therefore £415,150 (£65,550 + (16 x £21,850)).

Total pension input amount for the year is £27,664 (£415,150 – £387,486). This is less than the annual allowance of £40,000 for 2017-18 and therefore there is no annual allowance charge.

Lifetime allowance charge

There is no limit to the total level of benefits which an individual can receive from registered pension schemes during his or her lifetime. However, a charge to income tax known as the "lifetime allowance charge" will arise if total benefits exceed the lifetime allowance. Whenever pension benefits "crystallise" (e.g. when an individual starts taking a scheme pension) the value of the crystallised benefits is compared with the proportion of the lifetime allowance which remains unused. Any excess is chargeable to income tax. The lifetime allowance figures for tax years 2006-07 to 2017-18 are as follows:

2006-07	£1,500,000	2012-13	£1,500,000
2007-08	£1,600,000	2013-14	£1,500,000
2008-09	£1,650,000	2014-15	£1,250,000
2009-10	£1,750,000	2015-16	£1,250,000
2010-11	£1,800,000	2016-17	£1,000,000
2011-12	£1,800,000	2017-18	£1,000,000

Any excess of crystallised benefits over the available lifetime allowance is taxed at 55% if taken as a lump sum and at 25% otherwise. This tax charge falls jointly upon the individual and the scheme administrator. In practice, the tax will usually be paid by the scheme administrator and then deducted from the benefits paid to the individual.

Operation of the lifetime allowance

Whenever a "benefit crystallisation event" occurs, it is necessary to compare the value of the benefits that have crystallised with the proportion of the individual's lifetime allowance which remains unused after any previous such events. The main examples of a benefit crystallisation event are the payment of a lump sum and the commencement of a pension. Note the following points:

(a) The value of a lump sum is the amount paid to the scheme member. The value of a pension is generally equal to 20 times the amount of the pension which will be paid to the member during the first twelve months.

(b) On the first occasion that a benefit crystallisation event occurs, the value of the benefits that have crystallised is compared with the lifetime allowance as it stands on the date of the event. On a subsequent event, the value of the crystallised benefits is compared with the *proportion* of the lifetime allowance (if any) that remains after previous events. However, this proportion is applied to the lifetime allowance as it stands on the date of the subsequent event.

(c) If an individual becomes entitled to a scheme pension and a pension commencement lump sum from the same scheme on the same date, the payment of the lump sum is considered to be the earlier of the two events. This minimises the lifetime allowance charge, since the lifetime allowance is made available first to the lump sum (which would otherwise be taxed at 55%) rather than the pension.

EXAMPLE 7

Sharon is a member of two registered pension schemes. She receives no benefits from either of these schemes until 19 March 2009, when she takes a lump sum of £957,000 from one of her schemes. On 5 January 2018 she takes a lump sum of £530,000 from her other scheme. Calculate the lifetime allowance charge arising from these two events.

Solution

On 19 March 2009, the crystallised benefits absorb 58% of the lifetime allowance (which is £1,650,000 for events occurring during 2008-09). There is no lifetime allowance charge and 42% of the lifetime allowance remains unused.

On 5 January 2018, the crystallised benefits of £530,000 are compared with 42% of £1,000,000 (the lifetime allowance for events occurring during 2017-18). Crystallised benefits exceed the available allowance of £420,000 by £110,000. Therefore there is a lifetime allowance charge of £60,500 (55% of £110,000).

The lifetime allowance has now been fully used, so the full value of any further pension benefits will be subject to the lifetime allowance charge.

EXAMPLE 8

Stuart is a member of a registered pension scheme. He took no benefits from this or any other scheme until February 2018, when he received a lump sum of £320,000 and began to receive a pension of £52,500 per annum. Calculate the lifetime allowance charge arising from these events.

Solution

The value of the pension is £1,050,000 (20 x £52,500) so the total value of the benefits received is £1,370,000. This exceeds the lifetime allowance for 2017-18 by £370,000 and so there will be a lifetime allowance charge.

The lump sum is deemed to be the earlier of the two benefit crystallisation events, so it is the pension which has caused the lifetime allowance to be exceeded. Hence the excess is taxed at 25% and the lifetime allowance charge is £92,500 (25% of £370,000).

Summary

- In a defined benefits pension scheme, the benefits payable to members are usually based on final salary and length of service. In a money purchase scheme, the benefits payable to members are based upon the size of the pension fund built up during a member's working life.
- Registered pension schemes enjoy certain tax advantages when compared with unregistered schemes. A registered scheme's investment income is exempt from income tax. Any capital gains made on the disposal of scheme investments are exempt from capital gains tax. Tax relief is available in relation to contributions made by members and employers. Tax-free lump sums may be paid to members.
- Normal minimum pension age rose from 50 to 55 on 6 April 2010. Pension benefits from registered pension schemes must normally begin by the age of 75.
- The maximum amount of pension contributions on which an individual can claim tax relief in any tax year is equal to the greater of the individual's earnings for that year and £3,600. If earnings are less than £3,600, tax relief will be given on contributions beyond the level of earnings only if the pension scheme operates tax relief at source.
- Basic rate relief on an individual's pension contributions may be given by deduction at source. Relief at the higher rate and additional rate is then given by increasing the basic rate limit and higher rate limit by the gross amount of the contributions.
- Alternatively, tax relief may be given by deducting an employee's contributions from his or her gross pay before operating the PAYE system. Exceptionally, relief may be given by deduction from the individual's total income.

- In general, an employer's pension contributions are deducted when computing the employer's trading profit for the period of account in which the contributions are paid. However, tax relief on contributions which are unusually large may be spread over two or more periods.
- A tax liability will arise if an individual's total pension inputs for a tax year exceed the annual allowance for that year (which is reduced for certain high-income individuals). The excess is charged to income tax at marginal rate and this tax charge falls upon the individual concerned.
- A tax liability may arise when a benefit crystallisation event occurs. The most common examples of such an event are the payment of a lump sum to a member or the commencement of a pension. The value of the crystallised benefits is compared with the unused proportion of the lifetime allowance and any excess is charged to income tax. The tax charge is at either 55% or 25% (depending on whether the benefits are taken as a lump sum or a pension) and falls jointly upon the scheme administrator and the member concerned.

Exercises

14.1 State the maximum contribution to registered pension schemes on which an individual could obtain tax relief in 2017-18 if the individual's earnings for the year were:

(a) £120,000 (b) £1,200.

14.2 Freda is a member of a registered pension scheme which operates tax relief at source. She has income from self-employment of £60,000 in 2017-18 and makes pension contributions of £1,000 (gross) per month. Explain how tax relief will be given in relation to her pension contributions.

14.3 An employer's contributions into a registered pension scheme during the year to 30 June 2017 are £600,000. Explain how tax relief will be given on the contributions of £1,860,000 which the employer makes during the year to 30 June 2018.

14.4 Karen belongs to a number of registered pension schemes. Until tax year 2009-10 she had received no benefits from any of these schemes but in October 2009 she took a lump sum of £350,000 from one of her schemes. She received no further benefits until July 2017 when she took a lump sum of £1,120,000 from another of her schemes.

(a) Calculate the amount of any lifetime allowance charges arising in relation to either of Karen's lump sums.

(b) How would the situation change if the lump sum of £1,120,000 had been received in October 2009 and the lump sum of £350,000 had been received in July 2017?

14.5 Damon is a member of a defined benefit registered pension scheme. On retirement, he will receive an annual pension equal to 1/60th of final salary for each year of pensionable service. He will also receive a lump sum equal to 3/80ths of final salary for each year of pensionable service.

At the start of tax year 2017-18, Damon's annual salary was £360,000 and he had accumulated 20 years of pensionable service. By the end of the year his salary had risen to £390,000.

Damon's marginal rate of income tax for 2017-18 is 45% and he has no unused annual allowance brought forward from previous years. His "adjusted income" for the year is £427,500 and his "threshold income" exceeds £110,000. Calculate the annual allowance charge payable for 2017-18. (Ignore inflation).

***14.6** Edna's total pension input amounts for tax years 2014-15 to 2017-18 are as follows:

2014-15	£23,000
2015-16	£34,000
2016-17	£42,000
2017-18	£45,000

The annual allowance has been £40,000 since 2014-15. Edna has no unused annual allowance to bring forward from previous years and her "adjusted income" does not exceed £150,000 in any year. Her taxable income for 2017-18 (after deduction of the personal allowance) is £87,500.

Calculate the annual allowance charge for 2017-18 and the amount of any unused annual allowance carried forward to 2018-19.

***14.7** Irma is self-employed. Her trading income for 2017-18 is £64,880 and during the year she makes net contributions to a registered pension scheme of £6,000. Her only other income in 2017-18 consists of property income of £7,200.

Assuming that Irma is not a Scottish taxpayer, calculate her income tax liability for the year. How would the liability differ for a Scottish taxpayer?

Chapter 15

Payment of income tax, interest and penalties

Introduction

Interest is charged on income tax which is paid late. Conversely, interest may be added to repayments of income tax. The main purpose of this chapter is to identify the dates on which income tax is payable and to explain how the interest due on underpaid or overpaid tax is calculated. This chapter also considers financial penalties to which a taxpayer may become liable as a consequence of non-compliance with tax law.

Payment of income tax

Under the Self Assessment system (see Chapter 1) income tax which is not deducted at source is payable as follows:

(a) The taxpayer's income tax liability for the tax year in relation to all sources of income is aggregated. This tax liability is increased by the amount of any Class 4 National Insurance contributions (NICs) which are due for the year (see Chapter 16).

(b) Payments on account of the total liability (POAs) are due on 31 January in the tax year and on the following 31 July. For example, the POAs for 2017-18 are due on 31 January 2018 and 31 July 2018. Each POA is equal to 50% of the taxpayer's liability to income tax and Class 4 NICs for the *previous* tax year, less any tax which was paid by deduction at source (including tax paid by means of the PAYE system). Note that:

   (i) POAs are not required if the taxpayer's total liability to income tax and Class 4 NICs for the preceding year (less tax deducted at source) was under £1,000.

   (ii) POAs are also not required if more than 80% of the taxpayer's liability for the previous year was satisfied by deduction of tax at source.

   (iii) A taxpayer who believes that his or her liability for the current year will be less than in the previous year may claim to make reduced POAs. There are penalties for making such a claim fraudulently or negligently (see below).

(c) A balancing payment (or repayment) is normally due on 31 January following the end of the tax year. For example, the 2017-18 balancing payment is due on 31 January 2019. But note that:

  (i) If a return notice is issued late (i.e. after 31 October following the end of the tax year to which it relates) and this has not been caused by the taxpayer's failure to notify his or her chargeability to tax, the balancing payment is due three months after the date of the notice.

  (ii) If a self-assessment is amended by the taxpayer or by HMRC (or if a discovery assessment is raised) any additional amount payable is due 30 days after the date of its notification to the taxpayer or on 31 January following the end of the tax year, whichever is the later. However, this rule does *not* defer the date from which interest accrues on the additional tax.

  The amount of the balancing payment is equal to the income tax and Class 4 NICs liability for the year, less any tax deducted at source and less the POAs. The taxpayer's liability to Class 2 NICs (see Chapter 16) is added to this payment, along with any capital gains tax payable for the year (see Chapter 17).

(d) Taxpayers with employment income may request that a balancing payment which does not exceed £3,000 should be collected via the PAYE system. Any amount paid in this way is treated as if paid on the first day of the tax year in which the tax is collected. For instance, a balancing payment which is collected via PAYE during tax year 2017-18 is treated as if paid on 6 April 2017.

Interest is charged if any payment is made after the due date. Late payment penalties (see below) may also be imposed. Taxpayers receive regular statements from HMRC showing the amounts due, the amounts paid to date and the amounts of any interest and penalties.

EXAMPLE 1

(a) Warren's liability to income tax and Class 4 NICs for tax year 2016-17 was £17,200, of which £14,500 was paid via PAYE.

  (i) Compute his POAs for 2017-18 and state the dates on which these fall due.

  (ii) Compute the balancing payment for 2017-18 and state the due date of payment, given that Warren's liability to income tax and Class 4 NICs for 2017-18 is £19,300, of which £16,100 has been paid via PAYE.

(b) Diana's liability to income tax and Class 4 NICs for tax year 2016-17 was £3,400, of which £2,500 was deducted at source.

  (i) Compute her POAs for 2017-18 and state the dates on which these fall due.

  (ii) Compute the balancing payment for 2017-18 and state the due date of payment, given that Diana's liability to income tax and Class 4 NICs for 2017-18 is £11,400, of which none has been paid by deduction at source.

Ignore Class 2 NICs and capital gains tax.

Solution

(a) 84.3% of the liability for 2016-17 was paid via PAYE. This is over 80% and therefore no POAs are required for 2017-18. The remaining liability for 2017-18 of £3,200 (£19,300 – £16,100) is due for payment on 31 January 2019.

(b) 73.5% of the liability for 2016-17 was deducted at source. This is not over 80% but the remainder of the liability was only £900, which is under £1,000. Therefore no POAs are required for 2017-18. The liability of £11,400 for 2017-18 is due to be paid on 31 January 2019.

EXAMPLE 2

Barbara's liability to income tax and Class 4 NICs for 2016-17 was £26,000, of which £4,000 was deducted at source. Her liability for 2017-18 is £30,000, of which £1,000 has been paid by deduction at source. State the dates on which Barbara is required to pay her 2017-18 liability and compute the amount payable on each date.

Ignore Class 2 NICs and capital gains tax.

Solution

Barbara paid 15.4% of her 2016-17 liability by deduction at source. This is not over 80% and the remainder of the liability (£22,000) was not less than £1,000. Therefore POAs are required for 2017-18. The required payments are as follows

(i) 31 January 2018, POA £11,000 (50% of (£26,000 – £4,000))

(ii) 31 July 2018, POA £11,000

(iii) 31 January 2019, balancing payment £7,000 (£30,000 – £1,000 – POAs £22,000).

Digital tax accounts

As from April 2018, taxpayers who have digital tax accounts and update these accounts at least quarterly (see Chapter 1) will be able to adopt a "pay-as-you-go" system for tax payments. This will allow such taxpayers to choose more suitable payment patterns and to manage their cash flows better.

Direct recovery of tax debts

Legislation has been introduced which allows tax debts† owing to HMRC to be recovered directly from a taxpayer's bank and building society accounts. There must be a meeting with the taxpayer before such action is taken and there is a right of appeal against a direct recovery decision. Safeguards are in place to protect vulnerable taxpayers and to ensure that at least £5,000 remains in the taxpayer's accounts after a tax debt has been recovered.

† *HMRC may also collect tax debts of up to £17,000 through the PAYE system (depending on the size of the taxpayer's employment income) with or without the taxpayer's consent.*

Late payment penalties

In addition to the interest that is charged on tax paid late (see below), a taxpayer who makes a late balancing payment† may also incur a late payment penalty. Broadly, the late payment penalty system imposes a penalty equal to 5% of any tax not paid within 30 days of the due date, with two further 5% penalties for tax remaining unpaid six months and 12 months after the due date. The detailed rules are as follows:

(a) If all or part of a balancing payment remains unpaid more than 30 days after the due date, a penalty is charged equal to 5% of the amount unpaid.

(b) The "penalty date" (i.e. the date on which the first late payment penalty is charged) is the date which falls 31 days after the due date of payment.

(c) If any of the balancing payment is not paid within the five-month period beginning on the penalty date, there is another penalty equal to 5% of the amount still unpaid.

(d) Finally, if any of the balancing payment is not paid within the eleven-month period beginning on the penalty date, there is a further 5% penalty.

(e) If a taxpayer is liable to a late payment penalty, HMRC must issue the taxpayer with a penalty notice. Late payment penalties are due for payment within the 30-day period beginning with the day on which the penalty notice is served.

Note that the late payment penalty system does *not* apply to POAs.

† *Late payment penalties also apply to discovery assessments and amendments to self-assessments.*

EXAMPLE 3

Barbara (see Example 2 above) makes the following payments for 2017-18:

	£
31 January 2018	11,000
8 September 2018	11,000
17 February 2019	4,000
11 August 2019	2,000
5 February 2020	1,000

Compute the late payment penalties (if any) which Barbara would incur and state the dates by which these penalties should be paid.

Solution

- The first POA is paid in full and on time. The second POA is also paid in full but is paid late. However, late payment penalties do not apply to late POAs so there is no penalty.
- The penalty date for the balancing payment is 3 March 2019 (the date which is 31 days after the due date of payment)
- £3,000 of the balancing payment is not paid before the penalty date. Therefore there is a late payment penalty of £150 (5% of £3,000).

- The five-month period beginning with the penalty date starts on 3 March 2019 and ends on 2 August 2019. £3,000 of the balancing payment is still unpaid at the end of this period and so there is another late payment penalty of £150 (5% of £3,000).
- The eleven-month period beginning with the penalty date starts on 3 March 2019 and ends on 2 February 2020. £1,000 of the balancing payment remains unpaid at the end of this period and so there is a late payment penalty of £50 (5% of £1,000).

Assuming that penalty notices are issued on 3 March 2019, 3 August 2019 and 3 February 2020 respectively, the first £150 penalty is payable by 1 April 2019, the second £150 penalty is payable by 1 September 2019 and the £50 penalty is payable by 3 March 2020.

Interest on overdue income tax

Interest on overdue POAs, balancing payments and penalties is calculated as follows:

(a) In the case of late POAs and balancing payments, interest runs from the due date of payment up to the date on which the tax is actually paid.

(b) In the case of discovery assessments and amendments to self-assessments, interest runs from the date on which the balancing payment is due for the year to which the assessment relates (normally the 31 January which follows the end of that year) even though the tax itself might not be due for payment until a later date.

(c) Interest on a penalty runs from the due date of payment for that penalty (generally 30 days from its imposition).

(d) Interest is calculated on a daily basis at the official Bank of England rate plus 2.5% (currently 0.25% + 2.5% = 2.75% per annum). Apparently it is HMRC practice to use a denominator of 366 in such calculations, whether or not a leap year is involved.

EXAMPLE 4

Barbara (see Examples 2 and 3 above) pays all of her late payment penalties on 3 March 2020. Calculate the total interest payable by Barbara in relation to her income tax and Class 4 NICs for 2017-18, assuming an interest rate of 2.75% throughout.

Solution

(i) Interest on the second POA (39 days late) is £32.23 (£11,000 x 2.75% x 39/366).

(ii) The first £4,000 of the balancing payment is paid 17 days late. The next £2,000 is 192 days late and the final £1,000 is 370 days late. Interest is £61.76 ((£4,000 x 2.75% x 17/366) + (£2,000 x 2.75% x 192/366) + (£1,000 x 2.75% x 370/366)).

(iii) Interest on the first penalty (337 days late) is £3.80 (£150 x 2.75% x 337/366).

(iv) Interest on the second penalty (184 days late) is £2.07 (£150 x 2.75% x 184/366).

Total interest due is £99.86 (£32.23 + £61.76 + £3.80 + £2.07).

Interest on overpaid income tax

Repayments of overpaid POAs, balancing payments and penalties attract interest. This is calculated at the *greater* of 0.5% per annum and the official Bank of England rate. Such interest is referred to as *repayment interest* and is itself exempt from income tax.

Interest is calculated on a daily basis and runs from the "repayment interest start date" to the date on which repayment is made. The repayment interest start date is:

(a) as regards POAs and balancing payments, the *later* of the actual date of payment and the date on which the tax was due to be paid

(b) as regards income tax deducted at source (including PAYE), 31 January following the tax year for which the tax is deducted.

Repayments made by HMRC in relation to a tax year are attributed first to the balancing payment for that year, secondly in two equal parts to the POAs for that year and finally to tax deducted at source for the year. Note that:

(a) If a repayment is triggered by a claim to carry back a loss or a payment from a later year to an earlier year (e.g. if a trading loss is carried back or if a Gift Aid donation is carried back) interest on this repayment runs from the 31 January following the later year, *not* the earlier year.

(b) Penalties repaid to a taxpayer also attract interest, running from the date of payment to the date of repayment.

(c) Apparently it is HMRC practice to use a denominator of 365 when computing interest on a repayment, whether or not a leap year is involved.

(d) Repayment interest is not paid in relation to income tax that has been deliberately overpaid by the taxpayer. This rule prevents taxpayers from using HMRC as a source of tax-free interest.

Penalties

A taxpayer who fails to comply with statutory requirements† may become liable to a number of financial penalties, the most important of which are listed below. Some of these penalties are fixed in amount but HMRC often has the power to "mitigate" (i.e. reduce) the amount charged if it sees fit to do so. Whether or not a penalty is mitigated will usually depend mainly upon the seriousness of the taxpayer's offence and the degree to which the taxpayer has co-operated with HMRC. The main penalties are as follows:

† *The penalties charged in relation to failure to notify chargeability (see below), inaccuracies in a return or document and deliberate withholding of information are higher if offshore matters are involved. In some cases, the penalty could be as much as 200% of the amount of tax concerned.*

(a) **Failure to notify chargeability to tax**. An individual must notify HMRC if he or she is liable to income tax for a tax year, even if a notice requiring a return has not been issued for that year (see Chapter 1). Notification must be made within six months of the end of the tax year concerned.

The penalty regime which applies to a "failure to notify" is not confined to income tax but covers a range of taxes, including capital gains tax, corporation tax and VAT. Under this regime, the penalty for a failure to notify liability to income tax for a tax year is expressed as a percentage of the tax which (because of the failure) remains unpaid on 31 January following the end of that year. But no penalty is charged if the taxpayer has a reasonable excuse for the failure to notify. The applicable percentage is determined as follows:

(i) For a "deliberate and concealed" failure to notify, where the failure is deliberate and the taxpayer has attempted to conceal it, the percentage is 100%.

(ii) For a failure which is "deliberate but not concealed" the percentage is 70%.

(iii) Otherwise, the percentage is 30%.

These penalties may be reduced if the taxpayer discloses the failure. There are greater reductions if the disclosure is "unprompted" than if it is "prompted". A disclosure is unprompted if it is made at a time when the taxpayer has no reason to believe that the irregularity has been discovered or is about to be discovered by HMRC.

(b) **Late submission of a tax return**. The penalty regime which applies to the late filing of a self assessment tax return is explained below. This regime will eventually apply across a range of taxes. The late filing penalties are as follows:

(i) A £100 penalty is charged as soon as a tax return is late (by a single day). This applies whether or not the tax liability for the year has been paid and even if the taxpayer has no liability for that year or is owed a tax repayment for the year.

(ii) If a return is more than 3 months late, HMRC may charge a penalty of £10 per day whilst the return remains outstanding (up to a maximum of £900).

(iii) If a return is more than 6 months late, another penalty arises equal to the greater of £300 and 5% of the tax liability for the year.

(iv) If a tax return is more than 12 months late, a further penalty arises, again equal to the greater of £300 and 5% of the tax liability for the year. But if the taxpayer has deliberately withheld information from HMRC, the percentage used in the penalty calculation becomes 70% (not 5%). This rises to 100% if the withholding of information is deliberate and concealed. These higher penalties may be reduced if the taxpayer discloses the information which has been withheld.

The tax-geared penalties (i.e. penalties which are calculated as a percentage of the tax liability) have to be estimated by HMRC in the first instance. These penalties are then re-assessed when the taxpayer files the late return.

Note that none of the penalties listed above will be charged if the taxpayer has a reasonable excuse for failing to submit a return on time (e.g. serious illness).

(c) **Submission of an incorrect tax return**. A single penalty regime applies in relation to the submission of incorrect returns for the purposes of income tax and many other taxes. This common regime applies if an incorrect return leads to an understatement of the amount of tax due and the inaccuracy was either careless or deliberate. No penalty is charged if the taxpayer has taken reasonable care. The regime also applies if an assessment issued by HMRC understates the amount of tax due and the taxpayer fails to take reasonable steps to notify HMRC of this fact within 30 days.

The amount of any penalty under the regime is expressed as a percentage of the potential lost revenue. For a "deliberate and concealed" inaccuracy, the percentage is 100%. This percentage falls to 70% for an inaccuracy which is "deliberate but not concealed". Otherwise, the percentage is 30%. The percentage is also 30% in cases where the taxpayer has failed to notify HMRC of an under-assessment.

As with the "failure to notify chargeability" penalties (see above) these penalties may be reduced if the taxpayer discloses the infringement and there are greater reductions if the disclosure is unprompted than if it is prompted.

(d) **Fraud or negligence when claiming reduced POAs**. A taxpayer who makes a claim for reduced POAs and does so fraudulently or negligently may be subject to a maximum penalty equal to the difference between the POAs actually made and the POAs that should have been made.

(e) **Failure to keep records**. A taxpayer who fails to maintain or retain adequate records in support of the year's tax return may be subject to a penalty of up to £3,000.

(f) **GAAR penalty**. As from 15 September 2016, a penalty of 60% is applied in cases where a taxpayer's arrangements have been successfully counteracted by means of the general anti-abuse rule (see Chapter 1). The penalty is equal to 60% of the additional tax payable as a result of the counteraction.

In every case, the penalty described above is charged *in addition* both to the tax itself and to any late payment penalties or interest charged in relation to that tax.

Summary

- Under the Self Assessment system, income tax not collected at source or via the PAYE system is usually payable by means of two payments on account, followed by a balancing payment.
- Late payment penalties may be levied if a balancing payment is paid late and interest is payable on any tax paid late. Interest usually runs from the due date of payment up to the actual date of payment.
- Repayments of overpaid tax also attract interest, running from the date on which the tax was paid (or, if later, the due date of payment) up to the date of repayment.
- Financial penalties may be imposed for various breaches of the tax law.

Exercises

Any liability to Class 2 NICs and capital gains tax may be ignored in all of these exercises.

15.1 For each of the following taxpayers, state the dates on which the 2017-18 income tax is due to be paid and calculate the amount payable on each date. (Ignore Class 4 NICs).

(a) Guy's 2016-17 income tax liability was £1,600, of which £1,150 was paid via the PAYE system and £50 was deducted at source from savings income. His income tax liability for 2017-18 is £1,750, of which £1,310 is paid via PAYE and none is deducted at source.

(b) Marie's 2016-17 income tax liability was £6,730, of which £4,370 was paid via PAYE and £20 was deducted at source. Her 2017-18 liability is £6,580, of which £4,810 is paid via PAYE and £35 is deducted at source.

(c) Majid's 2016-17 income tax liability was £14,850, of which £11,990 was paid via PAYE and £110 was deducted at source. His 2017-18 liability is £16,110, of which £12,510 is paid via PAYE and none is deducted at source.

15.2 Dorothy's income tax and Class 4 NICs liability for 2016-17 was £24,600, of which £600 was deducted at source. Her liability for 2017-18 is £28,000, of which none is deducted at source. She made a first POA in respect of 2017-18 on 27 February 2018 and a second POA on 12 September 2018. She also made a balancing payment for the year on 21 February 2019. All of her payments were for the correct amount.

(a) Calculate the amount of any late payment penalties payable by Dorothy in relation to 2017-18.

(b) Assuming an interest rate of 2.75% per annum, calculate the amount of any interest payable by Dorothy in relation to 2017-18.

15.3 Jabran did not receive a notice to file a tax return for 2016-17 but he was aware that he had income which had not been assessed to tax. He notified HMRC of this fact on 2 October 2017 and a return notice was issued to him on 15 November 2017. He completed the return and submitted it with the necessary payment on 7 April 2018.

Explain the penalties and interest which Jabran might be required to pay.

***15.4** Frances paid income tax and Class 4 NICs of £47,000 in 2016-17, of which £19,000 was paid via the PAYE system. Her total liability for 2017-18 is £69,000, of which £21,000 is paid via PAYE. Her payments for 2017-18 are as follows:

	£
15 February 2018	14,000
14 September 2018	14,000
3 February 2019	16,000
15 December 2019	4,000

Calculate the late payment penalties and interest payable for the year, assuming that any penalties are paid on 15 December 2019 and that interest is charged at 2.75% p.a.

Chapter 16

National Insurance contributions

Introduction

National Insurance contributions (NICs) are payable by employees, by employers and by the self-employed. Contributions are collected by the National Insurance Contributions and Employer Office (NIC&EO) of HMRC and paid into a National Insurance Fund. This fund, supplemented if necessary by a grant from the Treasury, is then used to provide contributory social security benefits such as the state retirement pension.

The purpose of this chapter is to explain the circumstances in which NICs are payable and the way in which NICs are calculated.

Class 1 National Insurance contributions

Class 1 NICs are payable in relation to employees who are at least 16 years old. The employees themselves pay *primary* Class 1 NICs whilst employers pay *secondary* Class 1 NICs on their employees' behalf. Employees who continue to work after reaching state pension age pay no further primary contributions but employers must still pay secondary contributions in relation to such employees.

The amount of the Class 1 NICs payable in relation to an employee depends upon the employee's earnings. For National Insurance purposes, an employee's earnings consist of his or her gross pay *before* deducting pension contributions, charitable donations made via a payroll giving scheme or any other expenses borne by the employee. However, certain payments are excluded from earnings when calculating the liability to Class 1 NICs. Some of the main exclusions are:

(a) tips received directly from customers

(b) any business expenses which are paid for (or reimbursed) by the employer, including reasonable travel and subsistence expenses and incidental overnight expenses

(c) mileage allowances received from the employer if these are calculated at a rate which does not exceed the AMAP rate for the first 10,000 miles, regardless of the number of miles actually driven by the employee (see Chapter 7); but any excess forms part of the employee's earnings chargeable to Class 1 NICs

(d) suggestion scheme awards
(e) employer contributions to a registered pension scheme
(f) ex gratia compensation payments for loss of employment (subject to conditions)
(g) pensions and redundancy pay.

Benefits in kind which are not convertible into cash are generally not subject to Class 1 NICs. However, the *employer* will incur a liability to Class 1A NICs in relation to such benefits if they are chargeable to income tax (see below). If an employee's remuneration is paid in the form of non-cash assets such as gold bullion, gemstones or fine wines, a liability to Class 1 NICs arises if the assets are readily convertible into cash. Payments made in shares are generally liable to Class 1 NICs, unless they are "own company" shares provided under an approved share scheme or share option scheme (see Chapter 7).

Contribution periods

The main principles of the Class 1 National Insurance system are as follows:

(a) Primary and secondary Class 1 NICs are calculated according to the amount of an employee's earnings in a "contribution period". For those paid weekly or monthly, each week or month usually constitutes a contribution period. However, special rules apply to company directors (see later in this chapter).

(b) The liability to Class 1 NICs in a given contribution period is governed solely by the employee's earnings in that period and is totally unaffected by earnings in other periods. This is in contrast to the income tax PAYE system (see Chapter 7) which accumulates earnings over the year and calculates a tax liability each week or month based on the employee's total earnings for the tax year to date.

(c) If an employee has two or more employments in a contribution period, each of these employments is considered separately for the purpose of calculating the liability to Class 1 NICs. Earnings from two or more employments are aggregated only if the employments are with the same employer or with employers who "carry on business in association". The term "association" is not defined in the law relating to NICs but it is HMRC practice (when considering this question) to consider the interdependence of the employers concerned. Two or more employers are more likely to be associated for this purpose if they share facilities, personnel, customers etc.

(d) *Before 6 April 2016*, the rates at which Class 1 NICs were calculated depended upon whether or not the employee was "contracted out" of the State Second Pension (S2P). An employee who was contracted out of S2P paid lower Class 1 NICs but was not entitled to receive the State Second Pension on retirement. However, contracting-out was abolished as from 6 April 2016.

Primary Class 1 NICs

The primary Class 1 NICs payable by an employee for a contribution period falling during 2017-18 are calculated as follows:

(a) The employee's earnings in the period are compared with the *primary threshold*. The primary threshold for 2017-18 is £157 per week or £680 per month. No primary Class 1 NICs are payable for a contribution period if the employee's earnings in the period do not exceed this threshold.

(b) If earnings in the contribution period exceed the primary threshold, primary Class 1 NICs are payable at 12% on earnings between the primary threshold and the upper earnings limit (UEL). The UEL for 2017-18 is £866 per week or £3,750 per month.

(c) Any earnings beyond the UEL attract primary Class 1 NICs at 2%.

(d) These rules may be summarised as follows:

Weekly-paid:	
On the first £157	0%
On the next £709 (up to £866)	12%
On remaining earnings above £866	2%
Monthly-paid:	
On the first £680	0%
On the next £3,070 (up to £3,750)	12%
On remaining earnings above £3,750	2%

It is worth noting that the UEL (for all taxpayers) is aligned with the point at which higher rate income tax becomes payable by non-Scottish taxpayers. This point is reached when total income exceeds the sum of the personal allowance and the basic rate band. So for tax year 2017-18, the UEL for the whole year is £45,000 (£11,500 + £33,500). The UEL for a week is £866 (£45,000 ÷ 52) and the UEL for a month is £3,750 (£45,000 ÷ 12).

It is also worth noting that there is a lower earnings limit (LEL) as well as an upper earnings limit. The LEL for 2017-18 is £113 per week or £490 per month. The LEL has no effect on the amount of primary Class 1 NICs payable for a contribution period. But if an employee's earnings for a contribution period are less than the LEL, the employee is not credited with a contributions record for that period and this may affect his or her entitlement to certain social security benefits in the future.

EXAMPLE 1

(a) Compute the primary Class 1 NICs payable by the following weekly-paid employees for the week ending 11 August 2017:

(i) Employee A has earnings for the week of £105.

(ii) Employee B has earnings for the week of £140.

(iii) Employee C has earnings for the week of £320.

   (iv) Employee D has earnings for the week of £750.
   (v) Employee E has earnings for the week of £1,000.

(b) Compute the primary Class 1 NICs payable by the following monthly-paid employees for the month of August 2017:
   (i) Employee F has earnings for the month of £430.
   (ii) Employee G has earnings for the month of £600.
   (iii) Employee H has earnings for the month of £1,870.
   (iv) Employee I has earnings for the month of £3,200.
   (v) Employee J has earnings for the month of £5,800.

Solution

(a) (i) Earnings do not exceed the primary threshold, so primary contributions for the week are £nil. *Earnings are also less than the LEL, so the employee is not credited with a contributions record for the week.*
   (ii) Earnings do not exceed the primary threshold, so primary contributions for the week are £nil.
   (iii) 12% x (£320 – £157) = £19.56
   (iv) 12% x (£750 – £157) = £71.16
   (v) 12% x (£866 – £157) + 2% x (£1,000 – £866) = £87.76

(b) (i) Earnings do not exceed the primary threshold, so primary contributions for the month are £nil. *Earnings are also less than the LEL, so the employee is not credited with a contributions record for the month.*
   (ii) Earnings do not exceed the primary threshold, so primary contributions for the month are £nil.
   (iii) 12% x (£1,870 – £680) = £142.80
   (iv) 12% x (£3,200 – £680) = £302.40
   (v) 12% x (£3,750 – £680) + 2% x (£5,800 – £3,750) = £409.40

Secondary Class 1 NICs

The secondary Class 1 NICs payable by an employer in relation to an employee for a contribution period falling during 2017-18 are calculated as follows:

(a) The employee's earnings in the contribution period are compared with the *secondary threshold*. The secondary threshold for 2017-18 is £157 per week or £680 per month. No secondary contributions are payable if earnings in a contribution period do not exceed this threshold.

(b) If earnings in the period exceed the secondary threshold, secondary Class 1 NICs are payable at 13.8% on earnings above the threshold.

(c) These rules may be summarised as follows:

Weekly-paid:

On the first £157	0%
On remaining earnings above £157	13.8%

Monthly-paid:

On the first £680	0%
On remaining earnings above £680	13.8%

Note that employers are no longer required to pay secondary Class 1 NICs on earnings up to the "upper secondary threshold" (UST) for employees under the age of 21. The UST is currently set to the same figure as the UEL.

Furthermore, employers are not required to pay secondary Class 1 NICs on earnings up to the Apprentice UST (AUST) for employees who are apprentices and under the age of 25. The AUST is also currently set to the same figure as the UEL.

EXAMPLE 2

Compute the secondary Class 1 NICs payable in relation to each employee in Example 1. Assume in each case that the employee concerned is over 21 and is not an apprentice.

Solution

(a) (i)/(ii) Earnings do not exceed the secondary threshold, so secondary contributions for the week are £nil.

(iii) 13.8% x (£320 – £157) = £22.49

(iv) 13.8% x (£750 – £157) = £81.83

(v) 13.8% x (£1,000 – £157) = £116.33

(b) (i)/(ii) Earnings do not exceed the secondary threshold, so secondary contributions for the month are £nil.

(iii) 13.8% x (£1,870 – £680) = £164.22

(iv) 13.8% x (£3,200 – £680) = £347.76

(v) 13.8% x (£5,800 – £680) = £706.56

Employment allowance

In tax year 2017-18, most employers are able to offset an "employment allowance" of up to £3,000 per annum against their liability to secondary Class 1 NICs. This means that an employer whose liability to secondary Class 1 NICs does not exceed £3,000 for the year is not required to make any secondary contributions at all. The employment allowance is claimed as part of the payroll process through the RTI system (see Chapter 7).

However, the employment allowance is not available to companies with a single director and no other employees.

Directors' Class 1 NICs

The fact that NICs are calculated for each contribution period separately means that employees with identical annual earnings may pay very different amounts of primary contributions in the tax year, depending upon the distribution of their earnings over that year. Consider the following (rather extreme) example:

EXAMPLE 3

During 2017-18, an employee earns £4,000 per month.

(a) Calculate the total primary Class 1 NICs payable for the year.

(b) What would the total primary contributions be for the year if the employee received £48,000 in one month and nothing in the remaining 11 months?

Solution

(a) Primary contributions each month are equal to 12% x (£3,750 – £680) + 2% x (£4,000 – £3,750) = £373.40. This gives a total of £4,480.80 for the year.

(b) Primary contributions for the month in which the employee was paid £48,000 would be equal to 12% x (£3,750 – £680) + 2% x (£48,000 – £3,750) = £1,253.40.

Therefore the employee would save £3,227.40 in primary contributions (£4,480.80 – £1,253.40) if the entire year's salary were received in a single month.

Employees are not normally able to arrange for all of their year's earnings to be paid in one contribution period. However, company directors may well have sufficient influence to make such an arrangement. To counter this, the Class 1 contributions of company directors are calculated on an *annual* basis, regardless of the distribution of their earnings over the tax year. In effect, the entire year becomes a single contribution period. For 2017-18:

(a) The primary threshold and the secondary threshold are both £8,164.

(b) The upper earnings limit (UEL) is £45,000.

(c) The lower earnings limit (LEL) is £5,876.

EXAMPLE 4

Rework the previous example, given that the employee in question is a company director.

Solution

Regardless of the distribution of earnings over the tax year, primary contributions would be equal to 12% x (£45,000 – £8,164) + 2% x (£48,000 – £45,000) = £4,480.32.

Class 1A National Insurance contributions

Benefits in kind which are not convertible into cash are generally exempt from Class 1 NICs. However, such benefits give rise to a Class 1A contribution instead, *payable only by the employer* (not by the employee) if they are chargeable to income tax. For 2017-18, this contribution is calculated as 13.8% of the amount of the benefit in kind which is assessed on the employee for income tax purposes (see Chapter 8).

Note that the employment allowance of £3,000 (see earlier in this chapter) cannot be set against an employer's liability to either Class 1A NICs or Class 1B NICs (see below).

EXAMPLE 5

In 2017-18, George is provided with a petrol-engined motor car by his employer who pays for all fuel and other running costs. The car had a list price when new of £27,900 and has an emission rating of 143g/km. George's employer also pays his private medical insurance premium of £600 per annum.

Calculate the Class 1A contribution payable by George's employer for the year.

Solution

The employee benefits assessed on George for income tax purposes are:

	£
Car (18% + 9% = 27% x £27,900)	7,533
Fuel (27% x £22,600)	6,102
Medical insurance premium	600
	14,235

Therefore the Class 1A contribution payable by George's employer is 13.8% x £14,235 = £1,964.43.

Class 1B National Insurance contributions

From time to time, an employer may enter into a PAYE Settlement Agreement (PSA) with HM Revenue and Customs. The effect of such an agreement is that the employer pays the income tax liability of employees in relation to certain benefits in kind. In these circumstances, the employer is liable to make a Class 1B National Insurance contribution calculated (in 2017-18) as 13.8% of the sum of the benefits in kind and the associated tax which is payable under the terms of the PSA.

Class 2 National Insurance contributions

Class 2 NICs† are payable by self-employed people who are over 16 and under pensionable age. The contributions are payable at a flat rate (for 2017-18) of £2.85 per week. A self-employed person whose profit for the tax year is less than the "small profits threshold" (£6,025 for 2017-18) is not required to pay Class 2 NICs for that tax year but may do so voluntarily so as to maintain a full contributions record‡. Note that:

(a) For Class 2 NICs purposes, a self-employed person's profit for a tax year is equal to the amount of profit on which Class 4 NICs are payable for that year (see later in this chapter). If this is not less than the small profits threshold, Class 2 NICs are payable for each week or part-week during the tax year in which the person is self-employed.

(b) If a person has two or more businesses, the profits of all of them are aggregated when determining whether the person's earnings are less than the small profits threshold.

(c) Class 2 NICs are now collected through the Self Assessment system (see Chapter 15) along with income tax and Class 4 NICs. Payments on account (POAs) are not required for Class 2 NICs.

† *The Government has announced that it intends to abolish Class 2 NICs from April 2018.*

‡ *After the abolition of Class 2 NICs, self-employed persons whose profits are below the Class 4 lower profits limit (see below) will not be required to pay any NICs at all. In order to maintain a full contributions record, such persons will presumably have to make voluntary Class 3 contributions (see below) which are much more expensive than Class 2 contributions.*

EXAMPLE 6

(a) Alison has been self-employed for many years. Her profit for tax year 2017-18 is £5,600. Is she liable to pay Class 2 NICs for the year?

(b) Amanda starts her own business on 1 June 2017 and is self-employed throughout the remaining 45 weeks of tax year 2017-18. Her profit for 2017-18 is £7,200. Calculate the required Class 2 NICs for the year.

Solution

(a) Alison's profit for the year is less than the small profits threshold of £6,025. So she is not required to pay Class 2 NICs for 2017-18.

(b) Class 2 NICs for the year are £128.25 (45 × £2.85).

Class 3 National Insurance contributions

A person (employed or self-employed) whose earnings are too low in a contribution period to require payment of NICs may make a voluntary Class 3 contribution so as to maintain a full contributions record. For 2017-18, the Class 3 contribution is £14.25 per week.

Class 4 National Insurance contributions

In addition to the flat rate Class 2 liability described above, self-employed people who are over 16 and under pensionable age may also be liable to pay earnings-related Class 4 contributions. A self-employed person's Class 4 liability for a given tax year is based on the amount of trading income which is charged to income tax for that year. The Class 4 NICs are collected along with the income tax liability (see Chapter 15). Note that:

(a) The Class 4 liability is based on the person's trading income for the tax year *after* adjusting for capital allowances and trading losses but *before* deducting any pension contributions that are deducted from total income (see Chapter 14).

Trading losses which are set against the non-trading income of a tax year for tax purposes (see Chapter 12) are set instead against the first available trading income of that year or subsequent years for Class 4 purposes.

(b) If a self-employed person has more than one business, the earnings from all businesses for the year are aggregated.

(c) There is no liability to Class 4 NICs if trading income does not exceed the *lower profits limit* (£8,164 for 2017-18).

(d) If trading income exceeds the lower profits limit, Class 4 NICs are payable at 9% on profits between the lower profits limit and the upper profits limit. The upper profits limit for 2017-18 is £45,000. Any profits beyond the upper profits limit are charged to Class 4 NICs at 2%.

EXAMPLE 7

Calculate the Class 4 NICs payable in each of the following cases:

(a) Shawn has trading income for 2017-18 of £14,880.

(b) Catherine has trading income for 2017-18 of £50,000.

(c) Paul has trading income for 2017-18 of £7,500.

Solution

(a) 9% x (£14,880 – £8,164) = £604.44.

(b) 9% x (£45,000 – £8,164) + 2% x (£50,000 – £45,000) = £3,415.24.

(c) Paul's profits do not exceed the lower profits limit so Class 4 NICs for the year are nil.

Annual maximum contributions

An individual who has more than one employment will normally be required to make Class 1 contributions in respect of each employment. Similarly, an individual who is both employed and self-employed will normally be required to make Class 1 contributions in respect of the employment and Class 2 and Class 4 contributions in respect of the self-employment. In these circumstances the total NICs payable could become onerous, but relief is available in the form of limits on the amount of NICs payable by any one person in any one year. In practice, the calculation of these limits can be very complex but a simplified outline of the rules is as follows:

(a) **Maximum Class 1 and 2 contributions**. In any one tax year, the total of the Class 1 contributions payable by an individual *at the main rate* (currently 12%) plus any Class 2 contributions is limited to the amount of the Class 1 contributions which would be payable by a weekly-paid employee who had 53 weeks of earnings equal to the UEL. For 2017-18, this gives a maximum contribution of £4,509.24 (53 × 12% × (£866 – £157)). A refund is made if this limit is exceeded, but the refund calculation takes into account the fact that earnings above the primary threshold which do not attract 12% contributions should attract 2% contributions instead.

(b) **Maximum Class 1, 2 and 4 contributions**. A refund of *Class 4 contributions only* is made if the total main rate (12%) Class 1 contributions, Class 2 contributions and main rate (9%) Class 4 contributions paid by an individual in any one tax year exceed the amount obtained by adding 53 Class 2 contributions to the maximum main rate Class 4 contribution for the year. For 2017-18 this limit is equal to £3,466.29 (53 @ £2.85 + 9% × (£45,000 – £8,164)). The refund calculation takes into account the fact that profits above the lower profits limit which do not attract Class 4 contributions at 9% should attract Class 4 contributions at 2% instead.

EXAMPLE 8

(a) Sabrina has two employments throughout 2017-18. Calculate the refund of NICs due for the year if her regular monthly earnings from the two employments are:

(i) £850 and £1,250 (ii) £2,000 and £3,000 (iii) £4,000 and £4,500.

(b) Stephanie is employed at a monthly salary of £4,200. She also has a small business and pays 53 Class 2 NICs for 2017-18. She pays no Class 4 NICs. Calculate the refund of NICs due for the year.

(c) Stewart is self-employed and pays 53 Class 2 NICs for 2017-18. His trading income for 2017-18 is £39,380. He also receives directors' fees of £14,210 in the year. Calculate the refund of NICs due for the year.

Solution

(a) Sabrina will have paid *main rate* Class 1 NICs as follows:

	(i)	(ii)	(iii)
	£	£	£
First employment:			
12 x 12% x (£850 – £680)	244.80		
12 x 12% x (£2,000 – £680)		1,900.80	
12 x 12% x (£3,750 – £680)			4,420.80
Second employment:			
12 x 12% x (£1,250 – £680)	820.80		
12 x 12% x (£3,000 – £680)		3,340.80	
12 x 12% x (£3,750 – £680)			4,420.80
	1,065.60	5,241.60	8,841.60

In case (i), total contributions do not exceed the maximum, so no refund is due.

In case (ii), contributions exceed the maximum by £732.36 (£5,241.60 – £4,509.24) so Sabrina is entitled to a refund. However, the earnings which have given rise to the excess contributions are still subject to 2% contributions, so the refund is reduced by two-twelfths to £610.30.

In case (iii), Sabrina's contributions exceed the maximum by £4,332.36 (£8,841.60 – £4,509.24) so she is entitled to a refund of 10/12 x £4,332.36 = £3,610.30.

(b) Stephanie will have paid *main rate* Class 1 NICs and Class 2 NICs as follows:

	£
Class 1 (12 x 12% x (£3,750 – £680))	4,420.80
Class 2 (53 @ £2.85)	151.05
	4,571.85

This exceeds the maximum by £62.61 (£4,571.85 – £4,509.24). The refund can be made entirely out of Class 2 contributions so there will be no need to collect further 2% contributions on refunded main rate Class 1 contributions. The refund is £62.61.

(c) Stewart will have paid NICs as follows:

	£
Class 1 (12% x (£14,210 – £8,164))	725.52
Class 2 (53 @ £2.85)	151.05
Class 4 (9% x (£39,380 – £8,164))	2,809.44
	3,686.01

The total main rate Class 1 and Class 2 contributions are well within the maximum of £4,509.24. But the total of the main rate Class 1 contributions, Class 2 contributions and main rate Class 4 contributions exceeds the maximum of £3,466.29 by £219.72. Therefore Stewart is entitled to a refund of Class 4 contributions. However, the profits which have given rise to the excess contributions are still subject to 2% contributions, so the refund is reduced by two-ninths to £170.89.

Summary

- Primary Class 1 NICs are payable by employees. Secondary Class 1 NICs are payable by their employers. Class 1 NICs are calculated with respect to earnings in a contribution period and each contribution period is considered independently.
- In 2017-18, primary Class 1 NICs are payable at 12% on earnings that lie between the primary threshold and the upper earnings limit. Earnings that lie beyond the upper earnings limit attract primary Class 1 NICs at 2%. Secondary Class 1 NICs are payable at 13.8% on earnings that lie beyond the secondary threshold.
- The Class 1 NICs of company directors are assessed on an annual basis and are unaffected by the distribution of the director's earnings over the year.
- Class 1A NICs are payable by employers in relation to benefits in kind which are not convertible into cash and which are chargeable to income tax. Class 1B NICs are payable by employers in relation to PAYE Settlement Agreements.
- Class 2 NICs are payable at a flat rate by self-employed people whose profits are not less than the small profits threshold. Class 2 NICs are collected by means of the Self Assessment system, along with the person's liability to income tax and Class 4 NICs.
- Class 2 NICs are to be abolished as from April 2018.
- Class 3 NICs are paid voluntarily in order to maintain a full contributions record.
- Class 4 NICs are paid by self-employed people and are earnings-related. In 2017-18, Class 4 NICs are payable at 9% on profits between the lower and upper profit limits and at 2% on profits beyond the upper limit.
- There are annual maximum limits on the amount of NICs payable by an individual.

Exercises

It should be assumed in these exercises that all employees are over 21 and are not apprentices.

16.1 Compute the primary and secondary Class 1 NICs payable in relation to the following employees:

(a) A earns £170 for the week ending 23 June 2017.

(b) B earns £780 for the week ending 23 June 2017.

(c) C earns £930 for the week ending 23 June 2017.

(d) D earns £650 for the month of September 2017.

(e) E earns £3,300 for the month of September 2017.

(f) F earns £6,000 for the month of September 2017.

16.2 Joan is a company director. Her salary is paid on the last day of each month. Her gross salary throughout 2017 was £8,400 per month but she was awarded a 4% pay increase as from 1 January 2018. She contributes 10% of her gross salary to the company pension scheme and the company makes a further 15% pension contribution on her behalf.

She lives in accommodation provided by her employer and drives a company car. Her taxable benefits in kind during 2017-18 were £12,850.

Calculate the NICs payable by Joan and by her employer for 2017-18.

16.3 Mark starts his own business on 1 August 2017 and is self-employed for 36 weeks in tax year 2017-18. His trading profit which is assessed to income tax for 2017-18 is £9,250. Calculate the Class 2 NICs and Class 4 NICs payable by Mark for the year.

***16.4** Brenda is a company director and earns a regular monthly salary of £6,000. In December 2017 she received a £20,000 bonus. She is provided with a diesel-engined company car which has an emission rating of 198g/km and which had a list price when new of £26,000. The company pays all the running costs of the car, including fuel. Her BUPA subscription of £750 per year is paid by the company.

Calculate the NICs payable in respect of Brenda for 2017-18.

***16.5** Leonard is employed and received a gross salary of £3,335 per month during tax year 2017-18. He also has a small business and paid 53 Class 2 NICs for the year. His trading income for 2017-18 was £10,754.

Calculate the refund of NICs due to Leonard for the year (if any).

Review questions (Set A)

A1 Three brothers, Daniel, David and Derrick have been discussing their respective taxation affairs and how much they dislike paying tax. None of them are Scottish taxpayers.

Daniel's income for tax year 2017-18 consists of income from property of £47,500 and net debenture interest of £416.

David has an annual salary of £88,000. PAYE deducted from this salary was £28,800 for 2017-18. David paid 4% of his salary into an occupational pension scheme, with his employer contributing 6%. He also has the use of company car for the whole of the tax year. When new, the car cost his employer £34,800 but it had a list price of £37,000. David contributed £6,000 towards the cost of the car. It has a diesel engine and CO_2 emissions of 133g/km. The employer pays for all the running costs of the car (including all fuel) and David pays his employer £100 per month as a contribution towards private fuel. During 2017-18, David also received £2,240 in dividends.

Derrick has an annual salary of £53,000. PAYE deducted from this salary was £9,990 in 2017-18. He was given an interest-free loan from his employer of £12,000 on 6 June 2017 to fund a luxury cruise for his sixtieth birthday. Derrick repaid £8,000 of this loan in January 2018 and intends to pay off the remaining £4,000 in October 2018.

All three brothers are delighted that their parents are still alive, although both were born in 1931. The parents were married in September 1952. Their father has a private pension which amounts to about £30,000 per year and they both receive the state pension.

Required:

(a) Calculate the income tax payable by Daniel for 2017-18.

(b) Calculate the income tax payable by (or repayable to) David for 2017-18.

(c) Explain to David what changes he could make that would help him save tax.

(d) Calculate the income tax payable by (or repayable to) Derrick for 2017-18. You do not need to compute the loan interest using the daily method. Assume that the official rate of interest is 2.5% per annum.

(e) Explain to Derrick how he could have avoided paying tax on the interest-free loan.

(f) Calculate the total National Insurance contributions payable by both David and his employer for 2017-18.

(g) Explain how the married couple's allowance will operate in the situation of the father and mother. You are not required to complete any calculations. *(CIPFA)*

A2 Jeremy, who has been married for many years, was born in 1934 and receives a retirement pension of £23,460 per annum. He also receives dividend income of £7,500 per annum. In 2006 he purchased an annuity from which a monthly income of £325 (gross) is paid to him. The annuity was not purchased with assets held under a registered pension scheme. The capital element of each payment was agreed with HMRC to be £300 and income tax is being deducted from the income element.

Jeremy owns a furnished cottage which he rents to holidaymakers. In tax year 2017-18 it was let for 20 weeks at a weekly rental of £300.

The following expenditure was incurred:

	£	
Insurance (see note)	400	
Water rates and council tax	1,500	
Replacement of cooker	450	(very similar to previous cooker)

Note: An insurance premium of £400 for calendar year 2018 was paid on 1 January 2018. The insurance paid on 1 January 2017 was £360.

You are required:

To calculate the income tax payable by Jeremy for the year 2017-18, assuming that the property income is not assessed on the cash basis and that no elections have been made with respect to the married couple's allowance. *(ACCA)*

A3 Ae and Bee commenced in partnership on 1 July 2015 preparing accounts to 30 June. Cae joined as a partner on 1 July 2017. Profits have always been shared equally. The partnership's trading profits since the commencement of trading have been as follows:

	£
Year ended 30 June 2016	54,000
Year ended 30 June 2017	66,000
Year ended 30 June 2018	87,000

Dee commenced in self-employment on 6 April 2014. She initially prepared accounts to 5 April, but changed her accounting date to 31 July by preparing accounts for the four-month period to 31 July 2016. Dee's trading profits since she commenced trading have been as follows:

	£
Year ended 5 April 2015	35,160
Year ended 5 April 2016	32,880
Four months to 31 July 2016	16,240
Year ended 31 July 2017	54,120

Required:

(a) Calculate the trading income assessments of Ae, Bee and Cae for each of the tax years 2015-16, 2016-17 and 2017-18.

(b) Calculate the amount of trading profits that will have been assessed on Dee for each of the tax years 2015-16, 2016-17 and 2017-18.

(c) State the amount of Dee's unrelieved overlap profits as at 5 April 2018. *(ACCA)*

A4 In May 2017 Bernard, a self-employed plumber, and his son Gerald, a self-employed electrician, purchased 1,000 empty barrels from a Scottish whisky distillery. The barrels were over 100 years old and of no further use to the distillery. Bernard and Gerald sawed the barrels into halves and sold them to several local garden centres for use as ornamental flower tubs. Bernard and Gerald paid £10 per barrel to the distillery and sold a half-barrel for £8. Three-quarters of the barrels were sold by Bernard and Gerald in the summer of 2017 and the remainder in the summer of 2018.

You are required:

To prepare a list of points for consideration prior to writing a report to Bernard and Gerald on the liability to income tax on the profit generated by the venture. *(ACCA)*

A5 You are a trainee chartered certified accountant and your manager has asked for your help regarding a taxpayer who has made trading losses.

Sean has been in self-employment since 2007, but ceased trading on 31 December 2017. He has always prepared accounts to 31 December. His results for the final five years of trading were as follows:

	£
Year to 31 December 2013 - Trading profit	21,300
Year to 31 December 2014 - Trading profit	14,400
Year to 31 December 2015 - Trading profit	18,900
Year to 31 December 2016 - Trading profit	3,700
Year to 31 December 2017 - Trading loss	(23,100)

For each of the tax years 2013-14 to 2017-18, Sean has property business profits of £12,500. Sean has unused overlap profits brought forward of £3,600.

Required:

Identify the loss relief claims that are available to Sean and explain which of the available claims would be the most beneficial. You should clearly state the amount of any reliefs claimed and the rates of income tax saved. However, you are not expected to calculate any income tax liabilities. *Assume for the sake of simplicity that income tax rates, bands and allowances for all years are the same as in 2017-18.* (ACCA)

***A6** Roseanne starts business on 1 July 2017 and prepares accounts for the 16 months to 31 October 2018. The adjusted trading profit for this period is £37,440. Her only other income consists of bank interest of £500 per annum. In April 2018 she receives a notice to submit a tax return for 2017-18 but does not submit this return until 16 March 2019. The return is submitted electronically. Also on 16 March 2019, she pays all of the income tax and Class 4 NICs which fall due for payment on 31 January 2019.

Required:

(a) Calculate Roseanne's liability to income tax and Class 4 NICs for tax year 2017-18 and state the amount (or amounts) that fall due for payment on 31 January 2019. (*Ignore Class 2 NICs*).

(b) Calculate any possible interest and penalties payable by Roseanne, assuming an interest rate of 2.75% per annum.

***A7** Stephen is a UK resident taxpayer with two different sources of income. He works part-time as an IT consultant for a small number of clients, on a project management basis. A separate contract is drawn up for each project, specifying the deadline, expected output and the fee to be paid. Stephen uses his own laptop when necessary, and works from home most of the time.

Stephen also works two days a week (Thursdays and Fridays) for a nearby NHS Trust hospital where his wife (see below) works. He is given an office at the hospital, where he is required to be present between 8am and 6pm to work with the in-house IT team. In addition, the Trust provides 10 fully-paid days off in the year, and allows Stephen to invoice the Trust for the day even when he is sick.

Stephen's wife, Susan, is a pharmacist working in an NHS Trust hospital. Susan was born in 1974 and joined the hospital on 6 July 2017. Her gross pay for 2017-18 was £56,080 and income tax of £16,950 was deducted via PAYE.

Susan is provided with a motor car for both business and private motoring. Details of the cars provided during 2017-18 were as follows:

	Make	**List price**	**Emissions**	**Fuel**
		£	g/km	
6 July 2017 to 5 October 2017	Ford	13,700	91	Petrol
6 October 2017 to 5 April 2018	BMW	30,910	106	Petrol

Her employer paid for all of the running costs of both these cars but Susan contributed £150 per month for private use of the BMW car. She also reimbursed her employer for all of the private fuel used by the Ford motor car (but not the BMW motor car).

On 6 August 2017, the NHS Trust lent Susan £27,000 at an interest rate of 0.5% p.a. Susan repaid £18,000 of the loan on 6 March 2018.

Susan is provided with a mobile telephone and is allowed to use this telephone for both business and private calls. The NHS Trust did not have to pay for the telephone itself but paid call charges of £391 during the year (of which £128 related to private calls).

Susan's other income for 2017-18 consisted of gross pay from her previous employer of £17,130 (PAYE £3,150), dividends received of £7,300 and ISA interest of £240. She is not a Scottish taxpayer.

Required:

(a) Discuss and apply the criteria which may be used to determine whether Stephen should be regarded as employed or self-employed.

(b) Prepare an income tax computation for Susan for tax year 2017-18. If any of her income is not taxable, explain why this is the case. (Assume that the official rate of interest is 2.5%).

(c) Calculate both Employer's and Employee's National Insurance Contributions (NICs) payable in relation to Susan for 2017-18. *(CIPFA)*

***A8** Claud Chapperon is a self-employed wholesale clothing distributor who began trading on 1 July 2009. His summarised accounts for the year to 30 June 2017 are shown below (figures in brackets refer to notes).

	£	£
Sales (2)		400,000
Opening inventory (1)	40,000	
Purchases	224,000	
	264,000	
Closing inventory (1)	32,000	232,000
Gross profit		168,000
Wages and national insurance (3)	55,200	
Rent and rates	29,100	
Repairs and renewals (4)	3,490	
Miscellaneous expenses (5)	665	
Claud's own income tax and NICs	14,940	
Bad debts (6)	820	
Legal expenses (7)	1,060	
Depreciation	850	
Lease rental on Claud's car (8)	8,400	
Loss on sale of office furniture	60	
Gift Aid donations (9)	200	
Transport costs	3,870	
Interest (10)	990	
Running expenses of Claud's car (11)	2,000	
Premium on lease (12)	6,000	
Lighting and heating	1,250	
Sundry expenses (all allowable)	710	
Relocation expenditure (13)	2,395	132,000
Net profit		36,000

Notes:

1. The basis of both the opening and closing inventory valuations was "lower of cost or market value" less a general reserve of 50%.
2. Sales include £500 reimbursed by Claud's family for clothing taken from stock. The reimbursement represented cost price.
3. Included in wages are Claud's drawings of £200 per week and his wife's wages and secondary NICs totalling £16,750. His wife works full-time in the business.
4. The charge for repairs and renewals includes £3,244 for fitting protective covers over the factory windows and doors to prevent burglary.

5. Miscellaneous expenses comprise:

	£
Theft of money by employee	65
Political donation to Green Party	100
Gifts of 100 "Chapperon" calendars	500
	665

6. Bad debts comprise:

	£
Trade debt written off	720
Loan to former employee written off (not made for trade purposes)	250
Reduction in general allowance	(150)
	820

7. Legal expenses comprise:

	£
Defending action re alleged faulty goods	330
Costs re lease of new larger premises	250
Unsuccessful appeal against previous year's income tax assessment	200
Defending Claud in connection with speeding offence	187
Debt collection	93
	1,060

8. Claud's leased car had a retail price of £20,000 and was leased from 1 July 2016 to 30 June 2017. The car has emissions of 139g/km.

9. Gift Aid donations consist of £120 paid to the local children's hospital and £80 paid to Oxfam. Both payments were made on 30 April 2017.

10. Interest is as follows:

	£
Bank overdraft interest (business account)	1,020
Interest on overdue tax	130
Interest credited on NS&I a/c (see note 14)	(160)
	990

11. HM Revenue and Customs has agreed that one-third of Claud's mileage is private. Included in the charge for motor running expenses is £65 for a speeding fine incurred by Claud whilst delivering goods to a customer.

12. The premium was for a lease of six years. The lease began on 1 July 2016.

13. The relocation expenditure was incurred in transferring the business to new and larger premises.

14. Interest recently credited to the NS&I account is as follows:

	£
31 December 2016	160
31 December 2017	70

The following information is also provided:

(i) Capital allowances for the year to 30 June 2017 are £5,680.

(ii) Claud was born in 1961. He made net contributions of £11,800 to a registered pension scheme during 2017-18. His wife was also born in 1961.

(iii) Claud is a Scottish taxpayer.

You are required:

(a) To prepare a profit adjustment statement in respect of the period of account to 30 June 2017, showing the trading income for 2017-18.

(b) To calculate the Class 4 NICs payable by Claud for 2017-18.

(c) To prepare an estimate of Claud's income tax liability for 2017-18. *(ACCA)*

***A9** Iris (who is single) starts a business on 6 July 2017, preparing accounts to 5 April. Her adjusted trading loss for the nine months to 5 April 2018 is £15,000. However, she expects a trading profit of approximately £50,000 in the year to 5 April 2019.

Before starting her own business, Iris was in employment. Her recent employment income has been as follows

2013-14	£37,630
2014-15	£21,590
2015-16	£26,150
2016-17	£34,760
2017-18 (up to 5 July 2017)	£22,190

She has no other income in any year between 2013-14 and 2018-19 inclusive. She is not a Scottish taxpayer.

Required:

(a) Assuming for the sake of simplicity that tax rates, bands and allowances for all years are the same as those for 2017-18, calculate the effective percentage rate of tax relief that Iris would obtain if she claimed each of the following reliefs in relation to her trading loss:

- relief against total income for the year of the loss, *or*
- relief against total income for the previous year, *or*
- early trade losses relief, *or*
- carry-forward relief.

(b) Advise Iris as to the best course of action in relation to her loss.

***A10** Joseph Kent started business on 1 July 2015 as a joiner making conservatories. His tax-adjusted profits (before deduction of capital allowances) were as follows:

	£
Period to 31 December 2015	24,000
Year ended 31 December 2016	37,000
Year ended 31 December 2017	42,000

Capital additions and disposals were as follows:

		£
Additions		
1 July 2015	Plant and machinery	3,500
1 July 2015	Car (emissions 127g/km)	15,000
1 October 2015	Trailer	2,500
1 December 2016	Car (emissions 154g/km)	13,000
1 December 2017	Plant and machinery	2,400
Disposals		
1 December 2016	Car acquired 1/7/15	12,400
1 January 2017	Plant and machinery (at less than cost)	2,000

Private use of both cars has been agreed with HM Revenue and Customs at 20%. No claim is made to treat any of the assets as short-life assets.

Joseph's wife Sephora is a solicitor employed by a practising firm at a salary of £47,000 per annum. The following additional information is provided for 2017-18:

(i) A new petrol-engined car was provided for Sephora's use in August 2016. The list price at that time was £23,500. Of this amount, £4,000 was contributed by Sephora so that a better car could be provided. She was required to pay £25 per month towards the private use of the car but not towards the private fuel, all of which was provided by her employers. The car's emission rating is 132g/km.

(ii) Sephora has received a loan of £90,000 on the matrimonial home from her employers on which she pays interest at 0.25% per annum.

(iii) Sephora made a qualifying donation to the Oxfam charity on 1 July 2017 of £400 under the Gift Aid scheme.

(iv) Both Joseph and Sephora were born in 1979. They are not Scottish taxpayers.

You are required:

(a) To calculate Joseph's trading income for 2015-16 to 2017-18 inclusive.

(b) To calculate Sephora's income tax liability for 2017-18 (assuming an official rate of interest of 2.5% per annum). *(ACCA)*

Part 2

CAPITAL GAINS TAX

Chapter 17

Introduction to capital gains tax

Introduction

The next six chapters of this book are concerned with capital gains tax (CGT), which was introduced in 1965 with the aim of taxing any gains arising on the disposal of capital assets. Capital gains tax has undergone many changes since its inception and the changes that were made between 1965 and 1992 were consolidated into the Taxation of Chargeable Gains Act 1992. This Act has since been amended by subsequent Finance Acts.

Chargeable persons

A CGT liability may arise when a "chargeable person" makes a "chargeable disposal" of a "chargeable asset". The main categories of chargeable person are as follows:

(a) individuals who are resident in the UK

(b) business partners, who are each responsible for their share of the CGT due on the capital gains of a partnership

(c) the trustees of a trust or settlement

(d) the personal representatives of a deceased person.

Husbands and wives are assessed independently for CGT purposes, as are same-sex civil partners. The following are *not* chargeable persons for CGT purposes:

(a) companies and other corporate bodies, which pay corporation tax on their capital gains (not CGT) and so cannot normally incur a CGT liability†

(b) various other organisations including registered charities, community amateur sports clubs, local authorities, health service bodies, registered pension schemes and approved scientific research associations, all of which are generally exempt from CGT (subject to certain restrictions).

† *Although companies are generally not chargeable to CGT, a liability to CGT may in fact arise in relation to the disposal by a company of certain high-value residential property.*

Chargeable assets

All assets are regarded as chargeable assets except for those which are specifically exempted from CGT. The main exemptions are as follows:

(a) a taxpayer's principal private residence (see Chapter 21)

(b) motor cars, including vintage and veteran cars (but not personalised car registration plates); vehicles which are not covered by this exemption, such as vans, lorries and motor cycles, will generally fall within the scope of (d) below.

(c) items of tangible, movable property (referred to as "chattels") which are disposed of for £6,000 or less (see Chapter 19)

(d) chattels with a predictable useful life of 50 years or less ("wasting chattels") unless used in business and eligible for capital allowances (see Chapter 19)

(e) gilt-edged securities and qualifying corporate bonds (see Chapter 20)

(f) National Savings Certificates and Premium Bonds

(g) foreign currency (if acquired for private use)

(h) winnings from pools, lotteries, betting etc.

(i) decorations for valour (unless acquired by purchase)

(j) damages or compensation received for personal or professional injury

(k) life assurance policies (unless purchased from a third party)

(l) Individual Savings Accounts (ISAs) and Child Trust Funds (see Chapter 6)

(m) subject to conditions, shares in a Venture Capital Trust (see Chapter 6)

(n) up to £50,000 worth of shares acquired by an employee as the result of adopting "employee shareholder" status (see Chapter 7), subject to a lifetime limit of £100,000 on the amount of tax-exempt gains which may arise in relation to an employee shareholder agreement entered into after 16 March 2016.†

It is important to realise that neither a chargeable gain nor an allowable loss can arise on the disposal of an asset that is not a chargeable asset. This means that any gains made on the disposal of such assets are not taxable but it also means that any losses which arise will not usually attract tax relief.

However, losses arising on the disposal of Enterprise Investment Scheme (EIS) or SEIS investments, or on the disposal of investments which qualify for Social Investment Tax Relief (SITR) are eligible for tax relief even though gains on such disposals are not generally taxable (see Chapter 6).

† *This CGT exemption applies only to shares acquired under an employee shareholder agreement which was entered into before 1 December 2016.*

Chargeable disposals

The main and most obvious instance of a chargeable disposal occurs when a chargeable asset is sold. However, the sale of an asset in the course of trade (i.e. the sale of trading stock or inventory) does *not* constitute a chargeable disposal since any gain arising on such a sale is taxed as a trading profit (see Chapter 9).

Before CGT was introduced in 1965 there was a great incentive for taxpayers to show that the gain arising on the sale of an asset was a capital gain (not taxable) rather than a trading profit (taxable). This incentive diminished with the introduction of CGT. But it is still important to distinguish between capital gains and trading profits since the rules of computation for capital gains and trading profits are different, as are the rates of CGT and income tax (see later in this chapter).

As well as the sale of a chargeable asset, the following are also chargeable disposals:

(a) the sale of *part* of a chargeable asset

(b) the gift of all or part of a chargeable asset

(c) the loss or destruction of a chargeable asset

(d) the receipt of a capital sum derived from a chargeable asset (e.g. compensation received from an insurance company if an asset is damaged).

With regard to gifts, it is important to realise that CGT is basically a tax on the increase in value of an asset whilst owned by the taxpayer. This increase in value is chargeable to tax even if the taxpayer gives the asset away and receives nothing in return.

In general, the date on which a chargeable disposal is deemed to occur is the date on which ownership of the asset changes hands, regardless of the date on which any payment is made.

Non-chargeable disposals

The following types of disposal are *not* chargeable disposals and therefore any gains or losses arising on such disposals are exempt from CGT:

(a) gifts to charities and certain other bodies (e.g. art galleries and museums) and gifts of pre-eminent property to the nation (see Chapter 4)

(b) disposals caused by the death of the taxpayer.

Disposals between a husband and wife (or civil partners) who live together at any time during the tax year in which the disposal occurs *are* chargeable disposals. However, such disposals are deemed to occur at a disposal value such that neither a chargeable gain nor an allowable loss arises on the disposal (see Chapter 18). A similar treatment applies to:

(a) gifts of national heritage property, subject to certain undertakings being received by HMRC (e.g. with regard to reasonable public access)

(b) disposals of a company's shares which result in a controlling interest in that company being held by an employee ownership trust.

Basis of assessment

A person's CGT liability for a tax year is based upon the chargeable disposals made by that person during the tax year. For example, the 2017-18 liability is based upon chargeable disposals made between 6 April 2017 and 5 April 2018 inclusive. No liability to CGT arises until an asset is disposed of, so the mere fact that an asset has appreciated in value will not of itself trigger a CGT liability. The amount of a person's "taxable gains" for a tax year (i.e. the amount on which CGT is payable) is calculated as follows:

(a) The chargeable gain or allowable loss arising on each disposal made during the tax year is calculated separately (see subsequent chapters of this book).

(b) If total gains exceed total losses, the losses are subtracted from the gains to give the taxpayer's "net gains" for the year. If total losses exceed total gains, the gains are subtracted from the losses to give the "net losses" for the year.

(c) If there are net gains for the year, these are reduced first by any unrelieved losses brought forward from previous tax years or by any losses carried back on the death of the taxpayer (see later in this chapter).

(d) Net gains are then further reduced by the amount of the "annual exemption" for the year (£11,300 for 2017-18). The amount of any net gains which remain after the annual exemption has been deducted is the "taxable gains" figure for the year. If net gains are too low to allow the whole of the annual exemption to be deducted, taxable gains for the year are £nil and the balance of the annual exemption is lost.

(e) If there are net losses for the year, taxable gains for that year are £nil and the whole of the annual exemption is lost. The net losses may then be carried forward for relief in future years, as described later in this chapter.

Husbands, wives and civil partners are each entitled to the full annual exemption. This exemption is also available to the trustees of a settlement established for the benefit of a disabled person. For trustees of other settlements the annual exemption is lower (£5,650 for 2017-18). The personal representatives of a deceased person are entitled to the full annual exemption for the year of death and for the following two years.

EXAMPLE 1

Four taxpayers each make three chargeable disposals during 2017-18. Compute their taxable gains for the year (assuming that there are no unrelieved losses brought forward or carried back) if these disposals give rise to the following gains and losses:

(a) Taxpayer A has gains of £3,500, £4,100 and £5,950.

(b) Taxpayer B has gains of £5,700, £6,840 and a loss of £350.

(c) Taxpayer C has gains of £950 and £9,530 and a loss of £2,050.

(d) Taxpayer D has a gain of £8,950 and losses of £9,500 and £800.

Solution

(a) Total gains are £13,550 and there are no losses. Net gains are £13,550. Subtracting the annual exemption of £11,300 gives taxable gains for the year of £2,250.

(b) Total gains are £12,540. Total losses are £350 so net gains are £12,190. Subtracting the annual exemption of £11,300 gives taxable gains for the year of £890.

(c) Total gains are £10,480 and total losses are £2,050. Net gains are £8,430. This is less than the annual exemption of £11,300, so taxable gains for the year are £nil. The unused part of the annual exemption (£2,870) is lost.

(d) Total gains are £8,950 and total losses are £10,300. Net losses are £1,350. Taxable gains for the year are £nil and the whole of the annual exemption is lost.

Rates of CGT

For tax year 2017-18, there are two main rates of CGT. These are the *standard rate* of 10% and the *higher rate* of 20%. But the tax rates which apply to gains arising on the disposal of residential property (to the extent that these gains are not eligible for principal private residence relief) are 18% and 28% (see Chapter 21). Furthermore, a special rate of 10% applies to gains which qualify for "entrepreneurs' relief" (ER). In general terms, gains may qualify for ER if they arise on the disposal of a business (see Chapter 22).

These rates of tax are applied to the taxable gains which remain after capital losses and the annual exemption have been deducted. For individuals, the process is as follows:

(a) Gains which qualify for ER are always taxed at the ER rate of 10%.

(b) If the individual's taxable income for the year (see Chapter 2) exceeds the basic rate limit, gains which do not qualify for ER are taxed at the higher rate of 20% (or 28% in the case of residential property gains).

(c) If taxable income does not exceed the basic rate limit, any unused part of the basic rate band is first absorbed by gains which qualify for ER. Gains which do not qualify for ER are then normally taxed at the lower rate of 10% to the extent that they do not exceed any remaining part of the basic rate band and at 20% otherwise. But these rates are increased to 18% and 28% in the case of residential property gains.

The basic rate limit† for 2017-18 is usually £33,500 (see Chapter 2) but this may be increased for Gift Aid donations (Chapter 4) or pension contributions (Chapter 14).

(d) In general, capital losses and the annual exemption may be deducted from capital gains in such a way that the CGT liability is minimised. Similarly, any unused part of the basic rate band (after ER gains have been deducted) may be allocated between residential property gains and other gains in the most beneficial way.

The rate of CGT applicable to trustees and personal representatives is 10% for gains which qualify for ER, 28% for residential property gains and 20% for all other gains.

† *For this purpose, a Scottish taxpayer is treated as if he or she were not a Scottish taxpayer, so the applicable basic rate limit is the basic rate limit which applies in the remainder of the UK.*

EXAMPLE 2

Calculate the amount of CGT payable for 2017-18 by each of the following individuals. In each case, "taxable income" comprises the individual's total income, less reliefs which may be deducted from total income and less the personal allowance (see Chapter 2).

	Name	*Taxable income*	*ER gains*	*Residential prop. gains*	*Other gains*	*Allowable losses*
		£	£	£	£	£
(a)	A	71,000	nil	nil	12,500	nil
(b)	B	71,000	12,500	nil	nil	nil
(c)	C	47,500	32,800	15,700	nil	nil
(d)	D	52,700	27,600	nil	4,900	1,000
(e)	E	30,790	nil	11,700	nil	nil
(f)	F	31,700	nil	nil	20,300	400
(g)	G	23,100	4,000	17,000	8,500	2,200

Assume in each case that there are no Gift Aid donations or pension contributions.

Solution

(a) Taxable income exceeds the basic rate limit, so the "other" gains are taxed at 20%. CGT payable is (£12,500 – £11,300) x 20% = £240.

(b) Taxable income is not relevant since gains which qualify for ER are always taxed at 10%. CGT payable is (£12,500 – £11,300) x 10% = £120.

(c) The tax liability is minimised if the annual exemption is set against the residential property gains, since these are taxed at higher rates than gains which qualify for ER. Taxable income exceeds the basic rate limit, so CGT payable is (£32,800 x 10%) + ((£15,700 – £11,300) x 28%) = £4,512.

(d) To minimise the tax liability, the allowable losses of £1,000 are set against the "other" gains of £4,900. Similarly, the annual exemption is set first against these gains. The remaining £7,400 of the exemption must then be set against the gains which qualify for ER. CGT payable is (£27,600 – £7,400) x 10% = £2,020.

(e) After deducting the annual exemption, taxable gains are £400 and these consist of residential property gains. The unused part of the basic rate band is £2,710 (£33,500 – £30,790). This exceeds the taxable gains so CGT payable is (£400 x 18%) = £72.

(f) Taxable gains are £8,600 (£20,300 – £400 – £11,300) and these consists of "other" gains. The unused part of the basic rate band is £1,800 (£33,500 – £31,700). So the CGT payable is (£1,800 x 10%) + (£6,800 x 20%) = £1,540.

(g) The tax liability is minimised if the losses of £2,200 and the annual exemption of £11,300 are both set against the residential property gains, leaving £3,500 of these gains remaining (£17,000 – £2,200 – £11,300). The unused part of the basic rate band is £10,400 (£33,500 – £23,100) and ER gains absorb £4,000 of this.

If the basic rate band is allocated next to the residential property gains, CGT payable is (£4,000 x 10%) + (£3,500 x 18%) + (£2,900 x 10%) + (£5,600 x 20%) = £2,440.

If the basic rate band is allocated next to the "other" gains instead, CGT payable is (£4,000 x 10%) + (£6,400 x 10%) + (£2,100 x 20%) + (£3,500 x 28%) = £2,440.

The tax liability is unaffected by the allocation of the basic rate band and this will generally be the case in 2017-18, since the gap between the 10% and 20% rates is the same as the gap between the 18% and 28% rates.

Relief for capital losses

If a taxpayer has net losses for a year, the CGT liability for that year is £nil and the annual exemption is lost. The amount of the net losses may then be carried forward without time limit and set against the net gains of future years.

Losses carried forward must be offset against the first available net gains, but are offset only to the extent that those net gains exceed the annual exemption for the year in which they arise, so preventing the annual exemption from being wasted. Any losses remaining unrelieved are carried forward again to subsequent years. This method of preserving the annual exemption applies *only* to losses brought forward from a previous year. It is *not* possible to preserve the annual exemption by restricting the set-off of current year losses.

Since married couples and same-sex civil partners are taxed independently, the losses of one spouse (or partner) cannot be offset against the gains of the other spouse (or partner).

EXAMPLE 3

Three taxpayers each have £3,000 of capital losses brought forward. Calculate their taxable gains for 2017-18 if their total gains and losses for the year are as follows:

(a) Taxpayer A has gains of £8,300 and losses of £1,300.

(b) Taxpayer B has gains of £13,700 and losses of £700.

(c) Taxpayer C has gains of £17,400 and losses of £1,200.

Solution

(a) Net gains for the year are £7,000. This is less than the annual exemption of £11,300 so taxable gains for the year are £nil and the balance of the annual exemption is lost. There is no scope for relieving losses brought forward, so the entire £3,000 is carried forward to 2018-19.

(b) Net gains for the year are £13,000. This exceeds the annual exemption by £1,700 so £1,700 of the losses brought forward are relieved in 2017-18, giving taxable gains for the year of £nil. The remaining £1,300 of the losses are unrelieved and are therefore carried forward to 2018-19.

(c) Net gains for the year are £16,200. This exceeds the annual exemption by £4,900 so the entire £3,000 of losses brought forward are relieved in 2017-18, giving taxable gains for the year of £1,900. There are no unrelieved losses to carry forward.

Anti-avoidance rules relating to capital losses

TCGA 1992 contains the following anti-avoidance rules designed to prevent taxpayers from taking unfair advantage of the reliefs available in relation to capital losses:

(a) Capital losses incurred on a disposal to a connected person can be offset only against gains made on disposals to the *same person*, in the same or subsequent tax years. A taxpayer is deemed to be connected with a number of persons for CGT purposes, mainly relatives and business associates (see Chapter 18).

(b) A capital loss is not an allowable loss if it arises as a result of arrangements made by the taxpayer and a main purpose of those arrangements is to gain a tax advantage by creating an artificial capital loss.

Losses in the year of death

As stated earlier, disposals caused by the death of a taxpayer are exempt from CGT, although such disposals may give rise to an inheritance tax liability. But disposals made in the year of death (i.e. from 6 April up to the date of death) are *not* exempt from CGT and are taxed in the usual way, with a full annual exemption given for the year.

If a taxpayer suffers net losses in the year of death, such losses cannot (for obvious reasons) be carried forward. However, net losses incurred in the year of death may instead be carried back and set off against the net gains of the previous three years (most recent years first). As is the case with losses carried forward, losses carried back are set against a year's net gains only to the extent that those net gains exceed the annual exemption for the year in which they arise.

EXAMPLE 4

Sarah dies on 16 December 2017, having made net capital losses of £7,300 between 6 April 2017 and the date of her death. Her net gains in the previous three years (and the annual exemption for each of those years) were as follows:

	Net gains	*Annual exemption*
	£	£
2014-15	12,150	11.000
2015-16	3,300	11,100
2016-17	15,450	11,100

Calculate her taxable gains for 2014-15 to 2017-18 inclusive.

Solution

Since losses in the year of death are carried back to the most recent year first, it is easier to begin with the year of death and then work backwards.

(a) In 2017-18, Sarah has net losses. Her taxable gains for the year are therefore £nil and the annual exemption (available in full) is lost. The net losses of £7,300 may be carried back to 2016-17, 2015-16 and 2014-15, in that order.

(b) In 2016-17, Sarah's net gains of £15,450 exceed the annual exemption by £4,350 so £4,350 of the losses carried back are relieved in 2016-17, giving taxable gains for the year of £nil. The remaining £2,950 of the losses are carried back to 2015-16.

(c) In 2015-16, Sarah's net gains of £3,300 are less than the annual exemption of £11,100. Therefore taxable gains for the year are £nil and the balance of the annual exemption is lost. There is no scope for relieving losses carried back, so the £2,950 is now carried back to 2014-15.

(d) In 2014-15, Sarah's net gains of £12,150 exceed the annual exemption by £1,150 so £1,150 of the losses carried back are relieved in 2014-15, giving taxable gains for the year of £nil. The remaining £1,800 of the losses incurred in the year of death cannot be carried back any further and therefore cannot be relieved in any way.

Assuming that self assessments have already been made for 2014-15 and 2016-17, it will be necessary to revise these assessments to take into account the relief for losses carried back and to refund any CGT already paid for those years.

Relief for trading losses

If a taxpayer has claimed that a trading loss should be set against his or her total income for a tax year (or if no such claim can be made because total income for that year is zero) the taxpayer may further claim that any unrelieved part of the trading loss should be set against the capital gains of that year (see Chapter 12). If such a claim is made, the amount of the claim must be for the *lower* of the following two amounts:

(a) the amount of the unrelieved trading loss which is available for relief

(b) the "maximum amount", which is the amount of the taxable gains, *disregarding the annual exemption*, that would have been charged to tax for the year if the claim had not been made.

It is important to realise that the "maximum amount" is calculated as if the annual exemption simply did not exist. Not only is the annual exemption itself ignored in this calculation but so is the fact that capital losses brought forward might be restricted so as to preserve the exemption.

A trading loss which is set against capital gains is treated as a capital loss incurred in the year of the claim and is therefore relieved *before* giving relief for capital losses brought forward.

EXAMPLE 5

(a) Richard has net gains for 2017-18 of £17,500 and capital losses brought forward of £3,300. Calculate his taxable gains for 2017-18.

(b) Richard has unrelieved trading losses (eligible for relief against his capital gains in 2017-18) of £27,500. Re-calculate his taxable gains for 2017-18 if he claims that these losses should (as far as possible) be set against his capital gains.

(c) Now calculate the taxable gains for 2017-18 if the capital losses brought forward are £10,300 instead of £3,300.

Solution

(a) Without a trading losses claim for 2017-18, taxable gains for the year will be:

	£
Net gains	17,500
Less: Capital losses b/f	3,300
	14,200
Less: Annual exemption	11,300
Taxable gains	2,900

There will be no unrelieved capital losses to carry forward.

(b) A trading losses claim would have to be for the lower of:

(i) the unrelieved trading loss (£27,500)

(ii) the taxable gains, *disregarding the annual exemption*, that would be charged to tax if a trading losses claim were not made (£14,200).

Therefore the claim would be for £14,200. This would be relieved in priority to capital losses brought forward. Taxable gains for the year would be:

	£
Net gains	17,500
Less: Trading losses	14,200
	3,300
Less: Annual exemption (restricted)	3,300
Taxable gains	nil

The remainder of the annual exemption (£8,000) would be lost. There would be no scope for relieving any of the capital losses brought forward, so the entire £3,300 would be carried forward to 2018-19. This claim would seem to be wasteful, since trading losses of £14,200 are sacrificed in order to reduce taxable gains by £2,900 and preserve capital losses of £3,300 (a total of £6,200).

(c) Without a trading losses claim, taxable gains would be calculated as follows:

	£
Net gains	17,500
Less: Capital losses b/f (restricted)	6,200
	11,300
Less: Annual exemption	11,300
Taxable gains	nil

There would be unrelieved capital losses of £4,100 carried forward. The maximum amount of a trading loss claim is £7,200 (£17,500 – £10,300) so the claim would have to be for £7,200 and taxable gains would then be:

	£
Net gains	17,500
Less: Trading losses	7,200
	10,300
Less: Annual exemption (restricted)	10,300
Taxable gains	nil

The remainder of the annual exemption (£1,000) would be lost and the capital losses of £10,300 would be carried forward to 2018-19 in their entirety. The effect of the claim would be to preserve capital losses of £6,200 at the expense of sacrificing trading losses of £7,200. This might be worthwhile if Richard believes that he will have more chance of relieving capital losses than trading losses in future years.

Administration of CGT

The tax administration system which was described in Chapter 1 applies to CGT as well as to income tax. Note that:

(a) Taxpayers are normally not required to fill in the capital gains tax pages of their tax returns if both of the following conditions are satisfied:

   (i) total disposal proceeds for the year do not exceed four times the amount of the annual exemption (£45,200 for 2017-18)

   (ii) total chargeable gains for the year do not exceed the amount of the annual exemption (£11,300 for 2017-18).

   For this purpose, the term "total chargeable gains" means the total chargeable gains for the year *before* deduction of either current year losses or losses brought forward from previous years.

(b) Acquisitions of chargeable assets do not need to be entered on the tax return.

(c) A capital loss is not an allowable loss unless its amount is quantified and notified to HMRC. If the taxpayer submits a tax return for the year in which a loss is incurred, then notification must be made in that return. Otherwise, notification may be made by sending a separate notice to HMRC. Capital losses are not allowed unless they are notified to HMRC within four years of the end of the tax year concerned.

Payment of CGT

CGT is normally payable on 31 January following the end of the tax year to which the tax relates[†]. For instance, the date on which the 2017-18 CGT liability is normally payable is 31 January 2019. Payments on account of the CGT liability are *not* required.

If the proceeds of a disposal are received by the taxpayer in instalments over a period of more than 18 months, the taxpayer may make a claim for the CGT due in relation to the disposal to be payable over the period of the instalments or over an eight-year period, whichever is the shorter.

The regime of interest and penalties which was described in Chapter 15 applies to both CGT and income tax.

[†] *As from April 2019, any CGT which is due on the disposal of a residential property will be payable within 30 days of completion.*

Summary

- A liability to CGT may arise when a chargeable person makes a chargeable disposal of a chargeable asset. Individuals who are resident in the UK are chargeable persons. Companies are generally not chargeable persons.
- All assets are chargeable assets unless specifically exempted.
- A chargeable disposal occurs when all or part of a chargeable asset is sold (other than in the course of trade) or is given away, lost or destroyed.
- An individual's CGT liability for a tax year is based upon the chargeable disposals made by that individual during the year. For 2017-18, the first £11,300 of net gains are exempt from CGT.
- CGT for 2017-18 is generally payable at the standard rate of 10% or the higher rate of 20%. But gains on the disposal of residential property are taxed at 18% or 28% and gains which qualify for entrepreneurs' relief are always taxed at 10%.
- Net capital losses are carried forward and set against the net gains of subsequent years. Net losses incurred in the year of death may be carried back for three years.
- In certain circumstances, trading losses may be set against capital gains.
- CGT is normally payable on 31 January following the end of the tax year.

Exercises

17.1 Which of the following disposals might give rise to a CGT liability?

(a) the sale of antique furniture by a UK company

(b) the gift of shares from husband to wife (assuming that the couple live together)

(c) the gift of an oil painting to a charity

(d) the sale of an oil painting by a charity

(e) the sale of an oil painting by an art dealer

(f) the sale of an office building by a partnership.

17.2 Which of the following are chargeable assets for CGT purposes?

(a) shares in a limited company

(b) gilt-edged securities

(c) an antique table worth £20,000

(d) an antique chair worth £5,000

(e) a taxpayer's home

(f) a vintage Bentley.

17.3 An individual has capital losses of £2,500 in tax year 2017-18. There are no unrelieved losses brought forward from previous years. Compute the individual's taxable gains for 2017-18 if capital gains for the year are as follows:

either (a) £nil

or (b) £1,500

or (c) £8,950

or (d) £15,250.

17.4 In 2017-18, an individual has capital gains of £263,000 and allowable losses of £12,000. He has no unrelieved capital losses brought forward from previous years. His taxable income for 2017-18 (after deduction of the personal allowance) is £26,400 and he has made no Gift Aid donations or pension contributions. Calculate his CGT liability for the year, assuming that the gains of £263,000 comprise *either*:

(a) a single gain of £263,000 which qualifies for entrepreneurs' relief (ER), *or*

(b) a single non-ER gain of £263,000 arising on the sale of shares, *or*

(c) a single non-ER gain of £263,000 arising on the sale of residential property, *or*

(d) an ER gain of £205,700 and a non-ER gain of £57,300 on the sale of shares, *or*

(e) an ER gain of £205,700 and a non-ER gain of £57,300 on residential property.

17.5 An individual has capital losses brought forward from previous years amounting to £4,800. Compute the individual's taxable gains for 2017-18 if total gains and losses for the year are as follows:

either (a) gains £10,400, losses £1,000

or (b) gains £12,200, losses £300

or (c) gains £17,300, losses £nil.

17.6 John dies on 3 March 2018. Between 6 April 2017 and 3 March 2018, he has capital gains of £1,200 and capital losses of £15,400. His net gains in recent tax years (and the annual exemption for each year) have been as follows:

	Net gains	*Annual exemption*
	£	£
2013-14	52,700	10,900
2014-15	17,500	11,000
2015-16	13,900	11,100
2016-17	3,550	11,100

Explain how (and to what extent) John's net losses in 2017-18 will be relieved.

17.7 On what date is CGT for 2017-18 normally due for payment?

***17.8** Rosemary's capital gains and losses in recent years (and the annual exemption for each year) have been as follows:

	Gains	*Losses*	*Annual exemption*
	£	£	£
2014-15	6,500	12,700	11,000
2015-16	10,400	2,350	11,100
2016-17	13,900	nil	11,100
2017-18	20,200	7,300	11,300

There were no unrelieved losses to bring forward from 2013-14 or earlier. Compute her taxable gains for tax years 2014-15 to 2017-18 inclusive.

***17.9** In 2017-18, Ahmed has capital gains of £130,000 and allowable losses of £24,000. He also has capital losses brought forward of £4,700.

Ahmed's taxable income for 2017-18 (after deduction of the personal allowance) is £18,500. He makes Gift Aid donations of £8,000 during the year. Compute his CGT liability for the year assuming that his gains of £130,000 comprise *either*:

(a) a gain of £120,000 which qualifies for entrepreneurs' relief (ER) and a non-ER gain of £10,000 on the disposal of chattels, *or*

(b) an ER gain of £10,000 and a non-ER gain of £120,000 arising on the disposal of residential property, *or*

(c) an ER gain of £7,500, a non-ER gain of £70,000 on the disposal of residential property and a non-ER gain of £52,500 on the disposal of shares.

***17.10** Melissa is a sole trader. Her capital gains and capital losses for 2017-18 are £26,600 and £1,000 respectively. She also has capital losses brought forward from 2016-17 of £13,200 and unrelieved trading losses of £18,500 which are eligible for relief against capital gains in 2017-18.

Calculate Melissa's taxable gains for 2017-18, assuming that:

(a) a claim to relieve trading losses against capital gains is not made

(b) a claim to relieve trading losses against capital gains is made.

Chapter 18

Computation of gains and losses

Introduction

The computation of the gain arising on the disposal of a chargeable asset is basically a matter of subtracting the acquisition cost of the asset from its disposal value. However, it may be necessary to adjust the gain to take account of a number of other costs incurred by the taxpayer and the calculation becomes more complex if only part of the asset has been disposed of. Also, a different method of computation applies if the asset was acquired on or before 31 March 1982.

The purpose of this chapter is to explain the basic method of computation and to show how this method is modified for disposals of older assets.

Layout of a CGT computation

The computation of the chargeable gain or allowable loss arising on a chargeable disposal occurring during tax year 2017-18 is laid out as follows:

	£	£
Disposal value		xxx
Less: Incidental costs of disposal		xxx
		xxx
Less: *Allowable expenditure*:		
Acquisition cost of asset	xxx	
Incidental costs of acquisition	xxx	
Enhancement expenditure	xxx	
Cost of defending the owner's title to the asset	xxx	
Valuation fees	xxx	xxx
Chargeable gain or allowable loss		xxx

Each of the terms used in this layout is explained below.

Disposal value

If a disposal consists of the sale of an asset, disposal value is generally taken to be the proceeds of the sale. But if a sale does not constitute a bargain made at arm's length, the sale proceeds are ignored and disposal value is taken to be the market value of the asset on the date of the sale. This rule applies particularly to transactions between "connected persons". For CGT purposes, a taxpayer is connected to his or her:

(a) spouse (husband, wife or civil partner)
(b) relatives (brothers, sisters, ancestors, direct descendants) and their spouses
(c) spouse's relatives and their spouses
(d) business partners and their spouses and relatives.

Market value is also used as disposal value if a disposal takes the form of a gift. But disposals between spouses who live together are deemed to occur at a disposal value such that neither a gain nor a loss arises (see Chapter 17). This rule takes precedence over the usual rules concerning sales to connected persons and gifts.

In general, the market value of an asset is the amount it would fetch if sold on the open market. Listed ("quoted") shares and securities are valued for CGT purposes as follows:

(a) on a day that the Stock Exchange is open, the lower of the two closing prices quoted for the shares on that day, plus one-half of the difference between those two prices
(b) on a day that the Stock Exchange is closed, at the value calculated by rule (a) for the latest previous day on which it was open.

Incidental costs of disposal include legal fees, auctioneers' fees, advertising costs etc.

Allowable expenditure

The following expenditure may be set against disposal value when calculating the gain or loss arising on a disposal:

(a) the acquisition cost of the asset (or its market value on the date of acquisition if it was acquired by gift or otherwise than by way of a bargain made at arm's length)
(b) incidental costs of acquisition (e.g. legal fees)
(c) "enhancement expenditure", which is expenditure on making improvements to the asset, so long as that expenditure is still reflected in the state of the asset at the time of disposal (but the costs of mere repairs and maintenance are disallowed)
(d) costs incurred in defending the owner's title to the asset (generally legal costs)
(e) valuation fees necessarily incurred for CGT purposes.

If an asset is acquired as the result of a disposal between spouses who live together, the deemed acquisition cost for the spouse receiving the asset is equal to the deemed disposal value for the spouse who makes the disposal (see above).

EXAMPLE 1

(a) A chargeable asset was bought in June 2013 for £41,200 and sold in August 2017 for £73,350. Compute the chargeable gain.

(b) A chargeable asset was bought for £15,000 in August 2008. Legal costs of £500 were incurred when the asset was acquired. The owner of the asset incurred enhancement expenditure of £2,000 in May 2009 and £3,000 in June 2014. The asset was sold in July 2017 for £28,000. Legal costs of £700 were incurred on the sale. Compute the chargeable gain.

(c) A taxpayer bought a chargeable asset for £40,000 in February 2010. The asset was sold for £30,000 in October 2017. Compute the chargeable gain or allowable loss if:

   (i) the asset was sold in an arm's length transaction

   (ii) the asset was sold to the taxpayer's brother and had a market value of £45,000 on the date of the sale

   (iii) the asset was sold to the taxpayer's wife and had a market value of £45,000 on the date of the sale.

Solution

(a) The chargeable gain is (£73,350 – £41,200) = £32,150.

(b)

	£	£
Sale proceeds		28,000
Less: Incidental costs of disposal		700
		27,300
Less: Acquisition cost	15,000	
Incidental costs of acquisition	500	
Enhancement expenditure (£2,000 + £3,000)	5,000	20,500
Chargeable gain		6,800

(c)

	(i) £	(ii) £	(iii) £
Disposal value	30,000	45,000	40,000
Less: Acquisition cost	40,000	40,000	40,000
Chargeable gain/(allowable loss)	(10,000)	5,000	-

In case (iii), disposal value is set to £40,000 so as to ensure that neither a gain nor a loss occurs on this disposal to the taxpayer's spouse.

Part disposals

If only *part* of a chargeable asset is disposed of, only part of its cost can be allowed when computing the gain or loss. The allowable part cost is the full cost of the asset multiplied by the following fraction:

$$\frac{A}{A+B}$$

where: A is the value of the part disposed of (i.e. the disposal value), and

B is the value of the part remaining in the taxpayer's ownership.

This part disposal fraction applies not only to the acquisition cost of the asset but also to any other items of allowable expenditure which relate to the whole asset. But any item of expenditure which relates only to the part of the asset which has been disposed of should be allowed in full.

EXAMPLE 2

Peter buys a chargeable asset for £26,000 in May 2008. He sells a one-quarter interest in the asset for £12,000 in August 2017, incurring incidental costs of disposal of £500. The value of the other three-quarters interest in the asset in August 2017 is £40,000. Calculate the chargeable gain.

Solution

	£
Sale proceeds	12,000
Less: Incidental costs of disposal	500
	11,500
Less: Part cost:	
$\frac{£12,000}{£12,000 + £40,000} \times £26,000$	6,000
Chargeable gain	5,500

Notes:

(i) The fact that Peter has sold a one-quarter interest in the asset is irrelevant. What is relevant is that he has sold £12,000 worth out of an asset currently worth £52,000, as indicated by the part disposal fraction.

(ii) If Peter disposes of the remaining three-quarters of the asset at some future time, the remaining £20,000 of the cost (£26,000 – £6,000) will then be allowable.

(iii) The incidental costs of disposal are allowed in full since these relate solely to the part of the asset which has been disposed of.

Small part disposals of land

An exception to the usual part disposal rules occurs when a taxpayer makes a small part disposal of land. A part disposal of land is "small" if the land is freehold, or held on a lease with more than 50 years left to run, and the following conditions are met:

(a) If the disposal is caused by a compulsory purchase order, the disposal proceeds must not exceed 5% of the value of the whole piece of land. However, it is the practice of HM Revenue and Customs to treat disposal proceeds of £3,000 or less as small for this purpose, regardless of whether or not the 5% test is satisfied.

(b) If the disposal is not caused by a compulsory purchase order, the disposal proceeds must not exceed 20% of the value of the whole piece of land and the total proceeds of all disposals of land in the year of assessment (excluding small disposals caused by compulsory purchases) must not exceed £20,000.

A taxpayer who makes a small part disposal of land which satisfies these conditions may claim that the disposal should not be treated as a chargeable disposal but that the proceeds of the disposal should instead be subtracted from the acquisition cost of the land. This claim has the following consequences:

(a) No gain or loss arises on the small part disposal.

(b) Since the acquisition cost of the land is reduced, the gain arising on a subsequent disposal of the remainder of the land is automatically increased.

In effect, the gain arising on the small part disposal is deferred until the remainder of the land is disposed of. Fairly obviously, the taxpayer should not make such a claim if the gain arising on the small part disposal would be covered by the annual exemption for the year.

Note that these rules apply only to small part disposals of *land*, whereas the more general part disposal rules explained earlier in this chapter apply to all types of chargeable asset.

EXAMPLE 3

In July 2008, Malcolm bought a piece of land for £40,000. In June 2013 he sold part of the land for £11,000. This disposal was not caused by a compulsory purchase and was his only disposal of land in 2013-14. The value of the remainder of the land in June 2013 was £50,000. Malcolm had substantial capital gains in 2013-14, sufficient to absorb his annual exemption for the year, and therefore decided to make a small part disposal claim.

Calculate the chargeable gain arising in January 2018 when Malcolm sells the remainder of the land for £60,000.

Solution

The small part disposal claim in 2013-14 was valid since the total value of the land immediately prior to the disposal was £61,000 and the disposal raised £11,000 which is less than 20% of £61,000. Furthermore, the proceeds of all land disposals in the year did not exceed £20,000.

No gain or loss arises on the June 2013 disposal but the sale proceeds of £11,000 are subtracted from the acquisition cost of the land. The gain on the January 2018 disposal is therefore as follows:

	£
Sale proceeds	60,000
Less: Reduced acquisition cost (£40,000 – £11,000)	29,000
Chargeable gain	31,000

The effect of Malcolm's part disposal claim is that the whole of the gain arising on the two disposals taken together (£11,000 + £60,000 – £40,000 = £31,000) is charged to tax in tax year 2017-18, even though the first disposal took place in 2013-14.

Assets with negligible value

If the value of a chargeable asset has become negligible, the owner of the asset may make a "negligible value" claim. If this claim is accepted, the asset is treated as if it had been disposed of at its current, negligible value (giving rise to an allowable loss) and then immediately re-acquired at that value.

EXAMPLE 4

In September 2011, Gloria acquired 1,000 ordinary shares in a listed company for £7,000. Trading in the shares was suspended in December 2017 and Gloria claimed that the shares then had a negligible value of only 10p per share. This claim was accepted by HMRC. Compute the allowable loss.

Solution

	£
Deemed disposal value (1,000 x 10p)	100
Less: Cost	7,000
Allowable loss	(6,900)

If Gloria succeeds in selling the shares at some time in the future, their deemed acquisition cost for CGT purposes will be £100.

Assets held on 31 March 1982

CGT was originally introduced in 1965 and applied to disposals made on or after 6 April 1965, which was the "base date" for CGT. Gains which accrued before 6 April 1965 were not taxable. Therefore, if an asset was acquired before 6 April 1965 and disposed of after that date, only the part of the gain accruing after 6 April 1965 was taxable.

However, the CGT base date has since been changed to 31 March 1982. Therefore, if an asset which was held on 31 March 1982 is now disposed of, only the part of the gain accruing since 31 March 1982 is taxable. The calculation of the taxable part of the gain is achieved by means of a technique known as "rebasing" whereby the market value of the asset at 31 March 1982 is substituted for its acquisition cost in the CGT calculation.

Rebasing

Finance Act 2008 simplified the rebasing rules which apply to the disposal of assets held on 31 March 1982. The CGT treatment of such disposals is now as follows:

(a) The gain or loss arising on the disposal of an asset held on 31 March 1982 is calculated by comparing the asset's disposal value with its market value at 31 March 1982. Any enhancement expenditure incurred after 31 March 1982 is taken into account in the usual way when computing the gain or loss.

(b) The original acquisition cost of the asset is no longer relevant for CGT purposes and is entirely ignored. In fact, all costs incurred on or before 31 March 1982 (including any enhancement expenditure incurred up to that date) are ignored and are replaced in the CGT computation by the asset's market value at 31 March 1982.

(c) In effect, the owner of the asset is treated as if he or she had bought it on 31 March 1982 for its market value on that date.

Finance Act 2008 introduced a number of CGT reforms, including simplification of the rebasing rules as explained above. However, none of these reforms apply to companies. The rules which apply when a *company* makes a disposal of an asset held on 31 March 1982 are explained later in this book (see Chapter 24).

EXAMPLE 5

Alan bought a chargeable asset for £2,000 in April 1978. The asset was sold for £29,500 in January 2018. Compute the chargeable gain arising on this disposal if the asset's market value on 31 March 1982 was:

(a) £14,200 (b) £500 (c) £32,000

Solution

(a) The original cost of this asset is irrelevant and the gain or loss is calculated by means of rebasing. The chargeable gain is £15,300 (£29,500 – £14,200). Rebasing has worked in Alan's favour, since he is taxed on only £15,300 out of a total gain of £27,500 during his period of ownership of the asset.

(b) The chargeable gain is £29,000 (£29,500 – £500). Rebasing has not worked in Alan's favour, since he is taxed on £29,000 even though his total gain since 1978 is only £27,500. However, rebasing is mandatory and nothing can be done about this.

(c) There is an allowable loss of £2,500 (£29,500 – £32,000). Although Alan has enjoyed a total gain of £27,500 during his period of ownership of the asset, he is not taxed on this gain at all. Instead, he is granted an allowable loss of £2,500.

Part disposals of assets held on 31 March 1982

When a part disposal is made of an asset which was held on 31 March 1982, the part disposal fraction which would normally be applied to the cost of the asset when computing the chargeable gain arising on the disposal (see earlier in this chapter) is applied instead to the asset's market value at 31 March 1982.

The gain or loss arising on such a part disposal is calculated by comparing disposal value with the appropriate part of the asset's market value at 31 March 1982. If there has been enhancement expenditure since 31 March 1982, the appropriate part of that expenditure is also taken into account when computing the gain or loss.

EXAMPLE 6

Hilary bought a chargeable asset in November 1978 for £3,000. The asset had a market value on 31 March 1982 of £5,000. She sold part of the asset for £8,000 in November 2017, at which time the remainder of the asset was valued at £12,000. Compute the chargeable gain arising on this disposal.

Solution

	£
Sale proceeds	8,000
Less: Part market value at 31 March 1982:	
$\frac{£8,000}{£8,000 + £12,000} \times £5,000$	2,000
Chargeable gain	6,000

Note: Rebasing is mandatory. The acquisition cost of the asset is ignored.

Summary

- The disposal value of an asset is normally equal to sale proceeds, but if an asset is given away or is sold other than by way of a bargain at arm's length, the disposal value is normally deemed to be the market value of the asset on the date of disposal.
- Disposals between spouses who live together (including civil partners) are deemed to occur at a disposal value such that neither a gain nor a loss arises on the disposal.
- Allowable costs include an asset's acquisition cost, incidental costs, enhancement expenditure, costs of defending the owner's title and valuation fees.
- On a part disposal, the allowable part cost is calculated by multiplying the full cost by the part disposal fraction. Special rules apply to small part disposals of land.
- A taxpayer may claim that an asset has negligible value, so triggering a disposal which gives rise to an allowable loss.
- Rebasing applies on the disposal of an asset which was held at 31 March 1982. The gain or loss on disposal is calculated by comparing disposal value with the market value of the asset at 31 March 1982.
- Finance Act 2008 made a number of reforms to the capital gains tax system. These include a simplification of the rebasing rules. None of these reforms apply to disposals made by companies.
- The gain or loss arising on the part disposal of an asset held on 31 March 1982 is calculated by comparing disposal value with the appropriate part of the asset's market value at 31 March 1982.

Exercises

18.1 Carol purchased a holiday flat in December 2007 for £100,000. She spent £5,000 on installing central heating in February 2008 and a further £750 on repainting the interior of the flat in March 2008. The flat was never Carol's main residence.

She sold the flat at auction in February 2018 for £172,000, paying a 5% fee to the auctioneer. Legal costs were £400 in December 2007 and £500 in February 2018. Compute Carol's chargeable gain on the disposal of the flat.

18.2 David was given a chargeable asset in November 2010 at which time the asset had a market value of £7,500. He sold the asset in January 2018. Compute the chargeable gain or the allowable loss if his sale proceeds were:

(a) £14,950 (b) £6,350 (c) £25,780.

18.3 Edwina bought a chargeable asset in August 2007 for £240,000, paying acquisition costs of £12,000. In June 2013 she sold a one-quarter interest in the asset for £100,000, incurring disposal costs of £5,000. The remaining three-quarters interest in the asset was valued at £500,000 in June 2013.

(a) Compute the chargeable gain arising in June 2013.

(b) Also compute the chargeable gain arising in January 2018, when Edwina sold her remaining three-quarters interest in the asset for £520,000.

18.4 Francis acquired an oil painting for £11,500 in March 1979. He sold the painting for £87,500 in March 2018. Compute the chargeable gain or allowable loss arising on this disposal if the painting's market value on 31 March 1982 was:

(a) £10,000 (b) £15,000 (c) £100,000.

18.5 In June 2008, Gillian was given shares with a market value at that time of £6,000. In November 2015 she made a successful claim to the effect that these shares now had a negligible value of only £80.

(a) Compute the allowable loss.

(b) Compute the chargeable gain arising in March 2018, when Gillian sold the shares for £120.

***18.6** Jon bought a chargeable asset for £23,000 in May 1979. He incurred enhancement expenditure of £10,000 in June 1981 and a further £14,000 in July 1998. The asset was valued at £58,500 on 31 March 1982 and was sold for £185,000 in February 2018.

(a) Compute the chargeable gain.

(b) Now re-compute the gain, assuming that the person who bought the asset from Jon in February 2018 was his wife (who lives with him).

***18.7** Karen bought a house in 1990 for £42,000. In November 1991 she spent £18,000 on dividing the house into two self-contained flats. In September 2015 she sold one of the flats for £95,000, at which time the other flat was valued at £105,000. In January 2018 she sold the second flat for £110,000. Karen never lived in either of the flats.

Compute the chargeable gains arising on Karen's two disposals.

Chapter 19

Chattels and wasting assets

Introduction

A "chattel" is an item of tangible, movable property. A "wasting asset" is an asset with a predictable useful life not exceeding 50 years. If an asset is both a chattel and a wasting asset (e.g. a TV set) it is referred to as a "wasting chattel". Special capital gains tax rules apply to disposals of chattels, wasting assets and wasting chattels. The purpose of this chapter is to explain these rules.

The chattels exemption

The disposal of a chattel for £6,000 or less is exempt from capital gains tax. This rule removes from charge a great many trivial disposals and ensures that CGT is levied only if the disposal is material. The following points relate to the chattels exemption:

(a) This exemption applies only to chattels, not to assets in general.

(b) The exemption means that gains arising on the disposal of a chattel for £6,000 or less are not chargeable to CGT. It also means that losses arising on such disposals are not generally allowable. However, special rules apply to chattels acquired for more than £6,000 and disposed of for £6,000 or less (see later in this chapter).

(c) The £6,000 figure relates to the *gross* disposal proceeds. These are the proceeds before deducting incidental costs of disposal.

(d) If the gross disposal proceeds of a chattel exceed £6,000, the chargeable gain cannot exceed five-thirds† of the amount by which disposal proceeds exceed £6,000. This "marginal relief" ensures that taxpayers who dispose of chattels for more than £6,000 are not unduly penalised by the tax system.

† *The effect of the five-thirds formula is that disposals of chattels for £15,000 or less may benefit from marginal relief (depending upon the allowable expenditure). If disposal proceeds exceed £15,000, the marginal relief formula will always give a greater gain than the gain calculated in the normal way.*

EXAMPLE 1

In 2017-18, a taxpayer makes a number of disposals, as listed below. Which of these disposals would be exempt from CGT?

(a) An antique table sold for £5,000.

(b) A watercolour painting sold at auction. The auctioneer deducted his 10% commission from the selling price and sent the taxpayer a cheque for the remaining £5,670.

(c) A holding of shares sold for £4,500.

Solution

(a) The antique table is a chattel disposed of for £6,000 or less. Therefore the disposal is exempt from CGT.

(b) A watercolour painting is a chattel. The gross disposal proceeds must have been £6,300, since £6,300 less 10% = £5,670. The chattels exemption will not apply but the chargeable gain cannot exceed five-thirds of £300 (i.e. £500).

(c) A shareholding is not a chattel. Therefore the £6,000 exemption does not apply and the disposal will be chargeable to CGT.

EXAMPLE 2

In December 2017, Michael sells a piece of antique furniture for £6,360, paying incidental disposal costs of £320. He had acquired the furniture in January 2010 as a gift from his mother. Compute Michael's chargeable gain if the market value of the furniture in January 2010 was:

(a) £5,500 (b) £4,900

Solution

	(a)	(b)	
	£	£	
Sale proceeds	6,360	6,360	
Less: Incidental costs of disposal	320	320	
	6,040	6,040	
Less: Deemed acquisition cost	5,500	4,900	
Chargeable gain	540	1,140	(restricted to £600)

Notes:

(i) The maximum gain is £360 x 5/3 = £600. The gain of £540 in case (a) is less than £600, so the chargeable gain is £540.

(ii) In case (b), £1,140 exceeds £600, so the gain is restricted to £600.

Chattels disposed of at a loss

If a chattel is disposed of at a loss, there are two possibilities. Either:

(a) the disposal proceeds exceed £6,000, in which case the allowable loss is calculated in the usual way, or

(b) the disposal proceeds are £6,000 or less, in which case the chattels exemption applies and it appears that no allowable loss could arise.

However, if a chattel is acquired for more than £6,000 and then disposed of for less than £6,000, the chattels exemption is overruled and an allowable loss is available. But the amount of this loss is restricted to the amount that would arise if the disposal proceeds were exactly £6,000.

EXAMPLE 3

In March 2018, Naomi sells an oil painting which she had acquired many years previously for £10,000. Compute the allowable loss if she sells the painting for:

(a) £7,200 (b) £5,700

Solution

(a) Naomi has disposed of a chattel for more than £6,000, so the disposal is not exempt from capital gains tax. The allowable loss is calculated in the usual way as (£10,000 – £7,200) = £2,800.

(b) Naomi has disposed of a chattel for less than £6,000 and normally this disposal would be exempt from capital gains tax. However, since the asset was acquired for more than £6,000, a loss is allowed. This is calculated by substituting £6,000 for the disposal proceeds. The allowable loss is (£10,000 – £6,000) = £4,000.

Part disposals of chattels

A part disposal of a chattel may be made in one of two ways. Either:

(a) a part interest in a chattel may be disposed of, or

(b) for chattels forming a set, one or more of the items in the set may be disposed of.

Each of these forms of part disposal is considered below.

Disposal of a part interest in a chattel

If a disposal is made of a part interest in a chattel, this part disposal will be exempt from capital gains tax only if the value of the *whole* chattel immediately prior to the part disposal is £6,000 or less.

If the value of the whole chattel exceeds £6,000 the disposal is not exempt from CGT and the usual part disposal calculation is performed. However, the chargeable gain on the part disposal is limited to five-thirds of the amount by which the value of the whole chattel exceeds £6,000, multiplied by the usual part disposal fraction.

EXAMPLE 4

In October 2011, Jackie bought a chattel for £3,500. In October 2017 she sells a one-third interest in this chattel for £2,000. Compute the chargeable gain if the market value of the remaining two-thirds interest in October 2017 is:

(a) £4,000 (b) £5,000.

Solution

(a) The value of the whole chattel on the date of the part disposal is £6,000. Since this value does not exceed £6,000 the part disposal is exempt from CGT.

(b) The value of the whole chattel on the date of the part disposal is £7,000. Since this value exceeds £6,000 the part disposal is not exempt from CGT. The computation of the chargeable gain is as follows:

	£	
Sale proceeds	2,000	
Less: Part cost:		
$\frac{£2,000}{£2,000 + £5,000} \times £3,500$	1,000	
Chargeable gain	1,000	(restricted to £476)

Notes:

(i) The part disposal fraction is £2,000/(£2,000 + £5,000) which is 2/7ths.

(ii) If the whole chattel had been sold (for £7,000) the chargeable gain would have been restricted to (£7,000 – £6,000) x 5/3 = £1,667.

(iii) However, only 2/7ths of the chattel has been sold. So the gain is restricted to £1,667 × 2/7 = £476.

Disposal of part of a set

If a taxpayer acquires a set of chattels (e.g. a set of dining chairs) and then disposes of them individually, each disposal is regarded as a part disposal and will in general be chargeable to CGT only if the disposal proceeds of an individual item exceed £6,000.

However, a taxpayer who wished to dispose of a set of chattels with a total value exceeding £6,000 could use this rule to avoid capital gains tax by disposing of the items one by one (with each disposal raising less than £6,000). In order to prevent such tax avoidance, a series of disposals of chattels which form part of a set *to the same person or to persons connected with each other or acting together* are treated as a single transaction for capital gains tax purposes. If the individual disposals occur in different tax years, any gain which results from this treatment is apportioned between tax years in proportion to the sale proceeds of each disposal.

EXAMPLE 5

Andrew acquired a set of six dining chairs in January 2010 for £1,300. In March 2017 he sold three of the chairs to a friend for £5,200 (the other three chairs also being valued at £5,200 at that time). In August 2017 he sold the remaining chairs to the friend's brother for £5,300. Compute the chargeable gains arising on these disposals.

Solution

If it were not for the rule introduced above, neither of these disposals would be chargeable to CGT since neither of them raises more than £6,000. However, the two disposals are made to connected persons and are therefore to be regarded as a single transaction for CGT purposes. The total disposal proceeds are £10,500 (£5,200 + £5,300). This exceeds £6,000 so the disposals are chargeable. The computation is as follows:

	£	
Sale proceeds	10,500	
Less: Cost	1,300	
Chargeable gain	9,200	(restricted to £7,500)

The maximum gain is (£10,500 – £6,000) x 5/3 = £7,500. £9,200 is greater than this, so the chargeable gain is restricted to £7,500. The apportionment of this gain between the two disposals is as follows:

March 2017 disposal $\frac{£5,200}{£10,500} \times £7,500 = £3,714$ (taxed in 2016-17)

August 2017 disposal $\frac{£5,300}{£10,500} \times £7,500 = £3,786$ (taxed in 2017-18)

Wasting chattels

Chattels which have a predictable useful life not exceeding 50 years in length are referred to as "wasting chattels" and are generally exempt from CGT. Therefore the disposal of a wasting chattel will usually give rise to neither a chargeable gain nor an allowable loss.

An exception to this rule occurs in the case of movable plant and machinery used in business and eligible for capital allowances. Plant and machinery is always regarded as having a predictable useful life not exceeding 50 years and therefore movable plant and machinery is a wasting chattel. Unless the general chattels exemption applies, disposals of movable plant and machinery used in business and eligible for capital allowances are *not* exempt from CGT. One of two situations may arise on such a disposal:

(a) Disposal proceeds may be less than original cost. In this (the most likely) case, the allowable loss is reduced by the total capital allowances† which have been available on the asset. This will reduce the loss to zero.

(b) Disposal proceeds may be greater than original cost. In this case, the total of the available capital allowances on the asset is zero and therefore capital allowances have no effect on the computation, which will proceed in the usual way.

In fact, these rules also apply to fixed plant and machinery (i.e. plant and machinery that is not a chattel) if used in business and eligible for capital allowances.

It is worth noting that certain collectors' items such as antique clocks and watches and vintage motor cycles are regarded as plant and machinery. Consequently, these items are treated as wasting chattels, even though their useful lives may in fact considerably exceed 50 years. By virtue of this treatment, such items are exempt from CGT unless used in business and eligible for capital allowances.

† *The total capital allowances which have been available in relation to an asset are calculated as the difference between the cost of the asset and the disposal value which is shown in the computation of the gain or loss arising on the disposal.*

EXAMPLE 6

An item of movable plant and machinery is bought in February 2015 for £8,000 and used solely for trade purposes. Capital allowances are available in relation to this item. Compute the chargeable gain or the allowable loss which arises if the item is sold in July 2017 and the sale proceeds are:

(a) £5,500 (b) £6,500 (c) £7,500 (d) £8,500.

Solution

In case (a), sale proceeds do not exceed £6,000 so the disposal would seem to be exempt from CGT. However, the asset was acquired for more than £6,000 and sold for less than £6,000 so the chattels exemption is overruled. The computations are as follows:

	(a)	(b)	(c)	(d)
	£	£	£	£
Disposal value	6,000	6,500	7,500	8,500
Less: Acquisition cost	8,000	8,000	8,000	8,000
	(2,000)	(1,500)	(500)	500
Less: Available capital allowances	2,000	1,500	500	0
Chargeable gain/(allowable loss)	0	0	0	500

Notes:

(i) In case (a) the asset was acquired for more than £6,000 but sold for less than £6,000 so disposal proceeds are deemed to be exactly £6,000.

(ii) In cases (a), (b) and (c), available capital allowances are calculated as the difference between the disposal value used in the computation and acquisition cost.

(iii) In case (d), capital allowances are zero because the sale proceeds of the asset are greater than its cost. Disposal value exceeds £6,000 by £2,500, so the maximum gain is £4,167 (£2,500 x 5/3). £500 is less than this, so the chargeable gain is £500.

Wasting assets

A wasting asset which is not a chattel is *not* exempt from CGT. Typical examples of such wasting assets include:

(a) intangible assets such as copyrights, patents and options with lives not exceeding 50 years in length

(b) short leases

(c) fixed plant and machinery.

In general, the original cost of a wasting asset is deemed to waste away on a straight line basis over the asset's predictable life. The computation of the gain or loss arising on the disposal of such an asset is achieved by comparing the disposal value with the unexpired portion of the asset's cost at the time of disposal. But special rules apply to the disposal of a lease (see later in this chapter).

However, if a wasting asset which is not a chattel is used for business purposes and is eligible for capital allowances, the calculation of the gain or loss arising on disposal takes into account the full cost of the asset (not its unexpired portion). The required treatment is the same as that required for wasting chattels (see above).

EXAMPLE 7

In January 2008, Fiona acquired a 25-year copyright at a cost of £30,000. In January 2018 she sold the copyright for £35,500. Compute the chargeable gain.

Solution

When the copyright was bought it had a 25-year life. When it was sold there were 15 years remaining. Therefore the computation is as follows:

	£
Sale proceeds	35,500
Less: Unexpired portion of cost	
$\frac{15}{25}$ x £30,000	18,000
Chargeable gain	17,500

EXAMPLE 8

On 31 March 1978, Philip acquired a 45-year copyright at a cost of £75,000. The copyright was valued at £82,000 on 31 March 1982. On 31 March 2018, Philip sold the copyright for £47,000. Compute the chargeable gain.

Solution

Rebasing applies since the copyright was acquired before 31 March 1982. On 31 March 1982 there were 41 years of the copyright's life remaining. When it was sold there were five years of its life remaining. Therefore the CGT computation is as follows:

	£
Sale proceeds	47,000
Less: Unexpired portion of market value at 31 March 1982:	
$\frac{5}{41}$ x £82,000	10,000
Chargeable gain	37,000

Note:

The copyright is treated as if it had been bought for £82,000 on 31 March 1982 (with 41 years of its life remaining). The original cost of £75,000 is ignored.

Leases

For capital gains tax purposes, leases are classified into long leases (those of more than 50 years) and short leases (those of 50 years or less). A chargeable disposal may occur in connection with a lease in any of the following ways:

(a) A taxpayer who has a long lease on a property assigns that lease to someone else.

(b) A taxpayer who has a short lease on a property assigns that lease to someone else.

(c) A taxpayer who owns the freehold of a property (or has a long head-lease) grants a long lease (or long sub-lease) to someone else, the property eventually reverting to the taxpayer concerned.

(d) A taxpayer who owns the freehold of a property (or has a long head-lease) grants a short lease (or short sub-lease) to someone else, the property eventually reverting to the taxpayer concerned.

(e) A taxpayer who has a short head-lease on a property grants a shorter sub-lease to someone else, the property eventually reverting to the taxpayer concerned.

Each of these cases is considered below. If a property is (or has been) the taxpayer's main residence, the gain arising on the disposal of a lease on the property may be subject to the principal private residence exemption described in Chapter 21.

Assignment of a long lease

The assignment of a long lease is treated as a disposal of the whole asset and therefore causes no CGT difficulties at all. The computation proceeds in precisely the same way as the computation on the disposal of any other whole asset.

EXAMPLE 9

In August 2011, Jim acquired a 99-year lease on a flat for £170,000. In August 2017, he assigned the lease to Shirley for £212,000. The flat was never Jim's residence. Compute the chargeable gain.

Solution

The chargeable gain is simply £42,000 (£212,000 – £170,000). The fact that the lease is six years shorter by the time that Jim assigns it is of no consequence, since it is still a long lease (more than 50 years) on the date of assignment.

If the flat had been Jim's main residence for all or part of the period of ownership, the gain may have been reduced or eliminated by the principal private residence exemption.

Assignment of a short lease

A short lease is, by definition, a wasting asset. Therefore the computation of the gain arising on the disposal of a short lease should be achieved by comparing disposal proceeds with the unexpired portion of the lease's cost at the time of disposal.

However, unlike other wasting assets, the cost of a short lease is not deemed to waste away on a straight line basis. Instead, the cost of a short lease is deemed to waste away according to a table of percentages which is given in Schedule 8 of TCGA 1992 and is reproduced at the end of this chapter. The effect of this table is to write off the cost of a short lease slowly in the early years and more quickly in the closing years. The proportion of the cost† of a short lease which is allowed in the CGT computation on its disposal is:

$$\frac{\text{\% relating to number of years lease has left to run on disposal}}{\text{\% relating to original length of lease}}$$

If the lease was originally a long lease but the taxpayer has owned it for some years so that the lease now being assigned is a short lease, the denominator in the above fraction is taken as 100%, corresponding to "50 or more" in the Schedule 8 table.

Schedule 8 gives percentages for whole numbers of years only. If the duration of a lease is not a whole number of years, then the appropriate percentage is calculated from the table on a pro rata basis.

† *If any enhancement expenditure has been incurred, the proportion of this expenditure which is allowed in the CGT computation on disposal is equal to the Sch. 8 percentage for the number of years left on the date of disposal divided by the Sch. 8 percentage for the number of years left on the date of the enhancement expenditure.*

EXAMPLE 10

Jean acquired a 30-year lease on a property in July 2007 for £132,000. In July 2017 she assigned the lease to Lawrence for £145,000. The property was never Jean's residence. Compute the chargeable gain.

Solution

When the lease was acquired it had a 30-year life (Sch. 8 percentage 87.330%). When it was assigned there were 20 years remaining (Sch. 8 percentage 72.770%). Therefore the computation is as follows:

	£
Sale proceeds	145,000
Less: Unexpired portion of cost	
$\frac{72.770}{87.330} \times £132{,}000$	109,992
Chargeable gain	35,008

EXAMPLE 11

A taxpayer assigns a lease of duration 12 years and 5 months. Calculate the appropriate percentage for use in the CGT computation on the disposal.

Solution

The percentage for 12 years is 53.191%. The percentage for 13 years is 56.167%. The difference between these percentages is 2.976%. Therefore the appropriate percentage for a lease of duration 12 years and 5 months is 53.191 + (2.976 x 5/12) = 54.431%.

EXAMPLE 12

On 31 May 1981, Joan acquired a 45-year lease on a property for £38,000. The market value of the lease on 31 March 1982 was £35,000. Enhancement expenditure of £12,500 was incurred on 31 May 1991. On 30 November 2017 Joan assigned the lease to Giles for £65,000. The property was never Joan's residence. Compute the chargeable gain.

Solution

Rebasing applies since the lease was acquired before 31 March 1982. On 31 March 1982 there were 44 years and 2 months of the lease term remaining (Sch. 8 percentage 97.595 + (0.464 x 2/12) = 97.672%).

When the enhancement expenditure was incurred there were 35 years remaining (Sch. 8 percentage 91.981%). When the lease was assigned there were 8 years and 6 months remaining (39.399 + (3.755 x 6/12) = 41.277%). The computation is as follows:

	£
Sale proceeds	65,000
Less: Unexpired portion of market value at 31 March 1982	
$\frac{41.277}{97.672}$ x £35,000	(14,791)
Unexpired portion of enhancement expenditure	
$\frac{41.277}{91.981}$ x £12,500	(5,609)
Chargeable gain	44,600

Note:

The lease is treated as if it had been bought for £35,000 on 31 March 1982 (with 44 years and 2 months of its life remaining). The original cost of £38,000 is ignored.

Grant of a long lease

The grant of a long lease (or long sub-lease) out of a freehold (or a long head-lease) is treated as a part disposal for CGT purposes and the normal part disposal rules apply. The value of the part disposed of is usually equal to the proceeds of the disposal. The value of the part remaining takes into account both:

(a) the right of the taxpayer making the disposal to receive rents from the tenant, and

(b) the taxpayer's "reversionary interest", which is the right to take back the property when the lease (or sub-lease) finishes.

Grant of a short lease

The grant of a short lease (or short sub-lease) out of a freehold (or a long head-lease) is also treated as a part disposal for CGT purposes and therefore the part disposal rules apply again. However, part of the premium received on the grant of a short lease is assessable to income tax as property income (see Chapter 5) and therefore, in order to avoid double taxation, the disposal proceeds in the part-disposal computation are reduced by the amount of the premium which is assessable as property income.

EXAMPLE 13

Jeffrey acquired a freehold property in October 2009 for £234,000. In July 2017 he granted Jill a lease on the property for £160,000. The market value of the freehold after the lease had been granted was £200,000. The property was never Jeffrey's residence. Compute the chargeable gain, given that the lease granted to Jill was of duration:

(a) 99 years (b) 40 years.

Solution

(a) This is a part disposal with A = £160,000 and B = £200,000. The computation is as follows:

	£
Sale proceeds	160,000
Less: Part cost:	
$\frac{£160{,}000}{£160{,}000 + £200{,}000}$ x £234,000	104,000
Chargeable gain	56,000

(b) This is also a part disposal but £35,200 (£160,000 – (2% x £160,000 x 39)) of the disposal proceeds will be assessable as property income and this must be taken into account in the CGT computation. The computation is as follows:

	£
Sale proceeds (£160,000 – £35,200)	124,800
Less: Part cost:	
$\frac{£124,800}{£160,000 + £200,000}$ x £234,000	81,120
Chargeable gain	43,680

Note that the numerator of the part disposal fraction is taken as the disposal proceeds *after* deducting the property income assessment, whilst the denominator takes into account the disposal proceeds *before* deducting the property income assessment.

Grant of a short sub-lease out of a short head-lease

In essence, the grant of a short sub-lease out of a short head-lease is treated in a similar fashion to the assignment of a short lease, as discussed earlier in this chapter. As before, the TCGA 1992 Schedule 8 table of percentages is called into use to determine the part cost that should be deducted in the capital gains tax computation. But since the property will be returning to the original tenant when the sub-lease finishes, the proportion of the cost of the short head-lease which is allowed in the CGT computation on the granting of the sub-lease is equal to:

$$\frac{P1 - P2}{P3}$$

where:

P1 = % relating to the number of years left of the short head-lease when the sub-lease begins

P2 = % relating to the number of years left of the short head-lease when the sub-lease ends

P3 = % relating to original length of the short head-lease.

Since part of the premium received by the taxpayer on the grant of a short sub-lease will be assessable to income tax as property income, the capital gain arising is reduced by the amount of the property income assessment. However, this reduction cannot be used to convert a gain into a loss or to increase a loss.

EXAMPLE 14

In September 2011, Joanna acquired a 15-year lease on a property for £45,000. In September 2017 she granted a four-year sub-lease to Dean for £20,000. The property was never Joanna's residence. Compute the chargeable gain.

Solution

The computation of the chargeable gain is as follows:

	£
Sale proceeds	20,000
Less: Proportion of cost	
$\frac{43.154 - 26.722}{61.617}$ x £45,000	12,001
	7,999
Less: Property income assessment (£10,160)	7,999
Chargeable gain	nil

Notes:

(i) P1 = 43.154 (9 years), P2 = 26.722 (5 years) and P3 = 61.617 (15 years)

(ii) The property income assessment (see Chapter 5) is:

	£
Premium received	20,000
Less: £20,000 x (4 – 1) x 2%	1,200
	18,800
Less: Relief for premium paid:	
$\frac{4}{15}$ x (£45,000 – (£45,000 x (15 – 1) x 2%))	8,640
	10,160

(iii) The relief given for the property income assessment is restricted to £7,999 so as not to turn a gain into a loss.

Summary

- A chattel is an item of tangible, movable property. A wasting asset is an asset with a predictable useful life of 50 years or less. A wasting asset that is also a chattel is a wasting chattel.
- Chattels disposed of for £6,000 or less are generally exempt from CGT.
- If a chattel is disposed of for more than £6,000, the chargeable gain cannot exceed five-thirds of the amount by which disposal proceeds exceed £6,000.
- The allowable loss on chattels acquired for more than £6,000 and disposed of for less than £6,000 is restricted by substituting £6,000 for the disposal proceeds.
- Disposals of a part interest in a chattel are exempt from CGT if the value of the whole chattel is £6,000 or less.
- A series of disposals of chattels forming a set will be treated as a single transaction for CGT purposes if the disposals are to connected persons.
- Wasting chattels are exempt from CGT apart from movable plant and machinery used in business on which capital allowances are available.
- Wasting assets are not exempt from CGT. In general, the original cost of a wasting asset is written off over its predictable life using the straight line method. However, special rules apply to leases.
- An assignment of a long lease is regarded as the disposal of a whole asset.
- An assignment of a short lease is a disposal of a wasting asset. The original cost of a short lease is written off over its predictable life, using a table of percentages contained in Schedule 8, TCGA 1992.
- The grant of a long lease is treated as a part disposal.
- The grant of a short lease (or sub-lease) out of a freehold (or long head-lease) is treated as a part disposal. The part of the premium received which is taxable as property income is deducted from disposal proceeds in the CGT computation.
- The grant of a short sub-lease out of a short head-lease is a part disposal of a wasting asset. The Schedule 8 table is used to determine the allowable cost used in the CGT computation. The part of the premium received which is taxable as property income is deducted from the gain arising but cannot be used to convert a gain into a loss or to increase a loss.

Short lease amortisation table

(Schedule 8 of TCGA 1992)

Years	*Percentage*	*Years*	*Percentage*	*Years*	*Percentage*
50 or more	100	33	90.280	16	64.116
49	99.657	32	89.354	15	61.617
48	99.289	31	88.371	14	58.971
47	98.902	30	87.330	13	56.167
46	98.490	29	86.226	12	53.191
45	98.059	28	85.053	11	50.038
44	97.595	27	83.816	10	46.695
43	97.107	26	82.496	9	43.154
42	96.593	25	81.100	8	39.399
41	96.041	24	79.622	7	35.414
40	95.457	23	78.055	6	31.195
39	94.842	22	76.399	5	26.722
38	94.189	21	74.635	4	21.983
37	93.497	20	72.770	3	16.959
36	92.761	19	70.791	2	11.629
35	91.981	18	68.697	1	5.983
34	91.156	17	66.470	0	0

Exercises

19.1 Classify each of the following assets as either chattels, wasting assets or wasting chattels:

(a) A domestic washing machine.

(b) A gold ring.

(c) A personal computer.

(d) A 20-year lease on a building.

(e) A suit of clothes.

(f) An antique vase.

19.2 In October 2017 Keith sells an antique cabinet for £7,200. He incurs incidental costs of disposal amounting to £200. The cabinet cost Keith £2,300 in July 2009. Compute the chargeable gain.

19.3 In September 2017 Kevin sells a drawing for £2,000. He bought the drawing in February 2011 for £50,000 when it was thought (incorrectly) to be by a famous artist. Compute the allowable loss.

19.4 In January 2018 Karl sells a one-quarter interest in a chattel for £2,500. On the date of this sale, the remaining three-quarters interest is valued at £8,500. The chattel had cost Karl £3,850 in January 2009. Compute the chargeable gain.

19.5 In January 2015 Katrina buys an item of movable plant and machinery for use in her business. The plant costs her £50,000 and capital allowances are claimed. Compute the chargeable gain arising in March 2018 when she sells the plant, assuming that sale proceeds are:

(a) £65,000

(b) £38,000.

19.6 In June 2015 Katie acquired a 5-year option to buy a piece of land. The option cost her £10,000. In June 2017 she sold the option for £8,000. Compute the chargeable gain.

19.7 Katherine acquired a 40-year lease on a property on 31 August 1999 for £75,000. On 31 August 2017 she assigned the lease to Francesco for £97,500. The property was never Katherine's residence. Compute the chargeable gain.

***19.8** In March 2010, Sean acquired a pair of matching antique silver candlesticks at a cost of £4,000. In August 2017 he sold one of the candlesticks to James for £6,750. At that time the other candlestick was valued at £5,750. In September 2017 he sold the other candlestick to Julia for £5,800. Calculate the chargeable gain arising on these two disposals if:

(a) James and Julia are unconnected.

(b) James and Julia are a married couple.

***19.9** On 31 March 1980, Estelle acquired a patent with a 42-year life at a cost of £21,000. The patent was valued at £22,000 on 31 March 1982 and Estelle sold the patent on 31 March 2018 for £13,000. Compute the chargeable gain.

***19.10** In May 2009, Edward paid £350,000 to buy a 20-year lease on a flat. In November 2017 he granted a 5-year sub-lease on the flat to Petronella for £150,000. The flat was never Edward's principal private residence. Compute the chargeable gain.

Chapter 20

Shares and securities

Introduction

A disposal of shares or securities causes no CGT problems unless a taxpayer disposes of part of a shareholding which was built up over a period of time in a number of separate acquisitions. If this happens, it is impossible to identify the shares that have been disposed of, because shares of the same class in the same company are "fungible assets" (i.e. assets that cannot be individually distinguished). But the calculation of the gain or loss arising on the disposal cannot proceed until the cost of the shares has been established. Therefore TCGA 1992 specifies a set of *share identification* or *share matching* rules which are used to match disposals against acquisitions in these circumstances. The main purpose of this chapter is to explain these rules and to show how they are applied when calculating the gain or loss arising on a disposal of shares.

This chapter also explains the CGT rules relating to bonus issues, rights issues and capital distributions and outlines the CGT treatment of the share disposals which occur when one company is taken over by another company.

The share matching rules

For CGT purposes, disposals of shares or securities are matched against acquisitions of *the same class of shares in the same company* in the following order:

(a) First, against any acquisitions made on the same day as the day of the disposal.

(b) Next, against any acquisitions made during the following 30 days, matching with shares acquired earlier rather than later within that 30-day period. This rule is intended to counter the practice known as "bed and breakfasting", whereby shares are sold and then almost immediately re-acquired so as to trigger gains or losses for tax avoidance purposes.

(c) Finally, against shares forming the "Section 104 holding". This consists of a pool of all the shares of that class in that company that were acquired before the date of the disposal and which have not been matched against previous disposals.

It is important to note that the share matching rules which apply when a *company* makes a disposal of shares are different from those which apply for CGT purposes. The rules which have effect for corporation tax purposes are explained in Chapter 24.

EXAMPLE 1

Paul made the following acquisitions and disposals of ordinary shares in Crimmon plc:

Date		*Number of shares*
5 June 2011	acquisition	3,000
17 May 2012	acquisition	500
17 May 2012	disposal	800
9 June 2012	acquisition	200
13 March 2014	disposal	2,000
28 March 2014	acquisition	1,750
17 October 2017	disposal	1,000

No further shares were acquired during 2017. Against which acquisitions will each of the above disposals be matched?

Solution

(a) The 800 shares which were disposed of on 17 May 2012 are matched as follows:

- (i) first, against the 500 shares acquired on the same day
- (ii) next, against the 200 shares acquired in the next 30 days (on 9 June 2012)
- (iii) finally, against 100 of the shares that form the s104 holding; these are the 3,000 shares acquired on 5 June 2011 and there are 2,900 shares left in this holding after the 17 May 2012 disposal has been matched.

(b) The 2,000 shares disposed of on 13 March 2014 are matched as follows:

- (i) first, against the 1,750 shares acquired in the next 30 days (on 28 March 2014)
- (ii) finally, against 250 of the 2,900 shares that remain in the s104 holding (so there are 2,650 shares left in this holding after the 13 March 2014 disposal has been matched).

(c) The 1,000 shares disposed of on 17 October 2017 cannot be matched against shares acquired on the same day or during the following 30 days. Therefore these shares must be matched against 1,000 of the 2,650 shares that remain in the s104 holding.

The situation after these three disposals have been matched is that Paul is left with 1,650 shares in his s104 holding of ordinary shares in Crimmon plc.

The Section 104 holding

A taxpayer's "Section 104 holding" of shares of a certain class in a certain company is a pool containing any shares that were acquired before the date of the current disposal but which have not been matched against previous disposals. The name of this pool is derived from Section 104 of TCGA 1992, which provides the legal basis for its existence.

If it were not for the provisions of Section 104, it would be necessary to maintain detailed records of the date and cost of each individual share acquisition. However, the pooling arrangement provided by Section 104 eliminates the need to keep such detailed records. Instead, all that is required is a record of:

(a) the total number of shares in the s104 holding, and
(b) the total allowable expenditure in relation to those shares.

The allowable expenditure is normally equal to the cost (or CGT acquisition value) of the shares concerned. But if any of the shares in the s104 holding were acquired before 31 March 1982, their cost is replaced by their market value at that date. This is because rebasing applies to the disposal of assets held on 31 March 1982 and the cost of such assets is not relevant for CGT purposes.

Note that share acquisitions which are matched against same-day disposals or against disposals occurring within the previous 30 days (by virtue of the first two matching rules explained above) do not enter the s104 holding.

EXAMPLE 2

Pauline makes the following purchases of preference shares in Bassoon plc:

Date	*Number of shares*	*Cost* £
23 June 1980	1,000	1,000
14 May 1998	2,000	5,800
8 July 2017	3,000	8,700

The shares had a market value of £2 per share on 31 March 1982. There were no disposals on or before 8 July 2017. Show Pauline's s104 holding of preference shares in Bassoon plc at 8 July 2017.

Solution

	Number of shares	*Allowable expenditure* £
Acquired 23 June 1980	1,000	2,000
Acquired 14 May 1998	2,000	5,800
Acquired 8 July 2017	3,000	8,700
s104 holding c/f at 8 July 2017	6,000	16,500

Notes:

(i) The shares acquired before 31 March 1982 have been added into the s104 holding at their 31 March 1982 market value.

(ii) The three acquisitions forming the s104 holding have been combined into a single pool of 6,000 shares with total allowable expenditure of £16,500. It is now necessary to carry forward only these two "bottom line" figures, rather than the details of each individual acquisition.

(iii) On average, the allowable expenditure per share is £2.75 (£16,500 ÷ 6,000). When there is a disposal from the pool, this is the expenditure that will be allowed for each share that is disposed of (see below).

Disposals from the s104 holding

When there is a disposal of shares from the s104 holding, the number of shares that have been disposed of is deducted from the number of shares in the pool. It is then necessary to deduct a proportion of the allowable expenditure in the pool.

Strictly speaking, this proportion should be calculated using the part disposal fraction (see Chapter 18) which takes into account the value of the shares disposed of and the value of the remaining shares. In most cases, however, the value per share of the shares disposed of will be the same as the value per share of the shares that remain, so that the proportion of the allowable expenditure which should be deducted from the pool can be based upon the *number* of shares disposed of.

The gain or loss arising on a disposal from the s104 holding is calculated simply as the difference between the disposal value of those shares and the amount which has been subtracted from the allowable expenditure in the pool as a consequence of the disposal.

EXAMPLE 3

Paula makes the following acquisitions of ordinary shares in Indigent plc:

Date	*Number of shares*	*Cost*
		£
1 July 2010	5,000	6,300
2 August 2011	2,000	2,500
3 February 2014	1,200	2,300
4 January 2018	1,800	3,400

She sells 500 shares on 28 March 2018. No shares are acquired within the next 30 days.

(a) Show the s104 holding on 28 March 2018, just prior to and just after the disposal on that date.

(b) Compute the chargeable gain or allowable loss on the disposal if sale proceeds are:

(i) £1,300 (ii) £1,000 (iii) £700

Solution

(a) The s104 holding is as follows:

	Number of shares	*Allowable expenditure*
		£
Acquired 1 July 2010	5,000	6,300
Acquired 2 August 2011	2,000	2,500
Acquired 3 February 2014	1,200	2,300
Acquired 4 January 2018	1,800	3,400
	10,000	14,500
Sold 28 March 2018 (500/10,000ths)	(500)	(725)
s104 holding c/f	9,500	13,775

Notes:

1. The disposal in March 2018 must be from the s104 holding since it cannot be matched against shares acquired on the same day or within the next 30 days.
2. The disposal is 500 shares out of 10,000 shares. So 500 shares are deducted from the pool, along with 500/10,000ths (1/20th) of the allowable expenditure.
3. On average, the allowable expenditure in the pool is £1.45 per share and so the allowable expenditure deducted on the disposal (£725) is equal to 500 shares at £1.45 per share.

(b)

	(i)	(ii)	(iii)
	£	£	£
Sale proceeds	1,300	1,000	700
Less: Allowable expenditure	725	725	725
Chargeable gain/(allowable loss)	575	275	(25)

Bonus issues

A bonus issue occurs when a company issues free extra shares to its shareholders. The number of bonus shares received by a shareholder is generally in proportion to his or her existing shareholding. For instance, a "1 for 5" bonus issue would give each shareholder one free extra share for every five shares previously held.

For CGT purposes, a bonus issue is treated as a reorganisation of share capital and therefore bonus shares are deemed to have been acquired on the same date that the original shares were acquired. The required CGT treatment is to uplift the number of shares in each of the taxpayer's previous acquisitions so as to reflect the bonus issue. Since all of these previous acquisitions are generally held together in the s104 holding, the desired effect can usually be achieved by simply adding the bonus shares into the "number of shares" column of the s104 holding. The allowable expenditure associated with this holding is not affected, since bonus shares are issued free of charge.

EXAMPLE 4

Sherjeel made the following acquisitions of ordinary shares in Truculent plc:

Date	*Number of shares*	*Cost*
		£
27 September 2000	1,200	3,600
28 July 2002	800	2,800
3 February 2007	500	2,000
5 July 2011	300	1,500

On 1 September 2014, the company made a 1 for 10 bonus issue. Calculate the chargeable gain arising on 1 March 2018 when Sherjeel sold 1,400 shares for £6 each, assuming that he made no further acquisitions within the next 30 days.

Solution

The disposal cannot be matched against acquisitions on the same day or within the next 30 days, so it must come from the s104 holding. The s104 holding is as follows:

	Number of shares	*Allowable expenditure*
		£
Acquired 27 September 2000	1,200	3,600
Acquired 28 July 2002	800	2,800
Acquired 3 February 2007	500	2,000
Acquired 5 July 2011	300	1,500
	2,800	9,900
Bonus issue 1 September 2014	280	-
	3,080	9,900
Sold 1 March 2018 (1,400/3,080ths)	(1,400)	(4,500)
s104 holding c/f at 1 March 2018	1,680	5,400

The disposal proceeds are £8,400 (1,400 x £6). Therefore the chargeable gain is £3,900 (£8,400 – £4,500).

Note:

The 280 bonus shares increase the number of shares in the s104 holding but do not increase the allowable expenditure in that holding.

EXAMPLE 5

On 13 May 2012, Ruben acquired 400 shares in Xaron Ltd at a cost of £1,800. On 17 July 2017, the company made a 1 for 8 bonus issue and (on the same day) Ruben sold 50 shares in Xaron Ltd for £7 each. Compute the chargeable gain.

Solution

On 17 July 2017, Ruben acquired 50 shares in Xaron Ltd at zero cost. He also sold 50 shares in the company for £350. Under the "same day" rule, acquisitions and disposals made on the same day would normally be matched together. So (if this rule applied) the chargeable gain would be (£350 – £0) = £350.

However, the same day rule does not apply, because the 50 bonus shares are treated as if they had been acquired on 13 May 2012. This increases the number of shares in the s104 holding to 450 (with a cost of £1,800).

The allowable expenditure on the disposal of 50 shares from the s104 holding on 17 July 2017 is (£1,800 × 50/450) = £200 and the chargeable gain is (£350 – £200) = £150.

Rights issues

A rights issue occurs when a company offers its shareholders the right to buy extra shares. Rights issues are similar to bonus issues in that the number of shares offered to each shareholder is generally in proportion to his or her existing shareholding. But rights shares are not issued free of charge. Shareholders who are offered rights shares may either:

(a) ignore the rights issue (in which case there is no CGT impact)

(b) sell their "rights" (see later in this chapter)

(c) buy the shares which they are offered.

For CGT purposes, a rights issue is treated in a very similar way to a bonus issue. If a taxpayer buys rights shares, the number of shares in each of the taxpayer's previous acquisitions is uplifted to reflect the rights issue. But since rights shares are not free, it is also necessary to increase the allowable expenditure for each of these acquisitions.

Since all of the previous acquisitions are generally held together in the s104 holding, the desired effect can usually be achieved by adding the number of rights shares that have been acquired into the s104 holding and increasing the allowable expenditure of this holding by the acquisition cost of these rights shares.

EXAMPLE 6

Tina made the following acquisitions of ordinary shares in Hombus plc:

Date	*Number of shares*	*Cost*
		£
15 August 1993	500	1,250
23 January 2003	700	2,800

On 1 June 2014, the company made a 1 for 20 rights issue at £8 per share and Tina decided to buy the shares to which she was entitled. Calculate the chargeable gain arising on 12 November 2017 when Tine sold 840 shares for £7 each, assuming that she made no further acquisitions within the next 30 days.

Solution

The disposal cannot be matched against acquisitions on the same day or within the next 30 days, so it must come from the s104 holding. The s104 holding is as follows:

	Number of shares	*Allowable expenditure*
		£
Acquired 15 August 1993	500	1,250
Acquired 23 January 2003	700	2,800
	1,200	4,050
Rights issue 1 June 2014	60	480
	1,260	4,530
Sold 12 November 2017 (840/1,260ths)	(840)	(3,020)
s104 holding c/f	420	1,510

The disposal proceeds are £5,880 (840 x £7). Therefore the chargeable gain is £2,860 (£5,880 – £3,020).

Note:

The 60 rights shares increase the number of shares in the s104 holding and also increase the allowable expenditure in that holding.

Capital distributions

A capital distribution occurs when shareholders are repaid part of their share capital, usually when a company goes into liquidation. Unless the amount of the distribution is small (see below) a capital distribution is regarded as a part disposal for CGT purposes.

EXAMPLE 7

In March 2012, Vincent bought 10,000 ordinary shares in Apezium plc for £44,000. In June 2017, the company went into liquidation and Vincent received a first distribution of £0.50 per share. The market value of an ordinary share in Apezium plc just after this distribution was £0.75. Compute the allowable loss arising in June 2017.

Solution

The value of the part disposed of is £5,000 (10,000 @ £0.50) and the value of the part remaining is £7,500 (10,000 @ £0.75). The part disposal fraction is 5,000/12,500 which is equivalent to 2/5ths. Therefore the allowable expenditure for this disposal is 2/5ths of the allowable expenditure on the acquisition of the shares. The s104 holding is as follows:

	Number of shares	*Allowable expenditure* £
Acquired March 2012	10,000	44,000
Distribution June 2017 (2/5ths)	-	(17,600)
s104 holding c/f	10,000	26,400

The computation of the allowable loss is as follows:

	£
Disposal proceeds	5,000
Less: Allowable expenditure	(17,600)
Allowable loss	(12,600)

Sale of rights nil paid

Another example of a capital distribution occurs when a company makes a rights issue and a shareholder decides not to buy the shares concerned but instead to sell his or her rights to someone else (a "sale of rights nil paid"). When shareholders sell their rights they are *not* selling shares. What they are selling is the right to buy shares, often at an attractive price. The proceeds of such a sale are treated as a capital distribution. If the amount of money involved is small (see below) the amount received will be treated as a small capital distribution.

Small capital distributions

If the amount of a capital distribution is small when compared with the value of the shares concerned, the distribution is not treated as a disposal. Instead, the proceeds of the distribution are subtracted from the allowable expenditure relating to those shares. The effect of this is that the gain which would have been chargeable on the distribution is deferred until a subsequent disposal takes place. This is very similar to the treatment of small part disposals of land (see Chapter 18). Note that:

(a) A capital distribution is generally regarded as small if it consists of no more than 5% of the value of the company's shares just before the distribution. It is also HMRC practice to regard an amount of £3,000 or less as small for this purpose, even if the 5% test is not satisfied.

(b) Apparently HMRC will allow a small capital distribution to be treated as a disposal if this is to the taxpayer's benefit (e.g. if any gain is covered by the annual exemption).

EXAMPLE 8

In April 2014, Vanessa bought 100 shares in Entagon plc at a cost of £5 per share. The company went into liquidation and Vanessa received a first distribution of 40p per share in July 2017. The shares had a market value of £9.75 immediately after the distribution.

(a) Show how the distribution will be dealt with for CGT purposes.

(b) Calculate the chargeable gain arising in March 2018, when Vanessa received a second and final distribution of £9.82 per share.

Solution

(a) The value of the shares immediately prior to the distribution must have been £10.15 (£9.75 + £0.40). 40p is approximately 3.9% of £10.15 so the distribution ranks as a small capital distribution. The £40 received by Vanessa may be deducted from the £500 that she paid for her shares. This reduces the allowable cost on a subsequent disposal to £460.

(b) Assuming that the small capital distribution is not treated as a disposal, the s104 holding is as follows:

	Number of shares	*Allowable expenditure*
		£
Acquired April 2014	100	500
Distribution July 2017	-	(40)
	100	460
Disposal March 2018	(100)	(460)
s104 holding c/f	nil	nil

The gain arising on the disposal is:

	£
Disposal proceeds (100 @ £9.82)	982
Less: Allowable expenditure	460
Chargeable gain	522

Takeovers

A takeover occurs when one company acquires the shares of another company. Shareholders of the "target" company exchange their shares in return for cash, or shares of the acquiring company, or a combination of both cash and shares. The CGT treatment of such disposals is as follows:

(a) If a takeover is entirely for cash, the shareholders of the target company have sold their shares and have made chargeable disposals. The fact that shares have been sold as a consequence of a takeover is irrelevant and the gain or loss is computed in the usual way.

(b) If a takeover is entirely for shares (a "paper for paper" takeover), no chargeable disposals have taken place. A shareholder's newly-acquired shares in the acquiring company replace the shares originally held in the target company and are deemed for all CGT purposes to have been acquired on the same date and at the same cost as the original holding.

(c) If a takeover is partly for cash and partly for shares, a part disposal has taken place and a part disposal calculation is usually required. The value of the part disposed of is the amount of cash received and the value of the part remaining is the value of the shares received. However, if the amount of cash received by a taxpayer is no more than 5% of the total consideration (or no more than £3,000) the cash received may be treated as a small capital distribution.

EXAMPLE 9

In August 2011, Winston bought 8,000 shares in Hexico plc for £24,000. In October 2017 Zardac plc made a takeover bid for Hexico plc, offering the Hexico shareholders three shares in Zardac plus £1 in cash for every two Hexico shares. The offer was accepted on 29 October 2017 when the market value of shares in Zardac plc was £5 per share. Compute Winston's chargeable gain.

Solution

Winston received 12,000 shares in Zardac plc, worth £60,000, plus £4,000 in cash, a total of £64,000. The amount received in cash is 6.25% of the total and exceeds £3,000, so this cannot be treated as a small capital distribution. The s104 holding is as follows:

	Number of shares	*Allowable expenditure*
		£
Acquired August 2011	8,000	24,000
Distribution October 2017 (6.25%)	-	(1,500)
s104 holding after distribution	8,000	22,500
s104 holding (Zardac plc) c/f	12,000	22,500

The gain arising on the disposal is:

	£
Disposal proceeds	4,000
Less: Allowable expenditure	1,500
Chargeable gain	2,500

EXAMPLE 10

In June 2013, Darren bought 1,000 ordinary shares in Cubson plc for £8,400. In November 2017, Phere plc made a takeover bid for Cubson plc, offering two ordinary shares and one preference share in Phere for each ordinary share in Cubson. This offer was accepted on 21 November 2017 when the market value of ordinary shares in Phere plc was £4 per share and the market value of preference shares in Phere plc was £2 per share.

Show how Darren's cost of £8,400 should be allocated between the shares which he received by virtue of the takeover.

Solution

Darren received 2,000 ordinary shares worth £8,000 and 1,000 preference shares worth £2,000, giving a total consideration of £10,000. Since 80% of this total took the form of ordinary shares in Phere plc, these ordinary shares are deemed to have cost him 80% of £8,400 = £6,720. Similarly, the preference shares in Phere plc are deemed to have cost him 20% of £8,400 = £1,680. All of these shares are treated as if acquired in June 2013.

Gilts and qualifying corporate bonds

Gilt-edged securities and "qualifying corporate bonds" are not chargeable assets for CGT purposes. Therefore neither a chargeable gain nor an allowable loss can arise on their disposal. Note that:

(a) Gilt-edged securities ("gilts") are UK government securities such as Treasury Stock, Exchequer Stock etc.

(b) Qualifying corporate bonds consist of company debentures and other fixed-interest securities which are expressed in sterling and comprise a normal commercial loan.

(c) Gains and losses arising on the disposal of gilt-edged securities or corporate bonds by a *company* are assessed under the loan relationships rules for corporation tax purposes (see Chapter 23).

Summary

- Special matching rules are used to match disposals of shares and securities against acquisitions. Disposals are matched first against shares acquired on the same day as the disposal, then against shares acquired in the next 30 days and then against shares comprising the s104 holding.
- The s104 holding is a pool of shares of the same class in the same company that were acquired before the date of the current disposal but have not been matched against previous disposals. It is necessary to keep a record of the total number of shares in this pool and their total allowable expenditure.
- In general, the CGT effect of a bonus issue is to increase the number of shares in the s104 holding. Allowable expenditure is not affected. The CGT effect of a rights issue which is taken up by the shareholder is to increase both the number of shares and the allowable expenditure in the s104 holding.
- A sale of rights nil paid is treated as a capital distribution.
- A capital distribution is treated for CGT purposes as a part disposal unless it ranks as a small capital distribution, in which case the amount of the distribution is deducted from the acquisition cost of the shares concerned.
- If a takeover is entirely for cash, the shareholders of the target company have made chargeable disposals. If a takeover is entirely for shares, no chargeable disposals have taken place. If a takeover is partly for cash and partly for shares, a part disposal has occurred unless the amount of cash can be treated as a small capital distribution.
- Gilt-edged securities and qualifying corporate bonds are not chargeable assets for CGT purposes.

Exercises

20.1 A taxpayer makes the following acquisitions of preference shares in Muvex Ltd:

Date	*No of shares purchased*
10 August 2017	1,000
20 October 2017	200
1 December 2017	150

No further shares are acquired during 2017 or 2018. How will the following disposals be matched against these acquisitions?

(a) 250 shares sold on 20 October 2017

(b) 420 shares sold on 12 November 2017

(c) 300 shares sold on 1 April 2018.

20.2 Sandra acquired the following ordinary shares in Pincom plc:

Date	*No of shares*	*Cost*
		£
29 January 1995	1,000	4,000
13 August 1999	1,000	9,500
4 October 2011	2,000	22,500

On 26 June 2017, Sandra sold 700 of her shares in Pincom plc. Assuming that she acquired no further shares in the company during 2017, calculate the chargeable gain or allowable loss if her sale proceeds in June 2017 were:

(a) £8,400

(b) £6,300

(c) £5,200.

20.3 Jeremy acquired the following ordinary shares in Scarlon plc:

Date	*No of shares*	*Cost*
		£
19 September 2009	4,000	16,000
20 October 2011	2,000	12,000
21 November 2013	1,000	7,000
22 December 2017	3,000	24,000
13 January 2018	5,000	55,000

He made no further acquisitions during 2018. On 22 December 2017, he sold 10,000 shares in the company for £10 per share. Calculate the chargeable gain or allowable loss arising on this disposal.

20.4 William made the following acquisitions of preference shares in Pangol plc:

Date	*No of shares*	*Cost*
		£
17 February 2007	600	900
13 November 2011	200	400
9 October 2015	100	300

In January 2017, the company made a 1 for 4 bonus issue. In February 2018, William sold 450 shares for £4 per share. Calculate the chargeable gain, assuming that he made no acquisitions in the following 30 days.

20.5 Yvonne made the following acquisitions of ordinary shares in Ranghi plc:

Date	*No of shares*	*Cost*
		£
30 September 2006	2,000	1,200
1 December 2010	3,000	3,600

In January 2017, the company made a 1 for 5 rights issue at £1 per share and Yvonne decided to buy the shares which she was offered. In March 2018, she sold one-half of her shares in the company for £1.80 per share. Calculate the chargeable gain arising in March 2018, given that no further shares were acquired within the following 30 days.

20.6

(a) In November 2006, Yorick bought 6,000 ordinary shares in Togon plc for £30,000. In March 2018, the company went into liquidation and Yorick received a first distribution of £1 per share. The market value of an ordinary share in Togon plc just after this distribution was £2. Compute the allowable loss.

(b) In January 2010, Yolande bought 300 ordinary shares in Lippex plc at a cost of £1.20 per share. In May 2016, when shares in Lippex plc had a market value of £2 each, the company made a rights issue. Yolande sold her rights, realising £25. Compute the chargeable gain arising in November 2017 when Yolande sold all of her shares for £780, assuming that no further shares were acquired within the following 30 days.

20.7 In June 2016, Walter bought 10,000 shares in Ovod plc at a cost of £7 per share. In September 2017, Rundico plc made a takeover bid for Ovod plc, offering the Ovod shareholders eight Rundico shares plus £4 in cash for every five Ovod shares. The offer was accepted on 2 September 2017 when the market value of shares in Rundico plc was £4.50 per share. Compute Walter's chargeable gain.

***20.8** Suzanne acquired the following ordinary shares in Quarine plc:

Date	*No of shares*	*Cost*
		£
2 October 1979	200	600
10 January 1981	150	500
5 December 2001	400	1,420
8 November 2008	250	1,160
24 July 2017	300	1,400
10 August 2017	400	2,500
20 August 2017	350	2,600
31 August 2017	500	2,400

She made no further acquisitions. The shares were valued at £3.20 each on 31 March 1982. On 24 July 2017, Suzanne sold 1,200 shares for £7 per share. Compute the chargeable gain or allowable loss arising on this disposal.

***20.9** Saeed made the following purchases of ordinary shares in Hyban plc:

Date	*No of shares*	*Cost*
		£
24 August 1987	800	960
25 November 1992	1,200	1,440
26 February 1998	1,600	2,400
11 October 2007	400	800

In June 2014, the company made a 1 for 20 rights issue at £1.50 per share and Saeed took up the shares which he was offered.

Calculate the chargeable gain arising in November 2017, when Saeed sold 1,260 shares at £3 each. Assume that no further shares were acquired within the following 30 days.

***20.10** Susan made the following purchases of ordinary shares in Semicycle plc:

Date	*No of shares*	*Cost*
		£
11 January 2008	1,500	4,800
20 January 2015	1,140	5,700

In January 2018, the company went into liquidation and Susan received a first distribution of £2 per share. The market value of an ordinary share in Semicycle plc just after this distribution was £1. Compute the allowable loss arising in January 2018.

***20.11** On 9 May 2008, Steven bought 2,000 ordinary shares in Vexacon plc for £8,000. On 28 November 2013, he bought 500 ordinary shares in the company for £2,500.

In March 2018, Danstreet plc made a takeover bid for Vexacon plc. The shareholders of Vexacon were offered two shares in Danstreet plus £2 in cash for every Vexacon share. This offer was accepted on 21 March 2018 when the market value of shares in Danstreet plc was £4 per share. Compute Steven's chargeable gain or allowable loss.

Chapter 21

Principal private residence

Introduction

This chapter examines the CGT consequences of the disposal of a taxpayer's principal private residence. Although a principal private residence is not a chargeable asset for CGT purposes, a CGT liability may arise when a property is disposed of which has been used as a residence for only part of the period of ownership or which has been used partly as a residence and partly for other purposes.

Principal private residence

A dwelling which is a taxpayer's only or main residence is known as that taxpayer's principal private residence (PPR). A taxpayer's PPR is not a chargeable asset for CGT purposes. Therefore any gain which arises on the disposal of a PPR is not chargeable to tax and any loss which arises is not allowable. For a property to be regarded as a PPR, the taxpayer must actually occupy the property as a residence. Mere ownership is not sufficient. Furthermore, the term "residence" implies a degree of permanency and it is unlikely that the PPR exemption will apply to a property which has been used only as temporary accommodation. In *Goodwin* v *Curtis* (1998) a property which had been occupied by the taxpayer for only 32 days did not qualify as a residence.

The large majority of taxpayers own (at most) a single property and reside in that property, so that it is obvious that the property is the taxpayer's PPR. However, the following points may be relevant in more complex cases:

(a) A taxpayer may have only one PPR at any given time.

(b) A taxpayer who owns and lives in two (or more) properties may make an election to determine which property is to be regarded as the PPR. Such an election must be made within two years after the date from which it is to take effect. If no election is made, then the matter is decided by the facts of the case.

(c) A married couple who live together may have only one PPR between them. This rule also applies to civil partners who live together.

(d) The PPR exemption covers the residence itself together with grounds or gardens of up to half a hectare (5,000 square metres) in area. Larger areas may be included in the exemption if they are warranted by the size of the residence.

(e) The requirement that there must be actual residence in the property is relaxed if the taxpayer is required to live in job-related accommodation (see Chapter 8). In these circumstances, the PPR exemption is extended to any property which the taxpayer owns, so long as he or she intends to occupy the property as a main residence at some time in the future.

Partial exemption

If a property has been occupied as a PPR for only a part of the period of ownership, only a part of the gain realised on disposal will be exempt from CGT. The exempt part of the gain is equal to:

$$\frac{\text{length of period of residence}}{\text{length of period of ownership}} \times \text{whole gain}$$

The lengths of the periods of residence and ownership are usually calculated to the nearest month. Note the following important points:

(a) If the property was acquired before 31 March 1982, the period of ownership prior to that date and any period of residence prior to that date are ignored. This is because the base date for CGT is now 31 March 1982 (see Chapter 18).

(b) If a property has been the taxpayer's PPR at some time, the final 18 months† of ownership always count as a period of residence, whether or not the taxpayer was actually resident then (so helping taxpayers who move house and have difficulty in selling their previous residence). This rule applies even if the taxpayer claims another property to be his or her PPR during the 18 months.

† *For disposals made before 6 April 2014, the final 36 months of ownership were treated as a period of residence. This figure was reduced to 18 months by Finance Act 2014 but remains at 36 months for disabled persons and long-term residents in care homes.*

EXAMPLE 1

On 1 April 1986, Allan bought a house for £29,000. He lived in the house until 31 October 2015 when he bought another house and made this his principal private residence. The house he had bought in April 1986 was sold on 31 January 2018 for £145,000. Compute the chargeable gain.

Solution

In examples of this type it is necessary first to calculate the gain arising (ignoring any PPR exemption) and then to consider the PPR exemption as a second stage. The gain arising is as follows:

	£
Sale proceeds	145,000
Less: Cost of acquisition	29,000
Chargeable gain (before PPR exemption)	116,000

Allan owned the house for 31 years and 10 months (382 months). He was actually resident for 29 years and 7 months (355 months) and the final 18 months of ownership also count as a period of residence, making a total of 373 months during which the PPR exemption applies. The chargeable gain is therefore as follows:

	£
Total gain (as above)	116,000
Less: $\frac{373}{382}$ x £116,000	113,267
Chargeable gain	2,733

Deemed residence

The period of residence in a property is deemed to include certain periods when the taxpayer was not actually resident, so long as:

(a) there is a period of actual residence both at some time before the period of absence and at some time after the period of absence, and

(b) the taxpayer claims no other property to be a PPR during the period of absence.

These periods of "deemed residence" are as follows:

(a) any periods of absence during which the taxpayer is working in an employment, all the duties of which are performed *outside the UK* (or is living with a spouse or civil partner who is working in such an employment)

(b) a total of up to four years of absence during which the taxpayer is prevented from living in the PPR because he or she is employed *elsewhere in the UK* (or is living with a spouse or civil partner who is employed elsewhere in the UK)

(c) a total of up to three years of absence *for any reason*.

The requirement that the taxpayer must reside in the property at some time after the period of absence is waived if the absence is work-related and the terms of the employment prevent the taxpayer (or spouse or civil partner) from returning to the residence.

EXAMPLE 2

On 1 June 1995, Alice bought a house in Derby for £45,000.

- She occupied the house as her PPR until 1 May 1997 when she left to work in Exeter, living in rented accommodation.
- She returned to the house in Derby on 1 November 1998 and stayed until 1 July 2001 when she left to take up a post in the USA, again living in rented accommodation.
- She returned to Derby on 1 February 2004 and stayed until 1 June 2015 when she bought a house in Nottingham and made this her principal private residence.
- On 1 February 2018 she sold the house in Derby for £164,000.

Compute the chargeable gain.

Solution

	£
Sale proceeds	164,000
Less: Acquisition cost	45,000
Chargeable gain (before PPR exemption)	119,000

Alice's period of ownership of the house in Derby (a total of 272 months) can be broken down into the following periods:

(i)	1 June 1995 to 30 April 1997	23 months	Actual residence
(ii)	1 May 1997 to 31 October 1998	18 months	Working in UK
(iii)	1 November 1998 to 30 June 2001	32 months	Actual residence
(iv)	1 July 2001 to 31 January 2004	31 months	Working abroad
(v)	1 February 2004 to 31 May 2015	136 months	Actual residence
(vi)	1 June 2015 to 31 January 2018	32 months	Living in new PPR

Periods (i), (iii) and (v) are exempt since Alice was actually resident in the property during those periods. Period (ii) is exempt since Alice was working elsewhere in the UK, the four-year time limit has not been exceeded and she was resident in the property both before and after the absence. Similarly, period (iv) is exempt. The final 18 months of ownership are always exempt, which leaves the first 14 months of period (vi) to consider. During these 14 months Alice was claiming another property to be her PPR, so the period cannot count as a period of deemed residence and the gain arising during these 14 months is chargeable. The remaining 258 months benefit from the PPR exemption. The chargeable gain is therefore as follows:

	£
Total gain (as above)	119,000
Less: $\frac{258}{272}$ x £119,000	112,875
Chargeable gain	6,125

Letting relief

An extension to the PPR exemption, known as "letting relief", applies if a PPR has been let to tenants as residential accommodation. Typical situations are as follows:

(a) A property that is used entirely as a PPR for part of the period of ownership might be let to tenants during periods of absence by the owner. A chargeable gain will arise if the periods of absence are not entirely covered by the exemptions described above, but letting relief will then be available in relation to this gain.

(b) The owner of a property that has been used entirely as a PPR since it was originally acquired might now let part of the property to tenants whilst continuing to occupy the rest of the property as a PPR. In this case, the PPR exemption will generally cover:

   (i) the gain arising on the whole property in the final 18 months of ownership, and

   (ii) the remainder of the gain, to the extent that this is attributable to occupation by the owner of the property.

   The balance of the gain will be chargeable to CGT, but letting relief may then be available. In general, letting relief will *not* be granted if the part that has been let forms a dwelling which is entirely separate from the accommodation which forms the owner's residence (e.g. a self-contained flat with its own access from the road).

Letting relief is calculated as the *lowest* of:

(a) the gain which relates to the let part of the property or to the letting period

(b) the gain which is exempt because of the PPR exemptions

(c) £40,000.

EXAMPLE 3

In relation to the previous example in this chapter, assume now that Alice always let her Derby house when she was not resident there. Compute the chargeable gain.

Solution

The only chargeable period was a period of 14 months during which a gain of £6,125 arose and during which the property was let. Letting relief is available as the lowest of:

(a) The part of the gain which relates to the letting period (£6,125)

(b) The part of the gain which is exempt because of the PPR exemptions (£112,875)

(c) £40,000.

Therefore letting relief is £6,125 and the chargeable gain is reduced to £nil.

EXAMPLE 4

Alistair bought a house on 1 April 1997 for £125,000 and occupied the entire house as his principal private residence until 1 November 2005. As from that date, he rented the top floor (comprising one-half of the house) to tenants and retained the ground floor as his own residence. This arrangement continued until 1 October 2017 when he sold the house for £615,000. Compute the chargeable gain.

Solution

	£
Sale proceeds	615,000
Less: Original cost	125,000
Chargeable gain (before PPR exemption)	490,000

Alistair owned the house for a total of 20 years and 6 months (246 months). Exemption is available for the 103 months during which he occupied the whole property and for the final 18 months (a total of 121 months). He was resident in half of the property for the remaining 125 months, so 50% of the gain arising during these 125 months is also exempt. The other 50% is chargeable but letting relief is available. The chargeable gain is as follows:

	£	£
Total gain (as above)		490,000
Less: PPR exemption:		
£490,000 x 121/246	241,016	
£490,000 x 125/246 x 1/2	124,492	365,508
		124,492
Less: Letting relief, lowest of:		
(a) £124,492		
(b) £365,508		
(c) £40,000		40,000
Chargeable gain		84,492

Business use

If a property is used partly as a residence and partly for business purposes, the gain which is attributable to the part used for business purposes† is chargeable to CGT. No reliefs are generally available in relation to this gain. However, the usual exemption for the final 18 months of ownership of a PPR does apply to any part of a property which (at some time during the period of ownership) has been occupied as the taxpayer's main residence, even if that part of the property is used for business purposes during those 18 months.

† *The entitlement to full PPR exemption is not restricted if an individual sets aside a part of their residence for the use of an adult for whom they are caring under a local authority adult placement scheme, regardless of the fact that the income derived from this activity is generally treated as trading income.*

EXAMPLE 5

Ava bought a house on 1 July 1997 for £62,000. She occupied the entire property as her PPR until 1 August 2004 when she began using one-quarter of the house for business purposes. This continued until 1 November 2017 when she sold the house for £207,000. Compute the chargeable gain.

Solution

	£
Sale proceeds	207,000
Less: Acquisition cost	62,000
Chargeable gain (before PPR exemption)	145,000

Ava owned the house for 20 years and 4 months (244 months). For the first 7 years and 1 month (85 months) she occupied the entire house as her main residence. The PPR exemption applies to these 85 months and to the final 18 months of ownership (a total of 103 months). The PPR exemption also applies to three-quarters of the gain arising in the remaining 141 months. The chargeable gain is as follows:

	£	£
Total gain (as above)		145,000
Less: PPR exemption:		
£145,000 x 103/244	61,209	
£145,000 x 141/244 x 3/4	62,843	124,052
Chargeable gain		20,948

Summary

- A taxpayer's principal private residence (PPR) is exempt from CGT.
- A taxpayer with two or more residences may elect which property is to be regarded as his or her PPR. Such an election must be made within two years after the date from which it is to take effect.
- A married couple who live together may have only one PPR between them. This rule also applies to civil partners who live together.
- If a property has been occupied as a PPR for only a part of the period of ownership, only a part of the gain realised on disposal will be exempt from CGT.
- The final 18 months of ownership of a PPR always count as a period of residence.
- Subject to conditions, certain periods of absence are treated as periods of residence for CGT purposes. These include any time spent working abroad, up to four years spent working elsewhere in the UK and up to three years for any reason whatsoever.
- Letting relief of up to £40,000 may be available if a residence has been let to tenants as residential accommodation.
- If a residence is used partly for business purposes, the gain relating to the part used for business purposes is generally chargeable to CGT.

Exercises

21.1 Mohammed owns two properties - a flat in Central London and a country cottage in Sussex. In general he lives in his London flat during the week and spends the weekends in his Sussex cottage. Which of his two properties will be regarded as his principal private residence?

21.2 Melanie bought a house on 1 June 1986 for £31,000. The house was sold on 31 December 2017 for £173,000. Compute the chargeable gain arising in each of the following cases:

(a) Melanie occupied the house as her principal private residence throughout the period of ownership.

(b) Melanie occupied the house throughout her period of ownership with the exception of the period between 1 June 1993 and 31 May 1997 when she lived with a friend. During this time the house stood empty.

(c) As (b) except that the house was let as residential accommodation during Melanie's absence.

21.3 Rupert bought a house in Manchester on 1 November 1995 for £75,000. He occupied the house until 1 November 1999 when he left to work abroad for a year, moving back into the house on 1 November 2000. He stayed until 1 August 2004 when he left again, this time to work in Aberdeen, where he lived until his return on 1 November 2008. This time he stayed for three years, leaving on 1 November 2011 to go to live with a friend. He never returned to the house and it was sold on 1 March 2018 for £362,000. During his absences, Rupert always let his house and he claimed no other property to be his principal private residence. Compute the chargeable gain arising on the disposal.

21.4 Samantha bought a house for £47,500 on 1 August 1996 and occupied the house as her principal private residence. On 1 June 1998 she began to use one-fifth of the house for business purposes. Unfortunately her business eventually failed and on 1 June 2005 she ceased trading. From that date onwards she resided in the entire house until it was sold on 1 August 2017 for £165,000. Compute the chargeable gain.

*__21.5__ Terry bought a house for £65,000 on 1 June 1997 and occupied the house as his principal private residence. He lived in the house until 1 June 2003 when he went to stay with relatives in Australia, letting the house in his absence. He did not return until 1 June 2007, when he began using one-quarter of the house for business purposes and the other three-quarters as his residence. This arrangement continued until 1 June 2017 when he sold the house for £190,000. Compute the chargeable gain.

Chapter 22

CGT reliefs

Introduction

A taxpayer's capital gains tax liability may sometimes be reduced or deferred by taking advantage of various CGT reliefs. The main reliefs available are concerned with:

(a) damaged or destroyed assets

(b) replacement of business assets

(c) gift of business assets

(d) transfer of a business to a limited company

(e) disposal of a business ("entrepreneurs' relief")

(f) reinvestment into EIS shares

(g) loans to traders.

The purpose of this chapter is to explain, for each of these reliefs, the circumstances in which the relief is available and the way in which the amount of relief is calculated.

Damaged assets

If an asset has been damaged and insurance money or other compensation is received in consequence, the situation is usually treated as a part disposal. The value of the part disposed of (A) is the amount of money received and the value of the part remaining (B) is the value of the asset on the date that the money is received. Any money spent on restoration is treated as enhancement expenditure.

However, in certain circumstances, the taxpayer may elect that the situation should *not* be treated as a part disposal and that the amount of money received should instead be deducted from the allowable expenditure relating to the asset. This has the effect of increasing the gain arising on a subsequent disposal and is very similar to the CGT treatment of small capital distributions (see Chapter 20). The circumstances in which a part disposal may be avoided are as follows:

(a) All of the money received is applied to restoring the asset, or

(b) The asset is not a wasting asset and all the money received is applied to restoring the asset except for an amount which is small in comparison with the amount received and which is not reasonably required for restoration purposes, or

(c) The asset is not a wasting asset and the amount of money received is small in comparison with the value of the asset.

For this purpose, a sum is regarded as "small" if it does not exceed £3,000 or 5% of the amount with which it is being compared, whichever is the higher.

A part disposal calculation is unavoidable if only part of the money received is spent on restoring the asset and neither of the "small" tests is satisfied. However, the taxpayer may elect that the calculation should relate only to the amount which is received but not spent on restoration. If this election is made, the remainder of the money received is deducted from the allowable expenditure relating to the asset.

EXAMPLE 1

In July 2011, Laura bought an oil painting for £120,000. In October 2017, the painting was damaged by fire. In February 2018, Laura received compensation from her insurance company of £30,000. Compute the chargeable gain or allowable loss arising in each of the following circumstances:

(a) Laura spent none of the insurance money on restoration and the damaged painting was valued at £170,000 in February 2018.

(b) Laura spent £30,000 on restoring the painting in November 2017 and elected that the situation should not be treated as a part disposal.

(c) Laura spent £29,000 on restoring the painting in November 2017 and elected that the situation should not be treated as a part disposal.

(d) Laura spent £20,000 on restoring the painting in November 2017 and elected that the part disposal should relate only to the retained £10,000. The restored painting was valued at £200,000 in February 2018.

Solution

(a) This is a part disposal, with A = £30,000 and B = £170,000. The computation is:

	£
Disposal proceeds	30,000
Less: Part cost:	
$\frac{£30,000}{£30,000 + £170,000} \times £120,000$	18,000
Chargeable gain	12,000

The balance of allowable expenditure carried forward and used in the calculation of the gain arising on a subsequent disposal is £102,000 (£120,000 – £18,000).

(b) The entire amount received is spent on restoration so the election to avoid a part disposal is valid. The balance of allowable expenditure is:

	£
Incurred July 2011	120,000
Incurred November 2017	30,000
	150,000
Less: Received February 2018 (and not treated as a disposal)	30,000
	120,000

(c) The £1,000 retained is small in comparison with the amount received and therefore the election to avoid a part disposal is valid (so long as the £1,000 is not required for restoration purposes). The balance of allowable expenditure is:

	£
Incurred July 2011	120,000
Incurred November 2017	29,000
	149,000
Less: Received February 2018 (and not treated as a disposal)	30,000
	119,000

(d) By virtue of the election, the part disposal relates only to the retained £10,000, not to the entire £30,000 received. The computation is:

	£	£
Disposal proceeds		10,000
Less: Part original expenditure:		
$\frac{£10,000}{£10,000 + £200,000} \times £120,000$	5,714	
Part restoration expenditure:		
$\frac{£10,000}{£10,000 + £200,000} \times £20,000$	952	6,666
Chargeable gain		3,334

The balance of allowable expenditure carried forward in this case is:

	£
Incurred July 2011 (£120,000 – £5,714)	114,286
Incurred November 2017 (£20,000 – £952)	19,048
	133,334
Less: Received February 2018 (and not treated as a disposal)	20,000
	113,334

Without the election, the chargeable gain would be £11,739 (£30,000 – 30/230ths of £140,000). The balance of expenditure would be £121,739 (200/230ths of £140,000).

Destroyed assets

The loss or destruction of an asset is a chargeable disposal and usually results in a CGT computation in which disposal value is equal to the amount of any insurance money or other compensation received. However, if *all* of the money received is spent (within 12 months) on the purchase of a replacement asset, the taxpayer may claim that the disposal of the original asset should give rise to neither a gain nor a loss. The cost of the replacement asset for CGT purposes is then reduced by the gain which would have been chargeable on the disposal of the original asset if this claim had not been made.

If only *part* of the money received is spent on the purchase of a replacement asset, the taxpayer may claim that the chargeable gain on the disposal of the original asset should be restricted to the amount of money retained (so long as this is less than the gain). The cost of the replacement asset is then reduced by the balance of the gain that would have been chargeable if the claim had not been made.

EXAMPLE 2

Maurice bought an item of jewellery in November 2011 for £125,000. In 2017 the jewellery was stolen. As a result, Maurice's insurance company paid him £141,500 in May 2017. In June 2017 he spent £150,000 on the purchase of replacement jewellery and claimed that neither a gain nor a loss should arise on the disposal of the original jewellery.

(a) Compute the chargeable gain arising in March 2020 when the replacement jewellery is sold for £180,000.

(b) How would this computation differ if the jewellery bought in June 2017 had cost only £140,000 and Maurice had made an appropriate claim?

Solution

(a) Without a claim, the gain arising on the disposal of the original jewellery would be £16,500 (£141,500 – £125,000). The entire proceeds were spent on a replacement asset within 12 months so Maurice is entitled to make the claim. This reduces the deemed acquisition cost of the new jewellery to £133,500 (£150,000 – £16,500). The gain arising on the subsequent sale of the new jewellery is as follows:

	£
Disposal proceeds	180,000
Less: Deemed acquisition cost	133,500
Chargeable gain	46,500

(b) £1,500 (£141,500 – £140,000) of the gain on the original jewellery is immediately chargeable. The remaining £15,000 may be deducted from the acquisition cost of the new jewellery, reducing this cost to £125,000 (£140,000 – £15,000). The chargeable gain arising on the March 2020 disposal becomes £55,000 (£180,000 – £125,000).

Replacement of business assets

Subject to certain conditions, a taxpayer may claim that the gain arising on the disposal of a business asset (the "old asset") may be "rolled-over" against the cost of acquiring a replacement business asset (the "new asset"). The main effects of a claim for roll-over relief are as follows:

(a) The disposal of the old asset is deemed to give rise to neither a gain nor a loss.

(b) The cost of the new asset for CGT purposes is reduced by the gain which would have been chargeable on the disposal of the old asset if the claim for roll-over relief had not been made.

Full relief is available only if the disposal proceeds of the old asset are *wholly* applied in acquiring the new asset. If only *part* of the disposal proceeds are used to acquire the new asset, the effect of a claim for roll-over relief is that the chargeable gain on the disposal of the old asset is restricted to the amount of money retained (so long as this is less than the gain). The cost of the new asset is then reduced by the balance of the gain that would have been chargeable if the claim had not been made. The conditions which must be satisfied if a roll-over claim is to be accepted are:

(a) Both the old asset and the new asset must be drawn from the following list (though they need not both be the same type of asset):

  (i) land, buildings and fixed plant and machinery
  (ii) goodwill
  (iii) ships, aircraft, hovercraft, satellites, space stations and spacecraft
  (iv) milk, potato and fish quotas and certain EU agricultural quotas
  (v) Lloyd's syndicate rights.

(b) The old asset must have been used only for trade purposes throughout the period of ownership and the new asset must be taken into trading use immediately upon its acquisition. But where a taxpayer operates two or more trades, there is no requirement that the old and new asset should be used in the same trade.

(c) The new asset must be acquired during the period beginning one year before and ending three years after the date of disposal of the old asset.

(d) The taxpayer must claim the relief within four years of the end of the *later* of the tax year in which the old asset is disposed of and the tax year in which the new asset is acquired. It is not possible to restrict the amount of a claim so as to preserve the annual exemption.

Note that a similar relief is available to companies (which pay corporation tax on their chargeable gains). For companies, however, the list of assets which are eligible for this relief excludes intangible assets such as goodwill and quotas. These assets fall instead within the scope of the corporation tax intangible assets regime (see Chapter 23).

EXAMPLE 3

In May 2006, Janine bought a building for £187,525 for use in her business. In July 2017 she sold the building for £260,000 and, in the same month, bought another building for use in her business. Assuming that Janine claims roll-over relief, calculate the chargeable gain arising on the July 2017 disposal if the replacement building has a cost of:

(a) £270,000 (b) £240,000 (c) £185,000.

Solution

The gain on the disposal of the original building is computed as follows:

	£
Sale proceeds	260,000
Less: Acquisition cost	187,525
Chargeable gain	72,475

(a) The entire sale proceeds have been spent on a replacement building. None of the gain is immediately chargeable and the entire gain is rolled-over against the cost of the new building, reducing its allowable cost to £197,525 (£270,000 – £72,475).

(b) £20,000 of the sale proceeds have been retained. Therefore £20,000 of the gain is immediately chargeable. The remaining £52,475 may be rolled-over against the cost of the new building, reducing its allowable cost to £187,525 (£240,000 – £52,475).

(c) £75,000 of the sale proceeds have been retained. This exceeds the amount of the gain. Therefore the whole gain is immediately chargeable and no part of the gain may be rolled-over. The allowable cost of the new building is the full £185,000.

Replacement with a depreciating asset

If the new asset is a "depreciating asset" (i.e. a wasting asset or an asset which will become a wasting asset within ten years of the date of acquisition) the gain arising on the disposal of the old asset cannot be rolled-over and is *not* deducted from the cost of the new asset. Instead, the gain is temporarily deferred or "held-over" until it crystallises (i.e. becomes chargeable) on the *earliest* of the following three dates:

(a) the date on which the new asset is disposed of
(b) the date on which the new asset ceases to be used for trade purposes
(c) the 10th anniversary of the acquisition of the new asset.

Clearly, a gain which is held-over in these circumstances will become chargeable no more than ten years after the date of acquisition of the depreciating asset. However, if a suitable non-depreciating asset is acquired at any time before the earliest of the above three dates, the held-over gain may be transferred to this new asset, so converting a temporarily held-over gain into a permanently rolled-over gain.

EXAMPLE 4

In June 2017, Ian sold a freehold building for £200,000, realising a chargeable gain of £25,000. The building had been used only for trade purposes. In July 2017, he acquired fixed plant and machinery costing £220,000 and elected that the gain on the building should be held-over against the plant and machinery. Explain the way in which the held-over gain would be treated if:

(a) Ian sells the plant and machinery in October 2021.

(b) Ian sells the plant and machinery in March 2029.

Solution

Plant and machinery is always regarded as a wasting asset (see Chapter 19) so the plant and machinery acquired in July 2017 is a depreciating asset.

(a) The replacement asset is sold before the 10th anniversary of its acquisition and so the deferred gain becomes chargeable in 2021-22.

(b) The replacement asset is still in Ian's possession ten years after its acquisition, so the held-over gain of £25,000 crystallises in July 2027 and forms part of Ian's chargeable gains in 2027-28.

EXAMPLE 5

Imagine now that Ian (in the above example) buys another freehold building for business use in November 2020 and elects to transfer the held-over gain on the plant and machinery to the new freehold building. Explain the treatment of the held-over gain if the new building costs:

(a) £250,000 (b) £190,000.

Solution

(a) The entire proceeds of the sale of the original building have been invested in a new building so the whole held-over gain of £25,000 can be converted into a rolled-over gain, reducing the allowable cost of the new building to £225,000.

(b) £10,000 of the sale proceeds of the original building have not been invested in the new building and so cannot be rolled-over against its cost. This £10,000 will continue to be held-over against the plant and machinery and will become chargeable no later than July 2027. However, the remaining £15,000 is converted into a rolled-over gain, reducing the allowable cost of the new building to (£190,000 – £15,000) = £175,000.

Gift of business assets

The gift of an asset is a chargeable disposal and this is the case whether or not the asset is used in business. However, subject to certain conditions, a claim may be made for the gain arising on a gift of business assets to be held-over until the transferee disposes of the assets concerned. If such a claim is made, the transferor's gain on the disposal is reduced to zero and the transferee's deemed acquisition cost is reduced by the amount of the gain that would have been chargeable on the transferor if the claim had not been made. The conditions which must be satisfied are as follows:

(a) Both the transferor and the transferee must elect for the gain arising on the gift to be held-over. This election must be made within four years of the end of the tax year in which the gift is made.

(b) The gifted assets must consist of either:

  (i) assets used in a trade, profession or vocation carried on by the transferor or by the transferor's *personal company* (a company of which at least 5% of the voting rights are held by the transferor), or

  (ii) shares or securities of a trading company which is unlisted or which is the transferor's personal company (so long as the *transferee* is not a company).

If the gift is of shares, rather than of individual business assets, the gain arising on the disposal is apportioned between the amount which relates to chargeable business assets owned by the company on the date of the gift and the amount which relates to other chargeable assets (e.g. investments). Only the part of the gain relating to chargeable business assets is eligible for hold-over relief.

Sale for less than market value

Gift relief is also available if a business asset is sold for less than market value (typically to a connected person). But if the actual consideration received by the transferor exceeds the original cost of the asset (so that part of the gain has been realised) the amount of the gain which may be held-over is reduced by the excess of the actual consideration over the asset's cost.

EXAMPLE 6

In March 2018, Jonathan gives a business asset to his daughter. Jonathan acquired the asset for £25,000 in May 2012 and its market value on the date of the gift is £60,000. Both Jonathan and his daughter elect that the gain arising should be held-over.

(a) Compute the gain arising on the gift and the amount which may be held-over.

(b) How would the computation differ if Jonathan's daughter paid him £32,000 for the asset?

Solution

(a) The chargeable gain is £35,000 (£60,000 – £25,000). The whole of this gain may be held-over, reducing Jonathan's daughter's deemed acquisition cost to £25,000 (£60,000 – £35,000).

(b) The chargeable gain is still £35,000, since this is not a bargain made at arm's length and therefore disposal value is taken to be the market value of the asset on the date of disposal. However, £7,000 of the gain (£32,000 – £25,000) has been realised in cash, so the amount of the gain which may be held-over is reduced to £28,000. The remaining £7,000 of the gain is immediately chargeable. The daughter's deemed acquisition cost is £32,000 (£60,000 – £28,000).

EXAMPLE 7

In July 2008, Kathy paid £60,000 to acquire 90% of the ordinary shares of an unlisted trading company. In May 2015, she gave all of the shares to her son and both Kathy and her son elected that the gain arising on this gift should (as far as possible) be held-over. The net assets of the company on the date of the gift (at market value) were as follows:

	£
Goodwill	100,000
Freehold building (used only for business purposes)	150,000
Listed investments	50,000
Net current assets (none of which are chargeable)	40,000
Total net assets	340,000

(a) Compute the gain arising on the gift and the amount which may be held-over.

(b) Compute the gain arising in March 2018 when Kathy's son sells all the shares for £350,000.

Solution

(a) Presumably, the value of the shares on the date of the gift was 90% of £340,000 = £306,000. So the gain arising on the gift was £246,000 (£306,000 – £60,000).

The company's chargeable assets on the date of the gift were £300,000 of which £250,000 were chargeable business assets. So £246,000 x 250,000/300,000 = £205,000 of the gain was held-over whilst the remaining £41,000 was chargeable.

(b) The gain arising in March 2018 is as follows:

	£
Sale proceeds	350,000
Less: Deemed acquisition cost (£306,000 – £205,000)	101,000
Chargeable gain	249,000

Transfer of a business to a limited company

Subject to certain conditions, the gain arising on the transfer of a business to a limited company in return for shares in that company is held-over until the transferor disposes of the shares. If this relief applies, the gain arising on the disposal of the business is deducted from the deemed acquisition cost of the shares. The required conditions are:

(a) The business is transferred as a going concern.

(b) All of the assets of the business (other than cash) are transferred to the company.

(c) The consideration received by the transferor consists wholly or partly of shares in the company.

This relief (known as "incorporation relief") applies automatically, so there is no need for the transferor to make a claim. However, the transferor may elect that incorporation relief should *not* apply. One situation in which such an election might be made is when the gain concerned is covered by the transferor's annual exemption.

If incorporation relief applies and the consideration for a transfer consists only partly of shares, then only part of the chargeable gain is held-over. In these circumstances, the held-over gain is calculated as follows:

$$\frac{\text{value of the shares received}}{\text{total consideration received}} \times \text{whole gain}$$

EXAMPLE 8

In November 2017, Leroy transfers his business to a limited company in exchange for £50,000 in cash and shares which are valued at £600,000. The gain arising on the transfer is £260,000. Leroy does not elect to disapply incorporation relief. Calculate the amount of the gain which is immediately chargeable and the amount which is held-over.

Solution

The held-over gain is £260,000 x 600,000/650,000 = £240,000. The remaining £20,000 of the gain is immediately chargeable. The deemed acquisition cost of the shares is reduced to £360,000 (£600,000 – £240,000).

Entrepreneurs' relief

A relief known as "entrepreneurs' relief" (ER) may apply to gains of up to £10 million made by an individual on a "material disposal" of business assets. In order for this relief to be available, the individual must dispose of either:

(a) all or part of a business (including a share in a partnership) which the individual has owned throughout the period of one year ending on the date of the disposal, or

(b) assets used by a business at the time at which it ceases trading, as long as the business was owned by the individual (or by a partnership in which the individual was a member) throughout the year ending on the date of cessation and the assets are disposed of within three years of that date, or

(c) shares or securities in a trading company which, throughout the period of one year ending on the date of the disposal, has been the individual's personal company and of which the individual has been an officer or employee.

In case (a) above, it is important to realise that the disposal must be the disposal of either a whole business or a significant part of a business. Merely disposing of a business asset does not qualify for ER. The following points should also be noted:

(a) In the first two cases above, ER is available only in respect of disposals of "relevant business assets". These include goodwill but exclude assets held as investments.

(b) A trading company is "*a company carrying on trading activities whose activities do not include to a substantial extent activities other than trading activities*". HMRC will generally accept that a company is a trading company if no more than 20% of its activities are non-trading activities.

(c) A company qualifies as the individual's personal company for this purpose if the individual holds at least 5% of the company's ordinary shares and has at least 5% of the company's voting rights.

(d) The disposal of shares acquired through the exercise of an Enterprise Management Incentives (EMI) option is eligible for ER, subject to conditions (see Chapter 7).

Entrepreneurs' relief is given only if the individual makes a claim. Claims must be made by the first anniversary of the 31 January following the tax year in which the qualifying disposal is made. For example, if a disposal occurs during tax year 2017-18, an ER claim must be made by 31 January 2020.

Associated disposals

If an individual qualifies for ER on a disposal of shares or securities or on a disposal of a share in a partnership, relief may also be available in relation to "associated disposals". An associated disposal is the disposal of an asset which is owned by the individual but has been used in the business of the company or partnership concerned.

Entrepreneurs' relief rate (10%)

If an ER claim is made in respect of a qualifying disposal, any losses arising in relation to that disposal must first be deducted from the gains arising in relation to the disposal. The resulting amount is then subject to CGT at the "entrepreneurs' relief rate" of 10%.

The calculation of a taxpayer's CGT liability for a tax year may involve both gains which qualify for ER and gains which do not qualify. The taxpayer may also have capital losses in the year arising from non-ER disposals or capital losses brought forward from previous years. In these circumstances (as explained in Chapter 17):

(a) Non-ER capital losses, capital losses brought forward and the annual exemption may be set against gains in such a way that the CGT liability is minimised. This result is achieved if losses and the annual exemption are set first against non-ER gains (which may be taxable at 10%, 20%, 18% or 28%) and only then against ER gains.

(b) The unused part of the taxpayer's basic rate band (if any) is reduced by the amount of ER gains arising in the year. Any part of the basic rate band which still remains after this deduction is then available for non-ER gains.

The worked examples given in Chapter 17 illustrate these points.

The lifetime limit

Entrepreneurs' relief is subject to a "lifetime limit". A taxpayer may claim ER more than once but this limit restricts the total gains eligible for relief during the taxpayer's lifetime.

The relief was originally introduced on 6 April 2008 with a lifetime limit of £1 million. This limit was subsequently increased to £2 million as from 6 April 2010, to £5 million as from 23 June 2010 and to £10 million as from 6 April 2011.

If an individual makes qualifying gains in excess of the lifetime limit and that limit is subsequently increased, retrospective relief is not given for the excess of those gains over the previous limit. However, if the individual then has further qualifying gains at some time in the future, ER may be claimed in relation to gains of up to the amount by which the limit has increased.

EXAMPLE 9

Three taxpayers each wish to make an ER claim in relation to a qualifying disposal made during 2017-18. Their previous ER claims are as follows:

(a) Gemma made an ER claim in relation to a gain of £600,000 arising in June 2009.

(b) Robin made an ER claim in relation to a gain of £2,300,000 arising in May 2010.

(c) Joyce made an ER claim relating to a gain of £750,000 arising in October 2008 and a further ER claim relating to a gain of £6 million arising in September 2010.

For each of these taxpayers, calculate the remaining amount of the ER lifetime limit which is available in relation to qualifying disposals occurring on or after 6 April 2017.

Solution

(a) Gemma's claim in June 2009 did not exceed the lifetime limit (which was £1 million at that time) and so ER was available in relation to the whole of the gain. The remainder of the ER limit is now £9,400,000 (£10,000,000 – £600,000).

(b) Robin's qualifying gain in May 2010 exceeded the lifetime limit of £2 million, so ER would have been available in relation to only £2 million of that gain. Although the limit has since increased to £10 million, there is no possibility of retrospective relief in relation to the remaining £300,000 of the May 2010 gain. The remainder of the ER limit is now £8,000,000 (£10,000,000 – £2,000,000).

(c) Joyce's October 2008 claim was within the lifetime limit of £1 million and so ER was available for the whole of the gain. By September 2010, the lifetime limit had risen to £5 million, so ER was available in relation to £4,250,000 of the September 2010 gain. Although the limit has since increased to £10 million, there is no retrospective relief for the remaining £1,750,000 of this gain The remainder of the ER limit is now £5,000,000 (£10,000,000 – £750,000 – £4,250,000).

EXAMPLE 10

Calculate the CGT payable in respect of the following disposals, assuming in each case that the annual exemption is fully utilised against other gains, that there are no allowable losses other than those stated and that taxable income for 2017-18 exceeds the basic rate limit. Also assume that ER is claimed wherever possible.

(a) Wendy (who has never claimed ER before) sells her business in January 2018 and realises a chargeable gain of £720,000 in relation to relevant business assets. She has owned the business since 1991.

(b) Tom sells his business in March 2018. He realises a gain of £300,000 on the disposal of his business premises but incurs a loss of £120,000 on the disposal of his goodwill. He has owned the business for 15 years and has made no previous ER claims.

(c) In August 2017, Henry sells residential accommodation which he has been letting unfurnished to the same tenant since 2010. The gain on this disposal is £150,000.

(d) Since 2001, Brenda has been a director of a trading company and has owned 15% of its ordinary shares. She sells her shares in October 2017 and realises a gain of £12,500,000. During 2009-10 she had claimed ER in relation to a gain of £900,000 arising on the disposal of a business.

Solution

(a) £720,000 does not exceed £10 million, so the whole of the gain qualifies for ER. The gain is taxed at 10%, giving CGT payable of £72,000.

(b) The loss on the goodwill must be deducted from the gain on the premises before computing ER. Tom's net gains are £180,000. This figure is taxed at 10%, so CGT payable is £18,000.

(c) Henry's use of this property does not qualify as a trade and therefore ER is not available. ER would have been available if the letting of the property had qualified as the commercial letting of furnished holiday accommodation (see Chapter 5). CGT payable is £42,000 (£150,000 x 28%).

(d) The disposal in 2009-10 used up £900,000 of the lifetime limit, so £9,100,000 of the gain arising in October 2017 is taxed at 10% and the remainder is taxed at 20%. CGT payable is £1,590,000 (£9,100,000 x 10% + £3,400,000 x 20%).

Extension to long-term investors

Finance Act 2016 extended a form of entrepreneurs' relief to gains arising on the disposal of ordinary shares in unlisted trading companies by individuals (other than employees or officers of the company concerned). The shares must have been newly issued to the individual on or after 17 March 2016 and held for at least three years after 5 April 2016.

The rate of tax applicable to such gains is 10%. The total amount of gains eligible for this "investors' relief" is subject to a lifetime limit of £10 million. This limit is in addition to the £10 million lifetime limit which applies to entrepreneurs' relief generally.

Interaction of entrepreneurs' relief with other reliefs

A disposal which is eligible for entrepreneurs' relief may also qualify for the relief relating to a gift of business assets. But if a gift relief claim is made, no chargeable gain arises at the time of the disposal. Therefore an ER claim is inappropriate and cannot be made successfully. Similar comments apply to a disposal to which incorporation relief applies and a disposal which is the subject of a claim for rollover relief.

In all of these cases, the fact that no chargeable gain arises at the time of the disposal† means that the opportunity to benefit from ER in relation to that disposal is lost. Whether or not a subsequent disposal (e.g. a disposal of gifted assets by the transferee) will qualify for ER will depend upon the circumstances of that disposal and whether the necessary conditions are satisfied at that time for ER to be available.

† *However, a gain which is eligible for ER but is instead deferred into EIS or SITR investments (see below) remains eligible for ER when the gain becomes chargeable.*

Reinvestment into EIS shares

The gain arising on the disposal of *any* asset may be deferred if an amount of money *equal to the gain* is used to subscribe for shares which are eligible under the rules of the Enterprise Investment Scheme (see Chapter 6). Note the following points:

(a) The shares must be subscribed for during the period starting one year before and finishing three years after the disposal concerned.

(b) There is no requirement that income tax relief should be available in relation to the investment. It follows that the taxpayer does not have to be unconnected with the company concerned and that the amount of a deferred gain can exceed the maximum amount on which income tax relief is granted.

(c) The deferred gain usually becomes chargeable on the disposal of the EIS shares, but further deferral is possible if further EIS shares are then subscribed for.

(d) A similar deferral relief applies to gains that are reinvested into Social Investment Tax Relief (SITR) investments (see Chapter 6).

Furthermore, the gain arising on the disposal of *any* asset may be reduced for tax purposes by up to 50% of the amount invested through the seed EIS during the tax year in which the disposal takes place (see Chapter 6).

Loans to traders

If a taxpayer lends money to a trader and then finds that all or part of the loan is irrecoverable, the loss incurred may be treated as a capital loss and set against the taxpayer's capital gains. This relief is subject to the following conditions:

(a) the trader who has borrowed the money must be resident in the UK
(b) the money must have been borrowed for trade purposes
(c) the debt must be unsecured.

Subject to these conditions, the amount lost is treated as a capital loss of the year in which the taxpayer claims relief, though a claim may be backdated for up to two years if the debt was irrecoverable then. If relief is given and then all or part of the loan is recovered, the amount recovered is treated as a capital gain of the year in which recovery takes place.

Summary

- If the compensation received on the loss or destruction of an asset is spent on the purchase of a replacement, the taxpayer may claim that the disposal should give rise to neither a gain nor a loss. The gain which would have been chargeable is then subtracted from the cost of the replacement asset.

- The gain arising on the disposal of a business asset may be rolled-over against the cost of acquiring a replacement.

- If a business asset is replaced by a depreciating asset, the gain arising cannot be permanently rolled-over but may be temporarily held-over instead. This gain will become chargeable no later than 10 years after the replacement asset was acquired (unless the gain is transferred to a non-depreciating asset in the meantime).

- The gain arising on the gift of a business asset may be held-over until the transferee disposes of the asset.

- The gain arising on the transfer of a business to a limited company is held-over until the transferor disposes of the shares which were received in exchange for the assets of the business. The transferor may elect that this relief should not apply.
- Subject to certain conditions, entrepreneurs' relief is available in respect of gains of up to £10 million arising on the disposal of the whole or part of a business. Gains which qualify for entrepreneur's relief are taxed at only 10%.
- The gain arising on the disposal of any asset may be deferred if the amount of the gain is used to subscribe for shares eligible under the rules of the EIS.
- 50% of the gain arising on the disposal of any asset is exempt from CGT if an amount of money equal to the gain is invested through the seed EIS.

Exercises

22.1 In October 2007, Matthew bought a piece of rare porcelain for £10,000. The porcelain was damaged in early 2013 and in March of that year Matthew spent £3,850 on restoration work. In July 2013, Matthew's insurance company paid him £4,000 and Matthew successfully claimed that this should not be treated as a part disposal. He sold the porcelain in March 2018 for £23,500. Compute the chargeable gain.

22.2 In February 2009, Maria bought a diamond necklace for £13,500. In 2011 the necklace was stolen and, as a result, an insurance payment of £14,000 was received in February 2012. In the same month, Maria spent £14,750 on the purchase of a replacement necklace and claimed that the disposal of the original necklace should give rise to neither a gain nor a loss. Compute the chargeable gain arising in January 2018 when the replacement necklace was sold for £20,000.

22.3 In September 2008, Pamela bought a building for business use at a cost of £150,000. In September 2017 she sold the building for £261,400 and immediately bought another building, again for business use. Assuming that Pamela claims roll-over relief, calculate the chargeable gain arising in September 2017 if the cost of the new building is:

(a) £258,900 (b) £149,800 (c) £276,800.

22.4 In August 2017, Susannah (a sole trader) gave a business asset to her son. The asset had been bought by Susannah for £91,500 in July 2008 and enhanced in May 2009 at a cost of £34,500. The asset's market value in August 2017 was £215,000. Both Susannah and her son elected that the gain arising should be held-over.

Compute the amount of the held-over gain. Also explain how the situation would differ if Susannah's son had paid her £150,000 for the asset.

***22.5** In January 1981, Norman bought a freehold building for use in his business at a cost of £120,000. The building had a market value on 31 March 1982 of £125,000. In June 2013 he sold the building for £875,000 and in August 2013 he spent £720,000 on buying another building for use in his business. This building was sold in December 2017 for £730,000. Compute the gains arising on the disposal of each building (assuming that Norman claims roll-over relief).

***22.6** In May 2012, Ruth sold a freehold building which she had used exclusively for business purposes. The building was sold for £220,000, realising a chargeable gain of £42,500. In the following month, Ruth acquired fixed plant for £220,000 and elected to hold-over the gain on the freehold property against this plant and machinery. In August 2017, she acquired another freehold building for £205,000 and elected to transfer the held-over gain to this new building. Explain the treatment of the £42,500 gain.

***22.7** Calculate the CGT payable in relation to each of the following disposals, assuming in each case that the annual exemption is fully utilised against other gains, that there are no allowable losses and that ER is claimed wherever possible. The taxpayers concerned have made no previous ER claims.

(a) On 31 May 2017, Roger sold all of his shares in a trading company, realising a gain of £351,000. He has owned 25% of the company's ordinary share capital since March 2012 and has been a director of the company since June 2013.

(b) On 31 July 2017, Dennis sold his business (which he has owned since May 1990) and realised gains of £15,250,000 in relation to relevant business assets.

(c) On 31 August 2017, Denise sold her interest in a trading partnership and realised gains of £140,000 in relation to relevant business assets. She had been a member of the partnership for five years. Also on 31 August 2017, she sold a building which was owned by her personally but had been used by the partnership for business purposes since 2014. She realised a gain of £31,000 in relation to this building.

***22.8** In 2010, Shaun bought 20% of the ordinary shares of an unlisted trading company. The shares cost £140,000. He owned the shares until January 2018 when he gave all the shares to a friend. On the date of the gift, the shares had a market value of £500,000 and the company's assets were valued as follows:

	£
Freehold land and buildings	1,700,000
Goodwill	500,000
Investments	100,000
Motor cars	40,000
Net current assets	160,000

Calculate the chargeable gain, assuming that both Shaun and his friend elect that the gain arising should (as far as possible) be held-over.

Review questions (Set B)

B1 Mick Stone disposed of the following assets during tax year 2017-18:

(1) On 19 May 2017, Mick sold a freehold warehouse for £522,000. The warehouse was purchased on 6 August 2005 for £258,000, and was extended at a cost of £99,000 during April 2007. In January 2011, the floor of the warehouse was damaged by flooding and had to be replaced at a cost of £63,000. The warehouse was sold because it was surplus to requirements as a result of Mick purchasing a newly built warehouse during 2016. Both warehouses have always been used for business purposes in a wholesale business run by Mick as a sole trader.

(2) On 12 August 2017, Mick sold an acre of land for £81,700. He had originally purchased five acres of land on 19 May 2002 for £167,400. The market value of the unsold four acres of land as at 12 August 2017 was £268,000. The land has never been used for business purposes.

(3) On 24 September 2017, Mick sold 700,000 £1 ordinary shares in Rolling Ltd, an unquoted trading company, for £3,675,000. He had purchased 500,000 shares in Rolling Ltd on 2 June 2009 for £960,000. On 1 June 2014, Rolling Ltd made a 3 for 2 bonus issue. Mick has been a director of Rolling Ltd since 1 January 2009.

(4) On 19 January 2018, Mick made a gift of his entire holding of 24,000 £1 ordinary shares in Sugar plc, a listed investment company, to his son, Keith. On that date the shares were quoted on the Stock Exchange at 698p - 710p. The shares had been purchased on 8 May 2012 for £76,800. Mick's shareholding was less than 1% of Sugar plc's issued share capital, and he has never been an employee or a director of the company.

Required:

(a) Assuming that no reliefs are available, calculate the chargeable gain arising from each of Mick Stone's asset disposals during the tax year 2017-18.

(b) State which capital gains tax reliefs might be available to Mick Stone in respect of each of his disposals during the tax year 2017-18, and what further information you would require in order to establish if the reliefs are actually available and to establish any restrictions as regards the amount of relief.

(ACCA)

B2 Yvonne had the following transactions in the shares of Scotia plc:

			£
18 August 2005	Bought	3,000 shares	6,000
19 September 2012	Bought	2,000 shares	5,000
13 March 2018	Sold	5,000 shares	23,000
28 March 2018	Bought	1,000 shares	4,400

Sally's capital gains tax position in 2017-18 was as follows:

	£
Capital gains arising in the year	37,200
Capital losses arising in the year	6,000
Capital losses brought forward	11,500

You are required to:

(a) Calculate Yvonne's chargeable gain.

(b) Calculate Sally's CGT liability for 2017-18, assuming that her taxable income for the year (i.e. total income less reliefs and the personal allowance) was:

(i) £20,000 (ii) £30,000 (iii) £40,000.

Also assume that none of Sally's gains relate to the disposal of residential property or qualify for entrepreneurs' relief. She made no Gift Aid donations or pension contributions during 2017-18. *(ACCA)*

B3 In August 2017, Samuel sold 20,000 ordinary shares in WQZ Ltd for £8 each. He had bought shares in the company as follows:

12 August 2009	10,000	shares cost £12,500
8 October 2011	5,000	shares cost £8,200
21 February 2013	35,000	shares cost £86,300

WQZ Ltd is an unlisted trading company with an issued share capital consisting of 120,000 ordinary shares, all of which have equal voting rights.

Samuel has been a director of WQZ Ltd since 2011. He claims entrepreneurs' relief (ER) in relation to the share disposal in August 2017 and has never claimed ER before. He has no other disposals in 2017-18 and has no allowable losses brought forward

You are required to:

(i) Calculate the gain arising in August 2017.

(ii) Explain why this gain is eligible for entrepreneurs' relief.

(iii) Calculate Samuel's CGT liability for 2017-18 and state the due date of payment.

B4 In the year to 5 April 2018, Thomas More made the following disposals:

(i) A flat in a house that he had purchased on 1 December 2007 for £80,000. It had never been occupied as the main residence and had been consistently let during his period of ownership. The property had been converted into two flats in September 2008 at a cost of £32,000. The flat was sold for £142,000 on 1 December 2017 and out of this legal fees of £4,000 were paid. It was agreed that the value of the other flat was £130,000 in December 2017.

(ii) 20,000 shares which cost £111,700 in December 2008 and were sold for £150,000 in December 2017. (No shares were acquired within the next 30 days).

Required:

(a) Calculate the capital gains tax payable on the sale of the flat and the shares. There were no other chargeable disposals in the year and no capital losses brought forward from previous years. Assume that Mr More's taxable income for 2017-18 exceeds the basic rate limit.

(b) If you were told at the start of 2017-18 that Mr More intended making the above disposals and that his wife had capital losses of £30,000 brought forward (and did not intend to make any disposals in 2017-18) would there be any advice that you would consider giving to Thomas? *(Amended from AAT)*

***B5** On 30 June 2017 Jorge sold a house for £308,000. The house had been purchased on 1 January 2000 for £98,000 and used by Jorge as follows:

Months	
16	Occupied
18	Unoccupied – travelling overseas
24	Unoccupied – required to work overseas by his employer
11	Occupied
30	Unoccupied – required to work elsewhere in the UK by his employer
22	Unoccupied – travelling overseas
26	Unoccupied – required to work elsewhere in the UK by his employer
27	Occupied
7	Unoccupied – required to work overseas by his employer
14	Unoccupied – travelling overseas
15	Unoccupied – lived with sister
210	

Jorge let the house during all of his periods of absence. Throughout the period 1 January 2000 to 30 June 2017 Jorge did not have any other main residence. He also made the following disposals in 2017-18:

(i) On 30 September 2017 he sold a copyright for £8,200. The copyright had been purchased on 1 October 2015 for £7,000 when it had an unexpired life of 10 years.

(ii) On 6 October 2017 he sold a painting for £5,400. The painting had been purchased on 18 May 2013 for £2,200.

(iii) On 3 December 2017 Jorge sold two acres of land for £92,000. Jorge's father-in-law had originally purchased three acres on 4 August 2005 for £19,500 but died on 17 June 2012 and the land was inherited by Jorge's wife. On that date the three acres were valued at £28,600. Jorge's wife transferred the land to him on 14 November 2015. On that date the three acres were valued at £39,000. The market value of the unsold acre of land as at 3 December 2017 was £38,000.

Required:

Calculate Jorge's taxable gains for tax year 2017-18. *(ACCA)*

***B6** You have been consulted by Mr Christopher Rodrigues on two matters relating to capital gains tax. Extracts from his letter to you are:

"On 31 January 2018, I sold my shares in Fledgeby plc, a listed company. I had acquired them as follows:

1 January 2008	1,000	shares cost £4,200
19 June 2009	700	shares cost £2,950
31 December 2015	1,200	shares cost £5,620
11 August 2017	400	shares cost £2,100

I also took up a 1 for 4 rights issue at £3.50 per share on 31 May 2016. The shares were all sold for £38,000 on 31 January 2018 and I do not intend to buy any shares in the company in the future.

Also on 31 January 2018, I sold for £200,000 a plot of land that I acquired in January 1980 for £10,000. A friend has told me that the gain might be either a capital gain or a trading profit. But, as capital gains and trading profits are both taxed, it doesn't really matter which way it is dealt with."

Required:

(a) Calculate the chargeable gain arising on the sale of the shares in Fledgeby plc.

(b) Do you agree with the statement of the other taxation practitioner? Draft brief notes that will form the basis of the letter that you will write to Mr Rodrigues.

(Amended from AAT)

***B7** On 1 May 2003, Nigel acquired a 30-year lease for £20,000. He assigned the lease on 1 November 2017 for £75,000.

Kay purchased land in February 2009 for £20,000. She sold one-third of the land for £18,000 in March 2018 when the value of the remaining two-thirds was £60,000.

Shirley had the following dealings in the shares of Wingfield plc, a listed company:

			£
January 1981	Bought	4,000 shares	18,000
March 1995	1 for 4 rights issue	1,000 shares	7,000
November 1998	Bought	3,000 shares	24,000
January 2009	1 for 2 bonus issue	4,000 shares	-
March 2018	Sold	7,000 shares	56,000

The shares had a market value of £8 per share on 31 March 1982. No further shares were acquired during 2018.

You are required to:

(i) Calculate Nigel's chargeable gain.

(ii) Calculate Kay's chargeable gain.

(iii) Calculate Shirley's chargeable gain. *(ACCA)*

***B8** Gillian purchased 10,000 ordinary shares in Downtown plc in January 2012 for £20,000. In October 2017, Upmarket plc acquired the whole of the share capital of Downtown plc following a take-over bid. The terms of the take-over offer were:

One ordinary share in Upmarket plc, and

Two preference shares in Upmarket plc, and

£3 cash

for every five shares held in Downtown plc. The share prices of Upmarket plc immediately after the take-over were:

Ordinary shares £10 each, and

Preference shares £3 each.

You are required to:

Calculate Gillian's chargeable gain arising in 2017-18. *(ACCA)*

***B9** Joan has been a full-time director of Sunnybank Pursuits Ltd (a trading company) since 1998 and has owned 10% of the company's ordinary shares since 2000. She retired in February 2018 and gave all of her shares in the company to her daughter, Sylvia. The capital gain on the gift was £400,000 before deducting any reliefs. This was her only disposal in tax year 2017-18.

Joan does not claim entrepreneurs' relief in relation to this disposal but Joan and Sylvia have jointly elected that the capital gain arising on the disposal should be held-over.

The market values of the company's chargeable assets at the time that the shares were gifted were:

	£
Land and buildings	4,000,000
Plant and machinery	2,000,000
Goodwill	1,000,000
Listed shares	1,000,000

All items of plant and machinery cost more than £6,000 each and are valued at more than £6,000 each in February 2018.

You are required to:

(i) Calculate Joan's assessable capital gain in 2017-18.

(ii) Assuming that Joan is a higher-rate taxpayer in 2017-18, calculate the CGT that would have been payable in relation to this share disposal if there had been no hold-over claim but Joan had claimed entrepreneurs' relief instead. *(ACCA)*

Part 3

CORPORATION TAX

Chapter 23

Introduction to corporation tax

Introduction

The next six chapters of this textbook deal with corporation tax, which is the tax that companies pay on their profits. The purpose of this first chapter is to provide an introduction to the basic principles of corporation tax. Relevant legislation can now be found mainly in the Corporation Tax Act 2009, the Corporation Tax Act 2010 and the Taxation of Chargeable Gains Act 1992, as amended by subsequent Finance Acts.

Scope of corporation tax

UK resident companies are liable to corporation tax on their "taxable total profits", no matter where in the world those profits arise. Companies which are not UK resident are within the charge to UK corporation tax only if they trade in the UK through a permanent establishment or carry on a trade of dealing in UK land (see Chapter 32). Note that:

(a) A company's taxable total profits include both its income and its chargeable gains. The term "chargeable gains" is normally used in preference to "capital gains".

(b) The main source of income for most companies is likely to be trading income. But a company may also have other sources of income. These could include bank interest, loan interest, property income etc.

(c) In general terms, a company's income is computed in a broadly similar way to that of an individual. The main differences between the assessment of a company's income and an individual's income are explained later in this chapter. The way in which a company's chargeable gains are calculated is considered in Chapter 24.

For corporation tax purposes, the word "company" is taken to mean any corporate body or unincorporated association, excluding partnerships, local authorities and local authority associations. As well as limited companies, this definition includes clubs and societies, which are liable to corporation tax on their income from non-members.

Organisations that are generally exempt from corporation tax (subject to various conditions and limits) include registered charities and registered pension schemes.

Accounting periods

Corporation tax is charged in respect of "accounting periods" and it is very important to distinguish between accounting periods and periods of account. An *accounting period* is a period for which corporation tax is charged. A *period of account* is a period for which a company prepares a set of accounts.

Although accounting periods and periods of account are often the same thing, this is not always the case. An accounting period *begins* when:

(a) the company comes within the charge to corporation tax, or
(b) when the previous accounting period ends, so long as the company remains within the charge to corporation tax.

An accounting period *ends* on the *earliest* occurrence of any of a number of events. The main events which cause the end of an accounting period are:

(a) the expiration of 12 months from the beginning of the accounting period
(b) the end of a period of account
(c) the company starting or ceasing to trade
(d) the company ceasing to be within the charge to corporation tax
(e) the company becoming, or ceasing to be, UK resident
(f) the company entering administration or ceasing to be in administration.

These rules have the following general consequences:

(a) The length of an accounting period can never exceed 12 months.
(b) If a set of accounts covers a period of 12 months or less, the period of account forms a single accounting period and a corporation tax assessment is raised for this period.
(c) If a set of accounts covers a period of more than 12 months, the period covered by the accounts is broken down into two or more accounting periods, each giving rise to a separate corporation tax assessment. The first accounting period consists of the first 12 months of the period of account. The second accounting period consists of the next 12 months and so forth. If the period covered by the accounts is not an exact multiple of 12 months, the final accounting period will be of less than 12 months' duration.

EXAMPLE 1

Identify the accounting periods which relate to the following periods of account:

(a) Company A prepares accounts for the year to 31 December 2017.
(b) Company B prepares accounts for the six months to 31 October 2017.
(c) Company C prepares accounts for the sixteen months to 31 December 2017.
(d) Company D prepares accounts for the thirty months to 31 March 2018.

Solution

(a) The year to 31 December 2017 is a single accounting period.

(b) The six months to 31 October 2017 is a single accounting period.

(c) The sixteen months to 31 December 2017 is divided into two accounting periods - the 12 months to 31 August 2017 and the four months to 31 December 2017.

(d) The thirty months to 31 March 2018 is divided into three accounting periods. These are the 12 months to 30 September 2016, the 12 months to 30 September 2017 and the six months to 31 March 2018.

Taxable total profits

The main elements which are taken into account when computing a company's taxable total profits for an accounting period may be summarised as follows:

	£	£
Trading income	xxx	
Less: Trading losses brought forward	xxx	xxx
Income from property		xxx
Income from non-trading loan relationships		xxx
Non-trading income from intangible fixed assets		xxx
Chargeable gains	xxx	
Less: Allowable capital losses	xxx	xxx
		xxx
Less: Property business losses	xxx	
Deficits on non-trading loan relationships	xxx	
Trading losses relieved against total profits	xxx	
Relief for qualifying charitable donations	xxx	xxx
Taxable total profits (TTP)		xxx

Most of the elements listed above are explained in this chapter but chargeable gains are dealt with in Chapter 24 and losses/deficits are considered in Chapter 26. The corporation tax treatment of foreign income is covered in Chapter 32. Note that:

(a) A company cannot be an employee and so cannot have employment income.

(b) There is no corporation tax equivalent of the personal allowances which are available to individuals who pay income tax.

(c) Corporation Tax Act 2010 uses the term "taxable total profits" to refer to a company's profits which are chargeable to corporation tax. But the terms "chargeable profits" or "profits chargeable to corporation tax" (PCTCT) are also sometimes used.

Trading income

A company's trading income for an accounting period consists of its trading profit for that period, as adjusted for tax purposes. The starting point for the calculation is the company's pre-tax profit for the relevant period of account. This figure is then adjusted by excluding non-trading income and adding back disallowed expenses. The adjusted trading profit of a period of account lasting for more than 12 months is apportioned between the accounting periods of which it is composed (see later in this chapter). Capital allowances claimed for each accounting period are then deducted.

This process is very similar to the equivalent process which applies to self-employed individuals (see Chapter 9)†. However, the following points should be noted:

(a) When calculating a company's trading income, there is no need to disallow the private proportion of expenses. This is because a company does not have a private existence. Any private use *by employees* is treated simply as a cost of employing staff (who may then be liable to income tax on a benefit in kind). A similar argument applies if a company provides an employee with any other goods or services.

(b) For a company, appropriations of profit (which are disallowed) consist principally of dividends payable to shareholders and transfers to reserves.

(c) A company's Gift Aid donations are disallowed when computing trading income but are then treated as qualifying charitable donations and are deducted when calculating the company's taxable total profits.

(d) Legal and other fees payable by a company in connection with the raising of loan finance are dealt with under the loan relationships regime (see later in this chapter).

(e) Losses caused by the dishonesty of a director are disallowed.

(f) Accounts drawn up in accordance with either UK GAAP or International Financial Reporting Standards (IFRS) are generally valid for corporation tax purposes.

(g) Unlike individuals, companies are entitled to a special tax relief in relation to their research and development expenditure. Furthermore, a special corporation tax regime applies to a company's income and expenditure in relation to intangible assets. Both of these matters are explained towards the end of this chapter.

Corporation tax assessments are raised for accounting periods (not tax years) and so there is no need for any basis period rules. The basis period rules which apply to individuals (see Chapter 10) are completely irrelevant to companies. In particular, there are no special rules on commencement or cessation of trade or on a change of accounting date.

† *A corporation tax version of Chapter 9 is available on the website which accompanies this book. The website address is* www.pearsoned.co.uk/melville.

Capital allowances

A company's capital allowances are computed in much the same way as those of a self-employed individual (see Chapter 11)†. The only significant distinctions are as follows:

(a) Each accounting period ranks as a chargeable period when computing capital allowances for a company and so there is one capital allowances computation per accounting period. Since an accounting period cannot exceed 12 months in length, there will never be any need to scale *up* writing down allowances, but these are scaled *down* for accounting periods of less than 12 months.

(b) Changes to the capital allowances system that take effect for income tax purposes as from 6 April normally take effect for corporation tax purposes as from 1 April. For example, the fall in the emissions threshold for main pool motor cars from 130g/km to 110g/km will take effect for companies as from 1 April 2018 (not 6 April 2018).

(c) A company may claim only one AIA, regardless of the number of businesses which it carries on. A group of companies (i.e. a parent and its subsidiaries) may claim only one AIA for the entire group. This AIA may then be shared between the members of the group in any way that the group sees fit.

(d) Companies which invest in energy-saving or environmentally-beneficial plant and machinery that qualifies for a 100% FYA may be able to claim a *first-year tax credit* in relation to the expenditure, rather than using the FYA in the normal way. This tax credit takes the form of a cash payment from the Government and is generally equal to 19% of the relevant expenditure. However, the available first-year tax credits for a chargeable period are capped at the *greater* of:

    (i) the total of the company's PAYE and NICs liabilities for that period, and
    (ii) £250,000.

    First-year tax credits are intended primarily for companies which make a trading loss in the chargeable period and so have no trading profits against which to offset their FYAs. The first-year tax credits scheme will come to an end on 31 March 2018.

(e) 100% FYAs are available to trading companies which invest in plant and machinery for use in designated areas within Enterprise Zones. To qualify for this FYA, the expenditure must be incurred within eight years of the date of designation.

(f) When computing a company's plant and machinery capital allowances, there will be no need to make any private use restrictions. Any private use of assets by employees is treated as part of the cost of employing staff and capital allowances are available in full in relation to such assets (though the employees concerned may then be liable to income tax on a benefit in kind).

† *A corporation tax version of Chapter 11 is available on the website which accompanies this book. The website address is* www.pearsoned.co.uk/melville.

EXAMPLE 2

A company's income statement for the year to 31 December 2017 is as follows:

	£	£
Turnover		1,640,430
Cost of sales		827,390
Gross profit		813,040
Other income		24,000
		837,040
Less: Distribution costs	187,770	
Administrative expenses	341,920	529,690
Profit for the year (before tax)		307,350

Notes:

1. The other income of £24,000 consists of rents receivable.
2. Distribution costs are as follows:

	£
Depreciation of distribution vans	18,530
Loss on disposal of distribution van	990
General distribution costs (all allowable)	168,250
	187,770

3. Administrative expenses are as follows:

	£
Depreciation of office equipment	12,680
Profit on disposal of office equipment	(3,710)
Loss on disposal of investments	27,000
Trade debts written off	10,600
Increase in general allowance for doubtful debts	8,400
Customer entertaining	2,760
Staff entertaining	5,550
Gift Aid donations	10,000
Legal fees re acquisition of new freehold offices	4,500
Motor expenses (one-half private motoring by employees)	59,060
Patent royalties payable for trade purposes	20,000
Embezzlement by director	50,000
General administrative expenses (all allowable)	135,080
	341,920

Compute the company's trading income (before deduction of capital allowances) for the year to 31 December 2017.

Solution

		£	£
Profit per accounts			307,350
Less:	*Non-trading income*:		
	Income from property	24,000	
	Profit on disposal of office equipment	3,710	27,710
			279,640
Add:	*Disallowed expenses*:		
	Depreciation of distribution vans	18,530	
	Loss on disposal of distribution van	990	
	Depreciation of office equipment	12,680	
	Loss on disposal of investments	27,000	
	Increase in general allowance for doubtful debts	8,400	
	Customer entertaining	2,760	
	Gift Aid donations	10,000	
	Legal fees re acquisition of new offices	4,500	
	Embezzlement by director	50,000	134,860
Trading income (before capital allowances)			414,500

Notes:

(i) The Gift Aid donations are disallowed when computing trading income.

(ii) Motor expenses incurred in relation to private motoring by employees are allowable when computing trading income, so long as the employees work in the trade.

(iii) Patent royalties payable for trade purposes are allowable (see later in this chapter).

EXAMPLE 3

After deducting capital allowances for the year to 31 December 2016, the tax written down values of a company's plant and machinery were as follows:

	£	
General pool	112,500	
Special rate pool	14,700	(BMW car bought May 2015, 170g/km)

The company's next set of accounts covered the 15-month period to 31 March 2018. Plant and machinery bought and sold during this period were:

		£
18 March 2017	Bought plant	40,000
31 August 2017	Sold plant (cost £20,000 in 2013)	8,500
6 November 2017	Sold BMW motor car	11,300
6 November 2017	Bought Audi motor car (emissions 143g/km)	25,600
29 January 2018	Bought motor car (emissions 72 g/km)	7,100
12 March 2018	Bought plant	5,400
15 March 2018	Sold plant (cost £2,000 in November 2016)	2,200

Calculate the capital allowances available for the 15 months to 31 March 2018, assuming 20% private use of the BMW and Audi motor cars by a director of the company.

Solution

The 15-month period of account must be broken down into two accounting periods, which are the year to 31 December 2017 and the three months to 31 March 2018. Each of these accounting periods requires a separate capital allowances computation.

		Main pool	*Special rate pool*	*Allowances*
		£	£	£
y/e 31/12/17				
WDV b/f		112,500	14,700	
Acquisition (no AIA)			25,600	
			40,300	
Disposals		8,500	11,300	
		104,000	29,000	
WDA @ 18%		18,720		18,720
WDA @ 8%			2,320	2,320
		85,280		
Acquisition	40,000			
AIA @ 100%	40,000	0		40,000
WDV c/f		85,280	26,680	
Total allowances				61,040
1/1/18 - 31/3/18				
WDV b/f		85,280	26,680	
Disposal		2,000		
		83,280		
WDA @ 18% x 3/12		3,748		3,748
WDA @ 8% x 3/12			534	534
		79,532		
Acquisition	5,400			
AIA @ 100%	5,400	0		5,400
Acquisition	7,100			
FYA @ 100%	7,100	0		7,100
WDV c/f		79,532	26,146	
Total allowances				16,782

Notes:

(i) Capital allowances are not restricted for private use by an employee.

(ii) Maximum AIA is £200,000 for the year to 31/12/17 and (3/12 × £200,000) = £50,000 for the three months to 31/3/18.

Income from property

In general, a company's income from property (or "property business profit") is calculated in much the same way as an individual's income from property (see Chapter 5)†. But the following important distinctions should be noted:

(a) Interest payable on a loan taken out by a company for the purpose of buying or improving let property is dealt with under the loan relationships rules and is therefore disallowed when computing property income.

(b) The income tax rule that restricts tax relief on interest payable and other finance costs as from tax year 2017-18 (see Chapter 5) does not apply to companies.

(c) The loss reliefs available to a company which suffers a loss in relation to a property business are different from those available to an individual (see Chapter 26).

(d) Rent-a-room relief does not apply to companies.

(e) A company's property business profit must be calculated on the accruals basis. The cash basis is not available.

† *A corporation tax version of Chapter 5 is available on the website which accompanies this book. The website address is* www.pearsoned.co.uk/melville.

UK-REITs

Subject to a number of conditions, a listed UK company with property income comprising at least 75% of total profits and property business assets (plus cash) comprising at least 75% of total assets may apply to become a UK Real Estate Investment Trust (UK-REIT).

The qualifying property income of a UK-REIT is exempt from corporation tax. Capital gains made on the disposal of investment property are also exempt from corporation tax. Such companies must distribute at least 90% of their tax-exempt profits to their shareholders, deducting basic rate tax at source (see Chapter 2).

Income from non-trading loan relationships

Income from non-trading loan relationships consists mainly of bank and building society interest and any other interest receivable by a company. Such interest is assessed on the *accruals* basis. Note that companies generally receive interest gross (i.e. without deduction of income tax at source). In particular:

(a) Companies receive bank and building society interest gross.

(b) Interest received by a UK company from an individual or from another UK company (e.g. loan interest, debenture interest etc.) is also received gross.

The loan relationships rules are explained in more detail later in this chapter.

EXAMPLE 4

A company prepares accounts to 31 December each year and lets two properties to tenants. The following information relates to the year to 31 December 2017:

(a) Property A is owned by the company. The property was let from 1 January 2017 to 30 June 2017 at an annual rent of £9,600, payable monthly in advance. However, the rent due on 1 May and 1 June 2017 was not paid and the tenant then absconded. The company has now written off this rent as a bad debt.

Having advertised for a new tenant (cost £200), the company re-let the property from 1 September 2017 at an annual rent of £10,200, payable monthly in advance. The rent due on 1 December 2017 was not received until 3 January 2018.

Apart from advertising, the only other expenses incurred by the company in relation to Property A during the year to 31 December 2017 were:

	£
Minor repairs	230
Interest on loan to acquire the property	8,400

(b) Property B is a leasehold property which was acquired by the company on 1 October 2017. The company paid a premium of £120,000 for the grant of a 25-year lease but is not required to pay rent. As from 1 October 2017, this property was let to a tenant at an annual rent of £12,000. The first year's rent was paid in advance and the tenant also paid a premium of £40,000 for the grant of a 10-year lease.

No expenses were incurred in relation to this property during the year.

Calculate the company's property business profit for the year to 31 December 2017.

Solution

	£	£
Rent receivable:		
Property A £9,600 x 6/12 + £10,200 x 4/12		8,200
Property B £12,000 x 3/12		3,000
Premium received £40,000 – (£40,000 x 2% x (10 – 1))	32,800	
Premium paid 10/25ths x (£120,000 – (£120,000 x 2% x (25 – 1)))	24,960	7,840
		19,040
Less: Bad debt £9,600 x 2/12	1,600	
Advertising	200	
Repairs	230	2,030
Property business profit		17,010

Note that the loan interest is not deductible when computing property income but will be dealt with under the loan relationships regime.

Dividends received

Dividends received from other UK companies are paid out of profits which have already been subject to corporation tax. Therefore, to avoid double taxation, such dividends are not included in the taxable total profits of the receiving company.

Furthermore, most foreign dividends received by UK companies are now exempt from corporation tax (see Chapter 32) and are treated exactly as if they were dividends received from other UK companies. Accordingly, an exempt foreign dividend is not included in the taxable total profits of the receiving company.

Relief for charitable donations

Certain charitable donations and gifts are referred to as "qualifying charitable donations" and are deducted when computing a company's taxable total profits. Qualifying charitable donations are as follows:

(a) donations made by a company under the Gift Aid scheme (see Chapter 4)

(b) gifts of listed shares or securities to a charity

(c) gifts of land and buildings to a charity.

The Gift Aid donations that are deducted when computing taxable total profits for an accounting period are the donations actually *paid* during that period. Accruals and pre-payments are ignored. Similarly, the amount deducted in relation to gifts of assets is the market value of the assets given in the period. Unlike Gift Aid donations made by individuals (see Chapter 4) a company's Gift Aid donations are *not* grossed-up.

Charitable donations incurred by a company for trade purposes (and not within the Gift Aid scheme) are deductible when computing the company's trading income.

Gifts of pre-eminent property to the nation

A company which makes a gift of "pre-eminent property" to be held for the benefit of the public or the nation (e.g. a work of art) is entitled (subject to conditions) to a corporation tax reduction equal to 20% of the value of that property. If this tax reduction exceeds the company's corporation tax liability, then the liability is reduced to zero and the balance of the tax reduction is lost.

Loan relationships

A company is a party to a "loan relationship" if it is a debtor or creditor with regard to any debt which is a loan under general law. The main classes of debt to which the term refers are bank and building society deposits, bank overdrafts, Government securities ("gilts" or "gilt-edged" securities), corporate bonds (e.g. debentures) and other corporate debt. The tax treatment of income and expenditure relating to a loan relationship depends upon whether the relationship has been entered into for trade purposes. The loan relationships rules may be summarised as follows:

(a) **Trading loan relationships**. If a company has entered into a loan relationship for trade purposes, then:

    (i) Any interest payable (and any other cost relating to the debt) is treated as a trading expense.

    (ii) Any interest receivable (and other income relating to the debt) is treated as trading income. This will usually apply only if the company's trade is that of lending money.

(b) **Non-trading loan relationships**. If a company has entered into one or more loan relationships for non-trading purposes, then all of the "debits" and "credits" (costs and income) relating to such relationships are aggregated. Then:

    (i) If total credits exceed total debits, the net credits form part of the company's taxable total profits and are charged to corporation tax.

    (ii) If total debits exceed total credits, the net debits may be relieved in a variety of ways (see Chapter 26).

    Interest payable on underpaid corporation tax is treated as a non-trading debit. Similarly, interest receivable on a repayment of overpaid corporation tax is treated as a non-trading credit (see Chapter 25).

It is important to appreciate that the above treatment of costs and income relating to loan relationships applies to all such costs and income, *whether of a revenue or capital nature*. This means that the profit (or loss) arising on a disposal of Government securities or corporate bonds by a company is taxable (or allowable) even though such assets would not be chargeable assets for CGT purposes if held by individuals.

Accounting for loan relationships

The amount of income and expenditure brought into account for a loan relationship is calculated on the *accruals basis*. Any payments made net† of income tax are grossed up before being included in the corporation tax computation. Income tax deducted at source from such payments must then be accounted for to HMRC (see Chapter 25).

† *It should be assumed in all of the worked examples below that any payments made net of income tax have already been grossed up, so that the figures shown are the gross amounts.*

EXAMPLE 5

A manufacturing company has the following results for the year to 31 March 2018:

	£
Trading income	883,000
Income from property	14,200
Bank interest (amount received)	3,200
Interest on Government securities (amount received)	28,000
Dividends from UK companies	18,450
Chargeable gains	123,000
Gift Aid donation	24,000

The following information is also relevant:

(a) Bank interest of £1,100 was owing to the company at the end of the year. The corresponding amount at the start of the year was zero.

(b) The Government securities were acquired on 1 July 2017. Interest of £28,000 is payable to the company on 30 June and 31 December each year.

Compute the company's taxable total profits for the year to 31 March 2018.

Solution

	£
Trading income	883,000
Income from property	14,200
Income from non-trading loan relationships (£4,300 + £42,000)	46,300
Chargeable gains	123,000
	1,066,500
Less: Qualifying charitable donations	24,000
Taxable total profits (TTP)	1,042,500

Notes:

(i) The bank interest is income from a non-trading loan relationship and is assessed on the accruals basis. The amount that is charged to corporation tax for the year is £4,300 (£3,200 received + £1,100 accrued).

(ii) The interest on Government securities is income from a non-trading loan relationship and is assessed on the accruals basis. The income accrued in the year of £42,000 (£28,000 + £14,000) forms part of the company's total profits.

(iii) The dividends received do not form part of the company's total profits for corporation tax purposes.

(iv) The Gift Aid donation of £24,000 is a qualifying charitable donation.

EXAMPLE 6

A company produces the following income statement for the year to 31 March 2018:

		£	£
Gross profit brought down from trading account			762,950
Add:	Rental income (Note 1)	5,000	
	Loan interest receivable (Note 2)	2,600	
	Dividends received (Note 3)	18,750	
	Bank interest receivable (Note 4)	789	
	Patent royalties receivable (Note 5)	6,500	
	Profit on sale of building (Note 6)	6,000	39,639
			802,589
Less:	Operating expenses (Note 7)		568,912
Net profit for the year			233,677

Notes:

1. The property was let on 1 January 2018 at a rent of £20,000 per annum, payable annually in advance. The figure shown in the income statement represents the rent for the period 1 January 2018 to 31 March 2018. No allowable expenditure has been incurred in relation to the let property.
2. Loan interest of £1,950 was received during the year and a further £650 was owing to the company at the end of the year. None was owed to the company at the start of the year. The income statement shows the total of £2,600.
3. Dividends of £18,750 were received from other UK companies during the year.
4. Bank interest received in the year was £684. Of this, £100 was owed to the company at the start of the year. A further £205 was owing to the company at the end of the year but was not received until April 2018.
5. Gross patent royalties of £6,000 were received in the year and a further £500 was owing to the company at the end of the year. None was owed to the company at the start of the year. The income statement shows the total of £6,500. The patents are held for trade purposes.
6. The chargeable gain on the sale of the building is £2,350.
7. Operating expenses include:

	£
Directors' fees	100,000
Debenture interest (gross):	
Paid 1 January 2018	4,000
Accrued at 31 March 2018	2,000
Depreciation of tangible fixed assets	102,500
Customer entertaining expenses	2,400
Gift Aid donation paid in the year	750

All of the remaining operating expenses are allowable as trading expenses. The debentures were issued on 1 July 2017 for trade purposes. The company claims capital allowances for the year of £87,450.

Required:

(a) Compute the company's trading income for the year to 31 March 2018.

(b) Compute the company's taxable total profits for the year to 31 March 2018.

Solution

(a) The company's trading income is as follows:

	£	£
Net profit per accounts		233,677
Less: *Non-trading income*:		
Income from property	5,000	
Loan interest receivable	2,600	
Dividends received	18,750	
Bank interest receivable	789	
Profit on sale of building	6,000	33,139
		200,538
Add: *Disallowed expenses*:		
Depreciation	102,500	
Customer entertaining	2,400	
Gift Aid donation	750	105,650
		306,188
Less: Capital allowances		87,450
Trading income		218,738

(b) The taxable total profits for the year are:

	£
Trading income	218,738
Income from property	5,000
Income from non-trading loan relationships (£2,600 + £789)	3,389
Chargeable gain	2,350
	229,477
Less: Qualifying charitable donations	750
Taxable total profits (TTP)	228,727

Notes:

(i) The computation of the company's trading income is performed in the same way as that of an individual. The starting point is the net profit shown by the accounts. Non-trading income included in this net profit is subtracted and disallowed expenses are added back. The aim is to separate out the company's trading profit from the total net profit shown in the accounts. The debenture interest is an allowable expense since the debentures were issued for trade purposes. The patent royalties receivable are trading income since the patents are held for trade purposes.

It is extremely important to classify the company's profits correctly and to arrive at a separate figure for each category of profit (e.g. trading income, rents, interest, chargeable gains etc.). This analysis is necessary because different rules of assessment apply to each category of profit and is especially vital if the company has incurred any losses (see Chapter 26).

(ii) Property income is computed on the accruals basis.

(iii) The accrued loan interest forms part of the company's income from non-trading loans (assuming that the loan was not made for trade purposes). The remainder of this figure is bank interest, which is also assessed on the accruals basis.

(iv) Dividends received are not chargeable to corporation tax.

(v) The chargeable gain on the sale of the building is fully chargeable to corporation tax since the company is not entitled to the annual exemption (see Chapter 24).

(vi) The Gift Aid donation is a qualifying charitable donation.

(vii) It is assumed that the company has not elected into the "patent box" regime (see later in this chapter).

Long periods of account

As stated above, a period of account exceeding 12 months in length must be divided into two or more accounting periods, each of which will give rise to a separate corporation tax assessment. A company's income and gains† for a long period of account are allocated between accounting periods as follows:

(a) Trading profits (before deduction of capital allowances) are usually time-apportioned. Capital allowances are then computed separately for each accounting period.

(b) Property income is also usually time-apportioned.

(c) A net credit on non-trading loan relationships is allocated between accounting periods on the accruals basis.

(d) Chargeable gains are allocated to the accounting period in which the disposals occur.

(e) Qualifying charitable donations are allocated to the accounting period in which they are made.

In practice, the time-apportionment method which is normally used for trading profits and property income may be replaced by a more accurate method of allocation if one is available. For instance, if trading profits have been earned as a result of a small number of transactions and the profit arising on each transaction can be calculated individually, trading profits may be allocated between accounting periods according to the transactions occurring in each period.

† *Dividends received are allocated on the receipts basis. Although dividends do not form part of a company's taxable profits, this allocation may be important when determining whether or not the company is liable to pay corporation tax by instalments (see Chapter 25).*

EXAMPLE 7

A company makes up accounts for the 21 months to 30 September 2017. The company's results for this period of account are as follows:

	£
Adjusted trading profits (before capital allowances)	630,000
Non-trade loan interest receivable:	
Received 31 October 2016	600
Received 30 April 2017	600
Accrued to 30 September 2017	500
Chargeable gains:	
Disposal on 25 May 2016	2,300
Disposal on 12 December 2016	700
Disposal on 15 February 2017	10,500
Gift Aid donations:	
Paid 31 December 2016	4,000
Accrued to 30 September 2017	3,000

The loan interest receivable relates to a £12,000 loan made on 1 May 2016 at 10%. The company makes a £4,000 Gift Aid donation on 31 December every year. Show how the period of account will be divided into accounting periods and compute the company's taxable total profits for each accounting period. (Ignore capital allowances).

Solution

There are two accounting periods - the year to 31 December 2016 and the nine months to 30 September 2017. The taxable profits for each accounting period are as follows:

	12 mths to 31/12/16	*9 mths to 30/9/17*
	£	£
Trading income (12:9)	360,000	270,000
Income from non-trading loan relationship	800	900
Chargeable gains	3,000	10,500
	363,800	281,400
Less: Qualifying charitable donations	4,000	nil
Taxable total profits (TTP)	359,800	281,400

Notes:

(i) The loan interest is allocated on the accruals basis. Interest on the loan accrues at £100 per month so the interest for the period from 1 May 2016 to 31 December 2016 (eight months) is £800 and the interest for the period from 1 January 2017 to 30 September 2017 (nine months) is £900.

(ii) The chargeable gains are allocated according to the date of disposal and the Gift Aid donations are allocated according to the date of payment. The accrued donations are not deductible until the accounting period in which they are paid.

Research and development tax relief

Subject to certain conditions, small or medium-sized companies (SMEs) which incur research and development expenditure may claim tax relief on 230% of the amount of that expenditure. The expenditure must *not* be capital expenditure and must be relevant to the company's trade. Qualifying expenditure includes staffing costs, consumables (e.g. power, fuel and water) and payments to subcontractors.

For this purpose, the definition of a "small or medium-sized company" is based upon EU recommendations. Companies generally qualify as small or medium-sized if they have fewer than 500 employees and have either a turnover not exceeding €100 million or total assets not exceeding €86 million. Note that:

(a) In general, tax relief is given by deducting 230% of the qualifying expenditure when computing the company's trading income. If the effect of this deduction is to create or increase a trading loss, the company may (if it so wishes) claim a payment from HMRC equal to 14.5% of the "surrenderable loss". This is the *lower* of:

(i) the amount of the trading loss
(ii) 230% of the qualifying R&D expenditure.

If such a claim is made, the surrendered loss is then ineligible for the loss reliefs that are normally available in relation to a company's trading losses (see Chapter 26).

(b) There is a cap of €7,500,000 *per project* on the amount of expenditure in respect of which a small or medium-sized company may claim R&D tax relief.

"Above the line" tax credit for large companies

Until recently, large companies (i.e. non-SMEs) could deduct 130% of their qualifying research and development expenditure when computing trading income. However, this "super-deduction" ceased to be available from 1 April 2016. As from that date, large companies are allowed to deduct only 100% of their qualifying R&D expenditure when computing trading income. But such companies may then claim an "above the line" (ATL) 11% tax credit in relation to such expenditure. This tax credit operates as follows:

(a) The 11% tax credit is included as income when computing taxable total profits but is then deducted from the company's corporation tax liability for the period concerned. Assuming a corporation tax rate of 19% (see Chapter 25) the effect of the tax credit is to reduce the company's corporation tax liability by 8.91% of the R&D expenditure.

For instance, if R&D expenditure is £1m, the ATL tax credit is £110,000 and taxable profits increase by £110,000. The tax liability increases by £20,900 (19% × £110,000) but is then reduced by £110,000, a tax saving of £89,100 (8.91% of £1m).

(b) If the 11% tax credit exceeds the company's corporation tax liability for the period, the excess may (subject to conditions) be paid to the company by HMRC. Such payments are made net of corporation tax but the tax deducted may be set against the company's corporation tax liability in subsequent accounting periods.

Intangible fixed assets

A special tax regime applies to a company's income or expenditure in relation to intangible fixed assets (IFAs) such as patents, trademarks etc. In outline, the system is as follows:

(a) Subject to certain exclusions, tax relief is available for the cost of IFAs created or acquired by a company. The amount of relief is normally equal to the amortisation charged in the company's accounts. If an IFA is not amortised or is amortised over a very long period, the company may elect for a fixed rate tax allowance of 4% p.a.

(b) Capital allowances are not available to companies in respect of patent rights or know-how. Computer software falls within the IFAs regime unless the company elects for capital allowances to apply.

(c) A loss on the disposal of an IFA is eligible for tax relief. Similarly, a profit on the disposal of such an asset is taxable income. But if an IFA is disposed of for more than original cost and the disposal proceeds are re-invested in newly-acquired IFAs, the gain may be rolled-over against the cost of the new assets.

(d) Royalties payable or receivable for the use of IFAs (e.g. patent royalties) are within the scope of the IFAs regime and are dealt with on the accruals basis. Royalties which are paid or received net of basic rate income tax (see Chapter 25) are grossed up.

(e) If IFAs are held or used for trade purposes, the related income and expenditure is taken into account when computing trading income. If IFAs are held or used for non-trade purposes, the income and expenditure is aggregated to produce an overall non-trading gain or loss. A loss may be relieved in a number of ways (see Chapter 26).

Patent box

As from 1 April 2013, a company which owns a patent (and has significantly contributed towards the development of the patented invention) may elect into the "patent box" regime and so benefit from paying a lower rate of corporation tax on the amount of its trading income which is derived from exploiting the patent. Such income includes patent royalties and income derived from the sale of patented products or the sale of patent rights.

If a company elects into the patent box regime, this income is taxed at an effective rate of only 10%. This is achieved by making an additional deduction from the company's trading profit and then taxing this profit at the normal rate. For instance, if the normal rate of corporation tax is 19%, deducting 9/19ths of the patent box income from the company's profit (leaving 10/19ths) will achieve the desired result (since 10/19 × 19% = 10%).

The benefit of this regime has been phased in over a period of five years. Companies could claim only 60% of the additional deduction for the year to 31 March 2014 but this rose by a further 10% in each of the next four years. Therefore the full deduction can be made in the year to 31 March 2018 and in subsequent years.

Summary

- Corporation tax is charged on the worldwide profits of UK resident companies. Non-resident companies are liable to UK corporation tax only if they trade in the UK through a permanent establishment or carry on a trade of dealing in UK land.
- Corporation tax is charged in respect of accounting periods. The length of an accounting period can never exceed 12 months. A period of account which is longer than this is divided into two or more accounting periods.
- A company's taxable total profits consist of its income and chargeable gains, less any qualifying charitable donations.
- A company's trading income is calculated in a similar way to the trading income of an individual. However, special corporation tax rules apply to research and development expenditure and to income and expenditure relating to intangible fixed assets.
- A company's property income is assessed in a similar way to the property income of an individual. However, interest payable on a loan for the purchase or improvement of property is dealt with under the loan relationships rules.
- A company's income and expenditure relating to loan relationships entered into for trade purposes is taken into account when computing the company's trading income. Net credits on non-trading loan relationships form part of taxable total profits.
- Dividends received from other UK companies are not part of the taxable profits of the receiving company. Most foreign dividends are also exempt from corporation tax.
- A company's qualifying charitable donations consist mainly of Gift Aid donations. These are relieved on the payments basis.

Exercises

23.1 Identify the accounting periods relating to the following periods of account:

(a) year to 30 November 2017
(b) 1 October 2016 to 31 July 2017
(c) 1 January 2018 to 31 January 2018
(d) 33 months to 31 August 2017
(e) 1 April 2016 to 30 September 2017.

23.2 On 1 January 2018, a company receives gross debenture interest of £1,600 from another UK company and pays net debenture interest of £8,640 to individuals. Explain the corporation tax treatment of each of these items.

23.3 During the year to 31 March 2018, a company which qualifies as medium-sized spends £180,000 on research and development. This is qualifying expenditure under the R&D tax relief scheme. Explain the corporation tax treatment of this expenditure.

23.4 A company's accounts for the 17 months to 30 June 2017 include:

	£
Trading income	425,000
Debenture interest receivable:	
Received 31 October 2016	2,400
Received 30 April 2017	2,400
Accrued to 30 June 2017	800
Income from property (let since 2013)	9,010
Chargeable gains:	
Disposal on 31 January 2017	28,700
Disposal on 1 February 2017	49,760
Dividend received from UK company	10,000
Gift Aid donations:	
Paid 31 July 2016	6,000
Paid 31 January 2017	6,000

The debentures were acquired (not for trade purposes) on 1 May 2016. Interest is payable half-yearly on 30 April and 31 October. Show how the company's period of account will be divided into accounting periods and compute the taxable total profits for each accounting period. Ignore capital allowances.

23.5 A company has the following results for the year to 31 March 2018:

	£	£
Trading profits, after capital allowances		1,561,400
Bank deposit interest (account opened 1 April 2017):		
Received 30 June 2017		1,820
Received 31 December 2017		3,670
Accrued to 31 March 2018		1,980
Chargeable gain on sale of factory		531,000
Dividends received from UK companies		132,000
Deed of covenant payable annually to a charity:		
Paid 1 October 2017 for year to 30 September 2018	9,000	
Less: Prepayment	4,500	4,500

The charitable covenant began on 1 October 2017 and falls within the Gift Aid scheme. Compute the taxable total profits for the year.

***23.6** A company's income statement for the year to 31 March 2018 is as follows:

	£	£
Gross trading profit		383,870
Receivable from other UK companies:		
Dividends		4,000
Debenture interest (Note 1)		6,000
Bank interest receivable (Note 2)		2,600
Income from property (Note 3)		4,000
Profit on sale of investments (Note 4)		22,490
		422,960
Less:		
Distribution costs (all allowable)	97,500	
Administrative expenses (all allowable)	101,150	
Directors' fees	50,000	
Interest on bank overdraft	23,780	
Debenture interest payable (Notes 5, 8)	50,000	
Patent royalties payable (Notes 6, 8)	7,500	
Depreciation of tangible fixed assets	108,300	438,230
Net loss for the year		(15,270)

Notes:

1. The company acquired £240,000 of 10% debentures (for non-trade purposes) on 1 January 2018. Interest is receivable half-yearly on 30 June and 31 December. No interest was received during the year to 31 March 2018.
2. Bank interest receivable includes interest of £450 which had accrued at 31 March 2018 but which was not received until April 2018. There was no accrued interest at 31 March 2017.
3. The property was let on 1 December 2017 at a rent of £1,000 per month payable quarterly in advance on 1 December, 1 March, 1 June and 1 September. There were no allowable expenses in the year to 31 March 2018.
4. The agreed chargeable gain on the sale of the investments was £8,450.
5. £500,000 of 10% debentures were issued (for trade purposes) on 1 April 2017. The interest is payable (net of income tax) on 1 January each year.
6. As from 1 July 2017, the company is required to pay patent royalties of £10,000 per annum, deducting basic rate income tax at source. The net amount paid in the year to 31 March 2018 was £4,000. The royalties are payable for trade purposes.
7. Capital allowances of £32,700 are claimed for the year.
8. All figures given in the income statement are gross.

Compute the taxable total profits for the year.

Chapter 24

Corporate chargeable gains

Introduction

A company's taxable total profits for an accounting period include any chargeable gains which arise from disposals made during that period. The chargeable gains of a company are computed in a similar way to the capital gains of an individual, but there are some important differences between the rules which apply to companies and the rules which apply to individuals. The purpose of this chapter is to explain how the chargeable gains of a company are determined for corporation tax purposes. The relevant legislation is in the Taxation of Chargeable Gains Act 1992, as amended by subsequent Finance Acts.

Chargeable disposals and chargeable assets

A chargeable gain or allowable loss may arise if a company makes a chargeable disposal of a chargeable asset. A company's chargeable assets will usually consist of its tangible non-current assets (fixed assets) such as land and buildings, plant and machinery or investments, but certain assets are entirely exempt from the chargeable gains legislation. The main exemptions for a company are:

(a) motor cars

(b) items of tangible, movable property ("chattels") worth £6,000 or less

(c) chattels with a predictable useful life of up to 50 years ("wasting chattels") unless used in business and eligible for capital allowances

(d) gilt-edged securities and qualifying corporate bonds, which are dealt with by the loan relationships regime (see Chapter 23).

A chargeable disposal generally occurs when the whole or part of a chargeable asset is sold or given away. However, the gift of a chargeable asset to a charity is exempt.

Basis of assessment

The chargeable gains figure which is included in a company's taxable total profits for an accounting period is based upon the disposals made during that period. This figure is calculated as follows:

(a) The chargeable gain or allowable loss arising on each disposal is calculated.

(b) If total gains exceed total losses, the losses are subtracted from the gains to give net chargeable gains for the accounting period.

(c) If total losses exceed total gains, the chargeable gains figure for the accounting period is £nil. The net losses are then carried forward for relief in subsequent accounting periods (see Chapter 26).

Companies are *not* entitled to the annual exemption which is available to individuals who pay capital gains tax (CGT).

Computation of gains and losses

The chargeable gains and allowable losses of a company are computed in a similar way to those of an individual (see Chapters 18-22) but the following important distinctions should be noted:

(a) (i) The gain arising on the disposal of a chargeable asset by a company is reduced by "indexation allowance", which adjusts the gain to take account of inflation. Indexation allowance used to be available when calculating the capital gains of individuals for CGT purposes, but this is no longer the case.

(ii) Rebasing does not always apply when a company disposes of an asset acquired before 31 March 1982.

The way in which indexation allowance is calculated and the corporation tax treatment of assets acquired before 31 March 1982 are both explained below.

(b) The share matching rules that are used when a company makes a disposal of shares or securities are different from the equivalent rules that apply when such a disposal is made by an individual. The share matching rules which are used for corporation tax purposes are explained later in this chapter.

(c) The principal private residence exemption does not apply to companies.

(d) When a company disposes of an intangible asset, any gain or loss which arises is dealt with by the intangible fixed assets regime (see Chapter 23). Such disposals fall outside the scope of the tax on chargeable gains and cannot give rise to a chargeable gain or an allowable loss.

(e) Gift relief, incorporation relief, entrepreneurs' relief and EIS deferral relief do not apply to companies. But rollover relief is available on the replacement of tangible business assets (see Chapter 22) and "disincorporation relief" may be available if a company transfers certain business assets to its shareholders, who then continue to operate the business in an unincorporated form. Disincorporation relief is considered briefly at the end of this chapter.

Indexation allowance

Indexation allowance was introduced in 1982 with the intention of ensuring that capital gains caused by inflation should not be charged to tax.

Indexation allowance is calculated separately for each item of allowable expenditure shown in a computation. The indexation allowance available on an item of expenditure is equal to the amount of that expenditure multiplied by an *indexation factor*, which is computed according to the following formula and is rounded to three decimal places:

$$\frac{RD - RI}{RI}$$

where: RD is the Retail Prices Index (RPI) for the month of disposal, and
RI is the RPI for the month in which the expenditure was incurred.

A table of RPIs is given at the end of this chapter.

EXAMPLE 1

A company bought a chargeable asset (not a chattel) in June 2002 (RPI 176.2) for £1,200 and sold the asset in August 2017 (RPI 272.3) for £5,350. Compute the chargeable gain.

Solution

	£
Sale proceeds	5,350
Less: Acquisition cost	1,200
Unindexed gain	4,150
Less: Indexation allowance	
$\frac{272.3 - 176.2}{176.2} = 0.545 \times £1,200$	654
Chargeable gain	3,496

EXAMPLE 2

A company bought a chargeable asset in November 2000 for £15,000. Enhancement expenditure was £2,000 in January 2002 and £3,000 in June 2006. The asset was sold in February 2018 for £48,000. RPIs are as follows:

November 2000	172.1	January 2002	173.3
June 2006	198.5	February 2018	275.9

Compute the chargeable gain.

Solution

	£	£
Sale proceeds		48,000
Less: Acquisition cost	15,000	
Enhancement expenditure (£2,000 + £3,000)	5,000	20,000
Unindexed gain		28,000
Less: Indexation allowance:		
(i) on acquisition cost		
$\frac{275.9 - 172.1}{172.1} = 0.603 \times £15,000$	9,045	
(ii) on enhancement January 2002		
$\frac{275.9 - 173.3}{173.3} = 0.592 \times £2,000$	1,184	
(iii) on enhancement June 2006		
$\frac{275.9 - 198.5}{198.5} = 0.390 \times £3,000$	1,170	11,399
Chargeable gain		16,601

Notes:

(i) The three items of allowable expenditure were all incurred on different dates and therefore each attracts a different indexation factor.

(ii) The effect of indexation allowance is to convert each item of allowable expenditure to an equivalent amount as at the date of disposal. This removes the element of inflation from the calculation and calculates the chargeable gain in real terms.

For instance, there has been 60.3% inflation (indexation factor 0.603) between the date of acquisition of the asset and the date of its disposal. Therefore the company needs to make a gain of £9,045 (60.3% × £15,000) merely to maintain the purchasing power that it had when it originally acquired the asset. A similar argument applies to the two amounts of enhancement expenditure. In total, the company needs a gain of £11,399 to maintain its purchasing power. Any gain beyond this figure represents an increase in purchasing power and is therefore a gain in real terms.

Restrictions on indexation allowance

Note the following points about the indexation allowance:

(a) If RPI goes *down* between the month in which expenditure is incurred and the month of disposal, the indexation allowance available in relation to that expenditure is nil.

(b) No indexation allowance is available in respect of any incidental costs of disposal, even if they were incurred prior to the month of disposal.

(c) Indexation allowance cannot be used to convert a gain into a loss. Therefore, if the available indexation allowance (calculated in the normal way) exceeds the unindexed gain, the indexation allowance is restricted so as to give neither a gain nor a loss.

(d) Indexation allowance cannot be used to increase an unindexed loss. If there is an unindexed loss on a disposal then the indexation allowance is nil.

EXAMPLE 3

A company acquired a chargeable asset for £5,000 in February 2004 (RPI 183.8). The asset was sold in January 2018 (RPI 275.3). The asset was not a chattel. Compute the chargeable gain or allowable loss if the sale proceeds were:

(a) £9,000 (b) £5,500 (c) £4,800

Solution

	(a)	(b)	(c)
	£	£	£
Sale proceeds	9,000	5,500	4,800
Less: Acquisition cost	5,000	5,000	5,000
Unindexed gain or loss	4,000	500	(200)
Less: Indexation allowance			
$\frac{275.3 - 183.8}{183.8} = 0.498 \times £5,000 = £2,490$	2,490	500	nil
Chargeable gain or allowable loss	1,510	nil	(200)

Notes:

(i) In case (a), the indexation allowance can be given in full.

(ii) In case (b), the full indexation allowance would convert an unindexed gain of £500 into a loss of £1,990. Indexation allowance is restricted to £500 to prevent this.

(iii) In case (c) there is an unindexed loss, so indexation allowance is restricted to £nil.

Assets held on 31 March 1982

If an asset is disposed of which was acquired before 31 March 1982, only the part of the gain accruing since 31 March 1982 is charged to tax (see Chapter 18). The chargeable gain is usually calculated by means of the "rebasing" technique, whereby the market value of the asset at 31 March 1982 is substituted for its acquisition cost.

However, although rebasing now always applies for individuals, this is not the case for companies. Under corporation tax rules, rebasing does *not* apply if the rebasing calculation results in a greater gain than the calculation based on original cost.

In other words, for corporation tax purposes, the chargeable gain arising on the disposal of an asset acquired before 31 March 1982 is the *lower* of the gain based on original cost and the gain based on market value at 31 March 1982.

EXAMPLE 4

A company acquired a chargeable asset for £2,000 in April 1980 and sold the asset for £22,500 in September 2017. Compute the unindexed gain arising on this disposal if the market value of the asset at 31 March 1982 was:

(a) £4,200 (b) £500

Solution

(a) The unindexed gain over the entire period of ownership, based on the original cost of the asset, is £20,500 (£22,500 – £2,000). But the rebasing calculation gives a gain of only £18,300 (£22,500 – £4,200). This is less than the gain based on original cost so rebasing applies and the unindexed gain is £18,300.

(b) The rebasing calculation gives an unindexed gain of £22,000 (£22,500 – £500). This is more than the gain based on original cost so rebasing does not apply and the unindexed gain is £20,500.

Indexation allowance for pre-31 March 1982 assets

The rules for calculating the indexation allowance available to a company on the disposal of an asset held on 31 March 1982 are as follows:

(a) Indexation allowance is based on the change in RPI between March 1982 and the month of disposal. No further indexation allowance is available to compensate for the effects of pre-March 1982 inflation. This is why the table of RPIs given at the end of this chapter begins with the RPI for March 1982.

(b) In *both* the rebasing calculation and the calculation based on original cost, indexation allowance is calculated with reference to the *greater* of original cost and market value at 31 March 1982 (i.e. the same indexation allowance is given in both calculations).

EXAMPLE 5

Calculate the chargeable gain arising on the disposal described in the above example. RPIs are 79.44 for March 1982 and 272.9 for September 2017.

Solution

(a)

	Original cost	*Rebasing*
	£	£
Sale proceeds	22,500	22,500
Less: Original cost	2,000	
Market value 31/3/82		4,200
Unindexed gain	20,500	18,300
Less: Indexation allowance		
$\frac{272.9 - 79.44}{79.44} = 2.435 \times £4{,}200$	10,227	10,227
Chargeable gain	10,273	8,073

The rebasing calculation gives the lower gain, so rebasing applies and the chargeable gain is £8,073.

(b)

	Original cost	*Rebasing*
	£	£
Sale proceeds	22,500	22,500
Less: Original cost	2,000	
Market value 31/3/82		500
Unindexed gain	20,500	22,000
Less: Indexation allowance		
$\frac{272.9 - 79.44}{79.44} = 2.435 \times £2{,}000$	4,870	4,870
Chargeable gain	15,630	17,130

The rebasing calculation gives the higher gain, so rebasing does not apply and the chargeable gain is £15,630.

Losses on disposal of pre-31 March 1982 assets

If the rebasing calculation gives a gain and the original cost calculation also gives a gain, the chargeable gain is the *smaller* of these two gains. Similarly, if the rebasing calculation gives a loss and the original cost calculation also gives a loss, the allowable loss is the *smaller* of these two losses. Finally, if one of the calculations gives a gain and the other calculation gives a loss (or if either calculation gives a nil result) the situation is "no gain, no loss". In these circumstances there is no chargeable gain and no allowable loss.

EXAMPLE 6

A company acquired a chargeable asset (not a chattel) in 1979. The asset was sold in December 2017 (RPI 274.7) for £2,800. Compute the chargeable gain or allowable loss if the original cost of the asset and its market value on 31 March 1982 (RPI 79.44) were:

		Original cost	*MV at 31/3/82*
		£	£
either	(a)	3,500	4,000
or	(b)	350	450
or	(c)	200	900

Solution

(a)

	Original cost	*Rebasing*
	£	£
Sale proceeds	2,800	2,800
Less: Original cost	3,500	
Market value 31/3/82		4,000
Allowable loss	(700)	(1,200)

The rebasing calculation gives the higher loss, so rebasing does not apply and the allowable loss is £700. Indexation allowance was £nil in both calculations, since indexation allowance cannot be used to increase an unindexed loss.

(b)

	Original cost	*Rebasing*
	£	£
Sale proceeds	2,800	2,800
Less: Original cost	350	
Market value 31/3/82		450
Unindexed gain	2,450	2,350
Less: Indexation allowance		
$\frac{274.7 - 79.44}{79.44}$ = 2.458 x £450	1,106	1,106
Chargeable gain	1,344	1,244

The rebasing calculation gives the lower gain. Therefore rebasing applies and the chargeable gain is £1,244.

(c)

	Original cost	Rebasing
	£	£
Sale proceeds	2,800	2,800
Less: Original cost	200	
Market value 31/3/82		900
Unindexed gain	2,600	1,900
Less: Indexation allowance		
$\frac{274.7 - 79.44}{79.44} = 2.458 \times £900 = £2,212$	2,212	1,900
Chargeable gain	388	nil

The rebasing calculation gives a nil result, whilst the calculation based on original cost gives a gain. Therefore the situation is "no gain, no loss". Indexation allowance was restricted to £1,900 in the rebasing calculation so as to avoid converting a gain into a loss.

The rebasing election

A company may make an *irrevocable* election to the effect that gains and losses arising on all future disposals of assets held on 31 March 1982 should be calculated by the rebasing method, with no reference whatsoever to the costs incurred before 31 March 1982.

If this election is made, costs incurred before 31 March 1982 are completely ignored for all purposes, including calculation of the indexation allowance. Therefore indexation allowance will always be based upon market value at 31 March 1982, even if this is lower than the costs incurred before 31 March 1982.

Assets acquired before 6 April 1965

When the tax on chargeable gains was introduced, special rules applied to the disposal of an asset acquired before 6 April 1965. These rules no longer apply to individuals and are now rarely used for companies, as it becomes increasingly uncommon for a disposal to involve an asset acquired before 6 April 1965. Also, from the perspective of disposals made in the 21st century, the disposal of an asset acquired before 6 April 1965 must also be the disposal of an asset held on 31 March 1982. Therefore rebasing is available in relation to such disposals and rebasing will generally give a lower gain than the gain calculated according to the special rules mentioned above. However, these rules are still used for companies if they give the lower gain.

A summary of the treatment of assets acquired before 6 April 1965, together with a number of worked examples, can be found on the website which accompanies this book. The website address is www.pearsoned.co.uk/melville.

Disposals of shares or securities

The share matching rules which apply on a disposal of shares or securities by an individual were explained in Chapter 20 of this book. The main principle is that shares of the same class in the same company are pooled into the "Section 104 holding" and that disposals are generally matched against shares taken from this holding. Special rules apply if shares are bought and sold on the same day or if shares are sold and re-acquired within 30 days.

However, the share matching rules which are used when a *company* makes a disposal of shares or securities are not the same as the rules for individuals. A disposal of shares or securities by a company is matched against acquisitions in the following order:

(a) first, against acquisitions made on the same day

(b) next, against acquisitions made in the previous nine days (on a FIFO basis)

(c) next, against shares taken from the Section 104 holding, which (for companies) is the pool of shares acquired on or after 1 April 1982

(d) next, against the "1982 holding", which is a pool of shares acquired between 6 April 1965 and 31 March 1982 inclusive

(e) finally, against shares acquired before 6 April 1965 (on a LIFO basis).

These rules have to be more complex than their CGT equivalents because companies are entitled to indexation allowance and because rebasing does not always apply when a company disposes of a pre-31 March 1982 asset.

The Section 104 holding

A company's s104 holding of shares of a certain class in a certain company consists of the pool of shares which were acquired on or after 1 April 1982. Share acquisitions which are matched against disposals made on the same day or during the following nine days do not join the s104 holding.

The distinguishing characteristic of shares acquired on or after 1 April 1982 is that the indexation factor used on their disposal will differ according to the date of acquisition. If it were not for Section 104, it would be necessary to keep detailed records of the date and cost of each share acquisition made on or after 1 April 1982, so that indexation allowance could be calculated correctly on a disposal. However, the pooling system provided by Section 104 eliminates the need to keep these records. All that is required is a record of:

(a) the total number of shares in the pool

(b) their total cost

(c) their total *indexed cost*, which consists of total cost plus all indexation allowance due up to the date of the most recent "operative event". An operative event occurs whenever shares enter or leave the pool.

The indexed cost of the s104 holding is calculated as follows:

(a) The number of shares in the pool at 1 April 1985 (if any) is totalled and the cost of these shares is also totalled. The indexed cost of the pool at 1 April 1985 is calculated as total cost, plus an indexation allowance for each acquisition forming part of the pool, based on the change in RPI between the date of the acquisition and April 1985.

(b) On the occurrence of a subsequent operative event, the indexed cost of the pool is increased by reference to the change in RPI since the previous operative event (if any) or since April 1985 (if the previous event was before April 1985). TCGA 1992 does not require the indexation factor used in this calculation to be rounded to 3 decimal places. The pool is then adjusted as follows:

    (i) If the event is an acquisition, the number of shares acquired is added to the number of shares in the pool and their cost is added to the cost and to the indexed cost of the pool.

    (ii) If the event is a disposal, the number of shares disposed of is subtracted from the number of shares in the pool. It is then necessary to deduct a proportion of the cost and indexed cost of the pool. Strictly speaking, this proportion should be calculated using the part disposal fraction (see Chapter 18) which takes into account the value of the shares disposed of and the value of the shares remaining. In most cases, however, the value per share of the shares disposed of will be the same as the value per share of the shares remaining, so that the proportion to be deducted from the cost and indexed cost of the pool can be based upon the *number* of shares disposed of.

The unindexed gain (or loss) arising on a disposal from the pool is calculated as the difference between the disposal proceeds and the amount which has been subtracted from the cost of the pool as a consequence of the disposal. The indexation allowance due on the disposal is the difference between the amount subtracted from the cost of the pool and the amount subtracted from the indexed cost of the pool. As usual, indexation allowance cannot be used to create a loss or to increase a loss.

EXAMPLE 7

A company makes the following acquisitions of ordinary shares in JKL plc:

Date	*No of shares*	*Cost*	*RPI*
		£	
1 July 1983	5,000	6,300	85.30
2 August 1984	2,000	2,500	89.94
3 February 1997	1,200	2,300	155.0
4 June 2003	1,800	3,400	181.3

The company sells 500 shares on 8 July 2017 (RPI 271.7).

(a) Calculate the cost and indexed cost of the s104 holding on 8 July 2017, just prior to and just after the above disposal (RPI for April 1985 is 94.78).

(b) Compute the chargeable gain or allowable loss on the disposal if sale proceeds are:

(i) £2,000 (ii) £1,000 (iii) £700

Solution

(a) The cost and indexed cost of the s104 holding on 8 July 2017 are calculated as follows:

	No of shares	*Cost*	*Indexed cost*
		£	£
Bought 1 July 1983	5,000	6,300	6,300
Bought 2 August 1984	2,000	2,500	2,500
Add: Indexation to April 1985			
(a) $\frac{94.78 - 85.30}{85.30} = 0.111$			
0.111 x £6,300			699
(b) $\frac{94.78 - 89.94}{89.94} = 0.054$			
0.054 x £2,500			135
s104 holding at 1 April 1985	7,000	8,800	9,634
Add: Indexation to February 1997			
$\frac{155.0 - 94.78}{94.78}$ x £9,634			6,121
			15,755
Bought 3 February 1997	1,200	2,300	2,300
s104 holding at 3 February 1997	8,200	11,100	18,055

	No of shares	Cost	Indexed cost
		£	£
s104 holding at 3 February 1997	8,200	11,100	18,055
Add: Indexation to June 2003			
$\frac{181.3 - 155.0}{155.0}$ x £18,055			3,064
			21,119
Bought 4 June 2003	1,800	3,400	3,400
s104 holding at 4 June 2003	10,000	14,500	24,519
Add: Indexation to July 2017			
$\frac{271.7 - 181.3}{181.3}$ x £24,519			12,226
			36,745
Sold 8 July 2017 (500/10,000ths)	(500)	(725)	(1,837)
s104 holding c/f at 8 July 2017	9,500	13,775	34,908

Notes:

1. The indexation allowance calculated on operative events occurring after 5 April 1985 has not been rounded off to 3 decimal places.
2. The disposal in July 2017 must have come from the s104 holding since it cannot be matched against shares acquired on the same day or in the previous nine days.
3. The disposal is 500 shares out of a holding of 10,000. Therefore 500/10,000ths or 1/20th of the pool has been sold and so 1/20th of the cost and indexed cost are subtracted from the pool.
4. The cost of the shares disposed of is £725. Since the equivalent indexed cost is £1,837, the indexation allowance due on the disposal is £1,112 (£1,837 - £725).

(b)

	(i)	(ii)	(iii)
	£	£	£
Sale proceeds	2,000	1,000	700
Less: Cost	725	725	725
Unindexed gain or loss	1,275	275	(25)
Less: Indexation allowance (£1,112)	1,112	275	nil
Chargeable gain/(allowable loss)	163	nil	(25)

The 1982 holding

For a company, the 1982 holding is a pool of shares acquired between 6 April 1965 and 31 March 1982 inclusive. All of the shares in this pool attract the same rate of indexation allowance, based on the change in RPI between March 1982 and the date of disposal. This means that the calculation of this pool's value is much simpler than the calculation of the value of the s104 holding. All that is needed is a record of:

(a) the number of shares in the pool
(b) the total cost of these shares
(c) their market value at 31 March 1982.

When a disposal occurs, the number of shares in the pool is reduced and proportionate amounts are deducted from the pool's cost and from its market value at 31 March 1982. The gain or loss arising on the disposal is then calculated in the usual way, as for any disposal of a pre-31 March 1982 asset.

EXAMPLE 8

A company made the following acquisitions of ordinary shares in CDE plc:

Date	*No of shares*	*Cost*
		£
1 June 1970	1,000	3,000
30 October 1975	800	2,500
15 August 1981	900	3,100

The shares had a market value of £1.80 per share on 31 March 1982 (RPI 79.44). The company made no further acquisitions and sold 750 of the shares on 18 January 2018 (RPI 275.3) for £9,500. Compute the chargeable gain.

Solution

The sale of 750 shares on 18 January 2018 cannot be matched against any acquisitions made on the same day or during the previous nine days and there is no s104 holding. The next step is to match against the 1982 holding, as follows:

	No of shares	*Cost*	*MV 31/3/82*
		£	£
Acquired 1 June 1970	1,000	3,000	1,800
Acquired 30 October 1975	800	2,500	1,440
Acquired 15 August 1981	900	3,100	1,620
	2,700	8,600	4,860
Sold 18 January 2018 (750/2,700ths)	(750)	(2,389)	(1,350)
1982 holding c/f	1,950	6,211	3,510

The sold shares are deemed to have cost £2,389 and their market value at 31 March 1982 was £1,350. The calculation of the gain arising on the disposal is:

	Original cost	*Rebasing*
	£	£
Sale proceeds	9,500	9,500
Less: Original cost	2,389	
Market value 31/3/82		1,350
Unindexed gain	7,111	8,150
Less: Indexation allowance		
$\frac{275.3 - 79.44}{79.44}$ = 2.466 x £2,389	5,891	5,891
Chargeable gain	1,220	2,259

The rebasing calculation gives the higher gain, so rebasing does not apply and the chargeable gain is £1,220.

Bonus issues and rights issues

As explained in Chapter 20, bonus issues and rights issues are regarded as reorganisations of share capital and shares acquired as a consequence of such issues are not treated as acquisitions in the normal way. Instead, the required treatment of bonus shares and rights shares is to uplift the number of shares in each of the taxpayer's existing holdings. In the case of rights issues, it is also necessary to increase the cost of those holdings, since rights shares (unlike bonus shares) are not acquired free of charge.

This treatment applies to companies as well as to individuals, but one complication that may arise in the case of a company is that rights shares acquired after 31 March 1982 might join the 1982 holding. If this occurs, the cost of the rights shares is treated as enhancement expenditure and it is necessary (for indexation purposes) to keep a separate record of the cost and acquisition date of those rights shares.

EXAMPLE 9

A company made the following acquisitions of ordinary shares in Rujan plc:

Date	*No of shares*	*Cost*	*RPI*
		£	
15 August 1980	500	1,000	
23 January 1997	600	2,500	154.4

The market value of the shares on 31 March 1982 (RPI 79.44) was £2.50 per share. In June 2004 (RPI 186.8), Rujan plc made a 1 for 20 rights issue at £8 per share and the company decided to buy the shares it was offered. Calculate the chargeable gain arising in October 2017 (RPI 273.5) when the company sold 840 shares for £10 each.

Solution

The s104 holding:

	No of shares	Cost	Indexed cost
		£	£
Bought 23 January 1997	600	2,500	2,500
Add: Indexation to June 2004			
$\frac{186.8 - 154.4}{154.4} \times £2,500$			525
			3,025
Rights issue June 2004 (1 for 20)	30	240	240
	630	2,740	3,265
Add: Indexation to October 2017			
$\frac{273.5 - 186.8}{186.8} \times £3,265$			1,515
			4,780
Sold October 2017	(630)	(2,740)	(4,780)
s104 holding c/f	nil	nil	nil

The gain arising on the disposal of the s104 holding is:

	£
Sale proceeds (630 @ £10)	6,300
Less: Cost	2,740
Unindexed gain	3,560
Less: Indexation allowance (£4,780 - £2,740)	2,040
Chargeable gain	1,520

The 1982 holding:

	No of shares	Cost (original)	Cost (rights)	MV 31/3/82
		£	£	£
Acquired 15 August 1980	500	1,000		1,250
Rights issue June 2004 (1 for 20)	25		200	
	525	1,000	200	1,250
Sold October 2017 (210/525ths)	(210)	(400)	(80)	(500)
1982 holding c/f	315	600	120	750

The gain arising on the disposal from the 1982 holding is calculated on the basis that the company has sold an asset with a cost of £400 and a market value at 31 March 1982 of £500. The calculation also takes into account enhancement expenditure of £80 incurred in June 2004. The calculation of the gain is as follows:

	Original cost	Rebasing
	£	£
Sale proceeds (210 @ £10)	2,100	2,100
Less: Cost up to 31 March 1982	(400)	
Market value 31/3/82		(500)
Cost June 2004	(80)	(80)
Unindexed gain	1,620	1,520
Less: Indexation allowance		
$\frac{273.5-79.44}{79.44}$ = 2.443 x £500	(1,222)	(1,222)
$\frac{273.5-186.8}{186.8}$ = 0.464 x £80	(37)	(37)
Chargeable gain	361	261

The rebasing calculation gives the lower gain, so rebasing applies and the gain is £261. The total gain on the entire disposal of 840 shares is therefore £1,781 (£1,520 + £261).

Shares acquired before 6 April 1965

Special rules apply if a company disposes of shares which were originally acquired before 6 April 1965. However, these rules are now falling into disuse as it becomes increasingly uncommon for a disposal to involve shares acquired before that date.

A summary of the treatment of shares acquired before 6 April 1965, together with a number of worked examples, can be found on the website which accompanies this book. The website address is www.pearsoned.co.uk/melville.

Disposal of a substantial shareholding

A gain arising on the disposal of all or part of a "substantial shareholding" by an investor company which is a trading company† (or a member of a trading group) is exempt from corporation tax so long as certain conditions are satisfied. Similarly, any loss arising on such a disposal is not an allowable loss. The main conditions which must be satisfied are:

(a) The investor company has held a substantial shareholding in the investee throughout a 12-month period beginning not more than two years before the disposal.

(b) The investee is a trading company or the holding company of a trading group.

For this purpose, a company holds a substantial shareholding in another company if it holds at least 10% of that company's ordinary share capital and is entitled to at least 10% of that company's profits and assets.

† *The Government has proposed that the substantial shareholding exemption should be extended to investor companies which are not trading companies or members of trading groups.*

Disincorporation relief

A company which transfers a business to its shareholders (who will then continue to operate the business in an unincorporated form) may be able to claim disincorporation relief. The effect of this relief is that no corporation tax charge arises to the company on the transfer of land and buildings or on the transfer of goodwill. The main conditions that must be satisfied in order for this relief to be available are as follows:

(a) The company must transfer a business to some or all of its shareholders, who will then operate the business as a going concern. All of the assets of the business must be transferred (other than cash) and the total market value of the company's land and buildings and goodwill must not exceed a total of £100,000.

(b) The shareholders must have held their shares for at least the previous 12 months.

(c) A claim for relief must be made within two years of the date of the transfer.

If these conditions are satisfied, no chargeable gain will arise on the transfer of land and buildings and no tax charge will arise (under the intangible assets regime) in relation to the transfer of goodwill. Disincorporation relief is available in respect of transfers made between 1 April 2013 and 31 March 2018.

Summary

- A company's chargeable assets usually consist of non-current assets such as land and buildings, plant and investments. Non-chargeable assets include motor cars, chattels worth up to £6,000, wasting chattels, gilts and qualifying corporate bonds.
- A chargeable disposal occurs when the whole or part of a chargeable asset is sold or given away (unless given to a charity).
- If allowable losses for an accounting period exceed chargeable gains, the net losses are carried forward and relieved against chargeable gains in subsequent periods.
- Companies may claim indexation allowance.
- Rebasing does not always apply when a company disposes of an asset acquired before 31 March 1982. It is necessary to perform a calculation based on original cost as well as the rebasing calculation. The chargeable gain (allowable loss) is the lower of the two gains (losses) given by these calculations.
- When a company makes a disposal of shares or securities, the disposal is matched first against shares acquired on the same day, then against shares acquired in the previous nine days, then against the s104 holding and then against the 1982 holding.
- A gain arising on the disposal of a substantial shareholding by an investor company is exempt from corporation tax, subject to certain conditions.

Retail Prices Index (RPI)

(*Source*: Office for National Statistics)

	Jan	Feb	Mar	Apr	May	Jun	Jul	Aug	Sep	Oct	Nov	Dec
1982			79.44	81.04	81.62	81.85	81.88	81.90	81.85	82.26	82.66	82.51
1983	82.61	82.97	83.12	84.28	84.64	84.84	85.30	85.68	86.06	86.36	86.67	86.89
1984	86.84	87.20	87.48	88.64	88.97	89.20	89.10	89.94	90.11	90.67	90.95	90.87
1985	91.20	91.94	92.80	94.78	95.21	95.41	95.23	95.49	95.44	95.59	95.92	96.05
1986	96.25	96.60	96.73	97.67	97.85	97.79	97.52	97.82	98.30	98.45	99.29	99.62
1987	100.0	100.4	100.6	101.8	101.9	101.9	101.8	102.1	102.4	102.9	103.4	103.3
1988	103.3	103.7	104.1	105.8	106.2	106.6	106.7	107.9	108.4	109.5	110.0	110.3
1989	111.0	111.8	112.3	114.3	115.0	115.4	115.5	115.8	116.6	117.5	118.5	118.8
1990	119.5	120.2	121.4	125.1	126.2	126.7	126.8	128.1	129.3	130.3	130.0	129.9
1991	130.2	130.9	131.4	133.1	133.5	134.1	133.8	134.1	134.6	135.1	135.6	135.7
1992	135.6	136.3	136.7	138.8	139.3	139.3	138.8	138.9	139.4	139.9	139.7	139.2
1993	137.9	138.8	139.3	140.6	141.1	141.0	140.7	141.3	141.9	141.8	141.6	141.9
1994	141.3	142.1	142.5	144.2	144.7	144.7	144.0	144.7	145.0	145.2	145.3	146.0
1995	146.0	146.9	147.5	149.0	149.6	149.8	149.1	149.9	150.6	149.8	149.8	150.7
1996	150.2	150.9	151.5	152.6	152.9	153.0	152.4	153.1	153.8	153.8	153.9	154.4
1997	154.4	155.0	155.4	156.3	156.9	157.5	157.5	158.5	159.3	159.5	159.6	160.0
1998	159.5	160.3	160.8	162.6	163.5	163.4	163.0	163.7	164.4	164.5	164.4	164.4
1999	163.4	163.7	164.1	165.2	165.6	165.6	165.1	165.5	166.2	166.5	166.7	167.3
2000	166.6	167.5	168.4	170.1	170.7	171.1	170.5	170.5	171.7	171.6	172.1	172.2
2001	171.1	172.0	172.2	173.1	174.2	174.4	173.3	174.0	174.6	174.3	173.6	173.4
2002	173.3	173.8	174.5	175.7	176.2	176.2	175.9	176.4	177.6	177.9	178.2	178.5
2003	178.4	179.3	179.9	181.2	181.5	181.3	181.3	181.6	182.5	182.6	182.7	183.5
2004	183.1	183.8	184.6	185.7	186.5	186.8	186.8	187.4	188.1	188.6	189.0	189.9
2005	188.9	189.6	190.5	191.6	192.0	192.2	192.2	192.6	193.1	193.3	193.6	194.1
2006	193.4	194.2	195.0	196.5	197.7	198.5	198.5	199.2	200.1	200.4	201.1	202.7
2007	201.6	203.1	204.4	205.4	206.2	207.3	206.1	207.3	208.0	208.9	209.7	210.9
2008	209.8	211.4	212.1	214.0	215.1	216.8	216.5	217.2	218.4	217.7	216.0	212.9
2009	210.1	211.4	211.3	211.5	212.8	213.4	213.4	214.4	215.3	216.0	216.6	218.0
2010	217.9	219.2	220.7	222.8	223.6	224.1	223.6	224.5	225.3	225.8	226.8	228.4
2011	229.0	231.3	232.5	234.4	235.2	235.2	234.7	236.1	237.9	238.0	238.5	239.4
2012	238.0	239.9	240.8	242.5	242.4	241.8	242.1	243.0	244.2	245.6	245.6	246.8
2013	245.8	247.6	248.7	249.5	250.0	249.7	249.7	251.0	251.9	251.9	252.1	253.4
2014	252.6	254.2	254.8	255.7	255.9	256.3	256.0	257.0	257.6	257.7	257.1	257.5
2015	255.4	256.7	257.1	258.0	258.5	258.9	258.6	259.8	259.6	259.5	259.8	260.6
2016	258.8	260.0	261.1	261.4	262.1	263.1	263.4	264.4	264.9	264.8	265.5	267.1
2017	265.5	268.4	269.3	270.6	*270.8*	*271.1*	*271.7*	*272.3*	*272.9*	*273.5*	*274.1*	*274.7*
2018	*275.3*	*275.9*	*276.5*									

Note: RPIs for May 2017 and later months have been estimated by the author.

Exercises

24.1 A company made the following disposals during the year to 31 March 2018:

(a) A factory building was sold for £650,000 on 13 June 2017 (RPI 271.1). This building had cost £300,000 in August 2000 (RPI 170.5) and was extended in July 2002 (RPI 175.9) at a cost of £50,000.

(b) An office building was sold for £1,100,000 on 15 September 2017 (RPI 272.9) and was immediately replaced by another office building costing £1,050,000. The building sold in September 2017 had cost £600,000 in February 2002 (RPI 173.8). Rollover relief was claimed on the disposal of this building.

(c) A computer system was given to a charity on 14 July 2017 (RPI 271.7). This computer system had cost £5,000 in September 2012 (RPI 244.2) and had a market value of £500 in July 2017. Capital allowances had been claimed in relation to the computer system.

(d) A motor car was sold for £80,000 on 12 June 2017 (RPI 271.1). The car had cost £100,000 in June 2014 (RPI 256.3). Capital allowances had been claimed.

(e) An item of movable plant and machinery was sold for £30,000 on 16 September 2017 (RPI 272.9). This item had cost £70,000 in January 2011 (RPI 229.0) and capital allowances had been claimed in relation to the item.

(f) 8,000 ordinary shares in Exxak plc were sold for £80,000 on 18 December 2017 (RPI 274.7). Shares in Exxak plc had been bought as follows:

Date	*No. of shares*	*Cost*	*RPI*
		£	
22 November 2002	4,000	16,000	178.2
14 December 2006	6,000	30,000	202.7
12 December 2017	3,000	36,000	274.7

(g) Government securities were sold for £40,000 on 17 October 2017 (RPI 273.5). These securities had cost £45,000 in October 2011 (RPI 238.0).

Compute the chargeable gain or allowable loss arising on each of the above disposals and outline any other corporation tax consequences of each disposal. Also compute the net chargeable gains figure which should be included in the company's taxable total profits for the year to 31 March 2018.

24.2 PCC Ltd is a manufacturing company which prepares accounts to 31 December each year. The company made the following disposals of chargeable assets in the year to 31 December 2017:

(i) On 12 September 2017, 7,500 ordinary shares in Epsilon plc were sold for £9.50 each. PCC Ltd had bought ordinary shares in Epsilon plc as follows:

		£
14 January 1981	Bought 2,000 shares	4,000
27 June 1991	Bought 3,000 shares	15,000
10 March 2001	Bought 4,000 shares	28,000

The shares had a market value on 31 March 1982 of £2.50 per share.

(ii) On 9 October 2017, two watercolour paintings (which do not form a set) were sold at auction. In each case, the auctioneer charged a 10% commission. The paintings had been acquired for £2,000 each in September 2002 and had been hanging in the company's reception area ever since. The net sale proceeds of the paintings (after deducting commission) were £5,175 and £5,805 respectively.

(iii) On 1 June 2017, a short lease was assigned for £7,000. The lease was originally acquired as a 20-year lease on 1 January 2003 at a cost of £20,000.

(iv) On 25 November 2017, a freehold property was sold for £115,000. The building had been acquired in August 2004 for £50,000. In February 2017 the company bought fixed plant for £100,000.

PCC Ltd has not made (and does not intend to make) a "re-basing" election to the effect that assets acquired before 31 March 1982 should be treated as if acquired on 31 March 1982 at a cost equal to their market value on that date. However, the company does intend to make any other election which will reduce the amount of gains chargeable to corporation tax in the year to 31 December 2017.

On 1 January 2017, the company had capital losses brought forward of £7,145.

Required:

Compute the chargeable gain or allowable loss arising on each of the above disposals. Hence compute the net chargeable gains figure which should be charged to corporation tax for the year to 31 December 2017. Assume Retail Price Indices as follows:

March 1982	79.44	August 2004	187.4
June 1991	134.1	June 2017	271.1
March 2001	172.2	September 2017	272.9
September 2002	177.6	October 2017	273.5
January 2003	178.4	November 2017	274.1

Extracts from the short lease amortisation table given in Schedule 8 of the Taxation of Chargeable Gains Act 1992 are as follows:

5 years	26.722	6 years	31.195	20 years	72.770

(CIPFA)

***24.3** Timberlake Ltd prepares accounts to 31 March each year. The company made the following disposals of chargeable assets in the year to 31 March 2018:

(i) In February 2018, a rare Bentley motor car used by the company's Managing Director was sold for £750,000. This car had cost £300,000 in November 2003.

(ii) In October 2017, an office building was sold for £670,000. The building had been acquired in January 1979 for £100,000 and was extended in July 1981 at a cost of £10,000 and again in September 1988 at a cost of £40,000. The market value of the building on 31 March 1982 was £135,000.

(iii) In June 2017, a plot of land was sold for £120,000. This land had cost £42,000 in November 2003 and had been used for trade purposes.

In June 2004, the company had sold land for £50,000 and had made a claim for rollover relief in relation to this disposal. This land had cost £10,000 in October 1999 and had been used for trade purposes.

(iv) In August 2017, gilt-edged stocks bought for £100,000 in January 2008 were sold for £110,500.

(v) In June 2017, plant and machinery bought for £19,500 in June 2016 was sold for £22,500. In March 2018, plant and machinery bought for £16,000 in March 2014 was sold for £9,000. Capital allowances had been claimed in relation to both of these items.

(vi) In February 2018, the company sold 500 ordinary shares in Theta plc for £10 per share. Timberlake Ltd had bought ordinary shares in Theta plc as follows:

		£
June 2001	Bought 2,500 shares	12,500
January 2008	Bought 3,000 shares	18,000

Timberlake Ltd has elected that assets acquired before 31 March 1982 should be treated as if acquired on 31 March 1982 at a cost equal to their market value on that date. The company had capital losses brought forward of £156,200 on 1 April 2017.

Required:

(a) Compute the chargeable gain or allowable loss arising on each of the disposals made during the year to 31 March 2018. Assume Retail Price Indices as follows:

March 1982	79.44	March 2014	254.8
September 1988	108.4	June 2016	263.1
October 1999	166.5	June 2017	271.1
June 2001	174.4	August 2017	272.3
November 2003	182.7	October 2017	273.5
June 2004	186.8	February 2018	275.9
January 2008	209.8	March 2018	276.5

(b) Compute the chargeable gains figure which should be included in the company's taxable total profits for the year to 31 March 2018.

(CIPFA)

Chapter 25

Computation and payment of the corporation tax liability

Introduction

Having ascertained a company's taxable total profits for an accounting period (including any chargeable gains) the next step is to compute the corporation tax liability arising in that period. The purpose of this chapter is to describe the way in which the corporation tax liability is computed and to explain the system by means of which the tax is collected.

Corporation tax financial years

The rate of corporation tax is set for each *financial year*. For corporation tax purposes, a financial year (FY) runs from 1 April to 31 March inclusive and is identified by the year in which it begins. For example:

- FY2016 began on 1 April 2016 and ended on 31 March 2017
- FY2017 began on 1 April 2017 and ends on 31 March 2018

The fiscal year which applies to individuals (from 6 April to the following 5 April) is not relevant when dealing with corporation tax matters. Note that:

(a) If a company has an accounting period which coincides with a financial year (i.e. the year to 31 March) or is entirely contained within a financial year, the rate of corporation tax for that financial year is applied to the company's taxable total profits for the accounting period, giving the corporation tax liability.

(b) If an accounting period straddles 31 March, the taxable total profits for the period are time-apportioned between the two financial years involved and then charged to tax at the rates applicable in those two years. A simple time-apportionment is always made in these circumstances. This is different from the way in which the profits of a long period of account are allocated between accounting periods (see Chapter 23).

It may seem obvious that the apportionment referred to above will be required only if the rate of corporation tax has changed from one financial year to the next. In practice, however, the amount of tax payable for each financial year has to be calculated separately in order to ascertain the figures required for the company's tax return.

EXAMPLE 1

A company has taxable total profits of £5,000,000 for an accounting period. Explain how the corporation tax liability for this period will be calculated if:

(a) the accounting period is the 12 months to 31 March 2018

(b) the accounting period is the nine months to 31 January 2018

(c) the accounting period is the ten months to 31 October 2017.

Solution

(a) The 12 months to 31 March 2018 coincide with FY2017, so the taxable total profits of £5,000,000 will be taxed at the FY2017 rate.

(b) The nine months to 31 January 2018 are entirely contained within FY2017, so the taxable total profits of £5,000,000 will be taxed at the FY2017 rate.

(c) The ten months to 31 October 2017 are contained partly within FY2016 (3 months) and partly within FY2017 (7 months). The taxable total profits of £5,000,000 will be time-apportioned between FYs as follows:

FY2016	1 Jan 2017 to 31 March 2017	£5,000,000 x 3/10	= £1,500,000
FY2017	1 April 2017 to 31 Oct 2017	£5,000,000 x 7/10	= £3,500,000

The profits of £1,500,000 falling into FY2016 will be taxed at the FY2016 rate and the profits of £3,500,000 falling into FY2017 will be taxed at the FY2017 rate.

Rates of corporation tax

As from 1 April 2015†, there is a single rate of corporation tax (the "main rate") for each financial year. Main rates for FY2015 through to FY2020 are currently set as follows:

FY2015	20%	FY2016	20%	FY2017	19%
FY2018	19%	FY2019	19%	FY2020	17%

However, it is important to bear in mind that the main rates for FY2018 and subsequent years could be amended by future Finance Acts. Furthermore, it is not inconceivable that the main rate for FY2017 could be amended by a second Finance Act in 2017.

† *Prior to FY2015, there were two rates of corporation tax for each financial year. These were the main rate and the small profits rate. However, the gap between the main rate and the small profits rate had been declining for several years and in FY2015 the decision was taken to reduce the main rate to 20% and to abolish the small profits rate.*

‡ *The Northern Ireland Executive has been granted the power to set its own rate of corporation tax (subject to conditions) and it is expected that the main rate in Northern Ireland will fall to 12.5% in April 2018 so as to match the rate in the Republic of Ireland.*

EXAMPLE 2

Calculate the corporation tax liability of each of the following companies for the accounting period concerned:

(a) A01 Ltd has taxable total profits of £800,000 for the year to 31 March 2018.

(b) A02 Ltd has taxable total profits of £250,000 for the six months to 31 October 2017.

(c) A03 Ltd has taxable total profits of £1,600,000 for the year to 31 December 2017.

Solution

(a) The accounting period coincides with FY2017 so the applicable rate of corporation tax is the FY2017 main rate of 19%. The liability is £152,000 (£800,000 × 19%).

(b) The accounting period is entirely contained within FY2017 so the applicable rate of corporation tax is the FY2017 main rate of 19%. The corporation tax liability for the period is £47,500 (£250,000 × 19%).

(c) The first three months of the accounting period fall into FY2016 (main rate 20%) and the remaining nine months fall into FY2017 (main rate 19%). The liability for the year is (3/12 × £1,600,000 × 20%) + (9/12 × £1,600,000 × 19%) = £308,000.

Due date of payment

A company's corporation tax liability for an accounting period is generally payable by means of a single payment which is due nine months and one day after the end of the period. However, certain large companies are required to pay their corporation tax by instalments (see below). Electronic payment of corporation tax is now compulsory.

EXAMPLE 3

(a) A company prepares a set of accounts for the year to 31 July 2017. When is the corporation tax liability for this period due for payment?

(b) A company prepares a set of accounts for the 18 months to 31 December 2017. When is the corporation tax liability for this period due for payment?

(c) A company has taxable total profits of £360,000 for the nine months to 30 November 2017. Calculate the corporation tax liability for this period and state the date of payment

Assume in all cases that the company is not required to pay by instalments.

Solution

(a) The year to 31 July 2017 is a single accounting period. Corporation tax for the period is payable nine months and one day after 31 July 2017, which is 1 May 2018.

(b) This period of account breaks down into two accounting periods. These are the year to 30 June 2017 and the six months to 31 December 2017. Corporation tax for these two accounting periods is due as follows:

   (i) Corporation tax for the year to 30 June 2017 is payable nine months and one day after 30 June 2017, which is 1 April 2018.

   (ii) Corporation tax for the six months to 31 December 2017 is payable nine months and one day after 31 December 2017, which is 1 October 2018.

(c) The first month of the accounting period (March 2017) falls into FY2016 (main rate 20%). The remaining eight months fall into FY2017 (main rate 19%). Therefore the tax liability is (1/9 × £360,000 × 20%) + (8/9 × £360,000 × 19%) = £68,800.

   The liability of £68,800 is payable nine months and one day after 30 November 2017, which is 1 September 2018.

Payment by instalments

As mentioned above, large companies are generally required to pay their corporation tax by instalments. The main features of the instalments system are as follows:

(a) In general, a company is defined as a "large company" for an accounting period if it has augmented profits for that period which exceed £1,500,000. For this purpose, a company's "augmented profits" are its taxable total profits for the period concerned *plus* dividends received†. However, a large company is *not* required to pay tax by instalments for an accounting period if:

   (i) it has profits of £10 million or less for the accounting period and was not a large company in the 12 months preceding that period, or

   (ii) its tax liability for the period does not exceed £10,000.

   The limits of £1,500,000, £10 million and £10,000 are all scaled down for accounting periods of less than 12 months. Furthermore, the £1,500,000 and £10 million limits are reduced if the company has one or more related companies (see Chapter 28).

(b) Instalment payments are based on the company's own estimate of its corporation tax liability for the accounting period. When the tax liability for the year is finalised, the company is charged interest on any underpaid instalments and is paid interest on any overpaid instalments.

† *If a company belongs to a group of companies, any "intra-group" dividends received from other companies in the group are ignored when calculating augmented profits. See Chapter 28 of this book for more information on groups of companies.*

(c) For a 12-month accounting period there are four equal instalments. The first instalment falls due six months and 14 days from the start of the accounting period. The remaining three instalments then fall due at quarterly intervals. For instance, if the accounting period is the year to 31 December 2017, instalments fall due on 14 July 2017, 14 October 2017, 14 January 2018 and 14 April 2018.

If an accounting period is of less than 12 months' duration, the final instalment is always due three months and 14 days after the end of the period. Earlier instalments are due on the usual quarterly dates but only to the extent that those dates fall before the date of the final instalment. For instance, if an accounting period consists of the eight months to 30 September 2017, corporation tax is due in three instalments on 14 August 2017, 14 November 2017 and 14 January 2018.

In order to calculate the amount of each instalment, it is first necessary to multiply the corporation tax liability by 3/n, where n is the number of months in the accounting period. Each instalment is then equal to this figure, except that the final instalment may be lower than this in order to bring the total of the instalments to the correct amount.

EXAMPLE 4

A large company has a corporation tax liability of £720,000 for an accounting period. State the dates on which instalments are payable and compute the amount of each instalment if the accounting period is:

(a) the year to 31 March 2018 (b) the five months to 31 May 2017.

Solution

(a) Instalments are due on 14 October 2017, 14 January 2018, 14 April 2018 and 14 July 2018. Each instalment is equal to £720,000 x 3/12 = £180,000.

(b) Instalments are due on 14 July 2017 and 14 September 2017. The first instalment is equal to £720,000 x 3/5 = £432,000. The second and final instalment is £288,000, bringing the total to £720,000.

Payment by instalments (very large companies)

A "very large" company is defined as one with augmented profits which exceed £20m per annum. For accounting periods starting on or after 1 April 2019, the dates on which such companies are required to pay their quarterly instalments will be advanced by four months. So the instalments for a 12-month accounting period will fall due in the third, sixth, ninth and twelfth months of that period.

Accounting for income tax deducted at source

Certain payments made by companies are made net of basic rate income tax. These consist principally of patent royalties paid to individuals and loan interest paid to individuals. A company which makes such a payment must account to HMRC for the tax deducted at source. The gross amount of the payment then attracts tax relief under the appropriate heading in the company's corporation tax computation.

Similarly, a company may receive income net of basic rate income tax. This is now rare but one instance occurs when a company receives patent royalties from an individual. In such a case, the company reclaims the income tax suffered at source. The gross amount of the income is then charged to corporation tax.

Quarterly accounting system

Companies are required to make periodic (usually quarterly) returns to HMRC of income tax deducted from payments and income tax suffered on taxed income. Returns are made on form CT61. Nil returns are not required. Since it is now uncommon for companies to receive any taxed income, most of these returns will show only income tax deducted from payments. If this is the case, the company concerned must account for this income tax to HMRC within 14 days of the end of the return period. However, the procedure is rather more complex if the company also has taxed income.

Full details of the quarterly accounting system, together with several worked examples, can be found on the website which accompanies this textbook. The website address is www.pearsoned.co.uk/melville.

Shadow ACT

Until 6 April 1999, companies were obliged to pay Advance Corporation Tax (ACT) when paying dividends. Subject to certain conditions, the ACT paid for an accounting period was then treated as an advance payment of the corporation tax liability for that period, so reducing the amount of tax payable on the normal due date. ACT was abolished with effect from 6 April 1999 but some aspects of the ACT system are still relevant in a small number of cases. The present situation with regard to ACT (the "shadow ACT" system) is explained on website www.pearsoned.co.uk/melville.

Self Assessment

The system of Self Assessment for companies is similar in many ways to the equivalent system that applies for individuals (see Chapter 1). The main features of Corporation Tax Self Assessment (CTSA) are as follows:

(a) On the issue of an official notice by HM Revenue and Customs, a company must file a corporation tax return† for the accounting period specified in the notice, together with supporting accounts and computations. The return must normally be filed with HMRC by the *latest* of the following dates:

   (i) 12 months after the end of the accounting period specified in the notice

   (ii) 12 months after the end of the period of account in which the last day of the specified accounting period falls (but periods of account which last for more than 18 months are treated for this purpose as ending after 18 months)

   (iii) 3 months after issue of the notice.

   Most companies prepare their accounts to the same date each year and notices are usually issued within a few weeks of the end of each period of account, so that the required filing date is normally 12 months after the end of the period of account. There is nothing to prevent a company from submitting an early return. Online filing is now compulsory.

(b) The corporation tax return includes a formal self-assessment of the company's tax liability for the accounting period covered by the return. Unlike individuals, a company is *not* able to ask HMRC to calculate the tax liability.

(c) A company which is chargeable to corporation tax for an accounting period but has not received a notice requiring submission of a return must notify HMRC of its chargeability to tax within 12 months of the end of the period.

(d) HMRC has the right to amend a company's return (so as to correct obvious errors or omissions or anything else that is believed to be incorrect) within nine months of the date on which the return is filed. Similarly, the company has the right to amend its return and self-assessment within 12 months of the required filing date for that return.

   A company which believes that it has made an overpayment of corporation tax may make a claim for recovery of this overpaid tax (whether or not the alleged overpayment was caused by an error in a tax return). Such a claim must be made within four years of the end of the accounting period to which it relates. Depending upon the circumstances of the case, HMRC may or may not accept the claim.

† *As part of the "Making Tax Digital" project (see Chapter 1) online "digital tax accounts" are to be introduced for companies as from April 2020 and these accounts will replace the corporation tax return. In general, companies will be required to update their digital tax accounts quarterly. However, quarterly reporting will not apply to larger companies with more complex tax affairs. At present, it is expected that companies with annual turnover in excess of £10m will not be included in the quarterly reporting scheme and will continue to submit annual tax returns.*

(e) If HMRC wishes to open an enquiry into a company's tax return which is filed on or before the required filing date, then the enquiry must usually begin within 12 months of the date on which the return is filed. This means that the "enquiry window" for returns which are submitted early will close correspondingly early.

However, if a company's tax return is filed late or if the company amends its tax return, the deadline for starting an enquiry is extended to the quarter date (31 January, 30 April, 31 July or 31 October) which follows the first anniversary of the date that the return is filed or the amendment is submitted.

(f) Unless HMRC opens an enquiry into a company's tax return, the tax liability for the accounting period may usually be regarded as finalised when the enquiry window has closed. However, HMRC may raise a later "discovery assessment" if it is discovered that insufficient tax has been assessed.

The time limit for making a discovery assessment is normally four years after the end of the accounting period concerned. This increases to six years if the loss of tax has been caused by negligence on the part of the company (or a related person) and 20 years in the case of dishonesty.

(g) If a company fails to file a return by the required date, HMRC may make a determination of the amount of tax due. A determination can be displaced only if the company delivers the required return.

(h) A company is required to keep and preserve adequate records to substantiate the information entered on its tax return. These records must be retained for at least six years after the end of the accounting period concerned.

(i) Corporation tax appeals are dealt with in much the same way as income tax appeals (see Chapter 1). The tax avoidance disclosure regime which applies to income tax also applies to corporation tax.

Interest on underpaid and overpaid corporation tax

Interest on underpaid corporation tax generally runs from the date on which the tax should have been paid until the date on which it is actually paid. Interest on overpaid corporation tax generally runs from the date on which the tax was paid or (if later) the date on which it was due to be paid, until the date of repayment. Interest on overpaid corporation tax is calculated at a lower rate than interest on underpaid tax. Note that:

(a) It is HMRC practice to use a denominator of 366 when calculating interest on underpaid tax and a denominator of 365 when calculating interest on overpaid tax, whether or not a leap year is involved.

(b) Interest receivable on a repayment of overpaid corporation tax is taxable as a credit arising from a non-trading loan relationship. Similarly, interest payable on underpaid corporation tax is deductible as a non-trading debit (see Chapter 23).

(c) The interest rate which applies to underpaid instalments is generally lower than the normal rate during the period from the due date of the first instalment to the date which falls nine months and one day after the end of the accounting period.

Similarly, the interest rate applicable to overpaid instalments is generally higher than the normal rate during this period.

(d) If a company makes instalment payments on the assumption that it is a large company and this assumption later proves to be false, interest on any repaid instalments runs from the date on which a truly large company would have paid those instalments or (if later) the actual date of payment.

EXAMPLE 5

(a) A company calculates its corporation tax liability for the year to 30 September 2017 as £250,000 and pays this amount on the due date. The correct liability for the year eventually turns out to be £274,000 and the company pays a further £24,000 on 17 October 2018. Calculate the amount of interest payable by the company (assuming an interest rate of 2.75% per annum).

(b) A company calculates its corporation tax liability for the year to 30 November 2017 as £390,000 and pays this amount on the due date. The correct liability for the year eventually turns out to be only £333,000. The necessary repayment is made on 18 February 2019. Calculate the amount of interest payable to the company (assuming an interest rate of 0.5% per annum).

Neither company is a large company for the purposes of payment by instalments.

Solution

(a) The due date of payment for the year to 30 September 2017 is 1 July 2018 (i.e. nine months and one day from the end of the accounting period). Most of the corporation tax liability is settled on this date but the final £24,000 is not paid until 17 October 2018, which is 108 days late. Interest payable by the company is:

$$£24,000 \times 2.75\% \times \frac{108}{366} = £194.75$$

(b) The due date for the year to 30 November 2017 is 1 September 2018. The overpaid tax of £57,000 is paid on this date but is not repaid until 18 February 2019, which is 170 days later. Interest payable to the company is:

$$£57,000 \times 0.5\% \times \frac{170}{365} = £132.74$$

..lties

The main penalties which may be imposed in relation to corporation tax are as follows:

(a) **Late submission of tax return**. Penalties are charged if a company does not file its corporation tax return by the required date. These penalties are currently as follows:

  (i) If the return is up to three months late, a fixed penalty is charged of £100. This is increased to £500 for a third consecutive late return.

  (ii) If the return is over three months late, a fixed penalty is charged of £200. This is increased to £1,000 for a third consecutive late return.

  (iii) In addition to the above penalties, a further tax-geared penalty is charged if the return is submitted more than six months late. The penalty is expressed as a percentage of the amount of tax unpaid at the end of the six months, as follows:

  - If the return is made between six and 12 months late, the penalty is 10% of the tax unpaid six months after the return was due.
  - If the return is made more than 12 months late, the penalty rises to 20% of the tax unpaid six months after the return was due.

  It is important to note that a new penalty regime is being introduced in relation to late returns and late payment of tax (see Chapter 15). This regime will apply to a number of taxes but the date of implementation for corporation tax is not yet clear.

(b) **Failure to notify**. A penalty may be charged if a company which has not filed a tax return (and has not been issued with a notice requiring such a return) fails to notify HMRC of its chargeability to tax within 12 months of the end of the accounting period concerned. The penalty for a "failure to notify" is expressed as a percentage of the amount of tax which remains unpaid 12 months after the end of the period.

  As is the case for income tax (see Chapter 15) the applicable percentage varies from 30% to 100%, depending upon whether the failure to notify has been deliberate and/or concealed. The amount of any penalty is reduced if the failure is voluntarily disclosed and no penalty is charged if there is "reasonable excuse" for the failure.

(c) **Inaccurate tax returns**. A penalty may be charged if an inaccuracy in a tax return or other document leads to an understatement of the amount of corporation tax payable and the inaccuracy is either careless or deliberate. This penalty regime also applies if HMRC issues an assessment which understates the amount of tax payable and the company fails to take reasonable steps to notify HMRC of this fact within 30 days.

  As is the case for income tax (see Chapter 15) the amount of any penalty depends upon the company's degree of culpability and generally varies between 30% and 100% of the additional tax which becomes payable as a result of correcting the inaccuracy or understatement.

(d) **Failure to keep records**. A company which fails to keep and preserve adequate records is liable to a penalty of up to £3,000 per accounting period.

EXAMPLE 6

A company prepares accounts to 31 July each year. It calculates its corporation tax liability for the year to 31 July 2016 at £180,000 and pays this sum on 1 May 2017. The company is not large for the purpose of payment by instalments.

Despite being issued with a notice by HMRC in August 2016, the company fails to submit its return for the year to 31 July 2016 until 31 March 2018. The corporation tax liability for the year was finally assessed at £206,000. Calculate the penalties that would be charged.

Solution

The return was submitted eight months late and tax of £26,000 was still outstanding six months after the return was due. Assuming that the company is not a persistent offender, a fixed penalty of £200 would be charged, together with a tax-geared penalty of £2,600 (10% of £26,000). Interest would also be charged on the unpaid tax.

Summary

- A corporation tax financial year runs from 1 April to the following 31 March. If a company has an accounting period which straddles 31 March, the taxable total profits for the period are time-apportioned between the two financial years involved and then charged to tax at the rates applicable in those two years.
- There is a single rate of corporation tax for each financial year (the "main rate"). This fell from 20% to 19% in FY2017 and is due to fall to 17% in FY2020.
- The due date of payment for corporation tax is normally nine months and one day after the end of the accounting period. Large companies are required to pay their tax by instalments (usually quarterly).
- Interest is charged on underpaid corporation tax but this interest is deductible under the loan relationships regime as a non-trading debit. Similarly, interest is paid on refunds of overpaid corporation tax but this interest is taxable under the loan relationships regime as a non-trading credit.
- The system of Self Assessment for companies is similar in many ways to Self Assessment for individuals. However, a company must compute its own corporation tax liability and cannot require HMRC to calculate the tax due.
- Companies are usually required to file a corporation tax return within 12 months of the end of each period of account. Online filing is now compulsory. Late submission results in a penalty fine and there are penalties for various other infringements of the law relating to corporation tax.

Exercises

25.1 A company's taxable total profits for an accounting period are £3,200,000. Compute the corporation tax liability if the accounting period is:

(a) the year to 31 March 2017
(b) the year to 31 March 2018
(c) the year to 31 December 2017
(d) the ten months to 31 October 2018
(e) the ten months to 31 October 2017.

25.2 State the date (or dates) on which corporation tax is due for payment in relation to the following periods of account:

(a) the year to 31 March 2018
(b) the six months to 30 November 2017
(c) the 21 months to 30 June 2018
(d) the 27 months to 31 August 2018.

Assume in each case that the company concerned is not required to pay corporation tax by instalments.

25.3 (a) ABC Ltd has taxable total profits of £1,800,000 for the year to 31 March 2018. Taxable total profits were £1,600,000 for the year to 31 March 2017.

Calculate the company's corporation tax liability for the year to 31 March 2018 and state the date (or dates) on which this tax is due to be paid

(b) DEF Ltd has changed its accounting date from 31 December to 30 June. The first accounts to 30 June are for the six-month period to 30 June 2017. Taxable total profits for this six-month period are £960,000. Taxable total profits for the year to 31 December 2016 were £1,730,000.

Calculate the company's corporation tax liability for the six months to 30 June 2017 and state the date (or dates) on which this tax is due to be paid.

25.4 A company (which is not a member of a group) prepares a set of accounts for the year to 30 September 2017. Calculate the corporation tax liability for the year and state the date (or dates) on which this tax is due to be paid, in each of the following situations:

(a) Taxable total profits for the year are £4,500,000 and dividends received are £nil.
(b) Taxable total profits for the year are £1,250,000 and dividends received are £nil.
(c) Taxable total profits for the year are £1,250,000 and dividends received in the year are £300,000.

Assume in each case that the company was "large" in the year to 30 September 2016.

25.5 A company calculates its corporation tax liability for the year to 31 August 2016 as £120,000 and pays this amount on 1 June 2017. The company's corporation tax return is submitted during August 2017 and the tax liability for the year is finalised at £124,650. The balance of £4,650 is paid on 3 October 2017. The company is not a large company for the purposes of payment by instalments. Calculate the interest payable, assuming an interest rate of 2.75% per annum.

25.6 State the date (or dates) on which a "large" company would be required to settle its corporation tax liability for each of the following accounting periods:

(a) the eleven months to 31 May 2018
(b) the eight months to 31 August 2017
(c) the four months to 30 April 2018
(d) the month to 31 January 2018.

Assume in each case that the company's tax liability for the period exceeds £10,000 and that the company was also large in the previous 12 months.

***25.7** A company has the following results for the year to 31 March 2018:

	£
Adjusted trading profit, after deduction of capital allowances	360,284
Bank deposit interest (a/c opened 1 July 2017):	
Received 31 December 2017	9,957
Accrued to 31 March 2018	3,000
Dividend received in January 2018	24,300
Chargeable gains	295,327
Gift Aid donations:	
Paid 30 November 2017	30,000
Accrued to 31 March 2018	20,000

The company intends to make Gift Aid donations of £30,000 every six months, starting on 30 November 2017.

(a) Compute the company's corporation tax liability for the year.

(b) What would the tax liability have been if the above figures had related to the year to 31 January 2018 (and all the dates had been two months earlier)?

***25.8** A company (which is not a member of a group) has the following results for the 14 months to 31 December 2017:

	£
Adjusted trading profit, before deduction of capital allowances	1,413,510
Capital allowances claimed:	
Year to 31 October 2017	222,650
2 months to 31 December 2017	37,210
Chargeable gains:	
Disposal 12 May 2017	16,586
Disposal 6 November 2017	21,692
Building society interest:	
Received 31 December 2016	3,500
Received 31 December 2017	4,300
Dividend received on 25 September 2017	3,150

Accrued building society interest was £3,000 on 31 October 2016, £4,000 on 31 October 2017 and £nil on 31 December 2017.

Compute the company's total corporation tax liability for the 14-month period and state the date (or dates) on which this tax is due to be paid.

Chapter 26

Corporation tax losses

Introduction

At present, the tax reliefs available to a company which incurs a trading loss are similar to those available to individuals (see Chapter 12). Trading losses may be carried forward and set against future trading profits or may be set against the company's total profits for a specified period. *However, the Government has proposed a number of reforms to the corporation tax legislation relating to trading losses*. The main effect of these reforms is to offer more flexibility in the tax treatment of trading losses carried forward.

This chapter explains the tax reliefs that are currently available in relation to a company's trading losses and gives an outline of the proposed reforms. The corporation tax treatment of a company's non-trading losses is also considered in this chapter.

Relief for trading losses (existing legislation)

The rules which grant tax relief in relation to a company's trading losses are located in the Corporation Tax Act 2010. The main reliefs currently provided are as follows:

(a) **Carry forward of trade loss relief**. A trading loss may be carried forward and set against future profits of the same trade. This is the relief which takes effect if no other tax relief is claimed in relation to a trading loss.

(b) **Trade loss relief against total profits**. If a claim is made to this effect, a trading loss may be set against the company's total profits of:

  (i) the accounting period in which the loss arises (the "loss-making period"), and
  (ii) if the claim so requires, the 12 months prior to the accounting period in which the loss arises.

  Furthermore, a trading loss which is incurred in the 12 months before the company ceases to carry on that trade (a "terminal loss") may be set against the company's total profits of the preceding three years.

Each of these forms of loss relief is described below.

Carry forward of trade loss relief

Unless a company claims any other form of loss relief in relation to a trading loss, the loss is carried forward and relieved against the company's future trading profits†. Note that:

(a) Carry forward relief is given only against future *trading* profits.

(b) Furthermore, relief is given only against future trading profits arising from *the same trade* as that in which the loss was incurred. If a company ceases one trade and commences another, the losses of the old trade cannot be carried forward and relieved against the future profits of the new trade. Similarly, if a company carries on two trades simultaneously, a loss incurred in one of the trades cannot be carried forward and relieved against the future profits of the other trade.

(c) Relief must be given against the *first available* future trading profits.

(d) There are restrictions on the carry-forward of trading losses when there is a change in the ownership of a company (see later in this chapter).

† *The proposed reforms to the carry-forward rules are outlined later in this chapter.*

EXAMPLE 1

In the year to 31 March 2016, a company incurred a trading loss of £160,000 which was carried forward. The company's results for the next two years were:

	y/e 31 March 2017	*y/e 31 March 2018*
	£	£
Trading profits	110,000	1,850,000
Loan interest receivable	55,000	60,000
Chargeable gains	320,000	572,000

Compute the company's taxable total profits for the years to 31 March 2017 and 2018 and identify the tax rate(s) at which the loss is relieved.

How would the computation differ if all dates were moved forward by one year? How would the computation differ if all dates were moved back by one year?

Solution

	y/e 31 March 2017	*y/e 31 March 2018*
	£	£
Trading profits	110,000	1,850,000
Less: Trading losses b/f	110,000	50,000
Trading income	0	1,800,000
Income from non-trading loans	55,000	60,000
Chargeable gains	320,000	572,000
Taxable total profits (TTP)	375,000	2,432,000

Notes:

(i) In the year to 31 March 2017, trading losses are relieved to the fullest possible extent against the trading profits of the year. Taxable total profits are reduced from £485,000 to £375,000, saving corporation tax at 20% (the main rate for FY2016).

(ii) The trading losses of £50,000 which remain unrelieved cannot be offset against the loan interest or the chargeable gains of the year to 31 March 2017 but must be carried forward and relieved against the trading profits of the following year.

(iii) In the year to 31 March 2018, trading losses reduce taxable total profits by £50,000, saving corporation tax at 19% (the main rate for FY2017).

(iv) The total tax saved is £31,500 (£110,000 x 20% + £50,000 x 19%).

(v) If all dates were moved forward by one year, the trading loss would be incurred in the year to 31 March 2017 and would be relieved in the years to 31 March 2018 and 31 March 2019. The main rate for both of these years is 19%, so the total tax saved would be only £30,400 (£160,000 × 19%).

If all dates were moved back by one year, the trading loss would be incurred in the year to 31 March 2015 and would be relieved in the years to 31 March 2016 and 31 March 2017. The main rate for both of these years is 20%, so the total tax saved would be £32,000 (£160,000 × 20%).

(vi) It is worth noting that lower tax rates result in lower tax savings for a company which has incurred a trading loss.

Unrelieved qualifying charitable donations

As stated in Chapter 23, certain charitable donations and gifts made by a company rank as "qualifying charitable donations". These are:

(a) Gift Aid donations

(b) gifts of listed shares or securities to a charity

(c) gifts of land and buildings to a charity.

In general, qualifying charitable donations are deducted when computing a company's taxable total profits and so serve to reduce the company's corporation tax liability. But if a trading loss is incurred in a period in which charitable donations are made, the company's total income and gains for that period may be insufficient to cover its donations, in which case some or all of these donations will be unrelieved. A similar situation might arise if trading losses brought forward are set against the trading profits of the period.

In these circumstances, the tax saving that the unrelieved donations would normally have provided is permanently lost. Qualifying charitable donations are eligible for relief only in the accounting period in which they are made and cannot be carried forward for relief in subsequent periods or carried back for relief in previous periods.

EXAMPLE 2

A company has the following results for the three years to 31 March 2018:

	y/e 31/3/2016	*y/e 31/3/2017*	*y/e 31/3/2018*
	£	£	£
Trading profits/(losses)	(78,900)	36,300	64,900
Loan interest receivable	21,500	-	-
Gift Aid donations	1,000	1,000	1,000

Assuming that the trading loss of £78,900 is to be carried forward for relief against future trading profits, calculate the company's taxable total profits for each of the three years.

Solution

	y/e 31/3/2016	*y/e 31/3/2017*	*y/e 31/3/2018*
	£	£	£
Trading profits	-	36,300	64,900
Less: Trading losses b/f	-	36,300	42,600
Trading income	-	0	22,300
Income from non-trading loans	21,500	-	-
	21,500	0	22,300
Less: Qualifying charitable donations	1,000	-	1,000
Taxable total profits (TTP)	20,500	0	21,300
Trading losses c/f	78,900	42,600	-
Unrelieved charitable donations	-	1,000	-

Notes:

(i) In the year to 31 March 2016, the qualifying charitable donations of £1,000 are set against the loan interest. The £78,900 of trading losses are carried forward.

(ii) In the year to 31 March 2017, the trading income of £36,300 is used to relieve part of the trading losses brought forward, leaving £42,600 to carry forward. The qualifying charitable donations for the year are completely unrelieved.

(iii) In the year to 31 March 2018, trading losses brought forward are fully relieved. The remaining profits of £22,300 are then reduced by the qualifying charitable donations of £1,000, leaving taxable total profits of £21,300 for the year.

(iv) The company pays tax at the FY2015 main rate (20%) in the year to 31 March 2016 and at the FY2017 main rate (19%) in the year to 31 March 2018. So the Gift Aid donations reduce the tax liability for these two years by £200 and £190 respectively. In effect, these donations have cost the company only £800 in the year to 31 March 2016 and £810 in the year to 31 March 2018.

But the donations made in the year to 31 March 2017 have not reduced the liability for that year and so these donations have cost the company the full £1,000.

Trade loss relief against total profits

CTA 2010 allows a trading loss to be relieved against a company's total profits. This relief applies only if claimed and is available in two parts:

(a) A company may claim that a trading loss incurred during an accounting period should be relieved against the total profits of that accounting period (*before* deducting qualifying charitable donations).

(b) The company may then further claim that any part of the trading loss which remains unrelieved after a claim has been made under (a) above, should be relieved against the total profits of accounting periods falling wholly or partly within the 12 months prior to the loss-making period. Note the following points:

  (i) This relief is also given *before* deducting qualifying charitable donations.

  (ii) If more than one accounting period falls wholly or partly into the 12 months preceding a loss-making period, relief is given in later accounting periods in priority to earlier accounting periods.

  (iii) If an accounting period falls only partly into the 12 months preceding a loss-making period, the profits of that period are time-apportioned and relief is available against only the profits which fall into the specified 12 months.

Trade loss relief against total profits is voluntary. A company wishing to relieve a trading loss in this way must make an appropriate claim within two years of the end of the loss-making accounting period. A claim may be made under (a) above without a further claim under (b). But a claim under (b) cannot be made without a prior claim under (a).

A company may not specify how much of its trading loss should be relieved against total profits. The effect of a claim is to relieve trading losses to the fullest possible extent in each affected accounting period. Any part of the loss which remains unrelieved after relief has been given against total profits is eligible for carry-forward relief. If relief against total profits is not claimed, the entire loss is carried forward.

EXAMPLE 3

A company has the following results for the year to 31 December 2017:

	£
Trading loss	(112,500)
Income from property	14,000
Chargeable gains	103,000
Gift Aid donations	28,700

Assuming that a claim is made for the trading loss to be relieved against total profits, compute the company's taxable total profits for the year.

Solution

	£
Trading income	-
Income from property	14,000
Chargeable gains	103,000
	117,000
Less: Trade loss relief against total profits	112,500
	4,500
Less: Qualifying charitable donations	4,500
Taxable total profits (TTP)	0

Note:

Only £4,500 of the Gift Aid donations can be relieved. The remaining £24,200 is lost.

EXAMPLE 4

A company has the following results for the three years to 31 October 2017:

	y/e 31/10/15	*y/e 31/10/16*	*y/e 31/10/17*
	£	£	£
Trading profits/(losses)	112,500	110,700	(136,500)
Income from property	3,300	8,400	8,800
Gift Aid donations	2,000	2,000	2,000

Assuming that all possible claims are made to relieve the trading loss against total profits, calculate the company's taxable total profits for each of the three years.

Solution

	y/e 31/10/15	*y/e 31/10/16*	*y/e 31/10/17*
	£	£	£
Trading income	112,500	110,700	-
Income from property	3,300	8,400	8,800
	115,800	119,100	8,800
Less: Relief against total profits (a)	-	-	8,800
	115,800	119,100	0
Less: Relief against total profits (b)	-	119,100	-
	115,800	0	0
Less: Qualifying charitable donations	2,000	-	-
Taxable total profits (TTP)	113,800	0	0
Trading loss c/f	-	-	8,600
Unrelieved charitable donations	-	2,000	2,000

Notes:

(i) In the year to 31 October 2017, the claim for relief against total profits must be for the maximum possible amount of £8,800. This leaves nothing against which to relieve the Gift Aid donations and therefore they are lost.

(ii) The remaining £127,700 of the trading loss is eligible for relief against total profits of the year to 31 October 2016. The claim must be for the maximum possible amount of £119,100. This leaves nothing against which to relieve the donations, which are lost.

(iii) The trading loss may not be carried back any further. The computation for the year to 31 March 2015 is therefore completely unaffected by loss reliefs..

(iv) A total of £127,900 (£8,800 + £119,100) of the trading loss has been relieved against total profits. The remaining £8,600 is carried forward.

EXAMPLE 5

A company has the following results for the three accounting periods to 31 March 2018:

	y/e 30/6/16	*9 months to 31/3/17*	*y/e 31/3/18*
	£	£	£
Trading profits/(losses)	13,400	69,900	(122,800)
Chargeable gains	1,200	3,500	38,600

Assuming that all possible claims are made to relieve the trading loss against total profits, calculate the company's taxable total profits for each of the three accounting periods.

Solution

		y/e 30/6/16	*9 months to 31/3/17*	*y/e 31/3/18*
		£	£	£
Trading income		13,400	69,900	-
Chargeable gains		1,200	3,500	38,600
		14,600	73,400	38,600
Less: Relief against total profits (a)		-	-	38,600
		14,600	73,400	0
Less: Relief against total profits (b)	(1)		73,400	
	(2)	3,650		
Taxable total profits (TTP)		10,950	0	0
Trading losses c/f		-	-	7,150

Notes:

(i) £38,600 of the trading losses incurred in the year to 31 March 2018 are relieved against total profits of that period. This leaves losses of £84,200 which are eligible for carry-back relief. The carry-back period is the previous 12 months.

(ii) The nine-month accounting period to 31 March 2017 is entirely contained within the specified 12 months and so losses of £73,400 are relieved against total profits of that period. Losses relieved so far are now £112,000, leaving £10,800 still to be relieved.

(iii) Only three months of the year to 30 June 2016 fall into the specified 12 months. The maximum relief available is £3,650 (£14,600 x 3/12). The remaining £7,150 of the trading loss is carried forward.

Further points relating to relief against total profits

(a) A trading loss may be relieved against the total profits of an accounting period only if the loss-making trade is (or was) being carried on in that period.

(b) If more than one loss is eligible for relief against the total profits of an accounting period, earlier losses are relieved before later losses.

(c) Trading losses incurred by a company in the 12 months before the loss-making trade ceases may be carried back and set against total profits of the preceding three years.

(d) Relief against total profits is available only if the loss-making trade is being carried on "on a commercial basis" with a view to profit.

(e) In the case of *farming companies*, a loss is usually not eligible for relief against total profits if losses have also been incurred for the previous five years.

(f) There are restrictions on the carry-back of trading losses when there is a change in the ownership of a company (see below).

Repayments of corporation tax

If a claim to set a trading loss against total profits results in a repayment of corporation tax for an earlier accounting period, this repayment will attract interest. The amount of interest is calculated in the usual way (see Chapter 25) unless the accounting period for which repayment is being made began more than 12 months before the loss-making accounting period. In these circumstances, the interest is calculated as if the repayment were a repayment of tax for the loss-making accounting period itself.

EXAMPLE 6

A company which began trading on 1 April 2015 has no other income apart from its trading profits. Results for the first three accounting periods were as follows:

	y/e 31/3/2016	*6 months to 30/9/2016*	*y/e 30/9/2017*
	£	£	£
Trading profits/(losses)	180,000	120,000	(290,000)

All possible claims were made to set the trading loss of £290,000 against the company's total profits. All corporation tax was originally paid on the due date and the necessary repayment of corporation tax is made on 1 August 2018.

Calculate the amount of the repayment and the interest which will accompany this repayment, assuming an interest rate of 0.5% per annum.

Solution

The trading loss is relieved against the £120,000 profit of the six months to 30 September 2016 and then against the £90,000 profit of the six months to 31 March 2016. The loss of £80,000 which remains unrelieved is carried forward.

The company pays tax at the FY2016 main rate (20%) for the six months to 30 September 2016 and at the FY2015 main rate (also 20%) for the year to 31 March 2016. Therefore the loss relief claim will generate the following repayment:

		£
6 months to 30 September 2016	120,000 @ 20%	24,000
y/e 31 March 2016	90,000 @ 20%	18,000
Total repayment		42,000

Notes:

(i) The six months to 30 September 2016 did not begin more than 12 months before the loss-making period so interest on the £24,000 will run from 1 July 2017 (the due date of payment for the six months to 30 September 2016).

(ii) The year to 31 March 2016 began more than 12 months before the loss-making period so interest on the £18,000 will run from 1 July 2018 (the due date of payment for the loss-making period itself).

(iii) The repayment takes place on 1 August 2018. This is 396 days after 1 July 2017 and 31 days after 1 July 2018. Therefore the interest due is:

$$(\text{£}24{,}000 \times 0.5\% \times \frac{396}{365}) + (\text{£}18{,}000 \times 0.5\% \times \frac{31}{365}) = \text{£}137.84.$$

Anti-avoidance legislation

Specific anti-avoidance legislation exists to prevent the following manoeuvre, which would otherwise be very tax-efficient:

(a) Acquire a company with substantial amounts of unrelieved trading losses.

(b) Revive the loss-making trade.

(c) Set the company's pre-acquisition trading losses against its post-acquisition trading profits, so avoiding corporation tax.

The legislation referred to above provides that if there is a change in the ownership of a company and certain conditions are satisfied, trading losses arising before the change cannot be set against trading profits arising after the change. Nor can trading losses arising after the change be set against total profits arising before the change. The required conditions are that:

(a) a change in ownership has occurred at a time when the company's business has become negligible and then (at any time after the change) there has been a significant revival of the company's business, or

(b) a change in ownership and a major change in the nature or conduct of the company's business have both occurred within the same three-year period.

For this purpose, a change in ownership is deemed to occur if over half of the company's ordinary share capital is acquired either by one person or by a group of people, each acquiring at least a 5% shareholding.

Choice of loss relief

A company which incurs a trading loss must choose between carrying the loss forward against future trading profits or relieving the loss against the total profits of the current period and (possibly) the total profits of the previous 12 months. Some of the main criteria which will influence this choice are as follows:

(a) the likelihood and expected amount of future profits arising from the same trade as that in which the loss was incurred

(b) the company's cash flow situation (a cash shortage may dictate that loss relief should be obtained as soon as possible)

(c) the rates of corporation tax payable by the company in earlier accounting periods and the expected rates payable in future periods

(d) the possibility that qualifying charitable donations may be unrelieved

(e) in general, the desire to maximise the tax saved as a result of loss relief claims.

Proposed reforms to carry forward loss relief

As stated earlier, the Government has proposed a number of reforms to the corporation tax rules relating to trading losses carried forward. If implemented, these reforms would mostly affect trading losses incurred in accounting periods commencing on or after 1 April 2017. A trading loss incurred in an accounting period which straddles that date would be apportioned (usually on a time basis) into a "pre-1 April 2017" trade loss and a "post-1 April 2017" trade loss. The main features of the proposed reforms are as follows:

(a) A company would be able to claim that a trading loss incurred on or after 1 April 2017 should be set against the *total profits* of later periods. Furthermore, the company could stipulate the amount of loss relief (if any) claimed in each later period and there would be no obligation to relieve the loss at the earliest opportunity. This set-off would not be available unless the company continued with the loss-making trade in the later periods concerned. The trade would also have to be a "commercial" trade, carried on with a view to profit. Loss relief would be given *before* deduction of qualifying charitable donations.

In the case of "uncommercial" trades (not carried on with a view to profit) trading losses incurred on or after 1 April 2017 would be carried forward and automatically set against profits arising from the same trade in later periods. But the company could claim that only partial loss relief (or none) should be given in any such later period.

(b) As at present, a trading loss incurred before 1 April 2017 could be carried forward and relieved against future profits of the same trade. However, it would no longer be necessary to relieve the loss at the earliest opportunity and the company would be able to specify how much relief (if any) should be given in each later period.

(c) Trading losses carried forward to an accounting period in which the loss-making trade is terminated could be relieved against the total profits (for losses incurred on or after 1 April 2017) or trading profits (for losses incurred before 1 April 2017) of the terminating period and of the previous 36 months.

(d) A carried-forward trading loss incurred on or after 1 April 2017 would be eligible for group relief in later accounting periods (see Chapter 28).

(e) Finally, there would be a limit on the amount of carried-forward trading losses that could be relieved in any accounting period beginning on or after 1 April 2017. This limit would apply regardless of whether the losses concerned arose before or after that date. The limit would be equal to £5m plus 50% of the company's profits beyond the first £5m. In the case of a group of companies (see Chapter 28) the £5m "annual allowance" would apply to the whole group, not to each individual company.

At the time of writing, it is unclear whether these reforms (which were dropped from the March 2017 Finance Bill) will be re-introduced in a second Finance Bill later in the year. Further information will be posted as soon as possible on the website which accompanies this book. The website address is www.pearsoned.co.uk/melville.

Non-trading losses

A company may incur non-trading losses in a number of ways. The main classes of non-trading loss and the reliefs available for each are as follows:

(a) **Property business losses**. A loss incurred by a company on its property business is set against the company's total profits for the accounting period in which the loss occurs. To the extent that the loss cannot be relieved in this way, it is either:

   (i) carried forward† and set against the company's total profits in succeeding accounting periods (as long as the property business is still being carried on in those accounting periods), or

   (ii) relieved by means of group relief (see Chapter 28).

   Note that there are restrictions on the carry-forward of property losses when there is a change in the ownership of a company. These restrictions are similar to those relating to trading losses (see earlier in this chapter).

(b) **Net debits on non-trading loan relationships**. A deficit on a company's non-trading loan relationships (see Chapter 23) may be relieved in any of the following ways:

   (i) by set-off against the company's total profits for the accounting period in which the deficit occurs (*after* deducting any trading losses brought forward but *before* deducting any trading losses relieved against total profits and *before* deducting qualifying charitable donations)

   (ii) by group relief (see Chapter 28)

   (iii) by set-off against the company's income from non-trading loan relationships in the previous 12 months.

   Part of the deficit may be relieved in one way and part in another, if the company so wishes. Any part of the deficit for which relief is not claimed under (i), (ii) or (iii) above is carried forward† and set against non-trading profits (i.e. profits other than trading income) of subsequent accounting periods.

(c) **Non-trading losses on intangible fixed assets**. All or part of a non-trading loss on intangible fixed assets (see Chapter 23) may be relieved against the company's total profits for the loss-making period. Any part of the loss which is not relieved in this way and which is not relieved by means of group relief (see Chapter 28) is carried forward† and treated as non-trading expenditure of the next accounting period.

(d) **Capital losses**. Capital losses are relieved first against chargeable gains of the same accounting period and then against the chargeable gains of subsequent accounting periods. Capital losses cannot be relieved against any other form of income.

† *The proposed reforms to the carry-forward rules relating to trading losses (see earlier in this chapter) would also apply to property losses carried forward, non-trading loan relationship deficits carried forward and non-trading losses on intangible fixed assets carried forward.*

Summary

- A company's trading losses are carried forward for relief in subsequent accounting periods, unless the company claims trading loss relief against total profits.
- Qualifying charitable donations which cannot be relieved in the accounting period in which they are paid are lost and cannot be carried forwards or backwards for relief in subsequent or previous accounting periods.
- A company may claim that a trading loss should be relieved against the total profits of the loss-making accounting period. Any part of the loss which remains unrelieved after such a claim may be set against total profits of the previous 12 months.
- If a claim to relieve a trading loss against total profits results in a repayment of corporation tax for an earlier accounting period, this repayment will attract interest.
- Loss reliefs are also available in relation to property business losses, net debits on non-trading loan relationships, non-trading losses on intangible fixed assets and capital losses.

Exercises

26.1 A company has the following results for the three years to 31 May 2017:

	y/e 31/5/15	*y/e 31/5/16*	*y/e 31/5/17*
	£	£	£
Trading profits/(losses)	(32,200)	23,800	40,300
Gift Aid donations	400	500	600

Assuming that the trading loss is to be carried forward for relief against future trading profits, calculate the company's taxable total profits for each of the three years, showing the amount of losses carried forward at the end of each year. Also calculate the amount of tax saved as a result of trading loss relief.

26.2 A company has the following results for the year to 31 October 2017:

	£
Trading loss	(232,300)
Income from property	190,200
Chargeable gains	45,540
Gift Aid donations	24,000

Assuming that a claim is made to relieve the trading loss against total profits of the loss-making accounting period, calculate the taxable total profits for the year.

26.3 Which of the following statements is true?

(a) Capital losses may be carried forward and relieved against future trading profits.

(b) Trading losses may be carried forward for relief against future chargeable gains.

(c) Trading losses may be relieved against chargeable gains of the same period.

(d) Capital losses may be relieved against trading profits of the same period.

26.4 A company has the following results for its three most recent accounting periods:

	y/e 31/5/16	*eight months to 31/1/17*	*y/e 31/1/18*
	£	£	£
Trading profits/(losses)	59,700	73,600	(155,700)
Chargeable gains	8,400	-	48,700
Gift Aid donations	1,000	1,000	1,000

Assuming that all possible claims are made to relieve the trading loss against total profits, calculate the company's taxable total profits for each of the three periods.

26.5 A company's taxable total profits for the year to 30 June 2017 are £800,000. In the nine months to 31 March 2018, the company incurs a trading loss of £700,000 and has no other income or gains. There are no Gift Aid donations in either period.

(a) Explain the corporation tax effects of a claim to relieve the trading loss against total profits.

(b) Calculate the effective rate of tax relief obtained in relation to the trading loss if such a claim is made.

***26.6** A company has the following results for the four years to 31 March 2018:

	y/e 31/3/15	*y/e 31/3/16*	*y/e 31/3/17*	*y/e 31/3/18*
	£	£	£	£
Trading profits/(losses)	61,900	77,400	64,200	(172,500)
Chargeable gains/(capital losses)	(7,500)	4,300	2,700	5,700
Gift Aid donations	3,400	3,400	3,400	3,400

Calculate the total repayment of corporation tax (with interest) to which the company is entitled, assuming that:

(a) all possible claims are made to relieve the trading loss against total profits

(b) any repayment of corporation tax which is generated by these claims is made on 13 January 2019

(c) corporation tax for the three years to 31 March 2017 was all paid on the due dates

(d) the rate of corporation tax payable by the company for FY2014 was 20%

(e) the rate of interest paid on repayments of corporation tax is 0.5%.

Also explain how the situation would differ if the company had ceased trading on 31 March 2018 (computations are <u>not</u> required).

Chapter 27

Close companies and investment companies

Introduction

In general terms, a "close company" is one which is controlled by a small number of people and a "company with investment business" is one whose business consists wholly or partly of making investments. Special corporation tax rules apply to each of these types of company and the main purpose of this chapter is to explain the nature of these rules.

This chapter also considers the taxation consequences which should be borne in mind when deciding whether to trade as an unincorporated business or as a close company.

Close companies

The essence of a close company is that its affairs can be controlled and manipulated by a small group of people, possibly for tax-avoidance purposes. In fact, most companies in the UK are close companies. Certain anti-avoidance legislation exists in relation to close companies and the main points of this legislation are explained later in this chapter. The first step, however, is to provide a precise definition of the term "close company".

Definition of a close company

A close company is a UK resident company which satisfies certain conditions. The main instance of a close company is a company which is under the *control* of:

(a) five or fewer *participators*, or

(b) any number of participators who are also *directors* of the company.

The rights of a participator's *associates* are aggregated with that participator's own rights for the purpose of determining whether a company is a close company. Some important terms used in this definition are explained below.

Control

Persons are deemed to have "control" over a company if, taken together, they:

(a) own over 50% of the company's issued share capital, or

(b) have over 50% of the company's voting power, or

(c) would receive over 50% of the company's income, if it were all distributed, or

(d) would receive over 50% of the company's assets, if the company were wound up.

Participators

A "participator" is defined as someone who has a share or interest in the capital or income of the company. In many cases, a company's only participators are its shareholders, but other persons (e.g. option holders, loan creditors) might also rank as participators.

Directors

A "director", for this purpose, is any person:

(a) who occupies the position of director (whether called a director or not), or

(b) whose directions or instructions are normally obeyed by the directors, or

(c) who is a manager of the company and (possibly together with associates) controls at least 20% of the company's ordinary share capital.

Associates

The main "associates" of a participator are:

(a) the participator's business partners

(b) the participator's relatives

(c) the trustees of a settlement established by the participator or by his/her relatives.

For this purpose, a participator's relatives comprise his or her spouse (or civil partner), parents and remoter ancestors, children and remoter issue, brothers and sisters.

EXAMPLE 1

A company's issued share capital consists of 1,000 £1 ordinary shares, held as follows:

	No of shares		*No of shares*
David	200	Helen	50
Emma	50	Ian	30
Frederick	100	Jacqueline	40
George	50	Others (1 share each)	480

None of the shareholders are associated in any way and no shareholder is also a director.

(a) Is the company a close company?

(b) Would the company be a close company:

   (i) if David were Jacqueline's brother, or

   (ii) if Emma married Ian, or

   (iii) if David were Jacqueline's brother and Emma married Ian?

Solution

(a) The five largest shareholders own 45% of the share capital, so the company is not under the control of five or fewer participators. The company is also not under the control of its directors. Therefore the company is not a close company.

(b) (i) If David were Jacqueline's brother, her 4% holding would be aggregated with his and the five largest shareholders would control 49% (45% + 4%) of the share capital. The company would not be a close company.

   (ii) If Emma married Ian, his 3% would be aggregated with hers and the five largest shareholders would control 48% (45% + 3%) of the share capital. The company would still not be a close company.

   (iii) If David were Jacqueline's brother and Emma married Ian, the five largest shareholders would control 52% (45% + 4% + 3%) of the share capital. The company would then be a close company.

EXAMPLE 2

A company's issued share capital consists entirely of ordinary shares, held as follows:

	% holding	*Director*
Keith	7	Yes
Leonora	7	Yes
Martin	7	Yes
Norma	7	Yes
Oliver	7	Yes
Penny	16	No
Richard	4	No
Others (all non-directors owning under 1%)	45	
Total	100	

None of the shareholders are associated in any way.

(a) Is the company a close company?

(b) Would the company be a close company:

   (i) if Penny were a manager, or

   (ii) if Penny were Richard's daughter, or

   (iii) if Penny were both a manager and Richard's daughter?

Solution

(a) The five largest shareholders own 44% of the share capital, so the company is not under the control of five or fewer participators. The company is also not under the control of its directors, who own 35% of the share capital. Therefore the company is not a close company.

(b) (i) If Penny were a manager, she would not rank as a director since her shareholding is less than 20%. The situation would be unaltered and the company would not be a close company.

(ii) If Penny were Richard's daughter, then his 4% holding would be aggregated with hers and the five largest shareholders would control 48% (44% + 4%) of the share capital. The company would still not be a close company.

(iii) If Penny were both a manager and Richard's daughter, then her deemed 20% holding (16% + 4%) would make her a director. The six directors would control 55% of the share capital and the company would then be a close company.

Exceptions

Certain types of company are statutorily excepted from close company status, even if they are controlled by five or fewer participators or by the participator-directors. The main exception consists of listed companies with a substantial public interest. In order for this exception to apply, a company must satisfy all of the following conditions:

(a) The company's voting shares must have been both dealt in and listed on a recognised stock exchange within the 12 months prior to the date on which the company's status is being determined.

(b) The total voting power possessed by the *principal members* of the company must not exceed 85% of the total voting power.

(c) At least 35% of the company's voting power must be in the hands of the public.

For this purpose, a "principal member" is a shareholder who (possibly with associates) has more than 5% of the voting power of the company and is also one of the top five shareholders. If two or more shareholders, each holding more than 5%, tie for fifth place, there will be more than five principal members.

The "public" excludes the company's directors, their associates, pension schemes for the company's own employees and most principal members. But principal members which are non-close companies or pension schemes (apart from pension schemes for the company's own employees) *are* included within the definition of the public.

EXAMPLE 3

A company's issued share capital consists entirely of ordinary shares. These shares have been listed on a recognised stock exchange for many years and there have been frequent dealings in them within the last 12 months. The company's shares are owned as follows:

	% holding	*Director*
ABBQ Ltd (a non-close company)	13	-
DFFK Ltd (a close company)	7	-
Terry	8	Yes
Ursula	10	Yes
Vincent (a manager)	33	No
Wendy	4	No
Others (all non-directors owning under 1%)	25	
Total	100	

None of the shareholders are associated in any way. Is the company a close company?

Solution

At first sight, the company seems to be a close company. It is under the control of its directors (since Vincent ranks as a director) and it is also under the control of five or fewer participators. However, the company is listed on a recognised stock exchange and its shares have been dealt in within the past 12 months. Furthermore, its principal members (the top five shareholders, each owning more than 5% of the voting shares) hold only 71% of the company's voting power and the public (ABBQ Ltd, Wendy and the others) hold 42%. Therefore the company is excepted from being a close company.

Consequences of close company status

The main tax consequences† of close company status are as follows:

(a) Benefits in kind provided by the company to its participators or their associates are generally treated as distributions.

(b) Loans made to participators or their associates are assessed to tax.

Each of these consequences is explained below. Note also that special loan relationships rules apply if a close company enters into a loan relationship with one of its participators or with an associate of a participator.

† *Trivial benefits in kind provided to employees and costing no more than £50 each are exempt from income tax (see Chapter 8). However, an annual cap of £300 applies to the value of such benefits that can be received tax-free by a director of a close company.*

Benefits in kind provided to participators

Benefits in kind provided by a close company to its participators (or their associates) are generally regarded as distributions. The taxation effects of this are as follows:

(a) The cost to the company of providing the benefit is disallowed when computing its corporation tax liability.

(b) The company is deemed to have made a distribution equal to the amount of the benefit in kind which would have been assessed to income tax if the benefit had been received by an employee (see Chapter 8).

(c) The person receiving the benefit is taxed as if he or she had received a dividend of the same amount as the deemed distribution.

However, a benefit provided to a participator is *not* treated as a distribution if it is already assessable as employment income.

EXAMPLE 4

On 31 August 2017, a close company provides one of its shareholders with a holiday costing £3,600. This is charged as an expense in the company's income statement for the year to 31 March 2018. The shareholder concerned is not a director or employee of the company. Explain the tax treatment of this item.

Solution

The £3,600 is disallowed in the company's tax computation for the year to 31 March 2018. The company is deemed to have made a distribution of £3,600 and the recipient of the holiday is taxed as if he/she had received a dividend of £3,600.

Loans made to participators

If a close company makes a loan to a participator (or associate), the tax consequences are as follows:

(a) The company is required to pay an amount of tax which is calculated at 32.5% of the amount of the loan. This tax is payable nine months and one day after the end of the accounting period in which the loan is made. However, no tax is payable in relation to any part of a loan which is repaid to the company before the date on which the tax falls due.

(b) The tax paid when the loan was made is repaid to the company if the participator repays the loan or if the loan is written off. This tax repayment is made nine months and one day after the end of the accounting period in which the loan is repaid or written off.

(c) If a loan to a participator is wholly or partly written off, the amount written off is *not* treated as a debit arising under a loan relationship and therefore the company is denied tax relief in relation to this amount. Furthermore, the participator is deemed to have received income equal to the amount written off. This income is treated as if received net of income tax at the dividend ordinary rate (currently 7.5%).

The tax which is deemed to have been deducted at source from this income is not repayable to the participator, even if he or she is a non-taxpayer. However, further tax at the dividend upper (or additional) rate is payable on any part of the grossed-up income which, when added to the participator's other income, falls beyond the basic rate limit (or higher rate limit).

In the case of a participator who is also an employee, this tax charge takes priority over the usual rules which apply to employee loans written off (see Chapter 8).

(d) Certain loans are excluded from the treatment described above. These include loans made to a participator in the normal course of the company's business and loans not exceeding £15,000 made to a participator who is a full-time employee or director of the company, so long as that participator (with associates) has no more than a 5% interest in the company.

EXAMPLE 5

On 1 May 2017, a close company which prepares accounts to 31 March each year lends £30,000 to Ravi, who is one of its directors. No interest is charged on this loan. Ravi owns 18% of the company's ordinary share capital. Explain the tax treatment of this loan if:

(a) Ravi repays the loan in full on 15 February 2019

(b) Ravi repays £11,500 of the loan on 15 February 2019 and the remaining £18,500 is written off by the company on the same day.

Solution

Tax of £9,750 (32.5% of £30,000) is payable by the company on 1 January 2019. Since the loan is interest-free, it is treated as a beneficial loan and Ravi is subject to income tax on the related benefit in kind. As regards the eventual repayment or write-off of the loan:

(a) The tax of £9,750 is repaid to the company on 1 January 2020.

(b) The £9,750 is repaid on 1 January 2020 but the company cannot claim tax relief in relation to the £18,500 of the loan which has been written off.

Ravi is treated as receiving income in 2018-19 of £20,000 (£18,500 × 100/92.5), with tax deducted at source of £1,500. This is taxed in the same way as dividend income and so might give rise to further income tax at the dividend upper or dividend additional rates if Ravi's total income is sufficiently high.

Companies with investment business

A "company with investment business" is defined by the Corporation Tax Act 2009 as "*a company whose business consists wholly or partly of making investments*". The investment income of such a company will normally consist of:

(a) income from property

(b) net credits on non-trading loan relationships

(c) chargeable gains.

The company may also receive dividend income. But dividends other than non-exempt foreign dividends (see Chapter 32) are not chargeable to corporation tax. The expenses incurred by a company in relation to its investment business fall into two categories:

(a) expenses which are directly related to one of the company's sources of income and which may be set against that income (e.g. property expenses offset against property income, debits on non-trading loan relationships set against credits)

(b) management expenses, which are not related to any particular source of income but which may be set against the company's total income.

Note that only genuine management expenses are allowed. For example, in *L G Berry Investments Ltd* v *Attwooll* (1964), excessive directors' remuneration included in management expenses was disallowed.

To the extent that management expenses cannot be relieved in the accounting period in which they are incurred they may be carried forward (without time limit) to future periods. There are restrictions on the carry-forward of management expenses when there is a change in the ownership of a company. These restrictions are similar to those relating to the carry-forward of trading losses (see Chapter 26).

Choice of business medium

An individual who starts trading is faced with a choice between two alternatives:

(a) To trade as an unincorporated business, either as a sole trader or in partnership with others. In this case the individual is self-employed and the business profits are assessed to income tax as trading income.

(b) To trade as a limited company (probably a close company) with the individual concerned being a director and/or shareholder of the company. In this case, the company's profits are assessed to corporation tax and the individual's earnings and dividends from the company are assessed to income tax.

The choice between these two alternatives will be determined partly (though not solely) by taxation considerations. A full analysis of these considerations is beyond the scope of this book but some of the main factors which should be taken into account when deciding whether to trade as an unincorporated business or as a company include:

(a) the rates of income tax and corporation tax

(b) the NI contributions which are payable by the self-employed and by employees and employers

(c) the tax effects of distributing profits to the owner of the business

(d) the tax reliefs available on pension contributions

(e) the dates on which tax and NI contributions are due for payment

(f) the tax reliefs available in relation to trading losses

(g) the taxation of chargeable gains

(h) the tax treatment of loans made to the owner of the business.

Each of these factors is discussed below.

Rates of tax

The entire profits of an unincorporated business are charged to income tax, whether or not the profits are drawn out of the business. Rates of tax in 2017-18 are 20%, 40% or 45%, depending upon the owner's taxable income. A marginal rate of 40% applies if taxable income exceeds £33,500 (*£31,500 for Scottish taxpayers*). This is a relatively small sum. The 45% rate applies if the owner's taxable income exceeds £150,000.

By contrast, the profits of a company for FY2017 are always charged to corporation tax at the main rate of 19%, regardless of how large those profits are. Furthermore, the owners of a company can determine the amount of profits to be paid out as directors' remuneration and can therefore control the extent to which profits are assessed to income tax rather than corporation tax.

Note, however, that retaining profits in a company so as to minimise the tax liability in the short term will increase the value of the company's shares. This will result in an increased capital gains tax (CGT) liability in the longer term when shareholders dispose of their shares, though the gains made on such disposals might be eligible for entrepreneurs' relief and/or other CGT reliefs.

National Insurance

In 2017-18, the self-employed pay flat-rate Class 2 NICs of £2.85 per week. Class 4 contributions are also payable, calculated as 9% of profits between £8,164 and £45,000 and 2% of profits beyond £45,000.

The total amount of the Class 1 NICs payable in respect of directors' remuneration can be much higher than this. A director pays primary contributions at 12% on earnings between £8,164 and £45,000 and at 2% on any further earnings. In addition, the company pays 13.8% secondary contributions on all earnings in excess of £8,164. However, these secondary contributions are deductible when calculating the company's profits for corporation tax purposes.

Distribution of profits

The amount of income tax payable on the profits of an unincorporated business is entirely unaffected by the level of the owner's drawings. But the distribution of profits by a company (either as directors' remuneration or as dividends) has tax implications:

(a) The payment of directors' remuneration reduces the company's corporation tax liability at the expense of increasing the income tax liability of the directors concerned and creating a liability to both primary and secondary NICs.

(b) The payment of a dividend avoids the liability to NICs, but dividends are an appropriation of profit and are not deductible in the company's corporation tax computation. Furthermore, avoiding NICs will have an adverse impact on the shareholder's contributions record and this, in turn, may affect his or her entitlement to certain social security benefits in the future.

The decision as to whether to pay out a company's profits as directors' remuneration or dividends (or a mixture of both) is a complex one and should take into account the personal circumstances of the shareholders and directors as well as all of the factors listed above. A constraint which may need to be borne in mind is the need to pay sufficient remuneration to comply with National Minimum Wage regulations.

EXAMPLE 6

A close company which prepares accounts to 31 March each year is owned and managed by a single shareholder/director who is paid a salary of £5,000 per month. In addition to this salary, the company's owner intends to withdraw £20,000 from the company on 31 March 2018. Two approaches are being considered:

(a) that the company should make an extra salary payment to the owner, such that the total of this payment and the related secondary NICs will equal £20,000

(b) that the company should pay a dividend to the owner, such that the total of this dividend and the company's extra corporation tax liability (when compared with the other approach) will equal £20,000.

Consider the tax-effectiveness of each of these two approaches. Perform all calculations to the nearest £ and assume that the owner has no income apart from salary and dividends derived from the company.

Solution

	Extra salary £	*Dividend* £
Payments made by company:		
Salary	17,575	
Secondary Class 1 NICs @ 13.8%	2,425	
Corporation tax on £20,000 @ 19%		3,800
Dividend		16,200
Total payments	20,000	20,000
Amount received by owner:		
Gross salary	17,575	
Dividend received		16,200
Primary Class 1 NICs @ 2%	(351)	
Income tax @ 40%	(7,030)	
Income tax at nil rate (£5,000 @ 0%)		0
Income tax at upper rate (£11,200 @ 32.5%)		(3,640)
Income remaining after tax	10,194	12,560

Notes:

(i) The owner's regular salary is sufficient to ensure that any extra salary attracts primary Class 1 NICs at 2% and that any further income is subject to income tax at the higher rate (or the dividend upper rate).

(ii) In this example, the payment of a dividend is more tax-effective than the payment of extra salary, mainly because of the fact that dividends do not attract NICs. The total liability to tax and NICs is reduced by £2,366 (£2,425 + £351 + £7,030 − £3,800 − £3,640) and therefore income remaining after tax increases by £2,366.

Pension contributions

In 2017-18, a self-employed individual may obtain tax relief on pension contributions of up to £3,600 or 100% of self-employment income (whichever is the greater). Similarly, a company director may obtain tax relief on pension contributions of up to £3,600 or 100% of director's remuneration (whichever is the greater) whilst the company itself may make unlimited pension contributions on the director's behalf and deduct these contributions when computing taxable total profits. However, this deduction is available only if the contributions are paid wholly and exclusively for trade purposes.

Dividends do not rank as earnings and therefore dividends received are ignored when computing the maximum pension contributions on which an individual may obtain tax relief. Furthermore, a shareholder in a company is not (per se) an employee of that company. So a company cannot make employer's pension contributions in relation to one of its shareholders unless that shareholder is also a director or other employee.

Dates of payment of tax and NICs

A self-employed person must make payments on account of his or her liability to income tax and Class 4 NICs. These payments are due on 31 January in the tax year and on the following 31 July. The balance of the liability (if any) is payable on the following 31 January. Note that:

(a) Choosing an accounting date early in the tax year (e.g. 30 April) maximises the delay between earning profits and paying tax on them. For example, tax and Class 4 NICs on profits for the year to 30 April 2017 (basis period for 2017-18) are payable on 31 January 2018 and 31 July 2018 with a balancing payment on 31 January 2019.

(b) However, choosing an accounting date early in the tax year has the adverse effect of maximising the amount of overlap profits which are assessed twice on the commencement of trade.

(c) Class 2 NICs for a tax year are added to the balancing payment for that year.

In general, close companies will pay their corporation tax nine months and one day after the end of the accounting period. Income tax and Class 1 NICs in relation to directors' remuneration must be accounted for via the PAYE system.

Relief for trading losses

For both individuals and companies, trading losses may be carried forward and set against future profits of the same trade†. The main distinctions between trading loss reliefs for individuals and trading loss reliefs for companies are concerned with the opportunities to set such losses against total income:

(a) The trading losses of a self-employed individual may be set against that person's total income for the year of the loss, the previous year or both of these years.

In the case of a company, a claim to set trading losses against total profits of the previous 12 months cannot be made unless a claim has already been made to set trading losses against total profits of the current accounting period.

(b) Both for self-employed individuals and for companies, terminal losses incurred in the 12 months prior to a cessation of trade may be carried back for three years. For individuals, terminal losses may be relieved only against profits of the same trade (see Chapter 12). For companies, terminal losses are set against the company's total profits, not just profits of the same trade (see Chapter 26).

(c) In certain circumstances, the trading losses of an individual may be set against capital gains (see Chapter 12). A company receives a similar relief by virtue of the fact that a company's chargeable gains are automatically included in its total profits.

(d) Trading losses of an individual incurred in the opening years of a business may be relieved against total income of the previous three years. There is no equivalent relief for companies.

Note that a company's losses can be relieved only against the company's own income and gains, not against the income and gains of individual shareholders.

† *The Government has proposed that carried-forward trading losses incurred by a company on or after 1 April 2017 should be relievable against other forms of income as well as against trading income (see Chapter 26).*

Chargeable gains

If an unincorporated business disposes of a chargeable asset, any gain that arises is assessed to CGT on the owner of the business. The rate of tax for disposals occurring during tax year 2017-18 is usually 10% or 20%. The annual exemption is available.

The computational rules which apply when a company makes a chargeable disposal are somewhat different from those which apply for CGT. In particular, indexation allowance is available to companies but not to individuals. Gains arising in FY2017 are subject to corporation tax at 19%. No annual exemption is available. Gains retained in the company increase the value of the company's shares, so resulting in an increased CGT liability when shareholders eventually dispose of their shares. In effect a chargeable gain may be taxed twice, first to corporation tax and then to CGT.

Close company loans to participators

As explained earlier in this chapter, close companies must pay tax when making loans to participators. A tax charge of this type can sometimes be triggered accidentally if a director who is also a shareholder overdraws his or her current account with the company. These provisions have no relevance to unincorporated businesses.

Incorporation

If the initial choice is to trade as an unincorporated business, the trader may still consider incorporation at some future time. Some of the main tax consequences of incorporation are as follows:

(a) The transfer of the assets of a business to a company might give rise to a CGT liability. However, subject to certain conditions, the gains arising may be held-over until the shares which were acquired in exchange for the business assets are disposed of (see Chapter 22).

(b) If the company is under the control of the person who was previously the owner of the unincorporated business, assets which are eligible for capital allowances can be transferred at their written down values for capital allowances purposes, so avoiding the need for balancing adjustments (see Chapter 11).

(c) The transfer of assets to the company will not be treated as a supply for VAT purposes so long as the business is transferred as a going concern and the company is a taxable person at the time of the transfer (see Chapter 29).

(d) If the proprietor of the unincorporated business has unrelieved trade losses, these cannot be carried forward and used by the company. However, subject to certain conditions, such unrelieved losses may be relieved against the proprietor's income from the company (see Chapter 12).

Summary

- A close company is under the control of five or fewer participators or any number of participator-directors. The rights of a participator's associates are taken into account when determining whether or not a company is a close company.
- Certain types of company (mainly listed companies with a substantial public interest) are excepted from close company status.
- Benefits in kind provided to the participators of a close company are treated as distributions. Loans to participators are charged to tax.
- A company with investment business is a company whose business consists wholly or partly of making investments. Management expenses incurred by such companies are set against total income. Excess management expenses may be carried forward.
- The choice of business medium (unincorporated business or close company) may be made for tax reasons. But this is a complex decision and involves many aspects of the income tax, capital gains tax, NICs and corporation tax systems.

Exercises

27.1 Andrew Pearson is a shareholder of Andrew (Nottingham) Ltd. Which of the following (if any) are his associates when deciding whether the company is a close company?

(a) his sister
(b) his brother-in-law
(c) his nephew
(d) his father
(e) his partner in a firm of solicitors.

27.2 A company's share capital consists of 5,000 ordinary shares, held as follows:

	Number of shares
Sejanus (a manager)	900
Claudius (a director)	400
Agrippa (a director)	300
Cleopatra (a director)	300
Tiberius (a director)	200
Gaius (a director)	200
Ptolemy	190
Livia (the grandmother of Claudius)	190
Apicata (the wife of Sejanus)	120
Others (all non-directors owning 10 shares or less)	2,200
Total	5,000

Is the company a close company?

27.3 On 31 October 2017, a close company which prepares accounts to 31 March each year provides one of its full-time working directors with:

(a) an interest-free loan of £12,000 (the company does not provide loans in the ordinary course of its business)

(b) a season ticket for the opera, costing the company £1,800.

Explain the tax treatment of these two items, assuming that the director in question owns 10% of the company's ordinary share capital.

***27.4** On 19 April 2017, a close company (which makes up accounts to 31 March annually) lends £99,400 to Siobhan, who is a director of the company and who owns 30% of its ordinary share capital. The company does not provide loans in the ordinary course of its business. Siobhan pays a commercial rate of interest on this loan until 1 October 2018, when she repays £55,000. She then continues to pay a commercial rate of interest on the remainder of the loan until it is written off by the company on 31 March 2019. Explain the tax implications of these transactions.

***27.5** Glenda has been self-employed for many years, preparing accounts to 31 March each year. Her adjusted profits (after deduction of capital allowances) are currently running at approximately £80,000 per annum. She has no other income for tax purposes and she is not a Scottish taxpayer.

Glenda is now considering incorporation and would like to see a comparison of her current tax liability (including NICs) and the liability that would arise if she traded as a small company, with herself as the sole shareholder and director.

(a) Assuming that Glenda continues to operate as a sole trader and that her adjusted trading profit for the year to 31 March 2018 is £80,000, calculate the total liability to income tax and NICs for tax year 2017-18.

(b) Estimate the total liability to income tax, NICs and corporation tax that would arise for the year if Glenda formed a company and extracted £50,000 of the company's profit for the year either:

  (i) as a salary (so that her salary plus secondary NICs would total £50,000), or

  (ii) as a £50,000 dividend.

(c) In case (b), how would the total liability be affected if Glenda took £8,164 as a salary and the remainder of the £50,000 as a dividend?

Assume for the sake of simplicity that all director's remuneration and dividends are taken during tax year 2017-18. Perform all calculations to the nearest £.

Chapter 28

Groups of companies and reconstructions

Introduction

For corporation tax purposes, groups of companies are divided into a number of categories and each category enjoys certain tax advantages. These advantages may include:

(a) the transfer of trading losses and certain other deficits between group members

(b) the transfer of chargeable assets from one group member to another in such a way that no chargeable gain arises on the transfer.

However, group companies suffer certain tax disadvantages. These disadvantages include an increased likelihood of being required to pay corporation tax by instalments and a new proposed restriction on tax relief for interest payable (see below).

The main purpose of this chapter is to describe the categories of group which exist and the corporation tax rules which apply to each category. The tax implications of company reconstructions are also considered very briefly at the end of this chapter.

Related 51% group companies

Company A is a "related 51% group company" of Company B for an accounting period if, for any part of that period, either:

(a) Company A is a 51% subsidiary of Company B, or

(b) Company B is a 51% subsidiary of Company A, or

(c) Company A and Company B are both 51% subsidiaries of the same third company.

The full definition of "51% subsidiary" is given later in this chapter. But, in general terms, one company is a 51% subsidiary of another company if more than 50% of its ordinary shares are owned (directly or indirectly) by that other company.

If a company has one or more related 51% group companies in an accounting period, the profits limits of £1,500,000 and £10,000,000 which are used when determining whether the company must pay corporation tax by instalments (see Chapter 25) are both divided by (N + 1), where N is the number of those related 51% group companies.

Counting related 51% group companies

When counting the number of related 51% group companies which a company has for an accounting period, it is important to note that:

(a) A company is counted even if it was a related 51% group company of the company concerned for only part of the period. Furthermore, two or more related 51% group companies are counted even if they were related to the company concerned for different parts of the period but never simultaneously.

(b) Related 51% group companies which are dormant are ignored.

(c) Related 51% group companies are counted whether or not they are UK resident, even though overseas companies are generally outside the charge to UK corporation tax.

EXAMPLE 1

A Ltd owns 90% of the ordinary share capital of B Ltd and 70% of the ordinary share capital of C Ltd. C Ltd owns 70% of the ordinary share capital of D Ltd.

(a) Which companies are related 51% group companies of A Ltd?

(b) If B Ltd acquired 60% of the ordinary share capital of an overseas company, would this overseas company also become a related 51% group company of A Ltd?

Solution

(a) A Ltd directly owns more than 50% of the ordinary share capital of B Ltd and C Ltd, so B Ltd and C Ltd are both related 51% group companies of A Ltd.

A Ltd does not directly own any shares in D Ltd but it indirectly owns 49% of that company's ordinary share capital (70% x 70%). However, this is insufficient to make D Ltd a related 51% group company of A Ltd.

Therefore the related 51% group companies of A Ltd are B Ltd and C Ltd.

(b) Indirectly, A Ltd would own 54% of the overseas company's ordinary share capital (90% x 60%) so this overseas company would also become a related 51% group company of A Ltd.

EXAMPLE 2

E Ltd has taxable total profits of £800,000 for the year to 31 March 2018 and receives no dividends. The company owns 65% of the ordinary shares of F Ltd and 30% of the ordinary shares of G Ltd.

Calculate the corporation tax liability of E Ltd for the year to 31 March 2018 and state the date (or dates) on which this tax is due to be paid (assuming that the company was "large" for payment by instalments purposes in the year to 31 March 2017).

Solution

E Ltd has one related 51% group company (F Ltd). Therefore the £1,500,000 profit limit which is used when determining whether or not a company must pay corporation tax by instalments is reduced to [(£1,500,000 ÷ (1 + 1)] = £750,000. The company's augmented profit for the year exceeds this limit and therefore tax is payable by instalments.

The accounting period coincides with FY2017 so the applicable rate of tax is 19%. The liability is (£800,000 × 19%) = £152,000 and this is payable in four instalments of £38,000 each on 14 October 2017, 14 January 2018, 14 April 2018 and 14 July 2018.

EXAMPLE 3

S Ltd has taxable total profits of £120,000 for the six months to 30 September 2017 and receives no dividends. Until 1 June 2017, S Ltd had no related 51% group companies. However, on that date, its entire share capital was acquired by H Ltd. H Ltd has five other wholly-owned subsidiaries, two of which are dormant.

Determine whether or not S Ltd will be required to pay corporation tax by instalments for the six months to 30 September 2017.

Solution

S Ltd has four related 51% group companies (H Ltd and its three active subsidiaries) for this six-month accounting period. Therefore the profits limit which is used to determine whether or not the company must pay corporation tax by instalments is reduced to [(£1,500,000 × 6/12) ÷ (4 + 1)] = £150,000.

S Ltd has augmented profits for the period of £120,000. This does not exceed £150,000, so the company is not required to pay corporation tax by instalments for this period.

51% groups

The full definition of the term "51% subsidiary" (see above) is given in Corporation Tax Act 2010. This Act states that Company B is a 51% subsidiary of Company A only if *all* of the following conditions are satisfied:

(a) Company A owns (directly or indirectly) over 50% of the ordinary share capital of Company B, and

(b) Company A is entitled to more than 50% of the profits available to the ordinary shareholders of Company B, and

(c) Company A would be entitled to more than 50% of the assets available to the ordinary shareholders of Company B if Company B were to be wound-up.

Two companies are members of a 51% group if one company is a 51% subsidiary of the other or they are both 51% subsidiaries of a third company. Corporation tax provisions which relate specifically to 51% groups are as follows:

(a) Dividends received from a 51% subsidiary or fellow 51% subsidiary ("intra-group dividends") are disregarded when determining whether or not the company is liable to pay corporation tax by instalments (see Chapter 25).

(b) If at least one of the companies in a 51% group is liable to pay corporation tax by instalments, one of the group members may be nominated to pay all of the tax due by all of the group members. In these circumstances, instalments are based upon the estimated tax liability of the entire group. When the total liability of each group member is finally determined, the instalments already paid may be allocated between the group members in such a way as to minimise any interest payable.

EXAMPLE 4

A company with seven 51% subsidiaries has taxable total profits of £140,000 for the year to 31 March 2018. Dividends received in the year were £50,000. Calculate the corporation tax liability for the year and state the date (or dates) on which this tax is due to be paid, assuming that the company was "large" in the year to 31 March 2017 and *either*:

(a) all of the dividends received were intra-group dividends, *or*

(b) none of the dividends received were intra-group dividends.

Solution

(a) The company has seven 51% related companies and so must pay tax by instalments if augmented profits exceed £187,500 (£1,500,000 ÷ 8). Intra-group dividends are ignored so augmented profits are the same as TTP (£140,000) and instalments are not required. The liability of £26,600 (£140,000 × 19%) falls due on 1 January 2019.

(b) Augmented profits are £190,000, which exceeds £187,500. Instalments of £6,650 each fall due on 14 October 2017, 14 January 2018, 14 April 2018 and 14 July 2018.

Transfer pricing

For many years, the UK tax system has contained "transfer pricing" rules which prevent UK companies from gaining a tax advantage by carrying out transactions at artificial prices with connected companies overseas (see Chapter 32). The transfer pricing rules require companies to compute their profits for tax purposes as if such transactions had been carried out at the prices which would have applied between unconnected parties.

The original transfer pricing rules applied only to transactions with connected companies situated overseas, but these rules have now been extended to cover transactions between connected UK companies. Broadly, companies are connected for this purpose if one controls the other or they are under common control. The rules require an adjustment for tax purposes to the profits of the company which gains a potential tax advantage from the transactions and a corresponding adjustment to the profits of the other company.

Small and medium-sized companies are exempt from the transfer pricing legislation.

75% groups

Company B is a 75% subsidiary of Company A if the following conditions are satisfied:

(a) Company A owns (directly or indirectly) at least 75% of the ordinary share capital of Company B, *and*

(b) Company A is entitled to at least 75% of the profits available to the ordinary shareholders of Company B, *and*

(c) Company A would be entitled to at least 75% of the assets available to the ordinary shareholders of Company B if Company B were to be wound-up.

Two companies are members of a 75% group if one company is a 75% subsidiary of the other or they are both 75% subsidiaries of a third company.

The "UK related" members of a 75% group enjoy two main tax advantages†. These are the right to transfer certain losses and deficits between group members ("group relief") and the transfer of chargeable assets between group members in such a way that no chargeable gain arises on the transfer. These reliefs are described below.

A company is regarded as "UK related" if it is UK resident or if it carries on a trade in the UK through a permanent establishment.

† *However, if the proposed reforms to carry forward loss relief are implemented (see Chapter 26) the £5m "annual allowance" involved in the calculation of the maximum loss relief available in an accounting period would apply to the whole of a 75% group, not to each individual company.*

EXAMPLE 5

P Ltd is the parent company of a small group. All companies in the group are UK resident and all of the issued shares of each company are ordinary shares. Shareholdings within the group are as follows:

(a) P Ltd owns 80% of Q Ltd, 100% of R Ltd and 60% of S Ltd.

(b) Q Ltd owns 90% of T Ltd.

(c) S Ltd owns 70% of V Ltd.

Identify 51% subsidiaries and 75% subsidiaries within this group structure.

Solution

P Ltd owns (indirectly) 72% of the ordinary share capital of T Ltd (80% x 90%) and 42% of the ordinary share capital of V Ltd (60% x 70%). Therefore:

(i) Q Ltd and R Ltd are 75% subsidiaries (and 51% subsidiaries) of P Ltd.

(ii) S Ltd and T Ltd are 51% subsidiaries of P Ltd.

(iii) T Ltd is a 75% subsidiary (and a 51% subsidiary) of Q Ltd.

(iv) V Ltd is a 51% subsidiary of S Ltd.

Group relief

Group relief consists of the surrender of trading losses and/or certain other items by one member of a 75% group (the "surrendering company") to another member of the same group (the "claimant company"). The main items which may be surrendered are:

(a) trading losses and deficits on non-trading loan relationships

(b) property business losses, non-trading losses on intangible fixed assets and qualifying charitable donations.

Capital losses cannot be surrendered under the group relief rules, but a capital loss can in effect be transferred from one group company to another by a different means (see later in this chapter). Note the following points with regard to group relief:

(a) The surrender may be in whole or in part as best meets the requirements of the surrendering company and the claimant company. Trading losses and deficits on non-trading loan relationships may be surrendered even if they could instead have been set against the profits of the accounting period in which they are incurred. The other items are available for surrender only to the extent that (in aggregate) they exceed the surrendering company's gross profits for the period in which they are incurred.

For this purpose, a company's "gross profits" are its profits before deducting amounts which are eligible for group relief and before deducting losses or other amounts carried forward or back from any other period.

(b) A surrender may be made from subsidiary to parent, from parent to subsidiary or from subsidiary to fellow subsidiary.

(c) Only current-period† losses (or other items) are eligible for group relief. These must be set against the claimant company's profits for an *overlapping* accounting period. If the accounting periods of the surrendering company and the claimant company do not correspond exactly, group relief is available only in respect of the period of overlap between the two periods. The losses of the surrendering company and the profits of the claimant company are time-apportioned so as to determine the amounts which fall into the overlap period. A similar time-apportionment is required when a company joins or leaves a group part-way through an accounting period.

† *But if the proposed reforms to carry forward loss relief are implemented (see Chapter 26), trading losses incurred on or after 1 April 2017 and carried forward for relief in later accounting periods would be eligible for group relief in those periods.*

(d) The amount of losses and other items surrendered to a claimant company cannot exceed that company's "available profits" for the corresponding accounting period. Available profits are the company's profits *before* deducting any reliefs derived from a subsequent period but *after* deducting reliefs derived from a prior period or the current period. For example, the following items must be deducted when computing a company's available profits for group relief purposes:

- trading losses brought forward
- current-period trading losses which are relieved against total profits of the period (or which could have been relieved in this way)
- qualifying charitable donations for the period.

Note that group relief is given *before* relief for trading losses carried back.

(e) A group relief claim must be made within two years of the end of the claimant company's accounting period. Any amount paid to the surrendering company by the claimant company in return for the surrendered items is ignored for tax purposes so long as the payment does not exceed the amount of the surrendered items.

(f) There are restrictions on group relief if the surrendering company is UK related but is not UK resident. Restrictions also apply to the surrender of losses incurred by an overseas permanent establishment of a UK resident company (see Chapter 32).

(g) In certain circumstances, group relief may be claimed by UK parent companies in relation to losses incurred by their foreign subsidiaries (see Chapter 32).

EXAMPLE 6

Low1 Ltd is a wholly-owned subsidiary of High1 Ltd. Both companies are UK resident and prepare accounts to 31 March each year. Results for the year to 31 March 2018 are:

	High1 Ltd	*Low1 Ltd*
	£	£
Trading profit/(loss)	100,000	(180,000)
Chargeable gains	5,000	75,000
Gift Aid donations	12,000	-

Show how the trading loss sustained by Low1 Ltd may be relieved.

Solution

High1 Ltd has taxable total profits of £93,000 (£100,000 + £5,000 – £12,000). This sets a ceiling on the amount of group relief which may be claimed. The trading loss sustained by Low1 Ltd may be relieved in a number of ways. For example:

(a) The entire loss could be carried forward for relief in subsequent accounting periods.

(b) £75,000 of the loss could be relieved against the company's chargeable gains and the balance of £105,000 could then be carried forward. Alternatively, the remaining £105,000 of the loss could be relieved (as far as possible) against the total profits of Low1 Ltd for the previous 12 months.

(c) Group relief of anything up to £93,000 could be claimed and the balance of the loss then dealt with as above.

EXAMPLE 7

Low2 Ltd is a 75% subsidiary of High2 Ltd and both companies are UK resident. Recent results are as follows:

	High2 Ltd	*Low2 Ltd*
	£	£
Trading loss for year to 31 March 2017		(40,000)
Taxable total profits (before group relief):		
year to 31 December 2016	35,000	
year to 31 December 2017	56,000	

Compute the amount of group relief that may be claimed.

Solution

The accounting periods of High2 Ltd and Low2 Ltd do not correspond, so it is necessary to time-apportion profits and losses, as follows:

	1/4/16 - 31/12/16 *(9 months)*	*1/1/17 - 31/3/17* *(3 months)*
	£	£
(i) High2 Ltd profit	26,250	14,000
(ii) Low2 Ltd loss	(30,000)	(10,000)

The group relief available in each period is the lower of (i) and (ii). Therefore, High2 Ltd may claim that group relief of up to £26,250 should be set against its 2016 profits and that group relief of up to £10,000 should be set against its 2017 profits. The remaining £3,750 of the loss is not eligible for group relief.

Using group relief effectively

Group relief should be used to ensure that trading losses (and other eligible items) are relieved as tax-effectively as possible and that the group's overall tax liability is minimised. Points to bear in mind are:

(a) Claimant companies should consider claiming less than the full amount of capital allowances available for an accounting period, so maximising the profits available for group relief set-off.

(b) A company which has incurred a trading loss might lose tax relief on qualifying charitable donations if the loss is carried forward against future trading profits or set against the company's total profits. This loss of tax relief might be avoided if the loss is group-relieved instead.

(c) In an era of falling corporation tax rates, group-relieving a loss in the current period might result in a greater tax saving than carrying the loss forward for relief in subsequent accounting periods.

Transfer of chargeable assets within a group

If a chargeable asset is transferred from one member of a 75% group to another, the transfer is deemed to have occurred at a value giving rise to neither a gain nor a loss. When an asset which has been transferred between group members in this way is finally disposed of outside the group, the chargeable gain arising on the disposal is then (in effect) calculated with reference to the original cost of the asset to the group. Note that:

(a) The definition of a 75% group for this purpose is less rigorous than the definition given above in relation to group relief. A *capital gains group* consists of a principal company plus its 75% subsidiaries (as previously defined) plus the subsidiaries' 75% subsidiaries and so forth, subject to the over-riding requirement that the principal company must have more than a 50% interest in each member of the group.

(b) A 75% subsidiary which is part of a capital gains group cannot also be the principal company of another capital gains group.

EXAMPLE 8

J Ltd owns 80% of the ordinary share capital of K Ltd, which owns 80% of the share capital of L Ltd, which owns 80% of the share capital of M Ltd, which owns 80% of the share capital of N Ltd. All of these companies are UK resident. Which of the companies belongs to a capital gains group with J Ltd as the principal company?

Solution

At first sight, all five companies seem to belong to the capital gains group which has J Ltd at its head. However, J Ltd must have more than a 50% interest in each member of the group. J Ltd's actual interests in each member are as follows:

K Ltd	80%
L Ltd	80% x 80% = 64%
M Ltd	80% x 80% x 80% = 51.2%
N Ltd	80% x 80% x 80% x 80% = 40.96%

J Ltd's interest in N Ltd does not exceed 50%, therefore the capital gains group contains only J Ltd, K Ltd, L Ltd and M Ltd.

Since M Ltd is a member of this group it cannot also be the principal member of another capital gains group. So it is not possible for M Ltd and N Ltd to form a second capital gains group containing just those two companies.

Roll-over relief for capital gains groups

For the purposes of roll-over relief on the replacement of a business asset (see Chapter 22) all of the companies in a capital gains group are treated as a single company. This means that a gain arising on the disposal of a business asset by one member of a group can be rolled-over against the cost of a qualifying business asset acquired by any other member of the same group.

It is important to note that the qualifying business asset against which a gain is rolled-over must be an asset which has been newly acquired *by the group as a whole*. It is not possible to roll-over a gain against an asset which has been acquired by one group member from another.

Degrouping charge

A chargeable gain or allowable loss may arise in connection with an intra-group transfer if a company has a chargeable asset transferred to it from another group member and then leaves the group within six years of the date of the transfer. The company leaving the group (the "transferee company") is deemed to have sold the asset on the date of the intra-group transfer for its market value on that date (triggering a gain or loss) and then to have immediately re-acquired the asset on the same date and for the same amount.

The tax treatment of such a "degrouping" gain or loss depends upon the circumstances which have caused the transferee company to leave the group, as follows:

(a) If the transferee company has left the group because of a disposal of shares made by another company in the group, then:

  (i) any degrouping gain is added to disposal proceeds when computing the gain or loss arising on that share disposal, and

  (ii) any degrouping loss is treated as allowable expenditure when computing the gain or loss arising on that share disposal.

  The event that most frequently causes a company to leave a group is the disposal by a parent company of its shares in a subsidiary. Such a disposal necessitates the above treatment of degrouping gains or losses, so that (in effect) any such gains or losses arising when the subsidiary leaves the group are passed on to the parent.

  However, it is important to note that the disposal by a parent company of shares in a subsidiary is likely to qualify as the disposal of a "substantial shareholding". Since gains arising on such disposals are exempt from tax (see Chapter 24), this means that any degrouping gains arising in these circumstances would also be exempt.

(b) If the transferee company has *not* left the group because of a disposal of shares by another company in the group, then any degrouping gain or loss is treated as if it had arisen in the accounting period in which the transferee company leaves the group and is usually taken into account when computing the transferee company's corporation tax liability for that period. However, as explained later in this chapter, any gain or loss (including a degrouping gain or loss) may be treated for tax purposes as if it had accrued instead to another company in the group.

  These provisions would apply if (for example) a subsidiary company left a group because it had made a share issue and, as a result of that issue, its parent company no longer owned at least 75% of the subsidiary's shares.

EXAMPLE 9

S1 Ltd and S2 Ltd belong to the same capital gains group. In May 2014, S1 Ltd transferred a chargeable asset to S2 Ltd. This asset had originally cost £10,000 and its market value in May 2014 was £25,000. Indexation allowance of £1,350 would have been available in May 2014 If the asset had been sold outside the group. S2 Ltd (which prepares accounts to 31 December) leaves the group in March 2018.

(a) Calculate the degrouping gain arising on the departure of S2 Ltd.

(b) Explain the tax treatment of this gain.

Solution

(a) S2 Ltd is deemed to have sold the asset for £25,000 in May 2014 and then to have immediately re-acquired it for the same amount. The sale would have given rise to a chargeable gain of £13,650 (£25,000 – £10,000 – £1,350) so a degrouping gain of £13,650 arises when S2 Ltd leaves the group.

(b) The treatment of this gain depends upon the circumstances in which S2 Ltd has left the group. If this departure has been caused by a share disposal made by another member of the group (probably S2's parent), then £13,650 is added to disposal proceeds when calculating the gain or loss arising on that share disposal. Otherwise, the degrouping gain is treated as a chargeable gain of £13,650 accruing to S2 Ltd in the year to 31 December 2018.

Capital losses

Capital losses cannot be surrendered to another member of the group. This is in contrast to trading losses and certain other items which can be surrendered. At one time, the only way around this problem was to transfer assets between group members in such a way that chargeable gains and capital losses arose in the same company. Imagine that Company L and Company G were both members of a capital gains group, that Company L had capital losses and that Company G was about to dispose of an asset and realise a chargeable gain. Company L's capital losses could be set against this gain in the following way:

(a) Company G could transfer its asset to Company L (on a no gain/no loss basis).

(b) Company L could then dispose of the asset. The gain would be realised by Company L rather than Company G, so allowing Company L's losses to be set against it.

However a simpler procedure is now available. Two companies that are members of a 75% group may jointly elect that all or part of the gain (or loss) arising on a disposal by one of the companies should be treated as if it had been realised (or incurred) by the other company. This allows gains and losses to be brought together in the same company without having to actually transfer assets between group members. The election must be made within two years of the end of the accounting period in which the disposal occurs.

Pre-entry capital losses

A group which anticipates making disposals which will give rise to substantial chargeable gains might try to shelter those gains from tax by acquiring a "capital loss company". This is a company which has capital losses brought forward and/or assets which would realise capital losses on disposal. The intention of the acquisition would be to set these capital losses against the group's chargeable gains (by means of the procedure outlined above) and so reduce the group's overall corporation tax liability.

However, anti-avoidance legislation exists which prevents groups from gaining a tax advantage in this way. This legislation applies only if certain conditions are satisfied. The main conditions are as follows:

(a) There must be a change of ownership of the company concerned. This condition is satisfied if the company joins a group.

(b) The change of ownership must occur in connection with "arrangements", of which one of the main purposes is to secure a tax advantage.

If these conditions are satisfied, the anti-avoidance legislation applies and it is not possible to set the acquired capital losses against the group's chargeable gains.

Even if these conditions are *not* satisfied, there is in any case a restriction on the relief available in relation to a company's *pre-entry capital losses*. Pre-entry capital losses are defined as capital losses incurred by the company before joining a group. Such losses may be set only against gains arising on disposals of:

(a) assets which the company owned before it joined the group ("pre-entry assets"), or

(b) assets acquired by the company *from outside the group* since joining the group.

Consortia

A company is owned by a consortium and is known as a *consortium company* if at least 75% of its ordinary share capital is owned by other companies (which are known as *consortium members*) each of which:

(a) owns at least 5% but less than 75% of the consortium company's ordinary share capital, and

(b) is entitled to at least 5% of the profits available to the consortium company's ordinary shareholders, and

(c) would be entitled to at least 5% of the assets available to the consortium company's ordinary shareholders on a winding-up.

A 90% subsidiary of a consortium company is also a consortium company.

Group relief for a consortium

Group relief is available in either direction between a consortium member and a consortium company, so long as both companies are UK related and the consortium company is either a trading company or a company whose business consists wholly or mainly of holding shares in trading companies which are its 90% subsidiaries. Note the following points with regard to group relief for a consortium:

(a) The relief is restricted in proportion to the consortium member's shareholding in the consortium company. For instance, if CC Ltd is a consortium company and CM Ltd is a consortium member which owns p% of CC Ltd, then:

   (i) If CM Ltd is the claimant company, it may claim up to p% of CC Ltd's losses.

   (ii) If CM Ltd is the surrendering company, it may surrender to CC Ltd losses of up to p% of CC Ltd's profits.

(b) A group relief claim must be agreed by all the consortium members.

(c) The amount of a consortium company's trading loss which is available for group relief is the amount of that loss less any potential claim for relief against total profits of the loss-making period, whether or not such a claim is actually made.

EXAMPLE 10

The ordinary share capital of W Ltd (which is a trading company) is owned 30% by X Ltd, 25% by Y Ltd and 45% by Z Ltd. All companies are UK resident and prepare accounts to 31 March. Results for the year to 31 March 2018 are as follows:

	W Ltd	*X Ltd*	*Y Ltd*	*Z Ltd*
	£	£	£	£
Trading profit/(loss)	(62,000)	41,000	11,000	38,000
Chargeable gains	10,000	-	-	-

What are the maximum possible group relief claims which may be made?

Solution

W Ltd could claim that £10,000 of its trading loss should be set against its total profits of the loss-making period. Therefore, whether or not such a claim is made, the amount of the loss which is available for group relief is £52,000 (£62,000 – £10,000). This amount is shared between the consortium members in proportion to their shares in the consortium company, as follows:

	X Ltd	*Y Ltd*	*Z Ltd*
	£	£	£
Share of W Ltd available loss	15,600	13,000	23,400
Taxable total profits (before group relief)	41,000	11,000	38,000
Maximum group relief claim	15,600	11,000	23,400

Proposed restriction on interest relief

The Government has proposed that (as from 1 April 2017) there should be a limit on the amount of the interest expense that may be deducted when calculating the corporation tax liability of a "worldwide group". For this purpose, a worldwide group is a group defined as such by international financial reporting standards (IFRS).

Broadly, the proposed restriction would limit a group's deduction for interest payable (and similar items) to 30% of the group's taxable earnings before interest, tax, depreciation and amortisation ("EBITDA"). In general, the parent company of the group concerned would be required to file a "statement of allocated interest restrictions" which would set out the amount of the interest restriction that would be applied to each company in the group when computing that company's corporation tax liability.

However, a group with interest expense not exceeding a "de minimis" figure of £2m per annum would be exempt from the interest relief restriction.

Company reconstructions

If a company transfers a trade to another company, this ranks as a cessation of that trade and unrelieved trading losses incurred before the date of the transfer cannot normally be carried forward and set against the subsequent profits of the transferred trade.

But if a trade is transferred between two companies (both within the charge to UK corporation tax in respect of that trade) and at least 75% of the trade is effectively owned by the same persons both:

(a) at some time within the year before the date of the transfer, and

(b) at some time within the two years after the date of the transfer

then any unrelieved trading losses of the transferor company may be carried forward and set against subsequent profits (from the same trade) of the transferee company. For instance, this "succession of trade" relief would be available if a company created a 75% subsidiary and then transferred a trade to that subsidiary. However, this relief does not extend to non-trading losses or capital losses, neither of which can be carried forward from the transferor company to the transferee company.

Subject to certain conditions, the following provisions also apply to such "company reconstructions":

(a) For capital allowances purposes, assets are transferred at their tax-written down values, with no balancing adjustments.

(b) Chargeable assets are transferred to the transferee company on a no-gain, no-loss basis, as long as the transferor company receives no consideration for the assets and the assets remain within the scope of UK corporation tax.

Summary

- If a company has N "related 51% group companies", the profits limits which are used for payment by instalments purposes are divided by (N + 1).
- Transfer pricing rules apply to transactions carried out at artificial prices between group companies.
- Trading losses and certain other items may be surrendered between members of a 75% group. This is known as "group relief". Subject to certain conditions, group relief is also available between consortium members and consortium companies.
- Chargeable assets are transferred between members of a capital gains group on a no-gain, no-loss basis. However, a degrouping charge may arise if a group member has a chargeable asset transferred to it from another group member and then leaves the group within six years.
- Capital losses cannot be surrendered to another group member. However, two group members may elect that a gain or loss arising in one of the companies should be treated as if it had arisen in the other company.
- If a trade is transferred between two companies, the unrelieved trading losses of the transferor company may (subject to certain conditions) be carried forward and set against the subsequent trading profits of the transferee company.

Exercises

28.1 Arco1 Ltd and Arco2 Ltd are both 100% subsidiaries of Headco Ltd, which has no other subsidiaries. They are all UK resident. How will the relationship of the three companies affect the way in which they are taxed?

28.2 U Ltd has three subsidiaries (one of which is dormant) and has the following results for the year to 31 December 2017:

	£
Trading profits	485,000
Income from property	12,000
Dividends received from subsidiaries	128,000
Dividends received from non-group companies	30,000
Gift Aid donations	17,000

Compute the corporation tax liability for the year and state the date (or dates) on which this tax is due to be paid.

28.3 Bassnote Ltd is a wholly-owned subsidiary of Apexine Ltd. Both companies are UK resident and prepare accounts to 31 March each year. The results for the year to 31 March 2018 are as follows:

	Apexine Ltd	*Bassnote Ltd*
	£	£
Trading profit/(loss)	120,000	(90,000)
Trading losses brought forward	(42,000)	(19,000)
Income from property	7,000	3,000
Gift Aid donations	12,000	4,000

Calculate the maximum group relief that may be claimed for the year by Apexine Ltd.

28.4 A1 Ltd owns 90% of the ordinary share capital of A2 Ltd. A2 Ltd owns 80% of the ordinary share capital of A3 Ltd and 70% of the ordinary share capital of A4 Ltd. All companies are UK resident.

(a) Identify any 75% groups within this group structure.

(b) Which of these companies form a capital gains group with A1 Ltd as its principal company?

28.5 The ordinary share capital of PP Ltd (a trading company) is owned 32% by QQ Ltd, 35% by RR Ltd, 23% by SS Ltd. The remaining 10% is owned by various individuals, none of whom own more than 1%. All companies are UK resident and prepare accounts to 31 July. Results for the year to 31 July 2017 are as follows:

	PP Ltd	*QQ Ltd*	*RR Ltd*	*SS Ltd*
	£	£	£	£
Trading profit/(loss)	(96,000)	41,000	38,000	11,000
Chargeable gains	-	15,000	-	-
Income from property	12,000	6,000	11,000	4,000
Gift Aid donations	-	(3,000)	(2,000)	(1,000)

Compute the maximum possible group relief claims.

***28.6** T Ltd has owned 90% of the ordinary share capital of B Ltd for many years. Both are UK resident. Recent results for the two companies are as follows:

	T Ltd	*T Ltd*	*B Ltd*
	y/e 31/3/2017	*y/e 31/3/2018*	*y/e 30/11/2017*
	£	£	£
Trading profit/(loss)	880,000	130,000	(174,000)
Chargeable gains	25,000	13,000	3,000
Gift Aid donations	5,000	5,000	-

No dividends have been received by either company in any of these years and maximum group relief is claimed. Calculate the corporation tax which is payable by each company for each accounting period and state the due date (or dates) of payment.

Review questions (Set C)

C1 Tolbooth Ltd is a manufacturing company. It commenced trading on 1 April 2016 and prepared its first set of accounts for the 18 month period to 30 September 2017. As the accounting technician responsible for preparing the tax computation, you have extracted the following information from the audit file:

		£
(i)	Trading profits (before capital allowances)	690,000
(ii)	Rental income:	
	£20,000 per year from property rented on 1 April 2016.	
	Rent received annually in advance on 1 April.	
(iii)	Bank deposit interest:	
	Received 30 June 2016	200
	Received 31 December 2016	200
	Accrued to 31 March 2017	100
	Received 30 June 2017	1,200
	Accrued to 30 September 2017	445
(iv)	Plant and machinery purchased on 1 April 2016:	
	Factory machinery	121,000
	Motor car (125 g/km)	25,000
(v)	Gift Aid donations:	
	£5,000 every six months as from 31 December 2016	
	Paid 31 December 2016	5,000
	Accrued to 31 March 2017	2,500
	Paid 30 June 2017	5,000
	Accrued to 30 September 2017	2,500
(vi)	Chargeable gain on disposal 1 August 2017	8,300

Required:

(a) State how the first period of account to 30 September 2017 will be divided into accounting periods.

(b) Calculate the corporation tax liability for each accounting period.

(c) State the due date (or dates) of payment of the company's corporation tax liability for the 18 months to 30 September 2017.

(d) What difference would it make if the trading profit for the 18 months (before capital allowances) was £3,690,000 instead of £690,000?

(Amended from AAT)

C2 Quadrant Ltd has the following results for its three most recent accounting periods:

	y/e 30/6/16	*nine months to 31/3/17*	*y/e 31/3/18*
	£	£	£
Trading profit/(loss)	2,050,000	260,000	(895,000)
Loan interest receivable	51,600	39,000	28,700
Chargeable gains/(losses)	32,000	(3,000)	47,000
Gift Aid donations	10,000	8,000	5,000

Notes:

1. There were no trading losses brought forward on 1 July 2015.
2. Capital losses brought forward on 1 July 2015 were £67,300.
3. Following a bad trading result for the year to 31 March 2018, the company expects to return to making a sizeable trading profit in future years.

Required:

(a) Compute the company's corporation tax liability for each of the three accounting periods, assuming that no claims are made in relation to the trading loss.

(b) Compute the company's corporation tax liability for each of the three accounting periods, assuming that claims are made to relieve the £895,000 trading loss at the earliest possible opportunity. Also compute the amount of any trading losses carried forward.

(c) Calculate the amount of tax which would be saved in consequence of the claims referred to in (b) above. Would you recommend these claims?

(CIPFA)

C3 AA Ltd, BB Ltd and CC Ltd have the following results for the year to 31 March 2018:

	AA Ltd	***BB Ltd***	***CC Ltd***
	£	£	£
Trading profits	1,230,400	167,800	852,500
Interest receivable	16,300	-	15,000
Property income	-	5,000	-
Chargeable gains	46,400	13,600	37,300
Allowable capital losses	(2,900)	(77,400)	-
Dividends received	240,000	1,800	90,000
Gift Aid donations paid	5,200	1,000	4,800

None of these companies is a member of a group.

Required:

(a) Compute each company's corporation tax liability for the year and state the due date (or dates) of payment in each case.

(b) How would these liabilities and dates of payment alter if the above figures related to the year to 31 August 2017?

C4 VFD Limited (which is not a group company) has prepared a set of accounts for the ten months to 31 October 2017. These accounts show a profit before tax of £1,391,540. Relevant information is:

(i) Depreciation charged in the period was £149,365.

(ii) UK dividends received were £137,260.

(iii) The written down value of the company's plant and machinery at 1 January 2017 for capital allowances purposes was as follows:

	£
Main pool	148,300
Managing director's Volvo motor car (emissions 188g/km)	40,870

(iv) Additions and disposals were as follows:

January 2017	Sold machinery (original cost £75,000)	26,450
March 2017	Bought motor lorry	54,900
May 2017	Bought plant and machinery	126,720
July 2017	Sold Volvo motor car	35,090
July 2017	Bought Audi motor car (emissions 167g/km)	52,090

Required:

Calculate the corporation tax liability for the period ended on 31 October 2017 and state the date or dates) on which this is due for payment. *(CIPFA)*

C5 Antietam Ltd makes up accounts to 30 September annually. Results for the 12 months to 30 September 2017 are as follows:

	£
Trading profits (before capital allowances)	173,000
Capital allowances	32,000
Rental income	46,000
Chargeable gains	6,400
Dividends received	14,400

The company has capital losses brought forward from previous accounting periods of £1,400 and made a Gift Aid donation of £20,000 during the year.

Required:

(a) Calculate the corporation tax liability of Antietam Ltd for the year to 30 September 2017 and state the due date of payment.

(b) What difference would it make if you were told that the company has nine subsidiary companies and that all of the dividends received of £14,400 were paid to Antietam Ltd by its subsidiaries? *(Amended from AAT)*

***C6** Undulating Uplands Ltd is a UK resident manufacturing company and is not a member of a group. It had always made up accounts to 31 January but decided to change the year end from January to April. The company's results for the period from 1 February 2017 to 30 April 2018 are as follows:

	Notes	£
Adjusted trading profit		750,000
Dividends received	1	45,000
Bank interest received	2	13,800
Building society interest received	3	8,400
Gift Aid donations	4	16,000
Capital allowances on plant and machinery	7	65,000

The following additional information is available:

1. Dividends were received as follows:

	£
28 February 2017	7,200
31 May 2017	10,800
30 November 2017	9,000
31 March 2018	18,000

2. Bank interest was credited by Natland Bank plc as follows:

	£
21 February 2017	4,900
20 August 2017	3,900
21 February 2018	5,000

   Accrued interest was £4,500 on 31 January 2017, £4,300 on 31 January 2018 and £4,000 on 30 April 2018.

3. Building society interest was credited by Northshires Building Society as follows:

	£
31 May 2017	4,000
30 November 2017	4,400

   The account was opened on 1 February 2017 and closed on 30 November 2017.

4. The Gift Aid donations were paid as follows:

	£
15 July 2017	8,000
15 January 2018	8,000

5. The company had trading losses brought forward of £400,000 on 1 February 2017.

6. The company had capital losses brought forward of £15,000 on 1 February 2017.

7. The capital allowances figure of £65,000 comprised:

	£
12 months to 31 January 2018	39,000
3 months to 30 April 2018	26,000

8. In July 2017, the company bought a building for business use. This building cost £450,000. In March 2018, another building was sold for £350,000. This building had been bought in January 2003 for £150,000 and used exclusively for business purposes. An appropriate claim was made to minimise the chargeable gain arising on this disposal. (RPI was 178.4 in January 2003 and 276.5 in March 2018).

You are required:

To calculate the corporation tax liability for the period to 30 April 2018 and to state when this is payable (perform all calculations to the nearest month). *(ACCA)*

***C7** Q Ltd prepares accounts to 31 March each year. The company made the following two disposals of chargeable assets during the year to 31 March 2018:

(1) 1,250 shares in Hentic Ltd were sold on 28 June 2017 (RPI 271.1) for £25,000. Previous purchases and sales of shares in Hentic Ltd had been as follows:

		£	*RPI*
12 May 2001	Bought 2,000 shares	14,000	174.2
17 June 2004	Rights issue (1 for 10)	1,000	186.8
6 July 2008	Sold 1,000 shares	9,000	216.5
21 June 2017	Bought 600 shares	9,000	271.1

(2) The company's factory was sold for £437,500 on 4 March 2018 (RPI 276.5). This factory had been purchased on 11 April 2002 (RPI 175.7) for £285,000.

Note:

The factory purchased in April 2002 was a replacement for a previous factory which had been purchased for £200,000 on 3 January 1992 (RPI 135.6) and sold for £320,000 on 14 June 2002 (RPI 176.2). Rollover relief was claimed in relation to the June 2002 disposal.

Required:

(a) Calculate the chargeable gain arising on the sale of the shares in Hentic Ltd on 28 June 2017.

(b) Calculate the chargeable gain arising on the sale of the factory on 4 March 2018, assuming that a further factory was purchased on 6 November 2017 for £360,000 and that rollover relief is claimed in relation to the March 2018 disposal.

***C8** W Ltd owns 70% of the issued shares of X Ltd, 30% of the issued shares of Y Ltd and 80% of the issued shares of Z Ltd. All four companies are UK resident and all of the shares of each company are ordinary shares. Results for the year to 31 March 2018 for each company are as follows:

	W Ltd	*X Ltd*	*Y Ltd*	*Z Ltd*
	£	£	£	£
Trading profit/(loss)	210,000	(65,000)	35,000	(45,000)
Dividends paid in the year	-	30,000	18,000	27,000

Required:

(a) State (with reasons) which of X Ltd, Y Ltd and Z Ltd are "related 51% group companies" of W Ltd. Also explain how W Ltd might be affected by the fact that it has one or more related 51% group companies.

(b) Explain how the corporation tax computation of W Ltd for the year to 31 March 2018 is affected by the fact that it receives dividends from the other three companies.

(c) Calculate the maximum group relief that can be claimed by W Ltd for the year to 31 March 2018.

(d) Assuming that maximum group relief is claimed, calculate the corporation tax liability of W Ltd for the year to 31 March 2018 and state the date upon which this tax is due for payment.

***C9** Neil has been in business for many years preparing accounts to 5 April each year. His profits in a typical year (adjusted for tax purposes) are approximately £50,000 and his drawings are £3,000 per month (i.e. £36,000 per year). He has no other income and he is not a Scottish taxpayer.

Neil is now thinking of forming a company (wholly owned by himself) to run his business. If this happens, he would extract £36,000 per year from the company, either as a director's salary or as a dividend.

Required:

(a) Calculate the total amount of income tax and National Insurance contributions payable each year at present, with Neil operating as a sole trader.

(b) Calculate the total amount of corporation tax, income tax and National Insurance contributions that would be payable each year if Neil decides to incorporate and takes a monthly director's salary of £3,000.

(c) Calculate the total amount of corporation tax, income tax and National Insurance contributions that would be payable each year if Neil incorporates and takes a dividend of £36,000 per year.

Assume that the annual profits of the business continue to be £50,000. Use tax rates and allowances for tax year 2017-18 and corporation tax year FY2017 in your calculations and work to the nearest £.

***C10** P Ltd has owned 90% of the ordinary shares in S Ltd since 2005. Both companies are UK resident and both prepare accounts to 30 April each year. Results for the most recent two accounting years are as follows:

	P Ltd	*S Ltd*
	£	£
year to 30 April 2016		
Trading profit	85,000	120,000
Property income	9,000	-
Loan interest receivable	-	7,500
Dividend from S Ltd	27,000	-
Dividends from other companies	12,600	-
Gift Aid donations	10,000	3,000
year to 30 April 2017		
Trading profit	-	175,000
Trading loss	(108,000)	-
Property income	16,000	-
Loan interest receivable	-	8,000
Dividend from S Ltd	35,000	-
Dividends from other companies	8,100	-
Gift Aid donations	10,000	3,000

P Ltd has come to the conclusion that its loss-making trade will never return to profit. Accordingly, this trade is to be closed down with immediate effect and the company will commence a new trade during the year to 30 April 2018. This new trade is expected to yield annual profits of at least £200,000.

Required:

(a) Explain the alternative loss reliefs available in relation to the trading loss of £108,000 incurred by P Ltd for the year to 30 April 2017.

(b) Assuming that the most tax-efficient form of loss relief is chosen, calculate the corporation tax liability of each company for the year to 30 April 2016 and for the year to 30 April 2017.

Ignore the changes to the loss relief rules that have been proposed by the Government and which might take effect as from 1 April 2017.

Part 4

MISCELLANEOUS

Chapter 29

Value added tax (1)

Introduction

This is the first of two chapters on value added tax (VAT). Value added tax is an indirect tax which was introduced in 1973 (when the UK joined the EU) and which is charged on the supply of a wide variety of goods and services. Current legislation is to be found in the Value Added Tax Act 1994 (VATA 1994), as amended by subsequent Finance Acts.

At present, the underlying legislation on VAT takes the form of EU Directives, which are binding on the UK and dictate the results which UK legislation must bring about. After the UK leaves the EU, this will no longer be the case. It is possible, therefore, that the UK's departure from the EU may trigger significant changes to VAT law in the UK.

The principle of VAT

The basic principle of VAT is that tax should be charged at each stage of the production and distribution process but that the total tax due should be borne by the final consumer of the product. This is achieved as follows:

(a) Traders who are registered for VAT (see below) are required to charge VAT on their sales and must account for this *output tax* to HMRC, but

(b) such traders are allowed to recover from HMRC the *input tax* which they pay to their own suppliers, so that

(c) in effect, registered traders suffer no VAT and the total VAT is borne by the consumer at the end of the distribution chain.

EXAMPLE 1

A Ltd owns a quarry. It extracts stone from this quarry and sells it to B Ltd for £10,000 plus VAT. B Ltd converts all of the stone into paving slabs and sells these slabs to C Ltd for £18,000, plus VAT. C Ltd owns a garden centre, where the paving slabs are sold to the general public for a total of £32,000, plus VAT. Show how VAT is charged and collected at each stage of this process, assuming that VAT is to be calculated at 20% throughout.

Solution

	Cost price before VAT	*Input tax*	*Selling price before VAT*	*Output tax*	*Paid to HMRC*
	£	£	£	£	£
A Ltd	-	-	10,000	2,000	2,000
B Ltd	10,000	2,000	18,000	3,600	1,600
C Ltd	18,000	3,600	32,000	6,400	2,800
Total VAT charged					6,400

Note:

None of the three companies involved suffers any net VAT. In each case, the total of input tax paid to suppliers and the amount paid to HMRC is precisely equal to the output tax charged to customers. The final consumers, who are unable to reclaim the VAT which they pay, bear the total VAT of £6,400.

Taxable persons

Formally, UK VAT is chargeable when a *taxable supply* of goods or services is made in the UK by a *taxable person* in the course of business. The term "person" can refer to an individual, partnership or company, as well as to any other body which supplies goods or services in the course of business. There is no need for a profit motive to exist, just that goods or services are supplied for a consideration, so the term "person" can also refer to a charity, a club etc. A *taxable person* is a person making taxable supplies who is, or should be, registered for VAT. Persons must register if their turnover of taxable items exceeds a prescribed registration threshold and might register voluntarily even if turnover is below this threshold (see later in this chapter).

A taxable person should charge VAT to customers when making taxable supplies, must account for this output tax to HMRC and may reclaim the tax suffered on inputs. A person who is not a taxable person can neither charge VAT to customers nor reclaim input tax†.

† *The main national museums and art galleries are an exception to this general rule, in that they are allowed to reclaim input tax even though they provide free admission to the public and so do not operate a business. A similar rule applies to the non-business activities of certain charities (e.g. palliative care charities, search and rescue charities and air ambulance charities).*

Taxable supplies

A *taxable supply* is any supply of goods or services in the UK other than a supply which is specifically exempted from VAT. VAT is charged on a taxable supply at the standard rate of 20%, unless the supply attracts tax at the reduced rate (5%) or at the zero rate (0%).

The types of supply which are exempt from VAT and the types of supply which are taxable at the reduced rate or the zero rate are listed later in this chapter.

Supply of goods

A supply of goods is deemed to occur when the ownership of goods passes from one person to another. In general, a supply of goods will fall within the scope of VAT only if it is made for a consideration (i.e. in return for money or payment in kind) but the following are also deemed to be supplies of goods for VAT purposes:

(a) gifts of business assets on which input tax has been reclaimed, other than:
   (i) gifts made to any one person in any rolling 12-month period costing in total no more than £50
   (ii) gifts consisting of samples (where a "sample" is a specimen of a product which is intended to promote sales of that product)

(b) goods permanently taken out of a business for private use by the owner or an employee of the business, in respect of which input tax has been reclaimed.

The sale of goods on hire purchase terms is deemed to be a supply of goods but VAT is charged on the cash price of the goods, not the HP price.

Supply of services

Any supply which is made for a consideration but which is not a supply of goods is deemed to be a supply of services. However, a gift of services is not a taxable supply. The hiring of goods to a customer is a supply of services, not a supply of goods, since the ownership of the goods does not pass to the customer. A supply of services is also deemed to occur if the owner or an employee of a business:

(a) temporarily makes private use of goods owned by the business, in respect of which input tax has been reclaimed, or

(b) makes private use of services which have been supplied to the business, in respect of which input tax has been reclaimed.

However, the private use of a business motor car is generally not a taxable supply.

Self-supply

A "self-supply" occurs when a taxable person makes a supply to himself or herself. For example, a self-supply of a motor car occurs if a motor manufacturer produces a car and then uses it instead of supplying it to a customer. The Treasury is empowered to order that, for VAT purposes, self-supplied goods or services are regarded as both:

(a) a taxable supply made *by* the business, and

(b) a taxable supply made *to* the business.

The effect of such an order is that output tax must be accounted for in relation to the supply but that an equal amount of input tax is deemed to have been suffered. This input tax may then be irrecoverable in whole or part (see Chapter 30).

Exempt supplies

A supply of goods or services is an exempt supply if it falls within one of sixteen exemption groups. In summary, these exemption groups are as follows:

Group 1 The sale or lease of land and buildings, *other than*:

- (i) the sale (or lease for more than 21 years) of new and certain second-hand buildings for residential or charitable use (zero-rated)
- (ii) the sale of new or uncompleted commercial buildings or land to be used for their construction (standard-rated)
- (iii) the grant of gaming rights, fishing rights or timber rights; the provision of hotel and holiday accommodation, caravan and camping pitches, boxes and seats at a theatre or sports ground, parking facilities and facilities for the storage or mooring of aircraft, ships etc; the letting of sports facilities, self-storage facilities or hairdressing facilities (all standard-rated)
- (iv) any supply which would otherwise be exempt, but in respect of which an election has been made to waive exemption (the "option to tax")

Group 2 Insurance

Group 3 Public postal services provided by the Royal Mail

Group 4 Betting, gaming and lotteries

Group 5 Financial services (e.g. bank charges, stockbroking, underwriting)

Group 6 Education provided by schools, universities and further education colleges

Group 7 Health and welfare services

Group 8 Burial and cremation services

Group 9 Subscriptions to trade unions and professional bodies

Group 10 Sports competition entry fees paid to non-profit making bodies

Group 11 Disposals of works of art to approved bodies (e.g. the National Gallery)

Group 12 Certain fund-raising events organised by charities

Group 13 Cultural services

Group 14 Supplies of goods where input tax cannot be recovered

Group 15 Investment gold

Group 16 Supplies of services by groups involving cost sharing

The tax implications of a supply of goods or services being exempt are as follows:

(a) VAT cannot be charged on an exempt supply.

(b) A person who makes only exempt supplies cannot register for VAT, charges no output tax, is not a taxable person and cannot reclaim input tax.

(c) In effect, a person making only exempt supplies is in an identical position with regard to VAT as the final consumer at the end of a distribution chain.

Option to tax

The inability to reclaim input tax when making exempt supplies of land and buildings might lead the supplier to elect for the "option to tax" (see above). If such an election is made, the supplier charges output tax on the supply at the standard rate but may then reclaim input tax. The customer will of course have to pay VAT, but if the customer is also a taxable person then he or she will be able to reclaim the tax paid and therefore may not object to the arrangement.

Reduced rate supplies

A supply of goods or services is charged to VAT at the reduced rate of 5% if it falls within one of thirteen reduced-rate groups. These groups are as follows:

Group 1	Fuel and power supplied for domestic or charity use
Group 2	Installation of energy-saving materials in residential accommodation
Group 3	Grant-funded installation of heating or security equipment
Group 4	Women's sanitary products†
Group 5	Children's car seats and car seat bases
Group 6	Certain residential conversions
Group 7	Certain residential renovations and alterations
Group 8	Contraceptive products (unless exempt from VAT)
Group 9	Certain welfare advice or information (unless exempt from VAT)
Group 10	Installation of mobility aids for the elderly
Group 11	Smoking cessation products
Group 12	Static holiday caravans
Group 13	Passenger transport in small cable-suspended transport systems

† *These products are to be zero-rated as from a date yet to be announced.*

Zero rate supplies

A supply of goods or services is charged to VAT at the zero rate (0%) if it falls within one of eighteen zero-rate groups. These groups are as follows:

Group 1	Food (other than luxury foods and food supplied in the course of catering)
Group 2	Water and sewerage services unless supplied for industrial use
Group 3	Books, newspapers and journals (but stationery is standard-rated)
Group 4	Talking books and wireless sets for the blind and handicapped
Group 5	The sale (or lease for more than 21 years) of new buildings for residential or charitable use and second-hand buildings converted for residential use

Group 6	The sale (or lease for more than 21 years) of protected buildings that have been substantially reconstructed for residential or charitable use
Group 7	Certain categories of international services
Group 8	Passenger transport (but transport in vehicles seating less than 10 people and certain types of pleasure transport are standard-rated)
Group 9	Houseboats and static residential caravans
Group 10	Gold supplied by a central bank to another central bank
Group 11	Bank notes
Group 12	The dispensing of drugs and certain aids for disabled persons
Group 13	Exports
Group 14	Sales in tax-free shops before 1 July 1999
Group 15	The sale *by* a charity of donated goods and certain supplies made *to* a charity
Group 16	Children's clothing and footwear and protective boots and helmets
Group 17	Emissions allowances supplied before 1 November 2010
Group 18	Supplies made to a European Research Infrastructure Consortium (ERIC)

If goods or services fall within one of the above zero-rate groups but also fall within one of the exempt groups, zero-rating takes priority. The tax implications of a supply of goods or services being zero-rated are as follows:

(a) The supply is a taxable supply but the VAT due is calculated at 0%.

(b) A person who makes only zero-rated supplies is nonetheless making taxable supplies and must usually register as a taxable person if taxable turnover exceeds the prescribed threshold. Having registered (and this may be done voluntarily if taxable turnover is less than the threshold) the person will then be able to reclaim input tax.

The value of a supply

The *value* of a taxable supply is the amount on which the VAT charge is based and this is normally equal to the price (before VAT) charged for the supply. For example, if a standard-rated supply is made at a price of £1,000 plus VAT at 20%, the value of the supply is £1,000 and the "consideration" given for the supply is £1,200.

For standard-rated supplies, the VAT component of the consideration can be found by multiplying the consideration by the "VAT fraction". With a standard rate of 20%, this is 20/120 = 1/6th. Note that:

(a) If a supply consists of a gift of business assets, the value of the supply is deemed to be the price (excluding VAT) which the person receiving the gift would have to pay to purchase goods identical in every respect to the goods concerned. This rule also applies if assets are taken permanently out of a business for private use by the owner or an employee of the business.

(b) If the owner or an employee temporarily makes private use of business assets, the value of the resulting supply of services is generally based on the amount by which the assets have depreciated whilst being used for private purposes.

(c) If private use is made of services which have been supplied to the business, the value of the resulting supply of services is equal to an appropriate proportion of the value of the supply which was made to the business.

(d) If the consideration for a supply is paid in kind or if the supply is made to a connected person for less than market value, the value of the supply is taken to be the market value of the goods or services supplied.

EXAMPLE 2

(a) On 1 August 2017, a standard-rated supply is made with a value of £180. Calculate the VAT charged and the consideration for the supply.

(b) On 2 January 2018, a standard-rated supply is made for a consideration of £1,776. Calculate the VAT element and the value of the supply.

Solution

(a) The VAT charged is £36.00 (£180 x 20%) and the total consideration is £216.00.

(b) The VAT element is £296 (£1,776 x 1/6) and the value of the supply is £1,480.

Prompt payment discounts ("cash discounts")

If a customer is offered a discount in return for prompt payment (a "cash discount") the value of the supply is the VAT-exclusive price charged by the supplier, less any cash discount which is *actually taken* by the customer..

EXAMPLE 3

In June 2017, a standard-rated supply is made at a price of £4,000, plus VAT. The customer is offered a 3% discount if payment is made within 30 days. Calculate the value of the supply and the VAT charged on the supply if the customer:

(a) pays within 30 days (b) does not pay within 30 days.

Solution

(a) If the customer pays within 30 days, the value of the supply is £3,880 (£4,000, less 3%) and the VAT charged is £776 (£3,880 x 20%). The consideration is £4,656.

(b) If the customer does not pay within 30 days, the value of the supply is £4,000 and the VAT charged is £800 (£4,000 × 20%). The consideration is £4,800.

Mixed supplies

A "mixed supply" occurs if a mixture of goods and/or services is invoiced together at a single inclusive price. If all of the items in the mixture are chargeable to VAT at the same rate, the value of the supply and the related output tax can be calculated in the usual way. Otherwise, it is necessary to apportion the price charged between the various elements of the mixture in order to calculate the output tax due.

There is no standard way of achieving this apportionment but the method used must be fair and justifiable.

EXAMPLE 4

A VAT-exclusive price of £320 is charged for a mixed supply of goods. The goods concerned consist of standard-rated goods which cost the supplier £141 (excluding VAT) and zero-rated goods which cost the supplier £19. Calculate the output tax due, assuming a standard rate of 20%.

Solution

From the information given, the only way of apportioning the price of the mixed supply into the standard-rated element and the zero-rated element is to split the price according to the cost of each element to the supplier. On this basis, the value of the supply represented by standard-rated goods is £320 x 141/160 = £282. VAT at 20% of this figure gives £56.40. Therefore the total price charged should be £376.40.

Composite supplies

A "composite supply" occurs if a mixture of goods and/or services is supplied together in such a way that it is not possible to split the supply into its component parts. In this case, the nature of the supply as a whole must be considered in order to determine the rate of tax due (if any). For example, in the case of *Mander Laundries Ltd* (1973) it was held that the services of a launderette consist of a single, standard-rated supply of services, not a mixed supply of water, heat, hire of washing machines etc.

Imports and exports

At present, the VAT treatment of imports and exports depends upon whether the transactions involve goods or services and whether they are between the UK and a country which is not a member state of the EU or between the UK and another EU member.

After the UK leaves the EU, the VAT treatment of transactions between the UK and the remaining member states of the EU will presumably change. One possibility is that such transactions will be dealt with in the same way as transactions between the UK and non-EU countries (see below). However, this remains to be seen and will depend upon the outcome of lengthy negotiations that will take place as part of the UK's exit process.

Imports of goods to the UK from non-EU countries

VAT is charged on the import of goods from outside the EU at the same rate as if the goods had been supplied in the UK and must be paid by the person to whom the goods are supplied, whether or not that person is a taxable person. Note that:

(a) The VAT on imported goods is normally payable at the point of entry to the UK, but businesses which import goods may defer immediate payment and pay by direct debit once a month. HMRC will usually require a guarantee from an approved bank or insurance company before allowing an importer to defer payments in this way.

(b) For importers who are taxable persons, the VAT due on postal imports with a value not exceeding £2,000 may be deferred until the VAT return is submitted for the tax period which includes the date of importation.

(c) VAT suffered by taxable persons on imported goods may be treated as input tax.

(d) No VAT is charged on any consignment of goods (other than alcohol, tobacco and perfumes) which is imported from outside the EU and which has a value that does not exceed the "low value consignment relief" (LVCR) threshold of £15. This relief does not apply to mail order goods sent to the UK from the Channel Islands.

Exports of goods from the UK to non-EU countries

Exports of goods from the UK to non-EU countries are zero-rated.

Goods traded between EU countries

If a registered person in one EU country supplies goods to a registered person in another EU country and the customer's VAT registration number is obtained and shown on the sales invoice, then:

(a) The supply is zero-rated in the country of origin, so the supplier does not have to account for any output tax in relation to the supply.

(b) The customer must account for VAT on the "acquisition" (the term "import" is not used) at whatever rate is applicable to those goods in the destination country.

(c) The VAT suffered by the customer may then be treated as input tax.

If the customer's registration number is not known, or if the customer is not a registered person, the supplier will charge VAT at the rate applicable in the country of origin.

International services

International services are services which are supplied in the UK by an overseas supplier or supplied overseas by a UK supplier. The VAT treatment of international services depends upon the "place of supply" of those services. The general rules are as follows:

(a) Business to business (B2B) supplies are taxed at the place where the *customer* is established and it is the responsibility of the customer (not the supplier) to account for any output tax relating to such supplies. This is the "reverse charge" procedure.

(b) Business to consumer (B2C) supplies are taxed at the place where the *supplier* is established. For this purpose, a "consumer" is either a person who receives a supply of services for private purposes, or a charity etc. that has no business activities.

The main effects of these rules are as follows:

(a) If a UK business supplies services to a business customer located in an EU member state (but outside the UK) the supply is subject to the VAT rules of that member state and is outside the scope of UK VAT. If the customer is located outside the EU, the supply is outside the scope of VAT altogether.

(b) If a UK business supplies services to a non-business customer located overseas, the supply is subject to the normal UK rules (as if the customer had been in the UK).

(c) If a UK business *receives* services from overseas, the UK business must operate the reverse charge procedure and account for output tax at the appropriate rate for the services concerned. The VAT suffered by taxable persons as a result of this procedure is then treated as input tax. Input tax is generally recoverable, but certain classes of input tax are irrecoverable (see Chapter 30).

Note that supplies of telecommunications, broadcasting and other electronic services made by a business situated in one EU member state to a non-business customer situated in another EU member state are taxed in the member state in which the *customer* is located.

Reverse charge procedure within the UK

A reverse charge procedure similar to the one described above applies to certain supplies made within the UK. This procedure applies when a supply of *mobile telephones or computer chips* with a value of at least £5,000 is made within the UK to a VAT-registered person. Under this procedure, it is the responsibility of the purchaser (not the seller) to account to HMRC for the output tax due on the supply. The VAT suffered by the purchaser as a result of the reverse charge procedure may then be treated as input tax.

The aim of this procedure is to deal with so-called "missing trader" fraud, whereby VAT is charged on a supply but the supplier fails to account for this tax to HMRC and then cannot be traced. This type of fraud is commonly associated with the supply of mobile telephones and computer chips. The reverse charge also applies to emissions allowances and to wholesale supplies of gas and electricity or telecommunications services.

Registration

The total value of the taxable supplies made by a person is known as that person's *taxable turnover*. A person whose taxable turnover in a 12-month period exceeds the registration threshold (£85,000 from 1 April 2017) must register with HMRC. Online registration is now available. A person who registers is issued a VAT registration number which must then be quoted on that person's tax invoices (see next chapter). Note that:

(a) The registration threshold does not apply to businesses which do not have a UK establishment. Such businesses are required to register for UK VAT as soon as they make their first supply of goods or services in the UK, regardless of value.

(b) A person who is liable to register but who fails to do so is still a taxable person and is personally responsible for the output tax due in relation to supplies made since the date on which registration should have occurred.

When deciding whether or not the registration threshold has been exceeded, it is necessary to aggregate the taxable turnover from all of a person's business activities. The registration relates to the person, *not* to an individual business. It is important to bear in mind the definition of the word "person" for VAT purposes (see above) and to aggregate taxable supplies only if they are made by the same person.

EXAMPLE 5

(a) Jim is a sole trader with a taxable turnover of £75,000 per annum. Is he required to register with HMRC?

(b) Pearl and Dean are in partnership, operating a business with a taxable turnover of £100,000 per annum. Is anyone required to register?

(c) Julia is a sole trader with a taxable turnover of £60,000 per annum. She is also in partnership with Julie, operating a business with a taxable turnover of £70,000 per annum and sharing profits equally. Is anyone required to register?

Solution

(a) No. Jim's taxable turnover does not exceed the registration threshold.

(b) Yes. The partnership of Pearl and Dean is one "person" for VAT purposes and has a taxable turnover exceeding the registration threshold. Therefore the partnership must register.

(c) No. Julia as a sole trader is one person, whilst the partnership of Julia and Julie is another, quite separate, "person". Neither of these persons has a taxable turnover exceeding the registration threshold so neither of them is required to register.

Business splitting

"Business splitting" or "disaggregation" occurs when a business with a taxable turnover exceeding the registration threshold is divided into two or more smaller businesses, each operated by a different person and each with a taxable turnover not exceeding the registration threshold, in the hope of avoiding registration.

If this type of manoeuvre were successful, supplies could be made to customers without charging VAT and the administrative costs associated with making VAT returns and maintaining VAT records (see next chapter) could be avoided. The only disadvantage would be that input tax could not be reclaimed but in the case of a business with mainly exempt or zero-rated inputs this disadvantage would be slight.

However, if a business has been split artificially, HMRC may direct that the persons conducting the split businesses should be treated as a single taxable person for VAT purposes. In fact, this direction may be made even if the split businesses have never been operated as a single unit, so long as HMRC is satisfied that only one business really exists.

When to register

A person is required to register for VAT if, at the end of any calendar month, the value of that person's taxable supplies for the year ended on the last day of the month exceeds the registration threshold (£85,000 as from 1 April 2017). If the person has been making taxable supplies for less than twelve months, registration is required if the value of taxable supplies made to date is greater than the registration threshold. HMRC must be notified within 30 days of the end of the relevant month. Registration will then usually take effect after the end of the month following the relevant month. However, registration is not required if HMRC is satisfied that the person's taxable turnover for the following twelve months will not exceed the deregistration threshold (£83,000 as from 1 April 2017).

Registration is also required if there are reasonable grounds for believing that taxable turnover during the next 30 days alone will exceed the registration threshold. In this case, HMRC must be notified by the end of the 30-day period and registration will take effect from the beginning of that period.

For the purpose of deciding whether the registration threshold has been or will be exceeded, supplies consisting of the capital assets of the business are excluded from taxable turnover. However, such supplies normally receive no special treatment, so that the sale of a non-current asset will be a taxable supply unless the asset falls into one of the exemption groups.

EXAMPLE 6

Kevin begins trading on 1 January 2016. Taxable turnover during the first two years of trading is as follows:

2016	£	*2017*	£
January	1,800	January	6,800
February	2,100	February	5,400
March	2,800	March	6,100
April	2,600	April	7,600
May	2,400	May	8,100
June	2,900	June	7,900
July	3,300	July	8,200
August	3,500	August	7,900
September	4,200	September	8,800
October	5,500	October	8,100
November	6,900	November	8,300
December	8,200	December	9,700

The turnover in January 2017 includes £2,000 relating to the sale of machinery previously used in the trade. The VAT registration threshold was £82,000 until 1 April 2016 and £83,000 until 1 April 2017. State the date on which Kevin must register for VAT.

Solution

At the end of each month, cumulative taxable turnover during the previous 12 months (or since the start of trade, if less) are as follows:

2016	£	*2017*	£
January	1,800	January	49,200
February	3,900	February	52,500
March	6,700	March	55,800
April	9,300	April	60,800
May	11,700	May	66,500
June	14,600	June	71,500
July	17,900	July	76,400
August	21,400	August	80,800
September	25,600	September	85,400
October	31,100	October	88,000
November	38,000	November	89,400
December	46,200	December	90,900

The cumulative figure at the end of January 2017 is turnover for the months of February 2016 to January 2017 inclusive, less the £2,000 relating to the sale of a capital asset.

The registration threshold is passed at the end of September 2017. Kevin must notify HMRC by 30 October 2017. Registration will probably take effect from 1 November 2017.

Transfer of a business to an unregistered person

If a taxable person transfers a business as a going concern to a person who is not registered for VAT, supplies made by the business before the transfer date are deemed (for the purpose of deciding whether or not the transferee should register) to have been made by the transferee. So if the transferred business, together with any other business operated by the transferee, had a taxable turnover exceeding the registration threshold in the 12 months prior to the transfer, the transferee must register for VAT immediately.

Voluntary registration

A person making taxable supplies which do not exceed the registration threshold may nonetheless register for VAT voluntarily. This enables the person concerned to recover input tax but means that output tax must be charged when taxable supplies are made to customers. However, if the supplies are mainly zero-rated, or consist of standard-rate or reduced-rate supplies made wholly or mainly to customers who are themselves taxable persons, the fact that output tax must be charged will probably not deter customers.

Being registered for VAT will add to the administrative costs of running the business but this factor may be outweighed by the benefit of being able to recover input tax.

EXAMPLE 7

Lindsey is not registered for VAT. In the year to 31 March 2018, she has inputs costing £10,000 plus VAT at 20%. Her outputs total £35,000.

(a) How much profit does she make for the year?

(b) If she had registered for VAT voluntarily, how much profit would she have made?

(c) Does it matter whether the supplies that she makes are all:

- (i) zero-rated?
- (ii) standard-rated supplies made to VAT-registered businesses?
- (iii) standard-rated supplies made to the general public?

Solution

(a) Her profit is £23,000 (£35,000 – £12,000).

(b) If she had registered for VAT (and outputs had remained at £35,000) she would have been able to reclaim her input tax, giving a profit of £25,000 (£35,000 – £10,000).

(c) (i) If she makes only zero-rated supplies, voluntary registration has no effect on her selling prices and, therefore, no effect on her sales.

(ii) If she makes only standard-rated supplies to VAT-registered businesses, her prices will increase by 20% but her customers will be able to reclaim the extra tax paid and so there should be no effect on her sales.

(iii) If she makes only standard-rated supplies to the general public, increasing her prices may entail a loss of custom and she may prefer not to register.

Exemption from registration

HMRC may grant exemption from registration to a person making supplies which exceed the registration threshold, so long as these supplies are all zero-rated. An application for exemption might be made if the amount of input tax which could be reclaimed if the person were registered is small in comparison with the increased administrative costs associated with VAT registration.

Pre-registration input tax

VAT incurred before registration is not input tax. Nonetheless, it can be treated as input tax so long as certain conditions are satisfied. These conditions vary according to whether the VAT is incurred on a supply of goods or a supply of services:

(a) **Goods**. VAT suffered on a pre-registration supply of goods may be treated as input tax so long as the goods were supplied to the taxable person for business purposes within the four years prior to the date of registration and were not sold or consumed before that date.

(b) **Services**. VAT suffered on a pre-registration supply of services may be treated as input tax so long as the services were supplied to the taxable person for business purposes no more than six months before the date of registration.

Group registration

A group of companies may apply for the group to be registered as a single taxable person, rather than each company in the group being registered individually. Group registration has the following consequences:

(a) The input tax suffered by the group as a whole is set against the output tax charged by the group as a whole.

(b) One of the group companies is nominated as the "representative member" and takes responsibility for submitting VAT returns and accounting for VAT on behalf of the entire group. However, any other company in the group can be held liable if the representative member fails to pay the VAT which is due.

(c) Supplies between group members are not regarded as taxable supplies and are ignored for VAT purposes.

Individual group companies may register separately and choose not to join the VAT group. This may improve the cash flow position of a company with mainly zero-rated supplies which makes monthly VAT returns (see next chapter). It is also possible for a group of companies to form two or more VAT groups, with some of the companies belonging to one VAT group and some belonging to another.

Group registration offers tax avoidance opportunities in certain cases and HMRC may remove a company from a VAT group if avoidance is suspected.

Deregistration

Deregistration may be either voluntary or compulsory:

(a) A registered person may deregister voluntarily if HMRC is satisfied that taxable turnover, excluding supplies of capital assets, will not exceed the deregistration threshold (£83,000 from 1 April 2017) in the next 12 months.

(b) Compulsory deregistration is triggered when a registered person entirely ceases to make taxable supplies. The person must notify HMRC within 30 days that this has occurred and deregistration will normally take effect as from the date on which taxable supplies ceased.

(c) Deregistration is also compulsory on a change of legal status (e.g. when a sole trader admits a partner or when the business of a partnership is taken over by a company).

On deregistration, the person concerned is deemed to make a supply of all the tangible assets of the business and output tax is charged accordingly. However, assets on which no input tax was reclaimed are excluded from this deemed supply and the output tax due is not collected if it does not exceed £1,000 in total. The deemed supply does *not* take place if the business is sold as a going concern to another taxable person.

Summary

- VAT is chargeable when a taxable person makes a taxable supply of either goods or services in the course of business.
- A taxable supply is any supply of goods or services other than an exempt supply and may be charged to value added tax at either the standard rate, the reduced rate or the zero rate.
- A taxable person is a person who makes taxable supplies and who is (or should be) registered for VAT. A taxable person may be an individual, a partnership, a company, a charity, a club or an association.
- A person making taxable supplies which exceed the registration threshold must register with HMRC. A person making taxable supplies which do not exceed the threshold may register voluntarily.
- A taxable person must account to HMRC for the output tax charged to customers but may (in general) recover the input tax charged by suppliers.
- A person making only exempt supplies cannot charge VAT to customers and is unable to recover input tax.

Exercises

29.1 Classify each of the following supplies as either taxable at the standard rate, taxable at the reduced rate, taxable at the zero rate or exempt:

(a) a theatre ticket
(b) a loaf of bread
(c) bank charges
(d) electricity supplied for business use
(e) a taxi ride
(f) a taxation textbook
(g) gas supplied for domestic use
(h) a subscription to a professional body
(i) an insurance premium
(j) a new commercial building
(k) a meal in a restaurant
(l) a train ticket
(m) exports to a non-EU country
(n) writing paper.

29.2 A standard-rated supply is made in May 2017 at a price of £340, plus VAT. Calculate the VAT chargeable and the consideration for the supply if:

(a) no discount is offered
(b) a 2% discount is offered for prompt payment and the customer takes advantage of this discount
(c) a 2% discount is offered for prompt payment but the customer decides not to take advantage of this discount.

29.3 In each of the following cases, is anyone required to register with HM Revenue and Customs? If so, who?

(a) Lorna is a sole trader, making taxable supplies of £100,000 per annum.
(b) Mike owns two distinct businesses. One has a taxable turnover of £40,000 per annum and the other has a taxable turnover of £50,000 per annum.
(c) Pat and Phil are in partnership. Their taxable turnover is £60,000 per annum. Phil also owns another business with a taxable turnover of £45,000 per annum.
(d) JSmiCo Ltd has a taxable turnover of £250,000 per annum. The company's shares are owned entirely by John Smith and his wife.

29.4 Rosemary owns a business which has an annual turnover (excluding any VAT) of £90,000. Describe her VAT position if:

(a) she makes wholly exempt supplies
(b) she makes wholly standard-rated supplies
(c) she makes wholly zero-rated supplies.

29.5 Explain the VAT consequences of a UK business:

(a) buying goods from (or selling goods to) another EU country
(b) importing goods from a non-EU country
(c) exporting goods to a non-EU country.

***29.6** Answer the following questions:

(a) who should register for VAT?

(b) when should registration occur?

(c) what are the consequences of failing to register?

(d) when may a taxable person deregister?

(e) why might someone choose to register voluntarily?

***29.7** Sanjay began trading on 1 February 2017, selling standard-rated goods and services. He decided not to register for VAT voluntarily. His turnover (excluding VAT) for the first 16 months of trading was as follows:

2017	£	**2018**	£
February	2,550	January	10,080
March	3,660	February	7,920
April	3,880	March	6,780
May	4,240	April	5,100
June	4,860	May	4,890
July	5,290		
August	5,430		
September	6,320		
October	7,410		
November	11,050		
December	12,270		

In January 2018, he sold a machine (which had been used as a non-current asset) for £800. This is *not* included in the above turnover figures.

Sanjay is worried that his monthly turnover has started to fall and he is considering offering customer discounts in an attempt to reverse this trend.

Required:

(a) Explain the term "taxable person" for VAT purposes.

(b) State the circumstances in which VAT registration is compulsory and explain why some persons may choose to register voluntarily.

(c) State the date by which Sanjay would be required to register for VAT. Would registration be necessary if his monthly turnover for the remainder of 2018 seemed likely to continue on a downward trend?

(d) Explain the VAT consequences which would ensue if Sanjay began offering trade discounts or cash discounts to his customers.

(CIPFA)

Chapter 30

Value added tax (2)

Introduction

The previous chapter outlined the main principles of value added tax and explained the processes of registration and deregistration. This chapter is concerned with the procedures used to account for VAT to HMRC and the way in which the tax is administered. Other matters considered in this chapter include non-recoverable input tax, the VAT position of persons who make both taxable and exempt supplies and a number of schemes which exist in order to simplify the workings of the VAT system.

Accounting for VAT

At regular intervals (usually quarterly) registered persons must submit a VAT return to HMRC, showing input tax and output tax for the period covered by the return. Any excess of output tax over input tax is payable to HMRC. Any excess of input tax over output tax is repayable by HMRC. Note that:

(a) A VAT return must usually be submitted within one month and seven days of the end of the "tax period" to which it relates, together with any tax due. Online filing and electronic payment are now mandatory (subject to some minor exceptions).

(b) A registered person making supplies which are wholly or mainly zero-rated will be entitled to a VAT repayment in most tax periods. Such a person may opt to submit VAT returns monthly rather than quarterly, so speeding up tax repayments at the expense of making twelve returns per year rather than four.

Payments on account

A registered person who makes quarterly returns and whose annual VAT liability exceeds £2.3 million is obliged to make payments on account to HMRC. The first payment is due one month before the end of the quarter and a second payment is due at the end of the quarter. A balancing payment is made one month after the end of the quarter. All of these payments must be made electronically.

Each of the two payments on account is usually calculated as 1/24th of the total VAT liability for the previous year. However, the business may choose to pay its actual VAT liability for each month rather than the set POAs.

The tax point

The date on which a supply is deemed to occur is known as the "tax point" of that supply. The tax point of a supply determines:

(a) for outputs, the tax period in which the tax on that supply must be accounted for

(b) for inputs, the tax period in which the tax on that supply may be reclaimed

(c) the rate of VAT applicable to the supply (if VAT rates change).

For a supply of goods the "basic tax point" is the date on which the goods are removed or made available to the customer. For a supply of services the basic tax point is the date on which the services are performed. However, the actual tax point of a supply will differ from the basic tax point in the following circumstances:

(a) If the supplier issues a tax invoice or receives payment on a date which is earlier than the basic tax point, the actual tax point for the supply (or part of the supply) to which that invoice or payment relates is the date on which the invoice is issued or on which the payment is received, whichever occurs first.

(b) Otherwise, if the supplier issues a tax invoice within 14 days after the basic tax point, then the invoice date becomes the actual tax point.

HMRC may extend the 14-day rule mentioned above if asked to do so by a registered person who is genuinely unable to issue invoices within 14 days of the basic tax point.

Tax invoices

If a taxable person makes a taxable supply to another taxable person, a "tax invoice" must be issued. The main purpose of this invoice is to provide documentary evidence of the transaction, so allowing the person receiving the supply to reclaim the input tax related to that supply. The required contents of a valid tax invoice are:

(a) the invoice number, date and tax point

(b) the name, address and VAT registration number of the supplier

(c) the name and address of the customer

(d) for each invoice item, a description of the goods or services supplied

(e) for each description, the quantity of the goods or the extent of the services, the unit price, the amount payable (before VAT) and the rate of VAT applicable.

(f) the total amount due, before VAT

(g) the rate of any cash discount available

(h) the total amount of VAT chargeable.

A less detailed tax invoice may be issued if the consideration for the supply does not exceed £250. A less detailed tax invoice need show only:

(a) the name, address and VAT registration number of the supplier

(b) the tax point

(c) a description of the goods or services supplied

(d) the total amount payable by the customer, including VAT

(e) for each rate of VAT chargeable, the gross amount payable (including VAT) and the rate of tax which is applicable.

The issue of a tax invoice is optional if a supply is made to a customer who is not a taxable person. Retailers are not required to issue a tax invoice unless asked for one by the customer. A VAT invoice may be issued electronically as long as the customer agrees to electronic invoicing.

Accounting records

Every taxable person must keep such records as are required by HMRC. The main records which must be kept† are as follows:

(a) business and accounting records (including orders, delivery notes, business correspondence, purchases and sales books, cashbooks and other account books, till rolls, bank statements, paying-in slips and annual accounts)

(b) a VAT account

(c) a copy of each tax invoice issued

(d) all tax invoices received (although tax invoices are not required for payments of £25 or less relating to telephone calls, car park charges, toll charges or purchases made through coin-operated machines)

(e) documentation relating to imports and exports.

HMRC may also specify additional record-keeping requirements for all businesses of a particular description and (in cases where additional records might assist in identifying supplies on which VAT might otherwise go unpaid) for individual businesses.

All records must be retained for a period of six years or for such lesser period as HMRC may allow. HMRC is empowered to require a taxable person to provide their VAT records for inspection and is also empowered to inspect these records at the business premises.

† *The Government has proposed (as part of the "Making Tax Digital" project) that VAT accounting records should be kept electronically and that (as from April 2019) businesses should provide HMRC with summary VAT data which is generated automatically from these records. This data would be supplied quarterly and would effectively replace the VAT return.*

Special schemes

The VAT system offers a number of special schemes which are intended to simplify the workings of the VAT system, especially for smaller businesses. The main schemes are as follows:

(a) the cash accounting scheme
(b) the annual accounting scheme
(c) the flat-rate scheme for small businesses
(d) the flat-rate scheme for farmers
(e) the margin scheme for second-hand goods.

Each of these schemes is explained below. There are also several special schemes for use only by retailers. The "retail schemes" are briefly considered later in this chapter.

Cash accounting scheme

A registered person whose taxable turnover is not expected to exceed £1,350,000 in the next 12 months may opt to join the cash accounting scheme. Those who join this scheme account for output tax in the tax period in which *payment is received* from the customer and reclaim input tax in the tax period in which *payment is made* to the supplier. The tax point is ignored when allocating inputs and outputs to tax periods.

Joining this scheme allows a registered person to delay the payment of output tax to HMRC until the tax has actually been received from customers, which is beneficial if customers are given extended credit. The scheme also provides automatic relief for bad debts. On the other hand, input tax cannot be reclaimed until the tax has actually been paid to suppliers. A person may not join the cash accounting scheme unless:

(a) the person's taxable turnover (excluding sales of capital items) is not expected to exceed £1,350,000 in the next 12 months
(b) the person's VAT returns are up to date
(c) all amounts due to be paid to HMRC have in fact been paid, or the person has come to an arrangement for such payments to be made
(d) within the previous 12 months, the person has not been convicted of a VAT offence or assessed to a penalty for VAT evasion involving dishonest conduct.

A person who belongs to the cash accounting scheme must withdraw from the scheme at the end of a tax period if taxable turnover for the 12 months to date has exceeded £1,600,000. HMRC will allow such a person to remain in the scheme only if it can be demonstrated that the high turnover is not expected to recur and that taxable turnover for the next 12 months is expected to be no more than £1,350,000.

The cash accounting scheme cannot be used for supplies of goods and services which are invoiced before the supply is made or for supplies where payment is not due for more than six months after the date of the invoice.

Annual accounting scheme

A person with a taxable turnover which is not expected to exceed £1,350,000 in the next 12 months may apply to join the annual accounting scheme and submit only one VAT return per year. The scheme operates as follows:

(a) During the year the person makes nine interim payments to HMRC, each equal to 10% of the VAT liability for the previous year. These payments must be made by direct debit or by other electronic means and begin in the fourth month of the year.

(b) Optionally (and subject to HMRC approval) the taxable person may choose to make three interim payments in months four, seven and ten rather than the nine payments referred to above. In this case, each payment is equal to 25% of the VAT liability for the previous year.

(c) If a person joins the annual accounting scheme when first registering for VAT (or less than 12 months after registration), the interim payments are based initially upon the person's expected VAT liability for the year.

(d) At the end of the year the annual return is submitted together with a final payment consisting of the balance of the VAT liability. The return and payment must be made within two months of the end of the year.

(e) A person who operates the annual accounting scheme must withdraw from the scheme if taxable turnover exceeds £1,600,000 for the previous year.

The advantages of the scheme include a reduction in the number of VAT returns each year (from four to one) and more predictable cash flows. There is also more time at the end of the year in which to complete the required return and to pay any VAT which is due.

Flat-rate scheme for small businesses

An eligible business which is registered for VAT may opt to join the flat-rate scheme (FRS) for small businesses. This scheme enables a small business to calculate its VAT liability as a flat-rate percentage of total turnover and so avoids the need to keep detailed records of input tax and output tax. The FRS operates as follows:

(a) Output tax is charged to customers at the normal rate for the supply. Similarly, input tax is paid to suppliers at the normal rate. But the output tax charged to customers is not paid over to HMRC and (in general) input tax cannot be recovered.

(b) In each tax period, a flat-rate percentage is applied to the VAT-inclusive turnover for the period (including the value of any exempt supplies). The result of this calculation is the amount of VAT payable to HMRC for the period.

(c) The applicable flat-rate percentage depends upon the trade sector in which the business operates. With a standard rate of 20%, the flat-rate percentage currently ranges from 4% to 14.5%. But a special rate of 16.5% applies to certain "limited cost" businesses (e.g. labour-only businesses).

(d) Input tax on the purchase of capital assets costing at least £2,000 (including VAT) can be reclaimed in the usual way, in which case output tax must be accounted for in the usual way on the eventual disposal of the asset.

(e) The FRS can be used in conjunction with the annual accounting scheme. It *cannot* be used in conjunction with the cash accounting scheme or a retail scheme (see later in this chapter). However, the FRS offers an optional cash-based turnover method and an optional retailer's turnover method.

The FRS is available to businesses with a taxable turnover which is not expected to exceed £150,000 in the next 12 months. A business must normally leave the FRS if its VAT-inclusive income exceeds £230,000 during any 12-month period ending on an anniversary of the date that it joined the scheme.

Flat-rate scheme for farmers (Agricultural flat-rate scheme)

In general, a farmer making taxable supplies which exceed the registration threshold is liable to register for VAT in the normal way. Similarly, a farmer whose taxable supplies are below the threshold may register voluntarily. Since farmers make mainly zero-rated supplies, a farmer who is registered will usually receive regular repayments of input tax, at the expense of maintaining the necessary VAT records.

An alternative to registration is the flat-rate scheme for farmers. This scheme is available to farmers regardless of the size of their taxable turnover and is intended to reduce administrative costs. The scheme operates as follows:

(a) A farmer who joins the scheme does not register for VAT. This reduces administrative costs but deprives the farmer of the opportunity to reclaim input tax.

(b) In compensation, the farmer is allowed to add a flat-rate 4% to his or her selling prices and to retain this addition. The flat-rate addition may be charged only when selling designated goods or services to VAT-registered persons but applies even if the goods or services concerned would normally be zero-rated.

(c) From the point of view of a taxable person buying goods from a flat-rate farmer, the flat-rate addition is treated as input tax and may be reclaimed, subject to the usual rules and restrictions (see later in this chapter).

A farmer may not join this scheme if the total of the flat-rate additions which would be charged if the farmer were a member of the scheme exceeds the total amount of input tax which the farmer would otherwise be entitled to reclaim by £3,000 per annum or more.

Margin scheme for second-hand goods

In general, VAT is charged on the full value of goods sold, regardless of whether those goods are new or second-hand. However, subject to certain conditions, a taxable person selling second-hand goods may choose to sell them through the margin scheme and charge VAT only on his or her profit margin. The scheme operates as follows:

(a) Output tax is charged only on the seller's profit margin. This is the difference between the price at which the goods were obtained and their selling price. No output tax is charged to the customer unless the goods are sold at a profit.

(b) The seller's profit margin is deemed to be VAT-inclusive, so that the amount of tax due is calculated by multiplying this margin by the VAT fraction. Expenses incurred by the seller (e.g. the costs of restoration, repairs and spare parts) are ignored when establishing the amount of the profit margin.

(c) The buyer cannot reclaim the input tax suffered, even if he/she is a taxable person.

The main conditions which must be satisfied for the margin scheme to be used are that the goods concerned are second-hand and that they were acquired either on a supply on which no VAT was chargeable (e.g. from a member of the public) or from someone who also sold the goods under the margin scheme. The sales invoice must include an indication that the margin scheme has been applied.

EXAMPLE 1

An antiques dealer buys a table from a member of the public for £2,000. The dealer spends a further £750 (plus VAT) on restoration work and then sells the table for £5,000. Compute the output tax which must be accounted for in relation to this sale, assuming that the table is sold through the margin scheme.

Solution

Ignoring restoration costs, the dealer's margin is £3,000. The output tax due is therefore £3,000 x 1/6 = £500. Input tax on the restoration costs may be reclaimed in the usual way.

Retail schemes

Retailers are those who supply goods and services directly to the public. A retailer's sales will often consist of a very large number of relatively small transactions and in these circumstances it would sometimes be difficult and expensive to keep detailed records of each transaction for VAT purposes. In response to this problem, retail schemes have been devised which enable retailers to calculate their output tax in a fairly straightforward way. The standard retail schemes are as follows:

(a) point of sale scheme
(b) apportionment scheme 1
(c) apportionment scheme 2
(d) direct calculation scheme 1
(e) direct calculation scheme 2.

Full information on the detailed workings of the standard schemes is given on the website which accompanies this book. The website address is www.pearsoned.co.uk/melville.

Retailers with an annual taxable turnover exceeding £130 million cannot use any of these standard schemes. If such retailers wish to use a retail scheme they must negotiate an individual "bespoke retail scheme" with HMRC.

It should be noted that the growing use of information technology by large retailers and by many small retailers means that it is now much easier to record individual sales than it was when VAT was introduced in 1973. This means that the original rationale for the retail schemes has been diminished over the years. Accordingly, retailers may not use any of these schemes unless permitted to do so. HMRC permission will be granted only if a retailer cannot reasonably be expected to account for VAT in the normal way, so that the use of a retail scheme is strictly necessary.

Bad debts

If a taxable person uses the cash accounting scheme, the output tax relating to a supply is not accounted for until the consideration for that supply has been received and so automatic relief is given for bad debts. But persons who do not use the cash accounting scheme might account for the output tax relating to a supply before the consideration for that supply is received and then find that a bad debt has occurred. In these circumstances, a claim may be made for a refund of the VAT lost, so long as:

(a) goods or services have been supplied for a consideration and the related output tax has been accounted for to HMRC
(b) the value of the supply was no more than its open market value
(c) the debt has been written off in the books of account
(d) at least six months have elapsed since both the date of the supply and the date that payment was due
(e) the claim for bad debt relief is made within four years and six months from the later of the date of the supply and the date that payment was due.

A business that recovers input tax relating to a supply, but does not pay the supplier within six months of the date of supply or the date that payment was due (if later), must repay the input tax concerned to HMRC. This applies whether or not the supplier makes a claim for bad debt relief.

Non-deductible input tax

In general, a taxable person can reclaim the input tax relating to a supply so long as the supply is evidenced by a tax invoice and the goods or services involved are for use in the person's business. However, input tax is not reclaimable on certain types of supply, even though the supply is received in the course of business. The main examples of such non-deductible (or "blocked") input tax are:

(a) VAT on business entertainment for customers (other than overseas customers).

(b) VAT on the purchase of motor cars, apart from:

  (i) cars acquired by a car dealer, as stock in trade

  (ii) cars acquired for use by a driving school, car rental business or taxi business

  (iii) cars acquired *wholly* for business use

  If the input tax on the purchase of a car cannot be reclaimed, the subsequent sale of that car is an exempt supply.

(c) VAT on the purchase of second-hand goods that were sold under the margin scheme (see earlier in this chapter).

The VAT on goods or services which are not used at all for business purposes cannot be reclaimed. If goods or services are used partly for business purposes and partly for private purposes, then there are two possible treatments. Either:

(a) the input tax on the supply is apportioned and the business element of the tax is then reclaimed, or

(b) the whole of the input tax on the supply is reclaimed, but output tax is then accounted for in relation to the element of private use (the "Lennartz method").

The first treatment may be applied to supplies of either goods or services. The Lennartz method may be applied to supplies of goods (other than land and property, ships, boats and aircraft) but cannot usually be applied to supplies of services. Special rules apply to the private use of car fuel (see below).

Fuel for private motoring

If an employee or the owner of a business is provided with car fuel for private motoring, all of the input tax relating to fuel purchases by the business may be reclaimed but output tax must then be accounted for on the supply of fuel for private use. The amount of this output tax depends upon the car's level of carbon dioxide emissions (rounded down to the nearest 5g/km) and is determined by reference to a table of scale charges. As from 1 May 2017, the VAT-inclusive fuel scale charges are as follows:

Emission rating (g/km)	*Fuel scale charge 12 month period* £	*Fuel scale charge 3 month period* £	*Fuel scale charge 1 month period* £
120 or less	563	140	46
125	842	211	70
130	901	224	74
135	955	238	79
140	1,013	252	84
145	1,068	267	88
150	1.126	281	93
155	1,180	295	98
160	1,239	309	102
165	1,293	323	107
170	1,351	337	111
175	1,405	351	116
180	1,464	365	121
185	1,518	379	125
190	1,577	393	131
195	1,631	408	136
200	1,689	422	140
205	1,743	436	145
210	1,802	449	149
215	1,856	463	154
220	1,914	478	159
225 or more	1,969	492	163

With a standard rate of 20%, output tax is 1/6th of the scale charge. Scale charges do not apply if *no input tax at all* is reclaimed in relation to road fuel, whether used for business or private motoring and whether used in cars or in commercial vehicles. Scale charges may also be avoided if input tax is reclaimed only in relation to fuel used for business motoring and accurate records are kept from which this figure can be derived.

Note that the input tax suffered in relation to car repairs and maintenance is reclaimable in full (with no adjustment for private use) so long as the car is used for business purposes to some extent. However, only 50% of the input tax relating to car leasing charges is reclaimable if there is any private use of the car.

Partial exemption

As explained in the previous chapter, a taxable person who makes wholly taxable supplies may reclaim all input tax suffered (with the exceptions listed above). A person who makes wholly exempt supplies is not a taxable person and may reclaim no input tax at all.

A taxable person who makes partly taxable and partly exempt supplies is referred to as "partially exempt" and may reclaim part of the input tax suffered. The input tax which may be reclaimed for a tax period is the amount which is "attributed to taxable supplies". This amount is usually calculated as follows:

(a) Input tax suffered during the period on goods and services which are used exclusively for the purpose of making taxable supplies is attributed to taxable supplies and is reclaimable in full.

(b) Input tax suffered during the period on goods and services which are used exclusively for the purpose of making exempt supplies is attributed to exempt supplies and cannot be reclaimed at all.

(c) A proportion of any unattributed or "residual" input tax suffered during the period (on goods and services used for making both taxable and exempt supplies) is attributed to taxable supplies and may be reclaimed. This proportion is equal to:

$$\text{Residual input tax} \times \frac{\text{Value of taxable supplies}}{\text{Value of all supplies}}$$

The ratio of taxable supplies to all supplies is generally expressed as a percentage rounded up to the nearest whole number. But the percentage is rounded up to two decimal places if residual input tax is at least £400,000 per month (on average). When computing this ratio, certain supplies made by the person are omitted from the calculation, including self-supplies and supplies consisting of capital assets.

A taxable person may use the previous year's overall percentage to determine the provisional recovery of residual input tax in each tax period (see below) thereby avoiding the need to calculate a separate percentage for each period.

(d) If the total amount of input tax not attributed to taxable supplies for a tax period does not exceed a "de minimis" limit of £625 per month (on average) and is also no more than 50% of all the input tax for the period, then it is treated as being attributed to taxable supplies and is reclaimable in full.

Note that the calculation of reclaimable input tax for a tax period is only provisional. The calculation is performed again at the end of each year, taking into account input tax for the whole year and using a de minimis limit of £7,500 (12 × £625). Any difference between the amount of reclaimable input tax for the year and the amount calculated provisionally is an underpayment or overpayment of VAT and must be accounted for to HMRC.

The procedure described above is known as the "standard method" of computing reclaimable input tax for a partially exempt person. HMRC may approve or direct the use of an alternative method if this gives a more fair and reasonable result.

EXAMPLE 2

During the quarter to 31 December 2017, Nancy makes supplies as follows:

	£
Standard-rated supplies (excluding VAT)	120,000
Zero-rated supplies	80,000
Exempt supplies	50,000

She suffers input tax as follows:

Attributed to taxable supplies	7,500
Attributed to exempt supplies	8,500
Unattributed	12,000

Compute the VAT provisionally payable to HMRC for the quarter.

Solution

	£	£
Output tax		
Standard-rated supplies £120,000 @ 20%		24,000
Zero-rated supplies £80,000 @ 0%		0
		24,000
Input tax		
Attributed to taxable supplies	7,500	
Unattributed:		
$\frac{£120,000 + £80,000}{£120,000 + £80,000 + £50,000}$ = 80% x £12,000	9,600	17,100
Payable to HMRC		6,900

The input tax not attributed to taxable supplies for the quarter is £10,900 (£8,500 + 20% x £12,000). This is more than £625 per month on average and so cannot be reclaimed.

Simplified de minimis tests

A business which passes either of two "simplified tests" for a VAT period is able to avoid a full partial exemption calculation and can provisionally reclaim input tax attributable to both taxable and exempt supplies. The two tests are as follows:

(a) **Test 1**. Total input tax incurred does not exceed £625 per month (on average) and the value of exempt supplies is no more than 50% of the value of all supplies.

(b) **Test 2**. Total input tax incurred less input tax directly attributable to taxable supplies does not exceed £625 per month (on average) and the value of exempt supplies is no more than 50% of the value of all supplies.

These two tests may also be applied at the end of each year to determine whether or not the business is "de minimis" for the entire year.

As a further simplification, a business which was de minimis for the previous year may treat itself as provisionally de minimis for each VAT period in the current year and review its de minimis status only at the end of the current year. This simplification does not apply to businesses which expect to incur more than £1 million of input tax in the current year.

EXAMPLE 3

(a) During the quarter to 31 August 2017, Justin makes taxable supplies of £30,000 and exempt supplies of £20,000. Input tax incurred is £1,500. Does he pass either of the two simplified de minimis tests for the quarter?

(b) During the year to 31 March 2018, Margaret makes taxable supplies of £140,000 and exempt supplies of £60,000. Input tax incurred is £27,600, of which £22,800 is directly attributable to taxable supplies. Does she pass either of the two simplified de minimis tests for the year?

Solution

(a) Input tax averages £500 per month and exempt supplies are 40% of total supplies. Therefore Justin passes the first test and may provisionally reclaim all of his input tax for the quarter.

(b) Input tax averages £2,300 per month and so Margaret fails the first test. But total input tax less input tax directly attributable to taxable supplies averages only £400 per month and exempt supplies are 30% of total supplies. Therefore Margaret passes the second test and may reclaim all of her input tax for the year.

Administration of VAT

Overall responsibility for administration of the VAT system lies with the Commissioners for Revenue and Customs. HMRC has a number of dedicated specialist offices which deal with matters such as:

(a) VAT registration

(b) VAT accounting and debt management

(c) written enquiries relating to VAT.

There is also a network of local offices throughout the UK which deal with local VAT administration matters. HMRC officials from these offices may visit the business premises of registered persons in their area to check the accuracy of VAT returns and to ensure that the VAT system is being operated correctly.

VAT assessments

VAT is largely a self-assessed tax and so it is not normally necessary to raise formal VAT assessments. But HMRC may issue such an assessment if a taxable person has failed to make a VAT return or has made a return which is incorrect or incomplete.

VAT assessments cannot usually be raised any later than four years after the end of the tax period to which they relate, but this time limit is extended to twenty years if the taxable person has behaved dishonestly or fraudulently. Any claim for a refund of overpaid VAT must also be made within four years in most cases.

Appeals

A person who disagrees with an "appealable" VAT decision made by HMRC may ask for the decision to be internally reviewed. The person concerned also has the right of appeal to a tribunal. Appeals are permitted in relation to most VAT matters, but certain matters cannot be the subject of an appeal.

The internal review process and the appeals system are very similar to their direct tax counterparts (see Chapter 1). In summary:

(a) A request that an appealable HMRC decision should be reviewed must normally be made in writing within 30 days of the date of the decision. A request may be accepted later than this if the person concerned has a reasonable excuse for failing to meet the 30-day time limit.

(b) An internal review is carried out by an HMRC officer who has not previously been involved with the decision in question. The review is normally completed within 45 days. The review officer then writes to the person concerned to inform him or her of the review's conclusions.

(c) If no internal review is requested, an appeal to a tribunal may be made within 30 days of the date of the original decision. Otherwise, an appeal to a tribunal may be made within 30 days of the date of the review conclusion letter.

(d) Most VAT appeals are dealt with by the Tax Chamber of the First-tier Tribunal. The Tax and Chancery Chamber of the Upper Tribunal hears appeals against decisions made by the First-tier Tribunal.

(e) If either HMRC or the person concerned is dissatisfied with a decision made by the Upper Tribunal, a dispute on a point of law may be referred to the Court of Appeal.

Avoidance schemes

Businesses with a VAT-exclusive turnover of taxable supplies and exempt supplies which exceeds £600,000 p.a. are required to notify HMRC if they make use of certain designated VAT avoidance schemes which are listed on a statutory register. Similarly, businesses with a turnover exceeding £10 million are required to notify HMRC if they make use of schemes which bear certain hallmarks of VAT avoidance.

Penalties, surcharges and interest

The main penalties which may be imposed in relation to VAT are as follows:

(a) **Criminal fraud**. A person who attempts to evade VAT in such a way that his or her conduct amounts to criminal fraud may, on a summary conviction obtained before a magistrate, be imprisoned for up to six months. The person may also be required to pay a fine of up to £20,000 or three times the amount of tax evaded, whichever is the greater. If the conviction is on indictment, the person may be imprisoned for up to seven years and there is no limit to the size of any fine†.

(b) **Failure to notify**. A taxable person who fails to notify HMRC of his or her liability to register, or makes late notification, is liable to a penalty. This penalty is assessed in accordance with a penalty regime which applies to any failure to notify HMRC of a taxable activity. This penalty regime is not confined to VAT but covers a range of direct and indirect taxes‡.

Under this regime, the penalty for a failure to notify liability to register is calculated as a percentage of the "potential lost revenue". This is the amount of VAT for which the taxable person is liable between the date on which registration should have taken place and the date on which registration actually takes place. The percentage varies between 30% and 100%, depending upon the degree of culpability of the person in question but may be reduced if the person voluntarily discloses the failure to notify.

(c) **Incorrect VAT returns**. A taxable person who submits an incorrect VAT return is liable to pay a penalty. This penalty is assessed in accordance with a penalty regime which applies to the submission of incorrect tax returns generally and which covers a wide range of taxes‡. Under this regime, a penalty may be charged if an incorrect VAT return leads to an understatement of the amount of tax due and the inaccuracy was either careless or deliberate. A penalty may also be charged if a VAT assessment issued by HMRC understates the amount of tax due and the taxable person fails to take reasonable steps to inform HMRC of this fact within 30 days.

The amount of any penalty imposed depends upon the person's degree of culpability and will usually vary between 30% and 100% of the additional tax which is payable as a result of correcting the inaccuracy or the understatement. But these penalties are substantially reduced if the taxable person voluntarily discloses the inaccuracy or the failure to report an under-assessment.

† *In the Budget of March 2017, the Government proposed the introduction of a new penalty for "participating" in VAT fraud. This penalty would apply to businesses and company officers who enter into a transaction and who know (or should know) that the transaction is connected with the fraudulent evasion of VAT. The amount of the penalty would be 30% of the potential lost tax.*

This proposal was omitted from the shortened Finance Bill which became Finance Act 2017 before the General Election. However, it may be reintroduced in a later Finance Bill.

‡ *See Chapter 15 for further details.*

(d) **Default surcharge**. A "default" occurs if a taxable person submits a late VAT return and/or makes a late payment of VAT. In these circumstances, HMRC will usually issue a surcharge liability notice specifying a surcharge period running for 12 months from the last day of the tax period concerned. If a further default is made within this period, then:

- the surcharge period is extended to the first anniversary of the last day of the tax period to which the new default relates, and
- if the new default has resulted in any VAT not being paid on time, a default surcharge will be levied, calculated as the greater of £30 and a percentage of the tax paid late. The surcharge percentage is 2% for the first default within the surcharge period, 5% for the second default, 10% for the third default and 15% for the fourth and any subsequent default. However, surcharges are not imposed at the 2% or 5% rate for an amount of less than £400.

A surcharge period comes to an end only when no defaults have occurred for a continuous 12-month period. Note that special arrangements apply to businesses with a turnover not exceeding £150,000 per year. Such businesses are not issued with a surcharge liability notice on the first occasion that a default occurs but are offered help and support instead. However, a surcharge liability notice is issued if another default occurs within the following 12 months.

It is important to note that a new penalty regime is being introduced in relation to late returns and late payment of tax (see Chapter 15). This penalty regime will apply to a range of taxes and is being phased in over a period of several years. The date of implementation for VAT has not yet been determined.

(e) **VAT wrongdoing**. A VAT "wrongdoing" penalty is charged if a person makes an unauthorised issue of a VAT invoice. This situation would arise if VAT invoices were issued by a person who is not registered for VAT.

The amount of the penalty varies from 30% to 100% of the amount shown as VAT on the unauthorised invoice, with substantial reductions if the person concerned voluntarily discloses the wrongdoing.

(f) **Breaches of regulations**. A taxable person who fails to comply with sundry VAT regulations will initially receive a written warning from HMRC. If non-compliance is continued, the person is liable on a first offence to a penalty of £5 per day until the breach is remedied. The penalty rises to £10 per day on a second offence within a period of two years and again to £15 per day on a third or subsequent offence. The maximum penalty which may be charged is equal to 100 times the daily rate and the minimum penalty is £50.

Certain penalties may be mitigated (i.e. reduced or not charged at all) if the taxable person has a reasonable excuse for his or her conduct. As noted above, some penalties may also be mitigated if the person concerned has voluntarily disclosed any non-compliance and has co-operated fully with HMRC.

Interest

"Default interest" is charged on VAT which has been assessed (see above) or which could have been assessed but for the fact that payment was made before an assessment was raised. Such interest runs from the date on which the tax should have been paid to the date of payment. Conversely, if a taxable person makes an overpayment of VAT and this has been caused by an HMRC error, the person is paid interest on the tax that is refunded.

When a taxable person discovers that an error on a previous VAT return has resulted in an underpayment of VAT, default interest is not charged if the error is corrected in a later return. This is permissible as long as the error does not exceed the *greater* of £10,000 and 1% of taxable turnover for the return period, subject to a maximum of £50,000.

Repayment supplement

If a taxable person is entitled to a repayment of VAT for a tax period, this repayment is increased by a "repayment supplement" of 5% (or £50, if greater) so long as:

(a) the return for the relevant tax period is submitted on time, and

(b) the amount stated to be repayable in the return is either correct or does not exceed the correct figure by more than 5% or £250 (whichever is greater), and

(c) HMRC fails to issue written instructions for the repayment to be made within 30 days from the date on which the return was received.

Summary

- VAT is normally accounted for to HMRC on a quarterly basis, although a person who is entitled to a VAT repayment in most tax periods may submit monthly returns.
- The date on which a supply is deemed to occur is known as the "tax point".
- A tax invoice must normally be issued if a taxable person makes a taxable supply to another taxable person.
- There are several special schemes which simplify the workings of the VAT system. These include the cash accounting scheme, the annual accounting scheme, the flat-rate scheme for small businesses, the flat-rate scheme for farmers and the margin scheme. There are also several special schemes for retailers.
- The input tax suffered in relation to certain types of supply is not recoverable. Special rules apply to car fuel bought by a business and then used for private motoring.
- A person making a mixture of taxable supplies and exempt supplies is "partially exempt" and may reclaim only part of the input tax suffered.
- The VAT system is administered by HMRC. Penalties are imposed for non-compliance with VAT regulations.

Exercises

30.1 List the required contents of a valid VAT invoice.

30.2 With regard to value added tax, explain the main features of the cash accounting scheme and the annual accounting scheme.

30.3 The following information relates to the VAT return of Toucan Ltd for the three months to 30 November 2017. All figures are VAT-exclusive unless stated otherwise.

(i) Standard-rated supplies made to customers were £28,800. A cash discount of 2.5% was offered to customers who paid within 28 days and this discount was taken by customers who bought 50% of the supplies made during the quarter.

The figure of £28,800 includes a £1,600 sale made to a customer in September 2017. This customer went bankrupt in November 2017 and a bad debt of £1,600 was written off in the company's books on 30 November 2017.

On 15 November 2017, a customer was invoiced for £4,800 in relation to a sale of standard-rated goods. The customer paid for these goods on 4 December 2017 and the goods were made available to the customer on 10 December 2017. This sale is NOT included in the above figure of £28,800 and was NOT eligible for the 2.5% cash discount.

(ii) Standard-rated goods bought for resale or consumption cost £9,280. Standard-rated services cost £5,200.

(iii) On 1 September 2017, the company was charged VAT of £1,960 on the purchase of a motor car with emissions of 142g/km. Private use of this car by one of the company's employees accounts for 50% of its mileage. Maintenance charges in relation to the car were £280 for the quarter and fuel costs were £520. The company reclaims input tax on all car fuel.

(iv) In October 2017, the company bought a new non-current asset for a VAT-inclusive price of £14,100.

The company is now considering an application to join the flat-rate scheme for small businesses. Standard-rated sales are expected to run at £11,500 per month from now on and purchases of standard-rated items (other than non-current assets) on which VAT may be reclaimed are expected to be £5,500 per month. The company also anticipates the acquisition of a single non-current asset at a cost of £5,000 during 2018. All of these figures exclude VAT. The flat-rate percentage applicable to Toucan Ltd is 9.5%.

Required:

(a) Compute the VAT payable to (or repayable by) HMRC for the three months to 30 November 2017.

(b) Explain the main features of the flat-rate scheme for small businesses. Would Toucan Ltd be eligible to join this scheme? If so, would it be beneficial for the company to join the scheme?

(CIPFA)

30.4 Sebastian is self-employed. He drives a car with an emission rating of 198 g/km and he charges the cost of all the petrol used to his business bank account. In the quarter to 31 July 2017, he uses his car for both business and private journeys but does not keep detailed mileage records. The VAT-inclusive cost of all the petrol bought in the quarter is £798. How should Sebastian deal with petrol in his VAT return for the quarter?

***30.5** During the quarter to 31 December 2017, a taxable person makes the following supplies:

	£
Standard-rated supplies (including VAT)	326,400
Zero-rated supplies	88,000
Exempt supplies	440,000

Input tax for the quarter is £118,000, attributed as follows:

	%
Attributed to taxable supplies	35
Attributed to exempt supplies	40
Unattributed	25

Compute the VAT provisionally payable to or reclaimable from HMRC for the quarter.

***30.6** Tracey is a sole trader. She has the following transactions during the quarter to 31 December 2017 (all amounts shown are VAT-exclusive):

	£
Sales to UK customers:	
Standard-rated	34,475
Zero-rated	12,600
Exports of goods:	
To non-EU members	8,600
To EU members (all customers are VAT registered)	17,300
Purchases:	
Standard-rated	25,800
Zero-rated	6,200
Expenses:	
Wages and salaries	22,450
Car repairs	120
Insurances	260
Entertaining UK customers	420
Other expenses (all standard-rated)	9,700
Capital transactions:	
Purchase of new plant and machinery	8,000
Purchase of motor van	12,000

Tracey drives a car with an emission rating of 164 g/km and reclaims input tax on all of the fuel used by this car, whether for business or private motoring. She does not keep detailed mileage records. Calculate the amount of VAT due for the quarter.

Chapter 31

Inheritance tax

Introduction

This chapter provides a basic introduction to inheritance tax (IHT). An IHT liability can arise in a number of ways but the events which most commonly trigger such a liability are the transfer of assets on the death of their owner and the gift of assets during the lifetime of their owner.

IHT was introduced in 1986 to replace capital transfer tax. Current IHT legislation is to be found in the Inheritance Tax Act 1984 (originally the Capital Transfer Tax Act 1984) as amended by subsequent Finance Acts.

Transfers of value

The main situation in which a charge to IHT may arise is when a *transfer of value* of *chargeable property* is made by a *chargeable person*.

A transfer of value occurs when a transferor makes a "disposition" such that his or her estate is lower in value than it was before the disposition occurred. The value of a transfer for IHT purposes is equal to the reduction in the value of the transferor's estate. If the transferor also pays the IHT in relation to the transfer, this further reduces the value of the estate, so that the total value of the transfer is then equal to the amount of the disposition plus the associated IHT.

A disposition is a disposal of property or an interest in property. This includes disposals made during the lifetime of the transferor ("lifetime transfers") as well as disposals caused by the death of the transferor. However, certain dispositions are not regarded as transfers of value for IHT purposes and so cannot give rise to an IHT liability. The most significant of these dispositions are:

(a) dispositions without gratuitous intent (i.e. genuine commercial transactions which give rise to a loss and so cause a reduction in the value of the transferor's estate)

(b) dispositions made during the transferor's lifetime which are allowable expenditure for income tax or corporation tax purposes or which consist of pension contributions made by an employer for the benefit of employees

(c) dispositions made during the transferor's lifetime for the maintenance of his or her family (including spouses, civil partners, children and dependent relatives)

(d) dispositions caused by the fact that the transferor has died whilst on active service†.

† *This IHT exemption also applies to emergency services personnel and humanitarian aid workers. The exemption covers not only the estate of the deceased person but also any IHT that would normally be due on death in relation to transfers made during the person's lifetime (see below).*

Chargeable property

For IHT purposes, the word "property" refers to assets of any type and all property is chargeable property unless specifically excluded from charge. The main exclusions are:

(a) property situated outside the UK and owned by a person who is domiciled outside the UK (i.e. a person whose permanent home is situated outside the UK).

(b) government securities which give tax exemption to persons who are not resident in the UK and which are held by someone who is not UK resident

(c) "heritage property" designated as such by the Treasury, so long as undertakings are given with regard to maintenance of the property and the provision of public access

(d) certain decorations and other awards (e.g. medals for valour or gallant conduct) as long as these have never been disposed of in exchange for money or money's worth

(e) a reversionary interest in a trust or settlement, unless acquired by purchase (see later in this chapter for more information on trusts and types of trust).

Chargeable persons

An individual who is domiciled† in the UK (i.e. whose permanent home is in the UK) is a chargeable person and is liable to IHT in relation to all of his or her chargeable property situated throughout the world An individual who is not domiciled in the UK is liable to IHT only in relation to property situated in the UK. Note that:

(a) Husbands and wives (and civil partners) are assessed to IHT independently.

(b) A partnership is not a chargeable person. Each partner is individually liable to IHT in relation to his or her share of the partnership assets.

(c) A company is not a chargeable person. But the participators of a close company (see Chapter 27) may incur IHT in relation to transfers made by that company.

(d) A person who is entitled to an "interest in possession" in property which is held in a trust (see later in this chapter) is regarded for IHT purposes as owning the property concerned, as long as this interest existed prior to 22 March 2006.

† *An individual who is not domiciled in the UK on the date of a transfer may nonetheless be deemed to be domiciled in the UK on that date for IHT purposes. This applies if the individual has been domiciled in the UK at any time within the previous three years or has been resident in the UK for at least 17 of the most recent 20 tax years. The Government is proposing that the second of these criteria should be amended to "at least 15 out of the previous 20 tax years" (see Chapter 32).*

Exempt transfers

Certain transfers are wholly exempt from IHT. In other cases, an exemption or relief may reduce the value of a transfer for IHT purposes. The main exemptions and reliefs are:

(a) business and agricultural property reliefs (see later in this chapter)

(b) exemptions for transfers made to certain transferees (see below)

(c) exemptions available to the transferor (see below).

These exemptions and reliefs are applied to a transfer in the order given above.

Exemptions for transfers made to certain transferees

The following transfers are wholly exempt from IHT whether made on death or during the lifetime of the transferor:

(a) transfers to the transferor's spouse (husband or wife) or civil partner

(b) gifts to charities, community amateur sports clubs or qualifying political parties

(c) gifts made for national purposes to designated bodies (e.g. museums) and gifts of pre-eminent property to the nation (see Chapter 4)

(d) subject to conditions, transfers into a trust established for the maintenance, repair or preservation of designated heritage property or into an employee ownership trust.

Note that the spouse exemption is restricted if transfers are made by a UK domiciled transferor to a spouse or civil partner who is not UK domiciled (see Chapter 32). Note also that a transfer to a political party is exempt if *either* at least two members of that party were elected to the House of Commons at the last general election *or* one member of the party was elected and the party's candidates gained at least 150,000 votes at the election†.

† *The Government is proposing that this relief should be extended to parties with representatives in the devolved assemblies and to parties that have gained representatives through by-elections.*

Exemptions available to the transferor

The following exemptions are available in relation to lifetime transfers only:

(a) **Normal expenditure out of income**. Transfers consisting of "normal expenditure out of income" are wholly exempt from IHT. In order for a transfer to benefit from this exemption, HMRC must believe that the transfer is part of the normal expenditure of the transferor, is made out of the transferor's income (rather than capital) and leaves sufficient income to maintain his or her usual standard of living.

(b) **Small gifts**. Gifts to individuals with a value of up to £250 per transferee per tax year (from 6 April to 5 April) are wholly exempt from IHT. This exemption cannot be used to exempt part of a gift which has a value exceeding £250 and applies only if the value of all the gifts made to the transferee in a tax year does not exceed £250.

(c) **Gifts in consideration of marriage**. Gifts made to a bride or to a bridegroom in consideration of their marriage are exempt from IHT up to the following limits:

   (i) £5,000 if made by a parent of the bride or groom
   (ii) £2,500 if made by the grandparent or remoter ancestor of the bride or groom
   (iii) £2,500 if made by the bride to the groom or vice versa
   (iv) £1,000 in any other case.

   The above exemptions are per transferor per marriage and can be used to exempt part of the value of larger gifts. Similar rules also apply to gifts made on the registration of a civil partnership.

(d) **Annual exemption**. The first £3,000 of lifetime transfers made in any tax year (from 6 April to 5 April) is exempt from IHT. Note that:

   (i) If the total of the lifetime transfers made in a tax year exceeds £3,000, the exemption is set against the year's transfers in chronological order.

   (ii) Any unused part of the annual exemption may be carried forward to the following tax year (but no further) and set against the excess of that year's lifetime transfers over that year's annual exemption.

   (iii) Apparently it is HMRC practice to set the annual exemption against potentially exempt transfers (see below) as well as against chargeable lifetime transfers, even though potentially exempt transfers may never become chargeable to inheritance tax. There is some doubt as to whether this practice is statutorily correct but it has been followed in this book.

EXAMPLE 1

Tania makes no transfers during 2015-16. Her only transfers during 2016-17 and 2017-18 are as follows:

		£
2016-17		
June 2016	Gift to her son on his marriage	6,000
October 2016	Gift to her granddaughter	4,500
January 2017	Gift to Oxfam (a charity)	10,000
March 2017	Gift to a friend	100
2017-18		
July 2017	Gift to her nephew	1,000
August 2017	Gift to her cousin	3,500

Calculate the value of each of the above transfers after deduction of all the relevant exemptions. None of the gifts are regarded as normal expenditure out of income.

Solution

(AE = Annual exemption)

	Value before AE £	*AE for current year* £	*AE for previous year* £	*Value after AE* £
2016-17				
Gift to son on marriage (£6,000 – £5,000)	1,000	1,000	-	-
Gift to granddaughter	4,500	2,000	2,500	-
Gift to charity (exempt)	-	-	-	-
Gift to friend (exempt as a small gift)	-	-	-	-
	5,500	3,000	2,500	-
2017-18				
Gift to nephew	1,000	1,000		-
Gift to cousin	3,500	2,000		1,500
	4,500	3,000		1,500

Note:

£500 of the 2015-16 annual exemption remains unused but cannot be carried forward beyond 2016-17. The 2016-17 and 2017-18 annual exemptions are fully utilised.

Potentially exempt transfers (PETs)

If a lifetime transfer is not exempt from IHT as a result of the various exemptions listed above, the transfer will be either a "chargeable lifetime transfer" or a "potentially exempt transfer". Chargeable lifetime transfers are charged to IHT immediately. But potentially exempt transfers (PETs) are charged to IHT only if the transferor dies within seven years of the date of the transfer.

A potentially exempt transfer is a lifetime transfer made by an individual to any of the following:

(a) another individual

(b) a trust for the benefit of a disabled person

(c) a trust for the benefit of a bereaved minor (in certain cases).

Most lifetime transfers are in fact PETs. But lifetime transfers made to trusts other than those mentioned above are chargeable lifetime transfers.

Types of trust

The above definition of a PET makes reference to various types of trust. Trusts were introduced briefly in Chapter 6 but are explained again below:

(a) A trust (or settlement) is an arrangement whereby property is held by persons known as trustees for the benefit of other persons known as beneficiaries.

(b) If one or more persons are entitled to the lifetime use of the trust property or to the income generated by the trust property, those persons are "life tenants" and the trust is a trust with an "interest in possession" (IIP). A person whose interest in the trust property will not take effect until some future event occurs (e.g. the death of a life tenant) is said to have a "reversionary interest".

(c) A trust with no interest in possession is sometimes referred to as a "discretionary trust". The trustees of such a trust have the discretion to distribute as much or as little of the trust income to the beneficiaries as they see fit.

For IHT purposes, most trusts are classified as "relevant property trusts" and are subject to a special IHT regime. This involves a "periodic" tax charge on the trust property every ten years and an "exit" charge when property leaves the trust. Furthermore, lifetime transfers into a relevant property trust are chargeable lifetime transfers (not PETs).

However, trusts for the disabled and trusts for bereaved minors are generally not relevant property trusts. Such trusts are not liable to the periodic or exit charges and any lifetime transfers into such a trust are PETs.

EXAMPLE 2

Consider each of the following lifetime transfers and classify each one as either an exempt transfer, a PET or a chargeable lifetime transfer. Assume in each case that the transfer was made during 2017-18 and that the annual exemption for both the current year and the previous year have been set against earlier transfers.

(a) a gift of £10,000 made by a husband to his wife

(b) a gift of £20,000 made by a mother to her son on his marriage

(c) a gift of £50,000 made to a trust for the benefit of a disabled person

(d) a gift of £100,000 made to a relevant property trust.

Solution

(a) wholly exempt

(b) exempt £5,000; PET £15,000

(c) PET

(d) chargeable lifetime transfer.

IHT payable on chargeable lifetime transfers

The amount of IHT payable on a chargeable lifetime transfer depends upon:

(a) the value of the transfer (less any relevant exemptions), which must be grossed-up if the tax is paid by the transferor

(b) the rates of IHT in force on the date of the transfer

(c) the total (including the current transfer) of the gross chargeable lifetime transfers made during the seven years ending on the date of the current transfer.

Grossing-up

IHT is chargeable on the *gross* value of a transfer. This is the reduction in the value of the transferor's estate which the transfer has caused. If the transferee pays the tax due on a transfer, the gross value of the transfer is simply the amount received by the transferee (less any exemptions). However, if the tax due is paid by the transferor, the amount received by the transferee (less exemptions) is only the net value of the transfer and this must be grossed-up at the appropriate rates to find the gross value.

In general, any capital gains tax payable by the transferor in relation to the transfer is ignored when calculating the reduction in value of the transferor's estate.

Rates of IHT applicable to chargeable lifetime transfers

The rates of IHT applicable to chargeable lifetime transfers made during tax year 2017-18 are as follows:

Gross chargeable lifetime transfers for the seven years to date	*Rate of tax*	*Grossing-up fraction*
first £325,000 ("nil-rate band")	0%	nil
remainder after the first £325,000	20%	100/80

The rates of tax have been 0% and 20% for many years but the threshold beyond which 20% tax is payable is normally increased in each tax year, so increasing the width of the nil-rate band. However, this threshold has been frozen at £325,000† since 6 April 2009. Recent values of the IHT threshold have been:

Date of transfer	£
6 April 2006 to 5 April 2007	285,000
6 April 2007 to 5 April 2008	300,000
6 April 2008 to 5 April 2009	312,000
6 April 2009 to 5 April 2018	325,000

† *Finance (No. 2) Act 2015 provides that the IHT nil-rate band should remain at £325,000 until the end of tax year 2020-21. However, this provision could be overturned by subsequent legislation.*

For each transfer, the calculation of the tax due involves the following steps:

(a) The total gross value of previous chargeable lifetime transfers made during the seven years to date is brought forward.

(b) If the total brought forward has utilised the whole of the nil-rate band, tax is due at 20% on the gross value of the current transfer.

(c) If the total brought forward has not utilised the whole of the nil-rate band, the balance of that band is set against the current transfer. If this does not absorb the whole of the transfer, tax is due at 20% on the gross value of the remainder.

EXAMPLE 3

On 1 July 2017, Violet makes a chargeable lifetime transfer (after deduction of relevant exemptions) of £48,000. Her only previous chargeable lifetime transfer was made in 2013 and had a gross value (after exemptions) of £283,000. Calculate the IHT due if:

(a) the transferee agrees to pay the tax due

(b) the tax due is paid by Violet.

Solution

The total of transfers in the previous seven years is £283,000, leaving £42,000 of the nil-rate band to set against the current transfer.

(a) If the transferee pays the tax, the gross value of the transfer is £48,000 and the IHT due is £42,000 @ 0% + £6,000 @ 20% = £1,200. The total of gross transfers for the seven years to 1 July 2017 is £331,000 (£283,000 + £48,000).

(b) If Violet pays the tax, the net value of the transfer is £48,000. The gross value and the tax due are calculated as follows:

	Net	*Gross*	*Tax*
	£	£	£
£42,000 grossed up @ 0%	42,000	42,000	0
£6,000 grossed up @ 20%	6,000	7,500	1,500
Totals	48,000	49,500	1,500

The gross value of the transfer is £49,500 and the tax due is £1,500. The total of gross transfers for the seven years to 1 July 2017 is £332,500 (£283,000 + £49,500).

IHT payable on death

The IHT payable on death consists of:

(a) additional tax on any chargeable lifetime transfers made by the deceased person during the seven years ending on the date of death

(b) tax on any PETs made by the deceased person during those seven years

(c) tax on the estate of the deceased person as at the date of death, to the extent that the transfers made on death are not exempt from IHT.

Tax on chargeable lifetime transfers and PETs

The tax payable on death in respect of the chargeable lifetime transfers and PETs made in the seven years ending on the date of death is calculated as follows:

(a) The transfers are considered in chronological order with no distinction made between chargeable lifetime transfers and PETs.

(b) Tax is calculated on the gross value of each transfer using the IHT bands and rates in force *on the date of death* and taking into account any other chargeable transfers made *in the seven years ending on the date of the transfer* (including any PETs that have now become chargeable). Applicable rates of tax for deaths in 2017-18 are:

Gross chargeable transfers for the seven years to date	*Rate of tax*
first £325,000 ("nil-rate band")	0%
remainder after the first £325,000	40%

Note that the nil-rate band available on death in relation to a deceased person may be increased by a transfer of unused nil-rate band from a previously deceased spouse or civil partner (see later in this chapter).

(c) The tax calculated at (b) for each transfer may then be reduced by *taper relief*, depending upon the number of years which have elapsed between the date of the transfer and the date of death. Taper relief is given as follows:

Period between transfer and death	*Percentage tax reduction*
3 years or less	0%
Over 3 but not more than 4 years	20%
Over 4 but not more than 5 years	40%
Over 5 but not more than 6 years	60%
Over 6 but not more than 7 years	80%

(d) Finally, for each transfer, any tax paid during the lifetime of the transferor is subtracted, leaving a balance of tax due on that transfer. This tax liability is usually the responsibility of the transferee. No repayment is given if the lifetime tax paid in relation to a transfer exceeds the liability on death.

EXAMPLE 4

Wilson dies on 20 December 2017, having made only the following transfers during his lifetime:

		£
6 June 2007	Gift to daughter	50,000
4 March 2011	Gift to relevant property trust	516,400
11 January 2012	Gift to son on marriage	50,000

Calculate the IHT payable during Wilson's lifetime (if any) in relation to each of the above transfers, assuming that Wilson paid this tax himself. Also calculate any further IHT payable in relation to these transfers on Wilson's death.

Solution

The value of each gift after deduction of exemptions is as follows:

		Value before AE	*AE for current year*	*AE for previous year*	*Value after AE*
		£	£	£	£
2007-08	Daughter	50,000	3,000	3,000	44,000
2010-11	Relevant property trust	516,400	3,000	3,000	510,400
2011-12	Son (£50,000 – £5,000)	45,000	3,000	-	42,000

Lifetime tax liability

The gifts to Wilson's son and daughter were PETs and gave rise to no immediate tax liability but the gift to the trust was a chargeable lifetime transfer. There were no other such transfers during the seven years to date so the whole of the nil-rate band (£325,000 at that time) was set against the gift. The tax due was £46,350, calculated as follows:

	Net	*Gross*	*Tax*
	£	£	£
£325,000 grossed up @ 0%	325,000	325,000	0
£185,400 grossed up @ 20%	185,400	231,750	46,350
Totals	510,400	556,750	46,350

Tax liability on death

The June 2007 PET is more than seven years old at the time of Wilson's death. This PET is exempt from tax and can be completely ignored for IHT purposes. The tax due on the other two transfers is calculated as follows:

(i) *Transfer made on 4 March 2011*

The gross value of this transfer is £556,750 and there were no other chargeable transfers in the seven years to date (5 March 2004 to 4 March 2011). The tax due at the death rates applicable on 20 December 2017 is:

	£
£325,000 @ 0%	0
£231,750 @ 40%	92,700
	92,700
Less: Taper relief (6-7 years) @ 80%	74,160
	18,540

The lifetime tax paid on the transfer (£46,350) exceeds the tax liability calculated on death (£18,540). Therefore there is no further tax to pay on Wilson's death in relation to this transfer. However, there is no repayment of the excess of £27,810.

(ii) *Transfer made on 11 January 2012*

The gross value of this transfer is £42,000. Previous gross chargeable transfers in the seven years to date (12 January 2005 to 11 January 2012) were £556,750, completely absorbing the nil-rate band. Therefore the tax liability on death is:

	£
£42,000 @ 40%	16,800
Less: Taper relief (5-6 years) @ 60%	10,080
	6,720
Less: Lifetime tax paid	0
IHT payable by Wilson's son	6,720

Tax on the deceased person's estate

IHT on the deceased person's estate (to the extent that the transfers made on death are not exempt from IHT) is calculated using the rates of tax applicable on death. The calculation normally proceeds as follows:

(a) First, the nil-rate band is reduced by the total of gross chargeable transfers (including any PETs) made in the seven years ending on the date of death. Note that a deceased person's nil-rate band may be higher than usual because of a transfer of unused nil-rate band from a previously deceased spouse or civil partner (see below).

(b) The remainder of the nil-rate band (if any) is then set against the value of the estate and tax at 40% is calculated on the balance.

(c) The tax due is divided by the value of the estate and the result (expressed as a percentage) is the "estate rate" i.e. the average rate of tax borne by the estate.

However, a lower rate of IHT (36%) applies to an estate if at least 10% of the estate is left to charity. The figure to which the 10% test is applied is the value of the net estate after deducting all IHT exemptions, reliefs and any available nil-rate band, but adding back the amount left to charity. Note that the 36% rate does not apply when calculating the tax charge arising on death in relation to transfers made in the previous seven years.

EXAMPLE 5

Toby dies on 2 March 2018, leaving an estate valued at £400,000. None of the transfers made on death are exempt from IHT. Calculate the IHT due on the estate if the total of the gross chargeable transfers made by Toby in the seven years up to his death was:

(a) Nil (b) £125,000 (c) £370,000.

Solution

(a) £325,000 @ 0% + £75,000 @ 40% = £30,000. (Estate rate 7.5%)

(b) £200,000 @ 0% + £200,000 @ 40% = £80,000. (Estate rate 20%)

(c) £400,000 @ 40% = £160,000. (Estate rate 40%).

EXAMPLE 6

Rose dies on 10 July 2017, leaving an estate valued at £525,000. None of the transfers made on death are exempt from IHT apart from a bequest to the RSPCA (a charity). Rose made no chargeable transfers in the seven years prior to her death. Calculate the IHT due on the estate if the amount of the bequest to the RSPCA was:

(a) £10,000 (b) £30,000.

Solution

(a) The gift to charity is an exempt transfer and the nil-rate band is available in full, so IHT is due on £190,000 (£525,000 – £10,000 – £325,000). The total of this amount and the gift to charity is £200,000 and the gift is only 5% of this total. Therefore the lower rate does not apply and IHT due is £76,000 (£190,000 @ 40%).

(b) IHT is due on £170,000 (£525,000 – £30,000 – £325,000). The total of this amount and the gift to charity is £200,000 and the gift is 15% of this total. This is not less than 10% so the lower rate applies and IHT due is £61,200 (£170,000 @ 36%).

Transfer of unused part of nil-rate band

If one party to a marriage or a civil partnership dies and the amount that is chargeable to IHT on his or her death (including any transfers made in the previous seven years) does not use up all of the nil-rate band, the unused part of the nil-rate band may be transferred to the surviving spouse or civil partner for use on his or her death. Note that:

(a) The transferred part of the nil-rate band may be used only when the surviving spouse or civil partner dies. It is used when calculating any tax due on death in relation to transfers made in the seven years before the survivor dies and when calculating the tax due on the survivor's estate. It *cannot* be used to reduce the *lifetime* tax payable on any chargeable lifetime transfers made by the survivor.

(b) The amount available for transfer is calculated by determining the proportion of the nil-rate band which was unused when the survivor's spouse or civil partner died. This proportion is then applied to the amount of the nil-rate band which is in force on the date of the survivor's death.

EXAMPLE 7

Harriet died on 21 October 2017. Her husband had died previously and his estate on death (including transfers made in the last seven years of his life) had absorbed £177,840 of the nil-rate band at that time. Calculate the nil-rate band which is available when calculating the IHT due on Harriet's death, assuming that her husband died in:

(a) May 2006 (b) July 2008.

Solution

(a) When Harriet's husband died, the nil-rate band was £285,000. His estate absorbed £177,840 of this, leaving £107,160 (37.6% of the nil-rate band) unused. Therefore Harriet's nil-rate band on death is £325,000 + 37.6% of £325,000 = £447,200.

(b) When Harriet's husband died, the nil-rate band was £312,000. His estate absorbed £177,840 of this, leaving £134,160 (43% of the nil-rate band) unused. Therefore Harriet's nil-rate band on death is £325,000 + 43% of £325,000 = £464,750.

Main residence nil-rate band (from 6 April 2017)

As from 6 April 2017, an additional "main residence nil-rate band" (MRNRB) is available in relation to estates which include a residential property that has been the deceased person's main residence at some time, as long as the property is "closely inherited". In general terms, this means that the property has been left to the deceased person's direct descendants (children, grandchildren etc.). The MRNRB is taken into account only when calculating the IHT payable on the estate. It is *not* available when calculating any tax payable in relation to transfers made in the seven years before death.

The amount of the MRNRB is normally equal to the *lower* of the value of the property (net of mortgage debt) and the "maximum amount", which is being phased in as follows:

2017-18	£100,000	*2018-19*	£125,000
2019-20	£150,000	*2020-21*	£175,000

However, the maximum amount is increased if the deceased person's spouse or civil partner died previously and had unused MRNRB (see below). Furthermore, the maximum amount is reduced by £1 for every £2 by which the value of the deceased person's estate (before reliefs and exemptions) exceeds £2 million: Note that:

(a) Any unused proportion of the MRNRB is transferred to a surviving spouse or civil partner in the same way as the normal nil-rate band. A person will have unused MRNRB if he or she dies not owning a residence, or owns a residence but does not leave it to direct descendants, or leaves a residence to direct descendants with a value of less than the maximum amount.

(b) If entitlement to the MRNRB might be wholly or partly lost because the deceased person downsizes to a less valuable residence before death (or ceases to own a residence at all), any part of the MRNRB which would otherwise be lost is still available if assets of an equivalent value are left to direct descendants.

EXAMPLE 8

Desmond died on 18 July 2017, having made no transfers in the previous seven years. He left his entire estate to his wife Emily, including the family home valued at £420,000. Emily died on 9 May 2018, having made no transfers in the previous seven years. She left her entire estate to her daughter, including the family home valued at £430,000. Calculate the total nil-rate band available in relation to Emily's estate, assuming that neither her estate nor her husband's had a value in excess of £2 million.

Solution

(a) Desmond's estate was exempt from IHT (spouse exemption) so 100% of his nil-rate band was unused and Emily's nil-rate band is increased by 100% to £650,000.

(b) Desmond did not leave a main residence to his direct descendants, so 100% of his MRNRB was also unused. By the time of Emily's death, the maximum MRNRB had increased to £125,000. So Emily's MRNRB is increased by 100% to £250,000.

(c) The total nil-rate band available in relation to Emily's estate is therefore £900,000.

Quick succession relief

Quick succession relief (QSR) is available when property which is transferred on death was transferred to the deceased person within the previous five years and was charged to IHT at that time. The tax (if any) payable in relation to the transfer made on death is reduced by an amount which depends upon the gross value of the earlier transfer (G) and the amount of IHT paid on that transfer (T). The relief is calculated as:

$$\frac{G - T}{G} \times T \times QSR\%$$

The QSR percentage depends upon the length of the period between the earlier transfer and the date of death, as follows:

1 year or less	100%
Over 1 but not more than 2 years	80%
Over 2 but not more than 3 years	60%
Over 3 but not more than 4 years	40%
Over 4 but not more than 5 years	20%

Gifts with reservation

A "gift with reservation" is a gift of any property made in such a way that either:

(a) possession and enjoyment of the property is not *bona fide* assumed by the recipient of the gift at or before the start of the "relevant period", or

(b) the property is not enjoyed to the entire exclusion of the donor throughout the whole of the relevant period.

For this purpose, the "relevant period" is the period which ends on the date of the donor's death and which begins seven years before that date or (if later) on the date of the gift.

If there were no special rules relating to gifts with reservation, taxpayers would be able to divest themselves of property (so reducing the IHT charge on death) whilst continuing to benefit from that property. This is prevented by legislation which ensures that:

(a) property which is subject to a reservation at the date of the donor's death is treated as part of the donor's estate, and

(b) if any property ceases to be subject to a reservation before the donor's death, the donor is treated as having made a PET on the date that the reservation ceases to exist.

These rules are supplemented by regulations which deal with the possibility of a double tax charge arising if the gift is also a chargeable transfer.

Valuation

As stated at the beginning of this chapter, the value of a transfer for IHT purposes is equal to the reduction in value of the transferor's estate as a result of that transfer. In general, this is equivalent to the open market value of the transferred assets but this will not always be the case. For instance, if the transferor disposes of a small number of shares in a company, sufficient to convert a majority shareholding into a minority shareholding, it is likely that the true reduction in value of the transferor's estate will exceed the market value of the transferred assets. This aside, determining the market value of the transferred assets may in itself cause difficulty and special valuation rules are sometimes required.

Listed shares

For IHT purposes. shares which are listed on a recognised stock exchange (referred to as "listed shares" or "quoted shares") are valued at the *lower* of:

(a) the lower of the two prices quoted for those shares on the day of the transfer, plus one-quarter of the difference between these two prices (the "quarter-up" rule)

(b) the average of the highest and lowest prices at which bargains relating to those shares (if any) were recorded on the day of the transfer.

If listed shares are transferred on a non-working day (for which prices are unavailable) the shares are valued as if transferred on the last working day before the date of the transfer or the first working day after it, whichever gives the lower figure.

EXAMPLE 9

On 1 June 2017, Shirley gives 5,000 shares in a listed company to her daughter. Shares in the company are quoted at 189p - 197p on that date, with recorded bargains at 190p, 192p and 196p. Calculate the market value of the shares for IHT purposes.

Solution

The quarter-up rule gives 189p + 1/4 x (197p – 189p) = 191p. The average of the highest and lowest recorded bargains is 193p, so the shares are valued at 191p and the transfer has a market value of 5,000 x £1.91 = £9,550.

Related property

When calculating the value of a transfer for IHT purposes, the existence of any "related property" may be taken into account. Related property consists of property which:

(a) is owned by the transferor's spouse or civil partner, or

(b) is owned (or has been owned within the previous five years) by a charity, political party etc. as a result of an exempt transfer made either by the transferor or by his or her spouse or civil partner.

Under the related property rules, the property being transferred and the related property are valued together (as a whole) and then part of that value is apportioned to the property being transferred. These rules are intended to prevent taxpayers from avoiding IHT by fragmenting the ownership of an asset and will only be used if the valuation given by the related property rules is greater than the valuation that would be calculated normally.

EXAMPLE 10

Roy owns 3,500 ordinary shares in an unlisted company which has an issued share capital of 10,000 ordinary shares. Roy's wife owns a further 1,600 shares. Shareholdings in the company are valued as follows:

	£		£		£
500 shares	5,000	3,000 shares	33,000	3,500 shares	43,750
4,600 shares	64,400	5,100 shares	96,900		

Roy now transfers 500 of his shares to a relevant property trust. Calculate the value of this transfer for IHT purposes.

Solution

Ignoring related property, Roy's estate has reduced in value by £10,750 (£43,750 – £33,000) and this would normally be the value of the transfer. But taking related property into account, the value of the transfer is calculated as follows:

	£
Value of Roy's holding before the transfer (£96,900 x 3,500/5,100)	66,500
Value of Roy's holding after the transfer (£64,400 x 3,000/4,600)	42,000
Value of the transfer	24,500

Since £24,500 exceeds £10,750, the value of the transfer is £24,500.

Overseas property

Property situated outside the UK is valued in the appropriate foreign currency. This value is then converted into sterling, using the exchange rate for the day of the transfer which gives the lowest sterling value.

Business property relief

Business property relief of either 100% or 50% is available in relation to a transfer (made in the transferor's lifetime or on death) which meets *all* of the following conditions:

(a) the property transferred consists of "relevant business property"

(b) the business is a "qualifying business" (investment businesses do not qualify)

(c) the property has been owned by the transferor for at least two years, or has replaced other relevant business property, such that the combined period of ownership of both the original and replacement property is at least two years out of the five years preceding the date of the transfer.

The main categories of relevant business property, together with the applicable rates of relief, are as follows:

		Rate of relief
(a)	Property consisting of a business or an interest in a business	100%
(b)	Securities in an unlisted company which gave the transferor control of the company immediately before the transfer	100%
(c)	Shares in an unlisted company	100%
(d)	Shares transferred from a controlling holding in a listed company	50%
(e)	Land, buildings, plant and machinery which, immediately before the transfer, were used for business purposes by a partnership in which the transferor was a partner or by a company of which he/she had control	50%

(f)	Land, buildings, plant and machinery which, immediately before the transfer, were used in the transferor's business and owned by a trust of which the transferor was a life tenant.	50%

No relief is given in relation to "excepted assets". These are assets which have not been used for business purposes throughout the two years prior to the transfer and which are not required for the future use of the business.

Agricultural property relief

Agricultural property relief of either 100% or 50% is available in relation to a transfer of agricultural property (in life or on death) so long as that property has been either:

(a) occupied by the transferor and used for agricultural purposes throughout the two years preceding the transfer, or

(b) owned by the transferor throughout the seven years preceding the transfer and occupied by the transferor or someone else for agricultural purposes throughout those seven years.

For this purpose, agricultural property consists mainly of agricultural land and pasture, woodlands and associated buildings. Land managed according to the terms of certain wildlife habitat schemes (together with associated buildings) is also eligible for agricultural property relief. The rates of relief are:

(a) 100% if, immediately before the transfer, the transferor enjoys vacant possession of the property or the right to obtain it within the following 12 months

(b) Otherwise, 100% if the property is let on a tenancy starting after 31 August 1995 and 50% if the property is let on a tenancy starting before 1 September 1995.

These rates apply only to the "agricultural value" of the property. This is the value that the property would have if it could only ever be used for agricultural purposes. If a property qualifies for both business property relief and agricultural property relief, agricultural property relief is given first.

Administration of IHT

Inheritance tax is administered by HMRC. For chargeable lifetime transfers and transfers caused by the death of the transferor, an "account" must be delivered to HMRC, giving details of the transfers made and their value. Details of this procedure are as follows:

(a) **Chargeable lifetime transfers**. The transferor must deliver an account to HMRC within 12 months of the end of the month in which the transfer occurred. There is no need to deliver an account if the transfer is exempt or potentially exempt, or if:

  (i) for chargeable lifetime transfers consisting wholly of cash or quoted stocks and securities, the total of all chargeable transfers made in the seven years to date does not exceed the IHT threshold

  (ii) for chargeable lifetime transfers not consisting wholly of cash or quoted stocks and securities, the total of all chargeable transfers made in the seven years to date does not exceed 80% of the IHT threshold.

(b) **Death**. The personal representatives of a deceased person must deliver an account to HMRC within 12 months of the end of the month in which the death occurred. But there is no need to deliver an account if the person was UK-domiciled and:

  (i) the gross value of the estate, plus transfers made during the seven years prior to death, does not exceed the IHT threshold (or double this threshold if 100% of the nil-rate band was transferred to the deceased person on the prior death of a spouse or civil partner), and

  (ii) no more than £100,000 of the estate is situated outside the UK, and

  (iii) any trust assets included in the estate of the deceased person are held in a single trust and do not exceed £150,000 in value, and

  (iv) there have been no chargeable lifetime transfers or PETs made within the seven years to date, other than transfers consisting of cash, listed securities or land and buildings (and contents) with a total gross value not exceeding £150,000.

  If the deceased person was not UK-domiciled (and never had been) an account is not required so long as the value of UK assets transferred on death does not exceed £150,000 and these assets consist solely of cash, listed shares or listed securities.

When a transfer gives rise to an IHT liability, the HMRC Capital Taxes Office issues a notice showing the value of the transfer for IHT purposes and the amount of tax payable. Appeals may be lodged within 30 days of the date of the notice.

Payment of IHT

The IHT relating to a transfer is usually payable six months after the end of the month in which the transfer (or the death) occurred. However, the tax on chargeable lifetime transfers made in roughly the first half of the tax year (6 April to 30 September) is not payable until 30 April in the following tax year.

It is notable that the tax on a transfer is usually due for payment before the end of the 12-month period within which an account of the transfer must be delivered to HMRC. Since interest is charged on tax paid late, there is an incentive to deliver the account (and pay the tax due) on or before the due date of payment.

Summary

- The main occasion on which IHT is charged is when a transfer of value of chargeable property is made by a chargeable person. A transfer may be a lifetime transfer or a transfer made on death.
- The value of a transfer is equal to the reduction in value of the transferor's estate as a result of the transfer. The value of a transfer for IHT purposes may be reduced by business property relief and/or agricultural property relief.
- Transfers made to certain transferees (e.g. spouses, civil partners, charities and political parties) are exempt from IHT.
- Lifetime transfers comprising small gifts, gifts made out of income and gifts made on marriage or civil partnership are wholly or partly exempt from IHT. The first £3,000 of lifetime transfers made in any tax year is exempt from IHT.
- A potentially exempt transfer (PET) is not chargeable to IHT unless the transferor dies within seven years. A chargeable lifetime transfer may be charged to IHT when the transfer is made (depending upon the total of the transfers made in the previous seven years) and may attract additional tax when the transferor dies.
- The amount of IHT charged on the estate of a deceased person depends upon the size of the estate and the total of any chargeable transfers made in the seven years before the person's death.
- The IHT on a transfer is normally payable six months after the end of the month in which the transfer takes place.

Exercises

31.1 Phoebe made the following transfers during 2017-18:

		£
12 April 2017	Gift to grandson	50
17 May 2017	Gift to her nephew on his marriage	3,000
3 August 2017	Gift to her husband	25,000
31 October 2017	Gift to a relevant property trust	10,000
1 January 2018	Gift to the Labour Party	5,000

None of the gifts are regarded as normal expenditure out of income. Phoebe made no transfers at all during 2016-17. Calculate the value of each of her 2017-18 transfers after deduction of all the available exemptions.

31.2 Classify each of the following lifetime transfers as either exempt, potentially exempt, or chargeable:

(a) a gift to the transferor's favourite charity

(b) a gift to a relevant property trust

(c) a gift to the transferor's grandfather.

31.3 On 5 December 2017, Nicholas makes a gift of £80,000 (after deduction of all relevant exemptions) to a relevant property trust. His only previous chargeable lifetime transfers were in June 2008 (gross chargeable value £200,000) and July 2012 (gross chargeable value £281,000). Calculate the lifetime IHT payable in relation to the £80,000 gift and state the due date of payment:

(a) if the trustees pay the tax (b) if Nicholas pays the tax.

31.4 On 31 March 2011, Martha gave £500,000 to her daughter as a wedding present. On 1 April 2012 she gave £497,000 to a relevant property trust. Martha died on 1 January 2018, having made only these two transfers during her life.

(a) Calculate any lifetime tax due on each of the above transfers and state the due date of payment, assuming that Martha paid this tax herself.

(b) Calculate any further tax due on Martha's death in relation to these transfers and state the due date of payment. (Assume that there is no unused nil-rate band to be transferred from a previously deceased spouse or civil partner).

31.5 On 29 September 2017, Hyacinth makes a transfer consisting of 1,000 shares in a listed company. The shares are quoted at 572p - 588p on that date, with recorded bargains at 572p, 577p and 578p. Calculate the market value of the transfer for IHT purposes.

***31.6** On 12 November 2007, Hazel made a gross chargeable transfer to a relevant property trust of £266,000 (after deduction of exemptions). On 1 April 2013 she gave £300,000 to her grandson. These were her only transfers. She died on 17 December 2017.

Calculate the tax payable by her grandson as a result of Hazel's death. (Assume that there is no unused nil-rate band to be transferred from a previously deceased spouse or civil partner).

***31.7** Tony died on 11 July 2017, leaving an estate valued at £900,000. None of the transfers made on his death were exempt from IHT. He had made the following transfers during his lifetime:

		£
3 May 2009	Gift to relevant property trust (tax paid by trustees)	113,000
1 July 2010	Gift to daughter	185,000
1 August 2010	Gift to son	250,000
10 November 2011	Gift to relevant property trust (tax paid by Tony)	447,000

Calculate the tax payable as a result of Tony's death. (Assume that there is no unused nil-rate band to be transferred from a previously deceased spouse or civil partner and that Tony's residence was not left to a direct descendant).

Chapter 32
Overseas aspects of taxation

Introduction

The main purpose of this final chapter is to consider the way in which the UK tax system deals with the overseas income and gains of UK resident individuals and companies. The treatment of non-resident individuals and companies with income or gains arising in the UK is also briefly considered.

The chapter begins by explaining the factors which affect an individual's UK tax status and then continues with a brief review of the overseas aspects of income tax, capital gains tax and inheritance tax. Overseas aspects of corporation tax are dealt with towards the end of the chapter.

Residence and domicile

The extent to which an individual is chargeable to UK tax depends upon that individual's *residence* and *domicile*. These key concepts are explained below.

Note that an individual's *nationality* is usually not an important factor when determining that individual's UK tax status.

Residence

A statutory definition of the term "residence" was introduced in Finance Act 2013 and took effect as from 6 April 2013. The rules which determine whether or not an individual is UK resident are complex and require over 60 pages of detailed legislation. However, a summary of the main rules is as follows:

(a) An individual is UK resident for a tax year if he or she meets either the "automatic residence test" or the "sufficient ties test" for that tax year. If neither test is satisfied the individual is not UK resident for the year.

(b) The automatic residence test is met if the individual meets any of the "automatic UK tests" and does not meet any of the "automatic overseas tests".

(c) The most important automatic UK tests are as follows:

UK Test 1: the individual spends at least 183 days in the UK during the tax year

UK Test 2:

(i) the individual has a home in the UK during all or part of the tax year, *and*

(ii) spends at least 30 days in that UK home during the year, *and*

(iii) there is a period of at least 91 consecutive days (at least 30 of which fall within the tax year) in which the individual has that UK home and *either* has no home overseas *or* has one or more homes overseas but spends no more than 30 days in any of them during the tax year.

UK Test 3:

(i) the individual works full-time in the UK for a period of 365 days, *and*

(ii) all or part of that period falls within the tax year, *and*

(iii) more than 75% of the days in the 365-day period on which the individual does more than three hours of work are days on which he or she does more than three hours of work in the UK, *and*

(iv) there is at least one day in the tax year in which the individual does more than three hours of work in the UK.

(d) The most important automatic overseas tests are as follows:

Overseas Test 1:

(i) the individual was UK resident for one or more of the previous three tax years,

(ii) *but* spends less than 16 days in the UK during the tax year.

Overseas Test 2:

(i) the individual was UK resident for none of the previous three tax years, *and*

(ii) spends less than 46 days in the UK during the tax year.

Overseas Test 3:

(i) the individual works full-time overseas during the tax year, *and*

(ii) there are less than 31 days in the tax year on which the individual works for more than three hours in the UK, *and*

(iii) the individual spends less than 91 days in the UK during the tax year.

(e) The sufficient ties test examines ties to the UK under various headings (e.g. family ties) and determines the individual's residence status by counting the number of such ties. The test also takes into account the number of days spent in the UK during the tax year and the individual's residence status for the previous three years.

It is important to appreciate that the concept of UK residence normally applies to *whole* tax years and it is not usually possible to apportion a tax year into periods of residence and non-residence. However, such apportionment (or "split-year treatment") is permitted in certain cases. These include:

(a) *the year of departure*, if an individual who was UK resident for the previous tax year leaves the UK in order to work full-time overseas (and will be non-UK resident in the following tax year because he or she will meet the third automatic overseas test)

(b) *the year of departure*, if an individual who was UK resident for the previous tax year (and will be non-UK resident in the following tax year) leaves the UK to live abroad, so long as he or she had a home in the UK at the start of the tax year but ceases to have a home in the UK by the end of the tax year

(c) *the year of arrival*, if an individual who was not UK resident in the previous tax year comes to live or work full-time in the UK (subject to conditions).

If a tax year is apportioned into periods of residence and non-residence, any personal allowances to which the individual is entitled are available in full for that year.

EXAMPLE 1

Peter has had a home in the UK for many years and has always been UK resident. He has worked in the UK throughout his adult life but he retired in December 2016.

During tax year 2017-18 he takes a long round-the-world holiday. He maintains his UK home and does not establish a home overseas, but he is present in the UK for only 43 days during the tax year. Is he UK resident for tax year 2017-18?

Solution

Peter does not meet either the first or the third automatic UK test. However, he does meet the second automatic UK test and he does not meet any of the automatic overseas tests. Therefore he meets the automatic residence test and is UK resident for tax year 2017-18.

Domicile

An individual's domicile† is the country in which the individual has his or her permanent home. It is not possible to have more than one domicile at a time.

Individuals acquire a "domicile of origin" on birth. This is usually the domicile of the father or other person on whom the individual is dependent and is not necessarily the country of birth. Having reached the age of 16, an individual may then acquire a "domicile of choice", but such a domicile can only be acquired by settling in the chosen country.

If an individual acquires a domicile of choice, that domicile is also acquired by anyone under the age of 16 who is dependent on that individual. A domicile acquired in this way is known as a "domicile of dependency".

† *The Government has proposed that, as from 6 April 2017, individuals who have been resident in the UK for at least 15 of the past 20 years should be deemed domiciled in the UK for all tax purposes. Such individuals would no longer be "non-doms" and would no longer be able to use the remittance basis (see below). Also as from 6 April 2017, individuals born in the UK to UK-domiciled parents would no longer be able to claim "non-dom" status whilst resident in the UK.*

Income tax - general rules

The general rules governing an individual's liability to UK income tax are as follows:

(a) Individuals who are *resident* in the UK for a tax year are liable to pay UK income tax on all of their income for that year, including any overseas income. Note that:

   (i) Overseas employment income is taxed in accordance with the rules of ITEPA 2003 (see later in this chapter). Overseas trading income, property income and investment income are taxed by ITTOIA 2005.

   (ii) ITTOIA 2005 provides that the "relevant foreign income" of a UK resident who is not domiciled in the UK may be taxed only to the extent that the income is remitted to the UK (the "remittance basis"). The term "relevant foreign income" covers most of the forms of overseas income to which ITTOIA 2005 applies.

   In general, an individual who wishes that the remittance basis should apply for a tax year must make a claim to that effect. However, the remittance basis is automatically assumed to apply to an individual whose unremitted income and gains are less than £2,000 in the year concerned (unless the individual notifies HMRC that he/she does not wish the remittance basis to apply).

   (iii) Individuals who claim the remittance basis and have been UK resident for at least seven of the previous nine tax years are liable to an annual tax charge of £30,000. This increases to £60,000 for those who have been resident in the UK for at least 12 of the previous 14 years and to £90,000 for those who have been resident in the UK for at least 17 of the previous 20 years. Since this rule applies only to those who *claim* the remittance basis, it does not apply to individuals whose unremitted income and gains are less than £2,000 for the tax year.

   (iv) Personal allowances are generally available to UK residents. But individuals who claim the remittance basis are not entitled to personal allowances. Again, this rule applies only to those who *claim* the remittance basis.

   (v) Individuals who are taxed on the remittance basis may remit overseas income to the UK without incurring an income tax liability if this income is used to make a commercial investment in a qualifying business ("business investment relief").

(b) Individuals who are *not resident* in the UK are liable to pay UK income tax on their UK income only. Note that:

   (i) The UK property income of non-residents is usually payable after deduction of basic rate income tax by the letting agent or tenant.

   (ii) Personal allowances may be claimed by certain non-residents, principally those who are citizens of the European Economic Area (see Chapter 3).

(c) If a tax year is apportioned into periods of residence and non-residence, the above rules apply to the two periods as if they were separate tax years.

These general rules are subject to a number of exceptions, depending upon the type of income involved (see below).

Unremittable income

A UK resident who would normally be liable to income tax on income arising from an overseas source may make a claim to the effect that the income is "unremittable". Such a claim may be made if the income cannot be remitted to the UK because of:

(a) the laws of the country in which the income arises, or

(b) the executive actions of the government of that country, or

(c) the impossibility of obtaining foreign currency in that country which could be transferred to the UK.

The effect of the claim is that the income is not taxed in the year in which it arises but is taxed instead in the year in which it ceases to be unremittable (if that occurs).

Double taxation relief (DTR)

The rules given above are likely to lead to a number of situations in which income is taxed twice. For example, the overseas income of a UK resident will be taxed in the UK and might also be taxed in the country in which the income arises, depending upon that country's tax laws. Similarly, the UK income of a non-resident will be taxed in the UK and might also be taxed overseas. In order to avoid this situation, the UK has made "double taxation treaties" with many overseas countries. Typically, such a treaty might provide that certain forms of income should be exempt from income tax in the country of origin (or charged at a reduced rate) if receivable by a non-resident.

Unilateral double tax relief

Unless double tax relief is available (or prohibited) under the terms of a double taxation treaty with the country concerned, the UK tax system provides "unilateral double tax relief" for foreign tax suffered by a UK resident who receives overseas income. Overseas income which is received net of foreign tax is grossed-up and charged to UK income tax in the usual way, but the taxpayer is then given tax relief equal to the *lower* of:

(a) the amount of foreign tax suffered (the "withholding tax") and

(b) the amount of UK tax due on the overseas income.

The amount of UK tax due on the overseas income is equal to the difference between the tax due on the taxpayer's total income (including overseas income) and the tax which would be due if the overseas income were ignored. If the foreign tax suffered exceeds the UK tax due, part of the foreign tax suffered will be unrelieved.

Unilateral relief is available only if the taxpayer has taken all reasonable steps to minimise the amount of the foreign tax liability.

EXAMPLE 2

Vicky's income for 2017-18 consists of her UK salary of £45,270 and rents from overseas property (net of 30% withholding tax) of £3,500. Vicky is UK resident in 2017-18 and she is not a Scottish taxpayer. Calculate her UK income tax liability for the year.

Solution

Property income is £5,000 (£3,500 x 100/70). Therefore total income is £50,270 (£45,270 + £5,000) and taxable income is £38,770 (£50,270 – £11,500). The income tax liability is:

		£
33,500	@ 20%	6,700.00
5,270	@ 40%	2,108.00
38,770		8,808.00
Less:	Double tax relief, *lower* of:	
	(a) foreign tax (£1,500)	1,500.00
	(b) UK tax on foreign income (40% x £5,000) = £2,000	
UK income tax liability		7,308.00

Income from employment

Income from employment is taxed according to detailed rules contained in the Income Tax (Earnings and Pensions) Act 2003. Broadly, the extent to which an individual's income from employment is taxable depends upon the individual's residence status and whether the duties of the employment are performed in the UK or overseas. The rules are briefly summarised as follows:

(a) **Employee resident in UK**. Unless the remittance basis applies to the individual concerned (see below) the entire employment income of an individual who is UK resident is taxable on the receipts basis, regardless of whether the duties of the employment are performed in the UK or overseas.

(b) **Employee resident in UK (remittance basis)**. As explained earlier in this chapter, the remittance basis may apply to a UK resident individual who is not domiciled in the UK. If the remittance basis applies, then the extent to which employment income is taxable depends upon the individual's residence status in prior years. Broadly, the situation is as follows:

   (i) If the tax year concerned is one which immediately follows three consecutive tax years in which the individual was not UK resident, employment income that is classified as "foreign earnings" is taxed on the remittance basis. All other employment income is fully taxable (on the receipts basis). Foreign earnings are those which are in respect of duties performed wholly outside the UK.

(ii) Otherwise, employment income classified as "chargeable overseas earnings" is taxed on the remittance basis. All other employment income is fully taxable (on the receipts basis). Chargeable overseas earnings are those which are derived from a foreign employer in respect of duties performed wholly outside the UK.

(c) **Employee not resident in UK**. The employment income of an individual who is not resident in the UK is taxable (on the receipts basis) only to the extent that the income is in respect of duties performed in the UK.

Note that the income tax liability on any *foreign pensions* received by a UK resident is calculated on the full amount arising unless the remittance basis applies, in which case only the amount remitted to the UK is taxable.

Travelling and subsistence expenses

If the duties of an employment are performed abroad, the employee is resident in the UK and the earnings derived from the employment are not classed as "chargeable overseas earnings" (see above), then the following travel and subsistence expenses may be deducted from the employee's earnings for tax purposes:

(a) where duties are performed wholly abroad:

 (i) the costs of travelling abroad at the start of the employment and travelling back to the UK at the end of it

 (ii) the costs of overseas board and lodging provided or reimbursed by the employer to enable the employee to perform the duties of the overseas employment

(b) where duties are performed partly in the UK and partly abroad, travelling and subsistence expenses paid for or reimbursed by the employer (and assessable as earnings) relating to:

 (i) travel by the employee between the UK and the overseas place of work

 (ii) travel by the employee's spouse and minor children, if the employee is working abroad for a continuous period of 60 days or more, but limited to two return journeys per person per tax year.

Similar deductions to those described at (b) above are available to non-UK domiciled individuals who are working in the UK but these deductions are available for only five years, beginning with the date of arrival in the UK.

The 100% deduction for seafarers

If the duties of a *seafarer* who is resident in the UK are performed wholly or partly outside the UK throughout a continuous qualifying period of 365 days or more, a 100% deduction is given against all of the earnings for that period (including earnings relating to any work performed in the UK). In effect, the earnings attributable to such a qualifying period are exempt from UK income tax.

A qualifying period begins when an individual leaves the UK to work abroad as a seafarer and the period is treated as continuous even if the individual returns to the UK from time to time, so long as:

(a) no visit in the UK during the period lasts for more than 183 days, and

(b) on each day of return to the UK, the total number of days present in the UK since the period began is no more than one-half of the total length of the period so far.

The seafarers' earnings deduction (SED) is also available to seafarers who are not resident in the UK but who are resident in a state of the European Economic Area (see Chapter 3) other than the UK. Such seafarers are liable to UK income tax on duties performed in the UK (e.g. in the UK's territorial waters) but are now able to claim SED in relation to their earnings during a qualifying period.

Trading income

The extent to which the profits of a trade, profession or vocation are charged to UK income tax depends upon whether or not the owner of the business is UK resident and whether the business is carried on in the UK or overseas. The rules are as follows:

(a) Trading profits arising to a UK resident are charged to income tax wherever in the world the trade is carried on. Therefore UK residents are taxed on the profits of businesses which are carried on wholly or partly overseas.

(b) If a business is carried on wholly overseas, then income arising from that business ranks as "relevant foreign income" (see above). Therefore a UK resident who is not domiciled in the UK may claim that the income concerned should be taxed on the remittance basis.

(c) Trading losses arising from a business carried on wholly overseas may be carried forward in the usual way (see Chapter 12). Such losses are also eligible for terminal loss relief if incurred in the final year of trading. But "sideways relief" against total income is available only against overseas income which is not charged on the remittance basis and which consists of:

    (i) trading profits arising from a business which is carried on wholly overseas

    (ii) employment income ranking as "chargeable overseas earnings" (see above)

    (iii) overseas pensions.

(d) Trading profits arising to a non-UK resident are charged to income tax only if the trade is carried on wholly or partly in the UK or is a trade of dealing in UK land. In the case of a trade which is carried on only partly in the UK, the profits which are charged to income tax are the profits arising from the UK part of the trade.

Travelling and subsistence expenses

If a trade is carried on wholly overseas and the owner of the business is absent from the UK wholly and exclusively for business purposes, then the expenses listed below are allowable deductions when computing trading profits (so long as those profits are not taxed on the remittance basis):

(a) expenses incurred by the trader in travelling between the UK and the location of the overseas business

(b) overseas board and lodging expenses

(c) expenses relating to travel by the proprietor's spouse and minor children, if the proprietor is abroad for a continuous period of 60 days or more, but limited to two return journeys per person per tax year.

Income from property and investments

Income from property and income from savings and investments are charged to UK income tax according to the following rules:

(a) Income from property situated in the UK is taxable whether or not the person to whom the income arises is UK resident. Income from property situated overseas is taxable only if the person to whom the income arises is UK resident.

(b) Savings and investment income from a UK source is generally taxable whether or not the person to whom the income arises is UK resident. However, interest on UK Government securities is exempt from UK income tax if the recipient is not resident in the UK. Savings and investment income from an overseas source is taxable only if the person to whom the income arises is UK resident.

(c) Unless taxed on the remittance basis (see below), foreign savings income is eligible for the personal savings allowance and foreign dividends are eligible for the dividend allowance (see Chapter 2).

(d) Overseas property income and overseas savings and investment income generally rank as "relevant foreign income" (see above). Therefore a UK resident who is not domiciled in the UK may claim that these forms of income should be taxed on the remittance basis. However, overseas savings and investment income which is taxed on the remittance basis is taxed as if it were non-savings income and so cannot benefit from the starting rate for savings (0%), the savings nil rate, the dividend nil rate or the dividend lower, upper and additional rates (7.5%, 32.5% and 38.1%).

Capital gains tax - general rules

The general rules which govern an individual's liability to UK capital gains tax (CGT) are as follows:

(a) Individuals who are resident in the UK for a tax year are liable to CGT in relation to all disposals of chargeable assets which occur in that year, no matter where in the world the assets are situated. Double tax relief may be available.

(b) Individuals who are not UK resident are normally not liable to CGT at all, even in relation to disposals of assets situated in the UK†.

There are three main exceptions to these general rules:

(a) A non-UK domiciled individual who is resident in the UK is fully liable to CGT on the disposal of assets situated in the UK. However, gains arising from disposals of assets situated overseas may (in certain circumstances) be taxable only on the remittance basis. No annual exemption is available for a tax year in which an individual claims that the remittance basis should apply.

    Individuals who are taxed on the remittance basis may remit overseas gains to the UK without incurring a CGT liability if these gains are used to make a commercial investment in a qualifying business ("business investment relief").

(b) An individual who is not resident in the UK but who carries on a business in the UK is chargeable to CGT in relation to disposals of business assets situated in the UK.

(c) Individuals who acquire assets before temporarily leaving the UK (for up to five tax years) and then dispose of those assets whilst abroad remain chargeable to CGT in relation to these disposals. Gains arising in the tax year of departure are taxed in that year. Later gains are taxed in the year in which residence resumes.

A claim may be made to defer a CGT assessment relating to a disposal of overseas assets if it can be shown that the gain in question cannot be remitted to the UK. The conditions which must be satisfied in order that such a claim should be successful are the same as the equivalent conditions for income tax (see above). The taxpayer must show that the gain cannot be remitted to the UK because of either:

(a) the laws of the country in which the gain arises, or

(b) the executive actions of the government of that country, or

(c) the impossibility of obtaining foreign currency in that country.

If the conditions preventing remittance of the gain to the UK subsequently cease to exist, the gain is chargeable in the year in which this occurs.

† *As from 6 April 2015, gains made by non-residents on the disposal of UK residential property are charged to CGT. The amount of such a gain is generally calculated by comparing disposal value with the property's market value on 5 April 2015, but it is possible instead to time-apportion the gain arising over the entire period of ownership. Principal private residence relief is available if the property has been lived in at some time as the taxpayer's PPR.*

Inheritance tax - general rules

An individual who is domiciled in the UK is liable to inheritance tax (IHT) in relation to all of his or her chargeable property, wherever in the world that property is situated. An individual who is not domiciled in the UK is liable to IHT only in relation to property situated in the UK. The definition of "domicile" for IHT purposes is broader than the general definition given earlier in this chapter. An individual is treated as domiciled in the UK on the date of a transfer if that individual:

(a) was domiciled in the UK at any time within the previous three years, or

(b) was UK resident for at least 17 of the 20 tax years ending with the year in which the transfer takes place. *(As stated earlier, the Government has proposed that this should be changed to at least 15 of the last 20 years as from 6 April 2017).*

In general, transfers between spouses or civil partners are exempt from IHT. But transfers made by a UK-domiciled spouse/partner to a spouse/partner who is not domiciled in the UK are exempt only up to the amount of the nil-rate band (currently £325,000). As from 6 April 2013, a spouse or civil partner who is not domiciled in the UK may elect to be treated as domiciled in the UK for IHT purposes.

Corporation tax - general rules

A company's liability to UK corporation tax depends upon whether or not it is resident in the UK. A company is regarded as resident in the UK if it is incorporated in the UK or if its central management and control is situated in the UK. The general rules which govern a company's liability to UK corporation tax are as follows:

(a) A UK resident company is chargeable to UK corporation tax on all of its profits, no matter where in the world those profits are earned. Note the following points:

    (i) The profits of a trade conducted through a permanent establishment situated overseas (e.g. an overseas branch) are treated as trading income. Trading losses may be relieved as usual and group relief is generally available. But the losses of an overseas establishment may be surrendered only to the extent that those losses are not relievable in the overseas country.

    However, a company may now make an irrevocable election to the effect that the profits of *all* its overseas branches (including any chargeable gains) should be exempt from UK corporation tax. If this election is made, no relief will be available for foreign branch losses.

    (ii) Most foreign dividends received by UK companies are exempt from corporation tax (with certain exceptions) and are treated as if they were UK dividends.

    (iii) Gains arising on the disposal of overseas assets are generally chargeable gains and form part of the company's taxable profits.

(b) A non-UK resident company is chargeable to UK corporation tax if it carries on a trade through a UK permanent establishment or if it carries on a trade which deals in UK land. If a trade is carried on through a UK permanent establishment, the company is taxed on:

    (i) the trading profits of the UK establishment
    (ii) income from property in the possession of the UK establishment
    (iii) gains arising from the disposal of assets used by the UK establishment.

    The trading losses of a UK permanent establishment of a non-UK resident company may generally be set against any other profits of the establishment or may be carried forward against the establishment's future trading profits. As regards group relief:

    (i) An overseas company which is resident in the European Economic Area (EEA) may surrender the losses of a UK permanent establishment to UK resident group companies, so long as those losses are not relieved overseas. The establishment may also claim losses surrendered by UK resident group companies.
    (ii) An overseas company which is not resident in the EEA may surrender the losses of a UK permanent establishment to UK resident group companies only if those losses are not potentially relievable overseas (whether actually relieved or not).

    Assets transferred between a UK permanent establishment and a UK resident group company are transferred on a no-gain, no-loss basis, so long as the assets concerned remain within the charge to UK corporation tax.

Overseas subsidiaries

The profits of a non-UK resident subsidiary of a UK resident parent company may be subject to overseas tax but are not generally subject to UK tax unless the subsidiary is treated as a controlled foreign company (see later in this chapter). However, the UK resident parent company will be liable to corporation tax on any non-exempt income received from the overseas subsidiary (e.g. royalties) and the subsidiary does of course count as a "related 51% group company" (see Chapter 28).

As explained in Chapter 28, groups of companies enjoy a number of corporation tax reliefs, including (subject to certain conditions):

(a) transfer of trading losses and certain other items between group members
(b) transfer of chargeable assets between group members on a no-gain, no-loss basis.

These reliefs are generally available only to "UK related" companies (see Chapter 28) and do not usually apply to an overseas subsidiary. However, the losses of a subsidiary which is resident in the European Economic Area (EEA) or carries on a trade in the EEA may be surrendered to a UK company, but only after all possibilities of relief in any other country have been exhausted. In order to obtain relief against UK profits, the losses of the EEA subsidiary must be re-computed under UK tax rules.

Company migration

A UK resident company may wish to "migrate" overseas in order to escape paying UK corporation tax on its worldwide profits. This is only possible for companies which are incorporated outside the UK and involves moving the central management and control of the company from the UK to an overseas location. A company wishing to take this step must:

(a) notify HMRC of its intentions, specifying the date on which it intends to become non-resident, and

(b) provide HMRC with a statement of all the tax payable up to that date, specifying the arrangements which will be made to ensure that this tax is paid.

On the date that a company becomes non-resident it is deemed to make a disposal of all its assets at their market value on that date. This deemed disposal is likely to result in a sizeable chargeable gain, which is sometimes referred to as the "exit charge". However, this charge is not made in full in the following circumstances:

(a) If the company retains a permanent establishment in the UK, the deemed disposal does not include assets which are situated in the UK and which are used for trade purposes by that establishment.

(b) If the company is a 75% subsidiary of a UK resident company (termed the "principal company") the gains arising in connection with the deemed disposal of the company's *foreign* assets may be postponed, so long as both companies make an election in writing to that effect. The postponed gains will crystallise if:

    (i) within the following six years, any of the foreign assets are disposed of, or

    (ii) at any time, the company which is migrating ceases to be a 75% subsidiary of the principal company, or

    (iii) at any time, the principal company ceases to be UK resident.

    Any gains which crystallise are chargeable on the principal company.

Transfer pricing

A UK resident company might try to reduce its corporation tax liability by transferring goods or services at an artificially low price to an overseas subsidiary. This would have the effect of lowering the UK company's profits (which are liable to UK tax) and increasing the subsidiary's profits (which are not liable to UK tax).

However, this tax avoidance manoeuvre is blocked by "transfer pricing" legislation which requires that a true market price should be substituted for the transfer price in these circumstances and that the UK company should make the necessary adjustment when completing its self-assessment tax return (see Chapter 28). Small and medium-sized companies are generally exempt from the transfer pricing legislation.

Controlled foreign companies (CFCs)

A UK resident company which wishes to operate overseas may choose to do so through a separate non-UK resident company which is under its control (an overseas subsidiary).

Since the profits of a non-UK company are generally not chargeable to UK corporation tax, this would seem to be beneficial (especially if the operation is carried on in a country with low tax rates). Furthermore, any dividends paid by the overseas subsidiary to its UK parent would usually be tax-exempt. However, some of these tax advantages are lost if the overseas subsidiary ranks as a *controlled foreign company* (CFC).

As an anti-avoidance measure, the profits of a CFC are apportioned between its shareholders and profits that are attributed to a UK resident company are charged to corporation tax (the "CFC charge"). The main features of the CFC regime are as follows:

(a) A CFC is a company which is resident overseas but is under UK control. The CFC regime also applies to the overseas branches of a UK company which has elected that the profits of all its overseas branches should be exempt from UK corporation tax.

(b) No CFC charge arises if the CFC qualifies for one or more exemptions. The main exemptions (broadly) are:

   (i) **Exempt period**. The CFC regime does not apply to CFC accounting periods which end during the first 12 months in which a CFC is under UK control.

   (ii) **Excluded territories**. A CFC is exempt if it is resident in one of a number of excluded countries and satisfies certain other conditions.

   (iii) **Low profits**. A CFC is exempt if its accounting profits or its taxable total profits (calculated as if it were a UK company) do not exceed £50,000 or do not exceed £500,000, of which no more than £50,000 represents non-trading income.

   (iv) **Low profit margin**. A CFC is exempt if its accounting profits do not exceed 10% of its operating expenditure.

   (v) **Tax rate**. A CFC is exempt if it is subject to a level of overseas taxation which is equal to at least 75% of the corresponding UK tax (unless the CFC is resident in a country in which the local tax liability is determined under "designer rate" provisions which are intended to circumvent the CFC rules).

(c) If a UK company is required to pay a CFC charge in relation to its share of a CFC's taxable total profits, this charge is calculated at the average rate payable by the UK company for the accounting period in which the CFC's accounting period ends. But a UK company to which less than 25% of a CFC's profits are attributed is not required to pay a CFC charge at all.

The full CFC regime is extremely complex and involves many detailed rules. The basic aim of these rules is to ensure that the CFC charge applies only where necessary and should not apply in relation to genuine economic activities undertaken overseas, so long as there has been no artificial diversion of UK profits.

Double taxation relief for companies

Unless double tax relief is available (or prohibited) under the terms of a double taxation treaty with the country concerned, the UK tax system provides unilateral double tax relief for foreign tax suffered by a UK company which receives income from overseas.

Unilateral relief takes the form of a tax credit equal to the *lower* of the amount of foreign tax suffered and the amount of UK corporation tax payable on the foreign income. Any excess foreign tax is unrelieved (but see below).

EXAMPLE 3

In the year to 31 March 2018, a UK resident company had UK trading profits of £5,450,000 and overseas property income (net of 35% withholding tax) of £130,000. Compute the corporation tax liability for the year.

Solution

	UK	*Overseas*	*Total*
	£	£	£
Trading income	5,450,000		5,450,000
Property income £130,000 x 100/65		200,000	200,000
Taxable total profits (TTP)	5,450,000	200,000	5,650,000
Corporation tax @ 19%	1,035,500	38,000	1,073,500
Less: Unilateral DTR		(38,000)	(38,000)
Corporation tax due	1,035,500	-	1,035,500

The unilateral relief given is restricted to the UK tax due on the overseas income. The remaining £32,000 (£70,000 – £38,000) of foreign tax paid is unrelieved.

Unrelieved foreign tax

Unrelieved foreign tax arising in connection with trading income derived from an overseas permanent establishment (i.e. an overseas branch) may be carried back for up to three years or may be carried forward without time limit. Note that:

(a) When unrelieved foreign tax is carried back or forward, it is treated as if it were foreign tax paid in respect of the trading income of the same overseas branch in the accounting period to which it is carried. But if the rate of foreign tax suffered on such income is consistently higher than the UK tax rate, it is unlikely that there will be any scope for relieving unrelieved foreign tax from other accounting periods.

(b) These provisions are not relevant to a company which has elected that the profits of all its overseas branches should be exempt from UK tax (see earlier in this chapter).

Underlying DTR

If a UK resident company owns at least 10% of the voting power of an overseas company from which it receives a non-exempt dividend, then an additional form of unilateral double taxation relief, known as "underlying relief", is available. The idea of underlying DTR is to give relief for the foreign tax suffered on the profits out of which the dividend has been paid. Underlying relief is calculated by the formula:

$$\frac{D}{P} \times T$$

where: D = the gross dividend received

P = the profit available for distribution as shown in the accounts for the period to which the dividend relates

T = the overseas tax actually paid on the profits of that period.

However, since most foreign dividends received by UK companies are now exempt from corporation tax, underlying double tax relief applies only in the minority of cases where a company receives a non-exempt foreign dividend.

EXAMPLE 4

On 1 November 2017, a UK company receives a non-exempt dividend from an overseas company (in which it has 15% voting power) of £10,500, net of 30% withholding tax. The income statement of the overseas company for the year to which the dividend relates is:

	£
Profit before tax	400,000
Less: Provision for taxation liability	150,000
Profits after tax	250,000
Dividends	100,000
Retained profits c/f	150,000

The actual tax liability of the overseas company is finally agreed at £160,000. Compute the maximum unilateral double tax relief available in respect of the £10,500 dividend.

Solution

(i) D = £10,500 x 100/70 = £15,000. P = £250,000. T = £160,000

(ii) Withholding tax = £4,500

(iii) Underlying tax = $\frac{D}{P} \times T = \frac{£15,000}{£250,000} \times £160,000 = £9,600$

(iv) Maximum unilateral DTR = £4,500 + £9,600 = £14,100. Therefore the gross dividend is £24,600 (net £10,500 + tax £14,100).

Unilateral expense relief

A company may waive the right to claim unilateral "credit relief" (where DTR takes the form of a tax credit) and opt for unilateral "expense relief" instead. A company which opts for expense relief is assessed on the *net* foreign income, so that the foreign tax is treated as if it were an expense. Unilateral expense relief may be attractive if a company makes a claim to set a trading loss against its total profits, so that it has no corporation tax liability on the foreign income and cannot obtain any credit relief.

EXAMPLE 5

A UK company has a trading loss of £50,000 for the year to 31 March 2018. During the year, the company receives overseas property income (net of 40% withholding tax) of £12,000. Show the corporation tax computation for the year if:

(a) unilateral credit relief is claimed

(b) unilateral expense relief is claimed.

The company claims trading loss relief against total profits of the year to 31 March 2018.

Solution

	Credit relief	*Expense relief*
	£	£
Trading income	0	0
Property income (gross)	20,000	
Property income (net of foreign tax)		12,000
	20,000	12,000
Less: Trading loss	(20,000)	(12,000)
Taxable total profits (TTP)	0	0
Corporation tax liability	0	0
Unrelieved trading losses	30,000	38,000
Unrelieved foreign tax	8,000	nil

Notes:

(i) No unilateral credit relief is available since the overseas income is absorbed by the trading loss, leaving a UK tax liability of £nil.

(ii) Credit relief gives £8,000 of unrelieved foreign tax.

(iii) Expense relief eliminates the unrelieved foreign tax. The trading losses available for carry-back against total profits of the previous 12 months or carry-forward against future trading profits are increased by £8,000.

Interaction of charitable donations, loss reliefs and DTR

A company's taxable total profits are reduced by the qualifying charitable donations made in the accounting period (see Chapter 23) and by the amount of any trading losses relieved against the total profits of the period (see Chapter 26). Normally, it is sufficient simply to subtract donations and trading losses from the company's total income (and gains) without allocating these deductions to any particular source of income. But if unilateral double tax relief is claimed, such an allocation must be made so that the amount of UK tax payable on the foreign income can be calculated. This allocation may be made in any way that the company sees fit and should be done in such a way as to minimise the tax liability.

If any donations or trading losses are set against the foreign income, this will have the effect of reducing the UK tax due on that foreign income and so reducing the maximum unilateral DTR available. Therefore, donations and trading losses should be set first against UK income, then against foreign income.

EXAMPLE 6

In the year to 31 March 2018, a UK company has UK trading profits of £4,800,000 and overseas property income (net of 45% withholding tax) of £2,750,000. Gift Aid donations of £100,000 are made in the year. Compute the corporation tax liability for the year.

Solution

	UK	*Overseas*	*Total*
	£	£	£
Trading income	4,800,000		4,800,000
Income from property:			
£2,750,000 x 100/55		5,000,000	5,000,000
	4,800,000	5,000,000	9,800,000
Less: Donations	100,000	-	100,000
Taxable total profits (TTP)	4,700,000	5,000,000	9,700,000
Corporation tax @ 19%	893,000	950,000	1,843,000
Less: Unilateral DTR		(950,000)	(950,000)
Corporation tax liability	893,000	-	893,000

Notes:

(i) The donations are set against the UK income so as to maximise double tax relief on the overseas income.

(ii) DTR is limited to the UK tax due on the overseas income. Foreign tax paid is £2,250,000, of which £1,300,000 is unrelieved.

(iii) If the donations had been set against the overseas income, DTR would have been only £931,000 (£4,900,000 x 19%) and the tax liability would have been £912,000.

Diverted profits tax

As from 1 April 2015, large multinational companies may incur a liability to the diverted profits tax (DPT) if they divert profits away from the UK so as to avoid UK corporation tax. The main objective of this new tax is to counteract contrived arrangements used by large groups to divert profits from the UK which result in the erosion of the UK tax base. Broadly, a charge to DPT may arise if either:

(a) a company engages in artificial transactions which "lack economic substance" but which divert profits away from the UK, or

(b) a non-UK resident company carries on a trade in the UK but enters into arrangements which are designed to avoid the existence of a UK taxable presence (i.e. a permanent establishment in the UK).

If HMRC determines that the DPT should apply in a particular case, a notice must be issued to the company concerned, explaining the reasons for the charge. The notice should also state the amount of the charge and explain how it has been calculated. The company has 30 days in which to make representations to HMRC and HMRC then has a further 30 days in which to issue a charging notice (or to confirm that no charge is to be made).

DPT is charged at 25% of the amount of the diverted profits and is payable within 30 days of the issue of the charging notice. There are penalties for late payment.

Summary

- An individual's liability to UK income tax depends upon whether the individual is resident in the UK. Individuals who are resident in the UK for a tax year are liable to pay income tax on their worldwide income for that year. Non-residents are liable to income tax on their UK income only.
- Double taxation relief may be available if income is subject to both UK income tax and overseas tax.
- The extent to which an individual's income from employment is taxable in the UK depends upon the individual's residence status and whether the duties of the employment are performed in the UK or overseas.
- Trading profits arising to a UK resident are charged to income tax wherever in the world the trade is carried on. Trading profits arising to a non-resident are charged to income tax if the trade is carried on in the UK or is a trade of dealing in UK land.
- Income from UK property and investments is generally taxable in the UK whether or not the person to whom the income arises is UK resident. Income from overseas property and investments is taxable in the UK only if the person to whom the income arises is UK resident.

- Individuals who are resident in the UK for a tax year are liable to UK capital gains tax on their disposals throughout the world in that year.
- Individuals who are UK domiciled are liable to UK inheritance tax. The definition of "domicile" for IHT purposes is broader than the general definition.
- UK resident companies are liable to UK corporation tax on their worldwide profits. A non-UK resident company is liable to corporation tax if it carries on a trade through a UK permanent establishment or a trade of dealing in UK land.
- Most foreign dividends received by UK companies are exempt from corporation tax.
- The profits of a controlled foreign company may be apportioned between the controlling UK companies and assessed to corporation tax.
- Double tax relief for companies may take the form of credit relief, underlying tax relief or expense relief.
- A diverted profits tax (DPT) charge may arise if a company makes contrived arrangements to divert profits away from the UK and so avoid UK tax.

Exercises

32.1 (a) Jean-Paul is a Canadian citizen. He owns a house in Canada and regards Canada as his home but he lives in the UK for eight months during tax year 2017-18. During these eight months he tours the UK and visits friends and relatives but he does no work. Is he UK resident for tax year 2017-18? Is any of his income for the year liable to UK income tax?

(b) Pierre is a French citizen. He lives and works full-time in France but during tax year 2017-18 he spends three weeks in the UK on holiday. Is he UK resident for 2017-18? Is any of his income for the year liable to UK income tax?

(c) Carole has lived in the UK all her life and has a home in London. She retires in March 2017 and decides to spent the next 12 months travelling abroad. During tax year 2017-18 she takes several long holidays but she keeps her London home and does not acquire a home overseas. She spends 44 days in the UK during the tax year. Is she UK resident for 2017-18?

32.2 Amy is domiciled in the UK and has lived in the UK all her life. On 1 January 2017 she leaves to work in Australia for two years, returning on 31 December 2018. During her absence she makes no visits to the UK. Explain her UK income tax status for tax years 2016-17 to 2018-19 inclusive. (Ignore the sufficient ties test).

32.3 (a) Explain the concept of "domicile" for tax purposes.

(b) If an individual is UK resident, to what extent does the individual's domicile affect his or her liability to UK tax?

32.4 (a) How would a UK resident company proceed if it wished to "migrate" overseas? Why might this be a desirable step?

(b) A UK resident company may make an election to the effect that the profits of its permanent establishments situated overseas (i.e. its overseas branches) should be exempt from UK corporation tax. Why might a UK company decide not to make such an election?

32.5 Explain the term "controlled foreign company" (CFC). In what circumstances are the profits of a CFC chargeable to UK corporation tax?

32.6 Brist Ltd is a UK resident company which prepares annual accounts to 31 March. In the year to 31 March 2018, the company had a UK trading profit of £2,120,000 and received overseas property income of £98,000 (this figure is net of 30% withholding tax).

(a) Compute the company's corporation tax liability for the year and explain the treatment of any unrelieved foreign tax.

(b) Would the situation be any different if the overseas property income was replaced by trading income from an overseas branch?

***32.7** Donald is resident and domiciled in the UK. He is not a Scottish taxpayer. He has the following income in tax year 2017-18:

	£
UK trading profits	36,930
Income from UK property	5,000
Income from foreign property (net of 45% withholding tax)	2,200

Donald claims only the personal allowance. Compute the amount of income tax payable for 2017-18.

***32.8** A UK resident company has 19 subsidiaries, five of which are situated abroad. In the year to 31 March 2018, the company had the following results:

	£
UK trading profits	720,000
UK dividends received	40,000
UK chargeable gains	120,000
Overseas bank interest (net of 40% withholding tax)	10,800
Gift Aid donations paid	80,000

None of the dividends received were from any of the company's subsidiaries. Calculate the company's corporation tax liability for the year to 31 March 2018 and state the date (or dates) on which payment falls due.

Review questions (Set D)

D1 David Deans started trading as a painter and decorator on 1 July 2017. He has notified you of his turnover each month which, up to November 2017, has been as follows:

	£
July 2017	7,400
August 2017	8,600
September 2017	9,500
October 2017	10,700
November 2017	15,000

In anticipation of a meeting with Mr Deans, you have received a letter from him, of which the following is an extract:

"*In preparation for our meeting, I have some further information for you and some questions which I hope you will be able to answer for me. I anticipate that my turnover is likely to be £16,000 in December 2017 and £18,500 in January 2018. It must be reaching the time at which I need to be registered for VAT. Could you give me some idea of when this might be and whether I could delay it so as to improve my cash flow?*

Since starting business I have purchased substantial quantities of stock. Will I be able to recover any of the VAT I have paid?

In June next year, I intend to buy a new van and a new car for the business. Their cost, including VAT, will be £30,000 and £18,000 respectively. I assume that I will be able to recover the VAT on both items. The van will be used wholly for business and the car for both business and private use. The firm will pay for all the petrol used by both vehicles.

As yet, I have not suffered any bad debts but as the business expands there is always the risk that they might arise. Are there any special VAT arrangements to deal with them?"

Required:

Draft notes in preparation for the meeting with Mr Deans, responding to the queries which he has raised. *(Amended from AAT)*

D2 Larry died on 1 November 2017 leaving an estate valued at £300,000. He had never had a wife or civil partner and he left his estate to his best friend. On 1 October 2009 he had set up a discretionary trust and made a gross chargeable transfer to this trust of £275,000 (after deducting exemptions). His only other lifetime transfers were as follows:

12 March 2012	£60,000 to his mother
13 February 2013	£60,000 to his father
6 October 2014	£18,500 to his nephew (wedding present)
15 April 2016	£25,000 to a charity

Required:

Calculate the IHT payable (if any) on each of the four gifts and on the estate at death.

D3 A UK company has the following results for the year to 31 March 2018:

	£
Trading profits	175,000
Chargeable gains	23,000
Capital losses brought forward on 1 April 2017	18,000
Overseas property income (net of 15% foreign tax)	5,100
Overseas property income (net of 25% foreign tax)	6,375
Dividends received	nil
Gift Aid donations	7,500

Required:

Calculate the corporation tax payable for the year.

D4 A Ltd owns 85% of B Ltd and 60% of C Ltd. B Ltd owns 90% of D Ltd. The remaining 40% of C Ltd is owned by E Ltd. All these percentages represent holdings of ordinary shares and all companies are UK resident. Results for the year to 31 March 2018 are as follows:

	Trading profits (losses)	*Loan interest receivable*	*Overseas property income*	*Gift Aid donations*
	£	£	£	£
A Ltd	240,000	5,000	-	1,000
B Ltd	45,000	2,500	8,200	500
C Ltd	(30,000)	-	-	-
D Ltd	(25,000)	-	-	-
E Ltd	80,000	-	-	1,000

The overseas property income of B Ltd is the net figure after deduction of 18% foreign tax. A Ltd received a dividend of £17,000 from B Ltd on 31 December 2017.

Required:

Calculate the corporation tax payable for the year by all of these companies, assuming that maximum group relief is claimed for the trading losses and that double tax relief is given where appropriate.

***D5** Mrs Lammle, who is registered for VAT, has traded as a manufacturer of standard-rated items since 1 June 2001. She has decided to retire on 31 May 2017, her 65th birthday, and you are asked to finalise her tax position up to that date. You are provided with the following information:

(i) Mrs Lammle has always prepared accounts to 31 May each year. Overlap profits of £37,500 arose on commencement.

(ii) The last accounts will be for the year to 31 May 2017. Interim accounts have been prepared to 28 February 2017, revealing the following:

	£
Sales	100,200
Cost of sales	24,700
Gross profit	75,500
Expenses	29,000
Net profit	46,500

All of the above figures are net of VAT and contain no disallowable items.

(iii) For the last three months to 31 May 2017 (which is also the last VAT quarter), you have extracted the following figures from the accounting records:

	£
Sales:	
To UK customers	30,654
To overseas (non-EU) customers	8,000
Materials purchased:	
Standard-rated	4,098
Zero-rated	2,000
Exempt	800
Expenses:	
General (all standard-rated)	6,120
Wages	7,000
Hire of machinery	612
Business bank charges	500
Entertaining UK clients	400

All of the above include VAT if appropriate. There was no stock at 1 March 2017 and there is no outstanding stock left at 31 May 2017. All of the general expenses are allowable for income tax purposes.

(iv) The tax written down value of the plant and machinery carried forward after capital allowances had been calculated for the year to 31 May 2016 was:

	£
Plant and machinery main pool	12,375
Special rate pool (car with no private use)	5,250

No plant and machinery was acquired during the year to 31 May 2017.

(v) The business was sold as a going concern (to another taxable person) on 31 May 2017. The items sold were:

	£
Freehold shop	200,000
Freehold workshop	130,000
Goodwill	180,000
Plant (no item worth more than £6,000)	25,000
Car	6,000

The shop and the workshop were acquired on 1 June 2001 for £30,000 and £21,000 respectively. All of the items of plant were sold for less than original cost.

Required:

(a) Calculate the VAT due for the quarter to 31 May 2017.

(b) Calculate the final adjusted profit for the year to 31 May 2017, after deduction of capital allowances.

(c) Calculate Mrs Lammle's trading income for 2017-18.

(d) Calculate the capital gains tax due on the disposal of the business, assuming that entrepreneurs' relief is claimed. Mrs Lammle has made no previous claims for this relief, has no other disposals in 2017-18 and has no capital losses brought forward.

(Amended from AAT)

***D6** Quiver Ltd is VAT-registered. During the quarter to 31 March 2018, the company made the following supplies of goods and services:

	£
Standard-rated supplies (including VAT)	75,840
Zero-rated supplies	16,800
Exempt supplies	12,500

The company also suffered the following input tax during the quarter:

	£
Attributed to taxable supplies	5,210
Attributed to exempt supplies	860
Unattributed	2,470

The input tax which is attributed to taxable supplies includes £1,710 in relation to the purchase of a motor car on 1 January 2018 and a further £180 in relation to the fuel used by this car during the quarter. The car has emissions of 143g/km and is used for both business (70%) and private (30%) motoring and the company pays all fuel costs.

Unattributed input tax includes £620 of input VAT on UK customer entertaining costs and £590 of VAT on staff entertaining costs.

Required:

Calculate the VAT liability of Quiver Ltd for the three months to 31 March 2018 and explain why this calculation is provisional. *(CIPFA)*

***D7** Jimmy died on 14 February 2018. He had made the following gifts during his lifetime:

(1) On 2 August 2016, he made a cash gift of £50,000 to his grandson. This was a wedding present.

(2) On 14 November 2016, he made a cash gift of £800,000 to a trust. Jimmy paid the inheritance tax arising from this gift.

At the date of his death Jimmy owned the following assets:

(1) His main residence valued at £260,000.

(2) Building society deposits of £515,600.

(3) A life assurance policy on his own life. Proceeds of £210,000 were received from the insurance company following Jimmy's death.

Funeral costs amounted to £5,600. Under the terms of his will, Jimmy left £300,000 to his wife, with the residue of his estate to his nephew.

The nil rate band in tax years 2016-17 and 2017-18 was £325,000.

Required:

(a) Explain why it is important to differentiate between potentially exempt transfers and chargeable lifetime transfers for inheritance tax purposes.

(b) Calculate the inheritance tax payable as a result of Jimmy's death.

(ACCA)

***D8** P Ltd is the parent company of a small group. All of the companies in the group are UK resident apart from Q Corp., which is resident in an overseas country that is not part of the European Economic Area (EEA). Q Corp. does not trade in the UK or in any other EEA country. The following diagram represents holdings of ordinary shares:

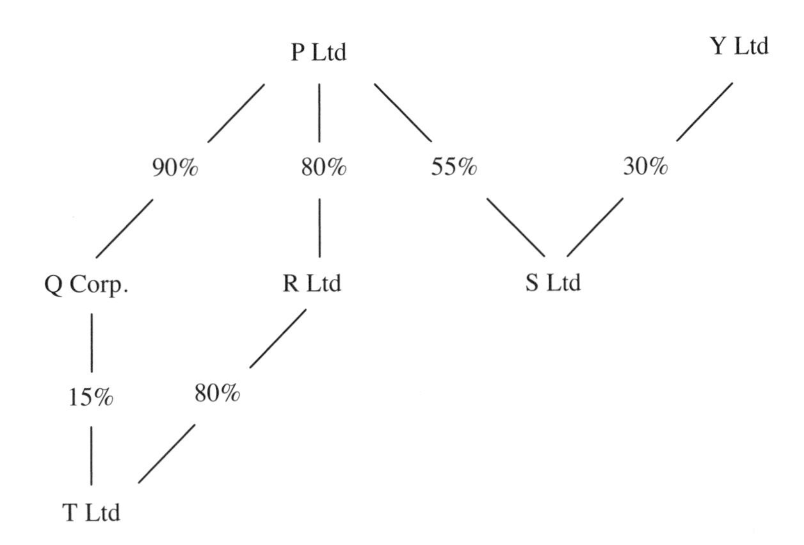

The trading profit or loss of each company for the year to 31 March 2018 is as follows:

		£			£
P Ltd	Profit	240,000	S Ltd	Profit	180,000
Q Corp.	Loss	(72,000)	T Ltd	Profit	56,000
R Ltd	Loss	(84,000)	Y Ltd	Loss	(95,000)

None of the companies had any other income or gains during the year or made any Gift Aid donations. No dividends were paid during the year.

Required:

(a) Identify the trading losses that may be surrendered to other companies in the group and the companies to which these losses may be surrendered.

(b) Calculate the corporation tax liability of each company for the year, assuming that group relief is claimed wherever possible.

(c) If any of the trading losses are not eligible for group relief, explain any alternative forms of relief that might be available.

Ignore the changes to the loss relief rules that have been proposed by the Government and which might take effect as from 1 April 2017.

Part 5

ANSWERS

Answers to exercises

Chapter 2

2.1

Non-Scottish taxpayers:

(a) £1,830 @ 20% = £366.00.

(b) £32,300 @ 20% = £6,460.00.

(c) £33,500 @ 20% + £34,333 @ 40% = £20,433.20.

(d) £33,500 @ 20% + £116,500 @ 40% + £170,000 @ 45% = £129,800.00.

Scottish taxpayers:

(a) £1,830 @ 20% = £366.00.

(b) £31,500 @ 20% + £800 @ 40% = £6,620.00.

(c) £31,500 @ 20% + £36,333 @ 40% = £20,833.20.

(d) £31,500 @ 20% + £118,500 @ 40% + £170,000 @ 45% = £130,200.00.

2.2

(a)

			Total	*Non-savings*	*Savings*
			£	£	£
Business profits			27,105	27,105	
Bank interest			720		720
Total income			27,825	27,105	720
Less: Personal allowance			11,500	11,500	
Taxable income			16,325	15,605	720
Income tax due					
Non-savings income	: Basic rate	15,605	@ 20%	3,121.00	
Savings income	: Nil rate	720	@ 0%	0.00	
		16,325			
Tax liability				3,121.00	

Taxable income does not exceed the basic rate limit, therefore the personal savings allowance is £1,000 and savings income of £720 is taxed at the savings nil rate. The income tax liability for the year would be the same for a Scottish taxpayer.

(b)

	Total	Non-savings	Savings
	£	£	£
Business profits	44,150	44,150	
Building society interest	930		930
Bank interest	570		570
Total income	45,650	44,150	1,500
Less: Personal allowance	11,500	11,500	
Taxable income	34,150	32,650	1,500

Income tax due

Non-savings income	: Basic rate	32,650	@ 20%	6,530.00
Savings income	: Nil rate	500	@ 0%	0.00
	: Basic rate	350	@ 20%	70.00
	: Higher rate	650	@ 40%	260.00
		34,150		
Tax liability				6,860.00

Taxable income exceeds the basic rate limit but does not exceed the higher rate limit, so the personal savings allowance is £500. Savings income of £500 is taxed at the savings nil rate. After this, there is £350 of the basic rate band remaining (£33,500 – £32,650 – £500) so the next £350 of the savings income is taxed at 20% and the remainder is taxed at 40%.

For a Scottish taxpayer, the liability on non-savings income would be (£31,500 × 20%) + (£1,150 × 40%) = £6,760, increasing the total liability by £230 to £7,090.

(c) Grossed-up loan interest is (£130,604 × 100/80) = £163,255. There is no non-savings income so the first £5,000 of savings income is taxed at the starting rate of 0%. However, taxable income exceeds the higher rate limit so the personal savings allowance is £nil.

The income tax liability is (£5,000 × 0%) + (£28,500 × 20%) + (£116,500 × 40%) + (£13,255 × 45%) which is a total of £58,264.75. Income tax deducted at source is £32,651 (£163,255 – £130,604) so income tax payable is (£58,264.75 – £32,651.00) = £25,613.75.

The computation would be unchanged for a Scottish taxpayer.

2.3

	Total	Non-savings	Savings	Dividends
	£	£	£	£
Self-employment income	28,880	28,880		
Income from property	15,730	15,730		
Bank interest	200		200	
Dividends	250			250
Total income	45,060	44,610	200	250
Less: Personal allowance	11,500	11,500		
Taxable income	33,560	33,110	200	250

Income tax due				
Non-savings income	: Basic rate	33,110	@ 20%	6,622.00
Savings income	: Nil rate	200	@ 0%	0.00
Dividend income	: Nil rate	250	@ 0%	0.00
		33,560		
Tax liability				6,622.00

Taxable income exceeds the basic rate limit but does not exceed the higher rate limit, so the personal savings allowance is £500. The dividend allowance is £5,000. Therefore all of the savings income and dividend income is taxed at 0%.

2.4

	Total	*Non-savings*	*Savings*
	£	£	£
Retirement pension	51,890	51,890	
Bank interest	620		620
Total income	52,510	51,890	620
Less: Personal allowance	11,500	11,500	
Taxable income	41,010	40,390	620

The personal savings allowance is £500, so £500 of the savings income is taxed at the nil rate. The tax liability is (£33,500 × 20%) + (£6,890 × 40%) + (£500 × 0%) + (£120 × 40%) = £9,504.00.

If the taxpayer had received £620 of dividends instead of the bank interest, these would all have been covered by the dividend allowance of £5,000 and taxed at 0%. The tax liability would have been reduced by £48 (£120 × 40%) to £9,456.00.

Chapter 3

3.1

(a) £11,500

(b) £7,500 (£11,500 – 1/2 × £8,000)

(c) (£11,500 – 1/2 × £30,000) gives a negative figure, so the personal allowance is £nil.

3.2

(a) Pamela's income exceeds £100,000 by £5,000, so her personal allowance is reduced by £2,500 from £11,500 to £9,000. Taxable income is £96,000 (£105,000 – £9,000) so the income tax liability is [(£33,500 × 20%) + (£62,500 × 40%)] = £31,700.

(b) With an income of £125,000, the personal allowance is reduced to £nil. Pamela's income tax liability is now [(£33,500 × 20%) + (£91,500 × 40%)] = £43,300.

(c) The £18,000 increase in salary from £105,000 to £123,000 (the point at which the personal allowance becomes zero) is effectively taxed at 60% and the remaining £2,000 of the increase is taxed at 40%. Therefore the tax liability rises by [(£18,000 × 60%) + (£2,000 × 40%)] = £11,600. This accounts for the difference between £31,700 and £43,300.

3.3

(a) The husband is entitled to the MCA because he and his wife were born before 6 April 1935. The full MCA of £8,445 is available, since the husband's income does not exceed £28,000.

(b) The husband is entitled to the MCA because he and his wife were born before 6 April 1935. His income exceeds the income limit by £40 (£28,040 – £28,000) so the MCA is reduced by £20 (1/2 × £40) to £8,425

(c) The husband is entitled to the MCA because he was born before 6 April 1935. His income exceeds the income limit by £6,400 (£34,400 – £28,000) so the MCA is reduced by £3,200 (1/2 × £6,400) to £5,245.

(d) The husband is entitled to the MCA because his wife was born before 6 April 1935. The full MCA of £8,445 is available, since the husband's income does not exceed the income limit of £28,000. His wife's income is disregarded for this purpose, even though the MCA is available solely by virtue of her age.

3.4

	(a)	(b)	(c)
	£	£	£
HUSBAND			
Net income	18,140	9,500	11,835
Less: Personal allowance	11,500	9,500†	11,500
Taxable income	6,640	0	335
Income tax			
£6,640 @ 20%	1,328.00		
£0 @ 20%		0.00	
£335 @ 20%			67.00
Less: MCA £8,445 @ 10%	844.50		
MCA £8,445 @ 10% = £844.50			67.00
(£777.50 transferred to wife)			
Tax liability	483.50	0.00	0.00
WIFE			
Net income	19,440	15,375	19,305
Less: Personal allowance	11.500	11,500	11,500
Taxable income	7,940	3,875	7,805
Income tax			
£7,940 @ 20%	1,588.00		
£3,875 @ 20%		775.00	
£7,805 @ 20%			1,561.00
Less: MCA £8,445 × 8/12 @ 10% (higher-income partner)		563.00	
MCA transferred from husband			777.50
Tax liability	1,588.00	212.00	783.50

† *In case (b), the husband cannot claim the marriage allowance because MCA is claimed for the year.*

3.5

	Total	*Non-savings*	*Savings*
	£	£	£
Retirement pension	10,480	10,480	
Income from annuity £912 × 100/80	1,140		1,140
Total income	11,620	10,480	1,140
Less: Personal allowance	11,500	10,480	1,020
Taxable income	120	0	120
Income tax due			
£120 @ 0% (starting rate for savings)	0.00		
Less: Tax deducted at source	228.00		
Tax repayable	(228.00)		

Toby cannot claim the MCA because his wife died before the start of the tax year. Even if he could claim the MCA it would be wasted, because his tax liability is already £nil.

3.6

(a) Brian's liability is (£25,000 – £11,500) × 20% = £2,700. Danny's liability is £nil.

(b) Brian's liability is reduced by £230 (£1,150 × 20%) to £2,470. Danny's PA becomes £10,350 (£11,500 – £1,150). This is still sufficient to cover his income so his liability remains at £nil.

(c) If Brian's total income were £50,000 he would be liable to income tax at the higher rate and so it would not be possible for Danny to transfer part of his personal allowance to him.

3.7

	Richard	*Patricia*
	£	£
Business profits	32,560	
Dividends		3,600
Less: Personal allowance	11,500	3,600
Taxable income	21,060	0
Income tax		
£21,060 @ 20%	4,212.00	
Less: MCA £6,165 @ 10%	616.50	
Tax liability	3,595.50	0.00

Notes:

(i) Richard's income exceeds the limit by £4,560. The MCA is reduced by £2,280 (1/2 × £4,560) to £6,165 (£8,445 – £2,280).

(ii) Patricia is entitled to a PA of £11,500 but can use only £3,600 of this. She cannot transfer any of her PA to Richard because MCA is claimed for the year.

Chapter 4

4.1

	£
Total income	26,205
Less: Payment £200 × 100/80	250
Net income	25,955
Less: Personal allowance	11,500
Taxable income	14,455
Income tax	
Tax borne @ 20%	2,891.00
Add: Tax deducted from payment	50.00
Tax liability	2,941.00

4.2

				(a)	(b)
				£	£
Total income				48,890	48,890
Less: Interest paid				1,600	
Net income				47,290	48,890
Less: Personal allowance				11,500	11,500
Taxable income				35,790	37,390
Income tax					
	(a)	(b)			
	33,500	33,500	@ 20%	6,700.00	6,700.00
	2,290	3,890	@ 40%	916.00	1,556.00
	35,790	37,390			
Tax liability				7,616.00	8,256.00

Paul's tax liability is reduced by £640 if he pays the interest. The cost of the interest to him is therefore only £960 (amount paid £1,600 less reduction in tax liability £640). In effect, the interest paid of £1,600 is reduced by tax relief at 40% (£640), leaving £960 as the cost to Paul.

4.3

Rose's net income is £11,225 (£11,250 – £25). This is covered by her personal allowance of £11,500 (of which £275 is wasted) so taxable income is £nil and the tax liability is zero. In fact the tax liability would also have been zero if the £25 payment had not been made, since Rose's total income is less than her personal allowance. The payment has had no effect on her tax liability and so tax relief on the payment is zero.

4.4

(a) 23% (b) marginal rate (c) 10% (d) 30%

4.5

(a) The donation is deemed to be made net of 20% income tax. Charities are not liable to income tax so the charity concerned recovers a further £240 (£960 × 20/80) from HMRC, making the donation worth £1,200 in total.

(b) If the taxpayer does not pay income tax for 2017-18 of at least £240, the income tax liability for the year will be increased to exactly £240.

(c) The taxpayer's basic rate and higher rate limits for 2017-18 are both increased by £1,200. This results in a tax saving of up to £240 (40% – 20% = 20% × £1,200) for a higher rate taxpayer and up to £300 (45% – 20% = 25% × £1,200) for an additional rate taxpayer.

4.6

	£
Dividends received	58,400
Less: Personal allowance	11,500
Taxable income	46,900
Income tax	
£5,000 @ 0%	0.00
£29,050 @ 7.5%	2,178.75
£12,850 @ 32.5%	4,176.25
Tax liability	6,355.00

Notes:

(i) The grossed-up Gift Aid donation is £550 (£440 × 100/80).

(ii) The basic rate band is extended by £550 to £34,050 (£33,500 + £550).

(iii) The first £5,000 of dividends are taxed at the dividend nil rate. The next £29,050 (£34,050 – £5,000) are taxed at the dividend ordinary rate and the remainder at the dividend upper rate.

4.7

	Matthew	*Widow*
	£	£
Non-savings income	29,260	20,895
Less: Gift of shares to charity		500
Net income	29,260	20,395
Less: Personal allowance	11,500	11,500
Taxable income	17,760	8,895
Income tax @ 20%	3,552.00	1,779.00
Less: MCA £7,940 @ 10%	794.00	
Tax liability	2,758.00	1,779.00

(See notes on next page)

Notes:

(i) The personal allowance is available in full in the year of death.

(ii) The grossed-up Gift Aid donation is £250.00 (£200 × 100/80).

(iii) MCA is available since Matthew was born before 6 April 1935 and is given in full in the year of death. Matthew's adjusted net income is £29,010 (£29,260 – £250) which exceeds the limit of £28,000 by £1,010. Therefore the MCA available is £7,940 (£8,445 – 1/2 × £1,010).

Chapter 5

5.1

Rental income for the year is £8,200 [(£8,000 × 9/12) + (£8,800 × 3/12)]. Interest payable of £3,075 (75% × £4,100) is deducted and therefore property income for 2017-18 is £5,125. The remaining £1,025 of the mortgage interest is treated as a tax reducer and will be relieved at 20%, as long as adjusted total income for the year is at least £1,025.

5.2

	£	£
Rents for the year £320 × 52		16,640
Less: Advertising costs	135	
Repairs and maintenance	590	
Insurance costs	730	
Replacement of refrigerator	335	
Mortgage interest (75% × £3,420)	2,565	4,355
Property income		12,285

Notes:

(a) "Replacement domestic items relief" is available in relation to the whole cost of the new refrigerator since it is substantially the same as the item which it replaces. Relief is also available for the costs of disposing of the old refrigerator. Total relief is (£325 + £10) = £335.

(b) Interest on a buy-to-let mortgage is (to some extent) a deductible expense when computing property income. But capital repayments are not deductible.

(c) The remaining £855 of the mortgage interest is treated as a tax reducer and will be relieved at 20%, as long as adjusted total income for the year is at least £855.

(d) If the tax year was 2018-19, only 50% of the mortgage interest for the year (£1,710) would be deductible. Property income for the year would be £13,140. The remaining interest of £1,710 would be treated as a tax reducer.

5.3

(a) Premiums received in relation to the granting of long leases (i.e. leases of more than 50 years) are not assessable to income tax.

(b) £12,000 – (49 × 2% of £12,000) = £240.

(c) £12,000 – (19 × 2% of £12,000) = £7,440.

5.4

The income tax assessment on the landlord is £12,300 (£15,000 – (9 × 2% of £15,000)). Therefore Jasper will be allowed an annual deduction from his trading profits of £1,230 for each of the ten years of the lease.

5.5

All three flats pass the 210-day test. However, Flat 1 does not pass the 105-day test and so will not be regarded as a furnished holiday let unless it can be averaged with one or more of the other flats. Possible averaging claims are:

(a) Flat 1 with Flat 2. This is no use since the average number of days let is only 103.

(b) Flat 1 with Flat 3. This is also no use since the average number of days let is only 104.

(c) Flat 1 with Flat 2 and Flat 3. This is beneficial since the average number of days let is 105.

Chapter 6

6.1

	Total	*Savings*	*Dividends*
	£	£	£
Bank interest	2,250	2,250	
Loan stock interest £14,520 × 100/80	18,150	18,150	
Dividends received	50,600		50,600
Total income	71,000	20,400	50,600
Less: Personal allowance	11,500	11,500	
Taxable income	59,500	8,900	50,600

Income tax due

Savings income	: Starting rate	5,000	@ 0%	0.00
	: Nil rate	500	@ 0%	0.00
	: Basic rate	3,400	@ 20%	680.00
Dividend income	: Nil rate	5,000	@ 0%	0.00
	: Ordinary rate	20,600	@ 7.5%	1,545.00
	: Upper rate	25,000	@ 32.5%	8,125.00
		59,500		
Tax liability				10,350.00
Less: Tax deducted at source (£18,150 – £14,520)				3,630.00
Tax payable				6,720.00

Notes:

(a) The basic rate band is extended to £34,500 (£33,500 + (£800 × 100/80)).

(b) There is no non-savings income so the first £5,000 of savings income is taxed at the starting rate. Since taxable income exceeds the basic rate limit, the personal savings allowance is £500 and the next £500 of savings income is taxed at the savings nil rate.

6.2

	Total	Non-savings	Savings	Dividends
	£	£	£	£
Retirement pension	10,886	10,886		
Bank deposit interest	480		480	
Dividends received	650			650
Total income	12,016	10,886	480	650
Less: Personal allowance	11,500	10,886	480	134
Taxable income	516	0	0	516

Taxable income consists entirely of dividends of £516. Since the first £5,000 of dividends are taxed at the dividend nil rate, the tax liability is zero. In fact the liability would still have been zero, even if the remaining £614 of the personal allowance (after using £10,886 against non-savings income) had been set against savings income and dividends in some other way.

Note: The ISA interest is exempt from tax.

6.3/6.4

See text.

6.5

	Total	Non-savings	Savings	Dividends
	£	£	£	£
Business profits	102,850	102,850		
Building society interest	410		410	
Dividends received	7,240			7,240
Total income	110,500	102,850	410	7,240
Less: Personal allowance	6,250	6,250		
Taxable income	104,250	96,600	410	7,240

Income tax due

Non-savings income	: Basic rate	33,500	@ 20%	6,700.00
	: Higher rate	63,100	@ 40%	25,240.00
Savings income	: Nil rate	410	@ 0%	0.00
Dividend income	: Nil rate	5,000	@ 0%	0.00
	: Upper rate	2,240	@ 32.5%	728.00
		104,250		
				32,668.00
Less: EIS relief (30% × £20,000)				6,000.00
Tax liability				26,668.00

Notes:

(a) Adjusted net income exceeds £100,000 by £10,500 so the personal allowance is reduced to £6,250 (£11,500 – 1/2 × £10,500).

(b) The personal savings allowance is £500, so all of the savings income is taxed at the nil rate.

Chapter 7

7.1

See text.

7.2

The basis of assessment for employment income is the receipts basis. The assessable income for 2017-18 is therefore £65,850 (£57,500 + £8,350).

7.3

(a) Free meals in the company canteen are exempt if available to all employees.

(b) Removal expenses of up to £8,000 are exempt if reasonable and incurred on first taking up an appointment or transferring to a new location.

(c) Long-service awards made in cash are taxable.

(d) A gift made in a personal capacity (rather than for services rendered) is exempt so long as it is reasonable in amount.

(e) The mileage allowance is exempt since it is less than the standard figure of 45p per mile for the first 10,000 miles. The employee has a deductible expense of £250 (2,500 × 10p).

(f) Employer contributions towards the additional household costs incurred by a homeworker are exempt from tax if supporting evidence is supplied to demonstrate that these costs have been incurred. Evidence would not be required if the contributions did not exceed £4 per week.

7.4

(a) Not generally deductible since not incurred in performing the duties of the employment. But there are exceptions to this rule in the case of site-based employees, employees undertaking business journeys from home and employees who are seconded to a temporary place of work.

(b) Deductible so long as necessarily incurred.

(c) Deductible if relevant to the employment.

(d) Deductible.

(e) Not deductible, even if worn only at the office. A suit provides warmth and decency and is therefore not purchased exclusively for the purposes of the employment.

(f) Not deductible unless reimbursed or paid out of a specific entertaining allowance. The expenses must also be wholly, exclusively and necessarily incurred.

Chapter 8

8.1

Annual value is £3,700 and there is an additional benefit of 2.5% × (£242,500 + £27,500 - £75,000) = £4,875, bringing the total to £8,575. However, there is 12% business use, which reduces the benefit by £1,029 (12% × £8,575) and the benefit is also reduced by the rent paid by Kim to her employer of £4,800 per annum. So the taxable benefit is £2,746 (£8,575 – £1,029 – £4,800).

8.2

The applicable percentage is 33% (18% + 12% + 3%) so the taxable car benefit is £7,986 (33% of £24,200). There is a further taxable fuel benefit of £7,458 (33% of £22,600).

8.3

(a) The amount outstanding at the end of the tax year is £12,000. Therefore the average amount of the loan between 1 June 2017 and 5 April 2018 is (£20,000 + £12,000)/2 = £16,000. The loan was in existence for ten months of the tax year, so the taxable benefit is equal to (£16,000 × 2.5% × 10/12) = £333.

(b) The taxable benefit is equal to (£20,000 × 2.5% × 7/12) + (£15,000 × 2.5% × 2/12) + (£12,000 × 2.5% × 1/12) = £379.

Chapter 9

9.1

The badges of trade are:

(i) subject matter
(ii) length of ownership
(iii) frequency of transactions
(iv) supplementary work
(v) reason for sale
(vi) motive

(see the chapter for an explanation of each of these).

9.2

(a) Expenditure must be incurred wholly and exclusively for the purposes of the trade.

(b) Expenditure fails the "remoteness test" if it has no connection with the trade. Such expenditure is disallowed. Expenditure fails the "duality test" if it serves both a business purpose and a private purpose. Such expenditure cannot be allowed in full. However, if the expenditure can be apportioned with reasonable accuracy, then only the private element is disallowed.

9.3

(a) allowable so long as the salary is commensurate with the work done
(b) not allowable when computing trading profits, but relieved under the Gift Aid rules
(c) not allowable (capital expenditure)
(d) allowable so long as the diaries carry a prominent advertisement for the business
(e) allowable
(f) not allowable (fails the duality test)
(g) not allowable (related to capital expenditure)
(h) probably allowable as a trade subscription
(i) not allowable (food, drink or tobacco)
(j) allowable (relates directly to trading).

9.4

(a) add £45 (b) add £15 (c) no adjustment required.

9.5

(a) Disallow 15% × £300 = £45.

(b) The amount assessed on the landlord is (£15,000 – (14 × 2% of £15,000)) = £10,800. So the amount allowable in each year is £720 (1/15th of £10,800) and the amount to be disallowed each year is £280 (£1,000 – £720).

9.6

	£	£
Net profit for the year		6,960
Add: *Disallowed expenditure*:		
Proprietor's salary	10,400	
Cost of new heating system	3,800	
Telephone (1/4th of £880)	220	
Motor expenses (1/5th of £3,250)	650	
Entertaining	520	
General allowance for bad debts	200	
Loss on sale of non-current asset	70	
Depreciation	2,500	18,360
		25,320
Less: *Non-trading income*:		
Rents receivable	1,200	
Bank interest receivable	80	
Profit on sale of non-current asset	310	1,590
Trading profit (before capital allowances)		23,730

Chapter 10

10.1

(a) 2017-18 (b) 2017-18 (c) 2019-20 (d) 2018-19

10.2

(a)

2015-16	Actual	1/7/15 to 5/4/16
2016-17	12 months to a/c date in year 2	y/e 30/6/16
2017-18	CYB	y/e 30/6/17
2018-19	CYB	y/e 30/6/18

There is an overlap period between 1 July 2015 and 5 April 2016.

(b)

2015-16	Actual	1/7/15 to 5/4/16
2016-17	Actual	6/4/16 to 5/4/17
2017-18	CYB	1/5/16 to 30/4/17
2018-19	CYB	y/e 30/4/18

There is an overlap period between 1 May 2016 and 5 April 2017.

(c)

2015-16	Actual	1/7/15 to 5/4/16
2016-17	First 12 months	1/7/15 to 30/6/16
2017-18	CYB	y/e 30/4/17
2018-19	CYB	y/e 30/4/18

There is an overlap period between 1 July 2015 and 5 April 2016. There is another overlap period between 1 May 2016 and 30 June 2016.

10.3

				£
2015-16	Actual	1/1/16 to 5/4/16	£27,300 × 3/18	4,550
2016-17	Actual	6/4/16 to 5/4/17	£27,300 × 12/18	18,200
2017-18	CYB	1/7/16 to 30/6/17	£27,300 × 12/18	18,200

There is an overlap period between 1 July 2016 and 5 April 2017 (9 months). The overlap profits are 9/18 × £27,300 = £13,650.

10.4

(a)	2015-16	CYB	y/e 31/1/16
	2016-17	CYB	y/e 31/1/17
	2017-18	End of previous basis period to date of cessation	1/2/17 to 31/5/17
(b)	2015-16	CYB	y/e 31/1/16
	2016-17	CYB	y/e 31/1/17
	2017-18	End of previous basis period to date of cessation	1/2/17 to 31/3/18
(c)	2016-17	CYB	y/e 31/1/17
	2017-18	12 months to normal a/c date	1/2/17 to 31/1/18
	2018-19	End of previous basis period to date of cessation	1/2/18 to 30/4/18

10.5

Year	*Basis period*	*Workings*	*Trading income* £
2013-14	1/6/13 to 5/4/14	£28,800 × 10/16	18,000
2014-15	1/10/13 to 30/9/14	£28,800 × 12/16	21,600
2015-16	y/e 30/9/15		19,900
2016-17	y/e 30/9/16		14,300
2017-18	y/e 30/9/17		13,800
2018-19	1/10/17 to 31/7/18	£11,100 – £10,800	300
			87,900

Notes:

(i) There is an overlap period from 1 October 2013 to 5 April 2014 with profits of 6/16 × £28,800 = £10,800. Therefore overlap relief of £10,800 is given in the tax year in which trade ceases.

(ii) The total of the trading income assessed to income tax is £87,900. This is equal to the total of the adjusted trading profits earned over the lifetime of the business.

Chapter 11

11.1

		Main pool	Allowances
		£	£
y/e 5/4/18			
WDV b/f		10,300	
Additions (ineligible for AIA)		8,000	
		18,300	
Disposals (£4,000 + £3,000)		(7,000)	
		11,300	
WDA @ 18%		2,034	2,034
		9,266	
Additions qualifying for AIA (£600 + £400)	1,000		
AIA @ 100%	1,000	-	1,000
WDV c/f		9,266	
Total allowances			3,034

Notes:

(i) Maximum AIA for the year is £200,000. The qualifying expenditure of £1,000 is well within this maximum.

(ii) The disposal value of the machinery sold in April 2017 is restricted to original cost.

11.2

		Main pool	Motor car (40% p.u.)		Allowances
		£	£		£
y/e 30/4/17					
Additions (ineligible for AIA)		13,500	15,000		
WDA @ 18%		2,430			2,430
WDA @ 8%			1,200	× 60% =	720
		11,070	13,800		
Additions qualifying for AIA	200,000				
AIA @ 100%	200,000	-			200,000
WDV c/f		11,070	13,800		
Total allowances					203,150

Notes:

(i) Total expenditure on plant and machinery (excluding cars) is £213,500 (£113,000 + £25,700 + £74,800). This exceeds the AIA maximum of £200,000, so the AIA claimed is £200,000 and the remaining £13,500 enters the main pool.

(ii) WDA for the car is calculated at 8% because it has emissions in excess of 130g/km.

The adjusted trading profit is now £60,000 (£263,150 – £203,150). Trading income for the first two tax years is as follows:

Year	*Basis period*	*Workings*	*Trading income*
			£
2016-17	1/5/16 to 5/4/17	£60,000 × 11/12	55,000
2017-18	y/e 30/4/17		60,000

The overlap period is 1 May 2016 to 5 April 2017. Overlap profits are £55,000.

11.3

		Main pool	*Special rate pool*	*Allowances*
		£	£	£
9 months to 31/12/17				
WDV b/f		178,400		
Additions (ineligible for AIA)			15,400	
Disposals		(3,400)		
		175,000		
WDA @ 18% × 9/12		23,625		23,625
WDA @ 8% × 9/12			924	924
		151,375		
Additions eligible for AIA	78,950			
AIA @ 100%	78,950	-		78,950
Additions eligible for 100% FYA	11,600			
FYA @ 100%	11,600	-		11,600
WDV c/f		151,375	14,476	
Total allowances				115,099

Notes:

(i) The Peugeot motor car is allocated to the special rate pool because it has emissions in excess of 130g/km.

(ii) The motor van is allocated to the main pool. Total additions to the main pool are £78,950 (£64,450 + £14,500). This figure is within the maximum AIA of £150,000 (9/12 × £200,000) which may be claimed for the period.

(iii) The low emission car attracts a 100% FYA.

(iv) WDAs are restricted because the chargeable period is only nine months long.

(v) Capital allowances on the two private use cars are £3,598 (see below).

(vi) Total capital allowances for the year are £118,697 (£115,099 + £3,598).

	Toyota (50% p.u.)		Saab (50% p.u.)		Allowances
	£		£		£
9 months to 31/12/17					
WDV b/f	18,200				
Additions (ineligible for AIA)			29,600		
Disposals	(15,000)				
Balancing allowance	3,200	× 50% =			1,600
WDA @ 18% × 9/12			3,996	× 50% =	1,998
WDV c/f			25,604		
Total allowances					3,598

Notes:

(i) The Saab motor car attracts WDA at 18% because its emissions do not exceed 130g/km.

(ii) WDA is restricted because the chargeable period is only nine months long.

(iii) The emission rating of the Toyota motor car is irrelevant (for this chargeable period) since it has been disposed of and so does not attract WDA in the period.

Chapter 12

12.1

(a) £nil.

(b) The loss will be carried forward and set against the first available profits of the same trade.

(c) The loss may be set against her total income of 2017-18 and/or 2016-17.

12.2

	2014-15	*2015-16*	*2016-17*	*2017-18*
	£	£	£	£
Trading income	-	4,710	6,210	14,810
Other income	10,000	10,000	10,000	10,000
Total income	10,000	14,710	16,210	24,810
Less: Trading losses b/f	-	(4,710)	(6,210)	(7,940)
Net income	10,000	10,000	10,000	16,870

12.3

(a)

Year	*Basis period*	*Workings*	*Trading income*
			£
2015-16	1/1/16 to 5/4/16	(£17,720 – £6,460) × 3/12	2,815
2016-17	y/e 31/12/16	£17,720 – £6,460	11,260
2017-18	y/e 31/12/17		nil

(b) The trading loss of 2017-18 is £9,800 (£7,480 + £2,320). A claim could be made to set this loss against total income in 2017-18 or 2016-17 or in both of these years:

   (i) A claim for 2017-18 is pointless since there is no income in that year.

   (ii) A claim for 2016-17 would reduce total income for that year to (£11,260 – £9,800) = £1,460 and so eliminate the very small income tax liability for the year. But the personal allowance would be almost entirely wasted.

   (iii) A claim for both years is pointless since a claim for 2017-18 is pointless.

   The 2016-17 claim would be less wasteful if Marcus declined to claim any capital allowances in either of the first two years of trading. Trading income for 2016-17 would become £17,720 and the 2017-18 loss would become £7,480. Claiming relief against total income in 2016-17 would then leave income of £10,240 for the year, which would absorb most of the personal allowance.

12.4

The losses eligible for early trade losses relief are:

Year	*Basis period*	*Workings*	*Trading loss* £	*Early trade losses claim*
2015-16	1/10/15 to 5/4/16	£(56,850) × 6/15	(22,740)	12-13 *to* 14-15
2016-17	1/1/16 to 31/12/16	£(56,850) × 12/15 – overlap £(56,850) × 3/15	(34,110)	13-14 *to* 15-16
2017-18	y/e 31/12/17		(32,660)	14-15 *to* 16-17

If all possible early trade losses relief claims are made, total income is:

	2012-13 £	*2013-14* £	*2014-15* £	*2015-16* £
Trading income	-	-	-	nil
Other income	25,100	25,250	26,400	13,450
Total income	25,100	25,250	26,400	13,450
Less: Early trade losses: 2015-16 loss	(22,740)			
2016-17 loss		(25,250)	(8,860)	
2017-18 loss			(17,540)	(13,450)
Net income	2,360	-	-	-

Notes:

(a) Personal allowances are totally wasted in 2013-14 to 2015-16.

(b) The loss incurred in 2017-18 has been only partly relieved. The remaining £1,670 of the loss (£32,660 – £17,540 – £13,450) is eligible for early trade losses relief in 2016-17 but there is no income in this year against which to set the loss. The loss will be carried forward and set against future trading profits.

Chapter 13

13.1

	Nickleby	*Copperfield*	*Drood*	*Total*
	£	£	£	£
1/1/17 - 31/3/17				
(£183,000 × 3/12 = £45,750)	15,250	15,250	15,250	45,750
1/4/17 - 31/12/17				
(£183,000 × 9/12 = £137,250)	27,450	54,900	54,900	137,250
Allocation of profit for the year	42,700	70,150	70,150	183,000

13.2

	Pickwick	*Snodgrass*	*Tupman*	*Total*
	£	£	£	£
Interest on capital	3,600	6,000	3,000	12,600
Salaries	40,000	-	30,000	70,000
Remainder (shared equally)	(6,700)	(6,700)	(6,700)	(20,100)
	36,900	(700)	26,300	62,500
Notional loss divided 36,900:26,300	(409)	700	(291)	-
Allocation of profit for the year	36,491	-	26,009	62,500

13.3

The allocation of profit for each period of account is:

	Dodson	*Fogg*	*Jackson*	*Total*
	£	£	£	£
y/e 30/6/15 (shared equally)	34,000	34,000	-	68,000
y/e 30/6/16 (shared 5:4:1)	44,000	35,200	8,800	88,000
y/e 30/6/17 (shared 5:4:1)	58,000	46,400	11,600	116,000

Each partner's trading income is:

Dodson

Year	*Basis period*	*Workings*	*Trading income*
			£
2014-15	1/7/14 to 5/4/15	£34,000 × 9/12	25,500
2015-16	y/e 30/6/15		34,000
2016-17	y/e 30/6/16		44,000
2017-18	y/e 30/6/17		58,000

Fogg

Year	*Basis period*	*Workings*	*Trading income*
			£
2014-15	1/7/14 to 5/4/15	£34,000 × 9/12	25,500
2015-16	y/e 30/6/15		34,000
2016-17	y/e 30/6/16		35,200
2017-18	y/e 30/6/17		46,400

Jackson

Year	*Basis period*	*Workings*	*Trading income*
			£
2015-16	1/7/15 to 5/4/16	£8,800 × 9/12	6,600
2016-17	y/e 30/6/16		8,800
2017-18	y/e 30/6/17		11,600

Note:

Dodson and Fogg each have overlap profits of £25,500. Jackson has overlap profits of £6,600.

13.4

(a) Trading profit of £117,460 for the year to 30 September 2016 is allocated Wardle £82,222, Jingle £23,492, Trotter £11,746. Trading profit of £136,540 for the year to 30 September 2017 is allocated Wardle £95,578, Jingle £27,308 Trotter £13,654. The partners' trading income is:

	Wardle	*Jingle*	*Trotter*
	£	£	£
2015-16 (6/12 × y/e 30/9/16)	41,111	11,746	5,873
2016-17 (y/e 30/9/16)	82,222	23,492	11,746
2017-18 (y/e 30/9/17)	95,578	27,308	13,654

(b) The bank interest of £200 for the year to 30 September 2016 is allocated Wardle £140, Jingle £40, Trotter £20. The bank interest of £220 for the year to 30 September 2017 is allocated Wardle £154, Jingle £44, Trotter £22. Each partner's bank interest is:

	Wardle	*Jingle*	*Trotter*
	£	£	£
2015-16 (6/12 × y/e 30/9/16)	70	20	10
2016-17 (y/e 30/9/16)	140	40	20
2017-18 (y/e 30/9/17)	154	44	22

(c) The loan interest of £1,240 (gross) for the year to 30 September 2016 is allocated Wardle £868, Jingle £248, Trotter £124. The loan interest of £1,360 (gross) for the year to 30 September 2017 is allocated Wardle £952, Jingle £272, Trotter £136. The gross amount on which each partner is charged to tax in 2016-17 (assuming time-apportionment between tax years) is:

	£
Wardle (£868 × 6/12 + £952 × 6/12)	910
Jingle (£248 × 6/12 + £272 × 6/12)	260
Trotter (£124 × 6/12 + £136 × 6/12)	130

Chapter 14

14.1

(a) £120,000.

(b) £3,600 (so long as at least £2,400 is paid to a scheme which operates relief at source).

14.2

She will pay net contributions of £800 per month, so obtaining relief at the basic rate. Her basic rate limit and higher rate limit will both be increased by £12,000.

14.3

Current year contributions are 310% of those in the previous year. This exceeds 210% so spreading may be required. The excess of current year contributions over 110% of previous year contributions is £1,200,000, which is between £1,000,000 and £1,999,999. Therefore this excess must be spread over the current period and the next two periods. Tax relief on contributions of £1,060,000 (£660,000 + £400,000) will be given in the year to 30 June 2018. Relief on contributions of £400,000 will be given in each of the years to 30 June 2019 and 2020.

14.4

(a) The first lump sum absorbs 20% of the 2009-10 lifetime allowance of £1,750,000. There is no lifetime allowance charge and 80% of the lifetime allowance remains unused. The second lump sum of £1,120,000 exceeds 80% of the 2017-18 lifetime allowance of £1,000,000 by £320,000. There is a lifetime allowance charge of £176,000 (55% of £320,000).

(b) The first lump sum now absorbs 64% of the 2009-10 lifetime allowance. The second lump sum is less than 36% of the 2017-18 lifetime allowance and therefore there is no lifetime allowance charge on either lump sum.

14.5

If Damon became entitled to payment of his pension and lump sum at the start of the tax year, he would receive an annual pension of £120,000 (£360,000 × 20/60) and a lump sum of £270,000 (£360,000 × 60/80). The value of his pension rights at the start of the year is therefore £2,190,000 (£270,000 + (16 × £120,000)).

If he became entitled to payment of his pension and lump sum at the end of the tax year, he would receive an annual pension of £136,500 (£390,000 × 21/60) and a lump sum of £307,125 (£390,000 × 63/80). The value of his pension rights at the end of the year is therefore £2,491,125 (£307,125 + (16 × £136,500)).

Total pension input amount for 2017-18 is £301,125 (£2,491,125 – £2,190,000). This exceeds the minimum annual allowance of £10,000 by £291,125. Therefore the annual allowance charge is £131,006.25 (45% of £291,125).

Chapter 15

15.1

(a) No POAs are required because the 2016-17 liability (less PAYE and tax deducted at source) was less than £1,000. A balancing payment of £440 (£1,750 – £1,310) is due on 31 January 2019. However, since this does not exceed £3,000, Guy may request that this payment should be collected via the PAYE system.

(b) The amount paid via PAYE and by deduction at source in 2016-17 (£4,390) was not more than 80% of the total liability for the year and the remainder (£2,340) was not less than £1,000. Therefore POAs are required for 2017-18. A first POA of £1,170 (one-half of £2,340) is due on 31 January 2018 and a second POA of £1,170 is due on 31 July 2018.

    A balancing *repayment* of £605 (£6,580 – £4,810 – £35 – £2,340) will be due by 31 January 2019. Marie could have made a claim to pay reduced POAs for 2017-18 if she had known that the POAs based on her 2016-17 liability were likely to be excessive.

(c) No POAs are required because more than 80% of the 2016-17 tax liability was satisfied by PAYE and deduction at source. A balancing payment of £3,600 (£16,110 – £12,510) is due on 31 January 2019.

15.2

(a) The balancing payment was not more than 30 days late so there are no late payment penalties.

(b) The first POA of £12,000 was paid 27 days late, the second POA of £12,000 was paid 43 days late and the balancing payment of £4,000 was paid 21 days late. The interest payable is:

	£
£12,000 × 2.75% × 27/366	24.34
£12,000 × 2.75% × 43/366	38.77
£4,000 × 2.75% × 21/366	6.31
	69.42

15.3

(a) Jabran notified HMRC of his chargeability to tax within the permitted six months and so incurs no penalty in relation to this notification.

(b) His tax return was due to be submitted to HMRC within three months of the issue date. He filed the return late (but not more than three months late) and so incurs a penalty of £100.

(c) The balancing payment was due three months after the issue date of the tax return. His payment was more than 30 days late and therefore he incurs a 5% late payment penalty.

(d) Interest is payable on the tax paid late and interest is payable on the late payment penalty if it is not paid within 30 days of the date of its imposition.

Chapter 16

16.1

(a) Primary : 12% × (£170 – £157) = £1.56
Secondary : 13.8% × (£170 – £157) = £1.79

(b) Primary : 12% × (£780 – £157) = £74.76
Secondary : 13.8% × (£780 – £157) = £85.97

(c) Primary : 12% × (£866 – £157) + 2% × (£930 – £866) = £86.36
Secondary : 13.8% × (£930 – £157) = £106.67

(d) Primary : nil (earnings do not exceed the primary threshold)
Secondary : nil (earnings do not exceed the secondary threshold)

(e) Primary : 12% × (£3,300 – £680) = £314.40
Secondary : 13.8% × (£3,300 – £680) = £361.56

(f) Primary : 12% × (£3,750 – £680) + 2% × (£6,000 – £3,750) = £413.40
Secondary : 13.8% × (£6,000 – £680) = £734.16

16.2

Class 1 NICs for a director are calculated on an annual basis. Pension contributions made by an employee are not deductible when calculating Class 1 NICs. However, any pension contributions made by an employer on behalf of an employee are not regarded as earnings for NICs purposes.

Gross pay for the year is (9 × £8,400) + (3 × £8,736) = £101,808.

Primary Class 1 NICs are 12% × (£45,000 – £8,164) + 2% × (£101,808 – £45,000) = £5,556.48.

Secondary Class 1 NICs are 13.8% × (£101,808 – £8,164) = £12,922.87.

Class 1A NICs (payable only by Joan's employer) are 13.8% × £12,850 = £1,773.30.

16.3

Mark's trading profit for 2017-18 (£9,250) is not less than the small profits threshold (£6,025) so he is liable to make Class 2 NICs of £102.60 (36 × £2.85). He is also liable to make Class 4 contributions of £97.74 (9% × (£9,250 – £8,164)). Therefore his total NICs liability is £200.34.

Chapter 17

17.1

(a) Companies are not chargeable persons, so the sale will not give rise to a CGT liability.

(b) Disposals between husband and wife who are living together are deemed to occur at a disposal value such that neither a gain nor a loss arises. So there will be no CGT liability on the gift.

(c) Gifts to charities are exempt from CGT.

(d) In general, charities are not chargeable persons and therefore disposals by charities do not give rise to a CGT liability (subject to certain restrictions).

(e) The sale is made in the course of trade. Therefore the profit arising will be a trading profit and not a capital gain.

(f) The partnership is not a chargeable person but the partners are. Any CGT liability arising on the disposal of the office building will be divided between them.

17.2

(a) Shares in a limited company are chargeable assets.

(b) Gilt-edged securities are not chargeable assets.

(c) A table is a chattel. Chattels disposed of for more than £6,000 are chargeable assets.

(d) A chair is a chattel. Chattels disposed of for £6,000 or less are not chargeable assets.

(e) A taxpayer's principal private residence is not a chargeable asset.

(f) Motor cars are not chargeable assets.

17.3

(a) Net losses are £2,500. The annual exemption is lost and taxable gains are £nil.

(b) Net losses are £1,000. The annual exemption is lost and taxable gains are £nil.

(c) Net gains are £6,450. The unused part of the annual exemption (£4,850) is lost. Taxable gains are £nil.

(d) Net gains are £12,750. The annual exemption of £11,300 is fully used and taxable gains are £1,450.

17.4

(a) Taxable gains are £239,700 (£263,000 – £12,000 – £11,300). Therefore the CGT liability is (10% × £239,700) = £23,970.

(b) The unused part of the basic rate band is £7,100 (£33,500 – £26,400). Therefore the CGT liability is (10% × £7,100) + (20% × £232,600) = £47,230.

(c) (18% × £7,100) + (28% × £232,600) = £66,406.

(d) The losses and the annual exemption are set against the gain of £57,300, leaving £34,000. The gain which qualifies for ER absorbs the whole of the unused part of the basic rate band so the CGT liability is (10% × £205,700) + (20% × £34,000) = £27,370.

(e) (10% × £205,700) + (28% × £34,000) = £30,090.

17.5

(a) Net gains are £9,400. £1,900 of the annual exemption is lost and taxable gains are £nil. The losses brought forward of £4,800 remain unrelieved and are carried forward to 2018-19.

(b) Net gains are £11,900. This exceeds the annual exemption by £600, so £600 of the losses brought forward are relieved and taxable gains are £nil. The remaining £4,200 of the losses brought forward are carried forward to 2018-19.

(c) Net gains are £17,300. This exceeds the annual exemption by £6,000, so all of the losses brought forward are relieved. Taxable gains are £1,200 (£17,300 – £4,800 – £11,300). There are no unrelieved losses to carry forward.

17.6

Net losses in 2017-18 are £14,200. The annual exemption is lost and taxable gains for the year are £nil. The net losses may be offset against the net gains of 2016-17, 2015-16 and 2014-15, in that order, to the extent that those net gains exceed the annual exemption. Relief is £nil in 2016-17, £2,800 (£13,900 – £11,100) in 2015-16 and £6,500 (£17,500 – £11,000) in 2014-15. Total relief is £9,300. The remaining £4,900 of net losses in 2017-18 cannot be relieved at all.

17.7

31 January 2019.

Chapter 18

18.1

		£
Sale proceeds		172,000
Less: Incidental costs of disposal:		
Auctioneer's fee	8,600	
Legal fees	500	9,100
		162,900
Less: Acquisition cost	100,000	
Incidental costs of acquisition:		
Legal fees	400	
Enhancement expenditure	5,000	105,400
Chargeable gain		57,500

(The repainting costs do not rank as enhancement expenditure).

18.2

	(a)	(b)	(c)
	£	£	£
Sale proceeds	14,950	6,350	25,780
Less: Deemed acquisition cost	7,500	7,500	7,500
Chargeable gain/(allowable loss)	7,450	(1,150)	18,280

18.3

(a)

	£
Sale proceeds (June 2013)	100,000
Less: Incidental costs of disposal	5,000
	95,000
Less: Part cost: $\frac{£100,000}{£100,000 + £500,000} \times £240,000$	(40,000)
Part incidental costs of acquisition: $\frac{£100,000}{£100,000 + £500,000} \times £12,000$	(2,000)
Chargeable gain	53,000

(b)

	£
Sale proceeds (January 2018)	520,000
Less: Remainder of cost (£240,000 – £40,000)	(200,000)
Remainder of costs of acquisition (£12,000 – £2,000)	(10,000)
Chargeable gain	310,000

18.4

	(a)	(b)	(c)
	£	£	£
Sale proceeds	87,500	87,500	87,500
Less: Market value 31 March 1982	10,000	15,000	100,000
Chargeable gain/(allowable loss)	77,500	72,500	(12,500)

Notes:

(i) The asset's cost is ignored, since the gain or loss is computed by means of rebasing.

(ii) In case (a), Francis is taxed on a gain of £77,500 even though his total gain over the entire period of ownership of the asset is actually only £76,000 (£87,500 – £11,500).

(iii) In case (c), Francis is granted an allowable loss of £12,500 even though he has made a gain of £76,000 during his period of ownership of the asset.

18.5

(a)

	£
Deemed disposal proceeds	80
Less: Deemed acquisition cost	6,000
Allowable loss	(5,920)

(b)

	£
Disposal proceeds	120
Less: Deemed acquisition cost (November 2015)	80
Chargeable gain	40

Chapter 19

19.1

(a) Wasting chattel. (b) Chattel. (c) Wasting chattel.
(d) Wasting asset. (e) Wasting chattel. (f) Chattel.

19.2

	£	
Sale proceeds	7,200	
Less: Incidental disposal costs	200	
	7,000	
Less: Acquisition cost	2,300	
Chargeable gain	4,700	(restricted to £2,000)

The gain is restricted to (£7,200 – £6,000) × 5/3 = £2,000.

19.3

	£
Deemed sale proceeds	6,000
Less: Acquisition cost	50,000
Allowable loss	(44,000)

19.4

	£
Sale proceeds	2,500
Less: Part cost:	
$\frac{£2,500}{£2,500 + £8,500} \times 3,850$	875
Chargeable gain	1,625

The maximum gain is (£11,000 – £6,000) × 5/3 × (£2,500/£11,000) = £1,894. The actual gain is less than this so the chargeable gain is £1,625.

19.5

	(a)	(b)
	£	£
Sale proceeds	65,000	38,000
Less: Acquisition cost	50,000	50,000
	15,000	(12,000)
Less: Available capital allowances	0	12,000
Chargeable gain or allowable loss	15,000	0

19.6

	£
Sale proceeds	8,000
Less: Unexpired portion of cost $\frac{3}{5} \times £10,000$	6,000
Chargeable gain	2,000

19.7

When the lease was acquired it had a 40-year life (Sch. 8 percentage 95.457%). When the lease was assigned there were 22 years remaining (Sch. 8 percentage 76.399%). Therefore the computation is as follows:

	£
Sale proceeds	97,500
Less: Unexpired portion of cost	
$\frac{76.399}{95.457} \times £75,000$	60,026
Chargeable gain	37,474

Chapter 20

20.1

(a)	20 October 2017	200	(bought on same day)
	10 August 2017	50	(s104 holding)
(b)	1 December 2017	150	(next 30 days)
	10 August 2017	270	(s104 holding)
(c)	10 August 2017	300	(s104 holding)

20.2

There were no acquisitions on the same day as the disposal or within the following 30 days, so the disposal must have come from the s104 holding. The s104 holding is as follows:

	Number of shares	*Allowable expenditure*
		£
Acquired 29 January 1995	1,000	4,000
Acquired 13 August 1999	1,000	9,500
Acquired 4 October 2011	2,000	22,500
	4,000	36,000
Sold 26 June 2017 (700/4,000ths)	(700)	(6,300)
s104 holding c/f	3,300	29,700

Note:

On average, the allowable expenditure in the pool is £9 per share. The allowable expenditure deducted on the June 2017 disposal (£6,300) is equal to 700 shares at £9 per share.

The gain or loss arising on the disposal is as follows:

	(a)	(b)	(c)
	£	£	£
Sale proceeds	8,400	6,300	5,200
Less: Allowable expenditure	6,300	6,300	6,300
Chargeable gain/(allowable loss)	2,100	0	(1,100)

20.3

The 10,000 shares disposed of on 22 December 2017 are matched as follows:

(a) The first match is against the 3,000 shares acquired on the same day as the disposal. These 3,000 shares were acquired for £24,000 and sold for £30,000 (3,000 × £10), so the chargeable gain on these 3,000 shares is £6,000.

(b) The next match is against the 5,000 shares acquired within the next 30 days. These 5,000 shares were acquired for £55,000 and sold for £50,000 (5,000 × £10), so the allowable loss on these 5,000 shares is £5,000.

(c) The third and final match is against 2,000 of the shares in the s104 holding. The s104 holding is as follows:

	Number of shares	*Allowable expenditure*
		£
Acquired 19 September 2009	4,000	16,000
Acquired 20 October 2011	2,000	12,000
Acquired 21 November 2013	1,000	7,000
	7,000	35,000
Sold 22 December 2017 (2,000/7,000ths)	(2,000)	(10,000)
s104 holding c/f	5,000	25,000

These 2,000 shares were acquired for £10,000 (the allowable expenditure deducted from the s104 holding on their disposal) and sold for £20,000 (2,000 × £10). Therefore the chargeable gain is £10,000.

Overall, the chargeable gain on the 22 December 2017 disposal of 10,000 shares is £11,000 (£6,000 – £5,000 + £10,000).

20.4

There were no acquisitions on the same day as the disposal or within the following 30 days, so the disposal must have come from the s104 holding. The s104 holding is as follows:

	Number of shares	*Allowable expenditure* £
Acquired 17 February 2007	600	900
Acquired 13 November 2011	200	400
Acquired 9 October 2015	100	300
	900	1,600
Bonus issue January 2017	225	-
	1,125	1,600
Sold February 2018 (450/1,125ths)	(450)	(640)
s104 holding c/f	675	960

The 450 shares which were disposed of in February 2018 were acquired for £640 (the allowable expenditure deducted from the s104 holding) and were sold for £1,800 (450 × £4). Therefore the chargeable gain is £1,160.

20.5

There were no acquisitions on the same day as the disposal or within the following 30 days, so the disposal must have come from the s104 holding. The s104 holding is as follows:

	Number of shares	*Allowable expenditure* £
Acquired 30 September 2006	2,000	1,200
Acquired 1 December 2010	3,000	3,600
	5,000	4,800
Rights issue January 2017	1,000	1,000
	6,000	5,800
Sold March 2018 (3,000/6,000ths)	(3,000)	(2,900)
s104 holding c/f	3,000	2,900

The 3,000 shares which were disposed of in March 2018 were acquired for £2,900 (the allowable expenditure deducted from the s104 holding) and were sold for £5,400 (3,000 × £1.80). Therefore the chargeable gain is £2,500.

20.6

(a) The value of the part disposed of is £6,000 (6,000 × £1) and the value of the part remaining is £12,000 (6,000 × £2) so there has been a 6,000/18,000 (1/3rd) part disposal. One-third is more than 5% and the amount received is more than £3,000, so this cannot be treated as a small capital distribution. The s104 holding is as follows:

	Number of shares	*Allowable expenditure*
		£
Acquired November 2006	6,000	30,000
Distribution March 2018 (one-third)	-	(10,000)
s104 holding c/f	6,000	20,000

The allowable loss is £4,000 (£6,000 – £10,000).

(b) The value of Yolande's shares immediately prior to the sale of rights was £600. £25 is less than 5% of £600, so the sale of rights ranks as a small capital distribution. Assuming that this distribution is not treated as a disposal, the s104 holding is as follows:

	Number of shares	*Allowable expenditure*
		£
Acquired January 2010	300	360
Distribution May 2016	-	(25)
	300	335
Sold November 2017	(300)	(335)
s104 holding c/f	-	-

The chargeable gain is £445 (£780 – £335).

20.7

Walter received 16,000 shares worth £72,000, plus £8,000 in cash, a total of £80,000. The amount received in cash is 10% of the total. This exceeds 5% and the amount exceeds £3,000. Therefore this does not rank as a small capital distribution and the situation must be treated as a part disposal. The s104 holding is as follows:

	Number of shares	*Allowable expenditure*
		£
Acquired June 2016	10,000	70,000
Distribution September 2017 (10%)	-	(7,000)
s104 holding after distribution	10,000	63,000
s104 holding (Rundico plc) c/f	16,000	63,000

The chargeable gain is £1,000 (£8,000 – £7,000).

Chapter 21

21.1

So long as Mohammed actually resides in both properties he may choose which is to be regarded as his PPR. Whichever property he bought and lived in first was automatically regarded as his PPR. After he bought the second property (and began residing in it) he could, if he wished, elect that this property should become his PPR for CGT purposes. He would do this if he thought that the gain arising on the disposal of the second property would exceed the gain arising on the disposal of the first property. The election would have to be made within two years after the date from which it is to take effect.

21.2

	£
Sale proceeds	173,000
Less: Acquisition cost	31,000
Chargeable gain (before PPR exemption)	142,000

The chargeable gain (before considering the PPR exemption) is £142,000. Considering each of the three cases individually:

(a) The house is not a chargeable asset and so the disposal is exempt from CGT. The chargeable gain is £nil.

(b) Melanie owned the house for 31 years and 7 months (379 months) and was absent for 48 months. There is no indication that the absence was work-related and this absence exceeds the permissible maximum "absence for any reason" by 12 months. Therefore the PPR exemption is £142,000 × 367/379 = £137,504 and the chargeable gain is £142,000 × 12/379 = £4,496.

(c) Letting relief is available and is the lowest of £4,496, £137,504 and £40,000, which is £4,496. This reduces the chargeable gain to £nil.

21.3

	£
Sale proceeds	362,000
Less: Acquisition cost	75,000
Chargeable gain (before PPR exemption)	287,000

Rupert's period of ownership (a total of 268 months) is broken down as follows:

(i)	1 November 1995 to 31 October 1999	48 months	Actual residence
(ii)	1 November 1999 to 31 October 2000	12 months	Working abroad
(iii)	1 November 2000 to 31 July 2004	45 months	Actual residence
(iv)	1 August 2004 to 31 October 2008	51 months	Working in UK
(v)	1 November 2008 to 31 October 2011	36 months	Actual residence
(vi)	1 November 2011 to 1 March 2018	76 months	Living with friend

Periods (i), (iii) and (v) are exempt (actual residence) and period (ii) is exempt (working abroad). Period (iv) exceeds the four-year maximum allowable for working in the UK but the remaining three months of this period are exempt as part of the 36 months allowed for any reason. The last 18 months of ownership are exempt but the remaining 58 months of period (vi) cannot be exempt since they are not followed by a period of actual residence. The chargeable gain is:

	£
Total gain (as above)	287,000
Less: PPR exemption:	
£287,000 × 210/268	224,888
	62,112
Less: Letting relief (lowest of £62,112, £224,888 and £40,000)	40,000
Chargeable gain	22,112

21.4

	£
Sale proceeds	165,000
Less: Acquisition cost	47,500
Chargeable gain (before PPR exemption)	117,500

Samantha owned the house for a total of 21 years (252 months). For 7 years (84 months) the house was used partly for business purposes. The computation of the chargeable gain is as follows:

	£	£
Total gain (as above)		117,500
Less: PPR exemption:		
£117,500 × 168/252	78,333	
£117,500 × 84/252 × 4/5	31,333	109,666
Chargeable gain		7,834

Chapter 22

22.1

The allowable expenditure in relation to the porcelain is £9,850 (£10,000 in October 2007, plus £3,850 in March 2013, less £4,000 received July 2013). The computation of the gain arising in March 2018 is:

	£
Sale proceeds	23,500
Less: Allowable expenditure	9,850
Chargeable gain	13,650

22.2

The gain arising on the theft of the original necklace would have been:

	£
Disposal proceeds	14,000
Less: Acquisition cost	13,500
Chargeable gain	500

The allowable cost of the new necklace is reduced to £14,250 (£14,750 – £500). The gain arising on its disposal is as follows:

	£
Disposal proceeds	20,000
Less: Deemed acquisition cost	14,250
Chargeable gain	5,750

22.3

The gain on the disposal of the original building is computed as follows:

	£
Sale proceeds	261,400
Less: Acquisition cost	150,000
Chargeable gain	111,400

(a) £2,500 of the sale proceeds have been retained. Therefore £2,500 of the gain is immediately chargeable. The remaining £108,900 may be rolled-over against the cost of the new building, reducing its allowable cost to £150,000 (£258,900 – £108,900).

(b) £111,600 of the sale proceeds have been retained. This exceeds the gain. Therefore the whole gain is immediately chargeable and no part of the gain may be rolled-over. The allowable cost of the new building is the full £149,800.

(c) The entire sale proceeds have been spent on a replacement building. Therefore none of the gain is immediately chargeable and the entire gain may be rolled-over against the cost of the new building, reducing its allowable cost to £165,400 (£276,800 – £111,400).

22.4

The amount of the held-over gain is computed as follows:

			£
Disposal value			215,000
Less:	Acquisition cost	91,500	
	Enhancement expenditure	34,500	126,000
Held-over gain			89,000

The son's deemed acquisition cost is £126,000 (£215,000 – £89,000). If he had paid his mother £150,000 for the asset, the held-over gain would be reduced by £24,000 (£150,000 – £126,000) to £65,000 and his deemed acquisition cost would be £150,000 (£215,000 – £65,000).

Chapter 23

23.1

(a) The year to 30 November 2017 is a single accounting period.

(b) The period from 1 October 2016 to 31 July 2017 does not exceed 12 months and is therefore a single accounting period.

(c) The period from 1 January 2018 to 31 January 2018 does not exceed 12 months and is therefore a single accounting period.

(d) The 33 months to 31 August 2017 is divided into three accounting periods. These are the 12 months to 30 November 2015, the 12 months to 30 November 2016 and the nine months to 31 August 2017.

(e) The 18 months to 30 September 2017 is divided into two accounting periods. These are the 12 months to 31 March 2017 and the six months to 30 September 2017.

23.2

Assuming that the debentures on which the company is receiving interest were acquired for non-trading purposes, the interest receivable is a credit on a non-trading loan relationship. The amount of debenture interest for the accounting period (computed on the accruals basis) is aggregated with any other debits and credits arising on non-trading loan relationships. Net credits are chargeable to corporation tax. Net debits are eligible for tax relief (see Chapter 26).

The income tax of £2,160 (£8,640 × 20/80) deducted from the debenture interest paid to individuals must be accounted for to HMRC. But the gross amount of interest payable for the accounting period (computed on the accruals basis) is allowed either as an expense when computing the company's trading income or as a debit when computing the net credit or debit arising from non-trading loan relationships (depending on whether or not the debentures were issued for trade purposes).

23.3

The company may deduct £414,000 (£180,000 × 230%) in relation to this R&D expenditure when computing its trading income for the year to 31 March 2018. If the effect of this deduction is to create or increase a trading loss, the company may claim a payment from HMRC equal to the *lower* of 14.5% of the trading loss and 14.5% of £414,000 (i.e. £60,030).

23.4

The 17 months to 30 June 2017 will be divided into two accounting periods. These are the 12 months to 31 January 2017 and the five months to 30 June 2017. The taxable total profits for each accounting period are as follows:

	12 months to 31/1/17	*5 months to 30/6/17*
	£	£
Trading income (time apportioned)	300,000	125,000
Debenture interest receivable	3,600	2,000
Income from property (time apportioned)	6,360	2,650
Chargeable gains	28,700	49,760
	338,660	179,410
Less: Qualifying charitable donations	12,000	-
Taxable total profits (TTP)	326,660	179,410

Notes:

(a) The debenture interest receivable is allocated on the accruals basis. Interest accrues at £400 per month. In the first accounting period, interest is due for the nine months from 1 May 2016 to 31 January 2017. In the second accounting period, interest is due for the five months from 1 February 2017 to 30 June 2017.

(b) The chargeable gains are allocated according to the dates of the disposals. Even though the two disposals are on consecutive days, they fall into different accounting periods.

(c) Dividends received do not form part of a company's taxable total profits.

(d) The Gift Aid donations are allocated according to the date of payment.

23.5

The taxable total profits for the year to 31 March 2018 are as follows:

	£
Trading income	1,561,400
Income from non-trading loan relationships (£1,820 + £3,670 + £1,980)	7,470
Chargeable gains	531,000
	2,099,870
Less: Qualifying charitable donations	9,000
Taxable total profits (TTP)	2,090,870

Notes:

(a) Interest receivable is taxed on the accruals basis.

(b) Dividends received do not form part of a company's taxable total profits.

(c) Gift Aid donations are relieved on the payments basis.

Chapter 24

24.1

(a) *Disposal of factory building*

		£	£
Sale proceeds			650,000
Less:	Acquisition cost	300,000	
	Enhancement expenditure	50,000	350,000
Unindexed gain			300,000
Less:	Indexation allowance:		
	(i) on acquisition cost		
	$\frac{271.1-170.5}{170.5}$ = 0.590 × £300,000	177,000	
	(ii) on enhancement expenditure		
	$\frac{271.1-175.9}{175.9}$ = 0.541 × £50,000	27,050	204,050
Chargeable gain			95,950

(b) *Disposal of office building*

		£
Sale proceeds		1,100,000
Less:	Acquisition cost	600,000
Unindexed gain		500,000
Less:	Indexation allowance:	
	$\frac{272.9-173.8}{173.8}$ = 0.570 × £600,000	342,000
		158,000
Less:	Rolled-over gain (£158,000 – £50,000)	108,000
Chargeable gain		50,000

£50,000 of the sale proceeds have been retained and therefore £50,000 of the gain is immediately chargeable. The base cost of the replacement building is reduced to £942,000 (£1,050,000 – £108,000).

(c) *Disposal of computer system*

There is no chargeable gain or allowable loss in relation to this disposal, since gifts to charity are not chargeable disposals.

The company's plant and machinery capital allowances computation for the year to 31 March 2018 will show a disposal of £500 and this will generate a balancing adjustment if the computer is being treated as a short-life asset (see Chapter 11).

Gifts of used plant and machinery to a charity are allowable as trading expenses and so there will be a deduction of £500 from the company's trading profit (see Chapter 9).

(d) *Disposal of motor car*

There is no chargeable gain or allowable loss in relation to this disposal, since cars are not chargeable assets

When the car was acquired it entered either the main pool or the special rate pool, depending upon its emission rating. A disposal value of £80,000 is subtracted from the relevant pool in the year to 31 March 2018.

(e) *Disposal of plant and machinery*

This plant and machinery is a wasting chattel. Wasting chattels are normally exempt assets but this item has been used in business and capital allowances have been claimed, so the exemption does not apply. However, the loss of £40,000 is reduced to £nil by capital allowances of the same amount.

The company's plant and machinery capital allowances computation for the year to 31 March 2018 will show a disposal of £30,000.

(f) *Disposal of shares in Exxak plc*

The disposal is matched first against the 3,000 shares acquired within the previous nine days. These shares cost £36,000 and were sold for £30,000, so there is an allowable loss of £6,000.

The remaining 5,000 shares of the disposal are matched with shares taken from the s104 holding, as follows:

	No of shares	*Cost*	*Indexed cost*
		£	£
Bought 22 November 2002	4,000	16,000	16,000
Add: Indexation to December 2006			
$\frac{202.7 - 178.2}{178.2} \times £16,000$			2,200
			18,200
Bought 14 December 2006	6,000	30,000	30,000
s104 holding at 14 December 2006	10,000	46,000	48,200
Add: Indexation to December 2017			
$\frac{274.7 - 202.7}{202.7} \times £48,200$			17,121
			65,321
Sold 18 December 2017	(5,000)	(23,000)	(32,661)
s104 holding c/f at 18 December 2017	5,000	23,000	32,660

These 5,000 shares were sold for £50,000 so the chargeable gain arising on their disposal is £17,339 (£50,000 – £32,661).

(g) *Disposal of Government securities*

There is no chargeable gain or allowable loss in relation to this disposal, since disposals of Government securities (or "gilt-edged" securities) by a company are dealt with by means of the loan relationships regime.

Assuming that the securities were not held for trade purposes, there will be a debit on non-trading loan relationships of £5,000.

Total chargeable gains are £163,289 (£95,950 + £50,000 + £17,339) and allowable losses are £6,000. Therefore net chargeable gains for the year to 31 March 2018 are £157,289.

24.2

(i) *Disposal of shares in Epsilon plc*

The s104 holding is as follows:

	No of shares	*Cost*	*Indexed cost*
		£	£
Bought 27 June 1991	3,000	15,000	15,000
Add: Indexation to March 2001			
$\frac{172.2-134.1}{134.1} \times £15,000$			4,262
			19,262
Bought 10 March 2001	4,000	28,000	28,000
	7,000	43,000	47,262
Add: Indexation to September 2017			
$\frac{272.9-172.2}{172.2} \times £47,262$			27,638
			74,900
Sold 12 September 2017	(7,000)	(43,000)	(74,900)
s104 holding c/f	0	0	0

These 7,000 shares were sold for £66,500 (7,000 × £9.50) so the unindexed gain arising on the disposal is £23,500 (£66,500 – £43,000). The available indexation allowance is £31,900 but this is restricted to £23,500 and the chargeable gain is zero.

The 1982 holding is as follows:

	No of shares	*Cost*	*MV 31/3/82*
		£	£
Bought 14 January 1981	2,000	4,000	5,000
Sold 12 September 2017	(500)	(1,000)	(1,250)
1982 holding c/f	1,500	3,000	3,750

Indexation allowance on this disposal is (272.9 – 79.44)/79.44 = 2.435 × £1,250 = £3,044. Rebasing gives the lower gain. The shares were sold for £4,750 (500 × £9.50). The chargeable gain is £456 (£4,750 – £1,250 – £3,044).

(ii) *Disposal of watercolour paintings*

The gross disposal proceeds of the paintings are £5,750 (£5,175 × 100/90) and £6,450 (£5,805 × 100/90) respectively. The first painting is disposed of for less than £6,000 and is exempt. The gain arising on the disposal of the second painting is as follows:

		£	
Sale proceeds		6,450	
Less:	Incidental costs of disposal	645	
		5,805	
Less:	Acquisition cost	2,000	
Unindexed gain		3,805	
Less:	Indexation allowance:		
	$\frac{273.5-177.6}{177.6}$ = 0.540 × £2,000	1,080	
Chargeable gain		2,725	(restricted to £450 × 5/3 = £750)

(iii) *Disposal of short lease*

When it was assigned, the lease had 5 years and 7 months left to run. The Sch. 8 percentage is 29.331 (26.722 + 7/12 × 4.473). The loss on the disposal is as follows:

		£
Sale proceeds		7,000
Less:	Cost (29.331/72.770 × £20,000)	8,061
Allowable loss		(1,061)

(iv) *Disposal of freehold property*

Assuming that the building and the plant are used for business purposes, all except £15,000 of the gain on the disposal of the building may be held over. The computation is as follows:

		£
Sale proceeds		115,000
Less:	Acquisition cost	50,000
Unindexed gain		65,000
Less:	Indexation allowance:	
	$\frac{274.1-187.4}{187.4}$ = 0.463 × £50,000	23,150
		41,850
Less:	Held-over gain	26,850
Chargeable gain		15,000

Total gains are £16,206 (£456 + £750 + £15,000). Allowable losses are £1,061 so net gains are £15,145. These are reduced by capital losses brought forward of £7,145 to £8,000.

Chapter 25

25.1

(a) The accounting period coincides with FY2016 so the applicable rate of corporation tax is the FY2016 main rate of 20%. The liability is (£3,200,000 × 20%) = £640,000.

(b) The accounting period coincides with FY2017 so the applicable rate of corporation tax is the FY2017 main rate of 19%. The liability is (£3,200,000 × 19%) = £608,000.

(c) The first three months of the accounting period fall into FY2016 (main rate 20%) and the remaining nine months fall into FY2017 (main rate 19%). Therefore the corporation tax liability is (£3,200,000 × 3/12 × 20%) + (£3,200,000 × 9/12 × 19%) = £616,000.

(d) The first three months of the accounting period fall into FY2017 (main rate 19%) and the remaining seven months fall into FY2018 (main rate also 19%). Therefore the corporation tax liability is (£3,200,000 × 3/10 × 19%) + (£3,200,000 × 7/10 × 19%) = £608,000.

(e) The first three months of the accounting period fall into FY2016 (main rate 20%) and the remaining seven months fall into FY2017 (main rate 19%). Therefore the corporation tax liability is (£3,200,000 × 3/10 × 20%) + (£3,200,000 × 7/10 × 19%) = £617,600.

25.2

(a) The year to 31 March 2018 is a single accounting period. Corporation tax is due nine months and one day after 31 March 2018, which is 1 January 2019.

(b) The six months to 30 November 2017 is a single accounting period. Corporation tax is due nine months and one day after 30 November 2017, which is 1 September 2018.

(c) The 21 months to 30 June 2018 breaks down into two accounting periods. These are the year to 30 September 2017 and the nine months to 30 June 2018. Corporation tax for the year to 30 September 2017 is payable on 1 July 2018. Corporation tax for the nine months to 30 June 2018 is payable on 1 April 2019.

(d) The 27 months to 31 August 2018 breaks down into three accounting periods. These are the year to 31 May 2017, the year to 31 May 2018 and the three months to 31 August 2018. Corporation tax for the year to 31 May 2017 is payable on 1 March 2018. Corporation tax for the year to 31 May 2018 is payable on 1 March 2019. Corporation tax for the three months to 31 August 2018 is payable on 1 June 2019.

25.3

(a) The accounting period coincides with FY2017 so the applicable rate of corporation tax is the FY2017 main rate of 19%. The corporation tax liability is (£1,800,000 × 19%) = £342,000.

The company is large for the accounting period (and was also large in the previous 12 months) so corporation tax is payable by instalments. There are four instalments of £85,500 each and they fall due on 14 October 2017, 14 January 2018, 14 April 2018 and 14 July 2018.

(b) The first three months of the accounting period fall into FY2016 (main rate 20%) and the remaining three months fall into FY2017 (main rate 19%). Therefore the corporation tax liability is (£960,000 × 3/6 × 20%) + (£960,000 × 3/6 × 19%) = £187,200.

The company is large for the accounting period since it has profits which exceed 6/12 × £1,500,000 = £750,000. The company was also large in the previous 12 months, so tax is payable by instalments. There are two instalments of £93,600 each and they fall due on 14 July 2017 and 14 October 2017.

25.4

The first six months of the accounting period fall into FY2016 (main rate 20%) and the remaining six months fall into FY2017 (main rate 19%).

(a) The company is large for the accounting period (and was also large in the previous 12 months) so corporation tax is payable by instalments. The tax liability is (£4,500,000 × 6/12 × 20%) + (£4,500,000 × 6/12 × 19%) = £877,500. There are four instalments of £219,375 each and they fall due on 14 April 2017, 14 July 2017, 14 October 2017 and 14 January 2018.

(b) The company is not large for the accounting period, since it has profits which do not exceed £1,500,000. The corporation tax liability is (£1,250,000 × 6/12 × 20%) + (£1,250,000 × 6/12 × 19%) = £243,750. This falls due nine months and one day after 30 September 2017, which is 1 July 2018.

(c) The company's augmented profits are (£1,250,000 + £300,000) = £1,550,000. This exceeds £1,500,000 so the company is large for the accounting period. The corporation tax liability of £243,750 (see (b) above) is payable in four instalments of £60,937.50 each on 14 April 2017, 14 July 2017, 14 October 2017 and 14 January 2018.

25.5

The due date of payment is 1 June 2017 (nine months and one day after 31 August 2016). The final payment of £4,650 was made on 3 October 2017, which is 124 days late. The interest payable is:

$$£4{,}650 \times 2.75\% \times \frac{124}{366} = £43.32.$$

25.6

In each case, the company must pay corporation tax by instalments and the final instalment is due three months and 14 days after the end of the accounting period. Earlier instalments are payable on the usual quarterly dates if they occur before the date of the final instalment.

(a) Instalments are due on 14 January 2018, 14 April 2018, 14 July 2018 and 14 September 2018. The first three instalments are each equal to 3/11ths of the corporation tax liability for the period. The final instalment is equal to the remaining 2/11ths of the liability.

(b) Instalments are due on 14 July 2017, 14 October 2017 and 14 December 2017. The first two instalments are each equal to 3/8ths of the corporation tax liability for the period. The final instalment is equal to the remaining 2/8ths of the liability.

(c) Instalments are due on 14 July 2018 and 14 August 2018. The first instalment is equal to 3/4ths of the corporation tax liability for the period. The second (and final) instalment is equal to the remaining 1/4th of the liability.

(d) The final (and only) instalment falls due on 14 May 2018 and is equal to the whole of the corporation tax liability for the period. It is not possible to fit in any earlier instalments since the first such instalment would normally have been payable on 14 July 2018.

Chapter 26

26.1

	y/e 31/5/15	*y/e 31/5/16*	*y/e 31/5/17*
	£	£	£
Trading profits	-	23,800	40,300
Less: Trading losses b/f	-	23,800	8,400
Trading income	-	0	31,900
Less: Qualifying charitable donations	-	-	600
Taxable total profits (TTP)	0	0	31,300
Trading losses c/f	32,200	8,400	-
Unrelieved charitable donations	400	500	-

Notes:

(i) Before trading loss relief, TTP for the year to 31 May 2016 would have been £23,300. The accounting period falls partly into FY2015 and partly into FY2016 (main rate 20% in both financial years) so tax saved is (£23,300 × 20%) = £4,660.

(ii) The first ten months of the year to 31 May 2017 fall into FY2016 (main rate 20%) and the remaining two months fall into FY2017 (main rate 19%). Therefore trading losses of £8,400 reduce the tax liability by (£8,400 × 10/12 × 20%) + (£8,400 × 2/12 × 19%) = £1,666.

(iii) An alternative approach to calculating the reduction in the tax liability for the year to 31 May 2017 is to calculate the liability with and without relief for trading losses.

Before deducting trading losses, TTP for the year would have been £39,700 and the tax liability would have been (£39,700 × 10/12 × 20%) + (£39,700 × 2/12 × 19%) = £7,873.83.

After deducting trading losses, the tax liability is (£31,300 × 10/12 × 20%) + (£31,300 × 2/12 × 19%) = £6,207.83, a saving of £1,666.

(iv) Total tax saved is (£4,660 + £1,666) = £6,326. This is an effective rate of tax relief of 19.65% on the trading loss of £32,200.

26.2

	£
Trading income	-
Income from property	190,200
Chargeable gains	45,540
	235,740
Less: Trade loss relief against total profits	232,300
	3,440
Less: Qualifying charitable donations	3,440
Taxable total profits (TTP)	0
Unrelieved charitable donations	20,560

26.3

Statements (a) and (d) are false. Statement (c) is true. Statement (b) is currently false but would become true if the proposed reforms to carry-forward relief were implemented. The relevant loss relief rules in Corporation Tax Act 2010 are as follows:

(a) Capital losses which are carried forward may be relieved only against future chargeable gains, not against future trading profits.

(b) At present, trading losses carried forward may be relieved only against future profits of the same trade, not against future chargeable gains. *However, if the proposed reforms to carry-forward relief are implemented, trading losses carried forward will be set against the total profits of later accounting periods (including the chargeable gains of those periods).*

(c) Trading losses may be relieved against total profits (including chargeable gains) of the accounting period in which the loss is incurred.

(d) Capital losses are relieved against chargeable gains of the same accounting period but not against trading profits of that period.

26.4

	y/e 31/5/16	*eight months to 31/1/17*	*y/e 31/1/18*
	£	£	£
Trading income	59,700	73,600	-
Chargeable gains	8,400	-	48,700
	68,100	73,600	48,700
Less: Trade loss relief (a)	-	-	48,700
	68,100	73,600	0
Less: Trade loss relief (b)	22,700	73,600	-
	45,400	0	0
Less: Qualifying charitable donations	1,000	-	-
Taxable total profits (TTP)	44,400	0	0
Trading losses c/f	-	-	10,700
Unrelieved charitable donations	-	1,000	1,000

Notes:

(i) The trading loss may be carried back for 12 months. The period to 31 January 2017 is wholly within these 12 months. But only four months out of the year to 31 May 2016 fall within the 12 months so maximum relief available in this year is £22,700 (£68,100 × 4/12).

(ii) Trading losses of £145,000 (£48,700 + £73,600 + £22,700) are relieved, leaving losses to carry forward of £10,700.

26.5

(a)/(b)

The main effects of a claim to relieve the trading loss against total profits are as follows:

(i) There are no profits in the loss-making period so the entire £700,000 is set against the profits of £800,000 for the year to 30 June 2017, reducing TTP to £100,000.

(ii) The first nine months of the year to 30 June 2017 fall into FY2016. The remaining three months fall into FY2017. Before loss relief, the tax liability for the year would have been (£800,000 × 9/12 × 20%) + (£800,000 × 3/12 × 19%) = £158,000.

(iii) After deducting loss relief, the tax liability for the year would be (£100,000 × 9/12 × 20%) + (£100,000 × 3/12 × 19%) = £19,750.

(iv) The tax saving is £138,250 (£158,000 – £19,750). On trading losses of £700,000, this represents an effective rate of tax relief of 19.75%.

(v) The corporation tax refund due for the year to 30 June 2017 carries interest dating from 1 April 2018 (or the date on which the tax was originally paid, if later).

Chapter 27

27.1

(a), (d) and (e) are associates, (b) and (c) are not.

27.2

The top five shareholders are Sejanus (with Apicata) 1,020 shares, Claudius (with Livia) 590 shares, Agrippa 300 shares, Cleopatra 300 shares and Tiberius 200 shares, totalling 2,410 shares. So the company is not under the control of five or fewer shareholders.

Sejanus is ranked as a director (since he is a manager and, with his wife, owns 20.4% of the share capital). So the directors are Sejanus (with Apicata) 1,020 shares, Claudius (with Livia) 590 shares, Agrippa 300 shares, Cleopatra 300 shares, Tiberius 200 shares and Gaius 200 shares, totalling 2,610 shares. The company is under the control of its participator-directors and is a close company.

27.3

(a) The director owns more than 5% of the company's share capital so the loan is taxable. The company must pay tax of £3,900 (32.5% of £12,000) by 1 January 2019 (unless the loan is repaid before then). Once paid, this tax is not refundable until nine months and one day after the end of the accounting period in which the loan is repaid or written off. The director will be subject to income tax on loan interest calculated at the official rate. If the loan is eventually written off (wholly or partly) the director will be taxed on the amount written off and the company will be denied any tax relief in relation to this amount.

(b) The director will be subject to income tax on a benefit in kind of £1,800. But if the ticket had been given to a shareholder who was not a director or other employee of the company, it would have been treated as a distribution. The cost of the ticket would have been disallowed in the company's accounts and the shareholder would have been charged to income tax as if he or she had received a dividend of £1,800.

Chapter 28

28.1

(a) Each company has two "related 51% group companies", so the profits limits used to determine whether or not corporation tax is payable by instalments are divided by (2 + 1) = 3. Therefore payment by instalments will be required for any of these companies which has profits (plus dividends received) exceeding £500,000 (£1,500,000 ÷ 3).

(b) When calculating the profits of Headco Ltd for payment by instalments purposes, dividends received from Arco1 Ltd and Arco2 Ltd are ignored.

(c) Transfer pricing legislation may apply to transactions between the companies, though small and medium-sized companies are generally exempt from this legislation.

(d) The companies form a 75% group, so trading losses and other items may be surrendered by one of the companies to either of the other companies.

(e) Chargeable assets are transferred between the companies on a no-gain, no-loss basis. A gain or loss arising in one company may be treated as if it had arisen in one of the other companies.

28.2

Dividends received are not charged to corporation tax (other than non-exempt foreign dividends). Therefore the taxable total profits of U Ltd for the year are:

	£
Trading profits	485,000
Income from property	12,000
Qualifying charitable donations	(17,000)
Taxable total profits (TTP)	480,000

The first three months of the accounting period fall into FY2016 (main rate 20%). The remaining nine months fall into FY2017 (main rate 19%). So the corporation tax liability for the year is (£480,000 × 3/12 × 20%) + (£480,000 × 9/12 × 19%) = £92,400.

U Ltd has two "related 51% group companies" (the two active subsidiaries). Therefore the usual £1,500,000 profits limit for payment by instalments purposes is divided by (2 + 1) = 3, giving a profits limit of £500,000.

Taxable total profits for the year plus dividends received (other than dividends from subsidiaries) are (£480,000 + £30,000) = £510,000. This exceeds £500,000, so U Ltd is "large" for the year to 31 December 2017.

If the company was also large for the year to 31 December 2016, the corporation tax liability of £92,400 is payable in four instalments of £23,100 each. These fall due on 14 July 2017, 14 October 2017, 14 January 2018 and 14 April 2018.

However, if the company was not "large" for payment by instalments purposes in the year to 31 December 2016, the corporation tax liability of £92,400 for the year to 31 December 2017 is payable nine months and one day after 31 December 2017, which is 1 October 2018.

28.3

Bassnote Ltd has current year trading losses of £90,000 and excess donations of £1,000, giving a total of £91,000. But Apexine Ltd has available profits of only £73,000 (£120,000 – £42,000 + £7,000 – £12,000) so the maximum group relief that may be claimed is £73,000.

28.4

(a) A1 Ltd owns 90% of A2 Ltd and (indirectly) 72% of A3 Ltd and 63% of A4 Ltd. So A1 Ltd and A2 Ltd form a 75% group. A2 Ltd and A3 Ltd form another 75% group.

(b) A1 Ltd, A2 Ltd and A3 Ltd form a capital gains group. A2 Ltd does not own at least 75% of A4 Ltd, so A4 Ltd is not a member of the capital gains group.

28.5

The trading loss of PP Ltd which is available for group relief is £84,000 (i.e. £96,000 less potential relief against total profits of £12,000). This is shared between the consortium members as follows:

	QQ Ltd	*RR Ltd*	*SS Ltd*
	£	£	£
Share of PP Ltd available loss	26,880	29,400	19,320
Available profits	59,000	47,000	14,000
Maximum group relief claim	26,880	29,400	14,000

Chapter 29

29.1

(a) standard rate
(b) zero rate
(c) exempt
(d) standard rate
(e) standard rate
(f) zero rate
(g) reduced rate
(h) exempt
(i) exempt
(j) standard rate
(k) standard rate
(l) zero rate
(m) zero rate
(n) standard rate.

29.2

(a) The value of the supply is £340. VAT charged is 20% of £340 = £68 and the consideration for the supply is £408.

(b) The value of the supply is £333.20 (£340 less 2%). VAT charged is 20% of £333.20 = £66.64 and the consideration for the supply is £399.84.

(c) The value of the supply is £340. VAT charged is 20% of £340 = £68 and the consideration for the supply is £408.

29.3

(a) Lorna must register since her taxable turnover exceeds the registration threshold.

(b) Mike must register since his aggregate taxable turnover exceeds the registration threshold.

(c) No-one need register. The partnership of "Pat and Phil" is not the same person as "Phil" so the turnover of the two businesses is not aggregated.

(d) The taxable "person" in this case is the company (not the shareholders) and therefore the company must register.

29.4

(a) She is not a taxable person, cannot register for VAT and cannot reclaim input tax.

(b) She is a taxable person and must register for VAT. She must account for output tax and may reclaim input tax.

(c) She is a taxable person and must register for VAT unless granted an exemption by HMRC. If she registers she may reclaim input tax. If she is granted exemption she will not be able to reclaim input tax but she will avoid the administrative burden associated with VAT registration.

29.5

(a) If a registered person in one EU country supplies goods to a registered person in another EU country, the supply is zero-rated in the country of origin but the customer accounts for VAT at the applicable rate in the destination country. If the customer is not a registered person, the supplier charges VAT at the applicable rate in the country of origin.

(b) VAT is charged on imports from non-EU countries at the same rate as if the goods had been supplied in the UK.

(c) Exports to non-EU countries are zero-rated.

See Chapter 29 for more details of the VAT treatment of imports and exports.

Chapter 30

30.1 & **30.2**

See text.

30.3

(a)

	£	£
Output tax:		
Standard-rated supplies ((£14,400 + (£14,400 × 97.5%)) × 20%)		5,688
Supply invoiced 15 November 2017 (£4,800 × 20%)		960
Fuel scale charge (1/6 × £252)		42
		6,690
Input tax:		
Standard-rated goods (£9,280 × 20%)	1,856	
Standard-rated services (£5,200 × 20%)	1,040	
Car maintenance (£280 × 20%)	56	
Car fuel (£520 × 20%)	104	
Non-current asset (1/6 × £14,100)	2,350	5,406
Payable to HMRC		1,284

Notes:

(i) Output tax is calculated on the selling price less any cash discounts actually taken.

(ii) Output tax is payable in relation to the sale to the bankrupt customer. Bad debt relief cannot be claimed until at least 6 months have elapsed.

(iii) The tax point of the £4,800 supply is the invoice date (earlier than the date of payment or the date on which the goods were made available).

(iv) Input tax cannot be reclaimed in relation to a car not used wholly for business purposes.

(b) The flat-rate scheme for small businesses (FRS) is available to businesses with a taxable turnover which is not expected to exceed £150,000 in the next 12 months. Toucan Ltd seems likely to satisfy this requirement. Membership of the scheme would allow Toucan Ltd to calculate its VAT liability as a flat-rate percentage of its total turnover and so avoid the need to keep detailed records of input tax and output tax. The FRS operates as follows:

(i) Output tax is charged to customers at the normal rate for the supply. Similarly, input tax is paid to suppliers at the normal rate. However, the output tax charged to customers is not paid over to HMRC and (in general) input tax is not recoverable.

(ii) In each tax period, a flat-rate percentage is applied to the VAT-inclusive turnover for the period. The result of this calculation is the amount of VAT payable to HMRC.

(iii) Input tax on the purchase of non-current assets costing at least £2,000 (including VAT) can be reclaimed in the usual way.

If Toucan Ltd joined the FRS, its average monthly VAT liability would be £1,311 (£11,500 × 120% × 9.5%). If the company did not join the scheme, the average liability would be £1,200 ((£11,500 - £5,500) × 20%). In both cases, input tax could be reclaimed on the expected non-current asset purchase of £5,000. It would appear, therefore, that Toucan Ltd would not benefit from joining the FRS unless administrative savings exceeded £111 per month.

30.4

Input tax reclaimed is £798 × 1/6 = £133.00. The scale figure for this car for a 3-month period is £408, so output tax of £408 × 1/6 = £68.00 must be accounted for. The only alternative would be for Sebastian to reclaim no input tax at all in relation to car fuel, but this would increase his VAT liability for the quarter by £65.00.

Chapter 31

31.1

	Value before AE	*AE for 2017-18*	*AE for 2016-17*	*Value after AE*
	£	£	£	£
Gift to grandson (exempt as a small gift)	-	-	-	-
Gift on marriage (£3,000 – £1,000)	2,000	2,000	-	-
Gift to husband (spouse exemption)	-	-	-	-
Gift to relevant property trust	10,000	1,000	3,000	6,000
Gift to Labour Party (exempt)	-	-	-	-
	12,000	3,000	3,000	6,000

31.2

(a) exempt (b) chargeable (c) PET.

31.3

The total of transfers brought forward in the seven years to date is £281,000, leaving £44,000 of the nil-rate band to set against the current transfer.

(a) If the trustees pay the tax, the gross value of the transfer is £80,000 and the IHT due is £44,000 @ 0% + £36,000 @ 20% = £7,200, payable on 30 June 2018.

(b) If Nicholas pays the tax, the net value of the transfer is £80,000. The gross value and the tax due are as follows:

	Net	*Gross*	*Tax*
	£	£	£
£44,000 grossed up @ 0%	44,000	44,000	0
£36,000 grossed up @ 20%	36,000	45,000	9,000
Totals	80,000	89,000	9,000

The tax due is £9,000, payable on 30 June 2018.

31.4

The value of each gift after deduction of exemptions is as follows:

		Value before AE	*AE for current year*	*AE for previous year*	*Value after AE*
		£	£	£	£
2010-11	Daughter (£500,000 – £5,000)	495,000	3,000	3,000	489,000
2011-12	Relevant property trust	497,000	3,000	-	494,000

Lifetime tax liability

The gift to Martha's daughter was a PET, so no lifetime tax was payable. The lifetime tax on the gift to the trust was £42,250, payable on 31 October 2012 and calculated as follows:

	Net	*Gross*	*Tax*
	£	£	£
£325,000 grossed up @ 0%	325,000	325,000	0
£169,000 grossed up @ 20%	169,000	211,250	42,250
Totals	494,000	536,250	42,250

Note that the nil-rate band used in the calculation of a lifetime tax liability is the nil-rate band on the date of the transfer, not the nil-rate band on the date of death. However, in this case, the nil-rate band was £325,000 on the date of the transfer and remained at £325,000 until the date of death.

Tax liability on death

(i) *Transfer made on 31 March 2011*

The gross value of this transfer is £489,000 and there were no other chargeable transfers in the seven years ending on the date of the transfer. Tax due at death rates for 1 January 2018:

	£
£325,000 @ 0%	0
£164,000 @ 40%	65,600
	65,600
Less: Taper relief (6-7 years) @ 80%	52,480
	13,120
Less: Lifetime tax paid	0
IHT payable by daughter on 31 July 2018	13,120

(ii) *Transfer made on 1 April 2012*

The gross value of this transfer is £536,250 and previous gross chargeable transfers in the seven years ending on the date of the transfer (2 April 2005 to 1 April 2012) were £489,000, using the whole of the nil-rate band. Tax due at death rates applicable on 1 January 2018:

	£
£536,250 @ 40%	214,500
Less: Taper relief (5-6 years) @ 60%	128,700
	85,800
Less: Lifetime tax paid	42,250
IHT payable by trustees on 31 July 2018	43,550

31.5

The quarter-up rule gives 572p + 1/4 × (588p – 572p) = 576p. The average of the highest and lowest recorded bargains is 575p, so the shares are valued at 575p each (£5,750 for 1,000 shares).

Chapter 32

32.1

(a) Jean-Paul meets the first automatic UK test and does not meet any of the automatic overseas tests. Therefore he meets the automatic residence test and is UK resident for tax year 2017-18. He is liable to pay UK income tax on all of his income for the year, including overseas income. However, he is not domiciled in the UK and so may claim the remittance basis. If he does this, his UK income (if any) will be fully liable to UK income tax but his overseas income will be liable only to the extent that it is remitted to the UK.

(b) Pierre does not meet any of the automatic UK tests. He meets the second and third automatic overseas tests. Therefore he does not meet the automatic residence test and he is not UK resident for the year unless he meets the sufficient ties test. Assuming this is not the case, he will be liable to pay UK income tax only on his UK income for the year (presumably £nil).

(c) Carole meets the second automatic UK test. She does not meet any of the automatic overseas tests. Therefore she is UK resident for tax year 2017-18. She will pay UK income tax on all of her income for the year (e.g. retirement pensions, investment income etc.). There appears not to be any overseas income but any such income would also be chargeable to UK income tax.

32.2

(a) *In tax year 2016-17*, Amy meets the first automatic UK test and does not meet any of the automatic overseas tests. Therefore she would normally be regarded as UK resident for the year. However, she is leaving the UK to work overseas (presumably full-time) and she will be non-UK resident in 2017-18 because she will meet the third automatic overseas test. In these circumstances, the split-year treatment applies. Amy will be treated as UK resident until 31 December 2016 and as non-UK resident for the remainder of the tax year.

She will receive the full personal allowance for 2016-17. Her income for UK tax purposes after 31 December 2016 will consist only of any income arising in the UK (e.g. rents from letting her house whilst away). Her Australian earnings will not be subject to UK tax.

(b) *In tax year 2017-18*, Amy meets none of the automatic UK tests and therefore she is not UK resident. Her Australian salary will not be subject to UK tax and she will be taxed only on her UK income (if any). As a citizen of the EEA, she is entitled to personal allowances.

(c) *In tax year 2018-19*, Amy is in the UK for 95 days. She meets none of the automatic overseas tests and presumably she meets at least the second automatic UK test. Therefore she would normally be regarded as UK resident for the year. However, she was not UK resident in the previous year and she is arriving to live and work full-time in the UK. The split-year treatment will apply and Amy will be treated as non-UK resident until 31 December 2018 but as UK resident for the remainder of the tax year.

She will receive the full personal allowance for 2018-19. Her income for UK tax purposes up until 31 December 2018 will consist only of any income arising in the UK. Once again, her Australian earnings will not be subject to UK tax.

32.3

(a) See text.

(b) If a UK resident is not UK domiciled, the remittance basis may apply so that foreign income is taxed only to the extent that the income is remitted to the UK. Similarly, gains arising from disposals of assets situated overseas may be taxed on the remittance basis. Also, an individual who is not domiciled in the UK is liable to inheritance tax only in relation to property which is situated in the UK. (See text for further details).

32.4

(a) See text.

(b) If a UK resident company makes this election, it applies to all of the company's overseas branches and is irrevocable. Although the profits of the company's overseas branches will be exempt from UK corporation tax, no tax relief will be available for any foreign branch losses that occur. A further disadvantage is that the company's overseas branches will fall within the controlled foreign company (CFC) regime and this may result in a CFC charge.

32.5

See text.

32.6

(a)	*UK*	*Overseas*	*Total*
	£	£	£
Trading income	2,120,000		2,120,000
Property income £98,000 × 100/70		140,000	140,000
Taxable total profits (TTP)	2,120,000	140,000	2,260,000
Corporation tax @ 19%	402,800	26,600	429,400
Less: Unilateral DTR		(26,600)	(26,600)
Corporation tax due	402,800	-	402,800

Double tax relief is restricted to the UK tax payable on the foreign income. The remaining £15,400 (£42,000 – £26,600) of foreign tax is unrelieved. This arises because the foreign tax rate exceeds the UK rate by 11% (11% × £140,000 = £15,400). The unrelieved foreign tax is lost.

(b)

If the overseas income consisted of trading income from an overseas branch, the unrelieved foreign tax of £15,400 could be carried back for up to three years or carried forward without time limit. The unrelieved tax would then be treated as foreign tax paid in respect of the overseas branch in the accounting period to which it was carried back or carried forward. If the UK rate of tax exceeded the foreign rate of tax in any such accounting period, this would offer an opportunity to relieve some or all of the unrelieved foreign tax.

However, the company may have elected that the profits of all of its overseas branches should be exempt from UK corporation tax. In this case, the overseas income would be totally ignored in the company's tax computation and there would be no relief for any foreign tax paid.

Answers to review questions

Set A

Question A1

(a)

	Total	*Non-savings*	*Savings*
	£	£	£
Income from property	47,500	47,500	
Debenture interest (£416 × 100/80)	520		520
Total income	48,020	47,500	520
Less: Personal allowance	11,500	11,500	
Taxable income	36,520	36,000	520

Tax due on non-savings income is (£33,500 × 20%) + (£2,500 × 40%) = £7,700.00. Daniel is a higher-rate taxpayer so the savings allowance is £500 and the tax due on savings income is (£500 × 0%) + (£20 × 40%) = £8.00. Tax borne is (£7,700.00 + £8.00) = £7,708.00, but tax deducted at source is £104.00 so tax payable is (£7,708.00 – £104.00) = £7,604.00.

(b) David's employment income is as follows:

	£
Salary	88,000
Less: Pension contributions (4%)	3,520
	84,480
Car (18% + 7% + 3%) = 28% × (£37,000 – £5,000)	8,960
Fuel 28% × £22,600	6,328
	99,768

Total income is £102,008 (£99,768 + £2,240) so the personal allowance is reduced by £1,004 to £10,496 (£11,500 – £1,004). Taxable non-savings income is £89,272 (£99,768 – £10,496) and the tax liability is (£33,500 × 20%) + (£55,772 × 40%) = £29,008.80. The dividends fall within the dividend allowance of £5,000 and are therefore taxed at the dividend nil rate. Tax payable is (£29,008.80 – £28,800.00) = £208.80.

(c) The £100 per month contributed towards private fuel is not deductible when calculating the taxable fuel benefit. It would be better if the £100 per month were payable for the private use of the car. It would then become deductible.

(d) The taxable benefit in relation to the beneficial loan is (£12,000 + £4,000)/2 = £8,000 × 2.5% × 10/12 = £167. Therefore total employment income is £53,167. The personal allowance of £11,500 reduces this to £41,667 and the income tax liability is (£33,500 × 20%) + (£8,167 × 40%) = £9,966.80. Tax repayable is (£9,990.00 – £9,966.80) = £23.20.

(e) There would have been no tax liability on the interest-free loan if it had not exceeded £10,000.

(f) Primary Class 1 NICs are ((£45,000 – £8,164) × 12%) + ((£88,000 – £45,000) × 2%) = £5,280.32. Secondary Class 1 NICs are ((£88,000 – £8,164) × 13.8%) = £11,017.37. The employer is also liable to Class 1A NICs of ((£8,960 + 6,328) × 13.8%) = £2,109.74.

(g) MCA is available because at least one of the couple was born before 6 April 1935 and they are legally married. The MCA will be claimed by the husband because they were married before 5 December 2005. The MCA for 2017-18 is normally £8,445 and results in a tax reduction of £844.50. But his income exceeds the limit of £28,000 so the MCA will be reduced by £1 for each £2 over the limit, down to a minimum of £3,260.

Question A2

	Total	*Non-savings*	*Savings*	*Dividends*
	£	£	£	£
Employment income	23,460	23,460		
Property income	3,680	3,680		
Annuity £25 × 12	300		300	
Dividends received	7,500			7,500
Total income	34,940	27,140	300	7,500
Less: Personal allowance	11,500	11,500		
Taxable income	23,440	15,640	300	7,500

Income tax due				
Non-savings income	: Basic rate	15,640	@ 20%	3,128.00
Savings income	: Nil rate	300	@ 0%	0.00
Dividend income	: Nil rate	5,000	@ 0%	0.00
	: Ordinary rate	2,500	@ 7.5%	187.50
		23,440		
				3,315.50
Less: MCA £4,975 @ 10%				497.50
Tax borne				2,818.00
Less: Tax deducted at source (£300 × 20%)				60.00
Tax payable				2,758.00

Notes:

1. Rents received are £6,000. Insurance is £370 (9/12 × £360 + 3/12 × £400). So total expenses are £2,320 (£370 + £1,500 + £450). Property income is £3,680 (£6,000 – £2,320).
2. Total income exceeds the MCA income limit by £6,940 so the MCA is reduced by £3,470 to £4,975 (£8,445 – £3,470).

Question A3

(a)

		Ae	Bee	Cae
		£	£	£
2015–16	1 July 2015 to 5 April 2016			
	£54,000 × 9/12 × 1/2	20,250	20,250	
2016-17	year ended 30 June 2016			
	£54,000 × 1/2	27,000	27,000	
2017-18	year ended 30 June 2017			
	£66,000 × 1/2	33,000	33,000	
	1 July 2017 to 5 April 2018			
	£87,000 × 9/12 × 1/3			21,750

(b)/(c)

		Dee
		£
2015-16	year ended 5 April 2016	32,880
2016-17	1 August 2015 to 31 July 2016	
	(£32,880 × 8/12) + £16,240	38,160
2017-18	year ended 31 July 2017	54,120

Overlap profits of £21,920 arise in respect of the eight months from 1 August 2015 to 5 April 2016.

Question A4

If the transactions are of a trading nature, the profits made by the partnership of Bernard and Gerald will be charged to income tax as trading income. The "badges of trade" will be used to decide whether they are trading, as follows:

(a) *Subject matter*. It appears that the subject matter of the transaction is of a type normally associated with a trading venture, rather than of a type more normally associated with investments or personal consumption.

(b) *Frequency of transactions*. There was only one purchase but there were several sales. The fact that sales were made to a number of different garden centres gives the impression of trading.

(c) *Length of ownership*. This was a fairly short-term venture. Most of the barrels had been sold within a few months and this again gives the impression of trading.

(d) *Supplementary work*. The barrels were sawn in half and Bernard and Gerald canvassed garden centres in the hope of finding customers. These activities constitute supplementary work and support the view that they were trading.

(e) *Motive*. It seems clear that the barrels were bought with only one view in mind - resale at a profit. This is a clear indicator of trading.

(f) *Acquisition*. The barrels were not inherited or gifted. They were purchased by Bernard and Gerald. This supports the view that they were trading.

It seems clear that this was an adventure in the nature of trade. Bernard and Gerald will be charged to income tax on their trading profits in tax years 2017-18 and 2018-19.

Question A5

(a) The year to 31 December 2017 forms the basis for tax year 2017-18, which is the final year of assessment for Sean's business. The trading loss of £23,100 for the year is increased by overlap profits of £3,600 to £26,700.

(b) The loss cannot be carried forward because the business has ceased trading. Therefore the only reliefs available are relief against total income and terminal loss relief.

(c) Sean could claim to relieve the trading loss against his total income of tax year 2017-18, tax year 2016-17 or both of those years. However, these claims would waste personal allowances. Total income for 2017-18 is £12,500. A loss relief claim for that year only would have to be for £12,500, leaving nothing against which to set the personal allowance. Similarly, total income for 2016-17 is £16,200 (£3,700 + £12,500) so a loss relief claim for that year only would also waste the personal allowance. A claim for both years would waste the whole of the personal allowance in one year and most of the personal allowance in the other year.

(d) The trading loss of £26,700 is eligible for terminal loss relief because it is incurred in the final 12 months of trading. The loss would be set against the trading profits (if any) of 2017-18, 2016-17, 2015-16 and 2014-15, in that order. Relief would be £3,700 in 2016-17, £18,900 in 2015-16 and £4,100 (£26,700 – £3,700 – £18,900) in 2014-15. Since Sean's property income absorbs the personal allowance in all of those years, there would be no waste of allowances and the loss would be relieved at basic rate (20%).

(e) Therefore the most beneficial way to relieve the trading loss is to make a terminal loss claim.

Set B

Question B1

(a)/(b)

(1) The cost of replacing the damaged floor is a repair. This is revenue expenditure not enhancement expenditure and is therefore not allowable in the computation of the chargeable gain. The gain is calculated as follows:

	£
Sale proceeds	522,000
Less: Allowable expenditure (£258,000 + £99,000)	357,000
Chargeable gain	165,000

Rollover relief will be available if the replacement warehouse was acquired no more than 12 months before 19 May 2017 but will be restricted if it cost less than £522,000. We need to know the cost and the precise acquisition date of the replacement warehouse.

(2) This is a part disposal. The fact that one-fifth of the land (in area terms) has been sold is not relevant and it is necessary to apply the A/(A + B) part disposal fraction. A is £81,700 and B is £268,000 so (A + B) is £349,700.

	£
Sale proceeds	81,700
Less: Cost (£167,400 × (£81,700/£349,700))	39,109
Chargeable gain	42,591

(3) The s104 holding is as follows:

	No of shares	*Cost*
		£
Bought 2 June 2009	500,000	960,000
Bonus issue 1 June 2014	750,000	-
	1,250,000	960,000
Sold 24 September 2017	(700,000)	(537,600)
s104 holding c/f	550,000	422,400

The chargeable gain is (£3,675,000 – £537,600) = £3,137,400. Entrepreneurs' relief may be available but this depends on whether Rolling Ltd is the taxpayer's personal company. We need to know whether he has held at least 5% of the company's ordinary shares (and voting rights) for the last 12 months. We also need to know whether he has made any previous ER claims and (if so) how much of the ER lifetime limit of £10m remains available.

(4) The shares are valued for CGT purposes at (698p + (710p – 698p)/2) = 704p. Therefore the market value of the shares on the date of disposal is (24,000 × £7.04) = £168,960 and the gain arising is (£168,960 – £76,800) = £92,160. There is no question of gift relief or entrepreneurs' relief because Rolling Ltd is not a trading company.

Question B2

(a) The disposal is matched first with the 1,000 shares bought in the following 30 days. These shares were sold for £4,600 (1,000/5,000 × £23,000) and were bought for £4,400, giving a gain of £200. The disposal is then matched with 4,000 of the shares in the Section 104 holding, as follows:

	No of shares	*Cost*
		£
Bought 18 August 2005	3,000	6,000
Bought 19 September 2012	2,000	5,000
	5,000	11,000
Sold 13 March 2018 (4/5ths)	(4,000)	(8,800)
s104 holding c/f	1,000	2,200

These 4,000 shares were sold for £18,400 (4,000/5,000 × £23,000) so the chargeable gain on their disposal is £9,600 (£18,400 – £8,800). The total chargeable gain is £9,800 (£200 + £9,600).

(b) Sally's net gains for 2017-18 are £31,200. Deducting losses brought forward of £11,500 leaves £19,700. Deducting the annual exemption of £11,300 leaves £8,400. The CGT payable is calculated as follows:

(i) Unused basic rate band is £13,500 (£33,500 – £20,000). This exceeds £8,400 so CGT payable is (10% × £8,400) = £840.

(ii) Unused basic rate band is £3,500 (£33,500 – £30,000). So the amount of CGT payable is (10% × £3,500) + (20% × £4,900) = £1,330.

(iii) There is no unused basic rate band. So CGT payable is (20% × £8,400) = £1,680.

Question B3

(i) The s104 holding consists of 50,000 shares at a total cost of £107,000. Therefore the gain on the August 2017 disposal is as follows:

	£
Sale proceeds	160,000
Less: Acquisition cost (2/5ths of £107,000)	42,800
Chargeable gain	117,200

(ii) The gain is eligible for entrepreneurs' relief because it arises on a disposal of shares in a trading company which (throughout the previous 12 months) has been Samuel's personal company and of which he has been an officer or employee. WQZ Ltd is his personal company because he owns at least 5% of its ordinary shares and has at least 5% of its voting rights.

(iii) Deducting the annual exemption of £11,300 leaves £105,900. The CGT liability is £10,590 (10% × £105,900). This is due for payment on 31 January 2019.

Question B4

(a) *Disposal of flat*

	£
Sale proceeds	142,000
Less: Incidental costs of disposal	4,000
	138,000
Less: Part cost: $\frac{£142,000}{£142,000 + £130,000} \times £80,000$	(41,765)
Part conversion costs: $\frac{£142,000}{£142,000 + £130,000} \times £32,000$	(16,706)
Chargeable gain	79,529

Disposal of shares

The chargeable gain is £38,300 (£150,000 – £111,700).

Total gains are £117,829 (£79,529 + £38,300). The CGT liability is minimised if the 2017-18 annual exemption is deducted from the gain arising on the disposal of the flat, leaving £68,229 (£79,529 - £11,300). CGT payable is [(28% × £68,229) + (20% × £38,300)] = £26,764.12.

(b) Mr More might consider the transfer of assets to Mrs More (at no gain, no loss). She could then dispose of them and any gain arising would be taxed in her name. For example, he could transfer the shares to her. If she then disposed of them and realised the gain of £38,300, this would be entirely covered by her losses brought forward and her annual exemption, so saving CGT of £7,660 (20% × £38,300).

Set C

Question C1

(a) The accounting periods concerned are the year to 31 March 2017 and the six months to 30 September 2017.

(b)

	y/e 31/3/17	*6 months to 30/9/17*
	£	£
Trading profits (time apportioned)	460,000	230,000
Less: Capital allowances:		
AIA £121,000 + WDA 18% × £25,000	125,500	
WDA 18% × £20,500 × 6/12		1,845
Trading income	334,500	228,155
Income from property	20,000	10,000
Income from non-trading loan relationships:		
£200 + £200 + £100	500	
£1,200 – £100 + £445		1,545
Chargeable gains		8,300
	355,000	248,000
Less: Qualifying charitable donations	5,000	5,000
Taxable total profits (TTP)	350,000	243,000
Corporation tax @ 20%	70,000.00	
Corporation tax @ 19%		46,170.00

Notes:

(i) The AIA maximum for the year to 31 March 2017 is £200,000.

(ii) The year to 31 March 2017 coincides with FY2016. Therefore corporation tax is payable at the FY2016 main rate of 20%.

(iii) The six months to 30 September 2017 are wholly contained within FY2017. Therefore corporation tax is payable at the FY2017 main rate of 19%.

(c) The due date of payment for the year to 31 March 2017 is 1 January 2018. The due date of payment for the six months to 30 September 2017 is 1 July 2018. In each case, the payment date is nine months and one day after the end of the accounting period.

(d) If trading profits were £3,690,000 for the 18 months (i.e. £3m higher than originally stated) then TTP for the two accounting periods would be £2m higher and £1m higher respectively. The revised tax liabilities would be £470,000 and £236,170.

The company would be "large" for payment by instalments purposes in both accounting periods since augmented profits would exceed £1,500,000 in the year to 31 March 2017 and £750,000 (6/12 × £1,500,000) in the six months to 30 September 2017.

However, the company was not large in the 12 months before the year to 31 March 2017 so the corporation tax for this year would still fall due on 1 January 2018. Corporation tax for the six months to 30 September 2017 would be payable in two instalments of £118,085 each on 14 October 2017 and 14 January 2018.

Question C2

(a)

	y/e 30/6/16	9 mths to 31/3/17	y/e 31/3/18
	£	£	£
Trading income	2,050,000	260,000	-
Income from non-trading loans	51,600	39,000	28,700
Chargeable gains	-	-	8,700
	2,101,600	299,000	37,400
Less: Gift Aid donations	10,000	8,000	5,000
Taxable total profits (TTP)	2,091,600	291,000	32,400
Corporation tax liability @ 20%/20%/19%	418,320	58,200	6,156

Notes:

(i) Capital losses carried forward at 30 June 2016 are £35,300 (£67,300 – £32,000). Therefore net chargeable gains for the year to 31 March 2018 are £8,700 (£47,000 – £35,300 – £3,000).

(ii) The first nine months of the year to 30 June 2016 falls into FY2015 (main rate 20%) and the last three months fall into FY2016 (main rate also 20%).

(b)

	y/e 30/6/16	9 mths to 31/3/17	y/e 31/3/18
	£	£	£
Trading income	2,050,000	260,000	-
Income from non-trading loans	51,600	39,000	28,700
Chargeable gains	-	-	8,700
	2,101,600	299,000	37,400
Less: Trading losses	525,400	299,000	37,400
	1,576,200	0	0
Less: Gift Aid donations	10,000	0	0
Taxable total profits (TTP)	1,566,200	0	0
Corporation tax liability @ 20%/20%/19%	313,240	0	0

Notes:

(i) Only three months of the year to 30 June 2016 fall into the 12 months prior to the loss-making period. Therefore loss relief in this year is restricted to £525,400 (£2,101,600 x 3/12).

(ii) Trading losses c/f are £33,200 (£895,000 – £37,400 – £299,000 – £525,400).

(c)

The reduction in the liability for the year to 30 June 2016 is £105,080 (£418,320 – £313,240) so the total tax saved as a result of the loss relief claims is £169,436 (£105,080 + £58,200 + £6,156). The amount of the loss relieved is £861,800 (£895,000 – £33,200). A tax saving of £169,436 on a loss of £861,800 represents an effective rate of relief of 19.66%. This is a higher rate of relief than can be expected in FY2018 onwards (with corporation tax rates set to be 19% or less) so the loss relief claims are recommended.

Question C3

(a)

	AA Ltd	BB Ltd	CC Ltd
	£	£	£
Trading profits	1,230,400	167,800	852,500
Income from non-trading loans	16,300	-	15,000
Property income	-	5,000	-
Chargeable gains	43,500	-	37,300
	1,290,200	172,800	904,800
Less: Gift Aid donations	5,200	1,000	4,800
Taxable total profits (TTP)	1,285,000	171,800	900,000
Corporation tax at 19%	244,150	32,642	171,000

The corporation tax liabilities of BB Ltd and CC Ltd are both due for payment on 1 January 2019 (i.e. nine months and one day after the end of the accounting period).

But AA Ltd has augmented profits of (£1,285,000 + £240,000) = £1,525,000 and this exceeds £1,500,000. So unless AA Ltd was not large in the previous 12 months, the company must pay tax by instalments. These instalments are due to be paid on 14 October 2017, 14 January 2018, 14 April 2018 and 14 July 2018. Each instalment is (£244,150 × 1/4) = £61,037.50.

However, if AA Ltd was not large in the previous 12 months, instalments are not required and the corporation tax liability of £244,150 is payable on 1 January 2019.

(b) If the accounting period is the year to 31 August 2017, the first seven months fall into FY2016 (main rate 20%) and the remaining five months fall into FY2017 (main rate 19%). The tax liability of AA Ltd becomes (£1,285,000 × 7/12 × 20%) + (£1,285,000 × 5/12 × 19%) = £251,646. Similarly, the tax liabilities of BB Ltd and CC Ltd become £33,644 and £176,250.

Corporation tax for the year to 31 August 2017 is normally payable on 1 June 2018. But for a company which is required to pay by instalments, the due dates are 14 March 2017, 14 June 2017, 14 September 2017 and 14 December 2017.

Question C4

		Main pool	SR pool	Allowances
		£	£	£
10 months to 31/10/17				
WDV b/f		148,300	40,870	
Additions (ineligible for AIA)			52,090	
Additions eligible for AIA	181,620			
AIA £200,000 × 10/12	166,667	14,953		166,667
Disposals		(26,450)	(35,090)	
		136,803	57,870	
WDA @ 18%/8% × 10/12		20,520	3,858	24,378
WDV c/f		116,283	54,012	
Total allowances				191,045

TTP is (£1,391,540 + £149,365 – £137,260 – £191,045) = £1,212,600. The corporation tax liability is (3/10 × £1,212,600 × 20%) + (7/10 × £1,212,600 × 19%) = £234,031.80.

This would normally fall due on 1 August 2018 but augmented profits are (£1,212,600 + £137,260) = £1,349,860. This exceeds (10/12 × £1,500,000) = £1,250,000 so the company is "large" for the accounting period. If it was also large in the previous 12 months, instalments are required.

The first three instalments are each equal to (3/10 × £234,031.80) = £70,209.54 and fall due on 14 July 2017, 14 October 2017 and 14 January 2018. The final instalment is the remaining £23,403.18 and this falls due on 14 February 2018.

Question C5

(a)

	£
Trading profits (£173,000 – £32,000)	141,000
Income from property	46,000
Chargeable gains (£6,400 – £1,400)	5,000
Qualifying charitable donations	(20,000)
Taxable total profits (TTP)	172,000

The tax liability is (6/12 × £172,000 × 20%) + (6/12 × £172,000 × 19%) = £33,540.00 and this is payable on 1 July 2018.

(b) The £1,500,000 profits limit which determines whether or not tax is payable by instalments is divided by (9 + 1) = 10, giving a limit of £150,000. Augmented profits (including dividends received but ignoring dividends from subsidiaries) are £172,000. This exceeds £150,000 so the company is "large" for the year.

Unless the company was not also large in the previous 12 months, the corporation tax liability is payable in four instalments of £8,385 (£33,540 × 1/4). These instalments fall due on 14 April 2017, 14 July 2017, 14 October 2017 and 14 January 2018.

Set D

Question D1

(i) Accumulative turnover up to the end of November is £51,200. This becomes £67,200 by the end of December and £85,700 (exceeding the registration threshold of £85,000) by the end of January. It will be necessary to notify HMRC within 30 days of the end of January 2018 and registration will probably take effect from 1 March 2018. Delay is inadvisable since there are penalties for delaying registration beyond the due date.

(ii) The input tax relating to stock held (i.e. not yet sold or consumed) on the date of registration may be reclaimed since it was supplied to Mr Deans within the four years prior to that date.

(iii) Input tax relating to the van is recoverable but not the input tax relating to the car. The input tax relating to all motor expenses, including all petrol, is recoverable but Mr Deans will have to account for output tax in respect of the fuel provided for private use. The amount of output tax due is calculated in accordance with scale charges which depend upon the car's emissions.

(iv) Bad debt relief is available so long as Mr Deans has written off the debt in his books and at least six months have elapsed since the date of supply. The cash accounting scheme would provide automatic bad debt relief.

Question D2

The value of each lifetime gift after deduction of exemptions is as follows:

		Value before AE	*AE for current year*	*AE for previous year*	*Value after AE*
		£	£	£	£
2011-12	Mother	60,000	3,000	3,000	54,000
2012-13	Father	60,000	3,000	-	57,000
2014-15	Nephew (£18,500 – £1,000)	17,500	3,000	3,000	11,500
2016-17	Gift to charity (exempt)	-	-	-	-

The first three gifts were PETs and the gift to the charity was an exempt transfer, so there was no lifetime tax liability in relation to any of these gifts. The tax liability on death is as follows:

(i) **Gift to mother**. Chargeable transfers in the previous seven years were £275,000, so the nil-rate band available is £50,000. IHT (before taper relief) is (£4,000 × 40%) = £1,600. Taper relief (5-6 years) at 60% is £960, so IHT due is £640.

(ii) **Gift to father**. Chargeable transfers in the previous seven years were (£275,000 + £54,000) = £329,000, so the nil-rate band available is £nil. IHT (before taper relief) is (£57,000 × 40%) = £22,800. Taper relief (4-5 years) at 40% is £9,120, so IHT due is £13,680.

(iii) **Gift to nephew**. Chargeable transfers in the previous seven years were (£275,000 + £54,000 + £57,000) = £386,000, so the nil-rate band available is £nil. IHT (before taper relief) is (£11,500 × 40%) = £4,600. Taper relief (3-4 years) at 20% is £920, so IHT due is £3,680.

(iv) **Estate**. Chargeable transfers in the previous seven years were (£54,000 + £57,000 + £11,500) = £122,500, so nil-rate band available is £202,500. IHT due is (£97,500 × 40%) = £39,000.

Question D3

	UK income	*Income net of 15% tax*	*Income net of 25% tax*	*Total*
	£	£	£	£
Trading income	175,000	-	-	175,000
Chargeable gains	5,000	-	-	5,000
Overseas property income	-	6,000	8,500	14,500
	180,000	6,000	8,500	194,500
Less: Gift Aid donations	7,500	-	-	7,500
Taxable total profits (TTP)	172,500	6,000	8,500	187,000
Corporation tax at 19%	32,775	1,140	1,615	35,530
Less: DTR	-	900	1,615	2,515
Corporation tax liability	32,775	240	0	33,015

Note: There is unrelieved foreign tax of [(£8,500 × 25%) – £1,615] = £510.

Question D4

A Ltd controls 75% or more of B Ltd (85%) and D Ltd (85% × 90% = 76.5%) so these three companies form a 75% group. C Ltd is a consortium company owned by A Ltd and E Ltd.

The trading loss incurred by C Ltd may be surrendered to A Ltd and E Ltd in proportion to their shareholdings in C Ltd. The trading loss incurred by D Ltd may be surrendered to A Ltd or B Ltd. Since both of these companies pay corporation tax at 19% for the year, the tax saving would be the same in both cases. It is assumed here that the loss is surrendered to A Ltd. The corporation tax liability of each company is as follows:

	A Ltd	*B Ltd*	*C Ltd*	*D Ltd*	*E Ltd*
	£	£	£	£	£
Trading income	240,000	45,000	-	-	80,000
Loan interest	5,000	2,500	-	-	-
Overseas property income:					
£8,200 × 100/82	-	10,000	-	-	-
	245,000	57,500	-	-	80,000
Less: Gift Aid donations	1,000	500	-	-	1,000
	244,000	57,000	-	-	79,000
Less: Consortium relief:					
60% × £30,000	18,000	-	-	-	-
40% × £30,000	-	-	-	-	12,000
	226,000	57,000	-	-	67,000
Less: Group relief	25,000	-	-	-	-
Taxable total profits (TTP)	201,000	57,000	0	0	67,000
Tax @ 19%	38,190	10,830	0	0	12,730
Less: DTR	-	1,800	-	-	-
Corporation tax liability	38,190	9,030	0	0	12,730

Notes:

(i) UK dividends received do not form part of the receiving company's taxable profits.

(ii) DTR is the lower of the foreign tax suffered (£1,800) and the UK tax on the foreign income (£10,000 × 19% = £1,900), which is £1,800. In general, Gift Aid donations are set against UK income so as to maximise DTR. However, in this case, even if the Gift Aid donations were set against the foreign income, this would still leave a UK tax liability on that income of £1,805 (£9,500 × 19%) so DTR of £1,800 would still be available.

(iii) If the D Ltd trading loss of £25,000 were surrendered to B Ltd (instead of A Ltd) this would be set against the UK income. Otherwise, DTR of £1,800 would be lost.

Index